Project Management

Information and
Technology for
Business COSC 111
Towson University

Objectives

- What is a Project
- Careers in Project Management
  - Certification
- Project Management Framework
- Project Management Knowledge Areas
- Project Management Tools

What is a Project

- A temporary endeavor undertaken to create a unique product or service
- Performed by People
- Constrained by limited resources (internal, external)
- Planned, executed, and controlled
- Temporary and Unique
  - Temporary in that every project has a definite beginning and a definite end.

Examples of Projects

- Class – identify examples of projects
  - List types of resources required
  - What are some constraints?
  - Why does it need to be planned and controlled?

Careers in Project Management

- What's available locally
- What do I need?
  - Degree – BS in either Project Management or Business Administration. Other degrees are acceptable with Project Management experience and/or Certification
- Graduate Studies in Project Management

What is Project Management

- The application of knowledge, skills, tool, and techniques to identify activities to meet project requirements
- The project team manages the work of the project, and the work typically involves:
  - Competing demands for scope, time, cost, risk and quality
  - Meeting stakeholder needs and expectations
  - Identifying requirements

What is Certification ?

- Recognized Certification from the Project Management Institute – better known as PMI
  - Certification
    - Rigorous study, and preparation for Exam
    - Some institutions, like Towson University offer preparatory seminars
      - Exam:
        - 200 Multiple Choice Questions
        - Must answer 137 correct to pass exam
        - Cost of Exam is $400 for non-member and less for members

Project Management Framework

- Project Management Context
  - Project Phases and the Project Life Cycle
  - Project Stakeholders
  - Organizational Influences
  - Key General Management Skills
  - Social-Economic-Environmental Influences
    - Weather, International Borders, Regulations

Project Phases and Life Cycle

- Each project phases is marked by one or more deliverable
  - A deliverable is a tangible, verifiable work product such as a working prototype.
- Project Life Cycle
  - Needs assessment or Feasibility Study to determine if the organization should undertake the project
  - Determine what project work should be done in each phase
  - Who should be involved in each phase
  - Project Work begins – cost and staffing increases up until about 75% of project completion
  - Cost and staffing decreases during the final phase to completion

Terms

- **Stakeholder:** Individuals and organizations that are actively involved in the project, or whose interests may be positively or negatively affected as a result of project execution or completion.
- **Project Manager:** the individual responsible for managing the project
- **Customer:** individual or organization that will use the project's product

Terms Continued

- **Performing Organization:** the enterprise whose employees are most directly involved in doing the work of the project
- **Project team members:** the group that is performing the work of the project
- **Sponsor:** individual or group within or external to the performing organization that provides the financial resources, in case or in kind for the project.

Organizational Structure

- The structure of the performing organization often constrains the availability of, or terms under which resources become available to the project
- Three main types
  - Functional
  - Projectized
  - Matrix
    - Weak
    - Balanced
    - Strong

Functional

- Each employee has one clear supervisor
- Staff members are grouped by specialty
- Project Scope usually limited to the boundaries of the function.
- Project Manager has little or no authority and can often be part time.
- Staff usually not assigned full time to project

Projectized Organization

- Most of the organization's resources are involved in project work
- Project Managers have a great deal of independence and authority
- Departments will generally report to the Project Manager

Matrix

- Blend of Functional and Projectized Organizations
  - Weak: Similar to Functional and the Project Manager's role is more like a coordinator, not all staff devoted to project
  - Balanced: Project Manager has more authority, working with Functional Managers and staff is temporarily devoted to project either full or part time
  - Strong: Full time project management with full time devoted project staff

Project Management Knowledge Areas

- As defined by PMI and found in the PMBOK
  - Publication by PMI which will document the accepted Project Management Body of Knowledge
    - Integration
    - Scope
    - Time
    - Cost
    - Quality
    - Human Resource
    - Communications
    - Risk
    - Procurement

		Project Plan Development	Project Plan Execution	Integrated Change Control	
	Initiation	Scope Planning & Definition		Scope Verification Scope Change Control	
		Activity Definition Sequencing, Duration Estimating, Schedule Development		Schedule Control	
		Resource Planning Cost Estimating and Budgeting		Cost Control	
		Quality Planning	Quality Assurance	Quality Control	
		Organizational Planning Staff Acquisition	Team Development		
		Communication Planning	Information Distribution	Performance Reporting	Administrative Closure
		Risk Planning and Identification Qualitative Risk Analysis Quantitative Risk Analysis Risk Response Planning		Risk Monitoring and Control	
		Procurement Planning Solicitation Planning	Solicitation Source Selection Contract Administration		Contract Closeout

Project Integration Management

- Includes the processes required to ensure that the various elements of the project are properly coordinated
- Project Plan – uses the outputs of all other planning processes or knowledge areas
  - **Project Plan Development** – integrating and coordinating all project plans to create a consistent, coherent document
  - **Project Plan Execution** – carrying out the project plan by performing the activities included therein
  - **Integrated Change Control** – coordinating changes across the entire project

Project Scope Management

- Includes the processes required to ensure that the project includes all the work required, and only the work required
  - **Initiation** – authorizing the project to begin
  - **Scope Planning** – developing a written scope statement
  - **Scope Definition** – Sub dividing the major project deliverables into smaller, more manageable components
  - **Scope Verification** – formalizing acceptance of project scope
  - **Scope Change Control** – controlling changes to project scope (unapproved changes is called Scope Creep"

Project Time Management

- Processes required to ensure timely completion of the project
  - **Activity Definition:** identifying the specific activities that must be performed to produce deliverable
  - **Activity Sequencing:** identifying interactivity dependencies
  - Activity Duration Estimating: estimating the amount of time (work units) to complete the task
  - **Schedule Development:** analyzing activity sequences, durations and resource requirements to create the schedule
  - **Schedule Control:** controlling changes to the schedule

Project Cost Management

- Includes the processes required to ensure that the project is completed within the approved budget
  - **Resource Planning:** Determine resources (people, material, equipment needed to complete the project
  - **Cost Estimating:** approximation of the costs of the resources required
  - **Cost Budgeting:** allocating the overall cost estimate to individual work activities
  - Cost Control: controlling changes to the project budget

Project Quality Management

- Processes required to ensure that the project will satisfy the needs for which it was undertaken
  - **Quality Planning:** identifying which quality standards are relevant to the project and how to satisfy them
  - **Quality Assurance:** evaluating overall project performance to provide confidence
  - **Quality Control:** monitoring specific project results to determine if they comply with relevant quality standards.

Project Human Resource Management

- Includes the processes required to make the most effective use of the people involved with the project.
  - **Organization Planning:** identifying, documenting, and assigning project roles, responsibilities, and reporting relationships
  - **Staff Acquisition:** getting the human resources needed assigned to and working on the project
  - **Team Development:** developing individual and group competencies to enhance project performance

Project Risk Management

- The systematic process of identifying, analyzing and respond to Project Risk
  - **Risk Management Planning:** deciding how to approach and manage risk activities
  - **Risk Identification:** determining which risks might affect the project and documenting their characteristics
  - **Qualitative Risk Analysis:** performing qualitative analysis of risks and conditions to prioritize their effects on project objectives
  - **Quantitative Risk Analysis:** measuring the probability and consequences of risks and estimating their implications for project objectives
  - **Risk Response Planning:** developing procedures and techniques to enhance opportunities and reduce threats to the project objectives
  - **Risk Monitoring and Control:** monitoring residual risks, identifying new risks, executing risk reduction plans, and evaluating their effectiveness throughout the project life cycle.

Project Procurement Management

- Includes the processes required to acquire goods and services, to attain project scope, from outside the performing organization.
  - **Procurement Planning**: determining what to procure and when
  - **Solicitation Planning**: documenting product requirements and identifying potential sources
  - **Solicitation**: obtaining quotations, bids, proposals
  - **Source Selection**: choosing from among the potential sellers
  - **Contract Administration**: managing the relationship with the Vendor
  - **Contract Closeout**: completion and settlement of the contract, including resolution of any open items

What is MS Project

- Define Resources
- Identify Project Activities
- Schedule Activities
- Sequence Activities
- Monitor Resource Costs
- Identify Project Deliverables
- Report on progress

Other Tools

- Using Excel to analyze
  - Quantitative Analysis
  - Qualitative Analysis
  - Project Budget
- MS Word for Project Templates
  - Change control form
  - Project Management Plans
  - Project Letterhead, Status Reports
  - Requisitions for Supplies
- MS Access
  - Track Project Risks
  - Track Project Issues
  - Track Project Action Items

Logical Relationships Between Activities

- Finish to Start – Work cannot **start** on a particular activity until the work of its successor is complete
- Finish to Finish – Work can begin but cannot be **completed** on an activity until the work of its successor is complete
- Start to Start – Work of the successor depends upon the **initiation** of the work of the predecessor
- Start to Finish – the completion of the successor is **dependent** upon the initiation of the predecessor

Other Terms

- Crashing – Taking action to decrease the total project duration
- Critical Path – The series of activities (tasks) that will determine the duration of the project
- Float – the amount of time an activity may be delayed without affecting the project end date
- Milestone – A significant event in the project, usually completion of a major deliverable
- Resource Leveling – adjusting activity scheduling based upon limited resource availability
- Work Breakdown Structure (WBS) – Represents the work of the project tasks in an organized structure which defines the total scope of the Project

Network Development Example
Precedence Diagramming Method

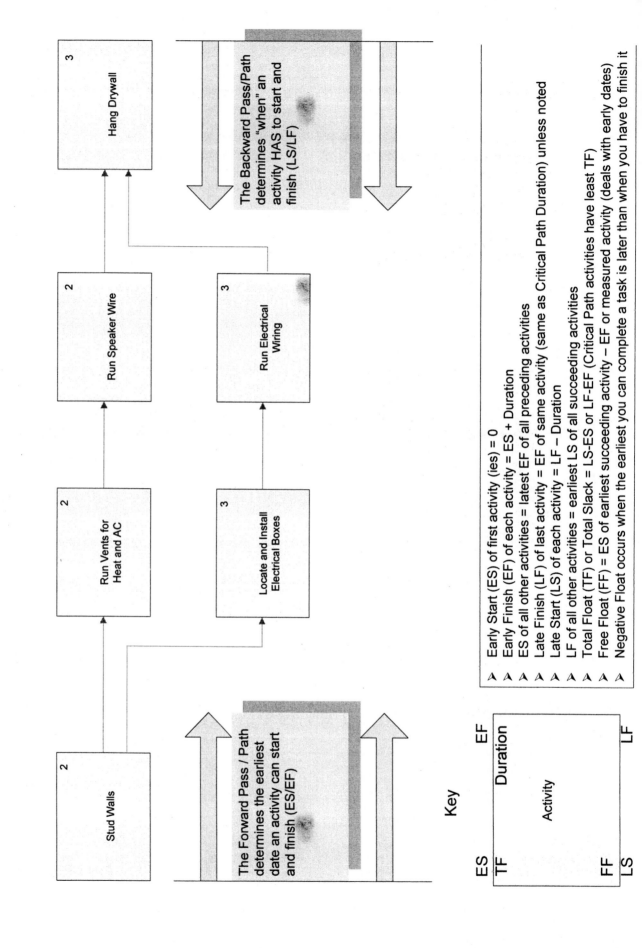

	2		
	Stud Walls		

	2				2		
	Run Vents for Heat and AC				Run Speaker Wire		

	3		
	Hang Drywall		

	3				3		
	Locate and Install Electrical Boxes				Run Electrical Wiring		

The Forward Pass / Path determines the earliest date an activity can start and finish (ES/EF)

The Backward Pass/Path determines "when" an activity HAS to start and finish (LS/LF)

Key

ES	Duration	EF
TF		
	Activity	
FF		
LS		LF

A Early Start (ES) of first activity (ies) = 0
A Early Finish (EF) of each activity = ES + Duration
A ES of all other activities = latest EF of all preceding activities
A Late Finish (LF) of last activity = EF of same activity (same as Critical Path Duration) unless noted
A Late Start (LS) of each activity = LF – Duration
A LF of all other activities = earliest LS of all succeeding activities
A Total Float (TF) or Total Slack = LS-ES or LF-EF (Critical Path activities have least TF)
A Free Float (FF) = ES of earliest succeeding activity – EF or measured activity (deals with early dates)
A Negative Float occurs when the earliest you can complete a task is later than when you have to finish it

Succeeding with Technology

ComputerSystemConceptsforRealLife

Ralph M. **Stair**

Kenneth J. **Baldauf**

THOMSON
COURSE TECHNOLOGY

Australia · Canada · Mexico · Singapore · Spain · United Kingdom · United States

THOMSON

COURSE TECHNOLOGY

Succeeding with Technology

by Ralph Stair and Ken Baldauf

Executive Editor: Mac Mendelson
Product Manager: Alyssa Pratt
Editorial Assistant: Amanda
  Piantedosi

Marketing Manager: Brian Boyle
Print Buyer: Laura Burns
Production Editor: Anne
  Valsangiacomo
Designer: Ann Small

Development Editors: Marilyn
Freedman, Laurie Brown
Cover Design: Abbey Scholz
Cover Image: Rakefet Kenaan
Compositor: Pre-Press, Inc.

For Lila and Leslie
—RMS

For Shani and Tyler
—KJB

BriefContents

Contents

2

HardwareDesignedtoMeettheNeed   46

3 **Software**Solutions**for**Personal and**Professional**Gain

4 TheInternet**and**World**Wide**Web

5

TelecommunicationsandNetworks 198

6   # **Database**Systems   244

7   E-commerce   290

8 Information, Decision**Support**, Artificial**Intelligence**, and **Special-Purpose**Systems

9 **Systems**Development   374

10 **Designing**Software**Solutions**

12 Societal and Ethical Issues in Computer Systems

Preface

You know your computer...
now what are you going to do with it?

Most students entering college have already had years of exposure to computers. Elementary and high school students use computers to write papers, create presentations, communicate with each other, conduct research, and entertain themselves. They understand the basics of computer use—how to turn them on and how to run popular applications. But today's technological world requires much more. Graduates entering the work force are often presented with technology that they have never before encountered. For example, individuals who land jobs with large businesses and organizations may work with virtual private networks, intranets, client/server networks, large databases—computer systems that assist large numbers of people in working effectively and efficiently together toward common goals. Graduates entering a medical profession will be stepping into a rapidly changing technical environment that is replacing nursing stations and large file storage facilities with database servers and tablet PCs connected to wireless networks. The computer has become a primary tool for graphic artists, musicians, individuals engaged in scientific research, criminologists, and most other professionals. These professionals work with all forms of computers: handheld, tablet, notebook, PC, server, mainframe, even super computers. Many professionals collaborate through computer networks of all kinds—personal area networks, local and wide area networks, wireless networks, intranets, extranets, and, of course, the Internet.

Even in our day-to-day personal lives we are called upon to learn new technologies that allow us to keep in closer contact with our friends and families and that provide more convenient access to information and entertainment. Text messaging with cell phones, digital cameras and camcorders, home Wi-Fi networks, and interactive TV are all wonderful technologies that require a significant investment in time for training.

Technological advances are difficult to keep pace with. This textbook will expose you to the most current and important technologies, assist you in understanding what makes them tick, and show you how they are being used to improve the way we work and live.

Welcome to the first edition of *Succeeding with Technology: Computer System Concepts for Real Life.*

Philosophy

Technology is changing the landscape of our professional and personal lives and offering us tremendous benefits. To take maximum advantage of these benefits, we must possess knowledge beyond word processors, spreadsheets, e-mail, and the Web. With so many technologies and devices in existence and new ones being developed every day, what should students know to succeed after college? This question is key to determining the path for an introductory computer course. The creation of *Succeeding with Technology* was guided by the philosophy that for students to prosper, they must grasp the underlying principles of the technologies that have an impact on our lives and understand how those principles are related to real-world activities. This textbook does not overwhelm you with descriptions of numerous inconsequential devices—no one is capable of gaining true understanding by memorizing long lists of technical terms. *Succeeding with Technology* is unique in providing straight-forward explanations of the principles that guide technological development, without overwhelming the reader with too much detail. An understanding of the principles provided in this book will translate to a practical understanding of the specific devices and practices in use today and in years to come.

The authors understand that technology in and of itself is not interesting to most people. What most people do find interesting are the exciting ways that technology is being used to improve our day-to-day lives, our professional productivity, society, and the world. For example, a supercomputer containing over 5,000 processors in and of itself may not interest someone. However, the story of how that computer is being used to simulate possible futures of our planet to help us avoid environmental disasters is of interest. The details of multimedia messaging service that connects cell phones with the Internet may not in itself be very interesting. However, being able to use a cell phone to snap a photo and email it to a friend is a valuable service in which many consumers are showing interest. *Succeeding with Technology* is unique in that it invests as much effort in showing how technology is used as it does in explaining how technology works. Every concept presented is backed up with practical examples of how it is making an impact on everyday life.

We are proud to introduce this unique textbook that takes readers beyond traditional computer literacy, beyond computer competence and fluency, to a deeper understanding of not only how digital technology works, but, more importantly, how it can be harnessed to improve your life.

Approach

Succeeding with Technology employs a different approach than the many computer concepts books currently on the market. It is a direct outgrowth of the trends that are causing the introductory computer course to change. From its high-impact graphic design to its content, the unique approach of this textbook is sure to engage and excite readers.

- Beyond PCs. We go beyond desktop PCs to provide coverage of the wide variety of computers and computer systems that are in use today. From cell phones to servers, from home wireless networks to virtual private networks, we cover all the latest technology that students are likely to encounter at home and at work.

- Focus on careers. This textbook contains a wealth of examples of how technology systems are used in different disciplines. Starting with Chapter 1, almost every page of this textbook contains exciting, current examples of how real people and organizations have used technology to achieve success.

- Speaks to students with varied skill levels. Although this textbook assumes that the reader has used a computer, the material is presented in a fashion that is sure not to leave anyone behind, while engaging even the most experienced computer user. Since this textbook focuses on concepts, not specific application skills, it does not assume a skill-level for the student, and therefore will speak to *all* students no matter what their skill level.

- Less jargon and fewer key terms. We include everything readers need to know and nothing they don't. Only important terms that students are likely to encounter in the real world appear in bold as key terms. When students are relieved of the need to memorize hundreds of key terms, they become free to understand more important fundamental concepts and gain practical knowledge that will last long past exam time.

- Important social issues explored. This textbook confronts important controversial issues head-on with complete coverage from all perspectives. P2P file sharing, the digital divide, students and plagiarism, violent video games, and many other current issues are explored, providing an excellent launching pad for class discussion. Social issues are touched on throughout the textbook, with special attention provided in chapter boxes and in the final chapter.

- Opportunities to explore beyond the textbook. We include references for the many examples that are provided in each chapter. Statistics and other factual data presented are also backed up with references to their sources. Teachers and students can use the references to follow up on stories and information, and learn more.

- Beyond the course. Because we have a stronger career focus than other concepts books, this textbook will be of interest to students from all majors. Because the detailed examples present a broad range of fields, students will get a good feel for what different careers involve. Through reading the examples, students can evaluate what careers and fields match their interests and talents.

FEATURES

Inspired by thousands of students who are well prepared to think about computer and technology systems and concepts, we've developed a set of features for this book designed to engage interest, show how to solve problems, and demonstrate what people can accomplish with computers. These features include Technology 360 boxes, Job Technology boxes, Community Technology boxes, Tech Edge boxes, and a Technology 360 Action Plan. Review the student section of this preface to see each element first hand as well as to learn more about what our learning tools offer your students. Here is a brief description of each of these features:

- Technology 360 boxes. These boxes open each chapter with a true-to-life scenario that students are likely to appreciate. In the scenario a person, not unlike a typical college student or recent graduate, is confronted with a situation that calls for the application of technical knowledge—the same technical knowledge that is provided by the chapter content. These boxes are intended to get the student thinking about the real-life application of the chapter topic. The scenario is revisited at the end of the chapter with an action plan that directly applies the chapter concepts to resolve the issues in the scenario.

- Job Technology boxes. These boxes highlight how technology is being used in a variety of jobs, fields, and career areas. Some of the fields touched on include medicine, physics, astronomy, biology, human resources, the military, telecommunications, entertainment, banking and finance, restaurants, retail, advertising, anthropology, the automotive industry, the computer and software industries, and many more.

- Community Technology boxes. These explore actual and potential problems related to the use of computer technology. Students are invited to think about issues such as the digital divide, how computer systems can be used to solve voting problems, protecting the environment and natural resources, spam, improving health care, taxing e-commerce, customer-sensitive advertising on the Web, violence in entertainment, privacy, waste, intellectual property, and more.

- The Tech Edge. These brief items focus on up-and-coming technology and technology that is already here, but is not commonly known about. The aim of this feature is to show students a broad range of the amazing things that are currently happening in our technology-driven culture. These are designed to get students excited about the technology and about learning more. Some topics include brain-computer interfaces, rapid manufacturing prototyping technology, plugged-in homes designed to help Alzheimer's patients, high-tech truck stops designed to reduce pollution, lobsters that advertise who caught them, and much, much more.

- Technology 360 Action Plans. These action plans follow up on the Technology 360 scenarios that open the chapter. Appearing at the end of the chapter, they show how the concepts taught throughout the chapter offer solutions to the problems encountered in the Technology 360 scenario at the beginning of the chapter.

- Careers index. At the back of the book, a unique index highlights the places in the book that discuss technology systems in different fields and careers. This special index makes it easy for students to find how computer systems are used in specific career areas throughout the textbook.

- End-of-chapter pedagogy. A wealth of end-of chapter material includes summaries tied to learning objectives, self-assessment tests, key term lists, review and discussion questions, lab and web exercises, virtual classroom activities, and teamwork exercises. A learning check provides students with a key that links end-of-chapter material to each learning objective. This rich array of study and review materials will help students retain concepts and use them beyond the course.

- End-of-book glossary. The book ends with a glossary of definitions for all bold-face key terms. Additional technical terms are also defined in the glossary for easy reference.

ENHANCING**THE**COURSE**WITH**THE**WEB**

In addition to having a well-designed set of learning features in the textbook, *Succeeding with Technology* takes advantage of how the World Wide Web opens many doors for engaging and meaningful online learning. We are committed to giving our readers every opportunity to build on and practice the lessons and concepts they have learned in the book via the Web, and we offer a robust Student Online Companion, at www.course.com/concepts/swt, with access to additional material, exercises, quizzes, and games that give students another way to test and build their knowledge of important concepts.

You can reinforce the lessons presented in this textbook with the Student Edition Labs and SAM Computer Concepts. Our site offers students free access to 30 different "Expand Your Knowledge" Student Edition Labs. Each lab enables them to practice real-world computer-based activities in a simulated environment. Different students learn in different ways, so these labs give each person the option to absorb these concepts in a variety of ways—through reading, observation, step-by-step practice, and hands-on application. Some of the exciting topics addressed in these labs include working with graphics, presentation software, networking basics, protecting your privacy online, visual programming, and project management.

SAM Computer Concepts goes a step further by allowing students to apply their knowledge in a hands-on application, and allowing instructors to administer customized lessons and generate dynamic reports. SAM Computer Concepts provides a total dynamic solution to your introductory computer course.

For more information on how to make SAM Computer Concepts Training and Assessment work for you, please visit www.course.com/sam or talk with your Course Technology sales representative.

TEACHING**RESOURCE**PACKAGE

Just as *Succeeding with Technology* goes beyond computer literacy and fluency to provide students with the information they need to use technology to achieve success, we also take the teaching resource package to the next level. The teaching package that accompanies this textbook offers many options for enhancing the course and enriching a student's learning experience. The package includes an Instructor's Manual, solutions, Exam View, distance learning content, PowerPoint presentations, and figure files.

The Instructor's Manual

The Instructor's Manual provides materials to help instructors make their classes informative and interesting. The manual offers several approaches to teaching the material, with a sample syllabus and comments on different components. It also suggests alternative course outlines and ideas for projects. For each chapter, the manual includes a chapter outline, learning objectives, lecture notes (including discussion topics) and teaching tips.

Solutions

We provide instructors with solutions to all of the end-of-chapter questions and problems. Solutions may also be found on the Course Technology Web site at www.course.com. The solutions are password protected.

ExamView®

This objective-based test generator lets the instructor create paper, LAN, or Web-based tests from testbanks designed specifically for this Course Technology textbook. Instructors can use the QuickTest Wizard to create tests in fewer than five minutes by taking advantage of Course Technology's question banks—or create customized exams.

Distance Learning Content

Course Technology, the premiere innovator in management information systems publishing, is proud to present online courses in WebCT and Blackboard, as well as at MyCourse 2.0 to provide the most complete and dynamic learning experience possible.

- MyCourse 2.0. MyCourse 2.0 is a flexible, easy-to-use management tool that gives instructors true customization over the online components of their course. It allows them to personalize their course home page, schedule course activities and assignments, post messages, administer tests, and much more. MyCourse 2.0 is hosted by Thomson Learning, allowing for hassle-free maintenance and student access at all times.

- Blackboard and WebCT Level 1 Online Content. If you use Blackboard or WebCT, the test bank for this textbook is available at no cost in a simple, ready-to-use format. Go to www.course.com and search for this textbook to download the test bank.

- Blackboard and WebCT Level 2 Online Content. Blackboard Level 2 and WebCT Level 2 are also available. Level 2 offers course management and access to a Web site that is fully populated with content for this textbook. Students purchase the Blackboard User Guide (ISBN 0-7895-6165-4) or the WebCT User Guide (0-7895-6163-8). The User Guides include a password that allows student access to Level 2.

For more information on how to bring distance learning to your course, instructors should contact their Course Technology sales representative.

PowerPoint Presentations

Microsoft PowerPoint slides are included for each chapter. Instructors might use the slides in a variety of ways, including as teaching aids during classroom presentations or as printed handouts for classroom distribution. Instructors can add their own slides for additional topics introduced to the class.

Figure Files

Figure files allow instructors to create their own presentations using figures taken directly from the textbook.

ACKNOWLEDGMENTS

Developing the first edition of any book is a difficult undertaking. We would like to thank our teammates at Course Technology for their dedication and hard work. Special thanks to Barrie Tysko, Senior Product Manager, Alyssa Pratt, Product Manager, and Jennifer Locke, Executive Editor, and Mac Mendelson, Executive Editor. We would also like to thank Kristen Duerr, Senior Vice President and Publisher. We would like to acknowledge and thank Marilyn Freedman and Laurie Brown, our Developmental Editors. They deserve special recognition for their tireless effort and help in all stages of this project. Anne Valsangiacomo, our Production Editor, guided the book through the production process. Abby Reip, Rachel Lucas, and Amee Peterson helped with the photos and illustrations. We would also like to thank Robin Ireland, who researched and wrote the Tech Edge elements that appear in the margins of every chapter. Finally, we would like to thank Jennifer Schmidt, who created our glossary.

We greatly appreciate the perceptive feedback from all of our reviewers who worked so hard to assist us, beginning with the proposal, and continuing through the completion of the first drafts, including:

Jim P. Borden, Villanova University
Nichol W. Free, Computer Learning Network
Alla Grinberg, Montgomery College
Joan Lumpkin, Wright State University
Bill Littlefield, Indiana University—Kelley School of Business
DeLyse Totten, Portland Community College
Therese Viscelli, Georgia State University
Elizabeth Spooner, Holmes Community College
Amy B. Woszczynski, Kennesaw State University

Ralph Stair would like to thank the Department of Information and Management Sciences, College of Business Administration, at Florida State University for their support and encouragement. He would also like to thank his family, Lila and Leslie, for their support.

Ken Baldauf would like to thank the Computer Science department at Florida State University for their support of this project, and his family for their support and patience throughout the writing process.

We are committed to listening to our adopters and readers and to developing creative solutions to meet their needs. We strongly encourage your participation in helping us provide the freshest, most relevant information possible.

We welcome your input and feedback. If you have any questions or comments, please contact us through Course Technology or your local representative, via e-mail at mis@course.com, via the Internet at www.course.com, or address your comments, criticisms, suggestions, and ideas to:

Ralph Stair
Ken Baldauf
Course Technology
25 Thomson Place
Boston, MA 02210

THE**AUTHOR**TEAM

Succeeding with Technology brings together an experienced author team. Ralph Stair has spent about 20 years teaching introductory computer courses. While at Florida State University, he developed market-leading information systems textbooks (*Principles of Information Systems* and *Fundamentals of Information Systems*) that were among the first to bring important upper-level information systems content to the introductory computer course used primarily in business schools. These popular textbooks are used around the world. Ralph Stair enjoys listening to people who use his textbooks and developing the best textbooks possible. The success of these textbooks allowed him to retire early from Florida State University to devote more time to research and writing. *Succeeding with Technology* is an outgrowth of his devotion to showing students how they can succeed with technology.

Managing the instruction of over 5,000 computer literacy students annually, Ken Baldauf brings additional practical experience and insight to the project. With a background in computer science, Ken started out teaching computer programming, but early on developed an interest in the impact of computers on society. This interest led him to head the computer literacy program at Florida State University. He has been instrumental in guiding computer literacy standards for Florida State University students. For the past five years he has assumed full responsibility for both the general computer literacy class and an introductory computer class for business majors. He has recently added an advanced computer literacy class to the curriculum. Ken has written several Windows textbooks, assisted in the development of Course Technology's TOM product, and contributed to the most recent editions of Ralph Stair's other books. *Succeeding with Technology* is the result of his many years of experience guiding students through the technology maze.

Feature**Walk**Through

What do you want to do? Where do you want to go? This textbook will tell you and show you how to use technology to get there. Regardless of your personal interests or career aspirations, this textbook will help you succeed with technology. It will help you achieve your personal and professional goals.

If you are like most students today, you've had some contact with computers. Perhaps you've been using computers in labs and at home since your days in elementary school. Or perhaps you've only worked with the computers at your local public library. Perhaps you haven't actually used a computer to do much at all, but you've played with game consoles or arcade games, used a self-service checkout at the grocery store, used an automatic teller machine, or used telephone directory assistance. If so, you've had some contact with technology systems.

How to turn on a computer may be obvious. Whether a Windows or Macintosh, computers are made to be user friendly these days. So are most word processing, spreadsheet, and other basic applications. The real challenge lies in knowing what to do with the computer—or any technology, for that matter—once you've gone beyond the basics.

This textbook presents concepts that are essential to success in our technology-driven culture. By opening this book, you are about to experience technology and its usefulness in a unique way—one that relates to your personal and professional goals. You will see how individuals use computers to improve and enhance their lives at work in a variety of fields and at home. Some will be students like you, learning to use technology in ways you haven't thought of before. If you master the concepts and tools presented in this book, your life will be easier and your success at whatever you attempt will be more likely.

Some of this book's features that will help you master computer and technology system concepts include:

LEARNING**OBJECTIVES**/CHAPTER**CONTENT**

Learning objectives and contents show you exactly what subjects will be covered in each chapter. Read this before you dive in so that you know what to expect.

After completing Chapter 1, you will be able to:

LEARNING OBJECTIVES	CHAPTER CONTENT
1. Describe the use of computer systems.	Using Computers to Achieve Individual and Organizational Goals
2. Discuss how computers are used in a variety of fields, and why studying computer systems can benefit you professionally and personally.	Careers and Computers
3. Define basic computer concepts.	Computers and the Internet
4. Discuss the components of any computer system and how they are used.	Computer Systems and Their Use
5. Explain how computer systems and applications can be developed and controlled.	Computer Systems Development, Security, and Control

WhyStudyComputers?

Jane Roberts faced the same dilemma as many college freshman. She had no idea what major to pursue. Although she had discussed career alternatives with her high school counselor, family, and friends, she still had difficulty choosing a major. She excelled in courses that suggested different majors than those aligned with her current interests.

A fellow student told Jane about the career center at the university and the computer systems available for use there. Jane decided to check it out, and found much of the information she needed to choose a major. A career counselor showed Jane how she could use user-friendly computerized questionnaires to relate her aptitudes, interests, and work environment preferences to various careers.

Once Jane decided on a career in which she could succeed and find fulfillment given her aptitudes, interests, and preferences, it was easy for her to determine a college major. Her professors then were able to help her decide on specific courses and internships that would enable her to find a good job on graduation and begin a successful start in her chosen career.

Jane's experience with computers at the career center sparked her interest in computers in general. She asked her major professors how computers were used in her chosen field so she could learn more and give herself an added advantage when entering the job market.

1. How did using a computer system make choosing a career and major easier for Jane?
2. What additional information might Jane be able to obtain about using computers in pursuing her major and planning her career?
3. How can students use Jane's experience to help plan their own careers?

Check out Jane's *Action Plan* at the conclusion of this chapter.

Introduction

Why study computers? As you will see throughout this book, computers can help you achieve your personal and professional goals. You can use computers to obtain and play the latest music, keep track of your expenses and develop a monthly budget, and obtain information about almost any topic. Today, computers are used in all career areas from anthropology to zoology. Computers are indispensable in computer science, business, engineering, science, the arts, the military, and many other fields. In this book, you will see thousands of examples of how individuals and organizations have used computers to achieve their goals.

This book will introduce you to basic computer concepts that every student should know. To realize the vast potential of computer systems, you will learn the latest about hardware, software, and the Internet. You will also learn about telecommunications and network systems, databases, electronic commerce and transaction processing, and information and decision support systems. Important information on computer systems development, multimedia, and ethical and societal issues will show you how computer systems can be acquired, used, and controlled to maximize their potential. Throughout Chapter 1 you will see why it is so important to study computer systems and their use.

Technology360 discusses people like you who face problems that can be solved with the help of technology. You will learn how they solve their problems using the concepts presented in the chapter when you get to the end of the chapter.

The Chapter Introduction welcomes you to the chapter. Learn what is most important in each chapter before you start reading.

Job Technology Boxes. These boxes highlight the use of technology on the job. Most major disciplines or careers are explored. These boxes cover applications in computer science, business, library science, engineering, the arts, history, medicine, and many, many other areas.

Community Technology Boxes. Explore actual and potential problems related to the use of computer technology. Learn more about the darker side of computer systems and controversial topics that have no simple solutions.

The Tech Edge. These brief news-based items tip readers off to a broad range of the amazing things that are currently happening in our technology-driven culture.

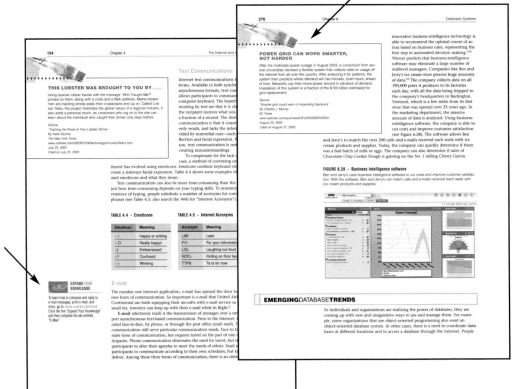

Expand Your Knowledge. These margin notes highlight opportunities to learn more about important topics through free access to 30 different "Expand Your Knowledge" Student Edition Labs. You can learn more about these labs on page xxii of the preface.

In addition to these special interest boxes, each chapter is loaded with fresh examples of individuals and organizations that have used technology to their benefit. On average, a chapter contains 20 to 40 current examples that explore a wide range of applications.

END-OF-CHAPTER**MATERIAL**

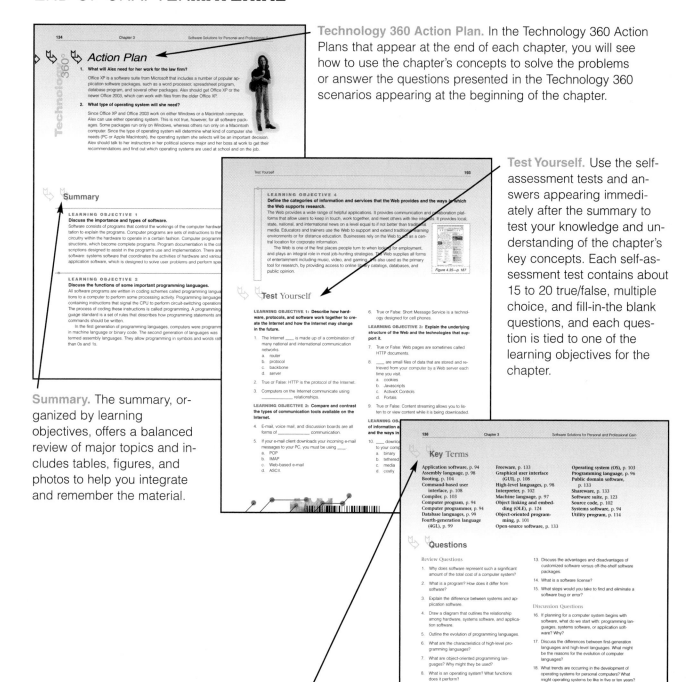

Technology 360 Action Plan. In the Technology 360 Action Plans that appear at the end of each chapter, you will see how to use the chapter's concepts to solve the problems or answer the questions presented in the Technology 360 scenarios appearing at the beginning of the chapter.

Test Yourself. Use the self-assessment tests and answers appearing immediately after the summary to test your knowledge and understanding of the chapter's key concepts. Each self-assessment test contains about 15 to 20 true/false, multiple choice, and fill-in-the blank questions, and each question is tied to one of the learning objectives for the chapter.

Summary. The summary, organized by learning objectives, offers a balanced review of major topics and includes tables, figures, and photos to help you integrate and remember the material.

Key Terms. The Key Terms list presents the most important technical terms used in the chapter. Each term is keyed to its location in the chapter.

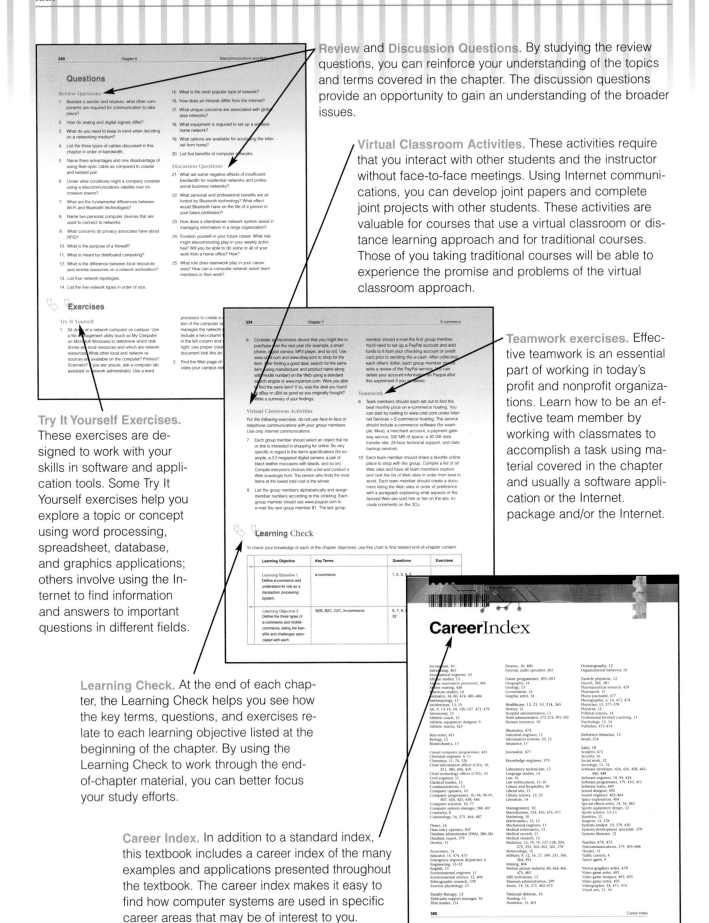

Review and **Discussion Questions.** By studying the review questions, you can reinforce your understanding of the topics and terms covered in the chapter. The discussion questions provide an opportunity to gain an understanding of the broader issues.

Virtual Classroom Activities. These activities require that you interact with other students and the instructor without face-to-face meetings. Using Internet communications, you can develop joint papers and complete joint projects with other students. These activities are valuable for courses that use a virtual classroom or distance learning approach and for traditional courses. Those of you taking traditional courses will be able to experience the promise and problems of the virtual classroom approach.

Teamwork exercises. Effective teamwork is an essential part of working in today's profit and nonprofit organizations. Learn how to be an effective team member by working with classmates to accomplish a task using material covered in the chapter and usually a software application or the Internet. package and/or the Internet.

Try It Yourself Exercises. These exercises are designed to work with your skills in software and application tools. Some Try It Yourself exercises help you explore a topic or concept using word processing, spreadsheet, database, and graphics applications; others involve using the Internet to find information and answers to important questions in different fields.

Learning Check. At the end of each chapter, the Learning Check helps you see how the key terms, questions, and exercises relate to each learning objective listed at the beginning of the chapter. By using the Learning Check to work through the end-of-chapter material, you can better focus your study efforts.

Career Index. In addition to a standard index, this textbook includes a career index of the many examples and applications presented throughout the textbook. The career index makes it easy to find how computer systems are used in specific career areas that may be of interest to you.

Tools**on**the**Web**

STUDENT**COMPANION**WEB**SITE**

We have created an exciting online companion for you to use as you work through this book, which will help you learn and practice new concepts every step of the way. This Web resource, which you can find at www.course.com/concepts/swt, includes the following features:

Useful Web Links

Access a repository of links to the home pages of the primary Web sites listed in each chapter of your book, for further research and exploration.

Practice Quizzes

Quizzes, created specifically for this site, allow you to test yourself on the content of each chapter and immediately see what answers you got right and wrong. For each question answered incorrectly, you are given the correct answer and the page in the textbook where that information is covered. Special testing software randomly compiles a selection of questions from a large database, so you can take each quiz multiple times with some new questions each time.

PowerPoint Slides

Get direct access to PowerPoint presentations that cover the key points from each chapter; a helpful study and review tool!

Computer Concepts Activity Center

Visit our concepts games activity center and play a number of fun games that help you absorb what you have learned in your course.

Interactive Key Terms

Each primary key term is listed with the definition hidden. View the term's definition by clicking that term. You can use these interactive terms as a study tool to test your technology vocabulary from each chapter.

Career Center

Many of you are searching now to learn about career possibilities for your future. Our Career Center helps you access information that will give you a chance to explore what you think you do and don't want to do, in technology-related fields and beyond! You will find a quick reference of the careers that are addressed in *Succeeding with Technology* and the pages of the book on which you can find those references. If one or more career possibilities catch your eye, you can read more about it in your book. Under general career headings, you will find links to interesting Web resources that pertain to the industry or career that interests you. This information can help you figure out what work you may want to do now or next.

Check out the site to see even more new tools beyond those listed here!

"Expand Your Knowledge" with Student Edition Labs

Your Student Companion Web site offers an additional exciting feature: free access to 30 different "Expand Your Knowledge" Student Edition Labs. Each lab enables you to learn real-world computer-based skills using activities in a simulated environment. If you are already familiar with some of the topics, use these labs to brush up on your skills.

Because different students learn in different ways, labs are built to give you the option to absorb concepts in a variety of ways—through reading, observation, step-by-step practice, and hands-on application.

In most chapters of your book, in the margins, you will see an element called "Expand Your Knowledge," which directs you to the Web site. Once you click the link on the Web site to the "Expand Your Knowledge" page, you can dive into the individual labs that pertain to the chapter that you are working on. Here is a table of contents, so that you know which labs are associated with which chapters:

Chapter	Lab	Chapter	Lab
1	Managing Files	7	E-Commerce
2	Using Input Devices Peripheral Devices Maintaining a Hard Drive Binary Numbers Understanding the Motherboard	8	
3	Using Windows Word Processing Spreadsheets Presentation Software Installing and Uninstalling Software Advanced Spreadsheets	9	Project Management
4	E-mail Creating Web Pages Connecting to the Internet Getting the Most out of the Internet Web Design Principles	10	Visual Programming
5	Networking Basics Wireless Networking	11	Working with Graphics Working with Audio Working with Video
6	Databases Backing up Your Computer Advanced Databases	12	Protecting your Privacy Online Keeping Your Computer Virus Free

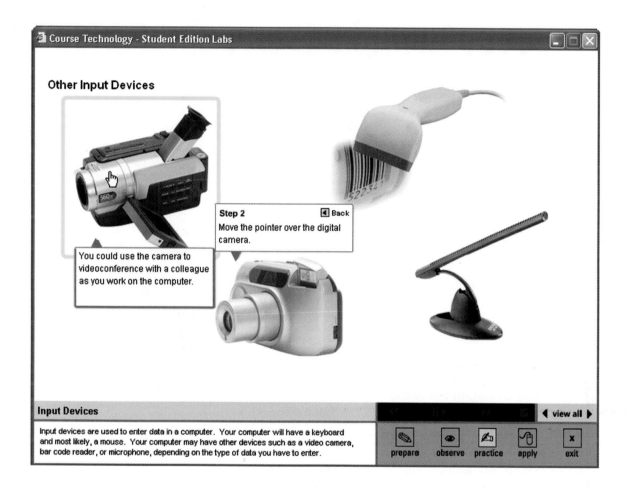

Course Technology - Student Edition Labs

Other Input Devices

Step 2 ◄ Back
Move the pointer over the digital camera.

You could use the camera to videoconference with a colleague as you work on the computer.

Input Devices ◄ view all ►

Input devices are used to enter data in a computer. Your computer will have a keyboard and most likely, a mouse. Your computer may have other devices such as a video camera, bar code reader, or microphone, depending on the type of data you have to enter.

prepare   observe   practice   apply   exit

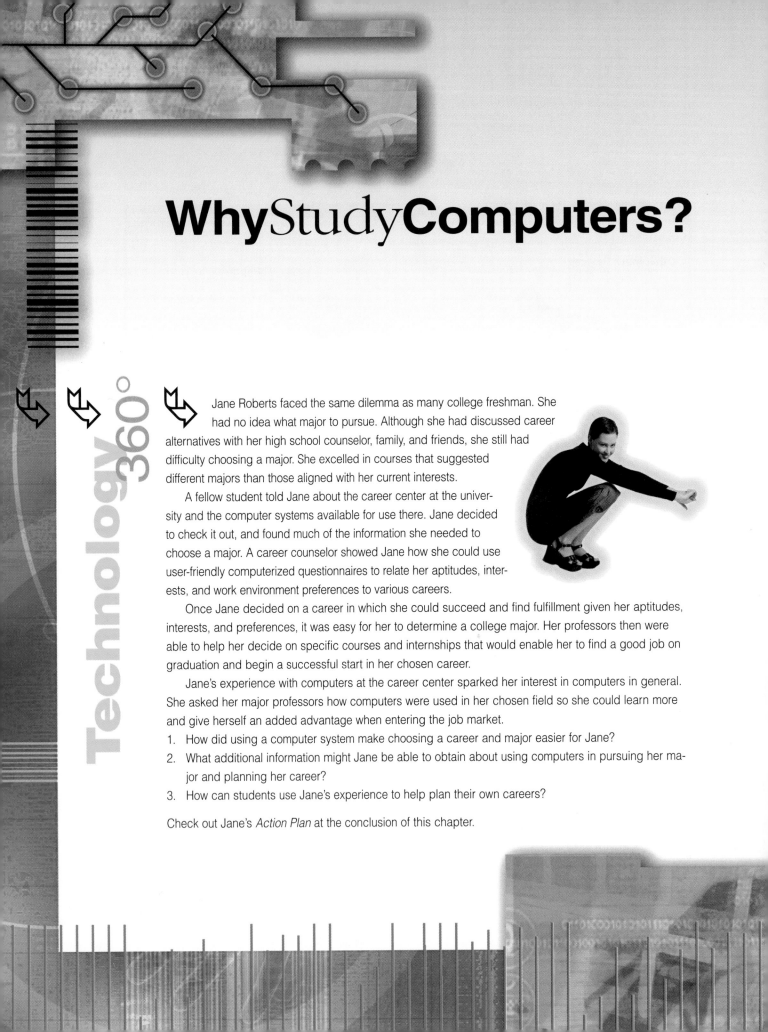

WhyStudy**Computers?**

Technology360°

Jane Roberts faced the same dilemma as many college freshman. She had no idea what major to pursue. Although she had discussed career alternatives with her high school counselor, family, and friends, she still had difficulty choosing a major. She excelled in courses that suggested different majors than those aligned with her current interests.

A fellow student told Jane about the career center at the university and the computer systems available for use there. Jane decided to check it out, and found much of the information she needed to choose a major. A career counselor showed Jane how she could use user-friendly computerized questionnaires to relate her aptitudes, interests, and work environment preferences to various careers.

Once Jane decided on a career in which she could succeed and find fulfillment given her aptitudes, interests, and preferences, it was easy for her to determine a college major. Her professors then were able to help her decide on specific courses and internships that would enable her to find a good job on graduation and begin a successful start in her chosen career.

Jane's experience with computers at the career center sparked her interest in computers in general. She asked her major professors how computers were used in her chosen field so she could learn more and give herself an added advantage when entering the job market.

1. How did using a computer system make choosing a career and major easier for Jane?
2. What additional information might Jane be able to obtain about using computers in pursuing her major and planning her career?
3. How can students use Jane's experience to help plan their own careers?

Check out Jane's *Action Plan* at the conclusion of this chapter.

After completing Chapter 1, you will be able to:

LEARNING OBJECTIVES	CHAPTER CONTENT
1. Describe the use of computer systems.	**Using Computers to Achieve Individual and Organizational Goals**
2. Discuss how computers are used in a variety of fields, and why studying computer systems can benefit you professionally and personally.	**Careers and Computers**
3. Define basic computer concepts.	**Computers and the Internet**
4. Discuss the components of any computer system and how they are used.	**Computer Systems and Their Use**
5. Explain how computer systems and applications can be developed and controlled.	**Computer Systems Development, Security, and Control**

Introduction

Why study computers? As you will see throughout this book, computers can help you achieve your personal and professional goals. You can use computers to obtain and play the latest music, keep track of your expenses and develop a monthly budget, and obtain information about almost any topic. Today, computers are used in all career areas from anthropology to zoology. Computers are indispensable in computer science, business, engineering, science, the arts, the military, and many other fields. In this book, you will see thousands of examples of how individuals and organizations have used computers to achieve their goals.

This book will introduce you to basic computer concepts that every student should know. To realize the vast potential of computer systems, you will learn the latest about hardware, software, and the Internet. You will also learn about telecommunications and network systems, databases, electronic commerce and transaction processing, and information and decision support systems. Important information on computer systems development, multimedia, and ethical and societal issues will show you how computer systems can be acquired, used, and controlled to maximize their potential. Throughout Chapter 1 you will see why it is so important to study computer systems and their use.

"A Generation Xer walks into his Baby Boomer Boss' office. 'What are all those books,' Generation Xer asks, pointing to a row of similar-looking volumes. 'The encyclopedia,' says the Baby Boomer Boss. 'Wow,' says the impressed Generation Xer. 'You mean somebody printed it out?'"[1] This anecdote by Joan Collier illustrates the extent to which computers have entered mainstream life. Although Baby Boomer bosses won't start retiring until 2011, most have been keeping up with technology. You will work for a boss who knows and expects you to know how to use computers within your field and industry.

On a daily basis, we all interact with **computers**—electronic devices used to perform calculations and other functions at high speed. Using computers to their full potential results in individuals with successful careers, organizations that reach their goals, and a society with a higher quality of life.

Today we live in an information economy. Systems based on computers are being used increasingly as a means to create, store, and transfer information. High-school students are using computers to acquire the latest music; investors are using computers to make multimillion-dollar decisions; financial institutions are employing them to transfer billions of dollars around the world electronically; and chemical engineers are using them to store and process information about chemical reaction rates to make stronger and lighter plastics. The University of California in San Diego is developing highway cameras integrated into a network of computers that can help direct traffic and save wasted fuel as a result (see Figure 1.1).[2] The new system produces traffic alerts to help commuters avoid congested areas. It is estimated that congested traffic and clogged roads can cost the largest cities billions of dollars in wasted fuel each year.

FIGURE 1.1 • Smart highways

In smart highways, computers, cameras, and networks are being used to reduce traffic congestion and save fuel.

Because computers have forever changed our society, our organizations, and our lives, we will present a framework for understanding computers and discuss why it is important to study them. This understanding will set the stage for future chapters of this text and will help you unlock the potential of computers to achieve individual and organizational goals.

USING COMPUTERS TO ACHIEVE INDIVIDUAL AND ORGANIZATIONAL GOALS

The different uses of computers are staggering. In almost every organization, from business to nonprofit charitable organizations, and in almost every career, computers have been used to achieve goals. But when you look closely at the functions

COMMUNITY /\/\/ TECHNOLOGY

Issues Box: Xylo, Inc. Creates Work/Life Solutions

As people become more involved with their careers, they often find it difficult to have enough time for a life outside their career. This is the work/life dilemma. College students experience this dilemma when they have to pass up an outing with friends to finish a class project due the next day. Working students have an even more complex dilemma because they have to balance school commitments, work commitments, and a personal life—the work/student/life dilemma. As we take on full-time careers and family responsibilities, the stakes in this balancing act become high.

Sometimes the way to resolve a dilemma involves letting people come up with their own creative solutions. If work is making it hard for employees to take care of even the basics of life, then maybe the solution is to help employees take care of those basic tasks while at work. The Web-based Xylo system helps organizations do just that. Xylo provides organizations with a custom designed, password-protected Web site tailored to fit the organization's objectives, culture, and values. The Web site offers employees direct access to a wide variety of relevant work/life information. It also includes a link to the organization's intranet for access from any computer with an Internet connection. The Web site is organized into three areas:

1. **Co-worker Connection.** Join a Company Team or Interest Group, Post a Classified Ad, and Join a Carpool
2. **My Company.** Company News, Company Links, Employee Birthdays, Suggestion Box, and Online Surveys
3. **Discounts & Services.** The Mall, Travel, Entertainment, Financial Matters, Healthy Living, and Family Matters

Some might argue that allowing employees to shop online during work hours is distracting and counterproductive. But, in the new work environment, many employers are finding that when they take an active role in helping employees handle work/life issues, employees become more content and the whole company benefits. Work/life solutions such as Xylo's exploit the benefits of modern-day telecommunications to build community, commitment, and contentment in the workforce.

Questions

1. What types of features would you like to see offered by Xylo or a similar service?
2. What types of industry would benefit most from a work/life solution such as Xylo's? Is there any type of business in which this solution might be inappropriate?
3. Are we moving to a point where we no longer differentiate between a professional life and personal life? Are there any hazards in doing so?

Sources
1. *"EDS Selects Xylo's Web-based Work/Life Solution,"* Business Wire, *November 6, 2001.*
2. *"Majority of Americans Find Work Meaningful and Purposeful,"* Business Wire, *www.xylo.com, October 30, 2001.*

performed by computers, you will see that all computers perform the same input, processing, output, and feedback functions. These functions help produce valuable information to help people improve productivity and quality and to help organizations achieve a competitive advantage.

Functions Performed by a Computer

A computer is used to collect (input), manipulate and store (process), disseminate (output) data and information, and provide a feedback mechanism (see Figure 1.2). These are the functions of any computer.

FIGURE 1.2 • The functions of a computer

A computer is used to input, process, and output data and information. Feedback is critical to the successful operation of a computer.

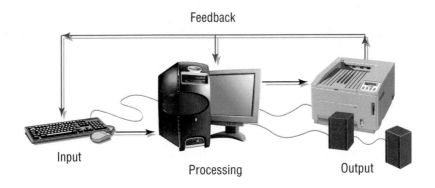

Feedback

Input

Processing

Output

Input.   *Input* can take many forms. In a 911 emergency response system, an incoming call would be considered an input. The output from a 911 emergency call could be a police car or ambulance dispatched to a specific location. In a computer designed to produce paychecks, employee time cards might be the initial input. Regardless of the system involved, the type of input is determined by the desired output of the system.

Processing.   In a computer, *processing* involves converting or transforming data into useful outputs. Processing can involve performing calculations, making comparisons and taking alternative actions, and storing data for future use. In the payroll example, hours worked for each employee must be converted into net pay. The required processing can first involve multiplying hours worked times the employee's hourly pay rate to get gross pay. If weekly hours worked are greater than 40 hours, overtime pay may also be determined. Then deductions are subtracted from gross pay to get net pay. For instance, federal and state taxes can be withheld or subtracted from gross pay; many employees have health and life insurance, savings plans, and other deductions that must also be subtracted from gross pay to arrive at net pay. In the 911 emergency call example, the incoming call can be converted into a specific address and the directions to get to that address.

Output.   In a computer, *output* involves producing useful information, usually in the form of documents, reports, and data for other applications. Outputs can include beautiful digital artwork, paychecks for employees, medical reports for doctors, weather forecasts, and music from a recording studio. Sometimes, output from one system can be used as input to control other systems or devices. For instance, output from a computerized fabrication system can cause one or more welding machines to make precision welds. Output can be produced in a variety of ways. For a computer, printers and display screens are common output devices.

Feedback.   In a computer, *feedback* is output that is used to make adjustments or changes to input or processing activities. Errors or problems might cause input data to need to be corrected or a process to be changed. A photographer, for example, might use software to place a photo of a beautiful sunset behind a picture of a sailboat. An error in combining the photographs might result in the sunset being inserted on top of the sailboat instead of in the background. This error can be corrected by changing how the photos are combined. Consider another example. Suppose that a restaurant hires a student to wait tables. At the end of the week, the number of hours worked is entered into a computer as 400 instead of 40 hours. Fortunately, most computers can check to make sure that data falls within certain predetermined ranges. For hours worked, the range might be from 0 to 100 hours. It is unlikely that an employee would work more than 100 hours for any given week. In this case, the computer would determine that 400 hours is out of range and provide feedback, such as an error report. The feedback is used to check and correct the input on the number of hours worked to 40. If undetected, this error would result in a very high net pay being printed on the paycheck! This type of valuable information can be critical, but how is valuable information generated and used?

Producing Valuable Information

Computers convert raw data into valuable information and other useful outputs. **Data** consist of raw facts, such as an employee's name and the number of hours he or she worked in a week, weather measurements from buoys deep in the Gulf of Mexico, the leading economic indicators for the last several months, inventory part numbers, and sales orders. As shown in Table 1.1, several types of data can be used to represent these facts. When these facts are organized or arranged in a meaningful manner they become information. **Information** is a collection of facts organized in such a way that they have additional value beyond the value of the facts themselves.

To be valuable to people and organizations, information should have the characteristics described in Table 1.2. If information is not accurate or complete, people and organizations can make poor decisions. If an inaccurate forecast of future demand in the job market indicates that demand for particular workers will be very high when the opposite is true, a student might prepare for a career that offers few job opportunities upon graduation. Furthermore, information that is not pertinent to the situation, is not delivered

TABLE 1.1 • Types of Data

Type	Description
Alphanumeric data	Numbers, letters, and other characters
Image data	Graphical images or pictures
Audio data	Sound, noise, or tones
Video data	Moving images or pictures

TABLE 1.2 • The Characteristics of Valuable Information.

Characteristics	Definitions
Accurate	Accurate information is error free. In some cases, inaccurate information is generated because inaccurate data is fed into the system. This is commonly called garbage in, garbage out (GIGO).
Complete	Complete information contains all of the important facts. For example, an investment report that does not include all important costs is not complete.
Economical	Information should be relatively economical to produce. Decision makers must always balance the value of information with the cost of producing it.
Flexible	Flexible information can be used for a variety of purposes. For example, information on how much inventory is on hand for a particular part can be used by a sales representative in closing a sale, by a production manager to determine if more inventory is needed, and by a financial executive to determine the total value the company has invested in inventory.
Reliable	Reliable information can be depended on. In many cases, the reliability of the information depends on the reliability of the data collection method. In other instances, reliability depends on the source of the information. A rumor that a politician might run for office may not be reliable.
Relevant	Relevant information is important to the decision maker. Information that one library had a record number of new Internet users may not be relevant to another library.
Simple	Information should be simple, not overly complex. Sophisticated and detailed information may not be needed. In fact, too much information can cause information overload, whereby a decision maker has too much information and is unable to determine what is really important.
Timely	Timely information is delivered when it is needed. Knowing last week's weather conditions will not help when trying to decide what coat to wear today.
Verifiable	Information should be verifiable. This means that you can check it to make sure it is correct, perhaps by checking many sources for the same information.

to decision makers in a timely fashion, or is too complex to understand may be of little value to an organization.

Productivity, Quality, and Competitive Advantage

Individuals and organizations use information to support their goals. This can increase productivity, enhance quality, and give an organization a competitive advantage. Universities often strive to increase the quality of their degree programs by making sure their courses are up to date and reflect the latest ideas and practices.

Productivity.   Developing computers that measure and control productivity is a key element for most organizations (see Figure 1.3). *Productivity* is a measure of the output achieved divided by the input required. A higher level of output for a given level of input means greater productivity; a lower level of output for a given level of input means lower productivity. Consider a counseling organization, where counseling productivity can be measured by the number of hours employees spent with clients divided by the total hours employees were paid for. For example, out of a 40-hour week, the typical employee may have spent 35 hours with clients. The counseling productivity is thus equal to 35/40, or .875. With administrative and other duties, a productivity level of .875 may be excellent. The numbers assigned to productivity levels are not always based on quantity; productivity may be based on factors such as quality or time. In either case, what is important is not the value of the productivity number, but how it compares to other time periods, settings, and organizations. A student might be able to increase his or her productivity in studying the day before a final exam from 6 hours (Productivity = 6 hours/24 hours or 25%) to 10 hours (Productivity = 10 hours/24 hours or 42%) by spending less time watching TV or talking to friends.

Once a basic level of productivity is measured, a computer can monitor and compare productivity levels over time to see if productivity is increasing. Then, corrective action can be taken if productivity drops below certain levels. In addition to measuring productivity, a computer can also be used within a process to significantly increase productivity.

FIGURE 1.3 • Using computers to increase productivity
By using computers, doctors can increase their productivity. In some cases, they are able to accomplish tasks with the help of computers that they would otherwise be unable to do.

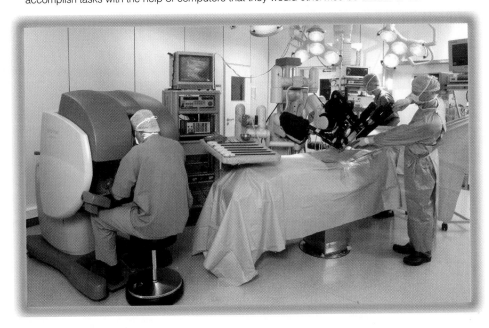

Quality. Low-quality products can turn organizations that once were the leaders in their field into laggards because of a perceived lack of quality. Without question, quality has been and will continue to be an important factor for all organizations.

The term quality has evolved over the years. In the early years of quality control, quality was concerned with meeting design specifications, that is, conformance to standards. An essay that followed all the rules of grammar might be considered high quality using this approach. If a product or service conformed to the designed or specified rules, such as the rules of grammar, it was considered high quality. However, a product or service can perform its intended function and still not satisfy customers' needs or be high quality. Today, *quality* means the ability of a product, including services, to meet or exceed customer expectations. This view of quality is totally customer oriented. A high-quality product will satisfy customers by functioning correctly and reliably, meeting needs and expectations, and by being delivered on time with courtesy and respect.

Competitive Advantage. A *competitive advantage* is a significant and long-term benefit. For an athlete, a competitive advantage might be obtained using a computer to analyze technique and training methods. For the military, a competitive advantage often results in a victory on the battlefield. For a nonprofit organization, the strategies for competitive advantage can result in reaching goals, such as better service or more outreach to society. For an artist or a professional photographer, a competitive advantage could be a new approach that is recognized for years or decades into the future.

Although it can be difficult to develop computers to provide a competitive advantage, a number of organizations have done so with success. A classic example is Sabre, a sophisticated computerized reservation system installed by American Airlines and one of the first computer systems recognized for providing competitive advantage. Travel agents used this system for rapid access to flight information, offering travelers reservations, seat assignments, and ticketing. Notice that the travel agents achieved an efficiency benefit from the Sabre system. Because Sabre displayed American Airline flights whenever possible, it also gave American Airlines a long-term, significant competitive advantage. With the Internet and free travel services, it can be difficult for travel companies to maintain a competitive advantage. Today, many people make their own travel arrangements through the Internet on sites such as www.travelocity.com.

CAREERSANDCOMPUTERS

Why study the use of computers in various fields? Regardless of what you study in school or what jobs you hold during your professional life, it is likely that computers will play a very important role in your success. Furthermore, you will find that the use of computers in one industry or field can be directly applied to other areas. Did you know that the same technology used to design downhill ski bindings was also used to develop the first clip-in bicycle pedals that are used today by all competitive bicycle riders? The same technology used to develop the posture of a downhill ski racer's position to cut through the wind was used to design and develop aerodynamic bicycle handlebars used in all triathlons today. As you read about the use of computers in various fields in this section and throughout the book, think of how you can use these examples to help you achieve your personal goals and career aspirations. You will find that an example of how computers are used in one field can be directly used in other fields.

Of course, it would be impossible to cover every career. In this section, we will give you a sampling of what is possible. We begin with the obvious: computer science.

Computer Science

Computer scientists design and build hardware, software, database systems, telecommunications, and Internet systems. Software engineers, for example, design and develop new programming applications. Of course, computer scientists use computers to help with the design process. Computer scientists are also responsible for conducting state-of-the-art research into topics such as artificial intelligence, robotic reasoning, electrical circuits, and fuzzy logic that could profoundly change our lives in the future.

Inside the computer industry, computer professionals work in areas such as design, manufacturing, sales, and services, often with a specific major product line. From a wide array of products, computer-systems professionals may choose to specialize in equipment designed for use within certain areas such as networks and telecommunications, multimedia systems, expert systems, or imaging technology. Others may choose to work in certain industry segments such as education, manufacturing, business, laboratories, engineering, and many other areas.

Computer personnel typically work in a computer department that employs a chief information officer (CIO), computer programmers, systems analysts, computer operators, and a number of other computer personnel. Computer personnel have a variety of job titles and responsibilities. The chief technology officer (CTO), for example, typically works under a CIO and specializes in hardware and related equipment and technology.[3] According to John Voeller, a CTO for the Black & Veatch engineering and construction company, "I don't just look at the technology of my enterprise. I look far beyond information technology at nanotechnologies, biotech, and other domains." In addition to technical skills, computer personnel also need skills in written and verbal communication, an understanding of organizations and how they operate, and the ability to work with people (users). The increased networking of PCs and availability of user-friendly software have created a need for end-user support specialists to work closely with users in getting the most from computers. In general, computer personnel are charged with maintaining the broadest enterprise-wide perspective.

Business

A variety of career opportunities exist in business, including management, marketing, accounting, finance, organizational behavior, human resources, leisure and hospitality, and information systems. All of these areas rely on computers to provide timely and accurate information to help business executives make decisions to increase profits or reduce costs. Computers are essential in producing business documents and reports, including payroll checks, inventory reports, tax documents, and many others. Many business schools have majors in management information systems to train future computer managers, such as the chief information officer.

Business organizations use computers for numerous functions. Computers are used by finance and accounting professionals to forecast revenues and business activities, determine sources and uses of funds, analyze investments, and perform audits. Sales and marketing departments use systems to develop new products, select production and distribution facilities, determine how to best promote products, and set prices. In manufacturing, computers are used to process orders, schedule production, control inventory levels, and monitor quality.

Computers have empowered employees in almost every career area. U.S. Microbics, Inc., an environmental solutions provider named one of the best companies to work for in San Diego, uses employee empowerment to focus on customer service.[4] The company has an employee profit sharing program and a belief that "none of us is as smart as all of us."

Computers allow people to work virtually anywhere at any time.[5] Bob Long, a field-sales support manager for Dow Chemical Company in Midland, Michigan, only spends about 10 percent of his time at his office. The rest of his time is spent on the move in airports, hotels, and cars, visiting customers and other sales representatives. Long even works from his 24-foot fishing boat, *Outcast*. He uses mobile computing systems and connections to the Internet to allow him flexibility and mobility.

Insurance

James D. Lester, III, senior vice president and chief information officer of a large insurance company has worked in the insurance industry for more than 20 years, after spending 35 years working in computer technology. Of the million and a half insurance applications that come in each year, 85 percent come in electronically, and 54 percent of those are processed and issued electronically in 24 hours using SmartApp software.[6] Insurance fraud and vehicle theft are no longer perpetrated primarily by small-time crooks but by organized crime rings using computers to falsify claim receipts, ship stolen vehicles throughout the world, and commit identity theft and fraud. The National Insurance Crime Bureau, a nonprofit organization supported by roughly 1,000 property and casualty insurance companies, uses computers to join forces with special investigations units and law enforcement agencies as well as to conduct online fraud-fighting training to investigate and prevent these types of crimes.[7]

Engineering

Engineering careers include aeronautical, mechanical, electrical, chemical, civil, industrial, and environmental engineering. Engineers use computers in design and operations (see Figure 1.4). In chemical engineering, for example, engineers use computers to design petroleum refinery operations to produce a variety of gasoline and diesel fuels using minimal energy requirements. Computers are also used to monitor and control petroleum refinery operations to make sure that sophisticated refinery towers and systems are efficiently and safely operating. Some universities use computers to design new aircraft and space vehicles. Computers

FIGURE 1.4 • Engineering design
The design of bridges and highways is enhanced through the use of computers.

are also used to make complex thermodynamics, power consumption, circuits and signal, and reactor design calculations, to name a few applications.

Library Science and Information Systems

Library science uses computers to quickly and accurately search and retrieve information. You can seek out information such as tables of statistics and documents at thousands of libraries, universities, government agencies, or large corporations. The Library of Congress Online Catalog is a database of approximately 12 million records about materials from the library's vast collection. Systems librarians work in public and academic libraries and are responsible for implementing and supporting library automation systems. They create digital library collections using tools such as servers, software, databases, protocols, and standards for Web-based systems.[8] Virtual reference services through e-mail, messaging, and video conferencing are having an impact on how librarians serve their patrons and on the design of libraries. Libraries of the future may have hands-on classrooms to teach users how to locate library resources and multimedia auditoriums. The Jean & Charles Schulz Information Center at Sonoma State University houses an automated retrieval system through which user requests are relayed by computer to an automatic crane, which locates materials and delivers them to a pickup station.[9] Librarians use computers to understand the needs of their patrons.[10] The role of librarian has been altered by the amazing use of computers.

Science and Mathematics

Chemistry, biology, mathematics, statistics, astronomy, physics, meteorology, environmental sciences, oceanography, sports science, and military science are just a few fields in science. Computers are used in all aspects of science. Dr. Charles Lieber, a Harvard University professor, is experimenting with nanoelectronics, a field that is a blend of chemistry and computer science.[11] His research is developing electronics and wires, as thin as four-atoms wide, which could change how computers work. Nanoelectronics is a subset of a larger field called nanotechnology that includes items that also operate at the atomic or molecular levels. New technologies that come out of these fields could cut resistance in wires and speed up chip operations.

Stephen Wolfram, the extraordinary particle physicist, started a company to sell Mathematica, a computation program that he wrote in the 1980s. His recent work in Cellular Automata (CA), mathematical systems in which patterns on grids are changed by successive applications of rules of transformation, explains how everything in the universe, including the workings of the human brain, may very well result from the application of simple rules. Although hard to understand, Wolfram's work takes the use of the computer to new highs.[12]

Brian Greene is a pioneer in string theory, which attempts to explain both large-scale physics and the physics of subatomic particles, in which a particle's location in space is not certain at any point in time, but is based on mathematical probability instead. Computers are used to analyze string theory equations.[13]

Advanced machines and computers have enabled medical research scientists to use protein sequencers and synthesizers to map the entire human genome.[14] Scientists have used computers to advance our knowledge so rapidly that we have a hard time keeping up. New technology moves us from theory to truth in every area of our lives.

Sports and Exercise

Computers have been used in all aspects of sports and exercise (see Figure 1.5). National Football League teams, for example, use computers to provide instant feed-

FIGURE 1.5 • **Computers in sports**

Subtle details, easily detected by the computer, aid coaches, medical personnel, and sports equipment companies in achieving their unique goals.

back. Computers are programmed to diagram and analyze offensive and defensive plays of teams and their opponents. The computer analyzes an opposing team's play from the past few games and predicts what the opponent will do in specific situations. The computer has also been used to design football equipment that reduces the chance of permanent paralysis or brain damage to players by analyzing films during which an injury takes place and producing graphs showing the force in pounds absorbed at points of the player's body at certain moments in time. Yet another use of the computer in sports is biomechanics, a familiar concept in Russian and East German athletics since the early 1960s. It has been used in the United States as well to coach its Olympic athletes. A computer programmed to watch athletes draws attention to factors too subtle to be detected by the human coach and shows athletes how to improve their techniques.

Medicine and Healthcare

Careers in medicine and healthcare include nursing, nutrition, exercise physiology, social work, psychology, family therapy, and medicine. Medical records and reports to hospital administrators, insurance companies, and government agencies are all produced by computers. Medical informatics, for example, is an area of medicine involved with storing medical records in a digital format on a national database. Computerized physician order entry (CPOE) enables physicians to place orders on the computer and notify nurses, laboratory technicians, pharmacists, clerks in accounting and anyone else involved immediately when the order is entered. When integrated with patient monitors and electronic messaging, physicians can receive and send messages and orders via e-mail.[15]

Some medical computers help doctors diagnose diseases and prescribe treatments. Specialized medical expert systems, software that is programmed to act like a team of expert doctors, can convert a patient's symptoms and problems into likely diseases, and include an estimate of the chances that the patient has each disease. Some medical expert systems also have the ability to suggest treatment options. In some cases, expert systems software explores possible diseases and treatments that might have been overlooked by even the best doctor.

Magnetic resonance imaging (MRI) machines are used in most hospitals today. Surgeons use the three-dimensional images produced by computer graphics to help them operate. They also use software to locate and remove some of the causes of seizures. Tests that detect cancer or measure chemical levels are performed using microchip-loaded probes that are threaded into the body via a catheter. Electronic sensors detect chemical changes in the lens of the eye that precede cataracts; this new treatment enables the use of drug intervention that may eliminate surgery. Specialists use video linkups to communicate treatment to emergency medical technicians. Dentists use intraoral video cameras to record and project images that are then logged as digital files into a database. The possibilities for the use of computers in medicine are endless.

The Arts

The use of computers in the arts surprises many people. Areas in fine and liberal arts appear to be beyond the use of computers. But this is not the case. History, English, anthropology, film studies, visual arts, geology, sociology, theater, mathematics, African studies, art history, Asian studies, classical studies, communications,

CAMERA, ACTION, PRESS SAVE

Directors of the movies *Shrek, Lord of the Rings,* and *The Lion, the Witch and the Wardrobe,* all used computers to create 3-D, animated storyboards to sell their scripts. Artists mapped out terrain, designed characters, and choreographed camera shots and scenes—all on disk. The storyboards also reduce filming time, which at $5,500 to 7,000 per hour, saves money, too.

Source:
"What's a Movie Before It's a Movie?"
By P.J. Huffstutter, Times Staff Writer
The Los Angeles Times
www.latimes.com/business/la-fi-previz6jul06,1,2523720.
story?coll=la-utilities-technology
July 6, 2003
Cited on July 21, 2003

American studies, language studies, literature, political science, dance, photography, and music all benefit from computers.

Computers have been widely used for producing art, music, and special effects in films such as *A.I.* and *Monsters, Inc.,* digital photography, and the ever-popular video games. Computers make it possible to film a scene, change it within the computer, and scan the altered images back onto a file to create an image undetectable by the human eye. Dinosaurs in the *Jurassic Park* films frightened audiences, while the heroine in *Final Fantasy* thrilled them because of the imagination of the computer professionals who created them.

Social Sciences

The social sciences include economics, geography, psychology, political science, sociology, and urban planning. In economics, computers are used to determine leading economic indicators, the Consumer Price Index used to monitor inflation, and a number of other indicators to monitor and control our economy. In geography, computers are used to map geographic areas. Police departments, emergency response teams, and the military use specialized geographic information systems (GISs) to precisely locate people and positions. In political science, computers are used in a wide variety of areas. The results of political surveys and polls are reported in the popular news almost daily. Computers are used in public elections. For example, Anieres, Switzerland uses computers and the Internet to allow its citizens to vote in local elections and referendums. Anieres, which is a suburb of Geneva, was the first city in Switzerland to use the Internet in a public, binding vote.[16] In the United States, online voting was used in the 2000 Arizona state Democratic primary, thought to be the first binding online election (see Figure 1.6).[17]

FIGURE 1.6 • Online voting in the 2000 Democratic primary
Kelsey A. Begaye, president of the Navajo Nation, used a laptop computer to cast an electronic ballot in the Arizona Democratic primary.

Education

Many companies, such as FedEx, are joining with colleges and universities to help prepare students for careers.[18] FedEx has opened a $23 million four-story facility, called the FedEx Technology Institute, in Memphis, Tennessee. Jim Phillips, chairman of the institute, hopes the new facility will show "mind-blowing" technologies and applications to college students and instructors. The institute is part of the University of Memphis and has the following programs: Center for Managing Emerging Technology, Center for Supply Chain Management, Center for Multimedia Arts, Center for Digital Economic and Regional Development, Center for Spatial Analysis, Center for Artificial Intelligence, Center for Life Sciences, and the Center for NG Transportation, Advanced Learning Center, and IT Research.

ClassLink Technologies, a high-tech start-up company in business for 5 years turned a profit last year selling computers to school districts. The company can link older computers, new computers, and home computers owned by students and teachers for sharing information and monitoring work. ClassLink technicians have installed systems in 30 districts throughout New Jersey, New York, Connecticut, and Pennsylvania reaching about 65,000 users.[19] High-school students with access to computers develop amazing skills quickly. For example, when a computer virus spread throughout a Massachusetts school system, infecting more than 700 computers, it was a group of high-school juniors who solved the problem and implemented the solution enabling the schools to get back to work.[20]

Using computers, students can earn college degrees from home by connecting to university resources, teachers, and other students through the Internet.[21] According to one student, "It's not for everyone, for sure. Some people need more interaction or to be right there with the teacher. There were times I felt like a hermit." For thousands of rural and urban high-school students in India, e-training introduces Web sites on history, math, news, entertainment, maps, and other areas.[22]

Architecture

Architecture uses all aspects of creativity, technical innovations, and cultural investigations in designing and constructing buildings, other structures, and surrounding areas, including landscaping. Architects often use computer-assisted design (CAD) and graphics software to develop, capture, and communicate architectural designs ideas (see Figure 1.7). Three-dimensional design software can be used to display design ideas with a high degree of realism. This technology allows owners and decision makers to take a computer-generated tour of buildings and the surrounding landscaping. CAD that enables architects and engineers to build projects digitally has added a fourth dimension—scheduling software. The new 4-D CAD tools are especially useful in the design and construction of complex projects allowing users to link 3-D building components with a computer-generated work schedule, resulting in savings in time and cost.[23]

FIGURE 1.7 • Computers in architecture
Computer-assisted design (CAD) software gives architects the ability to create and present architectural ideas with a high degree of realism.

Law Enforcement

Computers are used throughout law enforcement. Computers provide crime fighters with invaluable information on criminals, stolen vehicles, and missing persons. The Missing Child Act authorized the creation of a database to help local and state law enforcement authorities locate and identify the millions of children reported missing each year. The creation of a database of unidentified dead bodies has helped eliminate the uselessness of a family spending its life savings to search for a missing child whose body had already turned up in another state. Instead of a polygraph, computers can be used to "read" a voice, to detect the stress produced by lying, and to produce a voiceprint, which is as unique as fingerprints. Computers can be used to capture facial thermograms (systems of blood vessels), which, like fingerprints, are distinct and unique in each individual, and can be read using an infrared camera, a computer, and a database.

Dan Quealy, head of Ernst and Young's security and information technology practice in Dublin, and his team search through a company's computer files, documents, and e-mails to match potential criminals to crimes and produce proof for convictions in such cases as sexual harassment, pornography, computer fraud, and industrial espionage. Philip Curran, an investigator for Business Software Alliance (BSA) specializing in software piracy, helps track down crime syndicates who steal more than one-third of the software used in Western Europe.[24] Detective inspector Rick Adderly of West Midlands Police in the United Kingdom uses software to analyze high-volume crimes and identify burglars most likely to have committed them with up to 80 percent accuracy.[25]

Law

Computer technology is improving legal practice in two major areas. In one area, computers provide information on a firm's attorneys and staff, clients, billing, customer relationship management, and news items. iManage developed WorkSite to provide document management as well as collaboration with others using an intranet and the Internet. WorkSite presents relevant information on each client such as word-processing documents, e-mail, billing information, and images, in a single view accessible to everyone on the team. Computers are also used in the courtroom for evidence presentation and courtroom communications. Support services such as document imaging and management, graphics and animation for litigation, and electronic evidence management are all possible using the computer.[26]

The Government and the Military

Since the 1950s, computers have been used in compiling the census. Massive databases are part of most of the government's operations, such as the Internal Revenue Service. Pentagon activities, including security and nuclear defense, depend on computers. The space program would still be in the realm of science fiction without computers. The use of computers is important in every branch of the armed services including the Army, Navy, Air Force, Marines, and Coast Guard. Programs in military science, national defense, criminology, and law enforcement exist at many colleges and universities, and provide a variety of career opportunities.

As seen in the preceding sections, computers are used in almost every industry and field. The following sections introduce the computers and computer systems that are used in these industries and fields. This knowledge will help you understand the potential and scope of computers in today's world.

COMPUTERSANDTHEINTERNET

As mentioned earlier, a *computer* is an electronic device used to perform calculations and other functions at high speed. Computers, first developed in the early and mid-1900s, have two primary advantages over humans: speed and accuracy. Computers have the ability to make millions of calculations per second, whereas it can take human beings seconds to make just one calculation. In addition, computers can be highly accurate. If programmed correctly, they can continuously make calculations and comparisons without making a single mistake. Even the most careful human being will make an occasional mistake.

Hardware

Hardware includes all of the computer equipment used to input raw data, process it into something meaningful, and output the results. Computer hardware includes processing, storage, input, and output devices.

Processing and Storage. Processing devices include the central processing unit (see Figure 1.8), memory, and storage. Many of these components are placed on the *motherboard*, also called the *system board*, which is the main circuit board in the computer. Processing and storage devices are usually placed in a box, called the system unit, that houses and protects the processing and storage devices inside.

How fast a computer processes data and information depends on the speed of the central processing unit, and central processing unit speed is particularly important in processing video images.[27] Lifelike images of characters such as Gollum in the *Lord of the Rings* shows what is possible. An image-rendering technique is used by award-winning companies such as Mental Images of Germany and Pixar of the United States. The technology is also used to help design cars, such as those of Mercedes Benz.

One or more memory devices are needed to temporarily hold programs and data required by the CPU (see Figure 1.9). Memory, also called primary storage, is *volatile* storage because a loss of power to the computer means that the contents of memory is also lost or eliminated. Memory for the CPU is like a person's desk that holds only the current work or what is currently being processed.

A computer system also needs one or more larger storage devices that permanently hold programs and data. This type of storage is often called *secondary storage*. Permanent, or secondary, storage is *nonvolatile,* which means that you don't lose data and programs with a loss of power. Permanent storage devices are like a person's filing cabinets in an office or at home. Similarly to filing cabinets, permanent storage devices hold programs and data, whether or not the programs and data are currently being processed.

There are many different types of permanent storage devices, but the most common is the computer's hard disk. Computers can also use floppy disks; magnetic tape; high capacity disks that work with removable drives, such as a Zip drive; computer CDs (compact discs); or DVDs (digital video discs) (see Figure 1.10). To help prevent the unauthorized use and copying of movies, there is even an experimental self-destructing movie DVD with a built-in time limit that ranges from 8 to 60 hours. The movie stored on the DVD can only be viewed for a certain time after the DVD has been opened. After the time limit, the DVD turns a purple color and its contents are no longer available for viewing. One DVD contains the following warning, "Once you remove the DVD from its packaging, you only have 36 hours to watch it."

FIGURE 1.8 • Central processing unit

Faster processing speeds mean more sophisticated computing. This Intel® Pentium® 4 processor is fast enough to manipulate audio and video files, search large medical databases for research results, and process insurance claims for an insurance company. It is capable of carrying out over 9 billion instructions per second.

FIGURE 1.9 • Memory

Memory devices, such as this chip, store programs and data used by the central processing unit.

FIGURE 1.10 • Storage devices

Storage devices such as the hard disk, tape, CDs, and DVDs are used to permanently store data.

Input and Output Devices. Like in and out baskets for a person, input and output devices for a computer system are used to collect raw data and get it into the computer and to generate output and make it usable for people.

There are literally hundreds of different input devices. The most common ones are a *keyboard* and a *mouse* (see Figure 1.11). Input devices also include automatic scanning devices, equipment that can read magnetic ink characters on checks and other financial documents, joysticks, touch screens, microphones, and many other devices. The Scripps Institution of Oceanography, for example, developed a special underwater computer optical mouse to allow a diver as deep as 100 feet to control an underwater camera, which was normally controlled by a computer system and mouse on the surface.[28] The camera is used to record changes in the color of coral reefs with rising water temperatures. The mouse is the size of a brick and is made of plexiglass. The mouse pad is a piece of paper covered with plastic.

There are also hundreds of different types of output devices. The most common ones are display screens and printers. Some printers, for example, can print glossy 4 × 6 prints directly from a digital camera with or without a personal computer. Other output devices include high-quality stereo speakers for listening to music, plotters for drawing engineering diagrams, computer output microfilm (COM) for reading articles in libraries, and many others. At the University of California, Bernard Frischer, a history professor, uses a projector connected to a computer to display a simulation of the Roman Empire at 10:00 A.M. on June 21, 400 AD, a few decades before its collapse.[29] The computer system uses three projectors and a large screen to create a 3-D virtual view and bring history alive.

FIGURE 1.11 • Keyboard and mouse

Keyboards and mouse devices are the most common means for entering data into a computer.

Special-Purpose Hardware Instead of Surgery

There are truly remarkable special-purpose hardware devices that perform a variety of tasks. For example, patients can swallow a tiny capsule camera, which then takes pictures inside the body. The video pill contains an optical dome, a lens, a memory chip, and a transmitter with antenna. The camera pill is especially useful for looking at the intestine. According to an executive of Given Imaging, up until now "The 22 feet between the stomach and colon has been a black box." Ulcers, cancerous tumors, and even Crohn's disease are all possible problems in the intestines that can be more accurately diagnosed with the camera pill.

Recently approved by the Food and Drug Administration (FDA), the camera in a pill is an easy way to explore the intestine. Developed by a missile designer, the pill is often used after more conventional tests have failed. The camera pill, which is the size of a large vitamin pill, sends signals to electronic leads attached to a small device worn on the body. The camera takes about 60,000 flash pictures that are transmitted to the receiving device. Patients can engage in normal life activities—eating and moving–while the pill moves throughout the intestine. After 24 hours, the pill exits painlessly from the body, and the images

are uploaded to a computer system, where they are analyzed. Some liken the video images to the movie *The Fantastic Voyage.*

One young woman decided to try the video pill instead of an expensive surgery from which it would have taken six weeks to recover. The video pill found an ulcer that was causing her problems. The special-purpose device saved her time, pain, and money.

Questions

1. As a potential patient, what questions would you ask your physician about the video pill? Should insurance cover the cost of the video pill?
2. How do you feel new technologies such as this should be introduced to the public?
3. What types of technology do you think were used to develop the video pill?

Sources
1. *"To Avoid Surgery, Eat This Camera," by Marilyn Chase,* The Wall Street Journal, *August 15, 2002, p. D1.*
2. *"Collaboration Telemedicine," by Kolbasuk McGee,* InformationWeek, *June 10, 2002, p. 60.*
3. *"Surgeon Lends a Robotic Hand from 400 Km Away," Staff,* Electronics Weekly, *March 13, 2003, p. 8.*

Software

Software consists of programs and instructions given to the computer to execute or run. There are two types of software: application and system. *Application software* consists of programs that apply the power of computers to help perform tasks or solve problems for people, groups, and organizations (see Figure 1.12). People use application software to develop art work, work out dance routines, compute monthly budgets, complete and file tax returns, keep a list of items in their apartment or house, create beautiful color photos, compose music, play games, create letters and envelopes to send to friends and family during holidays, and perform many other useful tasks. Groups use application software to schedule meetings, work on joint projects, and even help make important decisions. Organizations use computers to do a variety of tasks, including paying employees, deciding where to explore for ancient ruins, determining the best legal strategy for an important client, designing fighter aircraft and training pilots to fly them, and designing a new manufacturing facility for cars and light trucks. Applications software can be purchased or developed.

System software is a collection of programs that interact with the computer hardware and application programs. One of the most important types of system

FIGURE 1.12 • **Application software**

Software applications can be used for a vast array of tasks, including word processing, keeping financial records, creating sophisticated artistic renderings, and writing music.

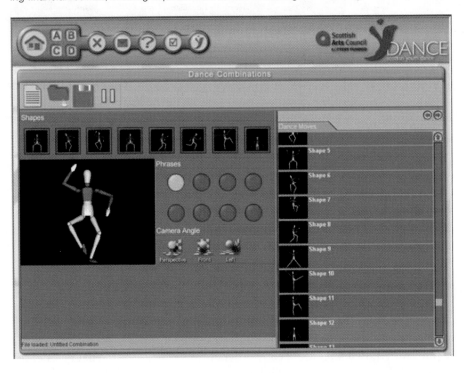

software is the computer's *operating system,* which controls all aspects of the computer. The operating system acts like a buffer between hardware and application software. Operating systems usually come with software, called *communications software,* to allow you to connect to other computers through the phone, cable, or satellites.

Software and the data used by software are stored in computer files. A **file** is a named collection of instructions or data stored in the computer or computer device. There are both *program files,* which contain instructions that can be run or executed, such as a word-processing program, and *data files,* which contain data and information, such as a word-processing document.

On most computers, filenames usually include an extension (*filename.ext*). The extension follows the filename and normally indicates the type of file. File extensions are separated from the filename by a period. The file extension "exe," for example, indicates an executable file or program that can be run. Wordprocessing. exe is an example of an executable file that you could run to start a word-processing program. The file extension "doc" represents a document file that contains data from Microsoft Word, a word-processing program; letter.doc is an example of a data file containing a document, such as a letter.

Internet

The **Internet** allows computers and other devices to be connected to other computers and a vast array of devices and services. People use the Internet for communication and information access. Some Internet applications include communication and collaboration, news, education and training, business, shopping and electronic commerce, banking and investment, employment and careers, and multimedia and entertainment (see Figure 1.13). A refrigerator made by the Korean company LG Electronics, for example, allows you to connect to the Internet

EXPAND YOUR **KNOWLEDGE**

To learn more about saving, opening, and organizing files and folders, go to www.course.com/swt. Click the link "Expand Your Knowledge" and then complete the lab entitled, "Managing Files."

FIGURE 1.13 • Employment opportunities via the Internet
Web sites provide a vast range of information to site visitors.

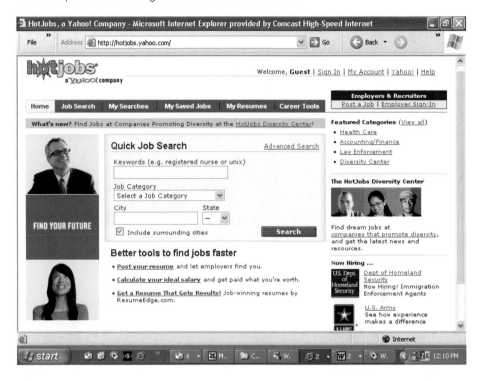

and make ice cubes.[30] With computer systems and equipment connected to the Internet from all continents and most countries, the Internet is the world's largest network. It is truly international in scope.

You can connect to the Internet in a variety of ways. People at home often use phone lines, cable from their local cable company, or satellite connections. Companies like America Online (AOL) and Microsoft Network (MSN) provide Internet access in addition to other services and features. These companies are called *Internet service providers (ISPs)*.

Most people use the *World Wide Web (WWW)* when they access the Internet. The Web, as it is often called, uses a graphical interface to make navigating through the Internet easy. Web sites on the Internet often start with www. For example, the Web address for the publisher of this book is www.course.com. The Web address for the University of Minnesota is www.umn.edu. The Internet is divided into top-level domains, such as .com and .edu. .com is used for commercial Web sites, whereas .edu is used for educational institutions. Web addresses are called *Uniform Resource Locators (URLs)*. When you visit a Web addresses, you start at the site's *home page*, which is the main page or starting place for that address. From the home page, you can go to other pages at that address or link to other addresses and other home pages. Some Internet sites, such as www.yahoo.com and www.google.com, are search engines that make finding information on the Internet much easier.

WELLNESS ON THE WEB

More than a business tool or a game closet, computers are now a highway to healthcare. A recent study by Pew Internet and American Life Project showed 80 percent of Internet users access the Web to research diet and nutrition, fitness, nonprescription drugs, treatments, procedures, diseases, and even mental health options.

Source:
"Con Artists See Gold in Do-Not-Call Registry"
Compiled by Vivian Marino
The New York Times
www.nytimes.com/2003/07/20/business/20PDIG.html
July 20, 2003
Cited on July 22, 2003

Types of Computers

Computers can range from very small, inexpensive devices for keeping dates and phone numbers to large, complex computers that make sophisticated weather forecasts (see Figure 1.14). Computer systems have been used for a wide variety of tasks. They have enabled disabled and homebound people to work in a number of areas such as accounting, bookkeeping, programming, and fields that permit outside contact via telecommunications and personal computers. The research and training center of the National Institute of Handicapped Research has developed an entire office environment that can be run by a quadriplegic using a computer-controlled system. The major types of computers include mobile and personal computers, workstations, servers, midrange and mainframe servers, supercomputers, and special-purpose computers.

Mobile and Personal Computers. **Mobile computers** are small, portable, and easy to use computer systems. *Personal digital assistants (PDAs), handheld computers, tablet PCs,* and *palmtop computers* are all examples of mobile computers. Part of this book was written using a handheld computer on an airplane. Although not as powerful as larger computers, mobile computers can be taken with you conveniently. Information and work done on a mobile device can be transferred easily to a personal computer using cables, a docking station, or a wireless connection. These computers cost from under $100 to about $1,000.

FIGURE 1.14 • Types of computers
Computers range from small handheld devices to large, expensive supercomputers.

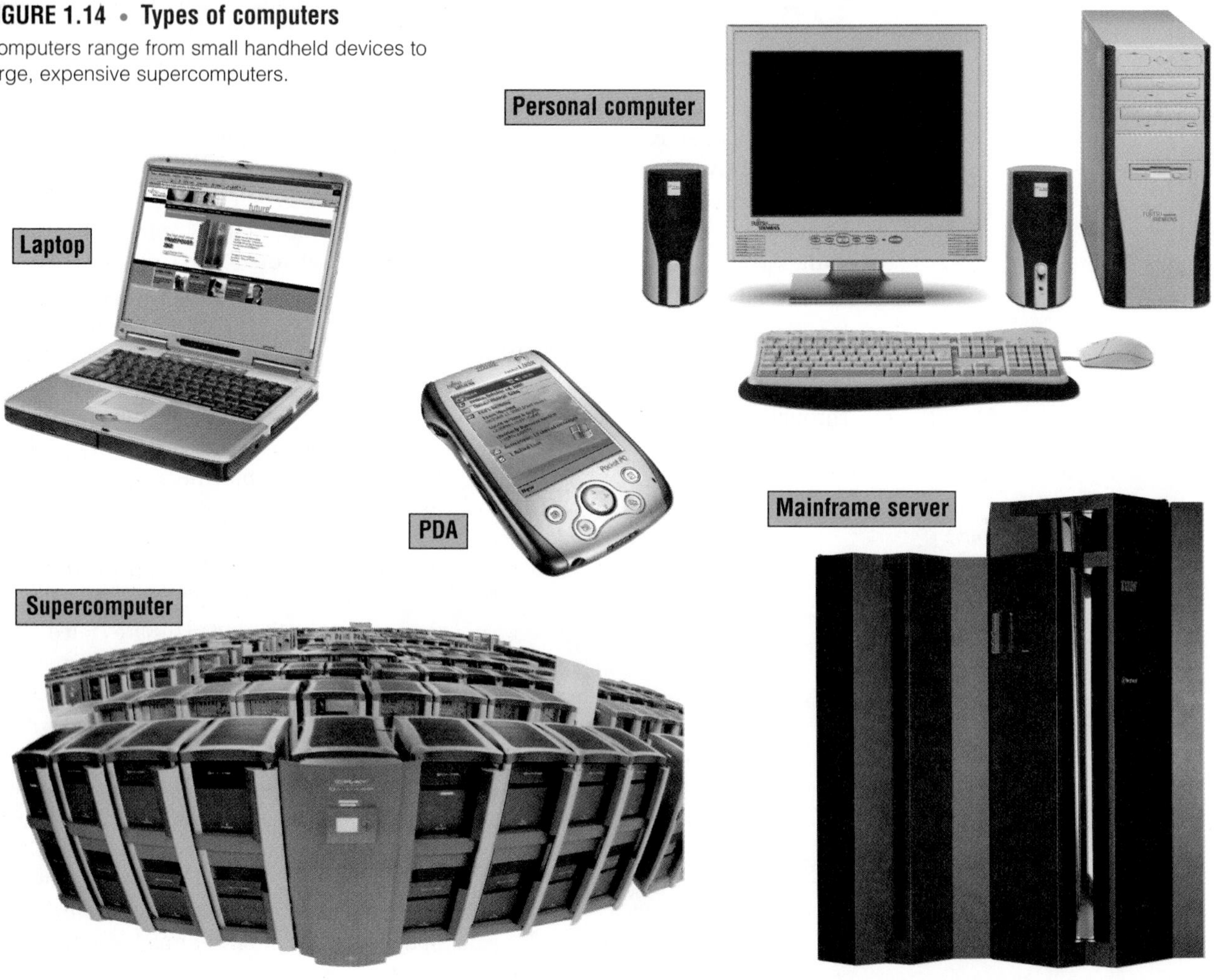

Personal computers are used by individuals, including students, scientists, small business owners, and the presidents of large organizations. It is estimated that over half of all U.S. households own personal computers. Personal computers typically cost from hundreds of dollars for a less powerful system to thousands of dollars for a more powerful model. The most popular types of personal computers are *laptop* (also called *notebook*) and *desktop* systems. Sales of laptop computers have grown dramatically in recent years. The Apple PowerBook laptop computer, for example, comes with a large 17-inch display screen for those who want a portable computer with a large display area. The Panasonic Toughbook has a magnesium case and steel-reinforced parts on the inside. It is used by military personnel, explorers, and others who need a rugged computer system. The keyboard resists liquids, and all openings on the computer can be sealed, making the entire device resistant to water, dust, and even sand.

Workstations. A **workstation** is a powerful desktop computer used to make sophisticated calculations or graphic manipulations. More powerful than a PC, workstations are used in engineering, graphics arts, movie production, and other areas where processing power is important. Workstations typically have multiple processors and large storage capacity. Silicon Graphics, for example, produces a variety of workstations that artists use to create special effects in movies. Workstations can cost tens of thousands of dollars.

Servers. A **server** is a computer sys-tem with hardware and software operating over a network or the Internet. A server often shares common resources, such as printers, disks, other input/output devices, and software. For example, a server can consist of 10 computers that share one printer, a few storage devices, and software on a network. Some servers are dedicated to a single use or operating system. *Web servers* are used to handle and coordinate traffic on the World Wide Web or the Internet. *Client servers* are used to coordinate clients (typically personal computers) connected together on a network. *UNIX servers* use the UNIX operating system, and *Linux servers* use the Linux operating system. Servers can cost thousands or tens of thousands of dollars.

Midrange and Mainframe Servers. **Midrange servers** are used by small businesses and organizations to perform business functions, scientific research, and more. Also called minicomputers, midrange servers are more powerful than personal computers. Midrange servers can handle multiple users connected to them at the same time. **Mainframe servers** are used by large organizations that require plenty of processing power and speed. Universities and large corporations use mainframe servers. Hundreds or thousands of people from around the world can be connected to a mainframe server at the same time. Midrange and mainframe servers can cost hundreds of thousands to millions of dollars.

Supercomputers. **Supercomputers** are the most powerful computers. The fastest supercomputer performs almost 36 trillion calculations per second, more than four times faster than the next fastest machine. U.S. companies, such as IBM, are racing to match or exceed the speed of this supercomputer. Sandia National Laboratories and Cray, Inc. plan to develop a supercomputer using an Advanced Micro Devices, Inc. chip.[31]

Supercomputers are used when the calculations are sophisticated and complex. A few universities use supercomputers to help their faculty perform research on weather forecasting, oceanography, and advanced mathematics. Some investment companies use supercomputers to handle trading and research, and some oil and gas exploration companies use them to help determine where to explore for oil and gas. Supercomputers cost millions of dollars; some cost more than $50 million.

Special-Purpose Computers. Mobile and personal computers, workstations, servers, midrange and mainframe servers, and supercomputers are *general-purpose computers*. They can be programmed and used for a wide variety of tasks or purposes. In contrast, *special-purpose computers* are developed and used for primarily one task or function. PlayStation is an example of a special-purpose computer used for playing realistic games on a TV set. *Kiosks* provide specific public information access to passersby. A *global positioning system (GPS)* installed in an automobile or boat pinpoints your current location and can direct you to a geographic goal (see Figure 1.15). People use *MP3 players* for listening to digital music files. *Digital cameras* and *video cameras* not only take pictures, but also can allow you to edit them, burn them to disk, and even send them to a friend. Other special-purpose computers are used to navigate space shuttles, target enemy forces with missiles and bombs, and control high-speed trains.

These basic computer concepts of hardware, software, and the Internet are important and increasingly being taught in elementary, middle, and high schools. But to get the most from a computer, you must go beyond these basic concepts to understanding more advanced computer systems and their use.

FIGURE 1.15 • Global positioning system

A GPS system is one type of special-purpose computer. It works in conjunction with satellites and mobile communication technology to dete-rmine and display your location on a map.

COMPUTERSYSTEMSANDTHEIRUSE

A **computer system** includes hardware, software, databases, telecommunications networks, people, and procedures that interact to perform some function. These components are illustrated in Figure 1.16. In this section, we'll investigate procedures, databases, telecommunications, and how people use these tools to achieve their goals.

FIGURE 1.16 • The components of a computer system

Computer systems consist of hardware, software, the Internet, databases, telecommunications, procedures, and the people who use them.

People are the most important element in most computer systems. *Computer systems personnel* include all the people who manage, run, program, and maintain a computer system. *Users* are students, lawyers, employees, engineers, nurses, and others who use computers to their benefit. Certain computer users are also computer systems personnel. **Procedures** include the strategies, policies, methods, and rules human beings use to operate a computer system. For example, some procedures describe when each program is to be run or executed in a medical research facility. Other procedures describe who can have access to certain facts in a database in a governmental agency. Still other procedures describe what is to be done in case of a disaster, such as a fire, earthquake, or hurricane.

This section introduces you to several information systems that perform important functions in our society: database systems, telecommunications and network systems, electronic commerce and transaction processing systems, management information systems, decision support systems, and artificial intelligence, expert, and special-purpose systems.

Database Systems

A *database* is an organized collection of facts and information. An individual can use a database to store and manipulate tax information, a list of friends and family members with phone numbers and addresses, a list of what is in that person's apartment or house for insurance purposes, a list of music CDs, and almost anything that can be placed into tables (see Figure 1.17).

Libraries use databases to store lists of books and articles that are available, governments use databases to store tax returns and a list of Social Security recipients, and universities use databases to store student grades and records. A business's database can contain facts and information on customers, employees, inventory, competitors' sales, and much more.

FIGURE 1.17 • Database

Databases help people organize and access data and information.

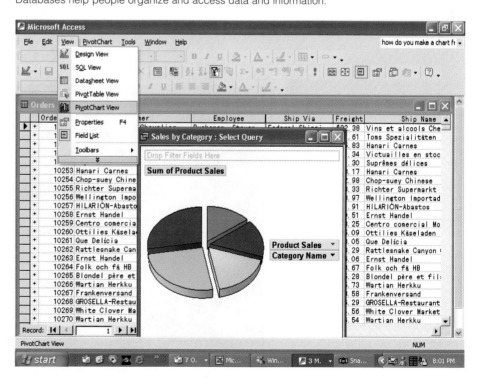

HAVE COMPUTER, CAN WORK

A computer and a telephone line give the disabled a new option for meeting professional goals and employers a new way to fulfill equal opportunity requirements: telecommuting. According to a study, the number of disabled people working at home jumped from 4.1 percent in 1997 to 7 percent in 2003. It is expected that number will rise to 10 or 20 percent in the next decade.

Sources:
"By Telecommuting, the Disabled Get a Key to the Office, and a Job"
By Eve Tahmincioglu
The New York Times
www.nytimes.com/2003/07/20/business/20JMAR.html
July 20, 2003
Cited on July 22, 2003
"Work At Home/Telework as a Reasonable Accommodation"
U.S. Equal Employment Opportunity Commission
www.eeoc.gov/facts/telework.html
Cited on July 22, 2003

Telecommunications and Network Systems

Telecommunication allows organizations to link computer systems together into effective networks. **Networks** can connect computers and computer equipment in a building, across the country, or around the world.

Telecommunications systems are an important yet often overlooked type of computer system. A **telecommunications system** is an organized collection of people, procedures, and devices used to share and transfer information. It may or may not contain a database component. In education, telecommunications systems power distance learning, which can bring new opportunities to students.[32] Students taking Television and the Modern Presidency at the University of Denver, are able to chat with former presidents, White House administrators, and Washington insiders. In a business organization, such systems include the telephone system, facsimile machines, and public address and emergency warning systems. Other examples of the use of telecommunications systems include teleconferencing and video conferencing systems, which allow people to share data, messages, and information instead of traveling to meetings. The key components of a video conferencing system are computer systems connected to other computer systems and a video system that transmits pictures from one location to another. The idea is to simulate a real face-to-face conference as much as possible. Doctors located across the world, for example, can consult on a difficult medical case (see Figure 1.18).

FIGURE 1.18 • Telecommuting
People and professionals can use computer systems to share information over long distances.

JOB TECHNOLOGY

Telecommunications and the Military

Telecommunications systems are being used increasingly during military conflicts. Using computers and satellite systems, coalition forces in the war against Iraq were able to hit targets precisely inside Iraq and in Baghdad. According to one officer, responding to a question about Mr. Hussein, "We tried to put one on his forehead last night."

Telecommunications systems are also being used to a greater extent in broadcasting military conflicts. Radio, TV, and newspaper reporters are using a vast array of computer systems and devices to bring the latest news and live pictures to the public.[33] Some people call this the age of digital reporting. Using laptop computers, satellite video phones, digital cameras, global positioning systems, and satellite transmission equipment that can beam stories anywhere in the world, reporters present the news. Because the cost of this equipment has fallen dramatically, even freelance jour-

nalists can now afford to purchase and use this high-tech equipment.

Questions

1. How have telecommunications systems contributed to the accuracy and timeliness of news reporting?
2. What are the advantages and disadvantages of the quantity of information generated by the news media?
3. In five years, how might telecommunications be used to report on wars?

Sources
1. *"Before Missiles Fly, Global Network Gleans,"* by David Cloud, The Wall Street Journal, *March 27, 2003, p. A1.*
2. *"Military Often Enlists Commercial Technology,"* Simon Romero, The New York Times, *March 10, 2003, p. 1.*
3. *"Navy, Marine Intranet Project Receives Go-Ahead,"* Staff, San Diego Union-Tribune, *December 12, 2002, p. C8.*

The computer systems components of hardware, software, the Internet, people, procedures, databases, telecommunications, and networks can be combined to accomplish many important tasks. One common task is to conduct electronic commerce and process routine transactions. Another is to provide people with information and decision support. These topics will be introduced next.

Electronic Commerce and Transaction Processing

Electronic commerce and transaction processing are common tasks for many people and organizations. People often buy products and services on the Internet using electronic commerce. Organizations typically process transactions, such as recording ticket sales at a concert or summarizing donations made to a religious group. Although electronic commerce and the processing of routine transactions, such as taking sales orders or sending out bills, can be done manually, computer systems can do the job faster, more accurately, and usually less expensively. In fact, the cost of some computer systems can be totally justified by the cost savings of performing routine transaction processing using the computer system.

Electronic Commerce. *Electronic commerce,* or *e-commerce,* involves conducting business or other transactions online, over the Internet or using other telecommunications and network systems. In a business setting, e-commerce can be *business to business (B2B), business to consumer (B2C),* or *consumer to consumer (C2C).* In addition to conducting business transactions, e-commerce can be used in many other areas. Using e-commerce technology, a team of musicians from all over the world can collaborate on a collection of songs and then sell them over the Internet.

A religious group can offer to give away free literature. A museum or art gallery can solicit gifts and donations, and an academic journal can offer the latest research results in biology before they are available in printed journals.

Transaction Processing Systems.

Processing routine transactions is an important application for any organization. A *transaction* represents an exchange, such as buying medical supplies at a hospital, downloading music on the Internet, or paying employees. A *transaction processing system (TPS)* is an organized collection of people, procedures, databases, and devices used to record completed transactions. Payroll is an example (see Figure 1.19). The primary inputs for a payroll TPS are employees' hours worked during the week and pay rate. The primary output consists of paychecks. Other outputs include various employee-related reports required by state and federal agencies, such as the Internal Revenue Service.

TPSs are absolutely essential for businesses, but they are equally important for other organizations. The U.S. government is perhaps the largest transaction processor in the world. Millions of Social Security checks are processed and sent out, and the Internal Revenue Service (IRS) processes millions of tax returns from individuals, corporations, trusts, and other entities every year. When you consider the military and all the other branches and agencies of the federal government, you realize how difficult it is to process all of its transactions in an accurate and timely fashion. Without computer systems, the federal government would not have the personnel or time to process all of its transactions.

Almost all organizations process transactions to some extent, whether using a computer system or manually. Think of all the transactions a typical college or university processes. Paying faculty and staff, processing student grades, paying for phone service and electric utilities, and keeping track of gifts and donations from alumni and others are just a few transactions that colleges and universities must process. Travel agencies, a small beauty shop, a small hockey team, charitable groups, career counselors, museums, and local nightclubs all have to process transactions.

FIGURE 1.19 • A payroll transaction processing system (TPS)
The inputs (employees' hours worked and pay rates) go through a number of procedures to produce output (paychecks).

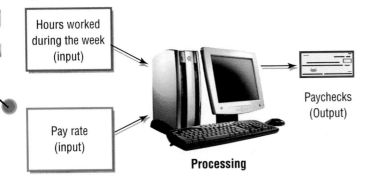

Hours worked during the week (input)

Pay rate (input)

Processing

Paychecks (Output)

Information, Decision Support, and Specialized Systems

Cost savings from an electronic commerce or transaction processing system can more than justify the expense of a complete computer system. But costs can only be cut so much. Information, decision support, and specialized systems offer benefits beyond cost savings. They offer almost unlimited potential for people and organizations to achieve their goals, such as finding the best insurance rate for a car, getting better service from a governmental agency, improving medical diagnosis, or increasing profits for a corporation.

Management Information Systems.
Most organizations realized that transaction processing systems were worth their cost in computing equipment, computer programs, and specialized personnel and supplies. They sped the processing of routine activities and reduced clerical costs. Although early TPSs were valuable, it soon became clear that the data stored in these systems could be used to help people make better decisions in their respective areas, including making better medical diagnoses of a sick patient, developing a better legal defense for a client, or planning a military campaign or invasion.

Management information systems (MIS) began to be developed in the 1960s and are characterized by the use of computer systems to produce important reports. A *management information system (MIS)* is an organized collection of people, procedures, databases, and devices used to provide routine information to managers and decision makers. The focus of an MIS is on operational efficiency. In a business setting, management information systems typically provide preplanned reports generated with data and information from the transaction processing system for marketing, production, finance, and other areas of business (see Figure 1.20).

FIGURE 1.20 • Management information system (MIS)

Functional management information systems draw data from the organization's transaction processing system.

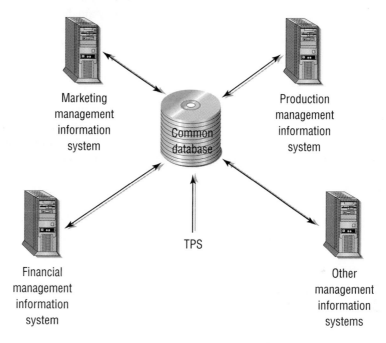

Decision Support Systems. By the 1970s and 1980s, dramatic improvements in technology resulted in computer systems that were less expensive but more powerful. People at all levels of organizations began using personal computers to do a variety of tasks; they were no longer solely dependent on the computer systems department for all their information needs. During this time period, it was recognized that computer systems could support additional decision-making activities. A *decision support system (DSS)* is an organized collection of people, procedures, databases, and devices used to support problem-specific decision making. The focus of a DSS is on decision-making effectiveness. Whereas an MIS helps an organization "do things right," a DSS helps a person "do the right thing." The overall emphasis is to support rather than replace decision making.

A DSS goes beyond a traditional management information system, which merely produces reports. A DSS can provide immediate assistance in solving complex problems that were not supported by a traditional MIS. Many of these problems are unique and not straightforward. For instance, a paleontologist might want to determine the best place to dig to possibly find dinosaur bones or an oil company might want to discover the best place to explore for oil. A person might use an Internet site such as www.progressive.com to get car insurance rates from Progressive and several other insurance companies. In London, the English National Opera used a DSS to help decision makers design an air-conditioning and air flow system during a $60 million renovation.[34] The DSS used a sophisticated model that analyzed air flow patterns and temperature gradients in the cooling system. Traditional MISs are seldom used to solve these types of problems; a DSS can help by suggesting alternatives and assisting in final decision-making.

Artificial Intelligence, Expert Systems, and Special-Purpose Systems.

In addition to MIS and DSS, organizations often use systems based on the notion of *artificial intelligence (AI)*, where the computer system takes on the characteristics of human intelligence. The field of artificial intelligence includes several subfields, one of which is expert systems. An *expert system (ES)* is an information system that can make suggestions and reach conclusions in much the same way that a human expert can. An expert system is an organized collection of people, procedures, databases, and devices used to generate expert advice or suggest a decision in an area or discipline. These computer systems are like human specialists with many years of experience in a field. In fact, they are developed in part through extensive interviewing and observation of such experts. For example, expert systems have been developed to search for oil and gas, to make medical diagnoses, and to assist in finding problems with electrical and mechanical devices. It is important to note that expert systems do not replace humans; they are programmed to behave in predesigned ways by human experts in a particular field. Medical expert systems, for example, do not replace doctors in making make medical decisions or diagnoses.

In addition to expert systems, there are other artificial intelligence and special-purpose systems (see Figure 1.21). A 911 emergency operator can use a *geographic information system (GIS)* to quickly locate a robbery victim who has just called for help. A hedge fund analyst can develop a *neural network* to help forecast or predict future stock and options prices. A computer scientist can develop a *fuzzy logic* system to help control a bullet (or high-speed) train, and an engineer can develop new software to help an industrial *robot* interpret visual images and navigate through a room of equipment. For example, after years of experimenting with a device like a chicken vacuum, engineers have developed a *special-purpose device* to help poultry companies catch about 150 chickens a minute. The robot-like device replaces about eight people and spares them from being scratched and befouled.[35]

FIGURE 1.21 • Special-purpose system

NASA's Mission Control Center in Houston, Texas is the hub through which all shuttle activity and decisions are determined.

COMPUTERSYSTEMSDEVELOPMENT, SECURITY, ANDCONTROL

In the preceding section, you saw how computer systems facilitate and enable the use of electronic commerce, transaction processing, information and decision support, and a variety of special-purpose functions. How do people and organizations assemble or create computer systems? How do they create or acquire the applications that power electronic commerce, transaction processing, information and decision support, or other systems?

Systems Development

Systems development is the activity of creating new or modifying existing systems. Systems development efforts can range from a small project, such as purchasing an inexpensive computer program to keep track of your monthly expenses, to a major undertaking, such as installing a $50 million system, including hardware, software, communications systems, databases, and new computer systems personnel to analyze complex geographic information. To improve its operations, for example, National Foot Care Program, Inc., launched a systems development improvement program, called the Quality Management and Improvement Program (QMIP).[36] The new program helps manage foot and ankle healthcare services for DaimlerChrysler's Medicare eligible retirees. Employees with foot and ankle sprains, breaks, or other foot and ankle problems can get treatment from National Foot Care. National Foot Care Program is the largest U.S. foot and ankle care provider and assists over 3,800 medical practitioners across the country.

Regardless of the size of the systems development project, the general activities in systems development are the same. They include systems investigation, analysis, design, implementation, and maintenance and review.

Systems Investigation   *Systems investigation* explores potential problems or opportunities in an existing system or situation. An existing system is examined to determine whether it is sufficiently satisfying the goals of the individual or organization. Systems investigation attempts to answer the question, "What is the problem, and is it worth solving?" The primary result of systems investigation is a set of problems or opportunities for which systems analysis is recommended. The U.S. Navy, for example, might conduct systems investigation to determine if its current computerized navigation system is still adequate or needs updating.

Systems Analysis   *Systems analysis* seeks to solve the problem or exploit the opportunity identified during systems investigation. It considers existing systems (if any), investigates alternative solutions to the problem, and explores the feasibility and implications of these solutions. In short, systems analysis attempts to answer the question "What must the computer system do to solve the problem?" The result of systems analysis is a listing of system requirements and priorities.

Systems Design   The purpose of *systems design* is to select and plan a system that meets the requirements outlined during systems analysis. Systems design seeks to answer the question "How will the computer system do what it must do to obtain the problem solution?" The primary results of systems design are outputs, inputs, and user interfaces; specifications for hardware, software, database, telecommunications, personnel, and procedural components; and explanations of how these components are related.

Systems Implementation   *Systems implementation* involves acquiring new systems or modifying existing ones according to the systems design and placing them into operation. Implementation includes hardware acquisition, software acquisition, personnel hiring and training, site preparation, data preparation, installation, testing, start-up, and operation. After systems implementation, the new or modified system will be in place and operating.

Corning Display Technologies Sheds New Light on the Systems Development Process

Corning Display Technologies, a branch of Corning Inc., is the world's leading supplier of the ultrathin glass substrates used to produce Active Matrix Liquid Crystal Displays (AMLCD)—the displays used for notebook computers, handheld devices, and more recently desktop computers.

Display glass is manufactured in two stages: The melting process takes raw silica and produces sheets of glass, and then a finishing line cuts those down to various sizes. Corning used a virtual model of the manufacturing process to experiment with methods of placing manufacturing operations at different locations. Since a melting line costs 10 times as much as a finishing line, Corning decided to leave its melting operations—one in the United States and one in Japan—unchanged, but break up its global finishing lines into several branch manufacturing units. Corning used the systems development process to help design and implement the new manufacturing operations.

The systems development project, 3 years old and in the final stages of deployment, has stayed on schedule

and under budget, and is paying for itself. The entire reorganization of Corning's manufacturing operations and systems development cost $750 million dollars.

Questions

1. What was the priority in Corning's approach to developing its new system? Why was the solution a success?
2. How could other industries use a similar approach?
3. How might this story have ended if Corning had not examined the efficiency of its system and simply added a new plant?

Sources
1. "Corning Inc.," Matthew Schwartz, Computerworld, *March 11, 2002.*
2. "Corning Begins Shipping GEN6 Glass for LCDs," Spencer Chin, Electronic Buyer's News, *June 30, 2003, p. 6.*
3. "Corning Sales up for First Time Since 2001," *Staff,* Electronic News, *April 28, 2003. www.computerworld.com.*
4. Corning Display Web site, *www.corning.com/ displaytechnologies/s.*

Systems Maintenance and Review The purpose of *systems maintenance and review* is to make any necessary changes to the system after it is installed and operational. Maintenance usually involves changes that are necessary to sustain the system; that is, to keep the system operating as efficiently, error free, and effectively as possible. Sometimes, substantial and expensive changes may be needed, such as acquiring a new computer system to analyze human DNA. Systems review is a periodic evaluation of the system to see if the original desired results are being achieved. In some cases, a systems review can restart the systems development cycle, beginning with systems investigation.

Program Development

Program development is the process of developing software solutions and services to address a specific need or problem. Professionals from all disciplines are finding themselves either called upon or inspired to participate in program development. A nurse may take it upon himself to design a more practical daily rounds schedule for the team of nurses on the floor he manages. A sales representative for a publisher may be asked to provide input to improve access to customer data while on the road. A sports fan may wish to compare and contrast team statistics to predict a Super Bowl winner. Each of these examples illustrates a need to develop a program. To develop any program, a fundamental understanding of problem-solving techniques and solution development is essential.

Programs can be custom developed or mass produced. *Custom-developed* programs are built or developed by individuals and organizations to address specific needs. For example, the 13 YMCAs in the San Antonio area contracted Sirius Computer Solutions to create a networked software solution that would allow them to better evaluate and coordinate the services they provide to the over 50,000 children and families of San Antonio.[37] "Thanks to Sirius, we were able to save money, break communication barriers, and manage programs on a consistent basis," said Liesen Benet, IT Director for YMCA, San Antonio area. Other software is mass produced and purchased *off-the-shelf* to meet the needs of a particular market. Most instructors and students, for example, purchase word-processing and spreadsheet programs that are mass produced by companies such as Microsoft. The market for this type of software is huge—estimated at $76.1 billion in 2003.[38]

Programs can be developed using a five-stage program development life cycle (PDLC). Understanding this development life cycle provides insight into the problem solving techniques used by professionals and shows how these techniques can be used by anyone to develop computer solutions for their own unique problems and needs. The five stages are problem analysis, design, coding, debugging and testing, and maintenance.

Problem Analysis. *Problem analysis,* the first stage of the PDLC, clearly defines problems by breaking them into their fundamental components; it is a divide-and-conquer approach. In this phase of the development cycle a problem or perceived need is logically organized so that it can be properly addressed. You clearly define the goals of your software in this stage.

Program Design. *Program design* makes use of logical thinking and algorithms to produce a detailed path to the goals defined in the problem analysis stage. An *algorithm* is a detailed procedure or formula for solving a problem. In the design stage, we learn to "think" like a computer. Learning how a computer executes a program can assist us in confronting life's challenges through a logical and methodical approach.

Program Coding. **Program coding** is the process of creating a program using a programming language to carry out predetermined algorithms (see Figure 1.22). The detailed algorithms created in the design stage are notated using the rules of a specific programming language.

Program Debugging and Testing. *Program debugging and testing* takes place prior to the release of software. Its goal is to ensure, as best as possible, that the software successfully accomplishes the goals for which it was designed. Debugging skills are essential not only for software manufacturers but also for end users. If a civil engineer developed a spreadsheet to analyze bridge stresses and structures, debugging and testing are critical or lives could be lost.

Program Maintenance. *Program maintenance,* the final stage of the development life cycle, is used to observe software in action and improve upon it if and when necessary. Often this stage leads back to the problem analysis stage, to address new issues and develop a new improved version of the software.

FIGURE 1.22 • Program coding

Programmers often first create pseudocode, which consists of the steps necessary for a program to complete a given task, written in plain English. The pseudocode is then translated into a programming language using programming code.

Pseudocode for the InitializeButton Click event procedure
InitializeButton
1. declare variables
2. verify that the user wants to initialize the file
3. if the user does not want to initialize the file
   display the message "File was not initialized" in a message box
else
   assign 20 spaces to the strParticipant field variable
   assign 15 spaces to the strCompany field variable
   open a random access file named participants.data
   repeat 20 times
      write a record to the participants.data file
   end repeat
   close the participants.data file
   display the message "File was initialized." in a message box
end if

Multimedia Applications and Production

Multimedia refers to the computer's ability to present and manipulate visual and audio media such as graphics, animation, video, sound, and music. Although early personal computers were considered tools for manipulating text and numbers, over time their capabilities have expanded to support the presentation and manipulation of multimedia data. Today's PCs have the processing speed and storage capacity to easily serve as a personal media center, storing and playing your favorite music and movies.

The digitization of sound, images, music, and video is what makes multimedia possible. *Digitization* is the process of representing information, in this case sound and images, with bits, 1s and 0s, that can be processed by a computer system.

Digital music and video have dramatically altered the entertainment industry. It is because of digitization that the computer industry and the entertainment industry are becoming tightly interwoven and overlapped. For example, the Internet has become a primary music distribution system, and cable television companies are supplying consumers with Internet connections. The integration of home computing equipment with home entertainment equipment has begun, and will become commonplace before long. Computers have become as important in supporting our entertainment needs as they are in assisting us in reaching our professional goals. When entertainment *is* a person's professional goal, technology has opened the door to many new possibilities.

Computers and the Internet have had a profound impact on the creative process of visual and musical artists. Musicians use digital processing to create new sounds and musical textures that broaden the scope of the music's affect on the audience. Through digital processing, old worn-out and damaged recordings can become new again. Using the Internet, musicians can collaborate to create music and recordings from distant and various locations. Advances in digital music recording technology have brought the price of high quality digital recording equipment down to the point where many musicians produce and record their own CDs in their own home studios. This ability for musicians to independently produce their own recordings and distribute them over the Internet or on CD has shifted some of the power in the music industry from recording company executives to the musicians.

Technology plays a strong role in the careers of most graphic artists. Illustrators, graphic designers, animators, videographers, and special effects artists make use of software that helps them create more effective artwork. Computer software automates many of the tedious and redundant tasks required in graphics and video production and allows the artist to create more complex and visually pleasing final products in a much shorter amount of time. Video production software running on powerful computers allows artists to bring imagined scenes to life that rival reality and trick the eye into believing that impossible experiences may indeed be possible.

The most complex form of multimedia allows artists to create virtual worlds for the audience to experience as though they were actually physically present in the world. Virtual reality is an increasing force in the entertainment industry as evidenced by IMAX theaters and the growing video game market. It is clear that many people enjoy immersing themselves in another world as a form of entertainment. The software tools used to create and

COMPUTERS HELP TREAT RSI

Cross a Yamaha grand piano with a video camera, a laptop computer, and special software, and you get a new way to diagnose and treat repetitive stress injuries among piano players. The technology, which can record more than 1,000 gradations in keystroke speed, could also be used to diagnose and treat similar injuries caused by violins or computer keyboards.

Source:
"Video-Computer Combo Helps Pianists Compensate for Stress Injury"
By Donald G. McNeil, Jr.
The New York Times
www.nytimes.com/2003/06/24/health/24PIAN.html
June 24, 2003

display the 3-D environments of virtual worlds are perhaps the most demanding on computer systems. However, today's PCs and home gaming systems provide the processing power that allows users to interact with virtual worlds that look as real as many of those presented in theaters.

Social, Ethical, and Security Issues

Although we will emphasize the positive aspects of computers throughout the book, there are potential social and ethical issues that need to be explored and addressed. These social and ethical issues are discussed in this section, including computer waste and mistakes, crime and fraud, privacy invasion, health concerns, and various ethical issues. This section also investigates how computer systems can be made more secure to protect them against some of the potential negative aspects of computerization.

Computer Waste and Mistakes   Individuals, organizations, and governments all waste computer system resources. Computer systems have been purchased and never or seldom used. Some corporate executives, for example, have purchased personal computers for their desk because they look good, but have never used them. Computer mistakes have cost companies and organizations billions of dollars. One stock trader, for example, made a mistake that cost his employer hundreds of millions of dollars. The stock trader made a typographical error in entering his trade into the computerized trading system (see Figure 1.23).

FIGURE 1.23 • **Costly mistakes in stock trading**

One typographical error made in a computerized trading system can cost millions of dollars.

Computer Crime   Computers can be used as a tool to commit crime or can be the object of the crime. As a tool, computers have been used in ingenious ways. In one scam, a bank employee stole a computer access number and transferred over $10 million to a foreign bank account in his name. Another example is the financial scandals that rocked the United States in the early 2000s.[39] In one case, a chief information officer (CIO) who was in charge of the computer system for a computer service firm was charged with assisting in a $15 million fraud. Although the CIO wasn't directly involved in the fraud, he helped the company get a favorable credit rating based on false accounting data. The CIO pled guilty to one count of federal bank fraud. He also lost his job.

Computers are also the objects of crime. If software on CDs, laptops, keyboards, display screens, and complete computer systems are left unsecured, they can be, and have been, stolen. People have had their laptop computers stolen in airport security lines with valuable financial and credit card information stored on the laptop's hard disk.

Computer systems can also help reduce crime.[40] A free computer center in Wellington, New Zealand has cut vandalism and given people in the community a sense of pride. When a pair of headphones disappeared from the center, the community rallied to make sure they were promptly returned.

Privacy   The issue of privacy deals with the collection and use or misuse of data. Data is constantly being collected on each of us and stored in large databases. This data is often distributed over easily accessed networks and the Internet without our knowledge or consent. A criminal can steal your Social Security number, date of

COMMUNITY /\/\~ TECHNOLOGY

Cell Phones with Digital Cameras—Bane or Benefit?

Television ads for cell phones with digital cameras show a young man in a cast laughing as a friend sends an image of another friend tumbling down a ski slope. Owners of these devices are enjoying this real-time visual communication worldwide. In Japan, where cell phones with cameras were first introduced, taking pictures with a cell phone is called "sha mail," where "sha" means to photograph in Japanese. One research company believes that the sales of phone cameras will be greater than digital cameras or cell phones alone.

The possibilities for such devices are expanding. For example, a young woman on a commuter train used her camera phone to take pictures of a man assaulting her and send them to the police who arrested the man on the next stop. Yet just as a useful tool like the computer has been used for theft, transmission of pornography, invasion of privacy, terrorist communications, and other unsavory and illegal purposes, some people are finding such uses for cell phones with digital cameras.

These phones, popular throughout Asia, are being used to take photos up women's skirts and in locker rooms. New Zealand may ban the use of phone cameras in swimming pools over concerns for "peeping toms" who can use the device for taking pictures in the showers or changing rooms. An enterprising use of

camera phones is photographing pages of interest from magazines and books to avoid purchasing them. Samsung Electronics is attempting to prevent industrial espionage by banning the use of these phones in their semiconductor and research facilities.

Questions

1. Should the government establish regulations to govern the use of phone cameras?
2. What rules should companies have regarding their use?
3. Does government regulation or company rules infringe on the rights of phone users?
4. What impact might regulation have on the sale of these phones?

Sources
1. *"Cell Phones Spreading Mischief," Yuri Kageyama,* The Associated Press, *reprinted in Summit Daily News, Thursday, July 10, 2003, B1.*
2. *"You Need This Gadget," Kay Itoi,* Newsweek, *December 23, 2002, p. 53.*
3. *"Phone Cameras to Outsell Film, Digital Cameras in 2003," Staff,* Photo Marketing Newsline, *March 26, 2003.*
4. *"Pools Move to Ban Cellphones," Heather Wright,* Infotech Weekly, *June 30, 2003.*

---

birth, and other personal information. With this information, committing a crime called *identity theft,* the criminal can access your financial records, steal your money, purchase products using your credit cards, and ruin your credit.

Computer Systems in the Work Environment. In the work environment, some people fear that humans will be displaced by computers, resulting in the loss of jobs. Some people also have health concerns. Can computer systems cause occupational stress? Some experts believe that long hours at a computer keyboard can cause repetitive motion disorder. Also called *repetitive stress injury (RSI),* the problems can include tendonitis, tennis elbow, the inability to hold objects, and sharp pain in the fingers. *Carpal tunnel syndrome (CTS),* which is an inflammation of the pathway for nerves that travel through the wrist (the carpal tunnel), is a problem for some people.[41]

Ethical Issues in Computer Systems Ethical issues are a concern with what is generally considered right or wrong. Some computer systems professionals believe that computers may create many opportunities for unethical behavior. A faculty member of a medical school falsified computerized research results to help get a promotion and a higher salary. In another case, a company was charged with using a Human Resources computer system to time layoffs and firings in order to avoid paying pensions to employees. More and more, the Internet is involved in cases of unethical behavior. For example, investors have placed false rumors or wrong information about a stock on the Internet to try to influence the price of the stock to make money.

Computer Security and Control   Individuals and organizations can install security and control measures to protect themselves against some of the potential negative aspects of computerization. For example, a number of software products have been developed to detect and remove viruses from computer systems. Some individuals and companies install *firewalls* (software and hardware that protects a computer system or network from outside attacks) to avoid viruses and prevent unauthorized people from gaining access to the computer system (see Figure 1.24). Identification numbers and passwords can also be used. There are a number of laws protecting people from invasion of privacy, including *The Privacy Act,* enacted in the 1970s. *Ergonomics,* the study of designing and positioning equipment such as computer systems, can help people to avoid health-related problems of using computer systems. In addition, many organizations have ethical codes of conduct to foster ethical behavior when using computer systems.

FIGURE 1.24 • Computer security

Some computer systems integrate advanced technologies like iris scans to verify that users accessing the system have proper clearance.

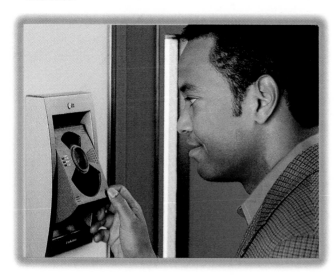

WHYSTUDY**COMPUTER**SYSTEMS?

Why study computer systems? From the examples and references in this chapter, it should by now be clear to you that computer systems are used in almost every field. Knowledge of computer systems will help you advance in your chosen career through online educational programs and up-to-date information on what's happening in your world. Computer systems can also enhance your personal life.

To adequately understand computer systems, you must acquire knowledge of computer concepts, computer systems and their use, and the development and control of computer systems. Knowledge of computer concepts is knowledge of computer equipment and how it functions. Knowledge of computer systems goes beyond the fundamentals of computer equipment and programs and involves knowledge of how data and information are used by individuals and organizations. Most important, however, knowledge of computer systems encompasses how and why this technology is applied. Finally, knowledge of computer systems development and control will show you how computer systems can be acquired and applied to realize your goals and aspirations. A powerful demonstration of how computer systems have been used in one industry could help you in your chosen field. You might find that the approach used to develop a decision support system used in the oil industry can also be used by a publishing company, a political campaign, a charitable organization, or even by the military or in government service. The possibilities are almost limitless.

Action Plan

1. How did using a computer system make choosing a career and major easier for Jane?

By using the computerized system in the career center, Jane was able to examine careers consistent with her aptitudes, interests, and work environment preferences. She was able to focus on a number of possible careers and choose the best for her. Once she decided on a career, it was simply a matter of choosing the college major most useful in pursuing that career.

2. What additional information might Jane be able to obtain about using computers in pursuing her major and planning her career?

Jane was able to use the Internet to monitor the job market, stay up to date on what was happening in her field, learn about continuing education programs, research prospective internships and jobs online and post her resume.

3. How can students use Jane's experience to help plan their own careers?

Students can check out their own schools' career centers for computerized career information and investigate careers of interest to them. If their schools do not have access to these systems, they can look for career centers in other schools in their area that might have them. They can use the Internet to explore career-related issues and ask their professors about how computers are used in various disciplines in which they have career interests.

Summary

LEARNING OBJECTIVE 1
Describe the use of computer systems.
Computer systems are sets of interrelated elements that collect (input), manipulate and store (process), and disseminate (output) data and information. Input is the activity of capturing and gathering new data, processing involves converting or transforming data into useful outputs, and output involves producing useful information. Feedback is a type of output that is used to make adjustments or changes to input or processing activities.

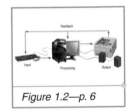

Figure 1.2—p. 6

In order to be valuable to managers and decision makers, information must have several characteristics. Information should be accurate, complete, economical to produce, flexible, reliable, relevant, simple to understand, timely, and verifiable. The value of information is directly linked to how it helps decision makers achieve their organization's goals.

Organizations use information to support their goals. This can increase productivity, enhance quality, and give an organization a competitive advantage. *Productivity* is a measure of the output achieved divided by the input required. *Quality* is the ability of a product or service to meet or exceed customer expectations. A competitive advantage can help an organization reach its goals, including higher profits, better service, or more outreach to society. Computer systems are used in almost every business and industry.

LEARNING OBJECTIVE 2
Discuss how computers are used in a variety of fields, and why studying computer systems can benefit you professionally and personally.

Most careers today involve the use of computer systems. These systems have impacted the structure of organizations, the way we do business, the types of jobs we hold, and the nature of work itself. Industries such as financial services, transportation, scientific research, retail, utilities, publishing, healthcare, and professional services could not function at their current level without computer systems. Knowledge of computer systems will help you on the job, and it will help you advance in your chosen career or field. Computer systems can also enhance your personal life.

Figure 1.5—p. 14

LEARNING OBJECTIVE 3
Define basic computer concepts.

A computer is an electronic device used to perform calculations and other functions at high speed.

Hardware includes all of the computer equipment used to input raw data, process it into something meaningful, and output the results. Computer hardware includes processing, storage, input, and output devices. Processing devices include the central processing unit, memory, and storage. A computer system also needs one or more, larger storage devices that permanently hold all programs and data. This type of storage is often called secondary storage. Permanent, secondary storage is non-volatile, which means that you don't lose data and programs with a loss of power. There are literally hundreds of different input devices. The most common ones are a keyboard and a mouse. There are also hundreds of different types of output devices. The most common ones are display screens and printers.

Figure 1.10—p. 20

Software consists of programs and instructions given to the computer to execute or run. There are two types of software, application and system. Application software applies the power of computers to help people, groups, and organizations solve problems. System software consists of programs that interact with the computer hardware and application programs. The computer's operating system controls all aspects of the computer, and acts like a buffer between hardware and application software.

Software and the data used by software are stored in computer files. Program files contain instructions that can be run or executed. Data files contain data and information.

The Internet allows computers and other devices to be connected to other computers and a vast array of devices and services. You can connect to the Internet through phone lines, cable from local cable companies, or satellite connections. The World Wide Web (www) uses a GUI interface to make navigating through the Internet easy. The Internet can be used for e-mail, electronic commerce, telecommuting, and many other applications.

Computers come in a variety of types and sizes. Mobile computers are small, portable, and easy to use computer systems. Personal digital assistants (PDAs), handheld computers, tablet PCs, and palmtop computers are examples of mobile computers. Personal computers are used by individuals. The most popular types are laptop (also called notebook) and desktop systems. A server is a computer system with hardware and software operating over a network or the Internet. A server allows multiple computers to share common computer resources, such as printers, disks, input/output devices, and software. Midrange servers are used by small businesses and organizations, and are more powerful than personal computers. Mainframe servers are used by large organizations that require plenty of processing power and speed. Supercomputers are the most powerful computers. They are used when a large number of computations are required or the calculations are sophisticated and complex. Special-purpose computers are developed and used for primarily one task or function.

Figure 1.13—p. 23

LEARNING OBJECTIVE 4

Discuss the components of any computer system and how they are used.

Computer systems consist of hardware, software, databases, telecommunications, procedures, and people. People are the most important element in most computer systems. Procedures include the strategies, policies, methods, and rules humans use to operate the computer system. A database is an organized collection of facts and information. Telecommunications allows organizations to link computer systems together into effective networks. Networks can connect computers and computer equipment in a building, across the country, or around the world.

Figure 1.16—p. 27

Electronic commerce, or e-commerce, involves conducting business or other transactions online, over the Internet, or using other telecommunications and network systems. In a business setting, e-commerce can be business to business (B2B), business to consumer (B2C), or consumer to consumer (C2C). A transaction represents an exchange. A transaction processing system (TPS) is an organized collection of people, procedures, databases, and devices used to record completed transactions.

A management information system (MIS) is an organized collection of people, procedures, databases, and devices used to provide routine information to managers and decision makers. The focus of an MIS is on operational efficiency. In a business setting, management information systems typically provide preplanned reports generated with data and information from the transaction processing system. A decision support system (DSS) is an organized collection of people, procedures, databases, and devices used to support problem-specific decision making. The field of artificial intelligence includes several subfields, one of which is expert systems. An expert system (ES) is an information system that can make suggestions and reach conclusions in much the same way that a human expert can. In addition to expert systems, there are other artificial intelligence and special-purpose applications.

LEARNING OBJECTIVE 5

Explain how computer systems and applications can be developed and controlled.

Systems development is the activity of creating new or modifying existing systems. Systems development efforts can range from a small project, such as purchasing an inexpensive computer program, to a major undertaking, such as installing a $50 million system, including hardware, software, communications systems, databases, and new computer systems personnel. The general activities in systems development include systems investigation, analysis, design, implementation, and maintenance and review. Program development is the process of developing software solutions and services to address a specific need or problem. Program development includes problem analysis, program design, program coding, program debugging and testing, and program maintenance.

Figure 1.22—p. 37

In addition to the positive aspects of computer systems, there are negative aspects, including computer waste and mistakes, crime and fraud, privacy invasion, health concerns, and various ethical issues. Complete computer systems have been purchased and never or seldom used. Computer mistakes have cost companies and organizations billions. Computers can be used as a tool to commit crime or can be the object of a crime. The issue of privacy deals with the collection and use or misuse of data. Health issues can include repetitive stress injury (RSI), which some experts think is caused by long hours at a computer keyboard Ethical issues deal with what is generally considered right or wrong. A number of security and control procedures can be used to prevent these negative aspects of computer systems or to deal with them if they occur.

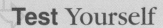

Test Yourself

LEARNING OBJECTIVE 1: Describe the use of computer systems.

1. What type of data is used to store numbers, letters, and other characters?
   a. analog
   b. digital
   c. alphanumeric
   d. simplex

2. What is used to make adjustments or changes to input or processing activities?
   a. output
   b. information
   c. feedback
   d. data

3. _____ is a measure of the output of a system achieved divided by the input required.

4. True or False: Today, quality means conformance to standards.

LEARNING OBJECTIVE 2: Discuss how computers are used in a variety of fields, and why studying computer systems can benefit you professionally and personally.

5. _____ design and build hardware, software, database systems, telecommunications systems, and Internet systems.

6. True or False: Computer systems have not been used to any extent in producing music.

7. True or False: The uses of computer systems in almost every field or career area are almost limitless.

LEARNING OBJECTIVE 3: Define basic computer concepts.

8. A(n) _____ is an electronic device used to perform calculations and other functions at high speed.

9. True of False: Processing devices include the central processing unit, memory, and storage.

10. _____ consists of programs and instructions given to the computer to execute or run.

11. What consists of a collection of programs to apply the power of a computer to help solve problems for people, groups, and organizations?
    a. application software
    b. system software
    c. utility software
    d. spreadsheet software

12. True or False: C++ and Visual Basic are examples of application software.

13. What allows computers and other devices to be connected to other computers and a vast array of devices and services?
    a. the CPU
    b. application software
    c. analog devices
    d. the Internet

14. A(n) _____ is a computer system with hardware and software operating over a network or the Internet.

LEARNING OBJECTIVE 4: Discuss the components of any computer system and how they are used.

15. True or False: A computer system is composed of hardware, software, the Internet, databases and telecommunications, people, and procedures that are configured to collect, manipulate, store, and process data into useful outputs.

16. People and organizations typically use software, called _____ to enter, organize, and manipulate data.

17. People buying CDs and books from a company over the Internet is an example of:
    a. C2C
    b. B2B
    c. B2A
    d. B2C

18. The focus of _____ is on operational efficiency.

19. A computer scientist can develop a _____ to help control a high-speed train.

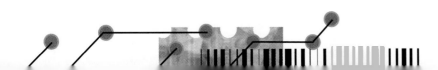

LEARNING OBJECTIVE 5: Explain how computer systems and applications can be developed and controlled.

20. What explores potential problems or opportunities with the existing system or situation?
    a. systems investigation
    b. systems analysis
    c. systems design
    d. systems implementation

21. True or False: The purpose of systems implementation is to select and plan a system that meets the requirements outlined during systems analysis.

22. _____ is a potential health problem that can be caused by long hours working on a computer keyboard.

23. True or false: Computers can be used as a tool to commit a crime or be the object of a crime.

Test Yourself Solutions: **1.** c. **2.** c. **3.** Productivity, **4.** F, **5.** Computer scientists, **6.** F, **7.** T, **8.** computer, **9.** T, **10.** Software, **11.** a. **12.** F, **13.** d. **14.** server, **15.** T, **16.** database management system (DBMS), **17.** d. **18.** a management information system (MIS), **19.** fuzzy logic, **20.** a. **21.** F, **22.** Repetitive stress injury (RSI) or carpal tunnel syndrome (CTS), **23.** T

 # Key Terms

computer, p. 4
computer system, p. 24
data, p. 7
file, p. 20
hardware, p. 17
information, p. 7
Internet, p. 20

mainframe server, p. 23
midrange server, p. 23
mobile computer, p. 22
network, p. 26
people, p. 25
personal computer, p. 23
procedures, p. 25

program coding, p. 33
server, p. 23
software, p. 19
supercomputer, p. 23
telecommunications system, p. 26
workstation, p. 23

 # Questions

Review Questions

1. How does information differ from data?

2. What is productivity? What is quality?

3. How can an organization achieve a competitive advantage?

4. Describe how five career areas can benefit from computer systems.

5. What is a computer?

6. What is the purpose of the computer's memory?

7. Describe the functions of the central processing unit.

8. Discuss popular input and output devices.

9. What is an Internet service provider?

10. List and describe the different computer types.

11. What is a computer system? Describe the components of a computer system.

12. What is a database management system (DBMS)?

13. Describe the various types of electronic commerce.

14. What is the difference between a transaction processing system and a management information system?

15. What is a decision support system (DSS)? An expert system?

16. What is the difference between systems analysis and systems design?

17. Give an example of a multimedia application.

18. Give several examples of computer crime.

19. What is identity theft?

20. What is repetitive stress injury?

21. Why is it important to study information systems?

Discussion Questions

22. What are the characteristics of valuable information? Give an example for each characteristic. Obtaining valuable information can involve trade-offs among these characteristics. Give example(s) of potential tradeoffs.

23. As part of a quality initiative, you decided a company needed a new computer system. The computer systems were brought in over the weekend. How should the new computer system be tested?

24. Go to one or more stores that sell computer hardware. Give an example of a hardware device that is not currently available that you would consider buying if it were available.

25. What career area or field is of interest to you? Describe how you could use one or more computer systems to advance your career in this area or field.

26. Describe how you could use management information and decision support to help you achieve your personal and professional goals.

27. Pick a hobby or an area that interests you. Describe how you would go through the systems development process to acquire a computer system to help you in this area of interest.

28. What social and ethical issues concern you the most? Which one is the most dangerous to you and society?

Exercises

Try It Yourself

1. Prepare a data disk and a backup disk to use for the lab and Web exercises throughout the text. Create one folder for each chapter in the textbook (you should have 12 folders when you are done). As you work through the Try It Yourself exercises and complete other work using the computer, save your assignments for each chapter in the appropriate folder. On the outside of each disk be sure to include your name, course, and section. On one disk write "Working Copy"; on the other write "Backup."

2. At one or more local computer stores, research your ideal personal computer system, including all hardware, software, databases, and so on. Using a spreadsheet, list the cost of each item and compute the total cost for the entire computer system.

3. Using the Internet, research a career area that interests you. (You can use a search engine, such as Yahoo.com or Google.com.) Using your word processor, prepare a report describing the number and types of computer systems occupations that are available in that career area. In addition, note how many other occupations require some computer systems technology and skills.

Virtual Classroom Activities

For the following exercises, do not use face-to-face or telephone communications with your group members. Use only Internet communications.

4. Use the Internet to research distance learning. What are the advantages of distance learning for a student? What are the disadvantages?

5. With a group or team, investigate invasion of privacy issues, including identity theft. What can you do to avoid invasion of your privacy? What new laws should be passed to protect people from the invasion of privacy?

Teamwork

6. Your first task is this: One member of the group must send an e-mail message to a second member of the group, giving an opinion on a current event. The second person should state an opinion in response and forward that message, including the first message, on to the third member of the group. Continue with this process until the last member of the group forwards the entire string of messages back to its originator. Print this final message and submit it to your instructor. It should

contain the names and comments of each member of the group.

7. Within your team, brainstorm about the characteristics of a good group or team member. Develop a contract to be used by your team to ensure that all members of the team will work hard to complete all teamwork assignments. Note that you can revisit this document and modify it if necessary. If you do, have all members initial the changes.

8. Your team should explore how a computer system can be used to obtain a competitive advantage in two or more career areas. You can use the Internet to search for ideas. Use your word-processing program to write a report on what you found.

Learning Check

To check your knowledge of each of the chapter objectives, use this chart to find related end-of-chapter content.

Learning Objective	Key Terms		Questions	Exercises
Learning Objective 1 Describe the use of computer systems	computer data	information	1, 2, 3, 13, 22	7
Learning Objective 2 Discuss how computers are used in a variety of fields and why studying computer systems can benefit you professionally and personally.			4, 25	3, 8
Learning Objective 3 Define basic computer concepts.	files hardware internet mainframe server midrange server mobile computer	personal computer server software supercomputer workstation	5, 6, 7, 8, 9, 10, 24	1, 4, 6
Learning Objective 4 Discuss the components of any computer system and how they are used.	computer system network people procedures telecommunications system		11, 12, 13, 14, 15, 26	2
Learning Objective 5 Explain how computer systems and applications can be developed and controlled.	program coding		16, 17, 18, 19, 20, 21, 23, 27, 28	5

Endnotes

1. Collier, Joan, "The X-Treme Generation Gap; Marketing to the New Consumer Age," *Florida Underwriters*, September 2002, p. 16.

2. Gross, Neil, "Highway Cameras That Can Direct Traffic," *Business Week*, November 18, 2002, p. 77.

3. Melymuks, K. "So You Want to Be a CTO," *Computerworld*, March 24, 2003, p. 42.

4. "U.S. Microbics, Inc. Wins Best Company Award," *PR Newswire*, January 3, 2002.

5. Shellenbarger, Sue, "Telework Is on the Rise," *The Wall Street Journal*, January 23, 2002, p. B1.

6. Klein, G. Barry, "The Automated Executive," *Technology Decisions*, September 2002, p. 56.

7. Bryant, Robert M., "Targeting Fraud in 2003: Creating Fraud Solutions . . . Now," *Claims Magazine*, p.39.

8. Breeding, Marshall, "What you can expect from the systems librarian," *Computers in Libraries*, Westport, January 2003.

9. Balas, Janet I., "Will there be libraries to visit in our future?" *Computers in Libraries*, Westport, October 2002.

10. Breeding, Marshall, "Monitoring the use of your Web site," *Information Today*, Medford, December 2002.

11. Hamilton, David, "The Nanotechnician," *The Wall Street Journal*, May 13, 2002, p. R17.

12. Levy, Steven, "Great Minds, Great Ideas," *Newsweek*, May 27, 2002.

13. Maiello, Michael, "Superstring Man," *Forbes*, February 4, 2002, p. 68.

14. Bylinsky, Gene, "Heroes of Manufacturing," *Fortune*, March 17, 2003, p. 124.

15. Versel, Neil, "Reaching Critical Mass; Between HIPAA Compliance and the Quality Push, Healthcare IT-with CPOE as a Huge Component-Is Coming into Its Own," *Modern Physician*, July 1, 2002, p. 13

16. "Swiss Town leads Way with Internet Voting," *CNN Online*, January 20, 2003.

17. Compton, Ann, "The Big Hit: Arizona Dems Flood On-line Voting Web Site," *abcNews.com*, March 10, 2000, http://abcnews.go.com/sections/politics/OnBackground/onbackground000313.html, cited September 18, 2003.

18. Brandel, Mary, "Home-Schooling–IT Talent," *Computerworkd*, January 27, 2003, p. 36.

19. McKay, Martha, "Hoboken, N.J., Company Sells Computers Systems to Schools," *Knight Ridder Tribune Business News*; Washington; March 2, 2003.

20. Goldstein, Michael, "Our Next-gen Techies," *Mass High Tech*; Burlington; January 6, 2003.

21. Williams, Reid, "Double-Clicking Toward a Degree," *Summit Daily News*, June 28, 2002, p. A8.

22. Staff, "Kalam Sets Young Dreams Soaring," *Businessline*; Islamabad; October 29, 2002.

23. Roe, Andrew, "Building Digitally Provides Schedule, Cost Efficiencies," *Construction Management*, Vol. 24B, No. 7, p. 29.

24. Staff, "The Net Detectives," *Business and Finance*, January 30, 2003, p.85.

25. Goodwin, Bill, "Burglars Captured By Police Data Mining Kit," *Computer Weekly*, August 8, 2002, p. 3.

26. Lamont, Judith, "Starting With the Basics: KM for Lawyers," *KM World*, September 2002, Vol. 11, No. 8, p. 12(2).

27. Goldsmigh, Charles, "German Visual Image Firm Is Honored for Film Graphics," *The Wall Street Journal*, February 26, 2003, p. B1.

28. Heun, Christopher, "Marine Mouse Takes IT to New Depths," *InformationWeek*, November 5, 2002, p. 20.

29. O'Sullivan, Mike, "Roman Forum Virtually Recreated in California," *Voice of American News*, January 31, 2003.

30. Mossberg, Walter, "New Refrigerator Surfs the Web," *The Wall Street Journal*, October 23, 2002, p. D1.

31. Clark, Don, "AMD Stages Supercomputer Coup," *The Wall Street Journal*, October 21, 2002, p. B4.

32. Jones, Rebecca, "Distance Learning Brings D.C. to Denver," *Rocky Mountain News*, February 10, 2003, p. 12A.

33. Nelson, Emily, "TV Crews Plan to Employ A Range of High-Tech Gear," *The Wall Street Journal*, March 12, 2003, p. B1.

34. Reina, Peter, "Modeling Helps Engineers Devise Cooling Fix," *Engineering News-Record*, April 1, 2002, p. 20.

35. Kilman, Scott, "Poultry in Motion," *The Wall Street Journal*, June 4, 2003, p. B1.

36. "National Foot Care Program Announces Launch of a Unique Program," *PR Newswire*, January 15, 2002.

37. "Sirius shapes up YMCA's communications infrastructure", *IBM News*, www-1.ibm.com/partnerworld/pwhome.nsf/mktgsale/nws_success_sirius.html accessed June 11, 2003.

38. Gaudin, Sharon, "Gartner Predicts Upturn in Software Sales", *Datamation*, March 17, 2003, http://itmanagement.earthweb.com/it_res/article.php/2110831 accessed June 11, 2003.

39. Nash, Kim, "CIO in Scandal," *Computerworld*, February 11, 2002, p. 24.

40. Strecker, Tom, "Computers Cut Vandalism," *New Zealand Infotech Weekly*, May 12, 2003, p. 6.

41. Smith, Steven, "Carpal Tunnel? Can't Blame The Computer," *Boston Globe*, June 24, 2003.

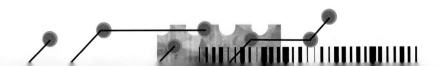

HardwareDesigned **to**Meet**the**Need

Marcus Bates recently graduated from college and started a new job as a graphic artist for Lamar Advertising. Now that he has steady income, Marcus wants to replace his four-year-old PC with a new computer. He realizes that there are a lot of purchasing options and that the decision will be a difficult one to make. He wants to make sure that he ends up with a device that perfectly suits his needs without wasting money on options that he doesn't need. Marcus uses his current computer for e-mail and instant messaging, Web browsing, managing his personal budget, basic word processing, multiplayer games, and sometimes for Lamar Advertising projects that he brings home. He is interested in trying out some of the new technology that he's heard about, specifically the ability to speak to the computer rather than typing and video phone over the Internet.

1. How should Marcus prepare for his purchasing decision?
2. What type of computer might best suit Marcus's needs?
3. How much processor speed, memory, and storage capacity does Marcus need?
4. What input/output devices would best suit Marcus's needs?
5. Are there any additional considerations to be made regarding this purchase?

Check out Marcus's *Action Plan* at the conclusion of this chapter.

After completing Chapter 2, you will be able to:

LEARNING OBJECTIVES	CHAPTER CONTENT
1. Understand how bits and bytes are used to represent text, values, colors, and sound and how digital data representation is changing our lives.	**The Digital Revolution**
2. Identify the functions of the components of a CPU, the relationship between the CPU and memory, and factors that contribute to processing speed.	**Integrated Circuits and Processing**
3. Identify different types of memory and storage media, and understand the unique properties of each.	**Storage**
4. Identify different types of input and output devices and how they are used to meet a variety of personal and professional needs.	**Input, Output, and Expansion**
5. Understand the decision-making process involved in purchasing a computer system.	**Selecting and Purchasing a Computer System**

Introduction

How can a person keep up with the ever-increasing momentum of technological innovation? If you tried to learn all the details of every new device, you would soon be overwhelmed. It makes better sense to first learn the underlying technology that all these devices share.

From large server computers that support the needs of thousands of users, to the smallest handheld computer, computing devices share certain characteristics. They all manipulate digital data, and they all share fundamental components: processing components, data storage, and input and output capabilities. By learning about these underlying principles and components, you will develop a better understanding of what computing devices are capable of and how you can benefit from those capabilities. You will become empowered to competently use information and communication devices, past, present, and foreseeable future.

A *computer system* is any device that supports four activities:

- **Input:** Capturing and gathering raw data
- **Processing:** Converting or changing raw data into useful outputs
- **Storage:** Maintaining data within the system temporarily or permanently
- **Output:** The results of the processing produced in a manner that is observable by human beings or used as input into another system

Although it is easy to see how PCs and other types of computers fit this definition, we sometimes overlook other electronic devices that also meet these criteria. For example, a digital cell phone accepts your voice as input, stores and processes sound-related data, and outputs an electronic signal. Other examples include CD, MP3, and DVD players, electronic fuel injection systems in automobiles, and a host of other devices with which we commonly interact.

This chapter looks in detail at hardware that supports the four activities of computer systems, starting with the most elementary concepts that are shared by all computing devices.

THE DIGITAL REVOLUTION

What do today's most popular cell phones, cameras, MP3 players, home entertainment centers, and even automobiles have in common with your personal computer? Digital electronics! Digital electronics is the force behind most of the technological innovation we are witnessing today. Digital cell phones, digital cameras, digital camcorders, digital surround-sound stereo, digital video disks (DVDs), digital cable TV, digital satellite radio, digital video recorders (such as TiVo), many current digital technologies include the word *digital* in their name. You can see a sampling of these devices in Figure 2.1. Other devices do not include the word digital in their name, including smart phones, HDTV (high-definition TV), global positioning systems (GPSs), and the wide array of new computers and computer applications, such as residential high-speed Internet access and wireless networking. Nevertheless, they are based on the same digital technology. It is clear that we are living in an increasingly digital society.

FIGURE 2.1 • Digital electronics

Notebook computers, cell phones, MP3 players, and a wide array of other devices are all based on the same digital technology.

We are in the midst of a digital revolution, and most experts agree that we've only seen the tip of the iceberg. It is impossible to guess how our lives will be affected by advances in technology over the next 5 or 10 years. By understanding the underlying principles of digital electronics, we can be better prepared to thrive in that future.

At the core of digital electronics is a most simple concept called the bit (short for **bi**nary dig**it**). A **bit** is the smallest unit of information used in computers. The word *binary*, from which bit is derived, describes a numbering scheme in which there are only two possible values for each digit: 0 and 1. All digital devices are based on the concept of representing data and information using bits, zeros and ones—a process called **digitization**. It is possible to digitize all recordable information: words, numbers, sound, music, and images, and in doing so to make the information easier to manipulate, duplicate, access, and share. To understand the importance of digitization, we must look at how computers use bits to represent data and information.

Bits and Bytes

A computer's design is based on a fundamental engineering principle: the switch. Switches have two possible states: on or off. It is from the two-state (binary) switch that the bit was born. Any object that can be judged as being in one of two different states can be used as a binary switch. For example, computers have three methods of implementing a binary switch: circuits that are either electrically charged or not charged (computer memory), magnetic particles that are arranged in one of two directions (hard disk), and a surface area that may or may not have a pit (CD). The two states of these binary switches are assigned meaning: charged=1, not charged=0, and so on.

How does a bit, that stores a 1 or 0, represent objects and ideas of importance to people, such as digital photographs and MP3 music? To answer this question, you must understand that 1 and 0 are simply symbols that have been arbitrarily chosen to represent the current state of the switch. We could just as easily say that a bit stores true or false, male or female, black or white, or any two units of information. Figure 2.2 illustrates how we can represent something useful by changing the 1s or 0s of bits to black or white areas in an image.

By itself, a bit is not all that useful. Most objects of value have more than two possible states. For instance, our eyes can discern over 16 million colors, not just black and white. How can we use a bit to represent 16 million colors? The answer is to combine it with many other bits.

By grouping bits together we create a wider range of possible 1 and 0 combinations. For example, a 2-bit group provides us with four possible combinations of 1s and 0s: 00, 01, 10, and 11. A 3-bit group allows us to represent eight different objects. With each additional bit that we add, we double the amount of objects or information that we can represent. Eight bits combined is called a **byte**. A byte—for example, 11000011—provides 256 different possible combinations of 1s and 0s. We could assign information to each of these combinations. For example, we could use a byte to represent 256 colors (see Figure 2.3). A simple equation illustrates the relationship between bits and the amount of information they represent: $2^b = i$, where b represents the amount of bits and i the amount of units of information. For example, $2^8 = 256$.

A byte is the standard unit of storage in digital electronics. To represent objects that have more than 256 possible

EXPAND YOUR **KNOWLEDGE**

To learn more about the ins and outs of binary numbers, go to www.course.com/concepts/swt. Click the link "Expand Your Knowledge" and then complete the lab entitled, "Binary Numbers."

FIGURE 2.2 • Using bits to represent something useful

By using the two states of a bit, its 1s and 0s, to represent black and white, we can create an image.

FIGURE 2.3 • Using bytes to represent something more useful

Three bytes can be used to represent photo-quality colors.

1. Example of byte
   codes and colors

```
10010010 11000011 10101010
10010010 11000111 10101010
10010010 11001111 10101010
10010010 11011111 10101010
10010010 11111111 10101010
10010011 11111111 19111911
10010011 11111111 00110101
10010011 11000011 11000110
10010111 11000011 10011000
10011111 11000011 11110000
10010011 11111011 00010001
10011010 11111111 10100001
10011110 11111111 11100110
10010111 11000011 11000011
10011111 11000011 00110011
10010011 11111011 11101011
```

2. Pixel color in image indicated
   by byte code in file

3. Image at proper resolution

states, we combine bytes together. For instance, we use 3 bytes (24 bits) to represent the over 16 million colors discernable to the human eye.

This approach to data representation can be considered a "look-up table" approach. Units of information are assigned to unique bit patterns to form a look-up table. For example, in a color look-up table, you might look up 10001111 to find that it represents light blue. A playing card table might show that 00001100 is the ace of spades. The text that we type on our computer keyboard is stored in bytes using a look-up table system. In the early days of computing, the computer industry agreed on a code for representing text characters and named it **American Standard Code for Information Interchange (ASCII)**.

ASCII is a prime example of an important concept called a *standard*. A standard is an agreed-upon way of doing something within an industry. ASCII is the agreed upon look-up table codes (more commonly called an ASCII chart) for character data.

Understanding the relationship between bits and the things they represent has practical applications. Want to buy a new digital camera? Understanding the difference between a 3-megapixel and 4-megapixel camera could save you $200, but you'll need to know about bits and bytes. Want to transfer CD music to your portable MP3-player? It helps to know about bits and bytes to determine the quality of the MP3 file you wish to create. Users of cell phones, computers, and computer networks all benefit from a clear understanding of how bits and bytes are used in digital electronics.

Kilo, Mega, Giga, Tera, and Peta

We abbreviate the word *byte* with *B* and *bit* with *b*. For example, we could write 3 B = 24 b. When discussing large quantities of bits and bytes we use the following prefixes:

- **Kilo:** roughly 1,000 (one thousand); actually 2^{10} (1,024)
- **Mega:** roughly 1,000,000 (one million); actually 2^{20} (1,048,576)
- **Giga:** roughly 1,000,000,000 (one billion); actually 2^{30} (1,073,741,824)
- **Tera:** roughly 1,000,000,000,000 (one trillion); actually 2^{40} (1,099,511,627,776)

So, 200 MB represents 200 million bytes, and 56 Kb represents 56 thousand bits. In casual conversation, we round these values to a thousand, million, billion, and trillion, but for more precise calculations you would use their actual value. You're most likely familiar with the prefixes kilo, mega, and giga as they are used to measure the capacity of disks and computer memory, as well as Internet connection speeds. As storage capacities and connection speeds continue to increase the use of tera as a prefix will become more common. Even the prefix *peta* (a quadrillion, or a thousand trillion) is increasing in use.

A petabyte of data is difficult to fathom. Think of it as the equivalent of 250 billion pages of text, enough to fill 20 million four-drawer filing cabinets. Or imagine a 2,000-mile-high tower of 1 billion diskettes.[1] Sound extreme? It's becoming commonplace for popular online services such as Google, AOL, Hotmail, and Yahoo! to maintain databases that are in the petabyte range[2].

Representing Values with Bytes: The Binary Number System

Bytes are treated differently depending on how they are used, just as we treat characters differently depending on how they are used. For example, when you see the symbols 322-2413 you treat them differently depending on what you are told about them. If this is a friend's phone number, you treat these symbols as characters representing buttons to press on your phone. If this is a math problem, you treat these symbols as numbers representing values in a subtraction equation.

The same is true with bytes. If you are shown a byte, 01000001, and are told that this is a byte from the e-mail message that you are composing, you would assume that this byte represents a typed character, and you could look up the character on an ASCII chart. If this byte were taken from a spreadsheet file, it could very well represent a value used in a calculation. However, it is not the decimal number 1,000,001, one million and one, it is the binary number 01000001 which is interpreted differently than a decimal number.

The **binary number system** is used in computer systems because like bits, the binary number system has only two numbers: 1 and 0. There are many number systems, all equal in power, and all supporting the same mathematical operations as our decimal number system. Computers represent quantities and values and carry out mathematical operations with binary numbers.

Because bytes can be used to represent values—binary numbers—computers are able to do some very useful things. Besides their use in performing calculations, binary numbers are used to represent digitized images and sound. Your favorite movie on DVD and songs on CD or MP3 are long lists of binary numbers interpreted by your media player.

Representing Images with Bytes

Using binary numbers we can represent images digitally. This simple fact has brought us flatbed scanners, digital cameras, digital camcorders, digital cable TV, the DVD movie, and digital video recorders. Not to mention phenomenal advances in movie production techniques. The fundamental technology behind all of these technologies rests on a small point of light or dot of ink called a pixel.

As illustrated previously in Figure 2.3, images are made up of a grid of small points called **pixels** (short for picture element). Pixel is a good term to remember as it has practical value when used to determine the quality of displays, printers, scanners, and digital cameras. Representing an image using bytes, is simply a matter of storing the color of each pixel in the image. Images stored in this manner are called **bit-mapped graphics** or *raster* graphics. Colors are expressed using numbers that represent combinations of intensities of red, blue, and green, 1 byte (256 levels of intensity) for each.

Simpler images, such as those used in clip art, can be represented using vector graphics. **Vector graphics** use bytes to store mathematical formulas that define all

the shapes in the image. Although vector graphics are impractical for representing photo-quality images, they are preferred for creating and storing drawings (see Figure 2.4). Vector graphics are easier to edit and manipulate than bit-mapped graphics and use far fewer bytes to store an image.

Animation and video are stored in the computer as a series of bit-mapped images called *frames*. When shown in quick succession, the frames create the illusion of movement. Television uses a rate of 30 frames per second (fps).

FIGURE 2.4 • Vector graphics

Vector graphics use bytes to store mathematical formulas that define all the shapes in an image.

Representing Sound and Music with Bytes

Digitizing sound has dramatically altered the music industry by replacing cassette tapes with higher-quality CDs and making it possible to share music files over the Internet. Digital sound is also responsible for digital PCS cell phones that provide higher sound quality and better security than traditional cell phones. Digital movies and television also make use of digital sound. How can such high-quality sound be encoded in the holes burned into the surface of a CD or DVD?

We digitize sound by representing it with numbers, and as we know, numbers can be represented with the 1s and 0s of the binary number system. In the natural world, sound is the displacement of air particles caused by vibration and sensed by the eardrum. We can quantify sound by measuring the amount of air particle displacement and charting it over time to create a graph, called an analog sound wave. The term *analog* refers to signals that vary continuously. An analog sound wave can be transmitted electrically using varying voltages of electricity as is done over a traditional telephone network. A sound wave can also be represented with numbers, digitally, through a process called sampling (see Figure 2.5).

To *sample* a sound wave, you measure its amplitude at regular time intervals; the shorter the time interval, the more accurate the reproduction of the sound. For example, the sampling rate for audio CDs is 44,100 samples per second, whereas the sampling rate of your voice on a digital cell phone is 8,000 times per second.

FIGURE 2.5 • Digitizing sound

A sound wave (1) is sampled by measuring its amplitude at consistent time intervals (2), digitally storing the amplitude values as numbers (3), then recreating the analogue wave from the numbers (4).

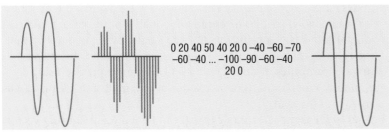

0 20 40 50 40 20 0 −40 −60 −70 −60 −40 ... −100 −90 −60 −40 20 0

1. Sound wave   2. Sampling   3. Digital storage   4. Recreated sound wave

Digital Hospitals

Hospitals are filled with state-of-the art medical equipment for monitoring patients' vital signs and assisting with medical procedures. Yet, many doctors and other healthcare professionals feel they are working in one of the last predigital industries. "Bellevue is an excellent hospital, but I think that a first-rate communications system would really enhance our ability to do our work. It just takes too long to get the data we need sometimes," says Sahid Samir, a resident at New York's Bellevue hospital.

Medical recordkeeping has come under critical scrutiny in recent years and is blamed for a considerable number of patient deaths. Many such accidents lead to medical malpractice suits. Some doctors are changing professions or relocating in order to avoid exorbitant malpractice insurance costs in their state.

This crisis in the medical profession is leading to the creation of the world's first all-digital hospitals. HealthSouth has teamed with Oracle to construct a 500,000-square-foot, 219-bed digital hospital in suburban Birmingham, Alabama. The Indiana Heart Hospital has partnered with GE Medical Systems to build an all-digital cardiac hospital in Indianapolis. Both hospitals promise to bring the same benefits to their patients: lower healthcare costs, greatly reduced human errors, and the best medical care available.

"We are so totally committed to a paperless, film-less, and wireless environment, that we won't even have nursing stations," said David Veillette, CEO of the Indiana Heart Hospital. "Instead, all of our caregivers will be able to input and retrieve information right at the patient's bedside."

The hospital medical records rooms typically filled with file cabinets containing patient records will be replaced by server computers. Nurses, doctors, and hospital technicians will be equipped with handheld computers and tablet PCs that will access patient records from the servers from anywhere in the hospital via a wireless network.

"Current health care trends, including nursing shortages, make the all-digital concept crucial," David Veillette, CEO of the Indiana Heart Hospital said. "The aging of the Baby Boomers means we have to find more efficient ways to take care of three times as many patients, with staffing levels that will be decreasing," he said. "The only way to do that is with information technology." With electronic records, hospital personnel won't have to struggle to read someone else's handwriting because data will be entered with a keyboard. Also, doctors and nurses won't have to search for paper files—reducing the possibility of errors, according to hospital officials.

HealthSouth is looking at 10 more cities where similar hospitals could be built.

Questions

1. What do you think would be the biggest challenge in launching an all-digital hospital? Digitizing the information? Choosing and installing the equipment? Training nurses, doctors, and technicians? Why?

2. What benefits will be available to patients and physicians if and when all medical recordkeeping is digitized?

3. What concerns may be associated with moving from paper recordkeeping systems to digital recordkeeping systems?

Sources
1. *"GE Medical Aids New All-Digital Cardiac Hospital in Indianapolis," by Rick Barrett,* The Milwaukee Journal Sentinel, *January 24, 2002.*
2. *"How Secure Is Digital Hospital?," Michelle Delio,* Wired News, *Mar. 28, 2001, www.wired.com.*
3. *"Nation's First All-Digital Heart Hospital Uses Information Technology to Battle Heart Disease,"* PR Newswire, *January 24, 2002.*
4. *www.gemedicalsystems.com*
5. *www.cpmc.columbia.edu/*

Sound represented as a series of numbers is called *digital sound* since it can be represented digitally using binary numbers and bits. Digital sound is used in audio CDs, a variety of other computer music formats, and digital phone communication, as well as other applications. It has tremendous advantages over analog sound in a number of ways. It can be duplicated and transmitted without any degeneration. It has a relatively limitless life span. It is easy to manipulate and process and can be encrypted for secure communications.

Digital phones and media players include an *analog-to-digital converter* (ADC) and a *digital-to-analog converter* (DAC) to translate sound and music back and forth between analog and digital signals.

Bits, Bytes, and Us

Digitization is the great equalizer of information. Whether the information is news or typed communication (text), music, photos, videos, or voice, it's all just a bunch of bits to the machine. This is the underlying principle of a trend called digital convergence. **Digital convergence** is the trend to merge multiple digital services into one device. At home, a single device can be used for audio and video entertainment, computing, information access, and voice, video, and text communications. At work, digital convergence can be used to combine voice, video, and text communications and information on a single network. On the road, digital convergence makes it possible to merge cell phone, PDA (personal digital assistant), MP3 player, and digital camera functionality into a single portable device, as you can see in Figure 2.6.

The digitization of information grants us power over that information. Learning the basic principles of digitization and binary data representation allows us to move beyond just knowing what buttons to push, to a deeper understanding of what is happening inside the machine and in our culture. Now, let's explore how computing devices manipulate bits and bytes to our advantage.

FIGURE 2.6 • **Digital convergence in your hand**

Handspring's Treo 600 Smart-Phone combines a digital cell phone, digital camera, and handheld computer in one device.

INTEGRATEDCIRCUITSANDPROCESSING

The ability to digitize information is at the heart of the digital revolution; however, digitized information is valueless without the ability to process it into useful forms. Processors are important components of all digital devices. CD and MP3 players process digitized music into analog sound, a digital cell phone processes voice sound waves into digital signals and back again, a digital cable TV receiver processes digital video into images on your television screen, and, of course, computers use software to processes data into useful information and services.

The quality of a processor typically reflects the quality of the computing device in which it resides. This is especially true in computers. New computer owners often boast about the speed of their system's processor. As aspects of computing move to increasingly divergent devices, we will no doubt gauge the quality of many devices by their processors.

This section provides a look at the technology used in today's processors, as well as how to measure the quality of a processor in order to make wise purchasing decisions. We'll look at important components that support the act of processing in integrated circuits, and how a special integrated circuit, called the central processing unit, works with other integrated circuits, called memory, to process data in computer systems.

Integrated Circuits

Computers use digital switches not only to store bits and bytes, but also to process them. We have learned that any object having two distinct states can be used as a digital switch. Over the years computers have used different devices as digital switches, progressing from physical switches and relays, to vacuum tubes, to transistors. The **transistor**, invented in 1947 at Bell Labs, has become the key ingredient of all digital circuits, including those used in computers. A transistor is composed of semiconducting material, typically silicon, that opens or closes a circuit to alter the flow of electricity. When electricity is flowing through a transistor it represents a 1; when it is not flowing it represents a 0. By combining transistors and using the output from one or more transistors as the input to others, computers control the flow of electricity in a manner that represents mathematical and logical operations.

Computers use transistors to process data by controlling the flow of electricity through opened and closed circuits. To store bits and bytes, computers combine transistors with capacitors. A *capacitor* is a passive electronic component that stores energy in the form of an electrostatic field. Transistors and capacitors are the building blocks for processing and storing bits and bytes.

In the late 1950s, Jack Kilby of Texas Instruments and Robert Noyce of Fairchild Semiconductor, developed a method to integrate multiple transistors into a single module called an **integrated circuit**. Integrated circuits, also called chips, are used to store and process bits and bytes in today's computers. The group of integrated circuits that work together to perform the processing in a computer system is called the **central processing unit (CPU)**. Today's technology is able to pack all the CPU circuits onto a single module smaller than the size of your smallest fingernail, called a **microprocessor**. The microprocessor and other supportive chips are housed on circuit boards where embedded pathways electronically join the chips together. The primary circuit board of a computing device is called the **motherboard** (see Figure 2.7).

FIGURE 2.7 • PC motherboard

All computing devices house their chips on a circuit board known as a motherboard.

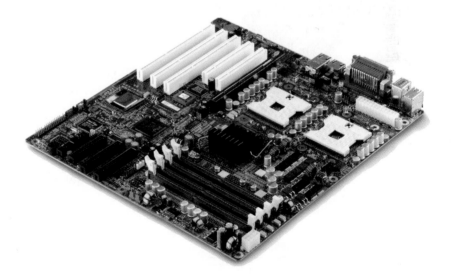

The Central Processing Unit and Random Access Memory

Processing is the act of manipulating data in a manner defined by programmed instructions. Computer programs contain lists of instructions for the processor to carry out. A processor is engineered to carry out a specific and finite number of instructions called its *instruction set*. When a computer runs a program, the processor progresses through the program's sequence of instructions, carrying out each instruction with specially designed circuitry, and jumping to various subsets of instructions as a user interacts with the program.

EXPAND YOUR
KNOWLEDGE

To learn more about the motherboard and its various components, go to www.course.com/swt. Click the link "Expand Your Knowledge" and then complete the lab entitled, "Understanding the Motherboard."

A CPU consists of three primary elements: the arithmetic/logic unit, the control unit, and registers. The **arithmetic/logic unit (ALU)** contains the circuitry to carry out instructions, such as mathematical calculations and logical comparisons. The **control unit** sequentially accesses program instructions, decodes them, and coordinates the flow of data in and out of the ALU, the registers, random access memory, and other system components such as secondary storage, input, and output devices. *Registers* hold the bytes currently being processed.

The CPU works closely with random access memory. **Random access memory (RAM)** is temporary, or *volatile*, storage that is cleared each time you turn off the computer. RAM stores data and program instructions waiting to be processed and the results of processing as bytes in addressed cells. RAM capacities in today's new PCs typically range from 128 MB to 512 MB. Data flows back and forth between the CPU and RAM across the system bus. The *system bus* consists of parallel pathways between the CPU and RAM capable of transporting several bytes at once. Figure 2.8 shows how the CPU, RAM, and the system bus work in concert to pass bits back and forth.

To understand the function of processing and the interplay between the CPU and RAM, let's examine the way a typical computer executes a program instruction.

FIGURE 2.8 • CPU, Bus, and RAM

Bytes travel between RAM and the CPU over the system bus.

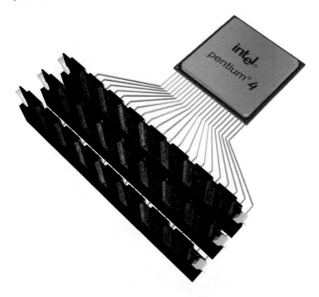

The Machine Cycle. The execution of an instruction involves two phases: the instruction phase and the execution phase. These two phases together make up the *machine cycle*. The time it takes for a computer to carry out one instruction is called *machine cycle time*.

Figure 2.9 shows the four steps in the machine cycle. In the instruction phase of the machine cycle, the computer carries out the following steps:

Instruction Phase
Step 1: Fetch instruction. The instruction to be executed is accessed from RAM by the control unit. The control unit stores the RAM address of the currently executing instruction.
Step 2: Decode instruction. The instruction is decoded, relevant data is moved from RAM to the CPU registers, and the stored address of the current instruction is incremented to prepare for the next fetch.

In the execution phase of the machine cycle, the computer carries out Steps 3 and 4:

Execution Phase
Step 3: Execute the instruction. The ALU does what it is instructed to do. This could involve making either an arithmetic computation or a logical comparison.
Step 4: Store results. The results are stored in registers or RAM.

FIGURE 2.9 • Execution of an instruction

The machine cycle is made up of the instruction phase and the execution phase, and consists of four steps: fetch, decode, execute, and store.

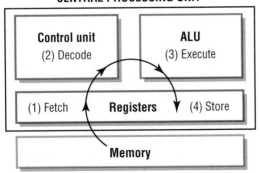

The instructions carried out by a processor are incredibly basic and highly detailed. For example, when running a calculator program, a simple addition such as 2 + 3 would take four keystrokes: "2", "+", "3", "=", and the result is displayed. However, the processor would execute five instructions per key stroke, a total of 20 instructions, to do a simple addition. Nineteen of those instructions are used to move the input data between computing components and around the processor, only one is used to perform the addition.

CENTRAL PROCESSING UNIT

Processors perform a variety of instructions on different types of data. For example, a digital to analog processor in a CD player reads bytes of digitized sound from a CD, and processes the digits into an output of analog sound—music. A digital camera accepts input from a camera lens and outputs a list of pixel color codes to a file. An e-mail program, translates keyboard data into ASCII characters, and forwards the collection of characters to an e-mail server for processing.

CPU Characteristics. The first consideration in selecting a computer is typically its speed—how quickly it can carry out tasks such as loading a program, opening a file, and writing to a CD. The speed at which a processor can carry out an instruction is governed by the system clock. Each CPU contains a *system clock* that produces a series of electronic pulses at a predetermined rate called the *clock speed*. Clock speed is measured in **megahertz (MHz)**, millions of cycles per second, or **gigahertz (GHz)**, billions of cycles per second. It is this specification that is always at the top of the list in computer advertisements, and contributes the most to the cost of the computer.

Faster clock speeds generate more heat in a system and require larger cooling systems. For this reason, you'll find that smaller devices generally have a lower maximum available clock speed, as illustrated in Table 2.1.

Although clock speed has a direct effect on overall system performance, it is not the only contributing factor. Other features of a processor's architecture can affect its performance. For example, different types of processors can process varying amounts of bits at a time. The number of bits that a CPU can process at once is called its *wordlength*. So a processor with a 32-bit wordlength and a 2-GHz clock speed is equal in performance to a 64-bit processor with a 1-GHz clock speed. Today's personal computers typically use wordlengths of 32 or 64 bits. The Apple G4 processor uses a wordlength of 128 bits. The larger the wordlength, the more powerful the computer.

TABLE 2.1 • Typical Clockspeeds in 2003

Machine Type	Clock Speeds
Handheld computer	33–400 MHz
Notebook PC	933 MHz–2 GHz
Desktop PC	900 MHz–3.06 GHz

Judging a computer's quality and speed by its specifications can be complicated. The public has been trained by marketing to judge computers by clock speed. However, today some personal computers with lower clock speeds outperform their competitors. For example, Apple claims that their G4 processor running at 1 GHz performs better than a Pentium processor running at 2 GHz.[3]

The true measure of processor performance is the amount of time it takes to execute an instruction. This measure is called **MIPS** for millions of instructions per second; a more precise measurement is called *FLOPS* for floating-point operations per second. Today's personal computers carry out billions of instructions per second, or operate in the **gigaflop** range. Supercomputers run in the *teraflop* (trillions) range. For example, IBM's ASCI White assists the U.S. government in simulating a nuclear detonation using massively parallel processing at 12.3 teraflops—12.3 trillion floating-point operations per second.[4] A human brain's probable processing power is around 100 teraflops, roughly 100 trillion calculations per second, according to Hans Morvec, principal research scientist at the Robotics Institute of Carnegie Mellon University. IBM's ASCI Purple, due out in 2004, will equal this power.[5]

We have learned a considerable amount about microprocessors. However, when we decide it is time to buy a new personal computer, we do not typically begin by comparing processors. We typically begin with more general considerations. Such as should I get a notebook computer or a desktop computer? Should I get an Apple or a PC? By deciding on computer type and platform, we typically align ourselves with a narrow range of processors from which to choose. In Chapter 1, we discussed the many types of computer systems available. Now, we will look at the concept of computer platform.

Computer Platforms. A computer's processor and operating system define its **computing platform**. There are many competing platforms for all types of computer systems. Table 2.2 lists some of the many computing platforms that exist today.

TABLE 2.2 • Characteristics of Computer Platforms

Processor	Operating System	Computer Type
Intel processor	Palm OS® 5.2.1	Handheld
Intel processor	Microsoft Pocket PC	Handheld
Intel Pentium (or compatible)	Microsoft Windows	Desktop, Notebook, Tablet
Intel Pentium (or compatible)	Linux	Desktop, Notebook, Tablet
G4 processor	Apple OS	Desktop, Notebook
1 or more UltraSPARC III processors	Solaris 8	Workstation, Midrange Server, Mainframe Server
Multiple POWER4 Processors	AIX® 5L	Mainframe Server, Supercomputer

Varying computer platforms support varying needs, and each has a unique look and feel. You can see a variety of computer platforms in Figure 2.10. The platforms of most interest to individuals are those associated with notebook and desktop personal computers. The two most popular personal computer platforms are *IBM-compatible* and *Apple*. The IBM-compatible platform includes all PCs manufactured to work like the IBM PC. This platform is sometimes called *Wintel* since these computers typically use the Microsoft Windows operating system and Intel or Intel-compatible processors. The original IBM PC platform uses easily obtainable components that any manufacturer can purchase. For this reason, hundreds of manufacturers make IBM-compatible computers. Apple has always used its own proprietary hardware, so there are no Apple-compatible computers.

Opinions on which platform is best vary depending on whom you ask. Some Apple users will tell you that Wintel computers are inferior and difficult to use, and some Wintel users make the same claim about Apple computers. Apple computers have a greater appeal to graphic artists and multimedia enthusiasts, the market that Apple seems to focus on. For example, Apple was the first to include a DVD+R drive with its home computer for video editing. Whenever pitting their processor against the competition, Apple does so by demonstrating speed in graphics processing, since that is what their processor is designed to do best. IBM-

FIGURE 2.10 • Desktop Computer Platforms

Varying computer platforms support varying needs, and each has a unique look and feel.

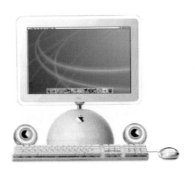

compatible computers have roots in business computing, but have grown to include all types of software. Since IBM-compatibles have a much greater market share than Apple, there is much more software available for them than for Apples. Apple has compensated by offering emulation software that enables its users to run both Apple and IBM-compatible software (at some cost in performance).

Comparing the performance of Apple computers to IBM-compatible computers is as difficult as comparing apples to oranges. As stated earlier, IBM-compatible computers use Intel (or Intel-like) processors. Intel processors are based on the *complex instruction set computer (CISC)* architecture, which includes many instructions in its instruction set and very fast system clocks. Apple computers use the Power PC processor engineered by Motorola, IBM, and Apple, which uses the newer *reduced instruction set computer (RISC)* architecture that works more efficiently with a smaller instruction set, but slower system clock. Because these architectures are dramatically different, you cannot compare them by clock speed. The only way to determine which one is faster is by running side-by-side comparisons of how quickly they accomplish processing tasks. These comparisons are called computer benchmarks.

Computer Benchmarks. When choosing a computer system, a shopper can judge a computer by the information provided by the manufacturer. However, such information is highly biased and somewhat untrustworthy. It is best to base purchasing decisions on unbiased and knowledgeable expert information, such as that provided in benchmark tests. **Benchmark** is a term for the side-by-side evaluation of competing products' performance. You can see an example of the results of a benchmark test in Figure 2.11.

FIGURE 2.11 • Benchmark tests
This chart shows the results of a handheld computer benchmark test by plotting the overall score earned against prices to illustrate the product that delivers the best deal.[6]

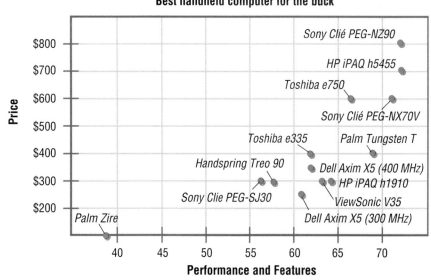

Computer benchmark tests are sponsored by manufacturers, computer magazines, and computer organizations. Examples include:

- Standard Performance Evaluation Corporation (www.specbench.org). This organization's mission is to establish, maintain, and endorse a standardized set of relevant benchmarks and metrics for performance evaluation of modern computer systems.

- PC Magazine Veritest (www.veritest.com/benchmarks/). This division of Ziff-Davis Media performs benchmark tests on current computer systems, and the test results are published in *PC Magazine.*
- Intel (www.intel.com/performance/resources/). This developer and manufacturer of computer components funds performance benchmarks for its own processors.

When reviewing benchmark test results, you should always consider the source and the details of the testing criteria.

Multiprocessing and Parallel Processing. Some computing tasks require more powerful computers. Individuals pursuing careers in motion picture special effects, animation, or other demanding graphics production areas will someday work on workstations with multiple processors to assist in graphics processing. Scientists running experiments with large quantities of data also require extra processing power. In Chapter 1, we learned about midrange and mainframe servers that support the computing needs of an entire organization. These computers also use multiprocessing.

As the name implies, *multiprocessing* is processing that occurs using more than one processing unit. The purpose: to increase productivity and performance. One form of multiprocessing involves using *coprocessors.* Typically used in larger workstations, coprocessors are special-purpose processors that speed processing by executing specific types of instructions, while the CPU works on another processing activity. Each type of coprocessor performs a specific function. For example, a math coprocessor chip is used to speed mathematical calculations, and a graphics coprocessor chip decreases the time it takes to manipulate graphics. A popular workstation for motion picture special effects specialists and animators is the Octane2 workstation from Silicon Graphics, Inc. (www.sgi.com/workstations/). It includes two CPUs and two graphics coprocessors: a vertex processing engine and an image and texture engine. A machine of this magnitude would be able to render a 3-D scene in minutes, when the same job might take hours on a typical PC.

Another form of multiprocessing is called *parallel processing*, which speeds processing by linking several microprocessors to operate at the same time, or in parallel. The challenge is not in connecting the processors, but making them work effectively as a unified set. Accomplishing this difficult task requires special software that can allocate, monitor, and control multiple processing jobs at the same time.

Massively parallel processing (MPP), used in supercomputers, involves using an even larger number of powerful processors operating together. For example, NEC built the *Earth Simulator* system (see Figure 2.12) in Japan that uses 5,120 processors to assist scientists in simulating possible futures for our planet to help us avoid possible environmental disasters.[7]

Physical Characteristics of the CPU. CPU speed is also limited by physical constraints. Most CPUs are collections of digital circuits imprinted on silicon wafers, or chips, each no bigger than the tip of a pencil eraser. In order to turn a digital circuit within the CPU on or off, electrical current must flow through a medium (usually silicon) from Point A to Point B. The speed at which the current travels between points can be increased by reducing the distance between the points.

Gordon Moore, cofounder of Intel, observed in 1965 that the continued increase in technological innovations was causing transistor

FIGURE 2.12 • Earth Simulator
The Earth Simulator system in Japan uses 5,120 processors to predict and plan for environmental disasters.

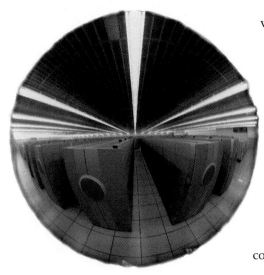

densities in an integrated circuit to double every 18 months. He predicted that this trend would continue. This prediction has come to be known as **Moore's Law** and over the years has proved true (see Figure 2.13). When transistor densities increase, so does the speed of the processor, since the electrons have shorter distances to travel. One interpretation of Moore's Law assumes that if transistor densities double, processor speeds will also double every 18 months. This has also proven true. This is helpful information as it allows us to predict how fast computers will be in years to come. It is anticipated that Moore's Law will continue to hold true for the next decade; however, at some point Moore's Law will fail due to the inherent physical limitations of silicon. Industry is researching alternatives to the silicon-based chip.

FIGURE 2.13 • Moore's Law

Moore's Law states that transistor densities in an integrated circuit double every 18 months.[8]

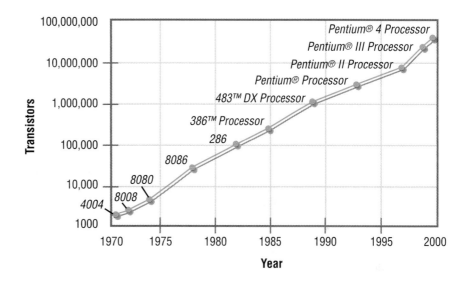

STORAGE

There have been tremendous developments in storage technologies in recent years. We are able to store more data in smaller devices and media for considerably less money than ever before. The large quantities of data that used to be chained to our desktop computers can now be easily taken with us wherever we go or copied and distributed to others. Consider the recordable CD (CD-R) that is similar to a floppy disk in use, size, and price, but stores nearly 500 times as much data. The public's use of CD-Rs to store music has had a tremendous impact on the music industry. Recordable DVDs are having the same impact on the motion picture industry. Storage technologies are affecting our personal and professional lives and society in general. Being aware of the storage options available to us provides us with opportunities that can improve our quality of life.

Storage has been defined as the ability to maintain data within the system temporarily or permanently. In the previous section, we discussed one form of temporary storage called RAM, sometimes called memory or primary storage. In this section, we will provide a more detailed look at the physical form of RAM, along with other storage circuits on the motherboard. We will then look at *secondary storage* devices that are used to store data more permanently than RAM while the computer is turned off.

Storage on the Motherboard

RAM is the largest store of data and program instructions on the motherboard. A few other forms of storage on the motherboard assist in improving computer performance and perform specialized tasks such as starting up the computer. Let's look at the physical circuit boards that make up RAM. You should find this information helpful when and if you decide to upgrade your computer. Let's also look at other forms of storage on the motherboard, including cache memory and ROM.

RAM SIMMs. We have discussed how RAM works hand-in-hand with the CPU to carry out program instructions. RAM exists as a set of chips grouped together on a circuit board called a *single in-line memory module*, or *SIMM*. RAM SIMMs are inserted into slots in the motherboard near the processor. A new computer typically comes with four RAM slots, two of which are occupied with SIMMs, as shown in Figure 2.14. This leaves two to use at a future date when you would like to add more memory to your system.

There are many different types of RAM: DRAM, SDRAM, RD-RAM, DDR-SDRAM, FPMRAM, EDO-RAM, BEDO-RAM—the list goes on and on. Each type of RAM reflects a manufacturer's effort to use a new technology to get data to the processor more quickly. When upgrading RAM, you should consult your computer documentation, or contact the manufacturer, to find out what type of RAM your computer uses. RAM modules are typically managed in pairs. In other words, to add 256 MB of memory to your computer, you would purchase two 128-MB SIMMs.

Besides RAM specifications, a computer shopper is likely to run into some other confusing memory specification. The two most prominent are cache size, as in "512K L2 cache for lightning-fast speed," and graphics card memory, as in "Advanced 128MB 9800 Pro graphics card." The following sections describe how these forms of memory affect system performance.

FIGURE 2.14 • **Motherboard RAM**

RAM SIMMs are inserted into slots in the motherboard near the processor.

Cache Memory. **Cache** (pronounced cash) **memory** is a type of high-speed memory that a processor can access more rapidly than RAM. Cache memory functions somewhat like a notebook used to record phone numbers. Although a person's private notebook may contain only 1 percent of all the numbers in the local phone directory, the chance that the person's next call will be to a number in his or her notebook is high. Cache memory works on the same principle: a cache controller makes "intelligent guesses" as to what program instructions and data will be needed next and stores them in the nearby cache for quick retrieval.

Three levels of cache are used in today's personal computers: L1, L2, and L3. The levels indicate the cache's closeness to the CPU. L1 is stored on the same chip as the microprocessor, L2 and L3 on separate chips. Cache sizes vary from processor to processor. A Pentium processor typically has a 512-KB cache. The PowerPC G4 processor uses a 2-MB cache. The larger the cache, the faster the processing.

Video RAM. **Video RAM** (VRAM) is used to store image data for a computer display. Video RAM acts as a buffer between the microprocessor and the display and is often called the *frame buffer*. When images are to be sent to the display, they are first read by the processor from RAM and then written to video RAM. From video RAM, the data is converted by a digital-to-analog converter into analog signals that are sent to the display. Most of today's PCs come equipped with 64 MB of VRAM; however, users who work with video, such as video producers, and gamers, need at least twice this amount. VRAM is typically not stored directly on the motherboard, but rather on a video circuit board, called a video card, that is plugged into the motherboard.

ROM. **Read-only memory (ROM)** provides permanent storage for data and instructions that do not change, like programs and data from the computer manufacturer. Since both the processor and RAM require electricity to store data, both are cleared and empty when a computer is initially powered up. The computer requires a place to permanently store the instructions needed to start up the computer and load the operating system into RAM. ROM fulfills this purpose.

In ROM, the combination of circuit states is fixed, and therefore the data represented by this combination will not be lost if the power is removed. ROM stores a program called the BIOS (basic input/output system). The BIOS stores information about your hardware configuration along with the boot program. The boot program contains the instructions needed to start up the computer. After running some system diagnostics, the boot program loads the operating system into memory and turns over control of the processor to the operating system. Many of today's computers use a *flash BIOS*, which means that the BIOS has been recorded on a flash memory chip, rather than a ROM chip. Flash memory is intended to store data permanently, like ROM, but can be updated with new revisions when they become available.

Handheld computers make extensive use of ROM not only to store the BIOS but also to store the operating system and applications that are included with the device. RAM, on these devices, is used to store data and additional software that the user may add.

JOB TECHNOLOGY

New Games Drive Users to Upgrade

Of all the software that runs on personal computers, you might find it hard to believe that among the most system-demanding are games.

With the arrival of graphically complex, highly anticipated games like Doom III, Half-Life 2, and The Sims 2, many gamers are finding that their old PCs can no longer cut it. To enjoy the full richness of these games, many consumers are shelling out $80 to $500 for a new video card. Many may also have to install more RAM. With some of the new games putting a lot of pressure on older CPUs, some gamers will decide it's time to buy a whole new PC.

The 3-D, eye-popping, almost photorealistic graphics of today's games verge on Pixar Animation Studios' (www.pixar.com) animation quality. The difference being that Pixar uses powerful banks of server computers to create movies such as *Finding Nemo*, whereas games rely on the processing power of one personal computer to draw the action to the screen in real time, 30 frames per second.

PC and PC hardware manufacturers, such as graphics card manufacturer ATI, are hoping that gamers flocking to upgrade will assist in the recovery of the PC market. According to ATI spokesman Chris Evenden,

the graphics hardware industry is a $2.5 billion business growing at an estimated 20 to 25 percent a year, compared with 5 to 10 percent growth for the PC industry overall. They attribute their high growth rate to the gaming industry. The last version of the system-demanding Half-Life game sold more than 8 million copies (including add-ons and expansion packs). And with gamers frothing at the mouth for the next version, and willing to spend some bucks to upgrade their hardware accordingly, ATI is seeing gold.

Questions

1. What other value can be found in PCs that allow you to move through photorealistic worlds, besides the entertainment value of games?
2. Name five career applications of this technology.
3. What components must gamers consider carefully when they purchase a PC?

Sources
1. *"Got Game? Might Need a New PC,"* Suneel Ratan, Wired News, *May. 15, 2003, www.wired.com.*
2. *"All-in-Wonder 9800 Pro Moves"* by Dave Salvator In; *"ATI's latest graphics/TV tuner/PVR entertainment card,"* PC Magazine, *June 9, 2003.*

EXPANDYOUR
KNOWLEDGE

To learn more about how to take care of your hard drive, go to www.course. com/concepts/swt. Click the link "Expand Your Knowledge" and then complete the lab entitled, "Maintaining a Hard Drive."

CMOS Memory. **CMOS memory** (pronounced see-moss, short for complementary metal-oxide semiconductor) provides semipermanent storage for system configuration information that may change. CMOS is unique in that it uses a battery to store data. CMOS is the reason that a PC is able to maintain the correct time and date even when it is not plugged in. In addition to keeping time, CMOS stores information about a computer system's disk drive configuration, start-up procedures, and low-level operating system settings. During the boot process, Windows users may be prompted to "Press F1 to enter setup." Pressing F1 would display the contents of CMOS. CMOS provides a service somewhere between RAM and ROM in that it is permanent like ROM, and doesn't go away when the computer is turned off, but can be changed like RAM.

Secondary Storage Technologies

Compared to RAM, secondary storage offers the advantages of permanence, greater capacity, and greater economy. On a megabyte-per-megabyte basis, most forms of secondary storage are considerably less expensive than RAM. Due to the electromechanical processes involved in using secondary storage, however, it is considerably slower than RAM.

When discussing secondary storage, we use the term *storage device* to refer to the device itself, the drive that reads and writes data. *Storage media* refers to the objects that hold the data, such as disks. The *storage capacity* of a storage medium is the maximum amount of bytes that it can hold. *Access time* refers to the amount of time it takes for a request for data to be fulfilled by the device. We select a storage device and media by examining the portability, storage capacity, and access time associated with the media and matching them to the task at hand.

Magnetic Media: Disks and Tapes. **Magnetic storage** devices use the magnetic properties of iron oxide particles to store bits and bytes more permanently than RAM. No physical storage medium can be genuinely permanent. It can be destroyed in any number of ways: fire, flood, sledge hammer. But if not abused, magnetically stored data will last years before naturally deteriorating. In magnetic storage, a surface is covered with a coating of particles that are organized into addressable regions (formatted). In the process of reading and writing data, a read-write head passes over the particles to determine, or set, the magnetic state of a given region. Two types of media use magnetic storage: disks and tapes. You can see a hard disk's storage surface and read-write heads in Figure 2.15.

Magnetic disks can be thin steel platters (hard disks) or Mylar film (floppy disks). When reading data from or writing data onto a disk, the computer can go directly to the desired piece of data by positioning the read-write head over the proper track of the revolving disk. Thus, the disk is called a *direct access* storage medium.

Magnetic disk storage varies widely in capacity and portability. Floppy disks are portable, but have a slower access time and lower storage capacity (1.44 MB) than fixed hard disks. Although more costly and less portable, fixed hard disk storage has a greater storage capacity and quicker access time. For these reasons, personal computers rely on the hard drive as the main secondary storage medium.

High-capacity diskettes, such as the Iomega Zip disk, and the Imation Superdisk allow you to store 69 to 83 times as much data as on a standard floppy disk in about the same amount of space. They accomplish this feat by packing the magnetic particles more densely onto the disk surface. Although these devices have gained in popularity, they still do not come as standard equipment on most computers. You need to purchase an Iomega Zip drive to use Zip disks, and a Superdisk drive to use Superdisks. High-capacity

FIGURE 2.15 • Hard disk drive
Hard disk drives store data on multiple stacked disks called platters that are read by read/write heads.

Platters

R/W heads

HOW MANY ANGELS ON THE HEAD OF A PIN?

Depends on how you store them. Currently data storage is confined by two dimensions. Out on the market within the next year, however, will be holographic memory, which stores data in three dimensions. Holographic techniques are anticipated to accommodate as much as 1,000 gigabytes on a CD-sized disk. By comparison, current DVDs can store less than 20 gigabytes. Data retrieval will be 60 times faster as well.

Source:
"Light on the horizon"
The Economist
www.economist.com/science/displaystory.cfm?story_id=1956881
July 31, 2003
Cited on August 4, 2003

disks cost a bit more than standard floppy disks. The release of writable CDs has significantly and negatively affected the market for these devices.

A *removable disk cartridge*, such as the Iomega Jaz disk, contains a hard disk within a removable cartridge. Although more expensive than fixed hard disks, removable disk cartridges combine hard disk storage capacity and floppy disk portability. Some people prefer removable hard disk storage for the portability and security it provides. It's ideal for graphic artists who deal with files too large to fit on floppy disks. Government agencies might also use removable disks cartridges to store top-secret files so that they are not left unattended.

Similar to the kind of tape found in audio or video cassettes, *magnetic tape* is a Mylar film coated with iron oxide. Magnetic tape is an example of a *sequential access* storage medium. If the computer needs to read data from the middle of a reel of tape, it must sequentially pass over all of the tape before the desired piece of data. This is one disadvantage of magnetic tape. When someone needs information, it can take time for a tape operator to load the magnetic tape on a tape device and get the relevant data into the computer.

Although access is slower, magnetic tape is usually less expensive than disk storage. For applications that require access to very large amounts of data, in a set order, sequential access is ideal. For example, government agencies, such as the U.S. Census Bureau, and large insurance corporations maintain too much data to store on regular hard drives. Magnetic tape provides a medium that can handle these large data sets. When these organizations conclude work on a data set, the tape is removed and stored, and a new tape takes its place. Magnetic tapes and tape cartridges are often used to back up disk drives and to store data off-site for recovery in case of disaster.

Optical Storage

Optical storage media, such as CDs and DVDs, store bits by using an optical laser to burn pits into the surface of a highly reflective disk surface (see Figure 2.16). A pit represents a 0, and the lack of a pit represents a 1. The 1s and 0s are read from the disk surface by using a low-power laser that measures the difference in reflected light caused by the pits (or lack thereof) on the disk. Audio CDs that store music, data CDs that store software, and DVDs that store motion pictures all use the same fundamental technology. The advantages of optical storage over magnetic storage

FIGURE 2.16 • CDs and DVDs comparison
Pits burned into the surface of the disk are what enable CDs and DVDs to store bits. DVDs are able to read and write much smaller pits than CDs, which allows them to store much more data.

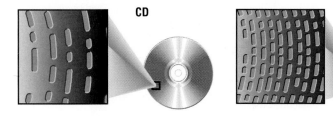

are in capacity and longevity. A CD can store up to 700 MB of data on an inexpensive, lightweight diskette. Data stored on magnetic media may begin to deteriorate in under 10 years, but data on a CD could last over 100 years.

The first optical media to be mass-marketed to the general public was the **compact disk read-only memory (CD-ROM)**, commonly referred to as a CD. Just like the ROM on your motherboard, once data has been recorded on a CD, it cannot be modified—the disk is read-only. Originally designed to store music, the CD soon replaced the cassette tape as the most popular form of music distribution, and migrated to more general data storage uses in the computer marketplace. The CD ideally satisfied the increasing storage demands of large software programs. Software that used to require dozens of floppy disks could be distributed on one inexpensive and convenient CD.

CD-ROMs are useful for storing all kinds of large data sets. J. Craig Venture, an entrepreneurial scientist who helped decode the human genome, has started a company that will decode your genome and send it to you on CD for a mere $500,000. Venter hopes ultimately to mass-produce gene CDs like so many Bruce Springsteen CDs that will stock the shelves of every general practitioner's office and be covered by insurance.[9]

A **digital video disk (DVD)** stores data in a fashion similar to CDs except that DVDs are able to write and read much smaller pits on the disk surface (see Figure 2.16) and sometimes write to and read from multiple disk layers. This vastly increases the amount of storage capacity from 700 MB on a CD to over 4.7 GB on a DVD. DVDs are the only disk with the capacity to store an entire digitized motion picture. An additional benefit of DVD drives is that they are *backward-compatible* with CD-ROMs, meaning that they can play CDs as well as DVDs.

Optical disk capacities will continue to increase, and access speeds will continue to decrease. Proof can be found in Sony's new blue-laser-based optical disk system that will store 23.3 GB on a standard size optical disk. Blue-laser systems are able to store more data than DVDs because of the shorter wavelength of blue light. The company plans to offer a 50-GB capacity version by 2005 and a 100-GB version at an unspecified point in the future.[10]

The popularity of the CD and DVD has soared since the introduction of recordable optical disks. A number of different writable CD and DVD devices are available today at reasonable prices. Since optical disks are inexpensive and have such high capacities, they are often more economical to use than high-capacity magnetic disks. Since this is relatively new technology, the manufacturers have not yet been able to agree on standards. Different manufacturers support different standards and formats. Because of this, CDs that you create on one device may or may not play on another device. Manufacturers use *R* to indicate that a media is recordable; that is, it can be written to once only. The process of writing to an optical disk is sometimes called burning. *RW*, for rewritable, is used to indicate that a disk can be rewritten numerous times just as you would a hard drive.

Currently, the most popular format for writable CDs is **CD-RW**, CDs that can be rewritten many times. There are two popular formats for rewritable DVDs, *DVD-RW* and *DVD+RW*. You can now find combo-drives that support both of these formats. CD-RW and DVD drives are also being combined and have become popular on new PCs. Be warned that no matter what format you choose, the CDs or DVDs that you create may not play on all players.

Other Storage Options

A **flash memory card** is a chip that, unlike RAM, is nonvolatile and keeps its memory when the power is shut off. Flash chips are small and can be easily modified and reprogrammed, which makes them popular in computers, cellular phones, digital cameras, and other products. When used in media devices such as digital cameras, camcorders, and portable MP3 players, flash memory cards are sometimes referred to as *media cards*. They serve media devices well, since they require a small storage device with high capacity. Compared to other types of secondary storage, flash memory can be accessed more quickly, consumes less power, and is smaller in size. The primary disadvantage is cost. A flash chip can cost almost three times more per megabyte than a traditional hard disk. Nonetheless, the market for flash chips has exploded in recent years.

USB storage devices are small flash memory modules about the size of your thumb, as you can see in Figure 2.17, that conveniently plug into the USB (universal serial bus) port, a common port found on most PCs, notebook computers, handheld computers, digital cameras, or MP3 players. They come in a range of stylish colors and some are even attached to key rings and double as a key fob. They store from 8 MB to over 1 GB of data.

FIGURE 2.17 • Keychain USB storage
USB storage comes in a variety of stylish colors and can store more than a gigabyte of data.

Evaluating Storage Media: Access Method, Capacity, and Portability

As with other computer system components, the access methods, storage capacities, and portability you require of secondary storage media are determined by your objectives. An objective of a credit-card company's computer system, for example, might be to rapidly retrieve stored customer data in order to approve customer purchases. A fast access method is critical to the success of the system. In a hospital setting, in which physicians are evaluating patients, portability and capacity might be major considerations in selecting and using secondary storage media and devices.

Storage media that provide faster access methods are generally more expensive than media that provide slower access. The cost of additional storage capacity and portability varies widely, but is also a factor to consider. In addition to cost, you may also need to address security issues. How should the secondary storage devices be controlled so as to allow only authorized people access to important data and programs?

Clearly the trend in storage media, as in most areas of technology, is toward smaller, more powerful (higher-capacity), and less expensive devices. The magnetic hard drive still reigns supreme as the choice for day-to-day large quantity storage due to its large capacity and low price. Writable optical disks are rapidly taking over the portable data storage market due to their high capacity and low price. Computer vendors are phasing out floppy drives by leaving them off new computers unless specifically requested by the customer, and CD-RW/DVD drives have taken over. Figure 2.18 and Table 2.3 illustrate the compelling reasons for choosing optical portable storage over magnetic storage.

FIGURE 2.18 • Comparing portable data storage media

The cost per MB of storage media is lowest for CD-RW and DVD-RW and highest for floppy disks. There are compelling reasons for choosing optical portable storage over magnetic storage.

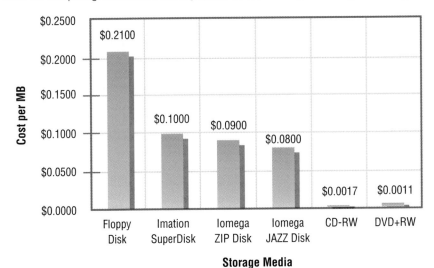

TABLE 2.3 • Comparing Data Storage Media

Storage Device	Capacity	Avg. Price per Disk	Cost per MB	Portable	Storage Type	Access Method	Use
Floppy Disk	1.44 MB	$0.30	$0.21	Y	Magnetic	Direct	Transport small files
Iomega ZIP Disk	100 MB	$9.00	$0.09	Y	Magnetic	Direct	Transport large or numerous files
Imation SuperDisk	120 MB	$12.00	$0.10	Y	Magnetic	Direct	Transport large or numerous files
Iomega JAZ Disk	1 GB	$80.00	$0.08	Y	Magnetic	Direct	Back up data files or treat as removable hard drive
CD-R	700 MB	$0.60	$0.0009	Y	Optical	Direct	Archive data and create music CDs
CD-RW	650 MB	$1.10	$0.0017	Y	Optical	Direct	Transport files, archive data, and create music CDs
DVD-R	4.7 GB	$3.00	$0.0006	Y	Optical	Direct	Archive data and create movie and music DVDs
DVD+RW	4.7 GB	$5.00	$0.0011	Y	Optical	Direct	Transport files, archive data, and create movie and music DVDs
Hard Drive	120 GB	$190.00	$0.0016	N	Magnetic	Direct	Permanent storage for programs and data
DLT Tape	110 GB	$164.00	$0.0015	Y	Magnetic	Sequential	Data intense industrial

INPUT, OUTPUT, AND EXPANSION

Users interact with computers through input and output (I/O) devices. Of all the computer components, I/O devices have the most direct impact on a user's computing experience. In order to accommodate a wide variety of data and the many environments in which data is processed, there are literally hundreds of different input devices on the market. By learning about input devices, we also learn what computers are capable of. Output devices connect directly with our senses. Al-

EXPANDYOUR
KNOWLEDGE

To learn more about other input devices as well as output devices, go to www.course.com/concepts/swt. Click the link "Expand Your Knowledge" and then complete the lab entitled, "Peripheral Devices."

though most output from a computer is visual, much is auditory, and some even affects our other senses. This section explores input and output and the different peripheral devices that users add to their computers to expand their functionality.

Input and Output Concepts

An **input device** assists in capturing and entering raw data into the computer system. Successful input devices must be easy to learn how to use, and effortless to manipulate. An **output device** allows us to observe the results of computer processing. In personal computer use, we typically use only a handful of I/O devices. There is a good chance that you have used a keyboard, mouse, display, and printer for much of your life. Using these devices is second nature to many people. New personal computing devices and product designs are challenging some of us to learn new techniques for input. Touch pads and TrackPoints are easy to get used to on notebook computers. Touch screens, stylus, and handwriting recognition may be a bit more challenging on handheld computers. These basic I/O devices are just the tip of the iceberg compared to all the devices used in industry. From drawing tablets used by graphic artists to magnetic ink character readers used by banks, a variety of input devices have been designed to accommodate the unique needs of professionals. The goal behind the design of such devices is always speed and functionality.

Speed and Functionality. Rapidly and accurately getting data into a computer system is the goal of most input devices. Some activities have very specific needs for output and input, requiring devices that perform specific functions. For example, several *New York Times* reporters use input devices that understand human speech to ease the stress of typing late-breaking stories.[11] The more specialized the application, the more specialized the associated system I/O devices. UPS had special electronic pads created for its drivers to use to collect customer signatures (see Figure 2.19). The pads improved the efficiency of UPS's recordkeeping.

The Nature of Data. *Human-readable* data can be directly read and understood by humans. A sheet of paper containing lists of customers is an example of human-readable data. By contrast, *machine-readable data* can be understood and read by computer devices and is typically stored as bits or bytes. Data on customers stored on a disk is an example of machine-readable data. Note that it is possible for data to be both human-readable and machine-readable. For example, both human beings and computer system input devices can read the magnetic ink on bank checks.

Source Data Automation. Regardless of how data gets into the computer, it is important that it be captured close to its source. *Source data automation* involves automating data entry where the data is created, thus ensuring accuracy and timeliness. Source-data automation is used by librarians who use scanners to check out and check in library materials. The moment a book is scanned at check out, its status will change in the online card catalogue to "checked out." Some rental-car companies use automated scanners that scan vehicles as they exit and enter the rental lot. The scanner collects data on the vehicle, including the mileage and gas gauge data, date, and time, and prepares a customer invoice before the customer returns to the counter.[12]

FIGURE 2.19 • UPS signature device

UPS drivers collect customers' signatures by having them sign an electronic pad that stores the signature electronically.

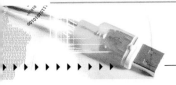

HOUSES THAT REMEMBER WHEN PEOPLE FORGET

The fastest growing group in the country is seniors over 80. This growth will soon overwhelm available care facilities and place the healthcare insurance industry in financial jeopardy. In response to that, Intel Corporation, working with the Alzheimer's Association, is designing technology for "plugged-in" homes that will help Alzheimer's patients live on their own by giving them automated reminders for simple tasks and monitoring them for off-site healthcare providers.

Source:
"Intel teams with Alzheimer's Association"
By R. Colin Johnson, EE Times
www.techweb.com/wire/story/OEG20030725S0020
July 25, 2003 (4:20 p.m. EST)
Cited on July 25, 2003

Hundreds of different input and output (I/O) devices exist. Many researchers feel that we are entering an era of **pervasive computing**, where everything and anything can be used for I/O.[13] Mark Weiser has written a number of papers on the topic of, what he calls, *ubiquitous computing*.[14] Ubiquitous computing presents a vision of the future in which computing saturates our lives to the point where it becomes unnoticeable and invisible. For example, writing is a ubiquitous component in today's society. Writing is so much a part of our environment that we don't notice it—the back of our breakfast cereal box, the advertisements on television, the billboards and signs on the way to work, newspaper headlines, magazine covers, all glimpsed and read, most unnoticed to our conscious mind. Picture computing in this framework, and you will understand ubiquitous computing. Some rather outrageous examples of pervasive and ubiquitous computing were presented at the Ideal Home Show in London. They included the Internet toilet roll browser that allows you to browse the Web while seated in your bathroom and prints using the paper on the toilet paper roll, and an Internet-enabled cutting board that contains a microprocessor-controlled system capable of browsing the Web (Figure 2.20).[15] Imagine being able to view recipes online while chopping carrots!

FIGURE 2.20 • Internet-enabled cutting board

The Internet-enabled cutting board contains a microprocessor-controlled system capable of browsing the Web.

Input Devices

Input devices can be classified as either *general purpose* or *special purpose*. General-purpose input devices are designed for use in a variety of environments. This category of input devices includes the standard keyboard and mouse. Special purpose input devices are designed for one unique purpose. An example of a special purpose input device is the pill-sized camera from Given Imaging that, when swallowed, records images of the stomach and the small intestine as it passes through the digestive system.[16]

Personal Computer Input Devices. Today's PCs are multimedia devices that can input (and output) data, such as text, audio, and video. Various input devices are used to capture these types of data, including keyboards, mice, microphones, digital cameras, and scanners.

A *computer keyboard* and a *computer mouse* are the most common input devices, used for entering data such as characters, text, and basic commands. A number of companies are developing new keyboards that are more comfortable, adjustable, and faster to use. For example, Microsoft's *ergonomic keyboard* is designed in such a way as to reduce the stress on your wrists common with traditional keyboards.

A computer mouse is used to direct the computer's activities by selecting and manipulating symbols, icons, menus, or commands on the screen. Different types of mice are available, including corded and cordless, one-, two-, or three- button, with scroll wheel and without. Some users prefer a trackball over a mouse. A *trackball* sits stationary and allows you to control the mouse pointer by rolling a mounted ball (see Figure 2.21). If you've ever tried to draw pictures using a mouse, you know how frustrating it can be. *Graphics tablets and pens* allow you to draw with a penlike device on a tablet to create drawings on your display.

FIGURE 2.21 • Trackball

A trackball provides an alternative to using a mouse for input.

Mobil Input Devices. Other methods for entering data are tailored for mobile computing. Notebook computers integrate the mouse either as a touch-sensitive pad below the spacebar (called a *touch pad*) or a nub in the center of the keyboard (called a *TrackPoint*). By moving your finger across the pad, or applying sideways pressure to the nub, you direct the mouse cursor on the screen.

Smaller mobile devices are doing away with the keyboard and mouse altogether. Handheld computers and tablet PCs use a **touch screen**, which allows you to select items on the screen by touching them with a **stylus**—a short penlike device, without ink. These devices translate characters written on the screen with a stylus into ASCII characters that can be stored and edited in a word-processing document.

Touch-sensitive screens are also used in **kiosks**. A kiosk is a special-purpose computing station made available to the passing public to access location-relevant information. For example, a new kiosk designed for use in churches accepts parishioners' donations (e-tithing) in cash, by check, or from a credit card and provides a tax receipt for the donation, along with a prayer (Figure 2.22).[17]

FIGURE 2.22 • Church kiosk

The interactive kiosks made by PlannedLegacy accept parishioners' donations (e-tithing) in cash, by check, or from a credit card and provide a tax receipt for the donation, along with a prayer.

Microphone Input Devices. Microphones take human speech as input, digitize the sound wave, and use **speech recognition** software to translate the input into text or commands. On the factory floor, equipment operators can use speech recognition to give basic commands to machines while using their hands to perform other operations. Speech recognition software can be used to take dictation, translating spoken words into ASCII text. *Voice recognition*, a similar technology, can be used by security systems to allow only authorized personnel into restricted areas.

Gaming Devices. Gamers enjoy specialized input devices that let them quickly react to game action. Most gamers prefer to use a **gamepad** device to control game characters; some people prefer the old-fashioned *joystick*. A gamepad is shown in Figure 2.23.

FIGURE 2.23 • Gamepad

Game enthusiasts use a gamepad device to control game characters in a virtual world.

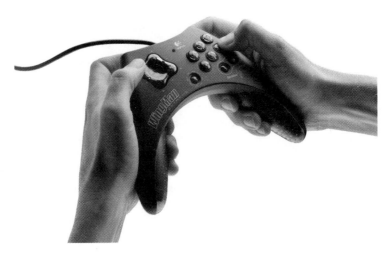

Digital Cameras. Many people are switching from film to digits as they discover the convenience of digital photography. A *digital camera* captures images through the camera's lens and stores them digitally rather than on film. The quality of a digital camera is typically judged on how many megapixels can be captured in an image. A traditional inexpensive film-based camera produces 1.2 megapixel images. You can buy a 2-megapixel digital camera for under $200, and a professional-grade 5-megapixel camera could cost as much as $1,500. As with most technology, prices in the digital camera market are rapidly dropping. Some cameras capture images on a flash memory card, and you can download the images to your PC using a USB cable; others store the photos directly on CD. Recently, cameras of megapixel quality have been added to some high-end cell phones.[18]

Many digital cameras, in addition to taking still images, allow you to capture short video recordings. If you are interested in longer video, you can purchase a camcorder. A bit more costly, *camcorders* allow you to take full-length digital video that you can watch on your TV, download to your computer, or transfer to CD, DVD or VCR tape. *Webcams* provide a lower-priced video camera for use as a computer input device. They are ideal for video conferencing over the Internet, as shown in Figure 2.24.

FIGURE 2.24 • Webcam

Webcams connect to your computer for video conferencing over the Internet.

Scanning Devices. You can input both image and character data using a scanning device. Both *page scanners* and *handheld scanners* can convert monochrome or color pictures, forms, text, and other images into bitmapped images. It has been estimated that U.S. enterprises generate over one billion pieces of paper daily. To cut down on the high cost of using and processing paper, many companies look to scanning devices as a way to help them manage their documents. Combined with *character recognition software*, a scanner can be used to transform document images into editable word-processing documents.

The field of biometrics uses a variety of scanning devices. *Biometrics* is the study of measurable biological characteristics. Biomet-

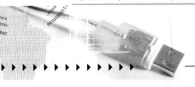

IT'S THE THOUGHT THAT COUNTS

Under development now are brain-computer interfaces (BCIs) that enable people who can't speak or move to do things like turn on a light or adjust the thermostat—just by thinking. BCIs interpret the pattern in the brain waves (EEG) and link to a computer with a special display that, in turn, performs the action. Eventually, more tasks will be possible as researchers identify the patterns specific to things like operating a wheelchair or using a word processing program.

Source:
"I Think, Therefore I Communicate"
By Lakshmi Sandhana
Wired News.com
www.wired.com/news/medtech/0,1286,59737,00.html
Wednesday, July 30, 2003
Cited on July 30, 2003

EXPAND YOUR **KNOWLEDGE**

To learn more about the mouse, keyboard, and other input devices, go to www.course.com/concepts/swt. Click the link "Expand Your Knowledge" and then complete the lab entitled, "Using Input Devices."

rics is becoming increasingly useful in the area of security as a tool for verifying a person's identity. Scanners and software can verify an individual's identity by examining biological traits, such as retinal or iris patterns, fingerprints, or facial features. First Financial Credit Union is using one such device to verify customer identity. The bank has installed kiosks at remote locations where customers are able to access all the services that a branch office would, including applications for new accounts and loans. The kiosks save the bank the cost of opening new branches. Fingerprint scans assure the bank that the customers making the transactions are who they say they are.[19]

Businesses and organizations use a number of special purpose scanners and optical readers to collect data. A *magnetic ink character recognition (MICR)*, device reads special magnetic-ink characters such as those written on the bottom of checks. *Optical mark recognition (OMR)* readers read "bubbled-in" forms commonly used in examinations, and polling (see box). *Optical character recognition (OCR)* readers read hand-printed characters. Point-of-sale (POS) devices are terminals, I/O devices connected to larger systems, with scanners that read codes on retail items and enter the item number into a computer system.

Output Devices

Computer output consists of the results of processing produced in a manner that is observable by human senses or that can be used as input into another system. Output can be visual—on a display or printed page—or audio—through speakers; in the case of virtual reality systems, output can even be tactile and olfactory to simulate the experience of being in a real environment (virtual reality is discussed in Chapter 8). Output from one system can be fed into another system as input. For example, consider the system that controls natural gas distribution throughout the U.K. One computer system monitors the pressure in the natural gas pipes that crisscross the country. The output from that system is fed into the computer system that regulates the flow of gas to maintain consistent and safe levels.[20]

Display Monitors. Remarkable progress has been made with display monitors, including those used with personal computers. With today's wide selection of monitors and displays, price and overall quality can vary tremendously.

The first consideration when selecting a display is typically size. Display size is measured diagonally and typically ranges from 14 to 17 inches for notebook computers to 15, 17, and 19 inches for desktop displays. There are of course extremes. For example, a 46-inch plasma display offered by Gateway, Inc. is intended for DVD movie viewing and driven by a personal computer. Display size is typically selected according to user need. If you use a lot of graphics applications, games, video, artwork, or like to multitask with many windows open on the screen at once, you'll want to go with a 17-inch or larger display size. If you mostly deal in text, e-mail, and Web pages, and wish to conserve desktop space, or go mobile, a smaller display size should suit your needs.

The quality of a screen is often measured in pixels. **Display resolution** is a measure of the amount of pixels on the screen. A larger number of pixels per

COMMUNITY TECHNOLOGY

Casting Your Vote

Input devices seem as though they would be a fairly benign topic. However, since the 2000 presidential election input devices have become one of the most controversial topics in voting history.

United States citizens take their right to vote seriously. It is the government's responsibility to assure its citizens that every vote is counted. In the 2000 elections, we all learned that counting every vote is not as easy as it sounds. The source of the problem had to do with the type of input devices used in some voting precincts.

Three main types of computerized voting systems are currently in use—punch card, mark-sense, and direct-recording electronic machines. None of these systems is flawless, but of the three the punch-card system stands out as being outdated and inaccurate.

Punch-card voting systems have been in use since the mid-1960s. Voters using them mark their ballots by punching holes in paper cards. The punch cards are fed into computerized counting machines either at local precincts or centralized tallying facilities.

There have been a large number of problems with these systems. The bits of paper that are removed when a card is punched, called chads, often do not become completely detached from their cards. These "hanging chads" can work their way back into place, blocking holes. Or, when severed from their cards as ballots are handled, they can work their way into holes punched in other ballots. The result is a voting catastrophe: some votes are not counted. In the very close 2000 presidential election, problems with chads led to thousands of votes having to be recounted by hand and serious questions as to who the next president should be. The outcome of the election was not settled for some weeks, leaving the country in an uproar.

Since then, state governments have invested heavily in new voting machines to replace the old-fashioned punch-card systems. Many of the punch-card systems are being replaced with mark-sense systems. Mark-sense ballots are paper ballots printed with circles, ovals, squares, or rectangles that voters fill in with a pen or pencil to mark their votes. Optical-scanning technology is used to detect the marks on each ballot. Other precincts are experimenting with direct-recording electronic (DRE) machines. DREs use computer terminals that allow voters to enter their votes by pressing buttons or touching images on a computer screen.

Internet-based voting is being used for some elections that have less political impact than a national presidential election. With Internet-based voting, voters cast their ballots from any Internet connected PC.

All voting technologies must perform two essential functions: ensuring that every vote is counted, and ensuring that only one vote is cast by each voter. The punch-card system caused concerns over the first function, but DRE machines and Internet-based voting systems cause concerns over the second function. Some people are concerned that since there is no printed receipt of a vote, these systems could be electronically manipulated to favor certain candidates without anyone ever knowing. Mark-sense systems seem to present the best solution since they cover both bases, but they do not provide convenient access to illiterate voters or some disabled voters. Some people feel that the ideal solution would be a DRE system that both electronically processes the vote and provides a printed ballot that can be used as a backup.

Questions

1. Which of the voting systems do you feel provides the most convenient access to all citizens? Why?
2. What considerations affect the decision-making process of precincts as they choose among voting systems?
3. Enumerate the benefits and drawbacks of an Internet-based voting system. How might the drawbacks be overcome?

Sources

1. "Election Automation—Types of computerized voting systems," accessed at the ACE (administration and cost of elections) project Web site, www.aceproject.org/main/english/em/emf02.htm, May 18, 2003.
2. "I Vote for High-Tech Balloting," Commentary by John Steele Gordon, Wall Street Journal, Nov 8, 2000.

square inch is considered to be a higher resolution of the image. A screen with a 1,024 x 768 resolution (786,432 pixels) has a higher level of sharpness than one with a resolution of 640 x 350 (224,000 pixels). The higher the resolution, the smaller the pixels and images they create. If you want to fit more on your display, you could do so by choosing a higher resolution. On the other hand, if you were suffering from eyestrain, you could choose a lower resolution that would increase the size of the objects on the display.

A **liquid crystal display (LCD)**, or **flat panel display**, is a flat display that uses liquid crystals—an organic, oil-like material—placed between two pieces of glass to form characters and graphic images on a backlit screen. Once used primarily as a laptop display, LCD displays are now being marketed to desktop PC users and are quickly displacing the old style CRT (cathode-ray tube) displays as their prices become competitive. The two primary choices in LCD screens are passive-matrix and active-matrix LCD displays. Passive-matrix displays are typically dimmer, slower, but less expensive. Active-matrix displays are bright, clear, and have wider viewing angles than passive-matrix displays. You can see the difference between a traditional CRT display and an LCD display in Figure 2.25.

FIGURE 2.25 • CRT and LCD displays

Compared to a traditional CRT display, LCD displays use much less desktop space.

LCD projectors are used for projecting presentations from your computer onto a larger screen. Typically costing thousands of dollars, these small portable devices are a must have item for people in businesses that require visually presenting ideas to audiences. Recently, budget LCD projectors have entered the market priced less than $1,000. LCD projectors can interface with most desktop, notebook, and even handheld computers.

Printers and Plotters. Printers and plotters produce *hard copy*—output printed to paper. A variety of printers with different speeds, features, and capabilities are available. The two most popular types of printers are color ink-jet printers and laser printers. *Laser printers* provide the cleanest output and are preferred in situations that demand professional-quality printed documents. Color laser printers are rather expensive, so many people settle for less expensive, lower-print-quality, color *ink-jet printer* or a black and white laser printer for home use.

LOSE YOUR GLASSES? JUST PRINT ANOTHER PAIR

Or fax your sister her birthday present. Both might well be possible soon with the progress occurring in a technology called rapid prototyping. RPs are 3-D printers that lay down layer after layer of material, even different materials using different print heads, until the specs have been matched. The systems have already dropped from $300,000 to $30,000, and it is rumored Hewlett-Packard has a machine in the works they will retail at $1,000.

Source:
"3-D Printing's Great Leap Forward"
By Daithí Ó hAnluain
Wired News
www.wired.com/news/technology/0,1282,59648,00.html
August 11, 2003
Cited on August 11, 2003

The latest trend in home printers is the photo printer. Sparked by low price digital cameras, *photo printers* have become a popular method for printing photo-quality images on special photo-quality paper.

The speed of a printer is typically measured by the number of *pages printed per minute (ppm)*. A printer's output resolution depends on the number of dots printed per inch. A printer with a *600 dot-per-inch (dpi)* resolution prints more clearly than one with a 300-dpi resolution.

Plotters are a type of hard-copy output device used for general design work. Businesses typically use plotters to generate paper or acetate blueprints and schematics, or print drawings of buildings or new products onto paper or transparencies.

Computer Sound Systems. Computer sound has functional and entertainment value in computer systems. Most of today's personal computer systems include at least low-quality speakers. The computer operating system and computer software use sound to cue the user to a system event. Some event-driven sounds are included to enhance the activity of using the computer; for example, the flourish of music that plays when Microsoft Windows starts up and shuts down. Other event-driven sounds are included to draw the user's attention to important information; for example, the beep that sounds when a warning dialog box is displayed, or the "You've Got Mail!" exclamation that is so familiar even to those who don't use AOL.

Sound systems also support media computer applications such as CD/MP3 music players and DVD movie players. The sound systems on most notebook and handheld computers are not of sufficient quality to support media, so users of such systems typically turn to headphones for high-quality sound.

Multimedia and gaming enthusiasts often purchase more expensive sound systems for their computers. For example, a surround sound system, with a subwoofer, can provide additional realism to games that use 3-D audio in a virtual reality simulation.

A computer's ability to output sound is particularly important to individuals who have limitations on their vision. Screen-reader programs such as JAWS, by the Freedom Scientific Corporation, read aloud the text displayed on the screen.

Special-Purpose I/O Devices

Many special-purpose input devices are designed to support scientific and medical research. For example, a new type of digital movie camera that uses ultrafast laser pulses is able to record things faster and smaller than ever. It is providing scientists with striking, 3-D color movies of atoms, molecules, and living cells in action. "We can watch the brain think, develop, age, deal with disease. We can see neurons grow inside the living brain," said Jeff Lichtman, a neurobiologist at the Washington University School of Medicine in St. Louis.[21] Chemists are using another new input device to track the motions of the particles—electrons, protons and neutrons—that make up an atom. To do so, they use an advanced laser strobe light that slices time into the shortest bits yet achieved—"attoseconds": a billionth of a billionth of a second.[22]

Computer scientists and musicians at the MIT Media Lab are experimenting with special input devices that allow children to compose and perform music without any musical instrument skills. The input devices include a drawing pad that plays music based on children's drawings, soft, squeezable, colorful instruments that let kids mold, transform, and explore musical material, and a variety of other devices that release the creativity in children. The output is beautiful and interesting music that reflects the child's creativity. "We designed the interconnectedness, immersive structure of Toy Symphony to let children unlock the expressive mysteries of music before learning the technical prerequisites".[23]

The area of virtual reality has produced a number of unique and interesting I/O devices. For example, the *virtual reality headset*, can project output in the form of three-dimensional color images. Spatial sensors in the headset act as input devices, and when you move your head, images and sounds in your headset change. Virtual reality devices (see Figure 2.26) already allow architects to design and "walk through" buildings before they begin construction. They allow physicians to practice surgery though virtual operations, and pilots to simulate flights without ever leaving the ground.

FIGURE 2.26 • Virtual reality I/O devices

This engineer uses a virtual reality headset to test a new manufacturing process prior to implementation.

Expansion

Most computers provide users with the means to add devices and expand their computers' functionality. A desktop computer user might wish to add a flatbed scanner, a notebook user might want to add a Webcam for video conferencing, and a handheld computer user might wish to add a folding keyboard for more convenient data entry. This section describes the most common methods of expanding a computer system.

Desktop Computer Expansion. One fact that has traditionally complicated system expansion is that peripheral devices use a variety of different types of cables and connectors. Desktop computers provide standard *ports* (sockets) for display, keyboard, printer, and mouse connectors, but have not easily accommodated the many other special-purpose cables and connectors. That trend is changing. Today's computers come with a number of **Universal Serial Bus (USB)** ports (see Figure 2.27). USB is a relatively new standard that was designed to accommodate a wide array of devices. In is not unusual to find six or more USB ports on a new computer into which you can plug the keyboard, mouse, and additional devices of your choice, such as handheld computers, digital cameras, portable MP3 players, network devices, joysticks, memory modules, and many others.

FIGURE 2.27 • Universal Serial Bus
Many of today's peripheral devices connect to the computer using the USB port.

More specialized peripheral devices may come with their own circuit board, called an *expansion board* or *expansion card*, to be installed in your computer. Installation of these devices is not as convenient as simply plugging in a USB connector, but typically is easy enough for most computer users to handle. The method of installing them varies from machine to machine, so users should consult their owner's manual for specific instructions. After removing the cover from your computer, you will see a bank of slots, *expansion slots*, that run across the rear of the computer's motherboard (see Figure 2.28); some slots may already contain cards. By viewing the card you wish to install, you should be able to determine which slot will accommodate the card. After installing the card according to instructions, the port on the card will be exposed at the back of the computer for use.

FIGURE 2.28 • Expansion slots
More specialized peripheral devices may come with an expansion card to be installed in the expansion slots on the motherboard of your computer.

An expansion card that is popular with professional and amateur videographers is the *FireWire* card. FireWire is a standard (IEEE 1394) used for fast video transfer from a camera to the computer. Once the card is installed, a cable is used to connect your digital camera to your computer so that video can be transferred for editing. FireWire comes standard on Mac computers.

After adding a device, either through a USB port or an expansion card, software will need to be installed to enable your computer to communicate with the new devices. The necessary software will be included on disk with the device.

Mobile Computer Expansion. Like desktop PCs, notebook computers include USB ports for convenient expansion. Notebook computers also provide *PCMCIA slots* that accept *PCMCIA cards*, shown in Figure 2.29, usually called *PC Cards*. PC Cards support a number of devices. For example, network adapters, modems, and additional storage devices, can all be purchased as PC Cards for notebook computers. Notebook computers also include ports to add a standard keyboard, mouse, printer, and display or LCD projector.

Handheld computers also have the ability to accommodate additional devices. For instance, your can connect a global positioning system (GPS) to a handheld computer, which when combined with GPS soft-ware can display your location on a map. Other options for handheld computers include wireless Internet access, Webcams, and LCD projectors. With the addition of a PCMCIA adapter, a handheld can support all the peripherals available to notebook computers.

FIGURE 2.29 • PC Card
Notebook computers offer expansion opportunities using PC Cards.

SELECTINGANDPURCHASINGACOMPUTERSYSTEM

Putting together a complete computer system is more involved than simply connecting computer devices. Take a moment to think about how car manufacturers build a car. They avoid installing a transmission incapable of delivering the engine's full power to the wheels. Instead, car manufacturers match the components to the intended use of the vehicle. Racing cars, for example, require special types of engines, transmissions, and tires. To select the right transmission for a racing

car, then, you must consider not only how much of the engine's power can be delivered to the wheels (efficiency and effectiveness), but also how expensive the transmission is (cost), how reliable it is (control), and how many gears it has (complexity). Similarly, you must assemble computer systems so that they are effective, efficient, and well balanced.

You should always base a computer system purchase on a careful study of the needs that it will address. Wyndham Resorts had issues with getting customers through the checkin and checkout process efficiently. To address the problem they equipped their hospitality staff with handheld computers (see Figure 2.30) and sent them out to check customers in at the curb or even when they arrived at the airport.[24] Other resorts have installed kiosks that allow customers to check in and out without the assistance of staff. Kiosks and handheld computers ideally address the specified problem—checking customers in and out as quickly and accurately as possible.

FIGURE 2.30 • Handheld computers in action

Wyndham Resorts decided that handheld computers were the best way to improve its checkin process.

Researching a Computer Purchase

Although businesses such as Wyndham Resorts employ IT (information technology) professionals to select and purchase computer systems to meet their business needs, individuals need to function as IT professionals when selecting their own personal computer systems. Purchasing a new computer system requires a considerable amount of research. The computer market changes so rapidly that no matter how much you know about computers, it will take some time to catch up with the current state of the market. Fortunately, many free resources are available to assist individuals in learning as much as they wish to know.

Browsing Web sites such as www.cnet.com and www.zdnet.com can help you decide on a computer type and platform. Browsing around your local computer store is another method of investigating the market. Be aware however, that what you see in the store is only a very small percentage of the computers and computer configuration options available to you online.

Once you have narrowed your decision down to a particular platform, it is time to start researching manufacturers. *Computer Shopper* magazine is available at most newsstands and includes hundreds of advertisements for PCs, notebooks, and handhelds, plus benchmark comparisons and product reviews. *MacWorld* magazine provides information on Apple desktop and notebook computers. Many computer industry magazines have information online as well.

Visiting manufacturers' Web sites can be very helpful. Viewing the PCs at www.gateway.com and www.dell.com can give you a good idea of the state of the market in terms of PC computer specifications and price. Check out www.apple.com for information on Apple desktop and notebook computers. Computer retailers such as www.cdw.com and www.mobileplanet.com provide a convenient format for shopping across a variety of computer types and manufacturers.

Portability versus Power

When beginning to plan the purchase of a computer system, typically the first issue you should consider is portability. How portable does your computer system need to be? Educators in Maine decided that laptop computers were just the thing

FIGURE 2.31 • Notebook computers in action

The Maine school system supplied their 7th graders with notebook computers to inspire learning.

FIGURE 2.32 • Tablet PC in action

With all the power and functionality of a notebook PC, the tablet allows you to take notes, while standing, walking, or sitting in meetings.

to inspire their seventh graders in the classroom (see Figure 2.31). In a controversial program, Maine purchased a notebook computer for every seventh grader in the state. Educators are impressed by how quickly students and teachers have adapted to laptop technology. Attendance is up. Detentions are down. Students are motivated to learn.[25] The portability and power of a notebook computer made this possible.

When purchasing your own computer you must analyze your own computing style and needs. Will you need access to information stored on your computer while you are away from your desk? How will you use your computer while you are at your desk and away? Portability is balanced with power and capacity. If you need extreme power while at your desk—for example to run virtual reality simulations or computer-aided design (CAD) software—you will need some type of desktop system; a notebook simply won't do. If your computing needs away from your desk are minimal, a handheld computer or combined PDA-cell phone should satisfy that need. If you don't need extraordinary power on the desktop, and your needs away from your desk are more substantial, then a notebook computer would allow you to use one device both at and away from your desk. A handheld computer might still be nice to have since you don't want to have to boot up your notebook just to retrieve a phone number or view your daily agenda. For people who use computers while on the go, a tablet PC could be the perfect solution. With all the power and functionality of a notebook PC, the tablet allows you to take notes, while standing, walking, or sitting in meetings (see Figure 2.32).

Interoperability

Once you've determined your portability needs, you need to consider how your device will interact with other computer systems. Will you be connecting to a corporate network where you work? If so, you will need to choose a device that is compatible and will be able to access the information that you need from work. Will you need access to the Internet? Internet connectivity becomes a bigger issue when dealing with mobile devices. We discuss these issues in Chapter 5. For now, be aware that such issues may have an impact on your computer selection.

Choosing a Manufacturer and Model

When choosing a manufacturer, Apple computer users have it easy. Since there is only one manufacturer of Apple computers, all an Apple user needs to decide on is model. IBM-compatible users need to compare specifications and prices from dozens of manufacturers, using the research techniques presented earlier in this section. A good place to begin is with the well-known manufacturers of good reputation. Talk with your friends, speak with your employer, and read reviews, until you feel confident in a particular manufacturer. Don't be lured by amazing deals. If it seems too good to be true, then there is probably substantial risk involved. For instance, you might find a very nice looking notebook computer with impressive specifications, manufactured by an unknown company, with a 1-year warranty, at an online clearance house for only $700. Although this offer sounds tempting, notebook computers typically need to be sent to the manufacturer for repairs once or twice during their lifetime. You'll be lucky to get a year out of this bargain notebook. It may have problems right out of the box, and the manufacturer may be nowhere to be found.

Next, you need to choose a processor, and the amount of memory and storage. In some devices, these choices are easy to make. For instance, the amount of choice you get when choosing a handheld computer is minimal. The choices are more complex for larger computers. Here, you will balance power against cost. You can pay a premium for the latest and greatest processor, or save substantially by purchasing at the next level below the state-of-the-art machine. Remember that the "latest and greatest" will be outdated—and drastically reduced in price—within 6 months. Also keep in mind that software demands increasing amounts of resources. A cheap computer may seem like a good deal today, but will probably not be able to support the applications of tomorrow—3 to 4 years down the road. Consider your future needs; will you be able to upgrade to a faster processor, add more memory, and add additional storage or upgrade storage?

The warranty that you select for your device is the most important component. For portable devices, a minimum of a 3-year warranty is best. Otherwise, consider how long it will be before you upgrade to a new computer, then assume that the computer you are currently purchasing will fall apart the day after the warranty expires. By assuming the worst, you will be prepared for the worst.

Choosing Peripherals

Finally, consider peripheral devices. What types best suit your needs? If you prefer using a keyboard for text input, and do a lot of it, you may want to consider an ergonomic design that will help prevent repetitive motion injuries. If you don't like to type, you may wish to explore speech recognition, so make sure that the computer you choose supports such an option. Think about unique applications that may require additional input devices, such as a gamepad, Webcam, or graphics tablet and pen. What type of printing will you be doing? Do you need professional quality output? Will you be printing digital photos? If the quality of printed output is important to your work, you may need to spend more on a printer than on your computer.

Purchasing decisions are typically constrained by a budget. You may need to make sacrifices in some areas to invest more in other, more critical areas.

Making the Purchase

Computer systems can be purchased online, over the phone, or in a local computer store. Purchasing one online from the manufacturer provides custom configuration options unavailable from local computer stores. Purchasing options include outright purchase (cash check, or credit card), lease, or financing. Computer store shoppers have the benefit of taking the newly purchased computer home with them. Online shoppers have to wait a week for delivery.

A purchase of this magnitude should always begin with a careful assessment of your information and computing needs—now and in years to come. Reasoned forethought—a skill required for dealing with computer, information, and organizational systems of all sizes—is the hallmark of true computer systems understanding.

Action Plan

1. How should Marcus prepare for his purchasing decision?

Marcus needs to list his specific computing needs at home and away from home. He needs to keep each activity in mind throughout the purchasing process, and make sure that the computer he purchases is able to support his needs.

2. What type of computer platform might best suit Marcus's needs?

Since this will be Marcus's primary computer, he will need something of substance: a desktop or notebook PC. Since Marcus is into computer games and graphic art, he will most likely want a large display, larger than a notebook computer would provide. He will need to choose between either the Apple or a Wintel platform. Since Marcus will be bringing some of his work home with him from Lamar, he should go with the same platform that is used at his work.

3. How much processor speed, memory, and storage capacity does Marcus need?

Interactive, 3-D gaming requires a fast processor. If Marcus is really into gaming he should go with the fastest processor available—3 GHz or faster with an Intel processor, 1.42 GHz in a Mac. If he is only mildly interested in gaming, he could save some money by going a notch down on processor speed to perhaps the speed that was fastest last year. His other interests do not require a state-of-the-art processor. Gaming also requires a significant amount of memory (512 MB recommended) but not necessarily a lot of storage (40 GB should suffice). However, if Marcus does any work with video editing or plans to store his music, or video files on his computer, he should get a large disk drive (160 GB). To sum up, if Marcus will be using his computer for gaming and multimedia, he should consider maximum processor speed, memory, and storage offered in top-of-the-line computer packages. Otherwise, he might save as much as $800 by going for a more basic package.

4. What input/output devices would best suit Marcus's needs?

As a gamer and artist, Marcus will want to get a large display, a color printer, a game controller, a drawing tablet, and a flatbed scanner. He will want to check with his employer to see what types of displays and drawing tablets they recommend and configure his home computer to be as similar to the one at work as possible. He should also purchase an upgraded video card with a significant amount of memory to smoothly run the gaming animation.

5. Are there additional considerations to be made regarding this purchase?

Since Marcus is new to speech recognition and video conferencing, he'll need to do some research to find out what hardware is required. Speech recognition runs best on a computer with a fast processor and lots of memory. If Marcus's computer meets those requirements, then all he needs to do is purchase an inexpensive microphone headset and speech recognition software. For video communication over the Internet, he'll need a broadband Internet connection and a Webcam. Since it sounds as though Marcus's job does not entail travel, he might not need much computing power on the road. Perhaps a PDA cell phone will suffice for his mobile computing needs. Marcus might also consider investing in a game system for his television. This might allow him to save some money by purchasing a more modest PC.

Summary

LEARNING OBJECTIVE 1

Understand how bits are used to represent text, values, colors, and sound and how digital data representation is changing our lives.

The digital revolution was sparked by the computer's ability to represent and manipulate information digitally, with 1s and 0s. The 1s and 0s used by computers are called bits. Each bit has two states that can be used to represent two units of information. When bits are combined they can represent an infinite amount of information ($2^b = i$, where b is the number of bits and i the units of information). Eight bits is a byte, which is the fundamental building block of binary data representation. We use kilobyte (KB), megabyte (MB), and gigabyte (GB) to represent a thousand, million, and billion bytes, respectively. We will see increasing uses of tera (trillion) and peta (quadrillion) as the need for huge data stores increases.

Units of information can be represented with bits in a standardized code by assigning each unit to a unique bit pattern using a "look-up chart." ASCII is a standardized code used in computers to represent character data. Bits can also be used to store values by using the binary number system. The binary number system uses 2 digits—0 and 1. Binary numbers are used for calculations, to represent color intensities in images, and to represent the amplitude of sound waves used to store digital music and sound. The process of transforming information such as text, images, video, music, and voice communications into bits is called digitization.

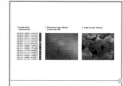

Figure 2.3—p. 50

LEARNING OBJECTIVE 2

Identify the functions of the components of a CPU, the relationship between the CPU and memory, and the factors that contribute to processing speed.

The CPU processes the data into information that is meaningful to people. The CPU's primary components are the control unit that fetches and interprets instructions, the arithmetic logic unit that carries out the instructions, and registers that store the bytes being processed. The CPU uses RAM as its primary storage. RAM provides the CPU with a working storage area for program instructions and data. Data flows back and forth between the CPU and RAM across the system bus.

The control unit in the CPU uses the four-step machine cycle to carry out program instructions: fetch instruction, decode instruction, execute instruction, and store results. Each processor has an instruction set, a finite number of instructions that it is designed to carry out. Clock speed, wordlength, and instruction set complexity all have an impact on the speed of processing. All activity in the system takes place in time with a processor's system clock. The faster the clock, the faster the processing. Clock speeds are measured in megahertz (MHz) and gigahertz (GHz). The number of bits the CPU can process at any one time is called its wordlength. Some computer systems use multiple processors to increase processing speed.

Moore's Law states that in silicon-based processors, transistor densities in an integrated circuit will double every 18 to 24 months.

Figure 2.8—p. 56

LEARNING OBJECTIVE 3

Identify different types of memory and storage media, and understand the unique properties of each.

RAM is volatile and temporarily stores data as long as there is an electrical current. ROM is more permanent storage that has its instructions hard wired into its circuitry. ROM stores the boot process that runs when the computer is powered up.

Magnetic and optical storage are two types of secondary storage that are used to store data and programs more permanently. Magnetic storage includes disks (random access) and tapes (sequential access). Optical storage includes CDs and DVDs, which are available in read-only disks and writable disks. Flash memory devices are becoming increasing popular as convenient portable storage for media data such as digital photos and music.

Figure 2.16—p. 65

LEARNING OBJECTIVE 4
Identify different types of input and output devices and how they are used to meet a variety of personal and professional needs.

People use input devices to provide data and instructions to the computer, and use output devices to receive results from it. General-purpose input devices include the keyboard and mouse for desktop computers, the touch pad and TrackPoint for notebook computers, and the touch screen for tablet and handheld devices. Scanners are used in a variety of industries to avoid data-entry errors by capturing data close to its source. Special-purpose input devices include gamepads, joysticks, tablets and pens, and Webcams.

Printers, plotters, and displays are the primary forms of output devices. Displays are selected by size and resolution. Traditional CRT monitors are losing market share to the leaner, cleaner LCD displays whose prices in recent years have dropped. Color ink-jet and black and white laser printers are popular for home and small business use, although color laser printer prices are dropping to the point of being more affordable.

Figure 2.25—p. 75

LEARNING OBJECTIVE 5
Understand the decision-making process involved in purchasing a computer system.

When selecting a computer system, you must first analyze your specific computing needs when at your desk and on the road. Select a computer type and platform that will support those needs. You may require one or two computers depending on your mobile computing needs. Options include desktop computers, notebook computers, tablet PCs, handheld computers (PDAs), and PDA-cell phones, with a tradeoff between power and portability.

Test Yourself

LEARNING OBJECTIVE 1: Understand how bits are used to represent text, values, colors, and sound, and how digital data representation is changing our lives.

1. Most computers use _____ to represent character data using bytes.
   a. hexadecimal
   b. kilobytes
   c. decimal notation
   d. ASCII

2. The _____ number system is ideal for digital systems since it has only two digits, 1 and 0.

3. True or False: 6 bits can represent 256 units of information.

4. _____ refers to the ability of one device to handle several different types of digital information, such as voice communications, character data, and music.
   a. digital revolution
   b. digital convergence
   c. digital communications
   d. digital ecomony

LEARNING OBJECTIVE 2: Identify the functions of the components of a CPU, the relationship

between the CPU and memory, and the factors that contribute to processing speed.

5. In the CPU, the _____ performs mathematical calculations, and the _____ sequentially accesses program instructions.

6. True or False: Data flows back and forth between the CPU and memory across the system bus.

7. Which of the following does not contribute to processor speed?
   a. clock speed
   b. ROM
   c. instruction set complexity
   d. wordlength

LEARNING OBJECTIVE 3: Identify different types of memory and storage media, and understand the unique properties of each.

8. When a computer is first powered on, the processor is fed instructions from _____.
   a. register storage
   b. RAM
   c. ROM
   d. secondary storage

9. True or False: The two types of optical storage are random access and sequential access.

10. Notebook computers use _____ cards as one method of connecting external devices.

LEARNING OBJECTIVE 4: Identify different types of input and output devices and how they are used to meet a variety of personal and professional needs.

11. _____ involves automating data entry where the data is created, thus ensuring accuracy and timeliness.
    a. keyboard input
    b. source data automation
    c. secure data entry
    d. special purpose device input

12. Most gamers prefer to use a _____ device to control game characters.

13. True or False: CRT displays are becoming more popular than the old-fashioned LCD displays.

LEARNING OBJECTIVE 5: Understand the decision-making process involved in purchasing a computer system.

14. True or False: Choosing a computer system requires a careful analysis of user needs.

15. The most important computer system component that you purchase is the _____.

16. The first consideration in selecting a computer system is _____.
    a. platform
    b. processor
    c. portability
    d. manufacturer

Test Yourself Solutions: 1. d. 2. binary, 3. F, 4. b. 5. ALU, control unit, 6. T, 7. b. 8. c. 9. F, 10. PC, 11. b. 12. gamepad, 13. T, 14. T, 15. warranty, 16. c.

Key Terms

American Standard Code for Information Interchange (ASCII), p. 50
arithmetic/logic unit (ALU), p. 56
benchmark, p. 59
binary number system, p. 51
bit, p. 49
bit-mapped graphics, p. 51
byte, p. 49
cache memory, p. 62
CD-RW, p. 66

central processing unit (CPU), p. 55
CMOS memory, p. 64
compact disk read-only memory (CD-ROM), p. 65
computing platform, p. 58
control unit, p. 56
digital convergence, p. 54
digital video disk (DVD), p. 66
digitization, p. 49
display resolution, p. 73
flash memory card, p. 66

gamepad, p. 71
giga, p. 50
gigaflop, p. 57
gigahertz (GHz), p. 57
input, p. 48
input device, p. 69
integrated circuit, p. 55
kilo, p. 50
kiosk, p. 71
liquid crystal display (flat panel display), p. 75
LCD projectors, p. 75

Questions

Review Questions

1. How many bits would it require to represent the 50 states in the United States?

2. How many colors can be represented by 1 bit?

3. Explain how bit-mapped images are stored.

4. Describe how digital music is captured and stored.

5. Describe the components of a machine cycle.

6. What is the difference between digital convergence and ubiquitous computing?

7. What factors affect processing speed?

8. What are the two most popular personal computer platforms? How do they differ?

9. Describe the various types of memory.

10. Explain the difference between sequential and direct access.

11. Describe various types of secondary storage media in terms of access method, capacity, and portability.

12. What factors determine the appropriate system output and input devices?

13. Discuss the speed and functionality of common input and output devices.

14. How do expansion techniques differ between notebook and desktop computers?

15. Describe the six steps of selecting and purchasing a computer.

Discussion Questions

16. The SmartPhone allows you to make phone calls, listen to digital music, and access text data, such as your calendar and address book. What other functionality would you like to see provided by a handy, all-in-one portable device? How can such a function be incorporated digitally?

17. Paper is difficult and expensive to organize, manipulate, and store over extended periods of time. In light of paper's drawbacks, discuss the impact(s) of various input and storage devices on organizations.

18. Contrast magnetic storage devices and optical storage devices. What are the advantages and disadvantages of each in terms of cost, control, and complexity?

19. Discuss where the various types of computers might be found in a typical large organization and what functions each type of computer might serve. How would these differ in a medium-sized organization?

20. List the activities that you do, or would do if you were able to, on computers both at your desk and away. What computer device(s) would best support your needs (PC, notebook, tablet PC, handheld)? What are your needs in terms of processor speed, memory capacity, and storage capacity? Provide your rationale.

Exercises

Try It Yourself

1. Use a spreadsheet to convert decimal into the binary number systems. Most spreadsheet applications have a function that will do this conversion automatically for you. For example Microsoft Excel includes a function named DEC2BIN. Create a chart that looks like this:

Decimal	Binary
1	1
2	10
3	11
4	100
5	101
6	110
7	111
8	1000
9	1001
10	1010

Example of function usage:

Decimal	Binary
1	=DEC2BIN(A2)
2	=DEC2BIN(A3)

Recall that the binary number system has only 2 digits (0 and 1). Create a second table in your spreadsheet that converts binary numbers to decimal (BIN2DEC). Type in binary values 1 through 10100 and use either a function or your brain to do the conversions. Use your tables to experiment with these number systems for better understanding.

2. You and two friends have decided to start your own business. You have secured a small business loan from the bank and leased some office space. Your partners have placed you in charge of purchasing desktop computers for the six employees of your company—the three owners and three clerical employees. None of the employees need a really fast processor, but the partners need larger amounts of memory and storage. The employees need the ability to archive data on a CD. All employees need a lot of work room on their desks so whatever you buy will have to take up as little desktop space as possible.

   Your budget is $10,000. You have already selected a vendor; now you need to decide on what should be included in each of the two types of systems: the owners' systems and the employees' systems. A price list for computer components appears in Table 2.4. Create a spreadsheet to find the best solution. Add a short memo explaining the rationale for your solution. Include the price of your owners' computers and your employees' computers and what components each will include. Also include the minimum and maximum price possible for a computer system.

3. What combination of the components listed in Table 2.4 would best suit your own personal computing needs at the lowest cost? Calculate the cost using a calculator program. Use a word processor to list the features and price of your computer. Search the Web and find a better deal from another source. Popular online vendors include www.dell.com, www.gateway.com, www.cdw.com, or you can look at Apple, http://store.apple.com. In your

TABLE 2.4 • PC Purchasing Options for Exercises 2 and 3

	Base Package $999	Upgrade Options		
Processor Speed	2.66 GHz	2.8 GHz add $566	3 GHz add $736	
Memory	512 MB	256 MB deduct $140	1024 MB add $280	
Hard Drive Storage	40 GB	80 GB add $60	160 GB add $110	
Portable Storage	DVD	CD-RW add $20	CD-RW/DVD add $69	DVD+RW add $150
Display	17" CRT	15" LCD add $260	18" LCD add $450	

word-processing document, list the features and price of the better deal that you found. Include a rationale for why you think it is a better deal.

4. Visit www.cnet.com and click Peripherals. In a word-processing document, list the subcategories of input/output devices that you find under:

   - Monitors
   - Printers
   - Scanners

   Now visit www.zdnet.com, click *Reviews & Prices,* then *All Products,* then *Peripherals,* and then Input Devices. Add the categories of Input Devices that are listed to your document. Looking over your complete list, mark those devices that would benefit you in your own computer use with an "X." Add a description of the types of activities you do that would require each marked item. In the case of monitors and printers, describe how you decided on the type.

5. Using common Web search engines, such as www.ask.com and www.google.com, find the name of the fastest supercomputer in existence. What is its name, who made it, how fast is it, and what is it used for? Do the same for the second fastest supercomputer. What is the difference between the two in speed and in age? Do these two computers support Moore's Law?

6. Consider the computing needs of your present or future career. Are there any special or unique hardware requirements? Use the Web to research this topic. Rank the following in order of importance for your professional computer system (most important being 1):

   ____ Portability
   ____ Network/Internet connection
   ____ Large high-quality display
   ____ Fast processor
   ____ Large amount of memory
   ____ Large-capacity hard disk drive
   ____ Large-capacity portable storage (Zip, CD-RW, and so on)
   ____ High-quality printer
   ____ Flatbed scanner
   ____ Digital camera
   ____ Special-purpose input device (provide description if applicable)

Virtual Classroom Activities

For the following exercises, do not use face-to-face or telephone communications with your group members. Use only Internet communications.

7. Assume that you are partners in a new business. Decide what business you are in. Assign each group member a role within the business. One member should act as company president and group leader. Choose a leader by casting electronic ballots. Each group member should be assigned a position in the new business. Each group member should then decide what type of computer he or she will need to do his or her job. Use the chapter content to decide what type of computer(s) will best suit your needs. Include processor speed, memory and storage types and capacities, along with I/O devices—the options discussed in this chapter. Justify your choices.

8. Each group member should go shopping on the Web to find the lowest priced system as defined in Exercise 7. Submit a detailed price breakdown to the group leader. The group leader should compile the data and total the cost of the new computer systems.

Teamwork

9. Identify the public and department-run computer labs on your campus. Divide them equally between team members. Each team member should visit his or her assigned labs and, either by observation or contact with the lab administrator, list the type of equipment used in the lab. Include processor speeds, memory capacity, storage types used on the computers, and manufacturer's name for all devices, including scanners, printers, and other peripherals. Reconvene and decide which lab on campus best meets students' needs. Write a report that summarizes your findings.

10. Assign each group member a particular computer component to research: processor, memory, storage, input device, and output device. Search the Web, periodicals, or computer stores for unique examples of such devices that were not included in this chapter. Compile your data to create a unique computer. The group with the most bizarre computer wins.

Learning Check

To check your knowledge of each of the chapter objectives, use this chart to find related end-of-chapter content.

Learning Objective	Key Terms		Questions	Exercises
Learning Objective 1 Understand how bits are used to represent text, values, colors, and sound, and how digital data representation is changing our lives.	binary number system bit bit-mapped graphics byte digital convergence digitization giga input	kilo mega output pixels processing storage tera vector graphics	1, 2, 3, 4, 16	1
Learning Objective 2 Identify the functions of the components of a CPU, the relationship between the CPU and memory, and the factors that contribute to processing speed.	arithmetic/logic unit (ALU) benchmark central processing unit (CPU) computing platform control unit gigaflop gigahertz (GHz) integrated circuit megahertz (MHz) microprocessor millions of instructions per second (MIPS) Moore's Law motherboard random access memory (RAM) transistor		7, 8, 9	5, 7, 8, 9
Learning Objective 3 Identify different types of memory and storage media, and understand the unique properties of each.	cache Memory CD-RW CMOS memory compact disk read-only memory (CD-ROM) digital video disk (DVD) flash memory card magnetic storage optical storage read-only memory (ROM) video RAM		10, 11, 12, 17, 18	7, 8, 9

	Learning Objective	Key Terms	Questions	Exercises
	Learning Objective 4 Identify different types of input and output devices and how they are used to meet a variety of personal and professional needs.	input device output device pervasive computing stylus touch screen	13, 14, 17	4, 7, 8, 9
	Learning Objective 5 Understand the decision-making process involved in purchasing a computer system.		15, 19, 20	2, 3, 6, 7, 8

Endnotes

1. "The Petabyte Frontier," CommWeb's *Telecom Weekly Bulletin*, February 28, 2002, *www.techtransform.com/id229.htm*.

2. "Supersize IT: From Megabytes to Petabytes," Mike Martin, August 26, 2002, *www.newsfactor.com/perl/story/19162.html*.

3. *www.apple.com/powermac/processor.html*.

4. "U.S. Activates World's Fastest Supercomputer: IBM's ASCI White," IBM Press Release, August 15, 2001, *www.ibm.com*.

5. "This Is Your Computer on Brains," Michelle Delio, *Wired News*, November 19, 2002, *www.wired.com*.

6. "Handheld Price/Performance Index," *PC Magazine* On-line, May 6, 2003, *www.pcmag.com/article2/0,4149,1016989,00.asp*.

7. "Japanese Computer Is World's Fastest, As U.S. Falls Back," Juhn Markoff, *NewYork Times*, April 20, 2002.

8. Moore's Law, Intel Website, Accessed September 12, 2003, *www.intel.com/research/silicon/mooreslaw.htm?iid=sr+moore&*.

9. "Burn Your Genes on CD – for $500,000," *Associated Press*, 2002, *www.cnn.com*.

10. "Sony announces blue-laser data storage format," Martyn Williams, *ComputerWorld* online, April 8, 2003, *www.computerworld.com/*.

11. "NewsTalk at the *New York Times*," Manua Janah, *Forbes ASAP*, December 5, 1994.

12. "A Car Pool That Really Works," Richard Morais, *Forbes*, December 19, 1994.

13. Centre for Pervasive Computing, *www.pervasive.dk/*.

14. *www.ubiq.com/weiser/*.

15. "Web goes down the toilet," BBC News, April 5, 2003.

16. *www.givenimaging.com*

17. "Kiosk Passes the Collection Plate," Charles Mandel, *Wired News*, May 07, 2003 *www.wired.com*.

18. "First megapixel camera cell phones unveiled," Martyn Williams, IDG News Service, April 8, 2003.

19. "Want Access? Give 'em the Finger," Lucas Mearian, *ComputerWorld*, January 28, 2002, *www.computerworld.com*.

20. "UK's Transco Selects Gensym's G2 Software; Large Gas Pipeline Company to Deploy Knowledge-Based Operator-Support Systems," *Business Wire*, February 6, 2002.

21. "Scientists track movement inside," Robert S. Boyd, *Milwaukee Journal Sentinel* (Wisconsin), May 5, 2003.

22. "Scientists track movement inside," Robert S. Boyd, *Milwaukee Journal Sentinel* (Wisconsin), May 5, 2003.

23. "MIT team helps kids compose symphonies," Azell Murphy Cavaan, *The Boston Herald*, March 30, 2003,

24. "Wyndham International Honored with Two Awards for Its Innovative Use of Information Technology," *Business Wire*, November 8, 2001.

25. "Laptops Win over the Skeptics, Even in Maine," Sarah Mahoney, *New York Times*, March 5, 2003.

SoftwareSolutions **for**Personal**and** Professional**Gain**

Alexandra Pollack is a second-semester freshman in college and working part time to help pay her expenses. She needs a new computer system, has saved for almost a year, and wants to make sure that she gets what she needs for the rest of college and her part-time job. One of her instructors advised her to decide what software she needs before she buys a new computer system.

Alex is majoring in political science and is interested in going to law school after she graduates. She is currently working as a clerk at a local law firm. The firm allows her to do some of her work from her dorm room, which is convenient for Alex. Working from her dorm room saves her a 25-minute drive and the cost of the expensive clothes she would need to work at the law firm's office. The law firm told her that she needs something called Office XP to do her work from home. A friend recommended that she consider getting Office 2003 instead.

Alex also enjoys music. She would like to be able to download music from the Internet and play the music on some type of portable device. She currently has an old CD player.

1. What will Alex need for her work for the law firm?
2. What type of operating system will she need?

Check out Alex's *Action Plan* at the conclusion of this chapter.

3

After completing Chapter 3, you will be able to:

LEARNING OBJECTIVES	CHAPTER CONTENT
1. Discuss the importance and types of software.	**An Overview of Software**
2. Discuss the functions of some important programming languages.	**Programming Languages**
3. Describe the functions of systems software and operating systems.	**Systems Software**
4. Describe the support provided by applications software.	**Application Software**
5. Discuss how software can be acquired, customized, installed, removed, and managed.	**Software Issues and Trends**

Introduction

Software is the key to unlocking the potential of any computer system and developing effective computer applications. Without software, the fastest, most powerful computer is useless. It can do nothing without instructions to follow and programs to execute. With software, people and organizations can accomplish more in less time.

All software is developed using a programming language. Programming languages have gone through a number of generations, and with today's languages, writing computer programs is easier and faster than it was 40 years ago. Programming languages are used to develop two basic types of software—system software and application software. System software makes computers run more efficiently, whereas application software helps people, groups, and organizations achieve their goals. Both types of software are discussed in this chapter. This chapter concludes with some important software issues, such as how to fix software bugs, software licenses, and copyrights.

In the early days of computing, when computer hardware was relatively rare and expensive, software costs were a comparatively small percentage of total computer system costs. The situation has dramatically changed today. Software can be 75 percent or more of the total cost of a particular computer system because (1) advances in hardware technology have resulted in dramatically reduced hardware costs; (2) increasingly complex software requires more time to develop, hence, it is more costly; and (3) salaries for individuals who develop software have increased due to the increased demand for their skills. In the future, as shown in Figure 3.1, software will constitute an even greater portion of the cost of the overall computer system. The critical functions software serves, however, make it a worthy investment.

FIGURE 3.1 • The importance of software

Organizations have greatly increased their expenditures on software as compared to hardware since the 1950s.

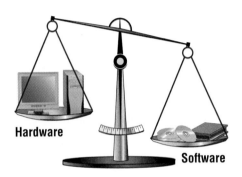

ANOVERVIEW**OF**SOFTWARE

One of software's most critical functions is directing computer hardware. As we saw in Chapter 1, *software* consists of computer programs that control the workings of the computer hardware, along with the *program documentation* used to explain the programs to the user. Today, program documentation is usually included in *Help* features or menus with the software package, on the Internet, or in manuals produced by the software manufacturer and others. **Computer programs** are sets of instructions or statements to the computer. Ultimately, these statements direct the circuitry within the hardware to operate in a certain fashion. **Computer programmers** are people who write or create these instructions or statements that become complete programs. Within the computer industry, they are called software engineers. *Program documentation* is the collection of narrative descriptions designed to assist in the program's use and implementation. Some documentation can be located within the program itself, whereas other forms of documentation are external to the program.

Systems and Application Software

There are two basic types of software: systems software and application software. **Systems software** is the set of programs that coordinates the activities of the hardware and various computer programs. Systems software is written for a specific set of hardware, most particularly the CPU. Recall from Chapter 2 that the particular hardware configuration of the computer system combined with the particular system software in use is known as the *computer platform*. The other type of software, **application software**, consists of programs written to solve problems

Discovering Planets with Better Software

For centuries, scientists have used telescopes to discover planets. To get less interference from the atmosphere, telescopes are often put on mountaintops or in earth orbit. But distant planets that are close to stars have been very difficult to find with telescopes. There simply isn't enough light to see them.

Discovering distant planets may require not better telescopes, but better software. "People thought we were a little crazy. When we told them we were going to look for planets around stars, they'd kind of look down at their shoes and scuffle a little bit," says astronomer Geoffrey Marcy. Because there were no off-the-shelf software packages available, Marcy and a team of astronomers wrote about 50,000 lines of software code to help find planets. They spent literally thousands of hours writing the code. The software used statistical analysis to compare what they expected with what they actually observed. It used to take 6 hours of computer time to analyze 10 minutes of observational data. With the new software and high-speed workstations, it now takes only 10 minutes to analyze the data.

Marcy, the director of the Center for Integrative Planetary Science at the University of California, Berkley, has found over 50 of the 86 known extra-solar planets. According to Frank Drake, chairman of the board of trustees of the SETI Institute, "It's one of the most important discoveries of the last 100 years."

Questions
1. How might software be used in other areas of science to make important discoveries?
2. Do you think there was any existing software that could have been used?

Sources
1. *"Scientists Develop Algorithms to Discover Extra-Solar Planets," Gary Anthes,* Computerworld, *June 3, 2002, p. 28.*
2. *"MARS: Where Beagles Dare," Staff,* Computing, *May 29, 2003, p. 1.*
3. *"A Faster, Better, Cheaper Way to Probe Space Failures," Jeff Hecht,* New Scientist, *November 16, 2002, p. 9.*

---

and help people and organizations achieve their goals. Application software applies the power of the computer to give individuals, groups, and organizations the ability to solve problems and perform specific activities or tasks.

How Software Works

Software usually consists of a number of files, ranging from a few to dozens or more. At least one of the files is an executable file with an .exe extension. Other files can store data. A text file typically has a .txt extension. Many word-processing files have a .doc extension. There are many ways to start or run executable files, including clicking icons with a mouse or typing commands into the computer. Either one of these actions causes an executable file to start running. When a program, such as a word processor, is started, instructions from the program are copied from the computer's disk drive, where they are permanently stored, in the computer's memory. Once in memory, the instructions are transferred to the processor and executed. As you create a document—for example, a term paper including text, bold terms, footnotes, and other features—the word-processing software obeys your commands and does what you wish (see Figure 3.2). When you are finished, you can close the program and stop it from running in memory in a variety of ways, such as clicking close buttons or entering commands, such as CLOSE or EXIT. When you close the program, it is removed from the computer's memory.

FIGURE 3.2 • Using word-processing software

Word-processing programs have many formatting features, such as **bold**, numbered lists, and even footnotes.

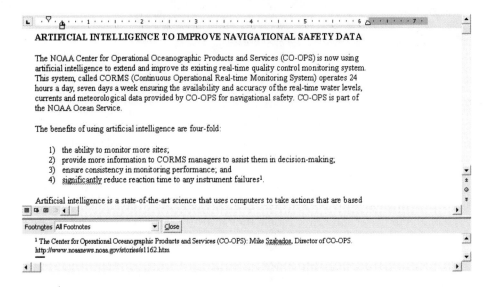

PROGRAMMINGLANGUAGES

All software, both systems software and application software, is written in coding schemes called programming languages. The primary function of a **programming language** is to provide instructions to the computer system so that it can perform a processing activity to achieve an objective or solve a problem. It's impossible to overemphasize the role of programming languages and software in problem solving and decision making and attaining individual and organizational goals. Because programming languages are becoming easier to learn and use, non-computer-people are increasingly writing their own programs. Students have written their own programs to help them complete homework assignments or class projects. Engineers have developed programs to design bridges, and corporate employees have written programs to help them on the job.

In the very early years of computing, writing computer programs was quite complex. The various switches and circuits comprising the computer hardware had to be manually set; that is, data was represented by physically switching various circuits on or off. In modern computers, however, the CPU works in conjunction with various software programs to control the physical state of the digital circuitry. In order for this to occur, the CPU must receive signals from the computer program that it can convert into actions (the switching of the circuits on and off.) Since these signals are not the actions themselves, but merely instructions that these actions should occur, they are called program code. *Program code* is the set of instructions that signal the CPU to perform circuit-switching operations. In the simplest coding schemes, a line of code will typically contain a single instruction such as, "Retrieve the data in memory address X." As discussed in Chapter 2, the instruction is then decoded during the instruction phase of the machine cycle.

As mentioned before, the writing or coding of instructions—that is, creating a computer program—is called *programming,* and the individual doing the writing or coding is called a *programmer.* The majority of people working with computer systems, however, are not programmers; they are users working with programs previously written by others.

Programmers work with programming languages, which are sets of symbols and rules used to write program code. Like writing a report or a paper in English, writing a computer program in a programming language requires that the programmer follow a set of rules. Each programming language uses a set of symbols that have special meanings, much as English uses the Roman alphabet. Each language also has its own set of rules, called the *syntax* of the language. The language syntax dictates how the symbols should be combined into statements capable of conveying meaningful instructions to the CPU. To some extent, programming involves translating what a user wants to accomplish into a code that the computer can understand and execute.

A *programming language standard* is a set of rules that describes how programming statements and commands should be written. A rule that "variable names must start with a letter" is an example. A variable is a quantity that can take on different values. Program variable names such as SALES, PAYRATE, and TOTAL follow the preceding rule because they start with a letter, whereas variables such as %INTEREST, $TOTAL, and #POUNDS do not.

Programming languages have evolved since the early days of computing, and they continue to evolve. As shown in Table 3.1, we think of the evolution of programming languages in terms of generations of languages. Let's take a look at how programming languages have changed.

TABLE 3.1 • The Evolution of Programming Languages

Generation	Language	Approximate Development Date	Sample Statement or Action
First	Machine language	1940s	00010101
Second	Assembly language	1950s	MVC
Third	High-level language	1960s	READ SALES
Fourth	Query and database languages	1970s	PRINT EMPLOYEE NUMBER IF GROSS PAY >1000
Beyond fourth	Natural and intelligent languages	1980s	IF certain medical conditions exist, THEN a specific diagnosis is made.

Machine Language: The First Generation

In the first generation of programming languages—**machine languages**—programmers wrote instructions in binary code, telling the CPU exactly which circuits to switch on and off. Each type of computer has its own machine language. Because machine language programs are written in binary code, they use only two symbols: 0 and 1; recall from Chapter 2 that these symbols are called bits. In machine language, a simple command to add two numbers could require several statements or lines of program code containing 0s and 1s. One line might retrieve the first number from the computer's memory. A second line of 0s and 1s might retrieve the second number from memory. As seen in Figure 3.3, a third line could add the two numbers. A fourth line might place the result back into another memory location.

Because programming in machine language is extremely difficult, very few programs are actually written in it. However, machine language is the only language capable of directly instructing the CPU. Thus, every non-machine-language program instruction must be translated into machine

FIGURE 3.3 • A simplified machine-language instruction

A machine language instruction consists of all 0s and 1s. Here are just a few elements of a single instruction.

00100101	00000010	00001101
Operation code (i.e., add, subtract)	Address location 1 (i.e., first number, to be added)	Address location 2 (i.e., second number, to be added)

language prior to its execution. This translation will be discussed more fully later in this chapter.

Assembly Language: The Second Generation

The second generation of programming languages attempted to overcome some of the difficulties inherent in machine-language programming by replacing the binary digits with symbols more easily understood by human programmers. **Assembly languages** use codes like ADD for add, MOV for move, and so on. Figure 3.4 shows a simplified assembly-language instruction that adds a number to a total. This second generation of languages was termed assembly language after the system programs used to translate them into machine code. These programs are called assembler programs, or assemblers.

FIGURE 3.4 • A simplified assembly-language instruction

An assembly-language instruction consists of symbols. Here is an example adding the contents of register 1 (R1) to a total (TOT).

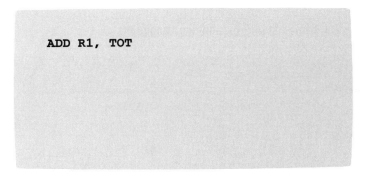

```
ADD R1, TOT
```

All languages beyond the first generation are called *symbolic languages* because their emphasis is on the use of symbols easily understood by human beings. For example, assembly language allows the exact location of the data in memory to be named according to their contents, for example, PAY for the location of data regarding pay rate. Previously, these memory locations were just binary-numbered addresses that required the programmer to remember or document their purpose. In addition, this movement toward a more symbolic, human-readable code allowed the programmer to focus on structuring a problem solution rather than on the complexities of writing instructions in binary code. Although a step above machine language in terms of sophistication, assembly language is still considered a low-level language.

High-level Languages: The Third Generation

The third generation of programming languages continued the trend toward greater use of symbolic code and away from specifically instructing the computer how to complete an operation. This third generation comprises high-level languages such as *BASIC (Beginners All-purpose Symbolic Instruction Code), COBOL (COmmon Business-Oriented Language),* and *FORTRAN (FORmula TRANslator).* A **high-level programming language** is one that uses English-like statements and commands. This type of language is easier to learn and use than machine and assembly languages because it more closely resembles the level of everyday human communication and understanding. High-level languages use statements such as PRINT TOTAL_SALES, READ HOURS_WORKED, and NORMAL_PAY=HOURS_WORKED*PAYRATE. In general, high-level programming languages have the following four characteristics:

1. Each statement in the language translates into several instructions in machine language. In other words, an instruction, such as READ SALES, might be converted into several instructions in machine language. In addition, high-level languages take the programmer one step further away from directing the actual operation of the computer. Although easier to use, high-level languages are not as efficient in terms of operational speed and memory utilization.

2. The language is English-like and uses abbreviations and words used in everyday communication. The syntax structure of this language is similar to verb-noun English constructions, and it uses familiar words to abbreviate instructions, such as READ, PRINT, RUN, LIST, and IF.

3. Each programming language has characteristics that make it appropriate for certain types of problems or applications. For example, COBOL has excellent file- and database-handling capabilities for manipulating large volumes of business data, whereas FORTRAN is better suited for scientific applications.

4. The language is relatively independent of a given computer hardware. This means that the same program can be used on a number of different computers by different computer manufacturers, with only small modifications, or no modifications at all.

Fourth-Generation Languages

A **fourth-generation language (4GL)** is a high-level programming language that is less procedural and more English-like than third-generation languages. It emphasizes what output results are desired more than how programming statements are to be written. As a result, many people with little or no training in computers and programming can use fourth-generation languages. Some of the features of 4GLs include:

• Query and Database Abilities. With some 4GLs, a user can give simple commands or perform simple procedures to retrieve information from a database. These commands are stated in the form of simple questions or queries. With a billing database written in a 4GL, for example, you can click on "AMOUNT" and enter ". $250" to get a listing of all bills that are greater then $250. These languages have been called query languages because they ask a computer questions in English-like sentences. Many of these languages also operate only on organized databases, and are thus called **database languages**. Some examples of queries in a fourth-generation database or query language are shown in Figure 3.5.

FIGURE 3.5 • Simple fourth-generation language instructions

```
PRINT EMPLOYEE NUMBER IF GROSS PAY > 1000
PRINT CUSTOMER NAME IF AMOUNT > 5000 AND
IF TIME DUE > 90
PRINT INVENTORY NUMBER IF ON HAND < 50
```

Fourth-generation languages can be used to print employee numbers for all employees with a gross pay that exceeds $1,000, print the name of all customers that owe more than $5,000 for more than 90 days, and print inventory numbers for all inventory items that have less than 50 units in stock.

- Code-generation Abilities. Some 4GLs use code-generation features, which automatically produce many of the programming statements and instructions required to gain a specific output result. In some cases, code generators can generate 90 percent or more of all statements for a particular programming project.
- Graphics Abilities. Creating, manipulating, and using graphics and illustrations can be easier and simpler with a 4GL than a lower-level language. For example, 4GLs can be used to develop trend lines and pie charts from data.

One popular fourth-generation language is a standardized language called *Structured Query Language (SQL),* which is often used to perform database queries and manipulations. Other 4GLs are used to develop programs for expert systems.

Languages beyond the Fourth Generation

After the fourth generation, it becomes more difficult to classify programming languages. Languages beyond the fourth generation include artificial intelligence languages, visual languages, and object-oriented languages.

Programming languages used to create artificial intelligence or expert systems applications are often called *fifth-generation languages (5GLs).* Artificial intelligence and expert systems are discussed later in the book. Fifth-generation languages are sometimes called natural languages because they use even more English-like syntax than 4GLs. They allow programmers to communicate with the computer by using normal sentences, as in the example shown in Figure 3.6. For example, computers programmed in fifth-generation languages can understand queries like: "How many athletic shoes did our company sell last month?" Fifth-generation languages have the potential to predict the weather, diagnose potential diseases given a patient's symptoms and current condition, and determine where to explore for oil and natural gas.

FIGURE 3.6 • **An example of a natural-language program**

```
GIVE ME A SORTED LIST OF
ALL SALES REPRESENTATIVES
LIVING IN DENVER AND
EARNING OVER $47,500
```

Visual languages use a graphical or visual interface for program development. Visual languages provide tools for the convenient development of GUI applications. Prior to visual languages, programmers were required to describe the windows, buttons, textboxes, and menus that they were creating for a GUI application by using programming language commands. With visual languages, the programmer drags and drops graphical objects such as buttons and menus from a toolbox onto an application form. Then, using a programming language, the programmer specifies the functions of those objects in a separate code window. *Visual Basic* was one of the first visual programming languages. Other languages with visual development interfaces include Visual Basic .NET and Visual C++ .NET (see Figure 3.7). *Visual Basic* and *Visual Basic .NET* can be used to develop applications that run under the Windows operating system.

FIGURE 3.7 • An example of a Visual Basic .NET program

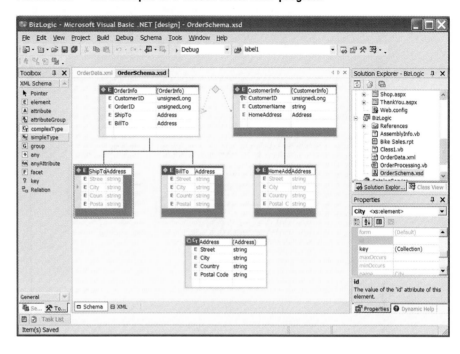

C++ is a powerful and flexible programming language used mostly by computer systems professionals to develop software packages. *Java* is a programming language developed by Sun Microsystems that can be run on any operating system and on the Internet. Java, which is discussed in Chapter 4, can be used to develop complete applications or smaller applications, called *Java Applets*. Visual Basic .NET, C++, and Java are also examples of objected-oriented languages, which are discussed next.

Object-oriented programming languages, such as Visual Basic .NET, C++, and Java, allow the creation and interaction of programming objects.[1] In object-oriented programming, data, instructions, and other programming procedures are grouped together. The items in such a group are called an object.

Building programs and applications using object-oriented programming languages is like constructing a building using prefabricated modules or parts. The object containing the data, instructions, and procedures is a programming building block. Unlike prefabricated building modules, however, the same objects (modules or parts) can be used repeatedly—millions of times if needed. Foliage Software Systems, for example, uses object-oriented programming to develop custom software packages for companies in avionics, financial services, and healthcare.[2]

This ability to reuse programming code is one of the primary advantages of object-oriented programming (see Figure 3.8). The instruction code within an object can be reused in different programs for a variety of applications, just as the same basic type of prefabricated door can be used in two different houses. Thus, a sorting routine developed for a payroll application could be used in both a billing program and an inventory control program. By reusing program code, programmers are able to write programs for specific application problems more quickly. National Security Group, Inc., for example, used object-oriented programming to create an insurance application for Computer Sciences Corporation. According to W. L. Brunson, president of National Security, "We were looking for new technology that would allow us to innovate and grow."[3] Object-oriented programming is also an excellent programming approach for database applications.

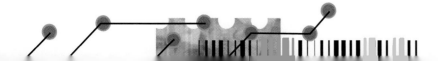

FIGURE 3.8 • Object-oriented programming

By combining existing program objects with new ones, programmers can easily and efficiently develop new object-oriented programs to accomplish organizational goals and personal goals.

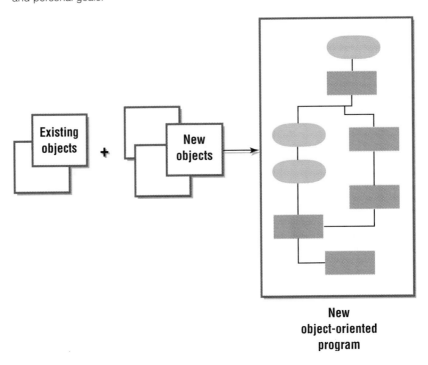

**New
object-oriented
program**

Programming Language Translators

Except for the first generation of programming languages, every programming instruction must be converted into machine language to be executed by the CPU. This translation is done by systems software called a *language translator*. A language translator converts a statement from a high-level programming language, such as the statement READ SALES, into machine language. The high-level program code is referred to as the **source code**; the machine-language code is referred to as the *object code*. Two types of translators are interpreters and compilers.

An **interpreter** is a language translator that converts each statement in a programming language, such as a Visual Basic program, into machine language and executes the statement, one at a time. An interpreter does not produce a complete machine-language program. After the statement executes, the machine-language statement is discarded, the process continues for the next statement, and so on (see Figure 3.9).

FIGURE 3.9 • How an interpreter works

An interpreter sequentially translates each program statement or instruction into machine language. The statement is executed and another statement is then translated. An interpreter does not produce a complete machine-language program.

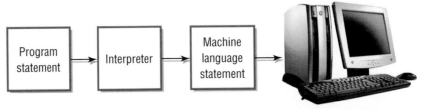

Statement execution

FIGURE 3.10 • How a compiler works

A compiler translates a complete program into a complete machine-language program (Stage 1). Once this is done, the machine-language program can be executed in its entirety (Stage 2).

Stage 1: Convert to machine-language program

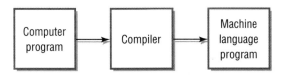

Stage 2: Execute machine-language program

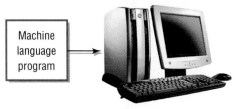

Program execution

A **compiler** is a language translator that translates a complete program, such as a C++ program, into a complete machine-language program (see Figure 3.10). The result is a program in machine language that can be run in its entirety. Once the compiler has translated a complete program into a machine-language program, the machine-language program can be run on the computer as many times as needed. With a compiler, program execution is a two-stage process. First, the compiler translates the program into a machine-language program; second, the machine-language program is executed.

Because compiled programs run faster than programs that have to be translated line by line by an interpreter, compilers are usually preferred for frequently run programs. Compiled programs are also often usable on different computer system platforms or operating systems. If a program is infrequently used, an interpreter may be a satisfactory language translator.

SYSTEMSSOFTWARE

Controlling the operations of computer hardware is one of the most critical functions of systems software. *Systems software* is a collection of programs that interacts with the computer hardware and application software programs, creating a layer of insulation between the two.

Operating Systems

An **operating system (OS)** is a set of computer programs that runs or controls the computer hardware and acts as an interface with application programs and users (see Figure 3.11). Operating systems can control one computer or multiple computers, or they can allow multiple users to interact with one computer. The various combinations of operating systems, computers, and users include:

- A Single Computer with a Single User. This is typical of a personal computer or a handheld computer that allows one user at a time.
- A Single Computer with Multiple Users. This is typical of larger, mainframe computers that can accommodate hundreds or thousands of people, all using the computer at the same time.

FIGURE 3.11 • Operating systems

An operating system (OS) is a set of computer programs that runs or controls the computer hardware and acts as an interface with application programs and users.

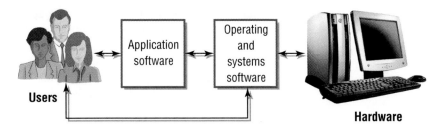

- Multiple Computers. This is typical of a network of computers, such as a home network that has several computers attached or a large computer network with hundreds of computers attached around the world.
- Special-purpose Computers. This is typical of a number of special-purpose operating systems that control sophisticated military aircraft, the space shuttle, some home appliances, and a variety of other special-purpose computers.

Although most computers use just one operating system, it is possible to have two or more operating systems stored on a single computer. When the computer starts, you are given the opportunity to choose which operating system you will use.

The operating system, which plays a central role in the functioning of the complete computer system, is usually stored on disk. For smaller computers, however, the operating system can be stored on a computer chip. After a computer system is started, or booted up, much of the operating system is transferred to memory. Once in memory, the operating system instructions are executed, or run. The operating system's collection of programs performs a variety of activities and functions, discussed below.

Common Computer Hardware Functions. Virtually all operating systems must perform certain tasks. For example:

- Starting the computer, often called **booting**. A *cold boot* is performed by pushing a start button or switch when the computer is not on. A *warm boot* is performed while the computer is currently running. For example, many computers have a *restart* procedure or button that when clicked performs a warm boot. During the booting process, a *power-on self test (POST)* is performed to make sure that the computer components are working correctly. The *basic input/output system (BIOS)* is activated from one or more computer chips to perform additional testing and to control various input/output devices, such as keyboards, display screens, disk drives, and various ports. Note that the computer can also be started from an operating system stored on a floppy disk, called a *recovery disk*. This can be done if there is a problem with the computer's hard disk and the computer is not booting correctly when turned on.
- Inputting data from a keyboard, a mouse, or some other input device.
- Reading data from and writing data to disk drives or other secondary storage devices.
- Outputting or writing information to the computer screen and printers. Because printers and similar devices are much slower than the computer's processor, operating systems often use *spooling,* whereby data is written from the processor to the hard disk or memory first in a buffer or queue area. The output is then transferred to the slower printer, freeing the processor for other tasks.
- Formatting floppy disks and other disks. Different operating systems often require different disk formats. Thus, before a disk can be used on a computer, it must be formatted. *Format* is a common function of an operating system.
- Configuring hardware devices. If a new printer is added, for example, the operating system can add the new printer to the computer using software called a *print driver.*

Hardware Independence. Look back at Figure 3.11, and notice that the application program can only communicate with the system hardware through the operating system. Because of this, the OS serves as a buffer or interface between the application program and the hardware. This function is, however, rather subtle and is intended to be transparent to the user. Transparent means that an activity or task happens automatically and does not have to be considered, understood, or known by the user.

Suppose that a computer manufacturer designs new hardware that can operate much faster than before. Let's further suppose that this new hardware functions differently from the old hardware, requiring different machine code to perform certain tasks. If operating systems did not exist, we would have to rewrite all of our application software to take advantage of the new, faster hardware. Fortunately, because many application programs usually share a single OS, we need to redesign only the OS layer so that it converts the same set of commands on the application side to the new group of instructions needed on the hardware side. Having an OS layer allows us to design many thousands of applications and use these applications on different types of hardware by adapting the OS.

Memory Management. The overall purposes of memory management are to control how memory is accessed and to maximize the use of memory and storage. The memory-management feature of many operating systems allows the computer to effectively execute program instructions and speed processing.

Controlling how memory is accessed allows the computer system to efficiently and effectively store and retrieve data and instructions and supply them to the CPU. Memory-management programs convert a logical request for data or instructions into the physical location where the data or instructions are stored. A logical view of data is the way a programmer or user thinks about data. With a logical view, the programmer or user doesn't have to know where the data is physically stored in the computer system. However, a computer understands only the physical view of data, which includes the specific location of the data in storage or memory and the techniques needed to access the data. You can think of these concepts as *logical versus physical access*. For example, the current price of product GIZMO might always be found in the logical location Gizmo$. If the CPU needed to fetch the price of GIZMO as part of a program instruction, the memory management program of the operating system would translate the logical location Gizmo$ into an actual physical location in memory or secondary storage, as shown in Figure 3.12.

Many operating systems use *virtual memory,* or *virtual storage,* which allows users to store and retrieve more data without physically increasing the actual storage capacity of memory. Virtual memory works by swapping programs or parts of programs between memory and one or more disk devices. The number of program segments that can be placed in memory depends on the size of the program

FIGURE 3.12 • The operating system controlling physical access to data
The user prompts the application software for specific data. The operating system translates this prompt into instructions for the hardware that finds the data the user requested. Having successfully completed this task, the operating system would then relay the data back to the user via the application software.

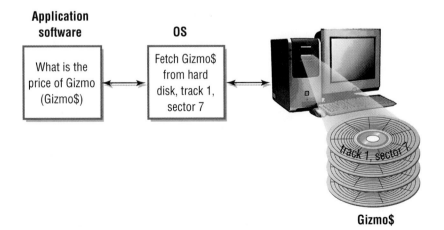

segments and overall memory capacity. Assume that you have written a program that consists of 10 pages of instructions. If you stored only a segment of this program, such as the first few pages, in memory, there might also be room for another program segment from some other program. In a sense, the computer stores only a few pages of a number of programs in memory, while the rest of these programs are stored on the disk, a concept called paging.

As you can see in Figure 3.13, four programs have been stored in memory. Portions of these programs may also be stored in virtual memory on the hard disk. What is the advantage of virtual memory? In general, computers using virtual memory can process more programs in a given amount of time than systems that do not use virtual memory. With virtual memory, only a few instructions are being executed for one program at any given moment. After these instructions are executed, a new subset of program instructions is transferred from storage to memory. In the meantime, the computer executes a few instructions from another program, and so on. Because the computer is only executing a few instructions at one time, the complete program does not need to be stored in memory. With more program segments, the CPU is less likely to have to wait for programs to be transferred from the disk to memory. This reduces CPU idle time and increases the number of jobs that can be run in a given time span. It is important to note that the physical size of memory remains the same. It only appears to be larger because more gets done in less time.

FIGURE 3.13 • A virtual memory system

Virtual memory is a process whereby partial programs are stored in memory. The remainder of the program is stored on disk.

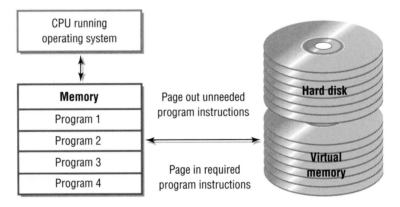

Processor Management. The OS also controls the operation of all processors within the computer system. As discussed in Chapter 2, the processor must retrieve each instruction, decode it, and then execute it. In addition, most operating systems permit several programs to be running at the same time, each requiring processor resources. For example, you may be entering text through a keyboard using a word-processing program, be connected to the Internet and playing the latest songs by using software that does this, have your appointments and calendar program open and running, and be printing the results from a tax preparation program, all at the same time. The operating system makes sure that all these programs access the computer's processor(s) in an efficient and effective manner. The operating system also makes sure that one program doesn't interfere with the operation of another program.

Today's operating systems permit one user to run several programs or tasks at the same time, which involves multitasking and multithreading, and allow several users to use the same computer at the same time, which is called time-sharing. *Multitasking* involves running more than one application at the same time. For example, a national sales manager might want to run an inventory control program, a spreadsheet program, and a word-processing program at the same time. With multitasking, he can share data and results among all three of the programs running. Spreadsheet results can be inserted into the inventory control program. Important tables and analysis from the inventory control program can then be inserted directly into the word-processing program. *Multithreading* is basically multitasking within a single application, that is, several parts of the program can be working at the same time. With multithreading, the national sales manager can work on two different spreadsheets at once, possibly printing one while entering data in another. As mentioned, *time-sharing* allows more than one person to use a computer system at the same time. For example, 15 research assistants in a school district can be entering survey results into a computer system at the same time. In another case, thousands of people may be simultaneously using an online computer service to get stock quotes and valuable news. Time-sharing works by dividing time into small slices, which can be a few milliseconds or less in duration. During a time slice, some tasks for the first user are done. The computer then goes from that user to the next. During the next time slice, some tasks for the next user are completed. This process continues through each user and cycles back to the first one. Because the time slices are small, it appears that all jobs or tasks for all users are being completed at the same time. In reality, each user is serially sharing the time of the computer with other users. Most operating systems for large computer systems, such as mainframes, allow for time-sharing.

Input, Output, Storage, and Peripheral Management. In a similar fashion, the operating system must also manage and coordinate the use of input and output devices, storage devices, and other peripheral equipment. Today's computers have keyboards, printers, display screens, and hard disk devices. Many have floppy disk drives, CD-ROM and DVD drives, joysticks, and a variety of other peripheral equipment. The operating system must manage all of the devices.

File Management. All computers store and manipulate files that can contain data, instructions, or both. Operating systems organize files into folders or directories. Folders and directories can hold one or more files. Files can be organized alphabetically, by size, by type, or even by the date they were created or last modified. In addition, operating systems allow files to be copied from hard disks to floppy disks, CDs, optical disks, and other media. This feature is essential for keeping accurate and current backup files. File management can protect certain files from unwanted users; one approach is to use secure passwords and identification numbers. File-management features also allow you to search for files in various folders or directories using keywords or even partial words.

Operating systems have file-management conventions that specify how files can be named and organized (see Table 3.2). In Windows, for example, filenames can be 256 characters long, both numbers and spaces can be included in the filename, and upper- and lowercase letters can be used. Windows and Linux don't permit certain characters, such as \, *, >, <, and some other characters, to be used in filenames. Operating systems also specify how files can be organized in folders or subdirectories. Organizing files into folders or subdirectories makes it much easier to locate files, compared to having all files in one large folder or directory.

TABLE 3.2 • Conventions or Rules for Filenames

Convention (Rule)	Windows	Macintosh	Linux
Length in characters	256	31	255
Case sensitive?	No	Yes	Yes
Can numbers be used?	Yes	Yes	Yes
Can spaces be used	Yes	Yes	No

Network Management. Many of today's operating systems, including ones for personal computers, allow multiple computers to be connected together, sharing disk space, printers, and other computer resources. From smaller PCs and Macintosh computers to huge networks of large, mainframe computers, network management features of today's operating systems allow computers to work efficiently and effectively together in clusters. Network management and operating systems will be covered in more detail in Chapter 5.

Providing a User Interface. One of the most important functions of any operating system is providing a user interface. A user interface allows one or more individuals to have access to and command of the computer system. The first user interfaces for mainframe and personal computer systems were command-based (see Figure 3.14). A **command-based user interface** requires that text commands be given to the computer to perform basic activities. For example, the command ERASE FILE1 would cause the computer to erase or delete a file called FILE1. RENAME and COPY are other examples of commands used to rename files and copy files from one location to another. Some mainframe computers still use a command-based user interface.

FIGURE 3.14 • Command-based interface

A command-based user interface uses text commands to get the computer to perform basic activities.

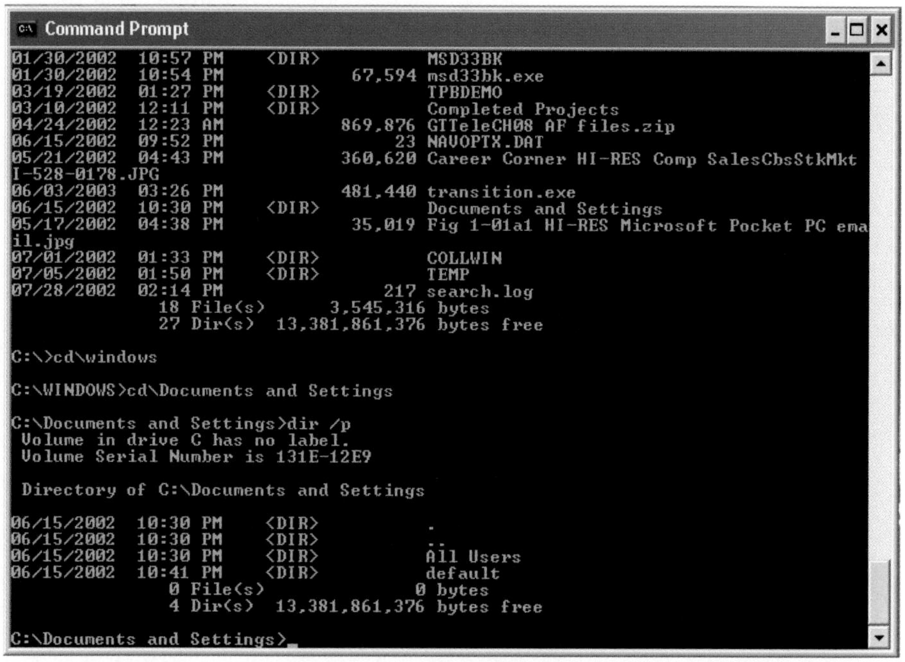

A **graphical user interface (GUI)** uses pictures or icons on the screen and menus to send commands to the computer system. Many people find that GUIs are easier to learn and use, because complicated commands are not required. With a mouse, the user can highlight and click a command to perform various operating system functions (See Figure 3.15).

Today, the most widely used graphical user interface is Windows by Microsoft. Alan Kay and others at Xerox PARC (Palo Alto Research Center, located in California) were pioneers in investigating the use of overlapping windows and icons as an interface. Some believe that Apple and Microsoft used this early GUI operating system as a model for their operating systems. As the name suggests, Windows is based on the use of a window, or a portion of the display screen dedicated to a specific application. The screen can display several windows at once. For this reason, all GUI environments are sometimes referred to as "windows" environments, even though they are not Microsoft products. The popularity of Microsoft's Windows is in part due to the many advantages of using any graphical user interface, as listed in Table 3.3.

FIGURE 3.15 • A graphical user interface (GUI)

A graphical user interface (GUI) uses pictures or icons on the screen and menus to send commands to the computer system.

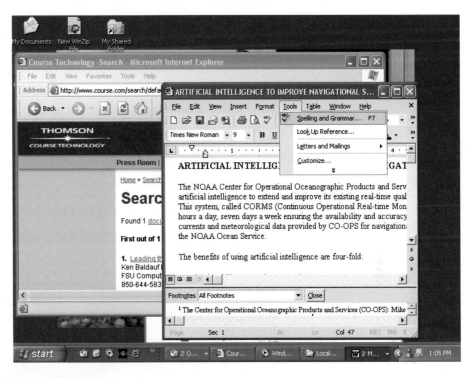

TABLE 3.3 • Advantages of a Graphical User Interface

- **Performing tasks in a GUI environment is intuitive.** To open a file, you click a file icon or symbol. To delete a file, you drag it to a wastebasket icon or press the delete key after the file has been highlighted. Deleting material in a word-processing program works much the same way; you highlight the material to be deleted and click a Delete command or press the Delete key.

- **The application interfaces are consistent.** They have the same appearance and general operation for opening and closing files, editing, moving, printing, erasing, saving, and so on. Once you learn the basics for one application, such as a word-processing program, the same basic commands and approaches work with other applications, such as spreadsheets or database programs.

- **The applications are flexible.** You can use either a mouse or the keyboard. In addition, you can save files in different ways, in different formats, and to different folders or directories by using different save options.

- **GUIs support multitasking.** With multitasking, the operating system can perform more than one activity or task at the same time. For example, it can print a document while it is opening up a spreadsheet program.

- **The applications can be easy to use.** Detailed, technical manuals describing complex commands are usually not needed. Some software companies, such as Microsoft, include assistance features, such as wizards, that help with the creation of tables and forms.

- **Mistakes can be corrected easily.** If you make a mistake, graphical user interfaces allow you to cancel or undo what you have done. Most menu boxes have a cancel option.

- **Confirmation is requested as a safeguard.** GUIs often ask you to confirm important operations, such as saving or deleting a file. Most have an OK or Yes option for you to check or click before an operation is carried out.

- **Windows operating systems allow object linking and embedding (OLE).** With OLE, you can copy or embed graphics from one program into another program or document, such as a word-processing report. You can also link many documents or files, such as reports developed in a word-processing program, to an original source document, such as a database program. When you make a link, you are actually referencing the original document or program. Changes are always made to the source document or program and transferred to the linked documents, such as one or more word-processing reports.

All operating systems can be considered either proprietary or portable (sometimes called generic). A *proprietary operating system* is one developed by a vendor for use with specific computer hardware. A *portable operating system* is one that can function with different hardware configurations. Portable operating systems play an important role in interoperability, the ability of devices and programs from different vendors to operate together. Because organizations often upgrade their computer hardware and software to support new activities, portability can be an important consideration in selecting an operating system.

Other Functions of Operating Systems. Operating systems perform a number of other important functions (see Figure 3.16). For example, they allow you to install new hardware and software easily. A feature called *plug and play (PnP)* allows you to attach a new hardware device and have it automatically installed and configured by the operating system. After PnP installs and configures the new device, it is ready to use.

FIGURE 3.16 • Other operating system functions

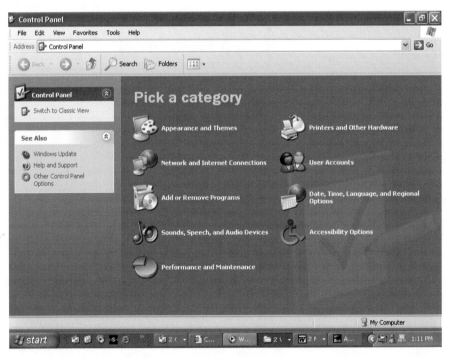

You can modify operating systems to make them more user-friendly. For example, visually or physically impaired people can use the accessibility options to make using the computer easier, and you can alter screen and mouse operations, change printer and modem operations, change the volume and tone of sound, and adjust how battery power is managed and used by laptop computers.

Operating systems typically come packaged with limited word processors, graphics programs, and games, such as solitaire, Minesweeper, and pinball. Some operating systems also come with Internet browsers and media players. Media Player by Microsoft, for example, can record TV programs, play music, and organize photos. The software also acts as a TV tuner.

The Evolution of Operating Systems

The early operating systems for computers were adequate, but did not provide many advanced functions or features. In the last several years, however, more ad-

EXPAND YOUR
KNOWLEDGE

To learn more about the Windows operating system, go to www.course.com/swt. Click the link "Expand Your Knowledge" and then complete the lab entitled, "Using Windows."

vanced operating systems have been developed. In addition to operating system software available for general-purpose computers, specialized operating systems are available for computers that are used in aircraft, military weapons, and other specialized devices. This section reviews selected computer operating systems available on general-purpose computers.

Older Operating Systems for PCs. One of the first operating systems (and the primary OS) for personal computers in the 1970s was Control Program for Microcomputers (CP/M). The original IBM Personal Computer, first introduced in the 1980s, used an OS by Microsoft called Personal Computer Disk Operating System (PC-DOS). IBM-compatible computers often used Microsoft Disk Operating System (MS-DOS) or a similar operating system. In the 1980s and 1990s, these operating systems were very popular for IBM PC and compatible systems. They were command-based operating systems, and used commands like COPY, RENAME, DIR for directory, and FORMAT.

Windows. Windows was originally designed to provide a GUI when used with DOS. As mentioned previously, the Windows operating system uses overlapping rectangles or windows that are displayed on the computer screen. Older versions of Windows include Windows 1, 2, 3, 95, 98, ME (for Millennium Edition), NT, and 2000. Newer versions of Windows, such as Windows XP, are fully functional operating systems that do not require DOS. Windows XP comes in a Home Edition and a Professional Edition. This newest version of the operating system can include security support when used with wireless networks. Windows is also easy to use and intuitive. You don't have to learn complex commands. Today, Windows is the most popular operating system for personal computers, with more than 80 percent of PCs using it.[4] See Figure 3.17.

FIGURE 3.17 • The Windows XP operating system
The Windows XP operating system is a recent version of Windows by Microsoft that comes in a Home Edition and Professional Edition.

Significant advances have been made with the newer Windows operating systems over some of the earlier versions, such as Windows 1.0, 2.0, and 3.0. With Windows 95, for instance, a taskbar at the bottom of the screen keeps track of all open applications and makes it easier to switch between applications during multitasking. A special file manager can be used to browse files. Networking several computers together was added as a feature to the Windows 95 operating system and all subsequent Windows operating systems.

Windows NT is also a complete GUI operating system, not just a shell, and can run DOS or Windows applications. Windows NT is a network operating system that allows personal computers and others to be connected in a network with telecommunications devices. Windows NT and Windows 2000 are often referred to as *network operating systems (NOS)* because they include security and network management features for networks and the servers that handle them.

Apple Computer Operating Systems. Although IBM-compatible system platforms traditionally use Windows operating systems and Intel chips (and are often called WINTEL for this reason), Apple computers typically use a proprietary Apple operating system and Motorola processors (see Figure 3.18). Like Windows, Apple operating systems have gone through revisions and changes to make them more useful. Some of the earlier Apple operating systems included Apple DOS and Mac-DOS. These early operating systems were command-based. Newer operating systems, such as OS X, are GUIs that are easy to learn and use. Simplicity does not mean that the operating system is less powerful, however. Macintosh operating systems offer many outstanding graphics and color abilities, virtual memory, and multitasking functions. They also have a "toolbox" of features that can be accessed by clicking icons with a mouse, including database access facilities.

FIGURE 3.18 • The Apple OS X operating system
The Apple OS X operating system offers outstanding graphics abilities.

UNIX. *UNIX* is a powerful operating system developed by AT&T for minicomputers. At the time of UNIX development in the 1970s, AT&T was not permitted to market the operating system due to federal regulations that prohibited the company from competing in the computer marketplace. All of this changed in the 1980s, when AT&T was broken up and many of the federal regulations preventing it from entering the computer marketplace were removed. Since then, UNIX has increased in popularity.

Today, UNIX is a leading portable operating system. Unlike Windows or Apple OS X, UNIX can be used on many computer system types and platforms from personal computers to mainframe systems. UNIX benefits organizations using both small and large computer systems, because it is compatible with different types of hardware and users have to learn only one operating system.

Although UNIX is traditionally a command-based operating system (see Figure 3.19), most users interact with a UNIX computer through a GUI interface that works much like Windows. In addition, there are several versions of UNIX. A UNIX program written for one computer might have to be modified to run on another computer system.

Linux. The *Linux* operating system was developed by Linus Torvalds in 1991. Linux uses a GUI (see Figure 3.20). Today, it is being used on computers from small personal computers to large mainframe systems. Unlike many other operating systems, Linux is an *open-source* software package, which means that users have access to the source code. The operating system is available free to users under a *General Public License (GPL)* arrangement. This is a big advantage of Linux compared to other operating systems such as Windows and Apple

FIGURE 3.19 • The UNIX operating system

UNIX is a command-based operating system, which can be more difficult to learn than GUI operating systems.

FIGURE 3.20 • The Linux operating system

Linux is an *open-source* software package, which means that users have access to the source code, and is available free to users.

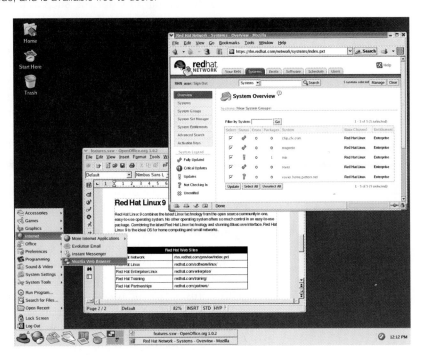

OS X. People can not only get copies of Linux free of charge, but they can also develop utilities, applications, and enhancements to the operating system.

Linux is available over the Internet and from other sources, including Red Hat Linux and Caldera OpenLinux. Many individuals and organizations are starting to use Linux. Galileo, the large travel and airline ticketing company, for example, uses Linux to run its Internet site.[5] "We are looking to deploy Linux wherever we can," says the chief technology officer for the company. Johns Hopkins University researchers are using the Linux operating system from Red Hat along with other application software to help analyze the impact of Atlantic currents on climate.[6] Panasonic is using Linux to run one of its high-speed television tuners.[7]

Operating Systems for Large Computer Systems. Larger computer systems and networks also require operating systems. For example, Microsoft Windows Server 2003 can be used to coordinate large data centers. The operating system also works with other Microsoft software products. It can be used to prevent unauthorized disclosure of information by blocking text and e-mails from being copied, printed, or forwarded to other people.[8]

Large mainframe computer manufacturers typically provide proprietary operating systems with their specific hardware. z/OS is a 64-bit operating system for IBM's large mainframe computers. MPE/iX is an operating system used by Hewlett-Packard's mainframe computers. Enterprise Systems Architecture/370 (ESA/370) and Multiple Virtual Storage/Enterprise Systems Architecture (MVS/ESA) are older operating systems used on large IBM mainframe computers.

Operating Systems for Small Computers and Special-purpose Devices. There are a number of operating systems for handheld computers. These operating systems are also called *embedded operating systems* because they are typically embedded in a computer chip. Embedded software is a $21 billion industry.[9] The popular Palm computer uses a Palm operating system. Microsoft has developed a number of operating systems for small computers, including Pocket PC, Handheld PC, and Windows XP Embedded for devices such as TV set-top boxes, small computers, and other devices. These operating systems allow handheld devices to be synchronized with PCs using cradles, cables, and wireless connections. Cell phones also use embedded operating systems. In addition, there are operating systems for special-purpose devices, such as computers on the space shuttle, in military weapons, and in some home appliances.

Utility Programs

Another type of systems software is a utility program. **Utility programs** are used to merge and sort sets of data, keep track of computer jobs being run, and perform other important routine tasks. Utility programs often come installed on computer systems; a number of utility programs can also be purchased. One utility program is even used to make computer systems run better and longer without problems.[10] Computer scientists at IBM and other companies are developing software to predict when a computer might malfunction and to take corrective action. The software can also help a network of computers share processing jobs to get more done in less time. Here is a brief sampling of some popular utility program features:

- Virus Detection and Recovery. Computer viruses from the Internet and other sources can be a nuisance or can completely disable a computer. Virus detection and recovery software can be installed to constantly monitor possible viruses that could enter the computer. If a virus is found, the software can eliminate the virus or "clean" the virus from the computer system, as shown in Figure 3.21. To keep the virus detection and recovery software current, it can be updated through the Internet to make sure the software checks for the latest viruses. Symantec and McAfee are examples of companies that make virus detection and recovery software.

FIGURE 3.21 • Virus detection and recovery software

Virus detection and recovery software is an important utility for anyone accessing the Internet and sharing files.

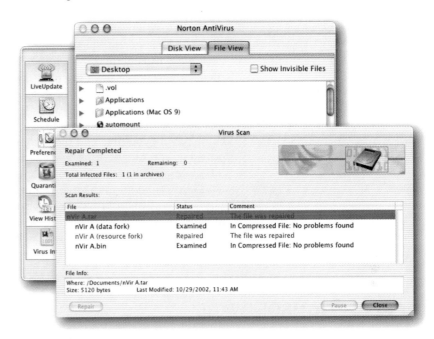

- **File Compression.** File compression programs can reduce the amount of disk space required to store a file or reduce the time it takes to transfer a file over the Internet. A popular program on Windows PCs is WinZip (www.winzip. com), which generates zip files. A zip file has a .zip extension and can be easily un-zipped to the original file. *MP3 (Motion Pictures Experts Group-Layer 3)* is a popular file compression format used to store, transfer, and play music. It can compress files to be 10 to 20 times smaller with near-CD-quality sound. Software, such as iTunes from Apple, can be used to store, organize and play MP3 music files.
- **Spam and Pop-up-ad Guards.** Getting unwanted e-mail (spam) and having annoying and unwanted ads pop up on your display screen while you are on the Internet can be frustrating and a big waste of time. There are a number of utility programs that can be installed to help block unwanted e-mail spam and pop-up ads, including Cloudmark SpamNet, IhateSpam, Spamnix, McAfee SpamKiller, and Ad-aware.[11]

FIGURE 3.22 • Norton disk utility

Disk diagnostic software, such as Norton's disk utility, can help detect disk problems and fix them.

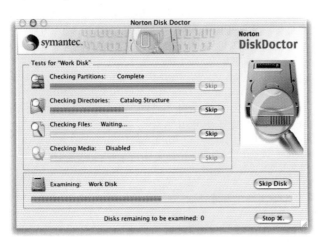

- **Disk Diagnostics.** A number of utility programs diagnose and fix hard disk problems (see Figure 3.22). This can involve scanning a disk for problems, fixing any problems, and defragmenting disks. *Defragmenting* involves rearranging files on a hard disk to increase the speed of executing programs and retrieving data stored on the hard disk. These types of disk diagnostic programs are available with many operating systems. They can also be purchased from companies that make utility programs, such as Symantec. Norton Utilities 2003 from Symantec, for example, can defragment a hard disk to make it run faster, recover deleted files, check for viruses, and clean infected disks.

- Disk Backup. A number of utilities can help you back up data and programs from a hard disk onto tape, writable CD-ROM drive, writable DVD drive, or other devices. These utilities can back up all data and programs or selected data and programs that may have changed since the last backup. BackUp MyPC, by Stomp, is an example of a backup utility for Windows PCs.
- Transferring Files. Transferring programs and files from an old computer to a new one is usually time consuming. Some people reinstall all programs and then copy data to CDs or floppy disks to transfer to the new machine. Utilities such as PC Relocator or Move2Mac automate this process. After installing utility software on the old and new machines and connecting both machines with a cable, it will automatically transfer programs and data files to your new machine, saving you time and the inconvenience of manually transferring your programs and files.
- Ink Saver. Inksaver from Strydent Software is an innovative software utility that reduces the amount of ink that is sprayed onto paper from ink-jet printers. Ink can be expensive for heavy ink-jet printer users. The software can reduce the ink used from 25 to more than 50 percent. At a 25 percent reduction in the ink used, the print is still fairly sharp, but the 50 percent ink reduction setting may not be clear enough for business documents.

APPLICATIONSOFTWARE

As discussed earlier in this chapter, the primary function of *application software* is to apply the power of the computer to give people, groups, and organizations the ability to solve problems and perform specific activities or tasks. When someone wants the computer to do something, one or more application programs are used. The application programs then interact with systems software. Systems software then directs the computer hardware to perform the necessary tasks. This concept was illustrated in Figure 3.11.

Of all the types of software, application software has the greatest potential to help an individual, a group, or an organization achieve its goals. Individuals can use application software to help advance their career or as entertainment. Groups and organizations use application software to help people make better decisions, reduce costs, improve service, or increase revenues. Let's look at each use of application software in more detail.

RAISING THE DEAD

Forensics experts now have a head start in identifying remains. With special software and a scanner, they can create a 3-D model of the skull and add flesh where, and to what degree, sex and ethnicity indicate. The software can also animate the 24 facial muscles used in expressions, "virtually" bringing the skull to life. Within hours police can have a "live" image of the deceased where previously it took weeks to produce even one 2-D drawing.

Source:
"Animation lets murder victims have final say"
By Anil Ananthaswamy
New Scientist *Print Edition*
www.newscientist.com/news/news.jsp?id=ns99994005
August 4, 2003
Cited on August 4, 2003

Application Software for Individuals

What kind of support application software provides for individuals depends on the function for which it was designed. For example, a graphics program such as PowerPoint can help a student make a presentation in class or help a sales manager develop an attractive sales presentation to give to the sales force at its annual meeting. Other programs can be used to edit and organize photographs. Apple Computer, for example, was one of the first PC companies to develop sophisticated photo-processing software.[12] The software from Apple, called iPhoto, allows digital camera users to find, organize, and share

JOB TECHNOLOGY

PixAround.com Brings 3-D Worlds to Your Desktop

Been working hard? How about a quick 10-minute break at a Mediterranean seaside resort? PixAround.com can bring that beach to your PC or Palm computer with such clarity that you'll almost be able to feel the spray on your face. Singapore-based PixAround is the world's leading provider of 360-degree interactive digital imaging (see Figure 3.23). The company has created software that will transform digital images from your camera or camcorder into a virtual environment for your computer.

PixAround's software is a popular tool in the real estate, travel and tourism, and hospitality industries. By clicking a mouse and dragging across an on-screen image, users can view an entire room as if they were actually standing in the middle of the room and turning a full circle. Using zoom buttons, users can zoom in to look at the details of a sculpture resting on a shelf in the corner. Travel agents use PixAround's product to give a prospective customer a feel for what it's like to be in the middle of a Las Vegas casino or resting on a beach in Bermuda.

Car dealers use PixAround's software to allow customers to rotate and examine a vehicle on the screen. By clicking and dragging across an image, users can rotate the car and scrutinize it from every angle—even the undercarriage and roof. The software is also valuable for customers who prefer to shop online rather than visiting the local mall. Being able to examine products from all angles reassures customers that they are purchasing a high-quality product.

Questions

1. Compare and contrast the impact of marketing using 360-degree interactive digital imaging with traditional Web marketing for real estate and other products.
2. List five products, other than those already mentioned, that could benefit from using 360-degree interactive digital imaging. What types of products are best suited for this technology? Why?
3. What features could PixAround add to its product to improve it? What features might make this virtual experience even more lifelike?

Sources
1. *"PixMakerPro—the 360 Degree Digital Imaging Solution for Professionals," http://pixaround.com, accessed June 2002.*
2. *"Customizable digital marketing solutions that allow marketers to do it their way," Staff,* PR Newswire, *May 28, 2002.*
3. *PixAround.com Web site, http://pixaround. com, accessed June 2002.*
4. *"CAD Software," Michael Burns,* PC World, *July 1, 2003, p. 82.*

FIGURE 3.23 • PixAround's 360-degree interactive digital imaging

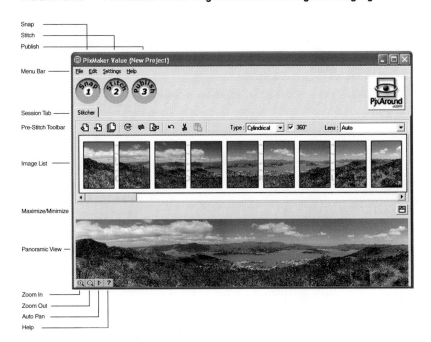

digital images (see Figure 3.24). After the success of iPhoto, several companies are now developing or marketing similar products, such as Picasa and Photoshop Album, for Windows PCs.

Common types of personal productivity applications include word processors, spreadsheets, database management systems, presentation graphics software, and personal information management software.

FIGURE 3.24 • Apple iPhoto photo-processing software

iPhoto allows digital camera users to find, organize, and share digital images.

Word-processing Applications. *Word processing* is perhaps the most highly used application software for individuals. Word by Microsoft is the most popular word-processing program and is available on both PCs and Macintosh computers (see Figure 3.25).

The features available on today's word processors are stunning. All of the common features you would expect are included, such as easy entry of text and formatting, the capability to develop attractive tables, spelling and grammar checking, and the generation of footnotes and endnotes. You can create numbered lists or bulleted lists in most word-processing programs. You can also insert photos, graphics, and drawings into documents from other programs. Today's word-processing programs also have features to easily generate a table of contents at the beginning of the text and an index at the end.

FIGURE 3.25 • A word-processing program

Word processing is perhaps the most highly used application software for individuals.

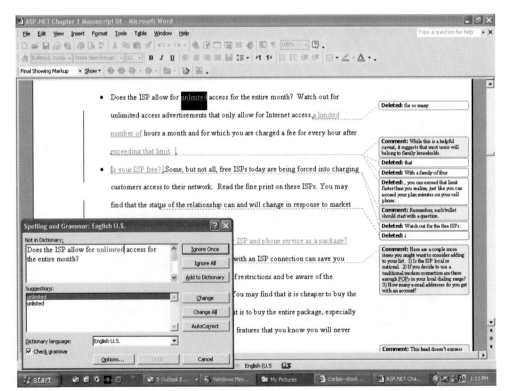

EXPANDYOUR
KNOWLEDGE

To learn how to get the most out of
your word processing application, go
to www.course.com/swt. Click the
link "Expand Your Knowledge" and
then complete the lab entitled, "Word
Processing."

You can use a word-processing application to help you communicate with others. It is easy to combine a list of names and addresses from a database with a form letter or letter template. The result can be hundreds or thousands of letters with all the names and addresses inserted from the database. Envelopes can also be printed with ease. Of course, you can also use a word processor to generate mailing labels, Christmas letters, notices to customers or clients, and resumes for potential employers. If you have access to the Internet, clicking an Internet address in a letter or other document can automatically connect you to the Internet, where you can get information or send e-mails to others.

Word-processing programs can be used with a team or group of people collaborating on a project. The authors and editors who developed this book, for example, used the "track changes" and "reviewing" features of Microsoft Word to track and make changes to chapter files. You can insert comments in or make revisions to a document that a coworker can review and either accept or reject.

Spreadsheet Applications. *Spreadsheet applications* are excellent for making calculations. A spreadsheet contains rows that are numbered and columns that are lettered. Cell D10, for example, is found in row 10 and column D. You can enter text, numbers, or complex formulas into a spreadsheet cell (see Figure 3.26). For example, you can have a spreadsheet automatically get the total or average of a column or row of numbers. Once you have entered numbers and formulas, you can perform *"what-if analysis."* If you have a budget spreadsheet containing your actual expenses for the last several months, you can change one number and immediately see the impact on your average monthly expenditures, your total for the month, and any other calculations that you have entered into your spreadsheet. In general, if you change a value in a spreadsheet, all the formulas based on the value are changed immediately and automatically.

EXPANDYOUR
KNOWLEDGE

To learn how to get the most out of
your spreadsheet application, go to
www.course.com/swt. Click the
link "Expand Your Knowledge" and
then complete the lab entitled,
"Spreadsheets."

FIGURE 3.26 • A spreadsheet program
Spreadsheet applications are excellent for making calculations, as seen in this screen.

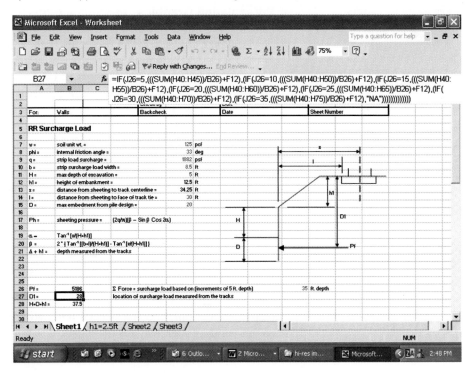

Spreadsheet applications have features to format cells with color, place headings in bold and italicized fonts, and insert attractive graphics. A variety of graphs and drawings based on data in the spreadsheet can be easily inserted into a spreadsheet. Three-dimensional pie charts, bar charts, line charts, and scatter diagrams can be generated automatically and placed anywhere in a spreadsheet. In addition, a number of drawing features allow you to insert boxes, text, arrows, lines, and many other graphic items.

Spreadsheet programs have many built-in functions for science and engineering, statistics, and business. The science and engineering functions include sine, cosine, tangent, degrees, maximum, minimum, logarithms, radians, square root, and exponents. The statistical functions include correlation, statistical testing, probability, variance, frequency, mean, median, mode, and much more. The business functions include depreciation, present value, internal rate of return, and the monthly payment on a loan, to name a few.

Optimization is another powerful feature of many spreadsheet programs. *Optimization* allows the spreadsheet to maximize or minimize a quantity subject to certain constraints. For example, a small furniture manufacturer that produces chairs and tables might want to maximize its profits. The constraints could be a limited supply of lumber, a limited number of workers that can assemble the chairs and tables, or a limited amount of various hardware fasteners that may be required. Using an optimization feature, such as Solver in Microsoft Excel, the spreadsheet can determine what number of chairs and tables to produce with labor and materials constraints in order to maximize profits. As another example, a company that produces dog food might want to minimize its costs, while meeting certain nutritional standards. Minimizing costs becomes the objective, while the nutritional standards are the constraints. Again, an optimization feature can determine the needed blend of dog food ingredients to minimize costs, while meeting the nutritional requirements of the dog food. These are just a few examples of the use of optimization in spreadsheets. Because of the power and popularity of spreadsheet optimization, some colleges and universities offer complete courses based on Solver in the Microsoft Excel spreadsheet. Most of these courses are in engineering and business schools.

Presentation Graphics. In addition to the limited graphics programs, such as painting and drawing software, that come with most operating systems, there are powerful *presentation graphics* programs that can be used for a variety of purposes (see Figure 3.27). Presentation graphics programs are almost essential for making presentations to professional groups and audiences that can vary from a few people to thousands of people. Physicians and medical personnel use presentation graphics to show the results of medical research at conferences. Forest-service consultants use presentation graphics to describe new forest management programs, and businesses almost always use presentation graphics to present financial results or new initiatives to executives and managers. Because of their popularity, many colleges and departments require students to become proficient with using presentation graphics programs. The people using presentation graphics are getting younger, much younger.[13] Fourth grade students, for example, used presentation graphics software to make presentations on sixteenth-century explorers in a history class.

Most presentation graphics programs, such as PowerPoint by Microsoft, consist of a series of slides. Each slide can be displayed on a computer screen, printed as a handout, or (more commonly) projected onto a large viewing screen for audiences. Powerful built-in features allow you to develop attractive slides and complete presentations. You can select a template for a type of presentation, such as recommending a strategy for managers, communicating bad news to a sales force, giving a training presentation, or facilitating a brainstorming session. The presen-

EXPAND YOUR
KNOWLEDGE

To learn more about advanced spreadsheet features, go to www.course.com/swt. Click the link "Expand Your Knowledge" and then complete the lab entitled, "Advanced Spreadsheets."

EXPAND YOUR
KNOWLEDGE

To learn how to get the most out of your presentation graphics application, go to www.course.com/swt. Click the link "Expand Your Knowledge" and then complete the lab entitled, "Presentation Software."

FIGURE 3.27 • A presentation graphics program

Presentation graphics programs are powerful tools that are becoming essential for the creation of professional presentations at both the small- and big-business level.

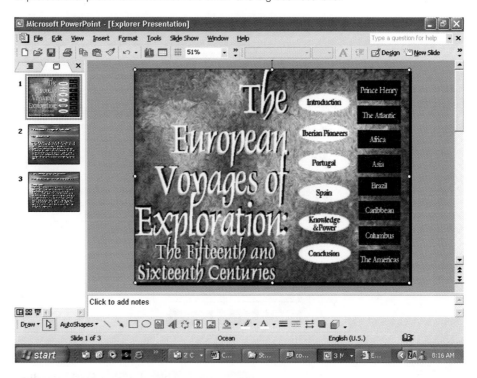

tation graphics program takes you through the presentation step by step, including applying color and attractive formatting. Of course, you can also custom-design your own presentation.

There are many outstanding features of presentation graphics programs. All types of charts, drawings, and formatting are available. Most presentation graphics programs come with many pieces of *clip art,* such as drawings and photos of people meeting, medical equipment, telecommunications equipment, entertainment, and much more. This clip art can be inserted into any slide. You can purchase additional clip art from other computer vendors and insert items into a slide. In addition, you can insert movie and sound clips into a presentation. Presentation graphics programs also have collaboration features that allow you to work with several people or groups around the world on a presentation.

Database Management Programs. *Database management* software can be used to store large tables of information (see Figure 3.28). Each table can be related. For example, a company can create and store tables that contain customer information, inventory information, employee information, and much more. Let's assume that a customer decides to place an order for two music CDs of a new artist, one for herself and one for a friend, by calling a sales rep she has worked with in the past. The sales rep can record the customer number, the inventory number for the new music CD, and the quantity, two CDs in this case. The database management software does the rest. First, the database takes the customer number and goes to the customer table to retrieve the name, address, and credit card information. With the employee number of the sales rep from the customer table, the database management software goes to the employee table to determine any sales commissions that should be paid to the sales rep. Next, the database management system takes the inventory number for the music CD and goes to the inventory table to get all the information about the music CD and make sure that there are at least two

FIGURE 3.28 • A database program

Database management software can be used to store large and varied tables of information and produce important documents and reports.

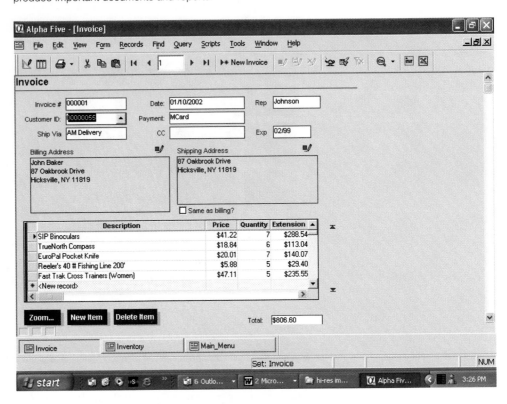

CDs in stock. Once all of this is done, the order can be processed and the two music CDs sent to the customer. All of this is done as a result of giving the customer number, inventory number, and quantity to the database management software.

Before database-management software existed, processing an order was done manually, requiring a lot of time and having the potential for making many mistakes. In addition to order processing, database-management software can be used personally to keep a record of expenses, a list of what is in your apartment or home, or a list of the members of a student government organization. Professionally, database-management software can be used to perform all business functions for a small business, including payroll, inventory control, order processing, bill paying, and producing tax returns. Database management systems can also be used to track and analyze stock and bond prices, analyze weather data to make forecasts for the next several days, and summarize medical research results.

Personal Information Managers. *Personal information managers (PIMs)* help individuals, groups, and organizations store useful information, such as a list of tasks to complete or a list of names and addresses. They usually provide an appointment calendar and a place to take notes. In addition, information in a PIM can be linked. For example, you can link an appointment with a sales manager that appears in the calendar with information on the sales manager in the address book. When you click the appointment in the calendar, information on the sales manager from the address book is automatically opened and displayed on the computer screen.

Personal information managers, such as Microsoft Outlook, can be used on handheld computers, laptops, or large-scale computers (see Figure 3.29). For example, you can take a handheld computer with you, make changes while trav-

FIGURE 3.29 • A personal information manager

PIMs can store information, organize and plan tasks, and even allow for note-taking.

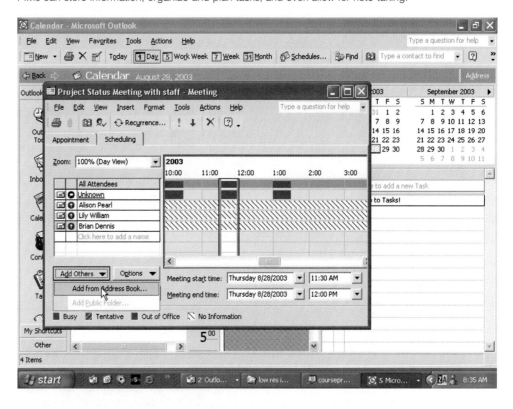

eling, and have the data automatically uploaded and synchronized with your main computer. This can be done with a docking station for your handheld computer. Of course, any changes you make to your PIM on your main computer can be automatically synchronized and transferred to a small, portable computer that you take with you.

Some personal information managers allow people to schedule and coordinate group meetings. If a computer or handheld device is connected to a network, the PIM data can be uploaded and coordinated with the calendar and schedule of others using the same PIM software on the network. Some PIMs can also be used to coordinate e-mails sent and received over the Internet.

Software Suites. A **software suite** is a collection of application software packages placed in a bundle. Software suites can include word processors, spreadsheets, presentation graphics, database management systems, personal information managers, and more (see Figure 3.30). It is even possible to select which software packages are part of the suite.

Office XP, a software suite from Microsoft, includes its word processor (Word), spreadsheet (Excel), database (Access), presentation graphics (PowerPoint), and personal information manager (Outlook). This suite of programs is available for both PCs and Apple Macintosh computers. Office 2003 is the latest version and is available with different software packages. The Enterprise Edition includes InfoPath, which allows people to create Web pages; Business Contact Manager; OneNote; for taking notes and drawing; and a desktop publishing tool.

Different versions of many software suites are often designed to work together. In other words, you can work in Office XP and share your work with others who are using Office 2003 or an older version of Office. Often, software is *upwardly compatible,* which means that a newer version of a software package can automatically read files from an older version of the same software.

FIGURE 3.30 • An example of a suite

Office XP, a software suite from Microsoft, includes a word processor (Word), spreadsheet (Excel), database (Access), presentation graphics (PowerPoint), and personal information manager (Outlook).

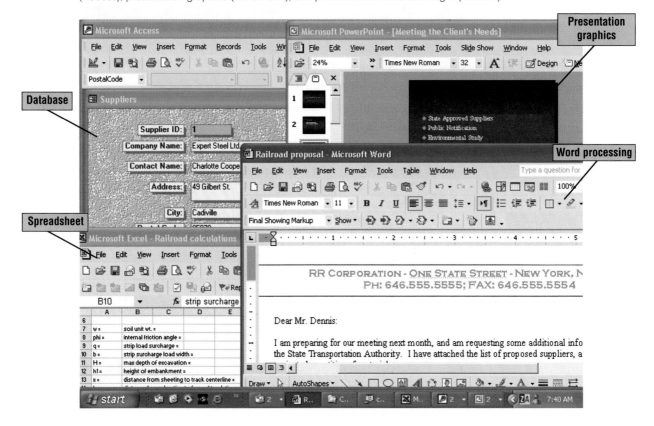

There are a number of advantages to using a software suite. The software has been designed to work similarly, so that once you learn the basics for one application, the other applications are easier to learn and use. With newer versions of some suites, files can be used on both PCs and Macintosh computers without a separate translation program. For example, you can create a word-processing document using a Dell computer with Windows XP, which is an IBM-compatible computer, transfer the file over the Internet, and use the same file on a Macintosh computer at a different location without any conversion or translation.

Applications can work together through **object linking and embedding (OLE)**. With this feature, you can *cut* or *copy* a figure, drawing, chart, table, or other item and *paste* it into another application. For example, you can copy a figure from a presentation graphics program and insert it into a word-processing or spreadsheet program. You can also *link* applications so a change in one will be linked and transferred to another, or you can *embed* an entire application inside another one. In addition to Office from Microsoft, other suites are available from Lotus (Smartsuite), Corel (WordPerfect Office for Windows and Linux systems), and Sun (StarOffice).

Buying software in a bundled suite is cost-effective: the programs usually sell for less money than they would cost individually. However, since there may be one or more weak applications in the suite, some people still prefer to buy separate packages.

HOME RECORDING STUDIOS ROCK

Home recording studio software cuts and pastes bits of sound just like a word processor, tuning up single instruments or entire bands. Musicians can set up a system at home for what just a couple of days in a professional studio would cost them—and it gives them complete creative control over their own work. An eight-track version of the software has already been downloaded nearly 2 million times.

Source:
"Recording software puts sound engineers in control—at home"
By Michael P. Regan
The Associated Press The Seattle Times
http://seattlepi.nwsource.com/business/132577_protools26.html
July 28, 2003
Cited on July 28, 2003

Integrated Software Packages. In addition to suites, some companies produce *integrated application packages* that contain several programs. For example, Works 2003 is one program that contains basic word-processing, spreadsheet, database, address book, a calendar, and some other packages. Although not as powerful as stand-alone software included in software suites, integrated software packages offer a range of capabilities for less money. Some integrated packages cost about $100.

Additional Application Software for Individuals

There are a number of other interesting and powerful application software tools for individuals. Some software contains multimedia features, discussed in detail in Chapter 11. In some cases, the features and capabilities of these application software tools can more than justify the cost of an entire computer system. Some of these programs are listed in Table 3.4, and you can see examples of some of them in Figure 3.31.

TABLE 3.4 • Examples of Additional Application Software

Type of Software	Explanation
Project management	Used to plan, schedule, allocate, and control people and resources (money, time, and technology) needed to complete a project according to a schedule. Project by Microsoft is an example of a project-management software package.
Financial management and tax preparation	Provide income and expense tracking and reporting to monitor and plan budgets. Some programs have investment-portfolio-management features. Tax-preparation software allows you to prepare federal and state returns. Many tax-preparation programs can get data from financial-management software packages. Quicken and Money are examples of financial-management packages. TurboTax is an example of a tax preparation program.
Web authoring	Create attractive Web pages and links. HomeSite and FrontPage are examples of Web-authoring tools.
Music	Creates, stores, and compresses music. Sibelius is a score writing software product available on PCs and Apple Macintosh computers and used around the world by music teachers, students, and professionals.[14] Starclass is another music-teaching software package that includes 180 lesson plans. MP3 is a commonly used music and sound compression standard that is used on many portable music players. MIDI is software that can be used to create and synthesize sound and music.
Photo and video editing	Stores, edits, and manipulates digital photographs and video clips. Moving Picture, for example, is a film-editing program that has been used by ABC, CBS, FOX, NBC, PBS, A&E, and other broadcasters.[15] Even large software companies are now investigating software to enhance a filmmaker's ability to store and manipulate digital images and sounds.[16] Microsoft, for example, may have invested as much as $500 million on research for new media software. Video editors are also becoming more powerful.[17] Adobe Premiere has a variety of editing tools, audio filters, and over 300 video templates that can be customized. The software can also generate sound tracks with a range of different tempos and modes. Other video-editing software includes Pinnacle Edition DV and Video Toaster.
Educational and reference	A number of exciting software packages have been developed for training and distance learning. University professors often believe that colleges and universities must invest in distance learning for their students.[18] Some universities offer complete degree programs using this type of software over the Internet. High-school teachers can use software, such as Plato, to determine what individual students need to perform better on state education examinations.[19]
Desktop publishing (DTP)	Works with personal computers and high-resolution printers to create high-quality printed output, including text and graphics. Various styles of pages can be laid out; art and text files from other programs can also be integrated into published pages. Adobe PageMaker is an example of a DTP package.
Computer-Aided Design (CAD)	Engineers, architects, and designers often use CAD to design and develop buildings, electrical systems, plumbing systems, and more. Autosketch, CorelCAD, and AutoCad are examples of CAD software.
Statistical	Performs a wide array of statistical tests. Colleges and universities often have a number of courses in statistics that uses this type of application software. Two popular applications in the social sciences are SPSS and SAS.
Entertainment	Games and leisure software can be used by itself or with other people while connected to the Internet. The games include adventure, sports, simulation, and strategy games. Sony Computer Entertainment, for example, uses a software program, called Virtually Human, to create "humanlike" characters.[20] The software is also used in medicine, dance, and drama to analyze human movement.

FIGURE 3.31 • Additional application software

Examples of specific software applications—computer-aided design, music, and statistical software—are shown here.

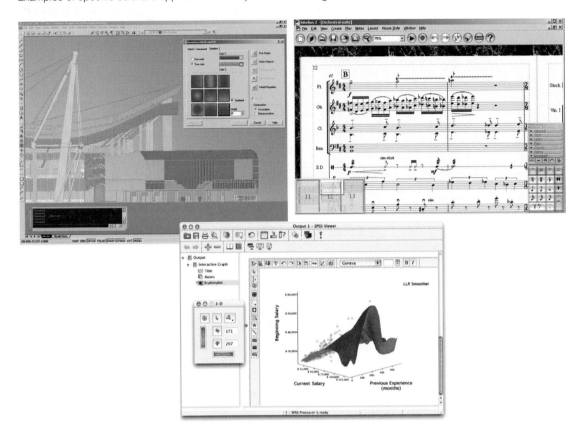

Application Software for Groups and Organizations

Application software is indispensable for groups and organizations. This software can be used to process routine transactions, provide information to help people make better decisions, and perform a number of specialized functions to handle unique but important tasks (see Figure 3.32). Application software is used in all areas of businesses. Monsanto, a chemical manufacturing company, used application software, called groupware, to let members of its agricultural chemical group work together in developing new products.[21] According to one company official, "We determined that this application has the potential to significantly increase the productivity of our engineering group by making programs more accessible to our young engineers."

Application software is used in almost every field. In fine arts, application software is being used to enhance art and film. IBM, for example, is developing software to help Sesame Street Productions convert thousands of episodes of the popular Sesame Street TV show from the old analog film format to a digital format.[22] The project "will save both time and money while it opens up new avenues for improving our abilities to create and generate revenues," says Sherra Pierre of Sesame Workshop. Landmark Theaters and Microsoft have teamed up to convert about 200 screens to a digital cinema system that makes film distribution and playback easier.[23] When completely imple-

FIGURE 3.32 • Application software for groups

Products such as groupware allow business associates easier access to collective data and each other.

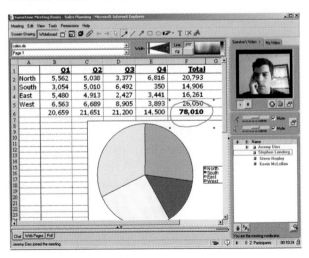

mented, Landmark will be the largest digital cinema theater installation in the United States. Application software is becoming so popular that there are contests for people who use the application software to create and display art.[24]

Routine Transaction Processing Software. Software that performs routine functions that benefit the entire organization can be developed or purchased. A fast-food chain, for example, might develop a materials ordering and distribution program to make sure that each fast-food franchise gets the necessary raw materials and supplies during the week. This materials ordering and distribution program can be developed internally using staff and resources in the company's Computer Systems Department or purchased from an external software company. Local, state, and national governments also need routine transaction processing systems. In Britain, for example, new application software has been developed for Camelot, the national lottery, to allow the sale of lottery tickets to be done on the Internet and using mobile phones.[25]

As discussed in Chapter 1, these routine processing systems are often called *transaction processing systems (TPSs)*. A few examples are shown in Table 3.5. Some computer vendors, such as SAP, package these important applications into a unified package called *enterprise resource planning (ERP)* packages.

TABLE 3.5 • Examples of Application Software for Routine Business Activities

Accounts payable	General ledger	Purchasing
Accounts receivable	Human resources management	Receiving
Asset management	Inventory control	Sales ordering
Billing	Invoicing	Scheduling
Cash-flow analysis	Order entry	Shipping
Check processing	Payroll	

Application Software for Information, Decision Support, and Specialized Purposes

As discussed in Chapter 1, routine transaction activities can store and generate a vast amount of data that can be transformed into useful information to help people or groups make better decisions. Although these systems are popular in businesses and corporations, they are also used in many other areas. Genetic researchers, for example, are using GenVision to visualize and analyze the human genome.[26] Music executives use decision support software to help pick the next hit.[27] One music producer in Barcelona says that the Hit Song Science software product picked Norah Jones as a success before she won a number of Grammy awards. The software also allows music executives to analyze clusters or groups of potentially successful music types.

Physicians also use software to make better decisions. Cancer is a major killer, second only to heart attacks for some age groups. About half of the 1.3 million Americans diagnosed with cancer each year undergo radiation, where x-ray beams are shot into the

WHICH AD WORKS BETTER WHERE?

According to Jupiter Research, more than $1.6 billion will be spent on Internet advertising in 2003. Previously marketers had no way to track advertising campaign results or connect sales with pay-per-click ads. A new software program now analyzes the response to Internet ads not only in a number of campaigns, but also across several platforms, giving marketers a tool they can use to keep track of how well their advertising dollars are performing.

Source:
"Overture to upgrade analytics software"
By Stefanie Olsen, Staff Writer
CNET News.com
http://news.com.com/2100-1024_3-5059162.html?tag=fd_top
August 1, 2003
Cited on August 2, 2003

body to kill the cancer cells. Sophisticated software is now being used to increase the cure rate.[28] The software analyzes up to 120 different scans of the cancer tumor to create a 3-D view of the tumor. The program then considers thousands of angles and doses of radiation to determine the best radiation program. The software analysis takes only minutes, but the results can save years or decades of life for the patient.

Table 3.6 presents some additional examples of applications for information, decision support, and specialized purposes.

TABLE 3.6 • Examples of Application Software for Information, Decision Support, and Specialized Purposes

Application Software for Information, Decision Support, and Specialized Purposes	Description
Management reporting software	A variety of reports can be produced from the data generated and stored from routine processing, including reports that are produced on a schedule, reports of exceptional or critical situations requiring immediate attention, and reports that are produced only when requested or demanded.
Groupware	Software to help groups of people work together more efficiently and effectively is often referred to as groupware. Groupware can support a team of managers working on the same production problem, letting them share their ideas and work via connected computer systems. Lotus Notes and Lotus Sametime are popular group software products by IBM that help people in distant locations work together by sharing schedules, notes, discussions, documents, and actual work on projects.
Decision support software	Special decision support systems (DSSs) can be developed to perform sophisticated qualitative and quantitative analysis for individual decision makers and managers. Software to help decision makers determine the best location for a new warehouse is an example.
Executive support software	This software is designed to support top-level executives and decision makers, such as generals in the military or presidents of companies.
Expert systems software	This software is programmed to act like an expert in a field such as medicine. Expert system software can be used to diagnose complex medical conditions in patients.
Artificial intelligence software	This software is programmed to have human-like intelligence. The software is used in robots, to simulate human thinking, to learn from new experiences, to handle imprecise and fuzzy information, and to perform a number of other specialized functions.

SOFTWARE ISSUES AND TRENDS

As software increases in importance, software issues become more significant. Acquiring, installing, and controlling the use of software are important. When to purchase new software and remove old software are also important issues. In addition, vendors are doing what they can to protect their software from being copied or duplicated by individual users and other software companies. Today, companies can copyright some software and programs, but this protection is limited. Another approach is to use existing patent laws. These and related issues will be explored in this section.

Acquiring Application Software

Individuals, groups, and organizations can either develop or customize a program for a specific application (called *proprietary software),* or purchase and use an existing software program (sometimes called *off-the-shelf software).* It is also possible to modify some off-the-shelf programs, giving a blend of off-the-shelf and customized approaches.

Customized Application Software. One option in acquiring application software is to make or customize software to deliver a specific problem solution. In some cases, this will result in in-house software development, during which the organization's computer personnel are responsible for all aspects of developing the

COMMUNITY /\\\\/\\ TECHNOLOGY

Using Application Software to Protect the Environment

Software has been used to help businesses cut costs and increase revenues. As seen throughout this chapter, software has been used to help engineers, scientists, musicians, artists, and many other individuals and organizations achieve their goals. But software can also be used to address many social issues, including protecting the environment.

From analyzing global warming to developing programs to protect forests from natural and man-made threats, software has been used to help monitor all aspects of our environment. Too often software has been used to assess the damage that has already been done to our environment. Today, we are seeing normal application software products used in business, science, and engineering include an environmental component. Architectural firms, for example, now have design software that includes an environmental impact analysis feature. The Athena Environmental Impact Estimator, for example, is application software for building design. In addition to helping architects determine what building materials are needed for a new project, the software computes and displays the possible environmental burdens of the project. Energy use (or misuse) can also be included as part of the analysis. Building for Environ-

mental and Economic Sustainability (BEES) is a software product that allows builders to analyze specific brand-name products. A builder can compare the environmental impact of using EcoWorx carpet tile versus similar products from Shaw Industries or other suppliers. About 80 products from 14 different manufacturers are included in the BEES software product.

Questions

1. How was software used to help protect the environment in the situations described?
2. How might similar software be used in other aspects of environmental protection?
3. Should federal and state governments pass laws to require software companies to include an environmental component in their software?

Sources
1. *"New Software Packages Allow Designers to Calculate the Environmental Burdens of Materials," Staff,* Architectural Record, *February 2003, pp. 174.*
2. *"Modern Architecture Calls for New Blueprint," Eric Lundquist,* eWeek, *March 10, 2003, p. 5.*
3. *"New Architecture Needed," John Dvorak,* PC Magazine, *November 19, 2002, p. M20.*

necessary programs. In other cases, customized software can be obtained from external vendors. For example, a third-party software firm, often called a value-added software vendor, may develop or modify a software program to meet the needs of a particular industry or company. A specific software program developed for a particular company or organization is called *contract software*. Some of the advantages inherent in in-house developed software include:

- The software usually meets user requirements. With customized software, you can get exactly what you need in terms of features, reports, and so on. Being involved in the development offers a level of control over the results. With off-the-shelf software, an organization might need to pay for features that are not required and never used. In addition, the software may not have all the required features, and ultimately require modification or customization.
- The software has more flexibility. Customized software enables an organization to have more flexibility in making modifications and changes.
- The software is problem-specific. With customized software, an organization gets programs that are easily tailored to a unique problem or task. This is usually not true of off-the-shelf software packages, which are designed for more general markets.

Along with these advantages, organizations must consider an important disadvantage of developing in-house customized software. If an organization chooses in-house development, it must acknowledge the time it takes to develop the required features. It can also be very expensive to develop in-house customized software, and getting a software package that meets organizational goals is not always accomplished.

Off-the-Shelf Application Software. Software can also be purchased, leased, or rented from a software company that develops programs and sells them to many computer users and organizations. Software programs developed for a general market are called general software programs or *off-the-shelf software packages,* since these programs can literally be purchased in packages "off the shelf" in a store.

Many individuals and organizations use off-the-shelf software. Most individuals and many organizations, for example, purchase software to perform word-processing, database functions, spreadsheet analysis, and other common activities. Purchasing, leasing, or renting off-the-shelf software offers a number of advantages, including:

- Lower costs. The software company is able to spread the software development costs over a large number of customers, hence reducing the cost any one customer must pay.
- Less risk. With an existing software program, you can analyze the features and performance of the package. If software is to be customized, there is more risk concerning the features and performance of the software that has yet to be developed.
- High quality. Many off-the-shelf packages are of high quality. In addition, a large number of customers or customer firms have tested the software and helped identify many of its bugs. There is, however, never an iron clad guarantee of high quality, particularly if the intended application is rather unique.
- Less time. Off-the-shelf software can often be installed quickly. It can take years or more to develop and install customized software.
- Fewer resources needed. If software is to be developed or customized in-house, it can take a complete staff of computer personnel. These additional resources are not needed if an organization uses off-the-shelf software.

Combining Customized and Off-the-Shelf Application Software. In some cases, individuals, groups, or organizations use a blend of external and internal software development. That is, off-the-shelf software packages are modified or customized by in-house or external personnel. A manufacturing company, for example, might want to acquire a powerful inventory control program to help reduce inventory costs. The company might also need to include specific inventory calculations for a few important inventory items. The best approach in this case might be to buy or lease off-the-shelf inventory software and to make the necessary changes to the inventory programs.

Some software companies encourage their customers to make changes to their software. Or in some cases, the software company supplying the necessary software will make the necessary changes for a fee. Other software companies, however, will not allow their software to be modified or changed by those purchasing or leasing it. As mentioned before, open-source software is free or inexpensive and can be changed or modified.

Installing New Software, Handling Bugs, and Removing Old or Unwanted Software

Software companies revise their programs and sell new versions every few years or more often. In some cases, the revised software can offer a number of new and valuable enhancements. In other cases, the software may use complex program code that

offers little in terms of additional capabilities. Furthermore, revised software can contain bugs or errors. Deciding whether or not to purchase the newest software can be a problem for organizations and individuals with a large investment in software.

Should the newest version be purchased when it is released? Some organizations and individuals do not always get the latest software upgrades or versions, unless there are significant improvements or capabilities. Instead, they may upgrade to newer software only when there are vital new features.

Installing New Software. Installing new software is usually straightforward (see Figure 3.33). Software for personal computers typically comes on CDs. Here is how you can install most software:

- Check the documentation to make sure that your computer meets the storage, processor, and memory requirements to run the software. This information, often called system requirements, is usually contained in the documentation that comes with the software. Information and documentation can also be placed on the outside of the box that contains the software. With some software, if you open the box, you cannot return it.
- Place the CD that contains the software in the computer's CD drive. In most cases, the software installation process will start immediately. If not, the instructions that come with the software will lead you through what is needed, depending on your computer and its operating system. Software can also be installed from floppy disks or over the Internet.
- Follow the installation instructions. You will likely be given choices during the installation. Most software products have standard or recommended installation settings.
- Once the software is installed, you might have to register or authorize the software before it can be used. This is usually done on the Internet.
- Check for updates. Some software, such as tax-preparation programs, offer updates to make sure you are using the latest version. In other cases, the Web site for the software company will post any bugs or problems with fixes or patches that you can install on your computer to eliminate potential problems. Some software packages have a large number of patches, which can take time to install. Updates are usually obtained over the Internet.

FIGURE 3.33 • Installing new software

These two screens show two points in the process of installing new software.

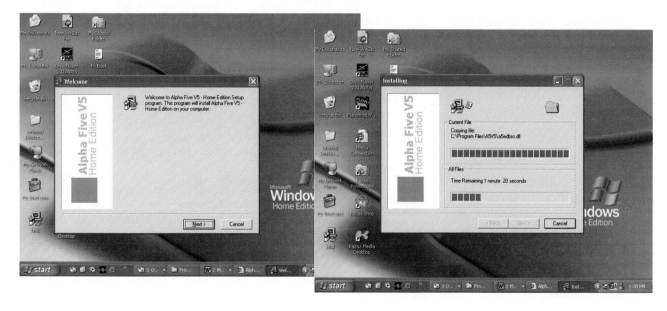

Handling Software Bugs. Software often has bugs, consisting of one or more defects or problems that prevent the software from working as intended or working at all. To maximize their revenues, software companies often release new software before it is completely and thoroughly tested. Here are some things you can do to overcome pesky software bugs:

- Be careful buying or acquiring the latest software before it has been completely tested and used by others. Some people would rather get software that is a year old or older to make sure that the errors have been found and fixed.
- After you install the software, check the *readme* files that may be included with the software. These files often contain last minute updates or disclosures, including bugs and how to deal with them.
- Register the software with the software maker. Software companies will often alert you if there is a problem or bug and give you steps to follow to eliminate it.

COMMUNITY ∿ TECHNOLOGY

Open-Source versus Proprietary Software

Increasing numbers of information systems developers are turning to Linux to power their systems. In Europe, oil company BP and Banca Commerciale Italiana are among the big companies that have moved to Linux. According to IBM, as many as 15 banks in central London are running Linux. Korean Air now does all its ticketing on Linux, and U.S. motor home manufacturer Winnebago also uses Linux. Most Linux adopters cite software licensing, hardware upgrade costs, and customizability as the primary reasons for the switch from other operating systems.

In the United States, the Walt Disney Company's animation division recently adopted Linux as its operating system of choice. In doing so they joined other major studios and special effects houses, including DreamWorks SKG, Pixar Animation Studios, Industrial Light and Magic, and Digital Domain. "For us, it's a move to less-expensive commodity technology systems," said John Carey, vice president for Walt Disney Feature Animation.

What lies behind an open-source system like Linux? The Free Software Foundation, associated with the GNU project that wrote Linux, argues that it is unethical to copyright and *own* software. It maintains that software should be freely shared and developed in a communal environment. Freely sharing the source code of operating systems like Linux and other software, they believe, promotes innovation in the development process. In contrast, those in the commercial software industry believe that a traditional business model is needed to

promote innovation in software development. It takes a significant quantity of money to employ top-notch software developers and programmers. Software manufacturers can invest hundreds of thousands of dollars in the development process. The businesses that provide us with this high-quality software could not remain afloat if they gave away their products.

Questions

1. Under the Free Software Foundation's philosophy, how would it be possible for software developers to earn a decent living?
2. What benefits do vendors like Microsoft offer their customers that might not be possible with uncopyrighted, free software?
3. The Free Software Foundation argues that copyrights are appropriate for printed material but inappropriate for digital media such as software. What do you think?

Sources
1. *"More Foreign Banks Switching to Linux," Matt Loney, ZDNet (UK), http://zdnet.com.com/2100-1103-887961.html, April 22, 2002.*
2. *"Disney Shifting to Linux for Film Animation," Steve Lohr, The New York Times, www.nytimes.com/2002/06/18/technology/18LINU.html?todaysheadlines, June 18, 2002.*
3. *"Linux Defined," Search390.com, http://search390.techtarget.com/sDefinition/0,,sid10_gci212482,00.html.*
4. *Free Software Foundation's Web site, www.fsf.org, accessed July 2002.*

- Check the Web site of the software vendor often. There can be updates that eliminate any known bugs. In addition, vendors often list bugs that have been found and offer patches or fixes that can be downloaded over the Internet.
- Check with popular PC magazines and journals. Popular PC magazines and journals often have articles on software bugs and possible solutions.
- If all else fails, carefully document exactly what happened when you found the bug and then contact the software vendor for a solution.

Removing (Uninstalling) Software. Removing or uninstalling unwanted software can be easy. Most operating systems have an Add/Remove Program feature to assist you. Note that this feature does not work with all software and that this feature does not always remove all elements of the program or software package. Some utility software packages can help eliminate unwanted elements of software you have removed. With some older computers, you can simply delete all the files in the program folder or subdirectory containing the program you want to remove.

Copyrights and Licenses

Most software products are protected by law using copyright or licensing provisions. Copyright and licensing provisions can vary. In some cases, you are given unlimited use of software on one or two computers. This is typical with many applications developed for personal computers. In other cases, you pay as you go. The more computers you use the software on, the more you pay the software vendor. This approach is becoming popular with software placed on networks or larger computers. Most of these protections prevent you from copying software and giving it to others without restrictions. As mentioned before, some software now requires that you *register* or *activate* it before it can be fully used. Registration and activation sometimes put unknown software on your hard disk that can monitor the activities and changes to your computer system. As discussed next, some software doesn't have restrictive copyright or licensing agreements.

Shareware, Freeware, Open Source, and Public Domain Software

Many software users are doing what they can to minimize software costs. Some are turning to **shareware** and **freeware**—software that is very inexpensive or free, usually for personal computers. Shareware may not be as powerful or as expensive as professional software, but some people get what they need at a good price. In some cases, you are given the opportunity to try the software before sending a nominal fee to the software developer. Some shareware or freeware software is in the public domain, often called **public domain software**. This software is no longer protected by copyright laws and can be freely copied and used.

Open-source software makes the source or machine code available to people. With this type of software, you can make changes to the software or develop your own software that integrates with the open-source software. Linux is an example of an open-source operating system (see Table 3.7). Some companies are also starting to reveal their source code. Microsoft, for example, decided to show government agencies the source code used to develop its Windows operating system to convince government agencies that the software is secure and safe.[29]

TABLE 3.7 • Examples of Open-Source Software

Software Type	Open Source Example
Operating System	Linux
Application Software	Open Office
Database Software	MySQL
Internet Browser	Mozilla
Instant Messaging	Jabber

Action Plan

1. What will Alex need for her work for the law firm?

Office XP is a software suite from Microsoft that includes a number of popular application software packages, such as a word processor, spreadsheet program, database program, and several other packages. Alex should get Office XP or the newer Office 2003, which can work with files from the older Office XP.

2. What type of operating system will she need?

Since Office XP and Office 2003 work on either Windows or a Macintosh computer, Alex can use either operating system. This is not true, however, for all software packages. Some packages run only on Windows, whereas others run only on a Macintosh computer. Since the type of operating system will determine what kind of computer she needs (PC or Apple Macintosh), the operating system she selects will be an important decision. Alex should talk to her instructors in her political science major and her boss at work to get their recommendations and find out which operating systems are used at school and on the job.

Summary

LEARNING OBJECTIVE 1
Discuss the importance and types of software.

Software consists of programs that control the workings of the computer hardware, along with the documentation to explain the programs. Computer programs are sets of instructions to the computer that direct the circuitry within the hardware to operate in a certain fashion. Computer programmers write or create these instructions, which become complete programs. Program documentation is the collection of narrative descriptions designed to assist in the program's use and implementation. There are two main categories of software: systems software that coordinates the activities of hardware and various computer programs and application software, which is designed to solve user problems and perform specific activities and tasks.

LEARNING OBJECTIVE 2
Discuss the functions of some important programming languages.

All software programs are written in coding schemes called programming languages, which provide instructions to a computer to perform some processing activity. Programming languages are sets of program code containing instructions that signal the CPU to perform circuit-switching operations.

The process of coding these instructions is called programming. A programming language standard is a set of rules that describes how programming statements and commands should be written.

In the first generation of programming languages, computers were programmed in machine language or binary code. The second generation of languages was termed assembly languages. They allow programming in symbols and words rather than 0s and 1s.

Figure 3.3—p. 97

The third generation consists of many high-level programming languages, including COBOL and FOR-TRAN, that use English-like statements and commands. Programs in these languages must be converted to machine language by language translators, but are easier to write than assembly or machine-language code.

A fourth-generation language (4GL) is less procedural and more English-like than third-generation languages. 4GLs include database and query languages such as Structured Query Language (SQL). Artificial intelligence and expert-system programming use fifth-generation languages (5GL). 5GLs are sometimes called natural languages because they use even more English-like syntax than 4GLs. High-level languages, from third- to fifth-generation, can be classified by their problem-solving characteristics.

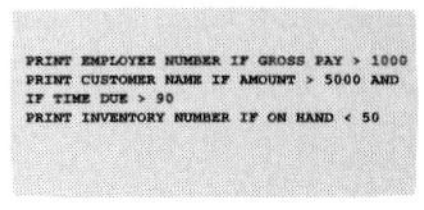

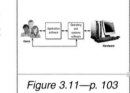

Object-oriented programming languages use groups of related data, instructions, and procedures called objects, which serve as reusable modules in various programs. These languages can reduce program development and testing time.

Figure 3.5—p. 99

LEARNING OBJECTIVE 3
Describe the functions of systems software and operating systems.

Systems software is a collection of programs that interacts with hardware and application software, creating a layer of insulation between them. Systems software includes operating systems, language-translation programs, and utility programs.

An operating system (OS) is a set of computer programs that runs or controls the computer hardware and acts as an interface with application programs. OSs convert an instruction from an application into a set of instructions needed by the hardware. The OS also serves as a buffer between application programs and hardware, giving hardware independence.

Figure 3.11—p. 103

A computer's operating system performs a number of important functions. Memory management involves controlling storage access and use by converting logical requests into physical locations and by placing data in the best storage space, perhaps in expanded or virtual memory. Processor management involves controlling the computer's processor or processors. The operating system also controls input, output, storage, and peripheral devices. Task management allocates computer resources through multitasking, multithreading, and time-sharing. Multitasking involves running more than one application at the same time. In multithreading several parts of a single application program can be working at the same time. Time-sharing allows more than one person to use a computer system at the same time. File management involves organizing files into folders or directories. Different operating systems have different file-management conventions. Network management allows multiple computers to work together.

An OS also provides a user interface. A command-based user interface uses text commands to send instructions; a graphical user interface (GUI), such as Windows, uses icons and menus. In addition, there are a number of other important operating system features, such as plug and play (PnP).

Figure 3.15—p. 109

Windows is a GUI used with newer computers. Newer versions of Windows, such as Windows XP, are fully functional operating systems that do not require DOS. OS X is a recent proprietary operating system for Apple computers.

UNIX is the leading portable operating system, usable on many computer system types and platforms. Linux is available free to users under a General Public License (GPL) arrangement. In addition, there a number of operating systems for larger, smaller, and special-purpose devices.

An interpreter is a language translator that converts each statement in a program into machine language and executes the statement. A compiler is a language translator that translates a complete program into a complete machine-language program. Utility programs include virus detection, file compression, spam guards, and disk diagnostics and backup functions.

LEARNING OBJECTIVE 4
Describe the support provided by application software.

Organizations can customize application software, buy existing programs off the shelf, or use a combination of customized and off-the-shelf application software. Each approach has advantages and disadvantages.

User software or personal productivity tools are general-purpose programs, including word-processing, spreadsheet, presentation graphics, database management programs, and personal information managers. A software suite is a collection of application software packages placed in a bundle. Some companies produce application software that contains several programs in one integrated package. Additional application software for individuals includes project management, financial management, tax preparation, Web authoring, photo and video editing, educational packages, desktop publishing, and many others.

Figure 3.27—p. 121

Software that helps groups work together is often called groupware. Routine transaction processing software includes accounts receivable, accounts payable, asset management, and many other applications. Software can also be purchased or developed for information, decision support, and specialized purposes.

LEARNING OBJECTIVE 5
Discuss how software can be acquired, customized, installed, removed, and managed.

Software issues and trends include acquiring software, installing new software, handling software bugs, removing software, copyrights and licenses, and the use of free or inexpensive shareware or freeware. Individuals, groups, and organizations can either develop or customize a program for a specific application (called *proprietary software*), or purchase and use an existing software program (sometimes called *off-the-shelf software*). It is also possible to modify some off-the-shelf programs, giving a blend of off-the-shelf and customized approaches. Being careful when buying software, checking readme files, registering software, checking the Web site for the software, checking popular PC magazines for fixes to software bugs, and contacting the software manufacturer are some of the ways to help find and solve software bugs.

Most software products are protected by law using copyright or licensing provisions. Some software companies give you unlimited use of software on one or two computers. People and organizations use shareware and freeware software to reduce software costs. Shareware may not be as powerful or as expensive as professional software, but some people get what they need at a good price.

Test Yourself

LEARNING OBJECTIVE 1: Discuss the importance and types of software.

1. _____ are sets of instructions or statements to the computer that direct its operation.

2. What is the collection of narrative descriptions about a computer program called?
   a. computer plan
   b. computer documentation
   c. computer platform
   d. application plan

LEARNING OBJECTIVE 2: Discuss the functions of some important programming languages.

3. True or False: The assembly language is an example of the first generation of programming languages.

4. COBOL is an example of a:
   a. first-generation language
   b. second-generation language
   c. third-generation language
   d. fourth-generation language

5. A programming statement, such as PRINT EMPLOYEE NUMBER IF GROSS PAY > 100 is an example of a _____ generation language.

6. True or False: Encapsulation means that functions or tasks are captured into an object.

LEARNING OBJECTIVE 3: *Describe the functions of systems software and operating systems.*

7. _____ is a collection of programs that interact with the computer and application hardware, creating a layer of insulation between the two.

8. Which of the following is not typically done with an operating system?
   a. control multiple computers
   b. control special-purpose computers
   c. manage the system software
   d. manage the memory function

9. _____ allocates computer resources to make the best use of system assets.

10. True or False: Multitasking involves running more than one application at the same time.

11. _____ allows more than one person to use a computer system at the same time.

12. Windows is an example of:
    a. a graphical user interface
    b. a command-based operating system
    c. a proprietary operating system
    d. an object-oriented operating system

13. True or False: OS X was one of the first operating systems for personal computers.

14. A(n) _____ is a language translator that converts each statement in a program into machine language and executes the statement.

LEARNING OBJECTIVE 4: **Describe the support provided by application software.**

15. True or False: Database programs can contain optimization features to minimize or maximize a quantity subject to constraints.

16. What type of application software would a physician use in a professional meeting or conference to present the results of a research study?
    a. word processing
    b. spreadsheet
    c. database
    d. presentation graphics

17. A(n) _____ helps individuals, groups, and organizations store useful information, including a list of tasks to complete, a list of names and addresses, and an appointment calendar.

18. Applications can work together through the use of
    a. compilers
    b. interpreters
    c. object linking and embedding
    d. groupware

19. Routine processing systems or applications are often called _____.

LEARNING OBJECTIVE 5: **Discuss how software can be acquired, customized, installed, removed, and managed.**

20. True or False: Individuals, groups, and organizations can develop or customize a program for a specific application. This is called proprietary software.

21. One way to help find and eliminate software bugs is to:
    a. check the OLE file
    b. check the readme file
    c. use the Add/Remove feature
    d. use the object-oriented error checking feature

22. True or False: Most software is protected by law using copyright or licensing provisions.

23. _____ makes the machine code available to users.

Test Yourself Solutions: **1.** Computer program, **2.** b., **3.** F, **4.** c., **5.** fourth, **6.** T, **7.** Systems software, **8.** c., **9.** Task management, **10.** T, **11.** Time sharing, **12.** a., **13.** F, **14.** interpreter, **15.** F, **16.** d., **17.** personal information manager (PIM), **18.** c., **19.** transaction processing systems (TPS), **20.** T, **21.** b., **22.** T, **23.** Open-source software

Key Terms

Application software, p. 94
Assembly language, p. 98
Booting, p. 104
Command-based user interface, p. 108
Compiler, p. 103
Computer program, p. 94
Computer programmer, p. 94
Database languages, p. 99
Fourth-generation language (4GL), p. 99

Freeware, p. 133
Graphical user interface (GUI), p. 108
High-level languages, p. 98
Interpreter, p. 102
Machine language, p. 97
Object linking and embedding (OLE), p. 124
Object-oriented programming, p. 101
Open-source software, p. 133

Operating system (OS), p. 103
Programming language, p. 96
Public domain software, p. 133
Shareware, p. 133
Software suite, p. 123
Source code, p. 102
Systems software, p. 94
Utility program, p. 114

Questions

Review Questions

1. Why does software represent such a significant amount of the total cost of a computer system?

2. What is a program? How does it differ from software?

3. Explain the difference between systems and application software.

4. Draw a diagram that outlines the relationship among hardware, systems software, and application software.

5. Outline the evolution of programming languages.

6. What are the characteristics of high-level programming languages?

7. What are object-oriented programming languages? Why might they be used?

8. What is an operating system? What functions does it perform?

9. What are the advantages of using a graphical user interface (GUI)?

10. What is a compiler? What is an interpreter?

11. Describe four utility programs. How might each be used?

12. What is a software suite? What is an integrated software package?

13. Discuss the advantages and disadvantages of customized software versus off-the-shelf software packages.

14. What is a software license?

15. What steps would you take to find and eliminate a software bug or error?

Discussion Questions

16. If planning for a computer system begins with software, what do we start with: programming languages, systems software, or application software? Why?

17. Discuss the differences between first-generation languages and high-level languages. What might be the reasons for the evolution of computer languages?

18. What trends are occurring in the development of operating systems for personal computers? What might operating systems be like in five or ten years?

19. When would you use an integrated software package versus a software suite?

20. Pick a career you would like to pursue. What types of application software might you find useful?

21. What advantage does an organization have if users build their own applications? Should users and computer system programmers choose the same development languages? Explain why or why not.

Exercises

Try It Yourself

1. Using a word-processing program, create a document that describes the top five application software packages for a career area of your choice. Give a brief description of each application software package and a description of how it might benefit you professionally.

2. Your department is adding eight new people. Before they arrive you need to acquire eight copies of personal computer software, both systems and application software. (Hardware had been purchased at an earlier time.) One of your responsibilities as department manager is to get bids from three local suppliers of computer software and determine what will be the total cost of acquiring this software for the eight additional employees. Use your spreadsheet software to analyze the costs of purchasing the software. Compute the total cost and the average cost per person.

3. Use the Internet to get information on object-oriented programming languages. You may be asked to send e-mail to your instructor about what you found.

Virtual Classroom Activities

For the following exercises, do not use face-to-face or telephone communications with your group members. Use only Internet communications.

4. Software is a key component of any distance learning system. Using the Internet or other sources, get information on two or more distance learning systems. You may be asked to write a report or send your instructor e-mail about what you found.

5. Groupware, software used to support group decision making, can be critical in making decisions in a group setting. Explore the use of groupware and group decision support systems software. You may be asked to write a report or send your instructor e-mail about what you found.

Teamwork

6. In a group of three or four classmates, interview three programmers or programmer/analysts from different businesses to determine what programming languages they are using to develop applications. How did these software developers choose the languages that they are using? What do they like about their own language and what could be improved? Which language would the programmers choose for software development if the decision were completely their own choice? It is possible that the programmers may each choose a different language. Considering the information obtained from the programmers, select one of these languages and briefly present your selection and the rationale for the selection to the class.

7. Freeware and shareware software packages are popular with many people. Have each team member investigate a freeware or shareware program, such as a word processor, a database program, or a spreadsheet program. Each team member should write a brief description of the software, including the features of the software versus the features of a normal commercial software package. The team should then write a description of the advantages and disadvantages of freeware and shareware in general.

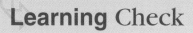

Learning Check

To check your knowledge of each of the chapter objectives, use this chart to find related end-of-chapter content.

Learning Objective	Key Terms		Questions	Exercises
Learning Objective 1 Discuss the importance and types of software.	application software computer program computer programmer	programming languages systems software	1, 2, 3, 4, 16	
Learning Objective 2 List and discuss the functions of some important programming languages.	assembly language fifth generation language (5GL) fourth-generation language (4GL) high-level programming language	machine language object-oriented programming language	5, 6, 7, 21	3, 6
Learning Objective 3 Describe the functions of systems software and operating systems.	booting command-based user interface compiler graphical user interface interpreter	object linking and embedding (OLE) operating system (OS) utility program	8, 9, 11, 12, 18	2
Learning Objective 4 Describe the support provided by application software.	object linking and embedding (OLE) software suite		13, 17, 19, 20	1, 2
Learning Objective 5 Discuss how software can be acquired, customized, installed, removed, and managed.	freeware open-source software public domain software shareware		10, 14, 15	2, 7

Endnotes

1. Hamilton, J.P. "New Book on Object-Oriented Programming with VB.NET," *M2 Best Books,* November 13, 2002.

2. Staff, "Foliage Software Systems Publishes White Paper on Avionics Software Development," *Business Wire,* April 9, 2002.

3. Staff, "National Security Selects Object-Oriented Insurance Administration System As Strategic Platform," *PR Newswire,* January 28, 2002.

4. Spanbauer, Scott, "Windows XPs Successor," *PC World,* March 2003, p. 32.

5. Staff, "Travel Web Services Take an Open Source Route," *Computer Weekly,* April 8, 2003, p. 4.

6. Staff, "IT Advances Research On Climate," *Information Week Online,* June 28, 2002.

7. Staff, "Panasonic to Supply Linux Development Platform and Operating System for Its Latest Broadband TV Tuner," *Electronic News,* April 21, 2003.

8. Clark, Don, "Microsoft Offers New Lock for Files," *The Wall Street Journal,* February 24, 2003.

9. Krishnadas, K. C. "India Pursues Global Role in Embedded Software," *Electronic Engineering Times,* April 14, 2003, p. 23.

10. Staff, "Computers Predict Their Own Future," *ORMS Today,* April 2003, p. 20.

11. Tynan, Daniel, "Natural-Born Killers," *PC World,* May 2003, p. 113.

12. Mossberg, Walter, "Two Windows Programs Make Flawed Attempts to Catch up to iPhoto," *The Wall Street Journal,* January 9, 2003, p. B1.

13. Kronholz, June, "PowerPoint Goes to School, *The Wall Street Journal,* November 12, 2002, p. B1.

14. Hugh, John, "Sound Advice for Software," *The Times Educational Supplement,* April 4, 2003, p. 25.

15. Staff, "StageTools Releases MovingPicture," *Millimeter,* March 10, 2003.

16. Williams, Elisa, "The Player," *Forbes,* October 28, 2002, p. 50.

17. Ozer, Jan, "Video Editors Battle for the High Ground," *PC Magazine,* September 12, 2002, p. 34.

18. Staff, "E Learning: The Challenges," *Computing,* May 1, 2003. p. 29.

19. Forelle, Charles, "The Never-Ending Exam," *The Wall Street Journal,* May 1, 2003, p. B1.

20. Strauss, Marise, "Virtually Human Creates Simulation from Dance," *Playback,* March 31, 2003, p. 14.

21. Staff, "Monsanto Puts a Friendly Face on Hard Software," *KMWorld,* February 2003, p. 28.

22. Crupi, Anthony, "Turning Muppets into Ditigal Assets," *Cable World,* April 14, 2003, p. 15.

23. Staff, "Landmark Theaters and Microsoft Create the Largest Digital Cinema in the United States," *Millimeter,* April 4, 2003.

24. Staff, "Digimations Art Contest," *Millimeter,* April 17, 2003.

25. Nash, Emma, "Camelot Installs New IBM System," *Computing,* May 1, 2003, p. 1.

26. Staff, Genomic Data Visualization Software, *Drug Discovery and Development,* February 1, 2003, p. 72.

27. Hecht, Jeff, "Talent-Spotting Software Predicts Cart Toppers," *New Scientist,* March 15, 2003, p. 17.

28. Brown, Erica, "Cancer in the Crosshairs," *Forbes,* October 28, 2002, p. 361.

29. Bank, David, "Microsoft to let Governments See Code," *The Wall Street Journal,* January 15, 2003, p. B5.

TheInternet**and** WorldWideWeb

Josh Greene has been using e-mail and the Web for as long as he can remember. His Web activities are so predictable that he imagines he has worn ruts in the paths he repeatedly travels. He has become disenchanted. His friend is really into downloading music files and movies on Kazaa, but Josh doesn't feel comfortable with that. He's heard that his school is really cracking down on file sharing, and he's concerned about picking up a virus, a common experience on Kazaa. Besides, Josh's computer takes f-o-r-e-v-e-r to download Web pages. Josh knows that the Web and Internet are evolving quickly and wonders how to keep up with what's new and exciting. Come to think of it, Josh isn't even sure about what the difference is between the Internet and the Web.

A number of Josh's friends have gotten new cell phones with all kinds of cool features. They send each other messages throughout the day. They always talk about cool stuff they found online and spend some evenings partying—on their computers! Josh's roommate is traveling to visit an online friend over the weekend. Josh is feeling a bit left out. Like it or not, Josh will be spending *his* evening online as he has a big research project due tomorrow. He's unable to get to the library so he plans on doing his research on the Internet but isn't sure where to start.

1. What online activities can Josh use to enrich his quality of life?
2. Which online activities are legal and safe, and which are not?
3. How should Josh conduct his research on his computer?

Check out Josh's *Action Plan* at the conclusion of this chapter.

LEARNING OBJECTIVES	CHAPTER CONTENT
1. Describe how hardware, protocols, and software work together to create the Internet and how the Internet may change in the future.	**Internet Technology**
2. Compare and contrast the types of communication tools available on the Internet.	**Internet Communications**
3. Explain the underlying structure of the Web and the technologies that support it.	**Web Technology**
4. Define the categories of information and services that the Web provides and the ways in which the Web supports research.	**Web Applications**

Introduction

We've learned how hardware and software work together to assist us in achieving our goals. This in itself is highly valuable. However, the true power of computing lies in connecting computing devices and users through the interconnected networks that make up the Internet. The Internet connects people on a global scale and provides us with a host of communication platforms, information, and services.

The Web is an Internet service that provides a user-friendly interface to resources on the Internet. It organizes and presents information on the Internet in a manner that is easier to navigate. More than any other technology, the Web has empowered individuals by providing a public forum on which to share ideas. It has leveled the playing field between small and large organizations and provided opportunities for some organizations that would otherwise never stand a chance of competing in a market. The Web, at any given time, can be viewed as a snapshot of the human condition. Anything of personal or professional interest to any person is represented here. The good, the bad, and the ugly. Thus, it has its share of controversy.

For students and professionals, the Web has become a primary source of information in support of scholarly research. Because of the vast amount of information and the lack of quality control, researchers must learn unique methods for sorting the wheat from the chaff. This chapter addresses all of these issues and much more!

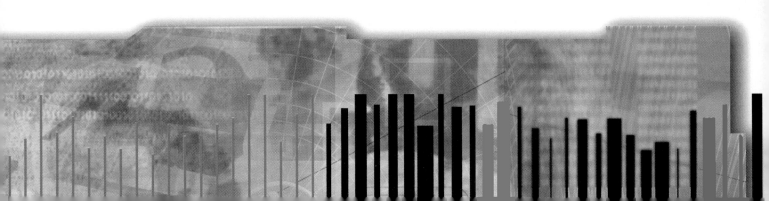

We are all familiar with the old phrase *two heads are better than one*. There is more wisdom to be learned from this phrase than you might think at first. If you take the phrase at face value, as a kind of simple accounting equation, two heads are better than one, just as two bags of gold are better than one. If you think about the phrase more deeply, however, you can gain more insight. When two individuals share their ideas, they are able to create greater ideas and solutions than either would be capable of creating independently, or even side by side. Today's most impressive engineering feats, such as the Mars Rover (see Figure 4.1), are possible only through the collaboration of many specialists. Communication is the key. Since each of us has unique knowledge and perceptions of the world, we can get a more complete and realistic image of the world by communicating and combining our knowledge and perceptions.

FIGURE 4.1 • Communication is the key
The Mars Exploration Rover is the product of the collaboration of many engineers and scientists.

The Internet provides a platform on which hundreds of millions of people combine and share knowledge and views. If two heads are better than one, hundreds of millions of heads sharing knowledge and unique perceptions is a powerful thing indeed. The Internet brings the power of community to computing.

The Internet provides the technology and physical connections between devices to support many applications, the most popular of which are e-mail and the Web. E-mail provides a convenient and low-cost form of communication over the Internet, while the Web provides a convenient method of sharing information and services over the Internet. The Web is not simply another name for the Internet, but rather one of many applications and services available on the Internet. People are using the Internet and its applications as a resource for communicating, learning, entertainment, and making new friends. We use it professionally to collaborate on projects. Businesses invest in the Internet to leverage competitive advantages. Products are marketed and sold over the Internet. Great works of creativity are published and distributed over the Internet. The Internet is highly regarded and a part of many of our daily lives, but what exactly is it?

INTERNETTECHNOLOGY

The Internet is relatively young and still in its early stages of development. New ways of using the Internet are being developed and introduced every day. In this section, we will provide a brief overview of the origins of the Internet, so that we can observe how it has come to be so influential. We examine the principles that govern the Internet so that we can be more knowledgeable about its capabilities and limitations.

A Brief History of the Internet

The *Internet* is a global, public, network of computer networks. A **computer network** is a collection of computing devices connected together to share resources such as files, software, processors, storage, and printers. Millions of privately owned networks are in existence around the world. Joining networks together into larger networks so that users on different networks can communicate and share data creates an *internetwork*. Today's Internet joins together networks of over 200 million computers, or *Internet hosts,* to create the world's largest internetwork (see Figure 4.2). To understand the Internet, you must examine its origins.

In 1957, computing was done primarily on large mainframe computers accessed from within an organization through a network of terminals. Government agencies, universities, businesses, and other organizations all used this type of networking environment. In that same year, the U.S.S.R. surprised the world by launching Sputnik, the first artificial earth satellite. The United States viewed the launch as a challenge. The following year President Eisenhower reacted by forming two government agencies under the Department of Defense (DoD) to advance space technologies, weapons, and, communication systems: the Advanced Research Projects Agency (ARPA) and the National Aeronautics and Space Administration (NASA). Many amazing achievements were to come from these organizations, but among those that had the most social impact were placing the first man on the moon and the Internet.

In 1969, ARPA commissioned ARPANET for research into networking. Its initial goal was to establish closer communications for research by connecting the computer networks of four research institutions: the University of California at Los Angeles, Stanford, the University of California at Santa Barbara, and the University of Utah. The goal was accomplished within the year. Once the groundwork was laid for successful communications between networks, ARPANET began growing at a rapid pace. Table.4.1 summarizes milestones in the development of the Internet.

FIGURE 4.2 • Internet hosts

This graph illustrates the distribution of Internet hosts around the world.

TABLE 4.1 • Internet Development Milestones

Year	Internet Hosts	Internet Milestone Event
1970	13	The first cross-country link was installed by AT&T to connect networks across the country.
1973	35	ARPANET went international as it expanded overseas to University College in London, England, and the Royal Radar Establishment in Norway.
1984	1,024	ARPANET was divided into two subnetworks: MILNET, for military needs, and ARPANET, for research.
1990	313,000	The ARPANET project was officially concluded, and "the Internet" was turned over to the public, to be managed by the Internet Society (ISOC).
1991	617,000	The Commercial Internet Exchange (CIX) Association was established to allow businesses to connect to the Internet.
1993	1,500,000	The first Web Browser, "Mosaic," was released to Internet users to an unprecedented enthusiastic reception.

With the birth of the Web, the Internet exploded, with a 341,634% annual growth rate in Internet hosts in following years (see Figure 4.3). Internet service providers began sprouting up all over the world to provide Internet service to businesses and homes. With increasing amounts of consumers flocking to the Web, businesses recognized it as a powerful new marketing and sales tool. The Internet's focus shifted from supporting solely academic and government interests to supporting public and commercial interests. Today there are over 700 million Internet users. The worldwide number of Internet users will top 1 billion in 2005[1]; that's ½ of the world's total population. In the U.S., 76% of the population is Web savvy, and more than half of U.S. citizens use the Web as part of their daily routine.[2]

FIGURE 4.3 • The growth of Internet hosts
With over 200 million Internet hosts supporting 700 million users today, and a growth rate of 20%, the worldwide number of Internet users will top 1 billion in 2005.

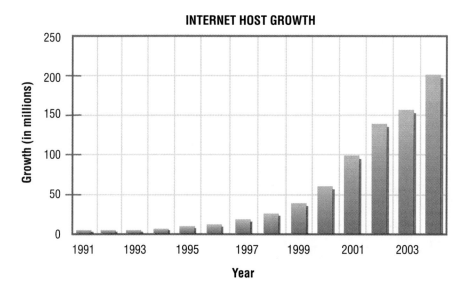

INTERNET HOST GROWTH

How Does the Internet Work?

The Internet is a combination of hardware, protocols, and software. The hardware provides the physical cables and devices that control and carry Internet data. **Protocols** are rules that ensure that participating devices are communicating in a uniform and manageable manner. Software allows users to interact with the Internet to access information and services. The following sections provide detailed explanations of the Internet's hardware, protocols, and software.

Internet Hardware. The hardware over which Internet traffic flows includes the Internet backbone, routers, and the computers that request and serve up information and services. The **Internet backbone** is made up of the many national and international communication networks that are owned by major telecommunications, or telecom, companies, such as MCI, AT&T, and Sprint—the same companies and networks that provide telephone service. These companies agreed to connect their networks so that users on all the networks could share information over the Internet. The cables, switching stations, communication towers, and satellites that make up these telecommunication networks provide the hardware over which Internet traffic travels. These large telecom companies are called network service providers (NSPs). Table 4.2 shows the percent of Internet traffic that each network service provider handles.

EXPAND YOUR
KNOWLEDGE

To learn more about how the Internet works, go to www.course.com/swt. Click the link "Expand Your Knowledge" and then complete the lab entitled, "Connecting to the Internet."

TABLE 4.2 • Network Service Providers

Market share of network service providers[3]

Network Service Provider	Percent of Internet Traffic Served
UUNET/WorldCom/MCI	27.9
AT&T	10.0
Sprint	6.5
Genuity	6.3
PSINet	4.1
Cable & Wireless	3.5
XO Communications	2.8
Verio	2.6
Qwest	1.5
Global Crossing	1.3

Figure 4.4 shows the North American portion of the AT&T global IP network, or backbone. Imagine 10 such backbone maps, each from different telecommunications companies, layered one on top of the other combined into one map—that is what the Internet backbone would look like.

FIGURE 4.4 • AT&T global IP network

The combined telecommunication networks, or backbones, of the major telecom companies, such as AT&T, make up the backbone of the Internet.

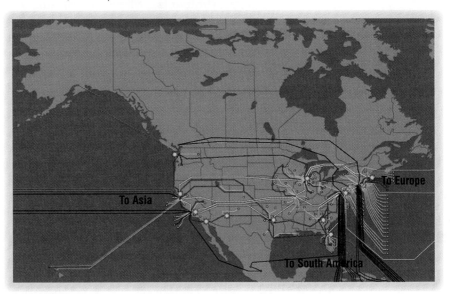

Network service providers enable Internet users to connect to their networks through utility stations called *points of presence* (PoPs). Points of presence include networking hardware that allows users to connect using dial-up connections and companies, such as Comcast (a cable company) and America Online to connect their Internet customers to the Internet backbone. MCI, for example, has more than 4,500 PoPs throughout North America, Europe, and the Pacific Rim, and incorporates more than 3.2 million dial-up modems.

Companies that provide users with access to the Internet through these PoPs are called **Internet service providers (ISP)**. There are hundreds of ISPs from local

to international levels. ISPs work as liaisons between Internet users and the telecommunications companies that own the backbones. They charge a monthly fee to Internet users and provide devices by which the user can connect to the Internet. Many companies, organizations, and institutions, work directly with the network service providers to connect their own organizations' networks directly to a PoP. Table 4.3 shows the number of people subscribing to the top 10 Internet service providers.

The Internet uses routers to make sure that information sent is routed to the intended recipient. **Routers** are special-purpose computing devices—typically small to large boxes with network ports—that manage network traffic by evaluating messages and routing them to their destination. Routers are typically located at network junctions, where one network is joined to another network. An e-mail message sent from New York to Los Angeles would pass from router to router until it reached its destination. Such an e-mail message might pass through as many as 20 routers along the way, but would reach its destination within a fraction of a second.

The physical building blocks of the Internet include the high-speed telecommunications networks that make up the Internet backbone, the network access points at which they connect, and the routers that manage the traffic traveling over the Internet. The Internet could not exist without this hardware. Equally important are the rules that govern the format of Internet traffic, which are called the protocols.

TABLE 4.3 • Top 10 Internet Service Providers[4]

Internet Service Providers	Estimated Subscribers
America Online	26,500,000
Microsoft Network	9,000,000
NetZero	8,600,000
Spinway	6,700,000
United Online	5,000,000
EarthLink	4,800,000
Excite@Home	3,700,000
Prodigy	3,500,000
1stUp.com	3,500,000
Freei.Net	3,200,000

Internet Protocols. Whether negotiating peace between nations at war, merging corporate infrastructures, or attempting to connect different types of networks, you must begin by striking common ground, and establishing policies and procedures. In networking, policies and procedures for finding common ground for communications between two devices are defined by protocols. The protocols for the Internet are the *Transmission Control Protocol* (TCP) and *Internet Protocol* (IP). Together these two protocols are commonly referred to as **TCP/IP.**

Data is transported over the Internet in packets. A data *packet* is a small group of bytes that includes the data being sent and a header containing information about the data, such as its destination, origin, size, and identification number. The Internet is a *packet switching* network. Internet applications, such as e-mail, divide up information, such as an e-mail message, into small packets in order to make efficient use of the network. Just as it is easier to move sand through a pipe than pebbles, it is easier to move packets over the Internet than large files. Upon arriving at their destination, the packets are reconstructed into the original message. Figure 4.5 illustrates the life of a packet on the Internet.

The Internet Protocol (the IP in TCP/IP) defines the format and addressing scheme used for the packets. Routers on the Internet use the packet header to direct the packet to its destination. The Transaction Control Protocol (the TCP in TCP/IP) enables two hosts to establish a connection and exchange streams of data. TCP guarantees delivery of data and also guarantees that packets will be delivered in the same order in which they were sent.

WIRELESS INTERNET ACCESS SAVES ON DIESEL FUEL, POLLUTION

Most long-haul truckers keep their engines running during the eight hours per day of federally mandated down time. A technology company in Tennessee has designed a new, high-tech truck stop that provides heat, air conditioning, phone service, and wireless Internet access in an effort to reduce the estimated two billion gallons of diesel fuel spent per year nationally, and the 36.2 million tons of pollution created by it.

Sources:
"Clean air at the Internet truck stop cafe
Hookup lets drivers turn off engine, go online at night"
By David R. Baker
San Francisco Chronicle
www.sfgate.com/cgi-bin/article.cgi?file=/chronicle/archive/2003/06/16/
BU222509.DTL&type=tech
Monday, June 6, 2003
Cited on July 3, 2003

FIGURE 4.5 • The life of a packet

Internet applications, such as e-mail, divide up information, such as an e-mail message, into small packets in order to make efficient use of the network. Upon arriving at their destination, the packets are reconstructed into the original message.

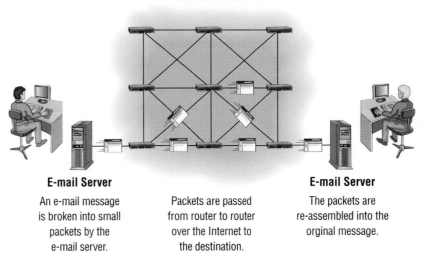

THE INTERNET

E-mail Server

An e-mail message is broken into small packets by the e-mail server.

Packets are passed from router to router over the Internet to the destination.

E-mail Server

The packets are re-assembled into the orginal message.

The Internet Protocol requires that all devices connected to the Internet have a unique IP address. An **IP address** consists of four numbers (0 to 255) separated by periods, such as 128.186.122.4. IP addresses can be *static,* permanently assigned to a particular computer, or *dynamic,* assigned to computers as needed. Computers that provide services, such as www.yahoo.com use static addresses, while computers that dial-up to connect to the Internet are assigned temporary IP addresses for the time that they are connected. The over 200 million Internet hosts cited earlier is actually a count of the number of assigned IP addresses. By using dynamic IP addresses, the Internet hosts can serve the over 700 million users.

IP addresses are represented in computers using binary numbers, 4 bytes divided by periods. For example:

```
11011000.00011011.00111101.10001001
```

By observing the binary representation, we can see that an IP address uses 32 bits. We know from Chapter 2 that 32 bits can represent 2^{32}, or almost 4.3 billion, possible IP addresses—enough to handle the 1 billion Internet users expected to be online by 2005. However, if you consider that eventually each user may need several IP addresses for several different devices or services, the 4-byte IP address may not be able to support the needs of the future. This is already an issue in China, Korea, and Japan, where they are rapidly using up the IP addresses that they have been assigned.[5] Changing to larger, IP addresses that can accommodate more users and more devices will require major infrastructure changes in the Internet.

Since people are more comfortable dealing with names than numbers, IP addresses are assigned associated English names called *domain names*. For example 128.186.6.14 is also known as www.fsu.edu. Domain names and IP addresses are managed by the Internet Corporation for Assigned Names and Numbers (ICANN) and can be purchased from accredited registrars (www.icann.org/registrars/accredited-list.html). The Internet uses the Domain Name System (DNS) to translate domain names into IP addresses. A database of addresses and names are stored on DNS servers. Internet services such as e-mail, and the Web, access DNS servers to translate the English addresses of people and Web sites to numeric IP addresses.

COMMUNITY TECHNOLOGY

Internet Cafes

The need to "stay connected" while traveling is causing some unlikely industries to get into the ISP business. *Internet cafes*, sometimes called *cybercafes*, provide islands of Internet connectivity for people away from their homes or offices.

Cruise ships are including Internet cafes as a service to their passengers. Passengers can use e-mail to communicate with friends and associates back home and save the costs of very expensive phone calls. They can also keep up with news and information on the Web. For an extra $100, Royal Caribbean will provide you with Connect@Sea, a service that provides 24-hour, unlimited access to the Internet from the privacy of your own stateroom or suite.

McDonald's, the company known for its Big Macs and Filet-o-Fish, is experimenting with providing Internet service to its customers in several cities. Customers who purchase an Extra Value Meal will get one hour of free high-speed wireless Internet access.

A young entrepreneur in Nepal plans to set up the world's highest cybercafe. Tsering Gyalzen is opening a facility at Mount Everest base camp that will allow climbers to go online before and after the big climb. Another type of high-altitude Internet will soon be available during air travel. Connexion by Boeing is equipping many passenger aircraft with the ability to offer passengers a high-speed Internet connection for in-flight Internet use.

What's next, the moon? Close; try Mars. The Mars Odyssey space vehicle included a transceiver that could eventually enable the use of the Internet on the distant planet. The transceiver would permit different Mars probes to communicate with each other and Earth stations. Eventually this technology could enable e-mail when we visit Mars.

Questions

1. The benefits of being able to access the Internet from a variety of locations are obvious. Are there any drawbacks?
2. Supplying customers with Internet access can be a costly investment that businesses must somehow pass on to customers in the form of fees or higher-priced merchandise. How much would you be willing to pay for an Internet connection while sipping coffee at Starbucks?
3. Throughout the course of your day, has there been any time that you could have benefited from an Internet connection to get some work done, where one did not exist? Where and when?

Sources
1. *"Cruise to exotic places and surf the Web,"* Miller, Stanley, JSOnline–Millwaukee Journal Sentinal, *June 24, 2002, www.jsonline.com accessed June 6, 2003.*
2. *"Wi-Fi Gets 'Super Sized,"* Singer, Michael, siliconvalley. internet.com, *March 11, 2003.*
3. *"High hopes for Everest cybercafe,"* Yogi, Bhagirath, BBC News, *February 15, 2003, http://news.bbc.co.uk/1/hi/world/ south_asia/2766087.stm, accessed June 6, 2003.*
4. *"Airlines to Offer Internet Access in '03,"* Bergstein, Brian, Associated Press, *Dec 15, 2002.*
5. *"E-Mail on Mars? Space Mission Could Be A Giant Step For Tech,"* Jesdanun, Anick, The Summit Daily News, *June 4, 2001, p 11.*

Many protocols are used on the Internet. Each service offered on the Internet—e-mail, the Web, instant messaging—has its own governing protocols. These protocols govern Internet communications, and are typically invisible to us as we work on the Internet; they work much like TCP/IP does. Although we don't see these protocols at work, they are essential in all Internet communications. Next, we will discuss how the software that we work with on the Internet provides us with the information and services that we find valuable.

Internet Software. Computers on the Internet communicate using client/server relationships. **Client/server** describes a relationship between two computer programs in which one program, the *client*, makes a service request from another program, the *server*, which provides the service (see Figure 4.6). A Web browser such as

FIGURE 4.6 • Client/server networking

Client/server applications, such as e-mail, the Web, and instant messaging, use a client application to connect to a shared server, which delivers the network service.

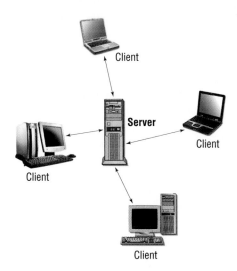

Internet Explorer, for example, is a client that requests a Web page from a Web server, such as www.monster.com. An e-mail program, such as Outlook or Eudora, is a client that connects to an e-mail server to retrieve e-mail messages. Instant messaging (IM) clients connect to IM servers to connect and communicate with other users on the Internet.

Server computers are typically powerful computers that can accommodate many simultaneous user requests. They are powered up 24 hours a day, 7 days a week to provide Internet services such as Web pages and e-mail service. The service performed by the server is defined by the type of server software it runs. A server running Web server software will reply to Web page requests, and a server running e-mail server software will govern the distribution of e-mail to and from the network. Different types of server software respond to requests that arrive at different ports on the server computer. **Ports** are logical addresses on the server that are associated with a specific service. For example, a server receives Web page requests on port 80 and domain name system requests on port 53; Gnutella, the technology used by popular file-sharing applications, uses port 6346. The client application requesting the service includes the correct port number in the outgoing packet headers. The server software accepting requests on that port number can be assured of the nature of the request.

In some cases a computer may act as both a client and a server, as happens in **peer-to-peer (P2P)** networking. In P2P communications, participants make a portion of their file system available to other participants to access directly (see Figure 4.7). In this relationship, an Internet user's personal computer acts as both server (as other users access files) and client (as the user accesses other's files). The Gnutella file-sharing system, which is at the heart of music sharing services such as Kazaa, makes use of P2P networking. Napster used a client/server system, which left the company liable for illegal file-sharing activities. Since P2P does not use a central server, it makes it more difficult to hold the company responsible for what users do with the software. However, by connecting users directly without a central server, users sacrifice speed and some level of safety. Providing access to your hard drive to thousands of strangers presents opportunities to hackers that they would ordinarily not have.

FIGURE 4.7 • Peer-to-peer (P2P) networking

P2P networking allows users to connect directly to communicate and share resources without the need for a central server.

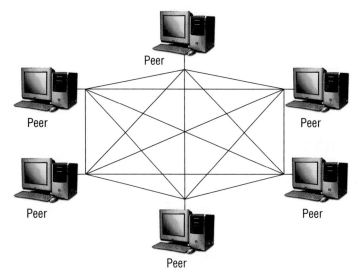

We see now that the Internet can be viewed conceptually as a multi-layer system. We've examined three layers that involve hardware, protocols, and software. Experts refer to the software portion of the Internet as the *application layer*. The protocol portion of the Internet, where client software communicates requests to servers using the packet-switching rules of TCP/IP, is called the *transport layer*. The hardware associated with the Internet is referred to as the *physical layer*. This general three-layer conceptual view of Internet technology is illustrated in Figure 4.8. Network specialists find it useful to use a more detailed, seven-layer model called the *Open System Interconnection (OSI) Model*. The OSI model provides network technicians and administrators with a deeper understanding of networking technology for designing and troubleshooting networks. For those of us just interested in using networks, however, the more general view provided here is enough to assist us in practical use issues, such as selecting an Internet service provider, working with Internet applications, protecting ourselves from hackers, and other issues that will be discussed as you progress through this book.

FIGURE 4.8 • Conceptual layers of the Internet

The Internet can be viewed conceptually as a multilayer system.

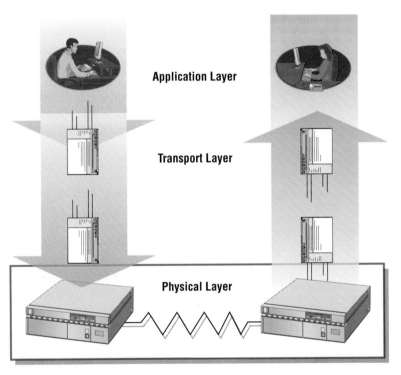

The Internet of today offers a wide assortment of communication options and information. The remainder of this chapter discusses the benefits of and techniques for getting the most out of the Internet, beginning with communication.

INTERNETCOMMUNICATIONS

In Chapter 2, we discussed how the digital revolution has brought us into the age of pervasive computing: we can have access to information wherever we go. Equally important and influential is the birth of *pervasive communications*, the ability to communicate with anyone through a variety of formats from anywhere anytime. Pervasive communications are the result of advances in wireless communications and Internet communications. This technology is fundamentally altering the ways in which personal and professional relationships are created and nurtured.

Synchronous and Asynchronous Communication

No current form of electronic communication can replace the quality and intensity of a face-to-face meeting. When we communicate face to face, we incorporate a number of conscious and subconscious communication tools. Spoken words combine with voice inflection, facial expression, and body language to communicate our thoughts. When we share a physical space, physiological variables are also at work during communication. These include the proximity of and distance between individuals, the environment itself, and unseen but unconsciously sensed characteristics of physical presence such as pheromones—chemical signals between individuals that are not consciously noted, yet have a subtle impact on individuals' behaviors and reactions.

Not all communications require the complexity and intensity of face-to-face communication. Much of our day-to-day communication requires only the transfer of information: "I'll pick you up at 8:00," "I agree to the terms of this contract," "Did you hear about Chuck and Grace?" When choosing a form and format of communication, we balance convenience against the quality of communication. From face-to-face quality down to leaving simple text messages, there is a wide range of options. Each communication option is appropriate for different situations, with some options being inappropriate in some situations.

There are two forms of electronic communication: synchronous and asynchronous. In **synchronous communication**, people communicate in real time. Phrases are transmitted from source to recipient as they are spoken or typed, and the recipient responds in kind (see Figure 4.9). Synchronous communication requires all participants to be engaged in communication at the same time. Telephone conversations, online chat, and instant messaging are examples of synchronous communication. **Asynchronous communication** allows participants to leave messages for each other to be read, heard, or watched, and responded to at the recipient's convenience (see Figure 4.9). Answering machines, voice mail, and e-mail are tools for asynchronous communication.

This section explores the communications options that are available over the Internet and accessible from a variety of computing and communications devices. It looks at how new forms of communication are influencing the way we live and conduct business. It also examines the capabilities and limitations of each communication tool to determine what is appropriate and what is not in today's world of e-communications.

FIGURE 4.9 • **Synchronous and asynchronous communication**

In synchronous communication, participants communicate in real time. In asynchronous communications, participants leave messages for each other, and they can respond to those messages at their convenience.

Synchronous
Birthday Greeting

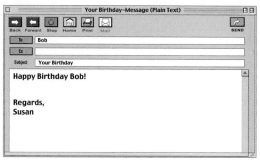

Asynchronous
Birthday Greeting

THIS LOBSTER WAS BROUGHT TO YOU BY . . .

Using special rubber bands with the message "Who Caught Me?" printed on them, along with a code and a Web address, Maine lobstermen are tracking whose plate their crustaceans end up on. Called Lobster Tales, the project illustrates the global nature of a regional industry. It also adds a personal touch, as consumers who log on to the site can learn about the individual who caught their dinner only days before.

Source:
"Tracking the Route of Your Lobster Dinner"
By Katie Zezima
The New York Times
www.nytimes.com/2003/07/24/technology/circuits/24lobs.html
July 24, 2003
Cited on July 25, 2003

Text Communications

Internet text communications take many forms. Available in both synchronous and asynchronous formats, text communication allows participants to communicate via a computer keyboard. The benefits of communicating by text are that it is cheap and fast; the recipient receives what you type within a fraction of a second. The downside of text communication is that it communicates only words, and lacks the information provided by nonverbal cues—such as voice inflection and facial expression. For this reason, text communication is notorious for creating misunderstandings.

To compensate for the lack of nonverbal cues, a method of conveying underlying sentiment has evolved using emoticons. *Emoticons* combine keyboard characters to create a sideways facial expression. Table 4.4 shows some examples of commonly used emoticons and what they mean.

Text communication can also be more time-consuming than the spoken word; just how time-consuming depends on your typing skills. To minimize the inconvenience of typing, people substitute a number of acronyms for commonly used phrases (see Table 4.5; also search the Web for "Internet Acronyms").

TABLE 4.4 • Emoticons

Emoticon	Meaning
:-)	Happy or smiling
:- D	Really happy!
:-}	Embarrassed
:-?	Confused
;-)	Winking

TABLE 4.5 • Internet Acronyms

Acronym	Meaning
L8R	Later
FYI	For your information
LOL	Laughing out loud
ROFL	Rolling on floor laughing
TTFN	Ta ta for now

EXPAND YOUR **KNOWLEDGE**

To learn how to compose and reply to e-mail messages, print e-mail, and more, go to www.course.com/swt. Click the link "Expand Your Knowledge" and then complete the lab entitled, "E-Mail."

E-mail

The number one Internet application, e-mail has opened the door to a relatively new form of communication. So important is e-mail that United Airlines and Continental are both equipping their aircrafts with e-mail service so that, for a small fee, travelers can keep up with their e-mail while in flight.[6]

E-mail (electronic mail) is the transmission of messages over a network to support asynchronous text-based communication. Prior to the Internet, we communicated face-to-face, by phone, or through the post office (snail mail). These forms of communication still serve particular communication needs. Face to face is the ultimate form of communication, but requires travel on the part of one or more participants. Phone communication eliminates the need for travel, but still requires participants to alter their agendas to meet the needs of others. Snail mail allows participants to communicate according to their own schedules, but takes days to deliver. Among these three forms of communication, there is an obvious need that isn't being met: an asynchronous communication that doesn't take days to deliver. E-mail meets that need. E-mail introduced a form of communication that is more convenient and less intrusive than face-to-face or phone communication, and much faster than snail mail. It is perfect for correspondence that does not require immediate dialogue.

E-mail Technology. E-mail uses client/server technology. E-mail clients communicate with e-mail servers to send and receive e-mail messages. E-mail messages, like the packets that carry them, include a header and a body. Sometimes e-mail messages can include an attached file (see Figure 4.10). The *e-mail header* includes technical information about the message: destination address, source address, subject, date and time, and other information required by the server. The *e-mail body* is an *ASCII text* message written by the sender to the recipient. The e-mail body may be presented as a text message or as an HTML document—a Web page. An e-mail message body cannot contain *binary data*—data that is intended for a processor to process. An **e-mail attachment** is typically a binary file or a formatted text file that travels along with an e-mail message but is not part of the e-mail ASCII text message itself.

FIGURE 4.10 • E-mail components

E-mail messages include a header and body, and sometimes an attached file.

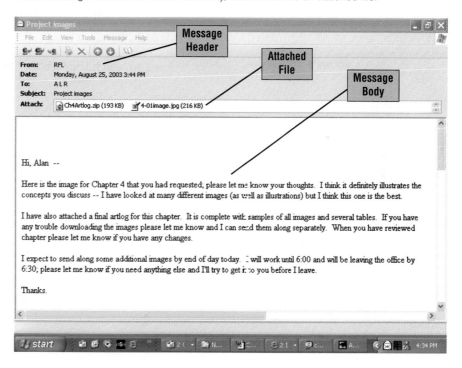

E-mail servers pass e-mail messages back and forth following the rules of the *Simple Mail Transfer Protocol (SMTP). The Multipurpose Internet Mail Extensions (MAPI)* protocol governs the transportation of e-mail attachments. An e-mail client, such as Outlook or Eudora, accesses e-mail from an e-mail server using either the Post Office Protocol (POP) or the Internet Message Access Protocol (IMAP). When you use the *Post Office Protocol (POP)* to access your e-mail, your incoming messages are transferred from the e-mail server to your PC for you to read and store. If you use *Internet Message Access Protocol (IMAP)* only the e-mail headers of your incoming messages are transferred to your PC. The actual messages are left on the server

where you can view them in your client window. *Web-based* e-mail stores your e-mail on a Web server, and you view the messages using your Web browser.

Broadcast E-mail. E-mail is ideal for sending, or *broadcasting*, messages to groups. Special interest groups, called *listservs*, create online communities for discussing topic-related issues via e-mail. E-mail sent to the listserv is forwarded to all members. The "Mom's Online Chat" listserv, for example, has over 12,000 subscribers who discuss issues of parenthood from a mother's perspective. Visit CataList at www.lsoft.com/lists/listref.html for a complete list of all public listservs. Many private clubs and organizations create listservs for their members to use for group communication. For example, the National Weather Service uses a listserv to help get the word out quickly when a tornado warning is in effect.

E-mail Newsletters. Another form of broadcast e-mail is subscription-based *newsletters*. E-mail newsletters can be general or specific in nature. For example, you can subscribe to the *New York Times* newsletter (www.nytimes.com) and receive the daily news in your e-mail box each morning (see Figure 4.11); the same articles delivered to the doorstep of New Yorkers in the print newspaper. You could subscribe to *ComputerWorld* (www.computerworld.com) and receive daily technology news. There are stock market reports, sports enthusiast newsletters, dog lovers' newsletters, the list goes on and on. These types of broadcast e-mail are like mailing lists, and they provide one-way communication. They do not allow subscribers to reply or contribute to the group as listservs do. Their purpose is to deliver news and information to interested people.

FIGURE 4.11 • The *New York Times* Newsletter

The *New York Times* newsletter subscription service delivers the daily news to your e-mail box.

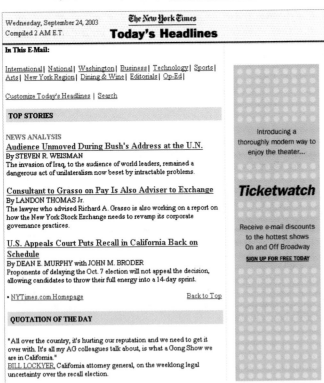

E-mail Issues. E-mail has its share of problems. Increases in the amounts of unsolicited e-mail, or **spam**, are driving Internet users to the limit of their patience. Laws are being proposed in both federal and state governments to place controls on advertising through e-mail.

E-mail can also be dangerous. Once you send an e-mail, there's no taking it back. Messages sent in anger can ruin a friendship. Employees have been fired for sending inappropriate e-mail to coworkers that are then forwarded to supervisors. Nearly everyone who uses e-mail has an embarrassing story to tell. Most of us quickly learn that e-mail should never be sent in anger. If you are angry, allow yourself time to cool off. Always remember that e-mail can and will be forwarded to just about anyone. E-mail can also be used as evidence in a court of law.

E-mail offers all the benefits and suffers from all the shortcomings of text-based asynchronous communications. Because of the lack of nonverbal cues, and intimacy, e-mail communication is inappropriate for intense or complicated discussions. It should be used for touching base, for communicating about light and superficial topics, or as a follow-up to previous voice or face-to-face conversations. Lengthy and deep e-mail messages should be reserved for your closest friends and family. Business-related e-mail should not be used for conversations that require a

COMMUNITY /\/\/\ TECHNOLOGY

Spam! Spam! Spam! Spam!

Spam is an aggravation for most Internet users, except perhaps marketers. Spam is unsolicited advertisements that arrive in your e-mail box. One explanation for it's being called spam is that it is named after a famous comedy skit performed by the British comedy troop "Monty Python" (see www.detritus.org/spam/skit.html). In the skit, restaurant customers can only order a menu item if it contains the processed meat. The restaurant goers are stuck with spam, just as we are stuck with junk e-mail.

Ryan Hamlin, general manager of Microsoft's anti-spam technology and strategy group believes that the spam problem is going to get worse. "Spam has reached epic proportions, and we are in a crisis situation," said Hamlin, who estimates that as much as 65% of total e-mail is spam. He believes that the situation has gotten so bad that some people are willing to give up e-mail if the spam situation does not get better. This is more than an inconvenience, he predicts that the filtering software and storage space required to deal with spam will cost us $18 billion in 2004.

The Anti-Spam Research Group (ASRG) believes that they have a solution. It includes several technologies, including:

- Simple authentication technology that will verify the sender of a message.
- "Trusted sender" technology to identify trustworthy e-mail senders.
- Reputation systems and interfaces that allow Internet users to identify good and bad e-mail sources.

Most of the technology industry is focused on the problem, since it threatens the industry itself. Federal and state governments are also interested since a remedy for spam is sure to please voters. The industry is coming up with technical solutions, while government is working to approve stiff penalties. With so many industrial and government entities working towards the same goal, there is an opportunity to implement solutions in a quick and effective manner. All involved seem to feel that spam will no longer be considered a problem by the end of 2005.

Questions

1. Track your daily e-mail over the course of a week. On average, what percentage of your daily e-mail is spam?
2. Of the spam that you receive, how much of it has some value to you?
3. Do you think that industry and government will provide an effective solution to stomp out spam? Why or why not?

Sources
1. *"Microsoft: Spam can be contained within two years, But it's going to get worse first," Joris Evers Joris,* IDG News Service, *May 30, 2003, www.computerworld.com accessed June 7, 2003.*
2. *"Major Internet Standards Group Working On Fast Plan To Can Spam," Mitch Wagner,* Internet Week, *May 25, 2003, www.internetweek.com/security02/showArticle.jhtml?articleID= 10100236 accessed June 7, 2003.*
3. *"Antispam measure gains steam in House," Declan McCullagh and Jim Hu,* ZDNet News, *May 23, 2003, http://zdnet.com.com/2100-1105_2-1009467.html accessed June 7, 2003.*

lengthy back and forth dialogue. An e-mail conversation that might require days of back and forth correspondences could be replaced by one brief phone call.

E-mail, in all its convenience, can be abused. Keep your e-mail messages short and to the point. Be aware that some people simply cannot or will not answer every e-mail they receive. If you don't get a reply about something that is important to you, pick up the phone; don't bombard the person with more e-mail messages.

Since e-mail is such a popular form of communication, many of us are finding ourselves buried in it. When you find yourself buried in e-mail, consider the following e-mail management strategy:

1. If you maintain multiple e-mail accounts, use *mail forwarding* to have your messages forwarded to one central account.
2. Use e-mail filters to filter out spam and other forms of less important broadcast e-mail and deposit them into appropriate folders for future review.
3. Check your e-mail every day. If your e-mail gets backlogged over a couple of days, scan through it from most recent to oldest.
4. When first reviewing new e-mail, do a quick scan, looking for messages that may require an immediate response and messages from individuals high on your priority list. Quick response times are a sure method of making a good impression.
5. Do not open any file attachments without first checking them with antivirus software, or the source of the e-mail to confirm that they are legitimate and do not contain a virus.
6. The goal of every e-mail session should be to reply, deal with, and file or delete all e-mail messages in your inbox. The only messages that you intentionally leave in your inbox should be those that require action ASAP. Your e-mail inbox can act as a to-do list.
7. E-mail that you wish to save for future reference should be sorted into folders by topic. For instance, you may have a folder for friends, another for humor, another for news, and others for various projects.

Discussion Boards and News Groups

Discussion boards, also called newsgroups, are similar to listservs, except that rather than using e-mail to facilitate discussion, they use a central *bulletin board* on the Internet. Users log on to the bulletin board to post, read, and reply to messages. Discussion boards can be public or private and created to support specific topics. For example, you may have a private discussion board for your class to use to post questions and comments regarding class material. Discussion boards are also used by private organizations. Some companies provide online assistance to their customers through Web discussion boards. For example, Macromedia (creators of the popular Web browser plug-in *Flash)* has an online customer support page that provides access to "Forums" for each Macromedia product where you can post questions. Tech support agents are online to answer the questions that are posted.

Usenet newsgroups maintain thousands of public discussion forums that are accessible using news reader software that connects to a Usenet server. But don't let the name fool you: Newsgroups do not provide news, but rather provide a forum for discussing news and other topics. You can find out more about Usenet at www.usenet.org. Many discussion boards have migrated from Usenet to the Web, and are accessed using a Web browser.

When using discussion boards and other forms of Internet communication there are some important rules of conduct to follow. First off, always check if the topic or question you wish to post has already been posted by another user. Duplicate posts are annoying for all participants. When posting or replying to a post always follow proper netiquette—network etiquette. *Netiquette*[7] is a set of rules of conduct for communicating online (see Figure 4.12).

FIGURE 4.12 • **Rules of netiquette**

Netiquette rules should be observed with e-mail, discussion groups, and all online communications. For more on netiquette, run a search at your favorite search engine on "netiquette"; you'll find an abundant amount of information.

RULES OF NETIQUETTE
Based on The Netiquette Home Page
(http://www.albion.com/netiquette/)

1 **Remember the human.**
Text-based communication makes it easy to forget that there is a person with feelings behind the words. Do unto others as you'd have others do unto you.

2 **Adhere to the same standards of behavior online that you follow in real life.**
Communicating online sometimes gives one a false sense of anonymity. Remember that your personal reputation is affected by what you say online.

3 **Know where you are in cyberspace.**
Different regions of the Internet require different levels of formality. Communicate with figures of authority or business colleagues with more formality than you would use with a friend.

4 **Respect other people's time and bandwidth.**
Do not waste the time of the people with whom you are communicating with redundant questions or needlessly lengthy dialog. Be brief and to the point.

5 **Make yourself look good online.**
Always present your best side.

6 **Share expert knowledge.**
Contribute your wisdom to the Internet community. Correct misinformation presented by others.

7 **Help keep flame wars under control.**
When insults are being hurled (flame wars), step in to intercede.

8 **Respect other people's privacy.**
Keep clear of rumors and speaking of others behind their backs.

9 **Don't abuse your power.**
The Internet is power. Use it for good rather than evil.

10 **Be forgiving of other people's mistakes.**
After all, we're only human. Remember that you were once a newbie (new user) too!

Chat

Internet **chat** involves synchronous text messaging between two or more participants. Participants log on to a chat server and send each other text messages in real time. As with most forms of group messaging, Chat forums are organized by topics. Some services call the various topic related forums *channels;* others call them *chat rooms.* The most popular public chat utility is called Internet Relay Chat

(IRC). IRC has thousands of channels. Any IRC participant can create a channel. At any given time there can be hundreds of thousands of users logged on to IRC. Each channel has a moderator empowered to control the dialog and even kick users out if they get unruly. Check www.irc.org for more information on IRC.

Other than moderators, chat and many forms of Internet communication are uncensored. If the Internet had a rating system, many chat rooms would be rated for adult use only.

As with most Internet technologies, chat is migrating to the Web. Many public and private chat Web sites are in use today. Two of the most popular are Yahoo!Chat (http://chat.yahoo.com) and AOL Chat (www.aol.com/community/ chat/allchats. html). For a unique chat experience check out www.worlds.com. Worlds.com provides a free software download that interacts with the Worlds server to create a virtual environment (see Figure 4.13). Participants in this chat environment select an *avatar,* a 3-D physical representation of themselves, which they navigate through the virtual world, chatting and interacting with other participants and their avatars. There's even a club where avatars can dance the night away.

Most chat programs allow you to chat in groups or one on one with a group member. Chat is a popular way of meeting new people on the Internet. However, you should be cautious when making a new acquaintance. The Internet population includes every type of person, including some people who are dangerous. Don't trust that anyone is necessarily who they say they are. Never give your real name, phone number, e-mail address, home address, or other private information to others on the Internet.

FIGURE 4.13 • World Chat
Chat participants navigate their avatars through a virtual world.

Instant Messaging (IM)

Instant messaging is a form of chat for one-on-one communications over the Internet. With instant messaging, participants build *buddy lists* or *contact lists,* that allow them to keep track of which people are currently logged on to the Internet. You can send messages to one of your online buddies, which opens up a small dialogue window on your buddy's computer and allows the two of you to chat via the keyboard (see Figure 4.14). Typical instant messaging software supports the following services:

- Instant messages. Send notes back and forth with a friend who is online
- Chat. Create your own custom chat room with friends or coworkers
- Web links. Share links to your favorite Web sites
- Images. Look at an image stored on your friend's computer
- Sounds. Play sounds for your friends
- Files. Share files by sending them directly to your friends
- Talk. Use the Internet instead of a phone to verbally speak with friends
- Streaming content. Look at real-time or near-real-time stock quotes and news

FIGURE 4.14 • Windows Messenger Instant Messaging
Instant messaging, another form of chat, allows participants to interact in one-on-one dialogues.

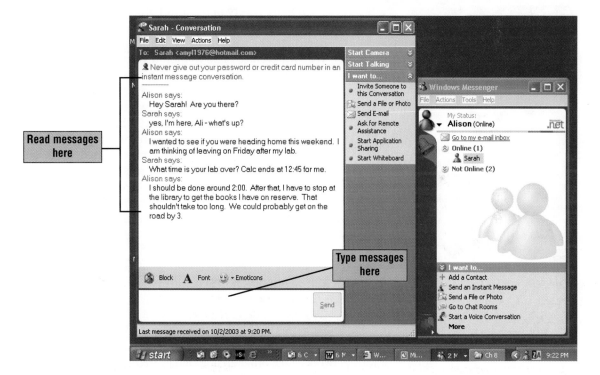

The four most popular instant messaging services are America Online Instant Messenger (AIM), MSN Messenger, ICQ (another AOL company), and Yahoo! Messenger. All four of these are free services to Internet users and provide client software that you can download for free. The downside is that each of these products is *proprietary*—they do not communicate with each other. So, if you use AOL Instant Messenger, you will be able to chat only with others using AOL Instant Messenger, not people using ICQ, MSN, or Yahoo! The proprietary nature of instant messaging may be changing however, because rivals Microsoft and AOL are working to interconnect their services.[8]

Instant messaging started out as a fun communication tool for personal use, but it is becoming a serious business tool. Business users are discovering that instant messaging improves productivity and saves money by allowing employees to participate in virtual conferences and collaborate on projects from any location.

Short Message Service (SMS) and Texting

Short Message Service (SMS) is a method of sending short messages, no longer than 160 characters, between cell phones. Using the alphanumeric keypad of the cell phone, users enter a short message and send it to a friend's cell phone (see Figure 4.15). The activity of sending text messages is called texting. Once a message is sent, it is received by a Short Message Service Center (SMSC), which must then get it to the appropriate mobile device. If the intended recipient is off line or out of range, the SMSC holds the message and delivers it when the recipient returns.

SMS is a digital technology and available only on digital cell phones. Most cell phones today make use of the digital Global System for Mobile Communications (GSM) network. It is predicted that the global GSM population will exceed one billion users in 2004. With the popularity of digital cell phone communication rising, cell phone texting is likely to become as popular as e-mail. In fact Internet communications and cell phone communications are beginning to merge. Some services allow messages to be sent from the Web to a cell phone and from cell phones to e-mail addresses.

FIGURE 4.15 • Texting with SMS

Many of today's popular cell phones support text messaging.

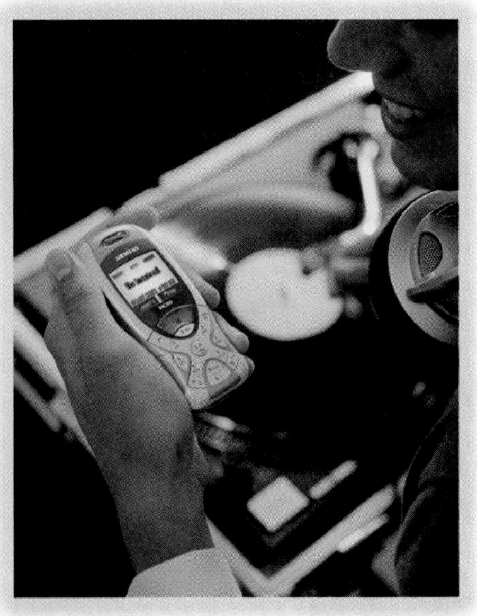

Texting is very popular in Europe and Japan, where many cell phone users view their phones more as a texting device than a voice device. In the United Kingdom, texting becomes more popular every year. An average of 55 million text messages were sent each day in mid-2003, almost twice as many as sent in 2001.[9] British banks are turning to texting to allow customers to interact with their accounts.[10] One study shows that, where offered, one in five bank customers makes use of texting to view bank statements and accounts and receive automatic alerts when their account is overdrawn. Texting is increasing in popularity in the United States and in businesses around the world. American Airlines has begun using text messaging to notify passengers if their flights are delayed. The New York Police Department is using text messaging to run license plate checks.

Because texting is limited in both the length of messages and the keyboard used to enter messages, the use of acronyms is abundant. In fact some text messages are so abbreviated that they are hardly understandable to the novice. Can you figure out what is being communicated with "UR2KIn2ME"? (It is "you are too kind to me.")

Voice Communications

Traditional telephone communications travel as analog signals over telecommunications networks. Like other analog signals that have been digitized, however, telephone communications will soon migrate from analog to digital. If you consider the benefits of digitization discussed in Chapter 2, and the fact that the Internet traverses the same networks as telephone communications, it makes sense that telephone communications would make the change from analog to digital and travel the network in packets, the same as Internet communications. The transition to digital transmission of voice via packets is already gaining momentum in the telephone industry. Sprint recently announced that "it has begun transforming its telephone network so voice calls are transmitted in packets—the same way that data move over the Internet. The move is designed to lead to a wide range of improved services for consumers, such as online voice-mail management".[11]

Once voice communications are fully converted to digital, the services offered by telephone systems and the Internet will intermingle. You will be able to access voice mail from your computer and e-mail on your phone. We will no longer think in terms of phones and computers, but rather in terms of communication devices that support voice, text, and video communications in both synchronous and asynchronous modes.

Video Communications

Video communications are becoming more prevalent as technology advances to support it. Although "video phones" have been anticipated since the 1950s, the computer industry is finally making the concept a reality. We learned in Chapter 2 that video consumes large quantities of bytes. Consider the display on your computer screen. Using 600 x 800 resolution and 16 bit color, it requires 960 KB to store the image on a computer screen. High-quality video, such as that used for television, displays 30 images, or frames, per second. Such video would require a data transfer rate of 230.4 Mb per second. This is a hundred times faster than high-speed Internet connections can support. To work around this limitation, video communications make use of small (3 to 4-inch) video windows, slower rates of frames per second (typically 15 fps or less), and sometimes fewer colors or monochrome images. Such sacrifices in video size and quality have made video communications a reality today. Video communications can take place over a standalone video phone, a TV-based video phone, or a PC-based video phone.

Standalone video phones provide video phone service over traditional phone lines. These devices follow the H.324 standard, and use computer modem technology to send digital signals over the analog phone network. Video phones may combine the phone and video display/camera in one unit or, as in the case of the "Beamer" Phone Video Station™ (PVS) offered by Vialta Inc. (see Figure 4.16), the display/camera unit may be sold separately and work in conjunction with your existing phone.

TV-based video phones use a set-top box equipped with a video camera and microphone that work in conjunction with a television set and phone line. *PC-based video phones* make use of the multimedia functionality of today's PC with an Internet connection. All that is required is a headset or speakers with a microphone, a video camera, or Webcam, and video communication software. Microsoft's Net-Meeting is a popular video communication program for the PC, and iChat AV is popular for use on Apple computers. Both products are free to download from the manufacturer's Web site.

FIGURE 4.16 • Video phone technology
The Vialta Beamer is a phone video station that works in conjunction with an existing phone over standard phone lines.

Although video communications have just recently become popular with home users for personal communications, this method of communication has been used in businesses for quite some time. The privately owned high-speed networks of the business community have provided the perfect platform for video conferencing.

Video conferencing is a technology that combines video and phone call capabilities along with shared data and document access. It is replacing the need for travel in many industries. Through high-speed Internet and private network connections, individuals are able to communicate with associates around the world in face-to-face meetings. Several products that support this technology over the Web—called *Web conferencing*—are on the market. Using Web conferencing, groups can see, hear, text chat, present, and share information in a collaborative manner.

Although not quite as powerful as video phone, some new cell phones are coming equipped with digital cameras and multimedia messaging service. *Multimedia messaging service (MMS)* allows mobile phone users to send pictures, voice recordings, and video clips to other cell phones or e-mail accounts. Mostly marketed as a novelty, these camera phones have potential for serious professional applications. For professions that benefit from or require the collection of on-site photos, camera phones can provide significant convenience. Insurance claim investigators, realtors, architects, construction supervisors, and crime scene investigators all could appreciate the convenience of snapping shots and e-mailing them to the home office or their own e-mail account for future reference. It is predicted that nearly 100 million people will subscribe to the MMS service by 2007.[12]

The ability to casually and secretly snap pictures with a device that doesn't look like a camera is causing some privacy concerns. The government in Victoria, Australia, has recognized inappropriate uses of mobile phone cameras. They have noticed a trend where photos of individuals are secretly taken and published on the Web. They are particularly concerned with issues of child pornography and are drafting laws to control the situation.[13]

WEBTECHNOLOGY

The World Wide Web was developed by Tim Berners-Lee in his research at CERN, the European Organization for Nuclear Research in Geneva, between 1989 and 1991 and released to the public in the form of the Mosaic Web browser in 1993. What he originally conceived of as an organizational tool to help keep track of his own personal documents has grown into an organizational tool that helps hundreds of millions of users share and access information through an intuitive graphical user interface. The **World Wide Web** (or just **the Web**) is a client/server Internet application that links together related documents from diverse sources providing an easy navigation system with which to find information.

The process of "linking together" documents from diverse sources requires three components:

1. A defined system for linking the documents
2. Protocols that allow different computers to communicate
3. Tools to assist in creating the documents and the links between them

Tim Berners-Lee came up with all three: hyperlinks for linking documents, the Hypertext Transfer Protocol (HTTP) along with server and client software to manage communications between different computers, and HTML, a language for creating and linking documents.

Over the past decade many new technologies have been developed that work with Berners-Lee's original Web technologies to deliver richer Web content—animation, video, music, and computer programs. This section covers the Web from the basics to state of the art technologies.

The Hyperlink Concept

The cornerstone of Tim Berners-Lee's World Wide Web is the hyperlink. A **hyperlink** is an element in an electronic document, a word, phrase or image, that when clicked, opens a related document. By relating documents to each other using hyperlinks, you form a Web of interrelated information that is logically arranged and easy to navigate (see Figure 4.17). Some differentiate between *hypertext,* text that acts as a link, and *hypermedia,* pictures or other media that act as links.

FIGURE 4.17 • Hyperlinks

By relating documents to each other using hyperlinks, you form a Web of interrelated information that is logically arranged and easy to navigate.

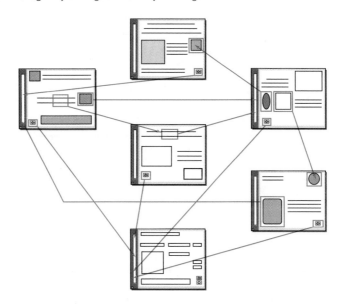

Hypertext Transfer Protocol (HTTP), Web Servers, and Browsers

Hypertext Transfer Protocol (HTTP) is the protocol used to control communication between Web clients and servers. A Web client, usually called a **Web browser**, is used to request Web pages from Web servers. A **Web server** stores and delivers Web pages and other Web services. Markup languages are used to create Web pages, and include commands that specify the format of the objects on a Web page. Web browsers interpret those commands to present the Web page content.

Web browsers are available for a number of different computing platforms. Desktop computers, notebook computers, and handheld computers all include Web browsers. Some cell phones now come equipped with Web browsers. Many popular Web sites are providing content in a stripped down form for convenient navigating on a small PDA or cell phone display. The Web is also available on televisions by using special Internet-connected set-top boxes. In the world of pervasive computing, Web interfaces are cropping up on all kinds of objects—from refrigerators to automobiles.

Uniform Resource Locator (URL)

A Web page location or address is represented by a **Uniform Resource Locator (URL)**. A URL indicates where a particular Web page resides on the Internet. Figure 4.18 identifies the different components of a URL.

FIGURE 4.18 • Components of a URL

The URL *http://www.course.com/cca/ch1/index.html* consists of several components.

Protocol	Web Server	Domain Name	Location on Server	Requested File
http://	www.	course.com/	cca/ch1/	index.html

The final portion of the domain name, .com, .edu, and so on, is called the *top-level domain (TLD)*. Top-level domains classify Internet locations by type or, in the case if international Web sites, by location. Table 4.6 lists some of the more popular top-level domains in use today. TLDs for international Web sites include abbreviations such as .cn for China, .au for Australia, and dozens of others.

TABLE 4.6 • Popular Top-Level Domains

TLD	Description
.com	Commercial business
.biz	Commercial business
.edu	Educational institution
.org	Nonprofit organization
.net	Networking service
.gov	Government agency
.name	Personal

It is becoming increasingly popular to create personal Web sites, under a personal domain name. For example, Jerry Jawalski could purchase the name jerry.jawalski.name, which includes the e-mail address jerry@jawalski.name, and the URL http://www.jerry.jawalski.name for as little as $15 per year. The price includes only ownership of the name; Jerry would still have to find a Web server on which to store his Web site.

EXPAND YOUR **KNOWLEDGE**

To learn more about how to create Web pages, go to www.course.com/swt. Click the link "Expand Your Knowledge" and then complete the lab entitled, "Creating Web Pages."

Web Markup Languages

The primary markup language that is used to specify the formatting of a Web page is called **Hypertext Markup Language (HTML)**. Web pages are sometimes called HTML documents. HTML uses tags to describe the formatting of a page. An **HTML tag** is a specific command indicated with angle brackets (< >) that tells a Web browser how to display items on a page. Figure 4.19 illustrates HTML code and how the browser interprets it. Note that commands act on the text between the opening command in brackets, and the closing command in brackets with a forward slash. Thus, <b>HTML</b> tells the browser to display the letters HTML in a bold font. Viewing the figure, can you guess what effect the <em> command has?

FIGURE 4.19 • Hypertext Markup Language (HTML)

The HTML code at the top is read by a Web browser, which displays the content on the bottom.

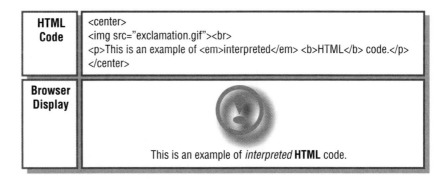

| HTML Code | ```
<center>
<img src="exclamation.gif"><br>
<p>This is an example of <em>interpreted</em> <b>HTML</b> code.</p>
</center>
``` |
| --- | --- |
| Browser Display | This is an example of *interpreted* **HTML** code. |

A number of newer Web markup languages are increasing in popularity. The one that most promises to change the landscape of the Web is Extensible Markup Language (XML). **XML** is a markup language for designing data classification to organize the content of Web pages and other documents. Although HTML provides a method of describing the format of a Web page, XML provides a method for describing and classifying the data in a Web page. Compare the HTML code and XML code in Figure 4.20. Although the XML code is simplified for the purpose of this example, it clearly illustrates how data is classified in XML code. In contrast, the HTML code says only how the data should look, and says nothing about the purpose of the data.

FIGURE 4.20 • XML

XML provides a method of describing or classifying data in a Web page.

Web Content	HTML Code	XML Code
Reebok® Classic Ace Tennis Shoe $49.95 Soft leather tennis shoe. Lightweight EVA molded midsole. Rubber outsole. China.	```<strong><font face="Verdana, Arial, Helvetica, sans-serif">Reebok® Classic Ace Tennis Shoe </font></strong> <strong>$49.95</strong> <table width="100%" border="1"><tr><td>Soft leather tennis shoe. Lightweight EVA molded midsole. Rubber outsole. China. </td></tr></table>```	```<product type="shoes"> <name> Reebok Classis Ace Tennis Shoe </name> <price>$49.95</price> <description> Soft leather tennis shoe. Lightweight EVA molded midsole. Rubber outsole. China. </description> </product>```

XML provides several advantages, to both Web content publishers and viewers. Publishers are able to use XML to separate data from Web page formatting. This is possible because XML Web content is implemented using several files: one that defines the structure of the data (product, name, price, and description), another that provides the actual data (Reebok, $49.95, and so on), and a third that defines the format of the presentation of the data in a Web browser. This method of organization offers great convenience to organizations that may change the content of a Web page frequently. For example, a news organization can use the same layout for their Web page, but change the data from day to day to reflect the latest news.
```

The structured data approach of XML provides convenience for Web browsing as well. Web searches become much easier when Web site content is classified and defined using XML tags. Imagine that the HTML and XML code in Figure 4.20 included many tennis shoes. It would be much easier for a search engine to find a match for "price < $60" in the XML code than in the HTML code.

XML has gained such approval from Web developers that the World Wide Web Consortium (W3C), the organization that develops and approves Web standards, is endorsing a successor to HTML called XHTML. *XHTML* embodies the best of both HTML and XML in one markup language. It is anticipated that XHTML will gradually replace HTML as the primary markup language of the Web.

Web Browser Plug-ins

HTML is a useful language for formatting text, adding color, and adding images to Web pages. However, HTML is not robust in its support of multimedia and user interaction. For that reason, there are plug-ins and helper applications.

A **plug-in** works with a Web browser to offer extended services—typically the ability to view audio, animations, or video. When a Web page contains content that requires a plug-in, you are typically provided with the opportunity to download and install the necessary tool at no cost, if you don't already have it. Macromedia's *Flash* is the most popular plug-in used today. Over 532 million copies have been downloaded for use by over 98% of Web users. Flash enables users to view animations and videos, and interact with games and other multimedia content (see Figure 4.21).

Many of the plug-ins available today address the issue of transferring large media files over the Web. The traditional method of viewing Web content is to request a file from a Web server by typing a URL or clicking a link, waiting while the file downloads to your computer, and then viewing the file in the Web browser window. The large size of audio and video files would leave users waiting for minutes, even hours, after they clicked a link before they could view the file. Some systems are able to reduce the wait by compressing the files to smaller sizes

FIGURE 4.21 • Flash computer games

Flash adds animation and interactivity to the Web.

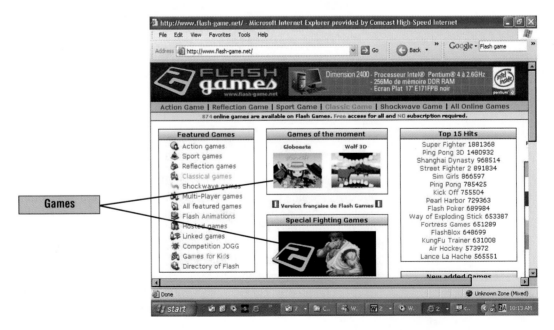

and storing the multimedia content in a more efficient manner. Another technique to deliver multimedia without the wait is called content streaming. With **content streaming**, sometimes called streaming media, streaming video, or streaming audio, the media begins playing while the file is still being delivered. Problems arise with this technique only when the speed of play outpaces the speed of delivery.

Programming the Web

More than just a tool for delivering information and multimedia, the Web also enables users to interact with data and programs. For example, through Web pages, users often interact with databases. Anytime you do a Web search, whether at Google or Amazon, a program running on the Web server takes your input and uses it to query a database. The results of the query are then displayed in the Web browser. The Web is being used in this capacity in private environments also. An organization may provide a method for its employees to access the corporate database through a Web page secured with a login prompt. Employees could then run queries from any Internet connection, just as if they were sitting in the office. The three most prevalent programming languages used to implement this type of interactivity are Java, JavaScript, and ActiveX.

Java is an object-oriented programming language that allows software engineers to create programs that run on any computer platform. This makes it the ideal programming language for the Web and the ability to program in Java is a highly regarded skill for programmers. Nearly 4,000 job ads at www.monster.com include references to Java. Java applications are commonly used on the Web to allow users to do everything from walk through a virtual world to view products in 3-D (see Figure 4.22) to calculate a mortgage payment.

JavaScript is similar to Java in that it provides functionality in Web pages. However, the two languages are very different. Java is a full-fledged programming language for all computing environments, but JavaScript was developed specifically for the Web and is more limited in nature. JavaScript code can be embedded directly into an HTML file to provide interactive Web pages. The effects of JavaScript code can be subtle, such as changing an image on a Web page when the mouse pointer moves over it. JavaScript can also be used to create more powerful programs that interact with data submitted by the user in a Web page form to pro-vide useful information.

Microsoft has created an alternative to JavaScript called *ActiveX*. ActiveX controls are included with some Web pages to provide interactivity or animation. You may have had warning messages pop up on your Web browser screen asking for your permission to install an ActiveX control. It's wise to avoid installing unsigned ActiveX controls from Web sites that you are unfamiliar with. "Unsigned" signifies that the ActiveX control is not registered—which in itself is not a danger. But an unsigned ActiveX control from an unknown source could contain a virus. ActiveX controls work only on Microsoft products. In other words, they are not supported by Web browsers other than Microsoft Internet Explorer.

FIGURE 4.22 • 3-D product viewer

Java applications allow viewers to rotate products on the screen for a complete 360-degree view. This Web page gives you a feel for driving a Mercedes SL55.

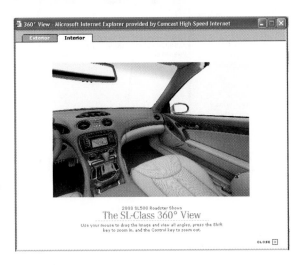

Cookies

Have you ever had a Web page greet you by name? It's becoming increasingly common for Web pages to recognize visitors and present content based on the visitor's interests. This is made possible through a technology called cookies.

Cookies are small text files that are stored on and retrieved from your computer by a Web server each time you visit a Web page (see Figure 4.23). Not all Web pages contain cookies, but many do. Cookies are typically used to store information about who you are and what your interests are. For example, www.weather.com includes a link asking, "Want us to remember your location?" If you click the link, it asks for your name, birth date, zip code, and an area of interest. After you submit this information, it is stored in a cookie on your computer. The next time you visit weather.com, the server retrieves the cookie and greets you with your name, local weather, and items of interest. If you make a purchase at Amazon.com, the next time you visit, rather than the generic welcome page, you see a page customized with your name and a list of products similar to the ones you previously purchased. For example, if you bought a cookbook on your last visit to Amazon, you will see advertisements for cookbooks and cooking supplies on your next visit (see Figure 4.24).

Some Web sites store information about visitors' interests in a database on the server. When a visitor arrives at the site, a cookie containing the visitor's ID number is collected, the ID number is used to access related data in the database, and the Web page is altered to reflect the visitor's preferences. Storing only a user ID number rather than the full user profile in a cookie is more economical and allows the Web publisher to analyze visitor patterns. Web publishers can gain considerable understanding about visitor interests by keeping track of the pages within the Web site that are visited and the amount of time the visitor spends on each page.

Cookies are typically used to offer convenience to users. However, some privacy advocates criticize cookies as gathering too much information about visitors and criticize companies for using that information in marketing. On the other

FIGURE 4.23 • Cookies in Internet Explorer
Cookies are files that are stored on and retrieved from your computer each time you visit a Web page.

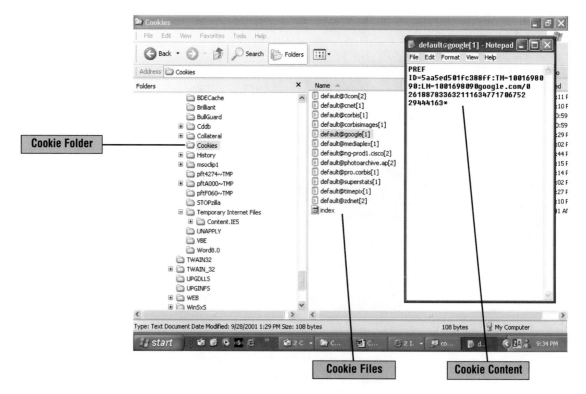

FIGURE 4.24 • The effect of cookies at Amazon.com

Cookies can assist a Web site in customizing your viewing experience.

hand, keep in mind that cookies can only store information that you yourself have entered into Web forms, and about the places that you visit while on the Web site.

Web browsers allow users to disable cookies. However, cookies are such an integral part of the Web that most Web sites assume that cookies are enabled, and some will even deny you access if you block cookies. If you disable cookies, or set your browser to request an okay before accepting a cookie, you will find that nearly all Web sites attempt to place at least one cookie on your computer either when you arrive at the site or when you click a link. Some Web sites will place as many as six or more cookies on your computer.

Search Engines, Subject Directories, and Portals

The fundamental purpose of the Web is to make it easier to find related documents from disperse sources by following hyperlinks. However, the Web has become so large that many complain of *information overload*; the inability to find the information you need due to the overabundance of unrelated information. In efforts to relieve us of the strain of information overload, Web developers have provided powerful tools to assist in organizing and cataloging Web content. This section provides a look at those tools.

A **search engine** is a valuable tool that enables us to find information on the Web by specifying words that are key to our topic of interest—*keywords*. Search engines scour the Web with bots (automated programs) called *spiders* that follow all Web links in an attempt to catalog every Web page by topic. The process is called Web *crawling*, and due to the ever-changing nature of the Web, it is a job that never ends.

One of the challenges of Web crawling is determining which of the words on any given Web page describe its topic. Different search engines use different

YOU ARE THERE

A technology company has created a new 3D distribution system for noncommercial portals they liken to an Internet version of the Public Broadcasting System. Their aim is to provide an open-source browser with access to reliable, educational information—from NASA to dolphin research—all in three-dimensional imagery.

Source:
"Portals in space"
By Paul Festa
CNET News.com
http://news.com.com/2008-1082_3-5056441.html?tag=lh
July 28, 2003
Cited on July 29, 2003

methods. Methods include counting word occurrences within the Web page, evaluating nouns and verbs in the pages title and subtitle, using keywords provided by the page's author in a <meta> tag, and evaluating the words used in links to the page from other pages. Once the search engine has a reasonable idea of a page's topic, it records the URL, page title, and associated information and keywords.

The next challenge facing a search engine, is determining which of the hundreds or thousands of Web pages associated with a particular keyword are most useful. The method of ranking Web pages from most relevant to least differs from search engine to search engine. Google uses a popularity contest approach. Web pages that are referenced from other Web pages are ranked higher than those that are not. Each reference is considered a vote for the referenced page. The more votes a Web page gets, the higher its rank. References from higher-ranked pages weigh more heavily than those from lower-ranked pages.

After finding, sorting, and ranking all the Web pages possible, a search engine stores the information in a database, and enables users to run keyword searches on the database. The database is continuously checked and refreshed so that it is an accurate reflection of the current status of the Web. When you search for a topic at any search engine, you are actually searching a database, and not the Web. Most search engines work hard to make sure that their database accurately reflects the Web's current state, but at times you will find that links presented in search results are no longer active.

A *meta search engine* allows you to run keyword searches on several search engines at once. For example, a search run from www.dogpile.com returns results from Ask Jeeves, FAST, FindWhat, Google, LookSmart, Overture, and other search engines.

A *subject directory* is a catalog of sites collected and organized by human beings. Yahoo.com, perhaps the most well-known Web site, provides a directory that divides Web topics into 14 general categories with many subcategories and levels of subcategories under each. Subject directories are often called subject trees because they start with relatively few main categories and then branch out into many subcategories, topics, and subtopics. Subject directories contain only a small percent of all existing Web pages, but because they are created by human beings—not bots—they are sure to contain relevant information. Subject directories are ideal for finding general information on popular or scholarly subjects. If you are looking for something more specific, you need to use a search engine.

Web portals are Web pages that serve as entry points to the Web. They typically include a search engine, a subject directory, daily headlines, and other items of interest (see Figure 4.25). They can be general or topic-specific in nature. Web portals are designed to be the first page that is displayed when you open your Web browser. Yahoo.com, lycos.com, and msn.com are examples of horizontal Web portals; horizontal refers to the fact that they cover a wide range of topics. Vertical Web portals focus on special interests groups. For example, the iVillage.com portal focuses on items of interest to women, and askmen.com is a vertical portal for men.

FIGURE 4.25 • **Portals**

Portals are entry points to the Web. iVillage.com is a vertical portal that appeals to women's interests.

Web Authoring Software

So far, we have discussed tools and technologies that assist people in viewing and using the Web. Before we leave the discussion of Web technology, we need to spend a moment discussing tools that assist people in creating Web pages.

Perhaps the best part of the Web is that anyone can put up a Web site. The Web is a great equalizer. In the real world, all people may be created equal, but they do not get equal air time and public exposure. In the Web world, all participants get the same opportunity to attract the Web community's attention. For as little as $6 a year, you can own your own domain name. For as little as $7 a month, you can rent space on a Web server. All you need to do is learn how to put together a Web site.

Creating a Web site does not take computer programming knowledge or knowledge of HTML. All it takes is something worth writing about, a good sense of visual design, and some Web authoring software. **Web authoring software** allows you to create HTML documents using a word-processor-like program. Rather than having to type out HTML tags to create Web page formatting, you add formatting using standard menu commands in a what-you-see-is-what-you-get (WYSIWYG) editor (Figure 4.26). *WYSIWYG* (pronounced wizzie-wig) implies that the Web page you design with the Web authoring software will look the same when published on the Web. When you save your Web page, the software creates the HTML file with the appropriate tags.

WYSIWYG editors are a great convenience for quickly creating Web pages. However, these editors fall short of automating all processes involved in Web production. A solid knowledge of HTML is a great benefit if you plan on creating and maintaining a Web site.

FIGURE 4.26 • WYSIWYG

In a WYSIWYG editor, like Dreamweaver, the Web page you design in the Web authoring software will look the same when published on the Web.

Although most people who use the Web do not have a Web site, it is likely that the percentage of people who do publish to the Web will continue to increase. The Web is an ideal way to share files with friends, family, business associates, and the world. You can use your Web site to share photos with family and friends, share your corporate mission statement with customers, or share your political philosophies with the world. The following section discusses the most common uses of the Web.

WEBAPPLICATIONS

EXPAND YOUR **KNOWLEDGE**

To learn more about Internet applications, including Web browsers, go to www.course.com/swt. Click the link "Expand Your Knowledge" and then complete the lab entitled, "Getting the Most out of the Internet."

The Web contains over 9 million unique Web sites. Of these 9 million, roughly half contain free and valuable information or services to the general public.[14] Although each Web site is unique, most can be classified under one of the following categories:

- Communication and collaboration
- News
- Education and training
- E-commerce
- Travel
- Banking, finance, and investing
- Employment and careers
- Multimedia and entertainment
- Information and opinion

This section explores each of these Web applications and how they benefit us personally and professionally.

Communication and Collaboration

Recall that many of the forms of digital communication have migrated to the Web. Most users access e-mail through the convenient Web interfaces of AOL or Hotmail. Discussion boards and chat rooms are in abundance on the Web. The Web itself is a communication medium, each Web page communicating the ideas if its author.

In the world of work, people use the Web as a communication link to their home offices while away. For example, attorneys at Shearman & Sterling use IBM's Websphere software platform to access all of the firm's information systems from their Web browser. Using the Web browser, attorneys can categorize their personalized content by topic area on tabbed pages, which resemble physical file folders, and organize their files, e-mail and other forms of information in "personal places." Similar "community places" provide areas for team collaboration.[15]

The Web also facilitates collaboration, by bringing together individuals with similar interests. A case in point is www.tonos.com (see Figure 4.27). Built for musicians, Tonos is an online destination for creating music, collaborating with others, showcasing work to the industry and the world, and accessing all the tools, tips, and services needed to further a musical career. In Tonos online studio musicians, songwriters, vocalists, and producers can team up online to create new music. Projects can start in many ways—with a lyric, a track, a melody, or a concept. Tonos member musicians sign on to projects and collaborate to produce finished products. Membership in Tonos may not be cheap, $129.95 annually, but entertainers like teen singer Melissa Bathory have found it worth the investment. Melissa's involvement with Tonos led to a big recording contract with Dream-Works Records.[16]

FIGURE 4.27 • Tonos online studio

Musicians can create music together in the Tonos online studio.

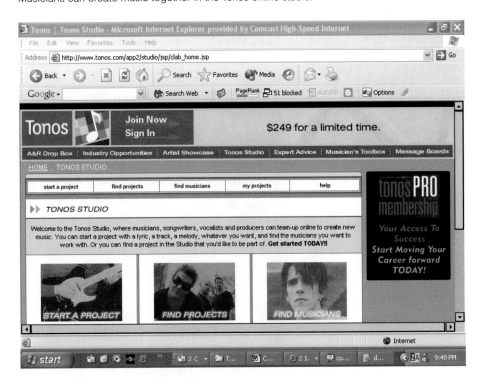

News

The Web is a powerful tool for keeping the public informed about local, state, national, and global news. It allows the public to actively research issues and become more knowledgeable. Traditional news media deliver the news through television, radio, and newspapers. These media provide only the news that they consider of interest to the general public. Items of special or unique interest may be bumped and replaced with more general stories. In contrast, the Web has an abundance of special interest coverage. It also provides the capacity to drill down into the subject matter. For example, during the war in Iraq, online news services provided news articles in text, audio, and video coverage. Clicking links allowed you to *drill down* and find out more about geographic regions by viewing maps; you could link to historical coverage of U.S./Iraqi relations, and you could learn about the battle equipment being deployed. The style of news coverage on the Web is influencing the way news is delivered on television. Major news networks are now dividing the television screen into multiple windows, to more fully present news stories.

Some television news networks are providing video clips of news events from their Web sites through a technology called webcasting. *Webcasting* takes advantage of streaming video technology and high-speed Internet connections to provide television-style delivery of information (see Figure 4.28). Webcasting expands the Web's ability to provide detailed news coverage and has the ability to transform Web news services into something resembling interactive TV.

Most city newspapers are accessible over the Web, and the major national news agencies, such as Reuters and the Associated Press also have a Web presence. You can get international news not only from U.S. news sources but also from other countries, providing a wide variety of perspectives on the news.

FIGURE 4.28 • Webcasting
Webcasting offers up-to-the-minute video clips of current news events.

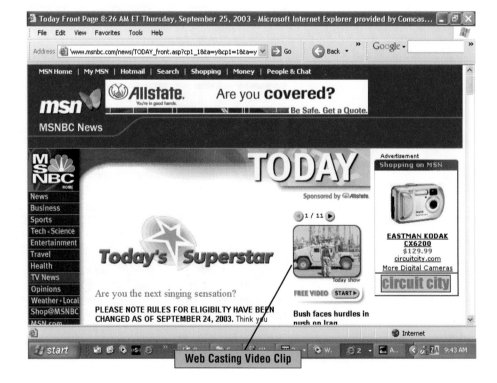

There are countless special interest news sources that provide industry specific news and information. Table 4.7 lists a small segment of the wide variety of industry specific news services available.

TABLE 4.7 • News Services on the Web

Industry	News Web Site
Biotechnology and Pharmaceutical	www.biospace.com/
Auto	www.auto.com/index/industry.htm
Airline, Airport, and Aviation	http://news.airwise.com/
Restaurant	www.nrn.com
Audio/Visual Communications	www.infocomm.org/
Hospitality	www.hotelnewsresource.com/
Customer Relations Management	www.crmdaily.com/
Oil Industry	www.oilonline.com/news/
Realty	www.realtor.org/
Textile, Apparel, Footwear	www.just-style.com/news.asp

Other Web sites provide a wide survey of industry-specific news from the major news sources. For example, Yahoo provides a categorized menu for industry news at http://biz.yahoo.com/industry/.

Education and Training

Educational institutions of all types and sizes are using the Web to enhance classroom education or extend it to individuals who are unable to attend.

Primary school education uses the Web to inform parents of school schedules and activities. Teachers give elementary school students research exercises in the classroom and at home that utilize Web resources. To make browsing safe for young users, *parental control* applications such as Net Nanny filter out adult content. By high school, students have integrated the Web into daily study habits. Teachers manage class Web pages that contain information and links for students to use in homework exercises.

Increasing numbers of college level courses are relying on the Web to enhance student's learning. Educational support products, such as Blackboard and WebCT, provide an integrated Web environment that includes virtual chat for class members; a discussion group for posting questions and comments; access to the class syllabus and agenda, student grades, and class announcements; and links to class-related material. Some course Web sites go as far as delivering filmed lectures using Webcasting technology. Such environments are used to complement the traditional classroom experience, or as the sole method of course delivery.

Conducting classes over the Web with no physical class meetings is called *distance education.* Many colleges and universities offer distance education classes, which offer a convenient method for nontraditional students to attend college. Nontraditional students include older students who have job or family obligations that might otherwise prohibit them from attending college. Distance education offers them a way of working through class material on a flexible schedule. Some schools are offering entire degree programs through distance education.[17]

Beyond traditional education, corporations such as NETg and SmartForce offer professional job-skills training over the Web (see Figure 4.29). Job seekers often use these services to acquire specialized business or technical training. Some of the training leads to certification. Certification verifies a person's skill and understanding in a particular area. It has become very important, especially for some technical skill sets, to assure an employer that a job applicant truly has the skills claimed. For instance, if you hire a certified Novell technician, you can be assured that that individual has the knowledge necessary to install and support your Novell computer network. Some corporations and organizations contract with NETg or SmartForce to provide on-the-job training for present employees to expand their skills.

FIGURE 4.29 • NETg

Professional job-skills training is available from corporations such as NETg without the need to ever step into a classroom.

E-commerce

The Web is an integral part of most business information infrastructures. It provides corporate information to employees, shareholders, the media, and the public. It can be and often is used as a primary interface to the corporate database. Its convenience and universal acceptance makes it the ideal platform for communications. It helps support communication among the links in an organization's value chain—the string of companies working together to produce a product. A value chain typically consists of the suppliers of the raw materials that are used to create a product, the manufacturing unit, transportation and storage providers, marketing, sales, and customer support. The Web acts as the glue that holds all of these units together by providing a central point of access to corporate information. The Web provides a convenient platform for marketing and selling products, and is very helpful in collecting marketing data. The Web strengthens communications with customers and improves overall customer satisfaction.

JOB TECHNOLOGY

Blogs and English 101

The Web has created a space for anyone to publish their writing for the world to read. Steven King was one of the first well-known authors to write specifically for the Web. Following his lead, many authors of fiction, nonfiction, poetry, and other formal writing styles have made their work available online. Communities of writers have used the Web to collaborate and to present work for critique. A new Web technology, called Web logs or blogs, has arisen to support the interaction between writers, readers, and critics.

A blog is a Web site that supports an active writer wishing to create an online identity and present a point of view. Blogs are used as a platform for controversial debate, for insight into a person's intimate reflections—similar to an online diary—or, in a more recent trend, as an educational tool to assist young writers in establishing their style.

Jeff Golub, who is an associate professor of English education at the University of South Florida, teaches future educators three central principles about encouraging student authorship: "Students will write when they have something to say, when they have an audience, and when they get feedback." Blogs provide the perfect medium for supporting all three needs.

Students enjoy sharing their ideas through writing on the Web. Consider, for example, Stesha, a 16 year old from Toronto who has published 436 entries in her diary on www.studentcenter.org. Nearly 2,000 people have viewed her work, many adding their own comments on what she has written. Above and beyond sharing points of view, blogs are ideal for education because they provide a means to share one person's writing with a group, and collect opinions and suggestions. At weblogg-ed.com you can find hundreds of links to Web sites devoted to journalism, literature, English composition, and other high-school and college writing courses. The Journalism 1 course at Hunterdon Central Regional High School organizes the entire class around a blog.

The Web site includes headline stories written by the students, links to outside news sources, all class information, educational links, and Web sites for each student in the course that include articles written, along with a discussion area for each article. Classmates and the teacher comment on each student submission. The best articles are published on the main page—which doubles as the school's newspaper. Students' obvious enthusiasm for the medium is reflected in their work.

So why hasn't this technology taken off in all schools? Since middle schools and high schools are responsible for the safety and well-being of their students, they must take extreme care with what student information is made public, and with what information their students are able to access. To protect their students, most schools need to limit blogs to their local network and in so doing drastically reduce the audience, undermining the purpose of the blogs. Each blog entry needs to be evaluated and at times censored. Limiting a student's power in this manner often frustrates the student and could eventually lead to apathetic feelings towards the technology. Once students are beyond high school, an increased amount of freedom makes blogs a more viable option.

Questions

1. What benefits do blogs provide for teachers and students over traditional methods of education?
2. Why are middle schools and high schools concerned about student safety in blogs?
3. Besides English and writing classes, what other classes could benefit from blogs?

Sources
1. *"Writing with Web Logs,"* Kristen Kennedy, Technology & Learning, *Feature; February 1, 2003, p 11.*
2. *"Booming blogs: www.kissyourshadow.com/index.php,"* Mairi MacLean, The Edmonton Journal, *Living; March 14, 2003, p C1.*
3. *www.weblogg-ed.com/ accessed June 8, 2003.*

The Web has dramatically changed the manner in which businesses do business and consumers shop for products. Doing business electronically over the Web and private networks is known as e-commerce. It is such an important topic that we have dedicated most of Chapter 7 to it.

ONLINE OPEN HOUSE

House hunters are using the Internet to search out shelter solutions. According to the National Association of Realtors, over 70 percent of the people looking for new homes use the Internet to find property. Listings are updated hourly, carry more information and better pictures on the property than any print publication, and a property can be viewed by anyone from anywhere in the world—often with the help, whether wanted or not, of friends and relatives.

Source:
"Web House-Hunts, 2¢ From All Over"
By Motoko Rich
The New York Times
www.nytimes.com/2003/08/07/garden/07TURF.html
August 7, 2003
Cited on August 9, 2003

Travel

The Web has had a profound affect on the travel industry and the way we plan and prepare for trips. From getting assistance with short trips across town to planning summer long holidays abroad, travelers are turning to the Web to save time and money, and overcome much of the risk involved in visiting unknown places.

Many of the success stories of the Web come from the travel industry. Web sites become successful when they uniquely fill a public need. Mapquest.com has certainly performed that function. Offering free street maps for cities around the world, Mapquest assists travelers in finding their way around town and between towns. Provide Mapquest with a departure location and destination, and it will show you the fastest route to take.

Travel Web sites such as travelocity.com, expedia.com, and priceline.com assist travelers in finding the best deals on flights, hotels, car rentals, vacation packages, and cruises (see Figure 4.30). Provided with dates and locations of travel, most travel Web sites will display the available flights and prices from which you can base your choice. Priceline.com takes a slightly different approach. It allows shoppers to name their own price, and then works to find an airline that will meet that price. Once flights have been reserved, travelers can use these Web sites to book hotels and a rental car.

FIGURE 4.30 • Travelocity.com

Travel Web sites such as travelocity.com assist travelers in finding the best deals on flights, hotels, car rentals, vacation packages, and cruises.

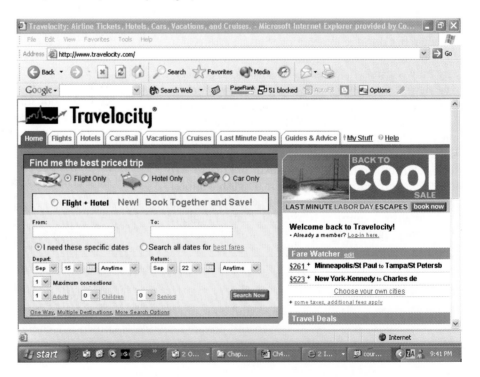

There are many special-purpose travel Web sites that assist individuals with particular needs. Some categories listed at Yahoo include backpacking, budget travel, disabilities, ecotourism, hitch hiking, train travel, traveling alone, traveling with pets, and vegetarian.

Employment and Careers

Web sites provide useful tools for people seeking employment and for companies seeking employees. Web sites such as careerbuilder.com and monster.com provide resources for choosing a career and finding a job. Most colleges have career and job placement services that make use of the Web to connect graduating students with employers. Consider the Web's role in the following job-hunting strategy:

1. Select a career. Use online references such as those at www.jobweb.com/catapult/default.htm to discover your personal strengths and weaknesses and map them to your ideal job.
2. Discover who the players are in your chosen career. Search the Web on a given career and industry title and see what companies are represented. Discover online trade journals and learn as much as you can.
3. Learn about the companies that interest you. Where better to start than the company's Web site? Many companies list career opportunities and provide you with information on how to apply.
4. Network with others in the field. There are many online industry-specific discussion groups and forums. Seek them out to make valuable contacts. You can start at www.hotjobs.com/htdocs/client/splash/communities/.
5. View job listings at general employment Web sites. Web sites such as www.hotjobs.com, www.joboptions.com, and www.careermosaic.com have large databases of job openings where you can search by profession or keywords. A complete list of the best of these sites can be found at www.quintcareers.com.
6. View job listings at industry-specific employment Web sites. There are hundreds of specialized job Web sites, from employment recruiters of all types to specialized job databank sites that focus on a specific industry.
7. Create an impressive Web site to represent yourself. Consider purchasing your own domain name—for example, www.janelle_johnson.com. Include an attractive welcome page with links to your resume and other details regarding your experience and skills. Employers like hard-copy resumes to be brief. At the bottom of your resume, you can add "Please visit www.janelle_johnson.com for more information." Make sure that your Web site is professional in appearance and content.

While searching for a way to earn money, don't be taken in by the many get-rich-quick scams that proliferate over the Web and through e-mail. Although there are many "work at home" offers on the Web, only a few are legitimate. You can get information about scams posing as business opportunities from the Federal Trade Commission.[18] In addition, the Internet Fraud Complaint Center, sponsored by the Federal Bureau of Investigation (FBI) and the National White Collar Crime Center (NW3C), provides information on how to spot Internet fraud and an online form for reporting Internet fraud.[19]

If you seek to be an entrepreneur, a number of resources on the Web can assist you with opening your own business. Entrepreneur.com offers valuable information for small business owners, as illustrated in Figure 4.31.

FIGURE 4.31 • **Entrepeneur.com**

For people who seek to be entrepreneurs, a number of resources on the Web can assist you with opening your own business.

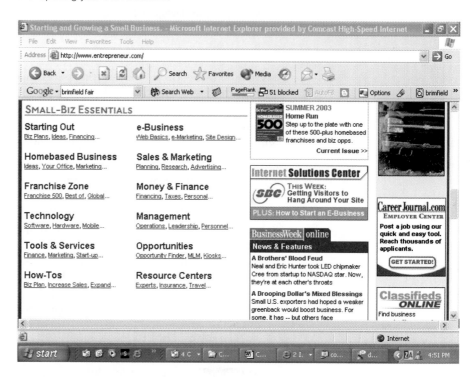

Multimedia and Entertainment

Faster Internet connection speeds and advances in streaming technology have brought a wide range of media and gaming applications to the Web. The Web has had a dramatic impact on the music and motion picture industries, causing unprecedented changes in marketing and distribution approaches. Many in the software industry are betting that online gaming will increase in its appeal across gender and age markets. As home entertainment equipment begins to merge with home computing equipment, the Web is anticipating the call to deliver entertainment.

Music. *Internet radio* is similar to local AM and FM radio except that it is digitally delivered to your computer over the Internet, and there are a lot more choices of stations. For example, msn.com provides access to hundreds of radio stations in over 35 musical genre categories. All that is required to listen to Internet radio is a media player such as the Real media player or Microsoft Windows media player. Some stations charge a subscription fee, but most don't.

Compressed music formats such as MP3 have made music swapping over the Internet a convenient and popular activity. File-sharing software such as Kazaa provides a convenient means by which consumers can copy and distribute music, often without consideration to copyright law (see Chapter 11). The result is a popular music distribution system that is largely illegal, impossible to control, and cuts deeply into the recording industry's profits. In addition, it is not always safe to swap files with strangers. One study discovered that 6% of all the music files downloaded from Kazaa are actually viruses renamed to look like MP3 files. Music industry giants have pulled together to win back customers by offering legal and safe alternatives to electronic music distribution that provide services and perks not offered by file-sharing networks at a reasonable price.

Several online music services are available. Apple's iTunes was one of the first online music services to find success.[20] The iTunes Music Store sold three million songs online to Apple computer users, at 99 cents each, in its first month. In Figure 4.32, Steve Jobs, CEO of Apple, announces the release of the Apple iTunes music service.

FIGURE 4.32 • Apple's iTunes music service

Steve Jobs, CEO of Apple, introduces iTunes—the music service that allows Internet users to download songs for listening on their Mac or PC, transferring to CD, or transferring to a portable device like the iPod pictured bottom right.

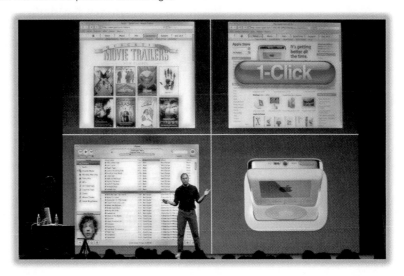

Within a year of its original release, Apple iTunes for Microsoft Windows was released to compete with other Windows-based music services such as Music-Match MX, PressPlay (which merged with a new, legitimate Napster music service), AOL MusicNet, and FullAudios Music Now.[21] These music services offer access to the catalog of the Big Five labels—Universal Music, Sony Music, Warner Music, BMG, and EMI, which together account for 80% of recorded music—over 300,000 songs. Music can be accessed from most music subscription services at three levels:

1. *Streamed music* is similar to Internet radio except that you get to select the songs and create your own play lists, which can be stored on the server for access from any Internet connected computer. Streamed music does not allow you to download the music files to your computer.
2. *Tethered downloads* allow you to download the actual music files to your computer and play them whenever you like using your media player. However, you cannot burn them to a CD or transfer them to a portable device.
3. *Portable downloads* transfer the music files to your computer, and you can then listen to them on demand, burn them to a CD, or transfer them to a portable device.

Most music services charge a monthly membership fee with the basic package priced between $8 and $10. The basic package typically includes unlimited streamed music and limited tethered downloads. More expensive packages add additional tethered downloads and portable downloads.

These new music services have their work cut out for them as they compete against the free file-sharing networks. A study done by Ipsos, a survey-based market research company, found that a quarter of all Americans over the age of 12 have downloaded a music or MP3 file from a file-sharing network.[22] Kazaa, the most popular file-sharing software, claims an audience of 140 million worldwide users. If any one of the new fee-based services could claim just 1% of that audience they would be considered a success. Ipsos' 2002 poll showed that 31% of file sharers are willing to pay for tunes. MusicMatch, PressPlay, MusicNet, and Music-Now are hoping that the extra services they offer will start a new trend back to a legitimate viable music distribution system.

Movies. The movie industry is also making the move to Internet distribution. The large size of video files has so far held video back from being as popular to swap on the Internet as music. However, with the increasing number of broadband connections, movie swapping is becoming increasingly popular. Warner Brothers was up in arms when it discovered that its film *The Matrix Reloaded* was being swapped on file-sharing networks within two weeks of the film's world premier.[23] A high-quality copy of the film was being downloaded by hundreds of people each day via a Web site that uses the file-sharing computer program BitTorrent. The Web site was subsequently taken down. It is assumed that either the movie was stolen by an inside source or someone sneaked a digital camcorder into a theater and recorded it off the screen. Disney was so concerned about movie pirating that they deployed metal detectors and night-vision goggles to select movie theater ushers to use during the opening weeks of *Finding Nemo*.[24]

Like the recording industry, the motion picture industry is undertaking both defensive and offensive tactics to thwart the trend towards illegal file sharing. One tactic is to develop a legitimate Internet distribution system. Movielink.com allows users to rent movies over the Internet (see Figure 4.33). You browse the

FIGURE 4.33 • Movielink.com

You can rent movies online at movielink.com.

movielink.com Web site for movies, just as you would look through a movie rental store. Movies rent for between $3 and $5 and are downloaded to your PC using the Movielink Manager software. You can view the movie on your PC or perhaps a laptop connected to your television set. You can hold onto the movie for 30 days, but once you begin watching it, you have only 24 hours before it removes itself from your computer. Needless to say, unless you have a fast Internet connection, and a way to view the movies you download on a large screen, this service probably won't satisfy you. However, as digital convergence leads to Internet integrated home entertainment centers—where home entertainment equipment merges with home computing and networking equipment—Movielink will be poised to provide what will then be a valuable service.

Games. The Web offers a multitude of games for individuals of all ages. From solitaire to massive multiplayer roleplaying games, there is a wide variety of offerings to suit every taste. Of course, the Web provides a medium for downloading single-player games to your desktop, notebook, handheld, or cell phone device (check www.download.com), but the power of the Web is most apparent with multiplayer games.

Multiplayer games allow you to interact with other users online (see Figure 4.34). There are a variety of types and platforms. Multiplayer games support from two to thousands of players at a time. They could be as simple as an online game of checkers. At the time of this writing, of the 123,453 people playing games at http://zone.msn.com/, 506 of them are playing checkers—253 simultaneous games. Meanwhile at the Ferion game network (another online gaming site) 78 players, of the 26,133 members are creating empires in space and exploring the virtual galaxy.

FIGURE 4.34 • **Endless Ages multiplayer game**
Multiplayer games connect Internet users and allow them to interact in a virtual world.

Multiplayer online games can be categorized into the following genres:

- Action. Fast-paced games requiring accuracy and quick reflexes
- Board. Games involving play on a virtual game board
- Card. These games involve the use of a virtual deck of cards
- Flight Simulation. Games that involve taking on the role of a pilot in a WWI biplane or a futuristic starship
- Multi-User Dimension or MultiUser Dungeon (MUD). Text-based games that make up for their lack of graphics with diverse and immersive game play
- Roleplaying Games (RPG). Games in which you take on the persona of a game character
- Sims (Simulations). Games in which you create your own character that lives in a simulated environment
- Sports. Games involving sports
- Strategy. Games that feature planning-, tactics-, and diplomacy-dominated game play
- Trivia/Puzzle. Games that require a good memory or problem-solving skills

Although most multiplayer games are free, some of the best have fees associated with them. You may need to purchase software, or pay monthly, yearly, or per play subscription fees.

Research on the Web

The connected world of the Web has, more than anything else, provided us with conveniently accessible answers to questions. Life is full of wonder. Throughout the course of the day, we might wonder about any number of experiences we have or observations we make. In days past, we might have gone home and searched for explanations in the family encyclopedia, or made a trip to the library.

More likely than not, however, we would have found that researching the question wasn't worth the bother, or that the question would simply pass from our minds. But today, we're connected to the world's largest encyclopedia, with most of us cracking it open every day. When we go online to check e-mail, we can take a moment to quickly run a search on something we were curious about sometime during the day. As the Web moves to cell phones and other handheld devices, we will be able to look up information at the moment a thought or question strikes us. This form of research is known as *curiosity-driven* research. Curiosity-driven research is responsible for most of the world's great inventions.

In another form of research, *assigned research,* we are given a topic to explore for the purpose of education. This type of research is common in college, and is often left open-ended. You are left to choose a topic, typically in a given subject area.

In order to provide an understanding of the stages of research required of most college students, we will imagine that you have been assigned a research project in one of your classes. As we work through the stages of your research, you will learn how the Web assists with each stage of the process from selecting a topic to citing resources.

Selecting and Refining a Topic. Selecting a topic is generally done through many stages of refinement. Some refinement may be done for us by a teacher or supervisor. For our imaginary research project, we will assume that you have full control of the topic selection. You begin by asking yourself the question "What in the universe would I like to explore?" Recall the subject directories found at Web portals like Yahoo that were noted earlier in the chapter. These Web portals are ideal for finding general information on popular or scholarly subjects. Sounds like a great place to start when looking for a topic. At www.yahoo.com, you look through the major headings, as shown in Figure 4.35.

FIGURE 4.35 • The Yahoo subject directory
Online subject directories are a great place to explore research topics.

Perhaps you have cultural interests; you enjoy monitoring social trends and issues, so you select the Society & Culture listings. From the long list of topics in this category, you might decide to investigate Issues and Causes—certainly there should be something of interest here. On the Issues and Causes page, you find a list of around 100 social issues. Perusing the list, you come across a social issue of personal interest: Genetic Engineering. Clicking this link, you find some Web page references on genetic engineering and some further refined subtopics: Agriculture, Cloning, Genetics, Institutes, Organizations. You pursue the Cloning option and find some general cloning links and yet another subtopic: Human Cloning. After following the Human Cloning link, and checking out some of the many pages on human cloning, you decide that this is an interesting topic with plenty of resources from which to draw and choose it as your research topic.

Notice that in the course of this process we have gone through four levels of subject refinement: Yahoo Directory > Society & Culture > Issues & Causes > Cloning > Human Cloning.

It is not unusual to back out at this point and try another path. It may take a dozen or more tries before you finally find something that interests you. Once you decide on a topic, you will continue to refine and refocus it as you learn more about it.

Sources of Information. In our example, you have already found a significant amount of information on your topic from the Web pages listed at Yahoo. Are the sources of this information reliable? Can you use them for your research paper? Although the Web has provided you with a convenient way of selecting a topic, and some surface information about our topic, to gain a deeper understanding, you should turn to more traditional forms of research. The library and online databases are a primary source of deep, trustworthy, authoritative information on most topics.

Many college campuses include a library. Even with the wealth of information available on the Web, libraries remain the most trustworthy of sources. The books, reference materials, journals, and other periodicals that are housed in your college or local library have undergone quality control evaluation to earn the right to sit on those shelves. Books and periodicals considered fundamental to any given field are typically stocked in the library. Library resources are professionally analyzed and categorized in a logical manner that is easy to navigate. Best of all, the most knowledgeable of researchers, librarians, are available to assist you with your project.

Because we are turning to the library, don't get the impression that we are leaving the Web behind. Most libraries have online card catalogs that can be searched to determine if it has any books or journal articles on your topic (see Figure 4.36).

FIGURE 4.36 • Library search page
Most college libraries use Web sites for keyword searches of books and journals.

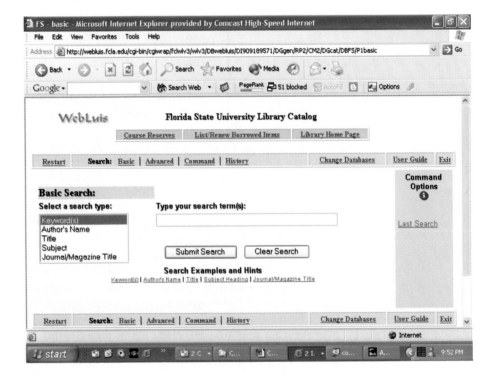

For example, a keyword search on "human cloning" may return 98 books and journal article titles such as:

Playing God?: genetic determinism and human freedom
Peters, Ted, 1941-; 2003
DIRAC SCIENCE LIBRARY QH438.7 .P48 2003 -- Not Checked Out

The listing shows that this book is relatively current and on the shelf. Clicking the title would provide more information about the book—perhaps even a brief overview (called an abstract) and the table of contents. Much of your initial library research can be done from your own PC. After finding interesting books and articles that are not currently checked out, print out your list and head to the library.

Besides online card catalogs, libraries typically provide links to public and sometimes private research databases on the Web. Online research databases allow visitors to search for information in thousands of journal, magazine, and newspaper articles. Information database services are valuable because they offer the best in quality and convenience. They provide full-text articles from reputable sources conveniently over the Web. College and public libraries typically subscribe to many databases to support the research of the community. One of the most popular private databases is LexisNexis Academic Universe. LexisNexis provides access to full-text documents from over 5,900 news, business, legal, medical, and reference publications, and you can access the information through a standard keyword search engine. The sources from which LexisNexis draws include:

- National and regional newspapers, wire services, broadcast transcripts, international news sources, and non-English language sources
- U.S. federal and state case law, codes, regulations, legal news, law reviews, and international legal information
- *Shepard's® Citations* for all U.S. Supreme Court cases back to 1789
- Business news journals, company financial information, SEC filings and reports, and industry and market news

A keyword search on "human cloning" for articles published within the last six months returns 125 full-length articles written on the subject. LexisNexis is a valuable and costly subscription, so if your school provides access, consider yourself fortunate.

After gaining deeper knowledge on your subject from library materials and online databases, you can return once again to the public Web to fill in the gaps. As you turn to the Web, you should do so with increased caution. Library and database sources typically come from reputable content and information providers. With Web content, things aren't always what they seem. A Web page posted by the Human Cloning Council (HCC) that proclaims the wonderful benefits of human cloning, may be a cover for a company that will benefit should human cloning be accepted. In the arena of Web research, you must follow up and check sources for validity.

Using a Web search engine you can search the Web for pages on your topic. Running a search on "Human Cloning" at Google brings up links to over 500,000 related Web pages—this is obviously a hot topic. Google attempts to present the search results in order of relevance. You might skim over the first few pages of results and investigate interesting links. You might also run a more detailed search. For example, "pros and cons of human cloning" brings up 6,000 pages.

After checking out books from the library, searching online databases, and scanning Web sites using a search engine, you should be close to being an authority on this subject. You know what human cloning is, the state of the science, the legal and ethical issues, and have read biased arguments on both sides of the issue. Now, it's time to compile your data and compose your research paper.

JOB TECHNOLOGY

Librarians Available Online 24/7

Frustrated by the number of hits you're getting on your Google searches? Homework deadline looming and can't find what you need on the Internet? REFERENCE LIBRARIAN TO THE RESCUE! Reference Librarians are using federal funding, the Web, and a software package called 24/7 Reference, to field questions from desperate knowledge seekers over the Web 24 hours a day, 7 days a week. Accessed from local library Web sites, like the Thomas Crane Public Library in Quincy, Massachusetts, users are invited to "Connect with a Librarian," welcomed with the slogan "A Professional Librarian, on Your Computer, at Your Convenience," and asked to fill out a short form. Included in the form is a text box in which you can state your question.

In a moment or two, a reference librarian greets you in a small chat window on the right side of the screen and uses the larger left portion of the screen to display Web sites that may assist you with your question. After a back and forth dialogue, and a librarian-run tour of Web sites, either the librarian is able to point you to useful Web resources or perhaps will advise you to visit your own local library. After you conclude your interaction with the librarian, a transcript of your dialogue is e-mailed to you so that you can refer to the Web sites the librarian showed you.

Unlike Internet search engines, which rely on computers to scour the Web, 24/7 Reference services use real reference librarians from libraries across the country. "I think the biggest benefit is that in an emergency when you need information for your personal life, for your school life, for your business life, you have someone you can count on who's trained to search," commented Linda Beeler, head of reference at Crane Library.

Questions

1. Which would you prefer to use, a Web search engine or an online reference librarian? Why?
2. What are the limitations of Web search engines when compared to a reference librarian?
3. What are the limitations of reference librarians when compared to the automated systems of Web search engines?

Sources
1. *"Online librarians have the answers you're looking for," Karen Eschbacher,* The Patriot Ledger *(Quincy, MA), March 14, 2003.*
2. *We Jumped on the Live Reference Bandwagon and We Love the Ride!" Glenda Schaake and Eleanor Sathan,* Information Today Inc., *April 2003, www.infotoday.com/cilmag/apr03/schaake_sathan.shtml accessed June 7, 2003.*
3. *24/7 Reference Web site, www.247ref.org/ accessed June 7, 2003.*

Citing Sources. An important component of your research paper is giving credit to your sources. If you quote directly from a source, make sure to enclose it in quotation marks and credit the source. Representing someone else's writing as your own is called **plagiarism.** Copyrighted material, also known as intellectual property, is protected by law and cannot be copied and presented as your own work. There are stiff penalties for copyright infringement in academic environments. You will find a passage similar to the following in most college's Academic Honor Systems or Codes of Conduct:

> Regarding academic assignments, violations of the Academic Honor Code shall include representing another's work or any part thereof, be it published or unpublished, as one's own. It shall also include presenting or submitting any academic work in a manner that impairs the instructor's ability to assess the student's academic performance. For example, plagiarism includes failure to use quotation marks or other conventional markings around material quoted from any source.[25]

A *citation* is how you formally recognize the source of a quotation in your paper. There are a variety of different citation styles, and different disciplines prefer different styles. You should check with your instructor as to which style he or she prefers.

Action Plan

1. **What enriching online activities can Josh use to improve his quality of life?**

   Josh can communicate with both his local and out of town friends online using e-mail, chat, and instant messaging. He can even meet other college students at www.collegeclub.com/ or www.student.com/. Josh can pick up a new cell phone and service that supports text messaging so that he can text with his friends. He can also involve himself in music and video clubs, and multiplayer gaming. Josh can keep up with the latest news from online news services, and use technology news services to find out what's new on the Internet and Web. Josh might decide to broaden his knowledge or skills in a given area by using online training. He might even work towards certification in order to gain an edge when it comes time to look for a job. In fact, in today's competitive job market, it's never too soon to start looking. Josh can start scanning the job sites to help decide on a career and see what's out there.

2. **What online activities are legal and safe, and which are not?**

   When accessing music and movies on the Web, Josh should know that ignoring copyrights can have serious consequences. Josh should also use caution when meeting new people online; not everyone is who they appear to be. Josh shouldn't travel solo to meet someone in person that he has met only online. When using material from the Web in his research paper, Josh should be sure to cite his sources, and never submit someone else's work as his own.

3. **How should Josh conduct research on his computer?**

   Josh could start looking for a topic at an online subject directory. Once he's selected a topic, he can research it using keyword searches at his school library's Web site, in the card catalogue, and in online databases. He can refine his topic and search as he learns more about it. Finally, he can use Web search engines to access public knowledge on the topic, being careful to consider the source.

Summary

LEARNING OBJECTIVE 1

Describe how hardware, protocols, and software work together to create the Internet and how the Internet may change in the future.

The Internet is the largest publicly owned network of networks. It was established in 1969 as the ARPANET under a government project named ARPA with a goal of connecting the computer networks of four universities. In 1990, it was turned over to the public to be managed by the Internet Society. The birth of the Web in 1993 led to an explosion in the Internet growth rate to the point that it connects over 200 million computers today.

The Internet combines hardware, protocols, and software to serve its users. Internet hardware consists of network backbones provided by the major telecommunication networks, routers that route packets of data to their destinations, and the computers that request and provide information and services. Internet service providers provide connections to points of presence on the Internet backbone for personal and professional use. The Internet is a packet switching network that makes use of rules, called protocols, to pass packets of data between computers.

The protocols of the Internet are TCP/IP. The Internet Protocol (IP) defines the format and addressing scheme used for the packets. Transaction Control Protocol (TCP) enables two hosts to establish a connection and exchange streams of data. The Internet uses IP addresses to identify hosts. Domain names are English representations of IP addresses. The Internet makes use of client/server software to supply users with the information and services they request. Server computers use port numbers to segregate the various types of service requests. Peer-to-peer communications do not use a central server, but rather allow Internet users to create connections directly between their computers.

Figure 4.4—p. 147

LEARNING OBJECTIVE 2
Compare and contrast the types of communication tools available on the Internet.

Internet-based communications can be classified as either synchronous or asynchronous, and are text-based, voice-based, or video-based. Forms of text communications include e-mail, discussion boards, chat, instant messaging, and Short Message Service (SMS), more commonly called texting. E-mail can be used to communicate with an individual or groups. E-mail sent to groups is called broadcast e-mail. Users can subscribe to listservs to correspond with others who share a particular interest. Some news providers offer a newsletter service, which automatically sends news to subscribers' e-mail boxes on a regular schedule. Because of the lack of nonverbal cues, e-mail is notorious for creating misunderstanding. E-mail messages include an e-mail header, body, and sometimes an attached file. E-mail can be accessed using POP, IMAP, or the Web.

In discussion boards and news groups, people use bulletin boards to post and respond to messages. Chat involves synchronous text messaging between two or more participants. Instant messaging is the most recent form of chat, and allows users to build buddy lists to keep track of and communicate with friends online. Texting is a technology that allows cell phone users to send short text messages to each other. Following the rules of netiquette, whenever you communicate with others on the Internet, reduces the chances for misunderstanding.

Figure 4.15—p. 162

Digital voice communication is creating a merger between Internet and telephone communications. This is particularly apparent in new cell phone technology, and the emergence of video phones.

LEARNING OBJECTIVE 3
Explain the underlying structure of the Web and the technologies that support it.

The Web makes use of the Internet's client/server technology to provide a medium for users to conveniently publish, view, and find information on the Internet. It uses Hypertext Transfer Protocol (HTTP) to allow Web browsers (clients) to access Hypertext Markup Language (HTML) documents, called Web pages, stored on Web servers. HTML documents use hyperlinks to connect to other HTML documents. HTML tags specify the document format and other commands from within HTML documents. Uniform Resource Locators (URLs) are Web page addresses that allow you to access a specific Web page on a server. XML and XHTML are new Web standards that allow for the storage and manipulation of structured data on the Web.

Web plug-ins work with Web browsers to offer extended services—typically the ability to view audio, animations, or video. Java, JavaScript, and ActiveX are programming languages that allow programs to be included in Web pages, which creates the ability for users to interact with Web content.

Figure 4.22—p. 169

Sometimes Web servers store a cookie, or a small text file, on your computer so that it can recognize you upon your next visit to a Web page. Cookies help Web pages present customized information to users.

Portals are Web pages that provide an entry point to the Web. They typically include headline news and information, along with a search engine and subject directory to help you find information on the Web.

Web authoring software allows you to create HTML documents in a WYSIWYG editor that works just like a word processor. With Web authoring software, you can generate attractive Web pages without having to know HTML.

LEARNING OBJECTIVE 4

Define the categories of information and services that the Web provides and the ways in which the Web supports research.

The Web provides a wide range of helpful applications. It provides communication and collaboration platforms that allow users to keep in touch, work together, and meet others with like interests. It provides local, state, national, and international news on a level equal to if not better than traditional media. Educators and trainers use the Web to support and extend traditional learning environments or for distance education. Businesses rely on the Web to act as a central location for corporate information.

The Web is one of the first places people turn to when looking for employment, and plays an integral role in most job-hunting strategies. The Web supplies all forms of entertainment including music, video, and gaming. It is also used as the primary tool for research, by providing access to online library catalogs, databases, and public opinion.

Figure 4.35—p. 187

Test Yourself

LEARNING OBJECTIVE 1: Describe how hardware, protocols, and software work together to create the Internet and how the Internet may change in the future.

1. The Internet ____ is made up of a combination of many national and international communication networks.
   a. router
   b. protocol
   c. backbone
   d. server

2. True or False: HTTP is the protocol of the Internet.

3. Computers on the Internet communicate using _____ relationships.

LEARNING OBJECTIVE 2: Compare and contrast the types of communication tools available on the Internet.

4. E-mail, voice mail, and discussion boards are all forms of _____ communication.

5. If your e-mail client downloads your incoming e-mail messages to your PC, you must be using ____.
   a. POP
   b. IMAP
   c. Web-based e-mail
   d. ASCII.

6. True or False: Short Message Service is a technology designed for cell phones.

LEARNING OBJECTIVE 3: Explain the underlying structure of the Web and the technologies that support it.

7. True or False: Web pages are sometimes called HTTP documents.

8. ____ are small files of data that are stored and retrieved from your computer by a Web server each time you visit.
   a. cookies
   b. Javascripts
   c. ActiveX Controls
   d. Portals

9. True or False: Content streaming allows you to listen to or view content while it is being downloaded.

LEARNING OBJECTIVE 4: Define the categories of information and services that the Web provides and the ways in which the Web supports research.

10. ____ downloads allow you to download music files to your computer, but not burn them to CD.
    a. binary
    b. tethered
    c. media
    d. costly

11. True or False: Web search engines are useful in deciding on a research topic.

12. Representing someone else's writing as your own is called _____.

Test Yourself Solutions: 1. c., 2. F, 3. client/server, 4. asynchronous, 5. a., 6. T, 7. F, 8. a., 9. T, 10. b., 11. F, 12. plagiarism

Key Terms

asynchronous communication, p. 153
chat, p. 159
client/server, p. 150
computer network, p. 145
content streaming, p. 169
cookie, p. 170
discussion boards, p. 158
e-mail, p. 154
e-mail attachment, p. 155
HTML tag, p. 166
hyperlink, p. 165
Hypertext Markup Language (HTML) , p. 166

Hypertext Transfer Protocol (HTTP), p. 165
instant messaging, p. 160
Internet backbone, p. 146
Internet service providers (ISP), p. 147
IP address, p. 149
Peer-to-peer (P2P), p. 151
plagiarism, p. 190
plug-in, p. 168
ports, p. 151
protocols, p. 146
routers, p. 148
search engine, p. 171

Short Message Service (SMS), p. 162
spam, p. 156
synchronous communication, p. 153
TCP/IP, p. 148
Uniform Resource Locator (URL), p. 166
video conferencing, p. 164
Web authoring software, p. 173
Web browser, p. 165
Web server, p. 165
World Wide Web, p. 164
XML, p. 167

Questions

Review Questions

1. What was the motivation behind the creation of the Internet?

2. What three components combined make up today's Internet?

3. What is the Internet backbone and who provides it?

4. What is the role of an ISP?

5. What are the responsibilities of a router?

6. How does P2P networking differ from client/server?

7. What is the difference between synchronous and asynchronous communication?

8. What is the number one use of the Internet?

9. Name the three methods of accessing e-mail from an e-mail server.

10. What is SMS and how is it used?

11. What do chat and instant messaging have in common? How do they differ?

12. Why is video conferencing so valuable?

13. What is the primary markup language and protocol of the Web?

14. What is meant by distance education?

15. What information and services can be found on the Web?

16. What are three common sources of information for research?

Discussion Questions

17. Describe how an e-mail message gets from your computer to your friend's computer.

18. What are the limitations of a 32-bit IP address and how might they be resolved?

19. What are the benefits and drawbacks of client/server architecture?

20. What are the benefits and drawbacks of P2P architecture?

21. Why might P2P networks be more hazardous, in terms of viruses and hackers, than client/server architectures?

22. What are the benefits and drawbacks of synchronous communication?

23. What are the benefits and drawbacks of asynchronous communication?

24. What is a common problem with communicating through e-mail? What can be done to help alleviate this problem?

25. What are binary files and why can't they be sent as e-mail?

26. Compare and contrast the benefits and shortcomings of IMAP and POP.

27. Discuss the importance of netiquette.

28. How will XML and XHTML change the nature of the Web?

29. Why are plug-ins necessary for some Web sites?

30. What are the pros and cons of Cookie technology?

31. How do search engines and subject directories differ? What types of scenarios does each support?

32. What is WYSIWYG, and why is it important to Web authors?

33. What is a concern of primary and secondary teachers when it comes to student Web use, and how can this concern be eased?

34. How is the Web used in job hunting?

35. Compare and contrast the pros and cons of library, database, and Web research.

Exercises

Try It Yourself

1. Use your favorite search engine to acquire the URLs of three online music services (you can select from those listed in this chapter) and pay each a visit. Create a spreadsheet that displays the features provided by each service at varying membership levels and their fees. Use formulas and functions to determine which service offers the best deal for your music needs. Write up your results using a word processor.

2. Use your favorite Web search engine to find several online travel services. Evaluate each of the services then, using a word processor, write up a summary of your impressions. Which service do you think is most helpful? Why?

3. Do a search on "plagiarism" at your favorite search engine. Study the search results and find answers to the following questions:
   a. How prevalent is plagiarism on college campuses?
   b. In what ways does the Web support plagiarism?
   c. What are colleges doing to fight plagiarism?

   Write up the results of your study using a word processor.

4. Visit www.opus1.com/www/traceroute.html. This Web site provides access to a program called Traceroute that allows you to view the path of a packet across the Internet. Traceroute returns the name of each router that the packet encounters on its journey. We will use this tool to trace the route of a packet from Tucson Arizona (the location of this Web server) to the Louvre in Paris France. 143.126.211.222 is the IP address of the Louvre's Web site. Type it in the textbox and click "Trace that puppy." The resulting list is the routers that your packet encountered on the way to the Louvre. How many routers (hops) did your packet visit? What can you discern from the router information? Can you guess who owns any of the routers and where they are located?

5. Search the Web for a biography on Tim Berners-Lee and use it to write a summary of his professional life.

Virtual Classroom Activities

For the following exercises, do not use face-to-face or telephone communications with your group members. Use only Internet communications.

6. Have each group member use a different search engine with the goal of finding the least expensive roundtrip airfare for a week in Jamaica. The flight

can depart from any airport within 100 miles of your present location. Define the departure and return dates of the trip. The person with the lowest fare is the winner and gets to delegate the work of writing up the team results.

7. Choose two instant messaging tools to download and evaluate. If you are unable to install software, you can substitute two Web-based chat utilities. Set up a date and time for all to log on to each tool and try it out. Carry out your evaluation live from within each tool conversing about the good and bad features. Write up reviews of each product.

Teamwork

8. Each team member should use a word processor to write a specific description of the e-mail serv-

ice(s) that you use to access your e-mail (POP, IMAP, or Web), and your level of satisfaction with your service. Team members should e-mail their papers to each other as attachments. As a group, determine which members are using appropriate e-mail services and which should switch. Write up the results of your discussion.

9. Have each group member go online in search of employment in his or her chosen field (if you don't have a chosen field, choose something of interest). Find a job posting in your field that lists the pay scale and job description. As a group, decide who found the best paying job and whose job sounds most satisfying. Write up your results.

Learning Check

To check your knowledge of each of the chapter objectives, use this chart to find related end-of-chapter content.

Learning Objective	Key Terms		Questions	Exercises
Learning Objective 1 Describe how hardware, protocols, and software work together to create the Internet and how the Internet may change in the future.	client/server computer network Internet backbone Internet service providers (ISP) IP address	peer-to-peer (P2P) ports protocols routers TCP/IP	1, 2, 3, 4, 5, 6, 18, 19, 20, 21	4, 5

Learning Objective 2
Compare and contrast the types of communication tools available on the Internet.
	asynchronous
	  communication
	chat
	e-mail
	e-mail attachment
	instant messaging
		Short Message
		  Service (SMS)
		spam
		synchronous
		  communication
			7, 8, 9, 10, 11,
			12, 22, 23, 24,
			25, 26, 27
				7, 8

Learning Objective 3
Explain the underlying structure of the Web and the technologies that support it.
	content
	  streaming
	cookie
	HTML tag
	hyperlink
	Hypertext Markup
	  Language
	  (HTML)
	search engine
		Uniform Resource
		  Locator (URL)
		Web authoring
		  software
		Web browser
		Web server
		World Wide Web
		XML plug-in
			13, 28, 29, 30,
			31, 32	

(continued)

	Learning Objective	Key Terms	Questions	Exercises
	Learning Objective 4 Define the categories of information and services that the Web provides and the ways in which the Web supports research.	plagiarism	14, 15, 16, 33, 34, 35	1, 2, 3, 6, 9

Endnotes

1 *Computer Industry Almanac,* www.c-i-a.com/pr1202.htm, accessed May 24, 2003.

2 *"The Ever-Shifting Internet Population: A new look at Internet access and the digital divide",* A report from the Pew Internet and American Life Project, www.pewinternet.org, April 16, 2003.

3. Pappalardo, Denise, "The ISP top dogs," *Network World Fusion,* accessed at www.nwfusion.com/newsletters/isp/2001/00846039.html, May 30, 2001.

4 Christenson, Nick, "Ranking Internet Service Providers by Size," accessed at www.jetcafe.org/~npc/isp/large.html, April 30, 2003.

5 Lui, John, "Asia running out of IP-address room," *ZDNet News,* May 28, 2003, zdnet.com.com/2100-1103_2-1010666.html?tag=fdfeed accessed June 8, 2003.

6 Wong, Edward, "United to Offer E-Mail and Data Access on Domestic Flights," *New York Times,* June 17, 2003.

7 "Netiquette Home Page," www.albion.com/netiquette/, accessed June 6, 2003.

8 "AOL, Microsoft Vow Messaging Cooperation," *The Associated Press,* June 4, 2003.

9 "UK Texting Takes Off," ThinkMobile.com, www.thinkmobile.com/News/00/69/49/, July 16, 2003.

10 "Businesses turn to texting", *BBC News,* December 9, 2002.

11 Shafer, Amy, "Sprint Voice Calls to Mimic Internet," AP News, May 27, 2003.

12 "IDC Pictures Srong Growth for MMS," MCommerce Times.com, : June 03, 2003.

13 "Phonecams spark children fears," AAP, AustralianIT.com, http://australianit.news.com.au/articles/0,7204,6873846%5e16123%5e%5enbv%5e,00.html, August 6, 2003.

14 OCLC Online Computer Library Center, Inc.—Office of Research, http://wcp.oclc.org/, accessed 6/2/2003.

15 "Shearman & Sterling shares knowledge to think big and think fast," IBM Software Success Stories Web site, www3.ibm.com/software/success/cssdb.nsf/cs/NAVO55JQVM?OpenDocument&Site=software, accessed May 1, 2002.

16 "DreamWorks Records Signs Deal with Tonos Musician Melissa Bathory," *City News Service,* December 30, 2002.

17 Online Degree Programs @ FSU, http://online.fsu.edu/student/degree/explore/program/.

18 For information on scams read the Federal Trade Commission's article entitled "Net Based Business Opportunities: Are Some Flop-portunities?" at www.ftc.gov/bcp/conline/pubs/online/netbizop.htm.

19 Internet Fraud Complaint Center (www1.ifccfbi.gov/index.asp).

20 Strauss, Neil, "Apple Finds the Future for Online Music Sales," *New York Times,* Section E , Page 1, May 29, 2003.

21 Black, Jane, "Web Music Gets Its Act Together," *BusinessWeek Online,* April 22, 2003, www.businessweek.com/technology, accessed June 8, 2003.

22 Menta, Richard, "Ipsos-Reid: More Americans Taste Tunes on Net," *MP3Newswire.net,* December 7, 2002, www.mp3newswire.net/stories/2002/tunetaste.html accessed June 8, 2003.

23 "Matrix sequel pirated online," *BBC News,* May 27, 2003.

24 "Night goggles to beat film piracy," *BBC News,* May 30, 2003.

25 FSU Academic Honor Code, FSU General Bulletin 2003-2004, http://registrar.fsu.edu/bulletin/undergrad/info/acad_regs.htm#AcademicHonorCode.

Telecommunications andNetworks

Technology 360°

Amanda Vicars works as a customer service representative for Microserve Software corporation. Microserve is based in Austin, Texas, but Amanda works from her home office in Greenfield, California. Amanda is comfortable with computers but is not a "techie." Her degree was in communications, and it was her communication skills, not her technical prowess that won her this job. However, she learned a lot in her training and is now proficient at looking up solutions in the online corporate database.

Amanda's first priority is to set up a home computer network capable of supporting the large amount of data and voice communications that it will be handling. She has a fairly new PC to serve as her workstation. However, she is using a dial-up Internet connection that is too slow to support her new work. The guidelines she was given during her training state that she will need a minimum of 1-Mbps Internet connection to be able to run database queries while communicating with customers on the phone. The connection needs to be reliable and secure, and will be used to connect to the Microserve virtual private network. Amanda has been given software to install on her PC that not only allows her to log in to the corporate network to access the database, but also allows her to seek assistance from customer service supervisors through a convenient chat utility.

To further complicate the situation, Amanda shares her house with a friend who at times will be sharing the Internet connection using a notebook computer.

1. How can Amanda find out what Internet services are available in her area? Once informed, what criteria should Amanda use in choosing an ISP?
2. What type of home network should Amanda set up to accommodate her own needs and those of her housemate? What equipment will she need to purchase?
3. What security precautions should Amanda take to insure the security of her home network and the Microserve corporate network?

Check out Amanda's *Action Plan* at the conclusion of this chapter.

LEARNING OBJECTIVES	CHAPTER CONTENT
1. Understand the fundamentals of data communications and the criteria for choosing a communications medium.	**Fundamentals of Telecommunications**
2. Explain how networking media, devices, and software work together to provide data networking services.	**Telecommunications Components: Networking Media, Devices, and Software**
3. List the different classifications of computer networks and their defining characteristics and understand how to set up a wireless home network.	**Networks and Distributed Computing**
4. Appreciate the benefits of computer networks in homes, organizations, and businesses.	**Networking Applications and Benefits**

Introduction

As personal computers empower individuals, networks empower groups. In an organization, teamwork is synonymous with success. The better the flow of information between group members, the more productive the group becomes at reaching goals more efficiently and effectively. Networks act as the circulatory system of an organization, and given this, an organization needs to ensure that the network can properly support its information and communications needs.

A network is fundamentally a communications system. In selecting the components of a network, you must consider the speed and capacity of the communications medium that carries the communications signal. The communications medium works in conjunction with communications devices and software to provide a data communications network. There are numerous types of networks, each supporting the unique needs of their environment. This chapter examines a variety of network types and their components to provide an understanding of how networks are used in businesses and homes to help us be more productive.

Just as the Internet is a public network that serves the information needs of the global population, smaller private networks serve the information needs of private organizations, businesses, and even individuals in homes. The Internet has been defined as a network of networks. In this chapter, we answer the questions: What *is* a network, and what is its value?

FUNDAMENTALS OF TELECOMMUNICATIONS

Communications may be defined as the transmission of a signal by way of a medium, from a sender to a receiver. The signal contains a message comprised of data and information. It is important to note two characteristics about communications. First, the message is not communicated directly; rather, it is communicated by way of a *signal*. Second, the signal itself goes through some *communications medium*, which is anything that carries a signal between a sender and receiver.

You can easily recognize these aspects of communications if you consider what happens when humans communicate (see Figure 5.1). When we talk to one another face to face, we send messages to each other. One person may be the sender at one moment in time and the receiver a few seconds later. The same entity, a person in this case, can be a sender, a receiver, or both. This is typical of two-way communications. The signals we use to convey these messages are our spoken words—our language. For communications to be effective, both sender and receiver must understand the signals and agree upon the way the signals are to be interpreted. For example, if the sender in Figure 5.1 is speaking in a language the receiver does not understand, or if the sender believes a particular word has one meaning and the receiver believes the word has some other meaning, effective communications will not occur.

FIGURE 5.1 • Human speech

In face-to-face situations, the transmission medium is the air.

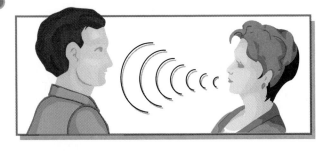

FIGURE 5.2 • Telephone communications

The transmission medium is the telephone lines.

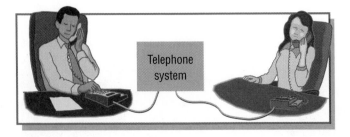

When we talk to one another, our speech causes vibrations in air molecules. In face-to-face communications, the transmission medium is the air. When we read, the transmission medium is the printed page. The traditional telephone converts a signal carried by the medium of air into an electronic signal carried over wires (another medium), and eventually converts it back into a signal carried by air (see Figure 5.2). A cell phone converts the sound waves created by your voice into a radio signal carried over air, which is received by a base station that transfers the signal to wires, and then perhaps to another cell phone over a radio signal.

As you consider the structure of computer systems, it is important to keep these fundamental communications concepts in mind. For example, establishing a communications link between two hardware devices requires that they "speak the same language," or that an "interpreter" of some sort play an intervening role. And, as we will discuss later in this chapter, the characteristics of the medium—in particular, the speed at which it can carry a signal—is an important consideration.

Telecommunications and Data Communications

Computing devices are able to communicate with each other via telecommunications and data communications systems. **Telecommunications** refers to the electronic transmission of signals for communications. Some telecommunications devices that we interact with on a daily basis include telephones, radios, TVs, and computers. *Data communications*, a specialized subset of telecommunications, refers to the electronic collection, processing, and distribution of data, typically between computer system hardware devices. A *telecommunications network* connects communications and computing devices. A *computer network* is a specific type of telecommunications network that connects computers and computer systems for data communications.

In this chapter we will discuss three components of telecommunications networks: networking media, networking hardware, and networking software. **Networking media** is anything that carries an electronic signal and creates an interface between a sending device and a receiving device. *Networking hardware devices* (or just *networking devices*) and *networking software* work together to enable and control communications signals between communications and computer devices. Usually networking hardware devices function as both sending and receiving devices. Figure 5.3 shows a general model of telecommunications. The model starts with a sending unit, such as a person, a computer system, a PC, a cell phone, or another device that originates the message. The sending unit transmits a signal to a networking device. The networking device can perform a number of functions, including changing or manipulating the signal. The networking device then sends the signal over a medium. The signal is received by another networking device that is connected to the receiving unit, a computer system, a PC, a cell phone, or another device that receives the message. The process can then be reversed.

FIGURE 5.3 • **General model of telecommunications**

Sending and receiving units use networking devices and media to communicate.

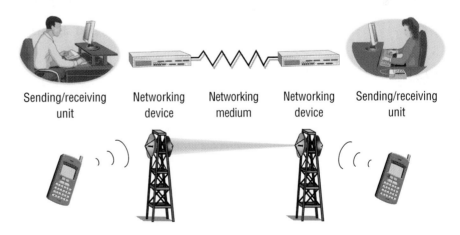

| Sending/receiving unit | Networking device | Networking medium | Networking device | Sending/receiving unit |

Advances in telecommunications technology are some of the most exciting developments in the field of computer systems today. These advances allow us to communicate rapidly with family, friends, and business associates, anywhere in the world. Telecommunications also reduce the amount of time it takes for groups to make decisions, facilitating faster group action and wasting less time. Consider how long it would take to complete a group project for school without the benefit of a telephone or e-mail.

Characteristics of Telecommunications

The characteristics of telecommunications components should be analyzed in terms of how they enable you to take advantage of opportunities or to solve problems. For example, you may find that you can get in an hour at the gym each day if you respond to e-mail during your hour-long daily commute on the bus or train, but this will require wireless access to e-mail. Perhaps the growth of your successful business is raising communications issues among your expanding workforce. This was the case for family-owned Construction One Inc., which at any given time might have 40 or 50 construction jobs going all over the country. They invested in a PCS wireless phone system that allowed job superintendents to communicate via phone or notebook computer, sharing problems and solutions, even transferring job site photos to the home office.[1] The owners of Construction One learned how an understanding of telecommunications components can help solve problems and maximize opportunities.

In order to select the best option from the wide array of telecommunications options available you must consider a number of important factors, such as signal types and transmission capacities. As you will see, one of the most important characteristics of a medium is the speed at which it can transmit signals (and hence data) in a given time period.

Types of Signals. If we measured the voltage on a telephone wire during a conversation, we would see something like Figure 5.4a. Notice that Figure 5.4a shows a signal that continuously changes over time. This type of continuous fluctuation over time between high and low voltage is called an **analog signal**. If we measured air pressure in Figure 5.4a instead of voltage, we would be representing a soundwave traveling through air. Thus, human speech is an analog signal. Recall from Chapter 2 that sound waves are analog signals. Since we represent the sound of our voice electronically over a phone line, it makes sense that this electronic signal would also be analog.

In contrast, if we measured the voltage on cables used to connect PCs, we would probably see something comparable to Figure 5.4b. The signal in Figure 5.4b at any given time is either high or low. This type of discrete voltage state—either high or low—is called a **digital signal**. The two states are used to represent the state of a bit, high for 1, and low for 0. It is convenient for computer hardware devices to communicate digitally because computer circuitry itself is digital.

FIGURE 5.4 • Analog and digital signals

An analog signal continuously changes over time. A digital signal has a discrete state—either high or low.

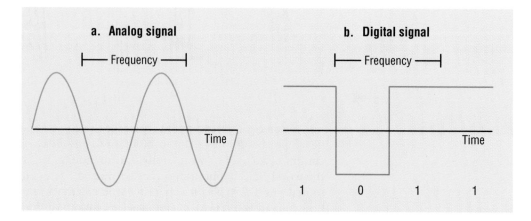

FIGURE 5.5 • Frequency

The speed at which a signal changes from high to low, the signal frequency, dictates the rate of speed at which data is delivered.

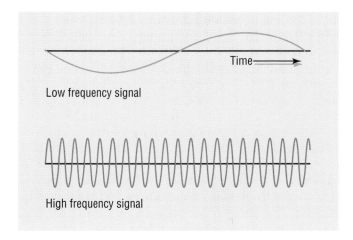

Low frequency signal

High frequency signal

The speed at which a signal can change from high to low is called the signal frequency (see Figure 5.5). The faster the signal frequency, the faster the data transmission. Signal frequency is measured in *hertz (Hz)*—cycles per second, and data transmission speed is measured in *bits per second (bps)*.

Transmission Capacities. Some uses of telecommunications can require very fast transmission speeds. For example, when the salesperson swipes your credit card at the checkout counter, your purchase information joins with thousands of others that are being routed to the credit-card company for approval. Such networks must handle high-volume traffic very quickly so as not to keep customers waiting. Other applications, such as connecting a home computer to an office computer to allow you to work at home a few days a week, do not require as much transmission capacity and speed. Residential networks typically have simple networking requirements. Business networking requirements are more complicated to calculate. Great care must be taken to ensure that the selected network components can support the organization's needs.

Some transmission media can accommodate more than one signal frequency at the same time. That is, both relatively low- and high-frequency signals can be sent simultaneously over a single medium. The range of signal frequencies that can be sent over a given medium at the same time is known as the **bandwidth**. Bandwidth, therefore, is a measure of transmission capacity. The larger the bandwidth, the greater the transmission capacity. A medium with a bandwidth of 100 Hz can transmit 10 times the number of bits as a medium with a bandwidth of 10 Hz. Figure 5.6 illustrates bandwidth as it relates to different environments and service levels.

FIGURE 5.6 • Bandwidth Options

A variety of different bandwidth services are available to suit a variety of residential and business needs.

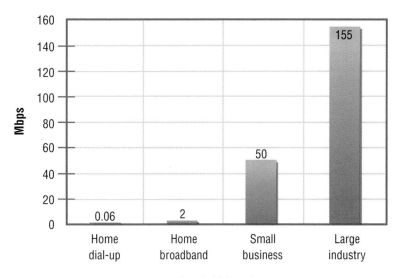

Bandwidth options

The medium's bandwidth, or capacity, constrains how many frequencies or channels can be used to send signals. Today's bandwidth options fall into one of two categories: narrowband or broadband.

Broadband media is significantly faster than narrowband. However, the minimum speed for a media to be considered broadband is hotly debated. Some telecommunications experts contend that broadband includes any media faster than 200 Kbps (kilobits per second), but others set the bottom limit of broadband at 2 Mbps (megabits per second). Michael Powell, the Chairman of the U.S. Federal Communications Commission (FCC), has stated that a clear, uniformly accepted definition of the term evades the FCC. "Whatever broadband is, it's fast—the Commission has defined it as 200 Kbs. I submit, however, that broadband is not a speed," Powell said. "It is a medium that offers a wide potential set of applications and uses. I think broadband should be viewed holistically as a technical capability that can be matched to consumers' broad communication, entertainment, information, and commercial desires."[2] Thus, *narrowband* would be considered anything below 200 Kbs, typically 56 Kbps, the speed of a traditional dial-up modem connection.

Not long ago, broadband data transfer speeds were only available at a premium price to businesses and organizations to support high-traffic data communications. Within the past few years, we have witnessed the introduction of affordable residential broadband service. Some politicians and business leaders are making efforts to bring broadband Internet acccess to every U.S. residence (see the Community Technology box). Residential broadband offers speeds as fast as 1.28 Mbps. Telecommunications companies offer businesses broadband services that support up to 155 Mbps. These types of broadband lines are used by large organizations, such as universities, credit-card companies, airlines, the military, and some government agencies.

The availability of broadband data communications is empowering professionals to become more effective in their chosen careers. Consider telemedicine, practicing medicine over telecommunications channels. The Charles R. Drew University of Medicine and Science is using telemedicine to bring healthcare to the innercity communities of Los Angeles.[3] In a pilot program, they networked an innercity clinic with their university for electronic consultations with ophthalmologists (eye doctors) in a service they call teleophthalmology. Clinicians at the innercity clinic interview patients, record digital images of the patient's eyes, and submit the patient record with images over the high-speed network to ophthalmologists at the university for review. Prior to the program, patients waited an average of three to 6 months for a routine eye exam. The teleophthalmology program cut the average consultation time from a half-hour to less than 5 minutes, allowing the clinic to catch up with its backlog of patients. Approximately 30 percent of patients in the program were diagnosed with sight-threatening conditions. Without broadband network connections and the teleophthalmology program, these individuals may have lost their sight. The program was so successful, that Charles R. Drew University of Medicine and Science received funding to open seven more clinics. They are also beginning a pilot program in telepsychiatry, which will allow patients to interact with psychiatrists through video conferencing over the high-speed network.

COMMUNITY /\/\/\ TECHNOLOGY

A National Broadband Policy?

Many professionals in the telecommunications industry and government believe that encouraging the provision of broadband Internet access to every home and business in America would provide a tremendous platform for economic growth and a catapult for innovation. John Chambers of Cisco Systems puts it this way: "Broadband should be a national imperative for this country in the 21st Century, just like putting a man on the moon was an imperative in the last century. In order to stay competitive, educate the workforce and increase productivity, the United States must have ubiquitous broadband." Mr. Chambers is a member of a high-powered group of industry leaders called the Technology Network, or TechNet. TechNet is lobbying for the development of a national broadband initiative with the goal of 100 Mbps to 100 million homes and small businesses by 2010. Considering that current popular broadband rates hover between 1 and 2 Mbps, this is quite a lofty goal. Lofty, but perhaps not unattainable with the proper backing.

A broadband Internet connection in every home and business would affect families, businesses, and society in general. It would provide new entertainment and e-commerce applications, enable an enriched exploitation of the Internet, as well as provide healthcare, education, and electronic government applications. Broadband would enable dramatically different patterns of network and communications usage that would have an impact on our lifestyles and businesses.

The FCC has recognized the benefits of widespread broadband and has developed its own national broadband initiative. The FCC has outlined a national policy with objectives that include:

- Promotion of the availability of broadband to all Americans
- Initiation of regulatory policies for broadband services
- Stimulation of investment and innovation in broadband technology

Other politicians are jumping on the broadband-wagon. Senator Joe Lieberman proposed a National Broadband Strategy in 2002 that calls for an FCC regulatory framework, tax credits and incentives to encourage broadband growth, and support and an organizational framework for further research and development.

The biggest challenge of delivering residential broadband is referred to as "the last mile." The infrastructure along the main backbones of the telecommunications networks can handle broadband, but the cables running to each household—the last mile of the telecommunications cable—are ill-equipped to handle the load. Massive and costly upgrades would be required to fulfill the goals of a national broadband policy.

Questions

1. In what ways would broadband in every home change the way you access information and communicate with friends and family?
2. Is it possible that the broadband-wagon is simply a ploy by politicians to get votes, and by telecommunications companies to build business? Or is this really an issue of importance?
3. Should the deployment of broadband be assisted by the federal government or should government leave industry to work it out on their own?

Sources
1. *"TechNet CEOs Call for National Broadband Policy,"* TechNet Press Release, Jan 15, 2002, www.technet.org/news/newsreleases_/2002-01-15.62.html.
2. FCC Broadband Web site, www.fcc.gov/broadband/Welcome.html.
3. *"Lieberman Joins Broadband Clamor,"* Roy Marc, Internet-News.com, *June 7, 2002,* www.isp-planet.com/news/2002/lieberman_020607.html.

TELECOMMUNICATIONSCOMPONENTS:NETWORKINGMEDIA, DEVICES,ANDSOFTWARE

Some telecommunications networks support voice communications, others support data communications, and still others support both voice and data. No matter what the type, the communications that take place on these networks require networking media, hardware, and software. This section compares and contrasts different types of network media, and the devices and software that support them.

Networking Media

Various types of communications media are used for telecommunications networks. Each type of medium exhibits its own set of characteristics, including transmission capacity and speed. In developing a network, the selection of media depends on the environment and use of the network. Media should be chosen to support the use, in the given environment at the least cost, taking into account possible future needs of the network. For example, computer users in a rental apartment would probably not be allowed to run network cables through walls and attic space to create a home network. They would need to select a wireless medium. However, wireless media may not have the capacity to support the video applications of a different user who wishes to run video programming from a digital video recorder to televisions around the house. This individual would need to run high-capacity cables. When a business invests in a network, it selects a network that will accommodate a reasonable amount of growth in both workforce and business needs without overestimating these requirements and wasting money.

Different communications media connect systems in different ways. Some media send signals along physical connections like wire, but others send signals through the air by light and radio waves.

Physical Cables. Physical cables range in bandwidth from narrow to broadband. Cables have an advantage over wireless options because some cables support much higher data transfer rates than wireless transmission can. The disadvantage of cables is their physical presence. Cables need to be laid, typically in an inconspicuous manner; they are run underground or inside walls. Depending on the environment, laying cable can take a considerable amount of time and effort. Three types of transmission cables are typically used to connect data communications devices: twisted-pair wire cable, coaxial cable, and fiber-optic cable.

Twisted-pair cable is, as you might expect, a cable consisting of pairs of twisted wires (see Figure 5.7). Twisted-pair is the type of cable that brings telephone service to your home. A typical cable will contain two or more twisted pairs of copper wire. The twist helps keep the signal from "bleeding" into the next pair. Because the twisted-pair wires are insulated, they can be placed close together and packaged in one group. Twisted-pair has traditionally been considered a narrowband medium, supporting speeds of only up to 56 Kbps. Dial-up modem connections use twisted-pair cable. More recent innovations have enabled twisted-pair to be used for broadband over short distances. It can support transfer rates of up to 7 Mbps, over distances of up to about 3.5 miles, at which point the signal begins to degrade. Devices called *repeaters* are sometimes used to boost the signal so that it can travel longer distances.

The primary advantage of twisted-pair wire cabling is that it is inexpensive to purchase and install. For large organizations, where cabling costs often represent over half the cost of many telecommunications installations, this advantage is significant. The principal disadvantage of twisted-pair wire cable is that it does not support data transfer rates as high as other forms of cabling.

FIGURE 5.7 • Twisted-pair cable

Twisted-pair cable, like that for home telephones, consists of pairs of insulated twisted wires bound together in a sheath.

FIGURE 5.8 • **Coaxial cable**

Coaxial cable, like that used for cable TV, consists of an inner conductor wire surrounded by insulation, a conductive shield, and a cover.

Figure 5.8 shows a typical coaxial cable. You may recognize this as the type of cable provided by cable television services, which connects to your television. A **coaxial cable** consists of an inner conductor wire surrounded by insulation, a conductive shield (usually a layer of foil or metal braiding), and a cover.

When used for data transmission, coaxial cable falls in the middle of the cabling spectrum in terms of cost and performance. It is more expensive than twisted-pair wire cable but less expensive than fiber-optic cable (discussed next). The construction of the coaxial cable provides better control of the signal than with twisted-pair cable, offering cleaner and crisper data transmission. It also offers a higher data transmission rate. For exceptionally high data transmission rates, however, you must look to fiber-optic cable.

Twisted-pair and coaxial cables transmit electrical signals over copper or other metal wires. In contrast, **fiber-optic cable**, which consists of thousands of extremely thin strands of glass or plastic bound together in a sheathing (a jacket), transmits signals with light beams (see Figure 5.9). These high-intensity light beams are generated by lasers and are conducted along the transparent fibers. These fibers have a thin coating, called cladding, which effectively works like a mirror, preventing the light from leaking out of the fiber. Such protection is not ensured with copper wire, where signals can sometimes bleed from one cable to the next, disrupting the signal.

Because it transmits via light rather than electricity, fiber-optic cable has some extraordinary abilities compared to other forms of cabling. Mostly it's fast. Fiber is capable of supporting tremendous data transfer rates—upward of 2.5 billion bps, or 32,000 long-distance phone calls simultaneously. Transmissions that take a little less than an hour over copper wires can be sent through optical fibers in under one second. Fiber is the choice for any situation that requires large amounts of data to be sent at high speeds. For example, Appalachian State University utilizes fiber-optic transmission equipment to facilitate a broadband cable television network that delivers 110 cable TV channels to the entire campus. Besides its high

FIGURE 5.9 • **Fiber-optic cable**

Fiber-optic cable, with the fastest data rate of all types of cable, transmits signals with light beams.

SEWERS DOUBLE AS CONDUITS FOR COMMUNICATIONS

Seattle, Albuquerque, and Indianapolis have all signed agreements with a company who has the perfect solution to installing fiber-optic cable without digging up the city streets to do so: use the existing sewer lines. Company employees will install stainless steel conduits in the larger pipes, and thread the cable through them. In smaller pipes, little robots will do the job. As an added bonus, the company will keep the city sewers clean.

Source:
"Seattle sewers to turn into fiber-optic arteries"
By Angel Gonzalez
Seattle Times
http://archives.seattletimes.nwsource.com/cgi-
bin/texis.cgi/web/vortex/display?slug=sewer26m&date=20030726&query=sewer
July 26, 2003
Cited on July 30, 2003

data transfer rates, fiber-optic cable has other advantages such as its small size, high reliability, and durability. It is also a secure media since the signal cannot be tapped into and stolen without notice. The only reason fiber is not being installed everywhere is its cost and the high cost of installation.

Microwave and Satellite Transmission.
Microwave and satellite transmissions are sent through the atmosphere and space. Although using these transmission media does not entail the expense of laying cable, the transmission devices needed to utilize them can be quite expensive. **Microwave transmission**, also called terrestrial microwave, consists of a high-frequency radio signal that is sent through the air. Microwave transmission is a line-of-sight medium, which means that a straight line between the transmitter and receiver must be unobstructed. Microwave transmissions can be sent through the air up to distances of approximately 30 miles. You often see microwave towers alongside interstate roads since the roads provide long straight unobstructed stretches of land (see Figure 5.10). Weather and atmospheric conditions can have an impact on the quality of a microwave signal. Typically, to achieve longer transmission distances, microwave stations are placed in a series—one station will receive a signal, amplify it, and retransmit it to the next microwave transmission tower. Microwaves can carry literally thousands of channels at the same time.

A **communications satellite** is basically a microwave station placed in outer space. Satellites receive a signal from one point on earth and then rebroadcast it at a different frequency to a different location (see Figure 5.11). The advantage of satellite communications is that it can transmit data quickly over long distances. This is important for companies that require high-speed transmission over large geographic regions. Problems such as the curvature of the earth, mountains, and other structures that block the line-of-sight microwave transmission make satellites an attractive alternative.

Most of today's satellites are owned by telecommunications companies that rent or lease them to other companies. However, several large companies are now using their own satellites for internal telecommunications. Some large retail chains, like Wal-Mart, use satellite transmission to connect their main offices to retail stores and warehouses throughout the country or the world. Holiday Inn has used satellites to improve customer service by sending the latest room and rate information to reservation desks throughout Europe and the United States. In addition to standard satellite stations, there are small mobile satellite systems that allow people and businesses to communicate. These portable systems have a dish that is a few feet in diameter and can operate on battery power anywhere in the world. This is important for news organizations that require the ability to transmit news stories from remote locations.

In the near future, satellites may be replaced by or complimented with other less expensive alternatives. For

FIGURE 5.10 • **Microwave towers**
Microwave signals require line-of-sight transmission.

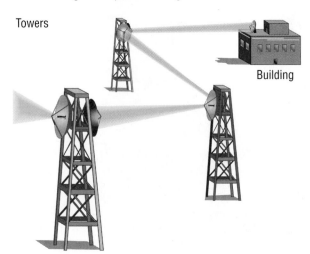

Towers

Building

FIGURE 5.11 • Satellite transmission

Communications satellites are relay stations that receive signals from one earth station and rebroadcast them to another.

example, NASA is funding a project hosted by AeroVironment that uses an unmanned, solar-powered airplane called Helios to serve the purpose of a satellite (see Figure 5.12).[4] Helios is capable of flying in the stratosphere, above commercial air traffic, for six months. One Helios plane could handle communications traffic for an entire metropolitan area.

FIGURE 5.12 • Satellite alternatives

The AeroVironment Helios can stay aloft for six months in the stratosphere delivering telecommunications signals.

Global Positioning System. The **global positioning system (GPS)** uses satellites to pinpoint the location of objects on earth. Using a GPS receiver, a network of 24 satellites, and a method of calculating locations called trilateration, a GPS system tells you the exact location of the receiver on the earth's surface. The GPS constellation of satellites orbit the earth in such a way that at any given time and location on earth, four satellites are visible to a GPS receiver. By measuring the distance from the receiver to each satellite, and calculating those distances with the known position of each satellite, the receiver is able to determine its location. Like the Internet, GPS was originally developed for national security and later extended for public use.

Early GPSs were expensive and used only in environments where determining your location was a matter of life and death, such as in far-traveling boats. Now, you can purchase a GPS receiver for as little as $150, and they are becoming increasingly popular in a variety of applications. Available as small handheld devices, add-ons for handheld computers, and as in-dashboard devices for automobiles, GPS systems are primarily used to assist travelers in getting from one place to another. GPS software is able to display a traveler's location on a city map and give suggestions for the shortest route to a destination (see Figure 5.13).

GPS has also been used to map the planet's surface. For example, a GPS receiver was taken to the peak of Mt. Everest in 1999 to determine the exact height of the mountain. It was measured to be 29,035 feet above sea level, 7 feet taller than the previously accepted height calculated in the 1954 Survey of India. The GPS also revealed that Mt. Everest is moving northeast at approximately 2.4 inches a year.

A newer application of GPS technology assists others in locating a person in danger. An amazing 359,000 children are kidnapped each year, with many more attempted kidnappings reported. The POMALS (peace of mind at light speed) company has developed a small, inexpensive GPS receiver called the ActivePak that parents can place in a child's backpack or pocket to allow them to track their child's location. Another GPS device for children (shown in Figure 5.14) is the Wherify watch GPS child locator.

To keep herself safe during late-night walks, Kursty Groves, a design student at the Royal College of Art in London, developed the Techno Bra, an undergarment device that is able to detect rapid jumps in heart rate caused by dangerous, distressing situations, and automatically alert the authorities with the location of the

FIGURE 5.13 • Handheld GPS receiver

A handheld GPS receiver pinpoints your exact location and displays it on a map.

FIGURE 5.14 • Useful GPS applications

GPS technology is being integrated into children's belongings, such as this wristwatch, to allow parents to track their child's location should the child become lost or in the case of a kidnapping.

victim using a GPS and cell phone all sewn into the undergarment. Other similar devices are being developed that monitor the health of individuals and notify rescue services if a heart attack or seizure occurs. GPSs provide us with convenience and safety; however, as with all technology that accesses personal data (such as a person's location at a given time), the use of GPS technology must not infringe on an individual's right to privacy.

Wireless Fidelity. **Wireless fidelity (Wi-Fi)** is a term used to describe wireless networking devices that use the 802.11 protocol. This protocol, developed by the Institute of Electrical and Electronics Engineers (IEEE), supports wireless computer networking within a limited range at broadband speeds of 4.5 Mbps to 11 Mbps. The well established 802.11b standard has recently been overshadowed by the new and faster 802.11g specification. The 802.11g specification allows Wi-Fi networks to transmit data at 54 Mbps. Wi-Fi technology uses wireless *access points* that broadcast network traffic using radio frequencies to computers equipped with Wi-Fi cards or adapters (see Figure 5.15). Wi-Fi has a range of 1,000 ft in open areas and 250 to 400 ft in closed areas. By positioning wireless access points at strategic locations throughout a building, campus, or city, Wi-Fi users can be continuously connected to the network and Internet, no matter where they roam. Wi-Fi has become increasingly popular for home networks. It provides an affordable and simple way to network home computers without the need to run cables.

Many new notebooks are coming equipped with Wi-Fi equipment thanks to Intel's Centrino technology. Centrino combines three technologies for convenient mobile computing: the Intel PRO/Wireless Network Connection, the Intel® Pentium® M Processor, and the Intel® 855 Chipset Family to offer fast processing, longer battery life, and wireless network connections. Having a Wi-Fi equipped notebook is useless however, unless you have an access point to connect to. Access points, commonly called hot spots, are popping up in many locations where people tend to congregate. In Chapter 4 you learned about Internet cafes, even some McDonald's, that provide hot spots for customer use. Your school may offer hot spots on campus for wireless network and Internet access. If you do a lot of traveling you may want to look into Boingo. Boingo is a subscription service that provides access to an increasing number of hot spots (2,600 at last count) in

EXPAND YOUR **KNOWLEDGE**

To learn more about wireless technology, go to www.course.com/swt. Click the link "Expand Your Knowledge" and then complete the lab entitled, "Wireless Networking."

FIGURE 5.15 • **Wi-Fi access points**

Wi-Fi access points are distributed around a geographic area to provide a network connection wherever you roam.

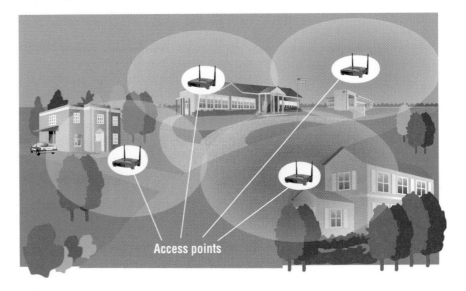

Access points

airports, hotels, cafes, coffee shops, and other public locations in over 300 cities and 43 states for around $21.95 per month.

Some cities, states, and even countries are providing hot spots for public use. The Polynesian Island of Niue in the South Pacific has claimed boasting rights for being the first country to offer free nationwide Wi-Fi Internet access service to its citizens and visitors.[6]

BlueTooth. Bluetooth technology is becoming quite well known. Go shopping for a new cell phone, handheld, or notebook computer, and there's a good chance that you'll find Bluetooth listed among the specifications. The Bluetooth specification was developed by the Bluetooth Special Interest Group (BSIG), a trade organization composed of leaders of the telecommunications, computing, and network industries, such as 3Com, Agere, Ericsson, IBM, Intel, Microsoft, Motorola, Nokia, and Toshiba. The Bluetooth SIG states their mission as "driving the development of a low-cost short-range wireless specification for connecting mobile products".[7] **Bluetooth** (named after a tenth-century Danish king) enables a wide assortment of digital devices to communicate wirelessly over short distances. Table 5.1 lists some Bluetooth-enabled devices.

TABLE 5.1 • Bluetooth-enabled Devices

Some Bluetooth-enabled Devices		
Personal computers	Mobile phones	Automobiles
Printers	Handheld computers	Microwave ovens
Keyboard/mouse	Digital cameras	Refrigerators
	Portable MP3 players	Washers/dryers
	Headphones and headsets	

Bluetooth-enabled devices communicate with each other in pairs. Up to seven devices can be "paired" simultaneously. The pairings may be created automatically or manually. The purpose is to allow pairings and communications to take place with minimal effort on the part of the user. For example, you might use a wireless headset to chat on a cell phone stored in your briefcase. Your handheld computer can be set to automatically synchronize with your personal computer when within range. Such automatic pairings allow personal information such as address books, e-mail, to-do lists, and active files to be shared and synchronized between all your information devices.

Bluetooth communicates at speeds of up to 1 Mbps within a range of up to 33 ft (see Figure 5.16). Bluetooth can also be used to connect devices to a computer network using access points like Wi-Fi. Bluetooth and Wi-Fi compete in some areas, but have unique qualities. Manufacturers are installing Bluetooth chips in a wide variety of communications and computer appliances to allow device-to-device connections. For example, six participants sitting around a conference table could exchange notes or business cards among their notebook, tablet, or handheld computers. In contrast, Wi-Fi focuses on connecting devices to a network and the Internet. Bluetooth devices can communicate directly with each other, whereas Wi-Fi devices communicate only through the nearest access point or hot spot. Wi-Fi has much faster data transfer speeds than Bluetooth.

FIGURE 5.16 • Bluetooth

Bluetooth-enabled devices communicate with each other wirelessly over short distances, up to 33 ft.

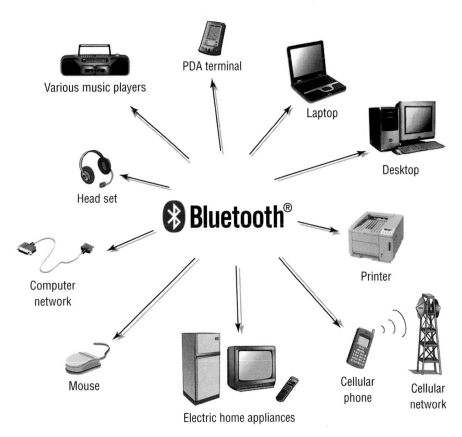

Infrared Transmission. Another type of wireless media, called *infrared transmission*, involves sending signals through the air via light waves. These light waves are longer than the visible spectrum but shorter than radio waves. Infrared transmission requires line-of-sight transmission and short distances. Your television remote control uses infrared to send signals to your television set. Infrared transmission can be used to connect digital devices such as handheld, notebook, and desktop computers. Most handheld and notebook computers include infrared ports, sometimes called *IrDA ports* for Infrared Data Association. External IrDA devices can be purchased and connected to desktop computers and printers. To transfer data between devices, you simply line up the infrared ports of the two devices within a couple feet of each other to create the connection. Once a connection is established, the operating system will provide instructions or a wizard to allow you to share files. Infrared is extremely slow compared to Bluetooth and Wi-Fi, and is expected to eventually be replaced in most applications by these newer, faster technologies. However, infrared is still used in many current models of handheld and notebook computers.

WIRED WORKS FOR KOREAN POLITICIAN

Over 70 percent of the population in South Korea is connected to broadband. The enthusiastic adoption of the technology is changing everything from marriages to politics. In 2003, supporters of a candidate who was losing by 11 A.M. on election day sent out over 800,000 e-mails to mobile phone users, urging them to vote. Three hours later the candidate moved into the lead and won the election.

Source:
"Korea's Weird Wired World"
By Benjamin Fulford
Forbes.com
www.forbes.com/technology/free_forbes/2003/0721/092.html
July 21, 2003
Cited on July 21, 2003

Cellular Transmission. In cellular transmission, a geographic area is divided into cells. A base station, equipped with a tower and a small building that houses the radio equipment, is placed at the center of each cell. As a cell phone user moves from one cell to another, the system judges the cell phone's location based on its signal strength, and passes the phone connection from one cell tower to the next. The signals from the cells are transmitted to a receiver and integrated into the regular phone system. Cellular phone users can thus connect to other cell phone users or anyone who has access to regular phone service (see Figure 5.17).

FIGURE 5.17 • Cellular transmission

As a cell phone user moves from one cell to another, the system judges the cell phone's location based on its signal strength, and passes the phone connection from one cell tower to the next.

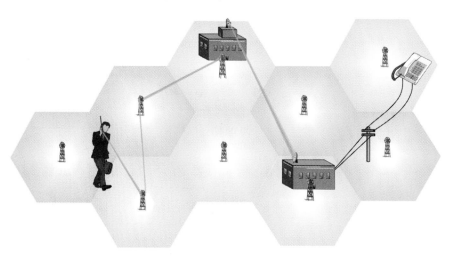

The mobility of cell phone communications is finding important uses in the healthcare industry. Sunnybrook Health Science Centre found cell phones to be the solution to their patient call response issues.[8] Toronto's Sunnybrook is the largest veteran's hospital in Canada. When surveyed, Sunnybrook patients expressed concern over the amount of time it took for caregivers to respond to a call. Investigation revealed that caregivers were responding to patient calls in under 5 minutes, but 5 minutes could seem like 15 or 20 to a resident in need of immediate attention. After extensive research Sunnybrook found a solution in technology that connected patient help buttons to cell phones carried by the caregivers. Now, when a Sunnybrook patient presses the call button, the system rings the cell phone of the caregiver responsible for that patient, and within seconds the patient is communicating with the caregiver over a speaker phone while the caregiver is en route to physically assist the patient.

Networking Devices

A telecommunications networking device can be one of various hardware devices that support electronic communications. Not long ago many of these devices were of interest only to network technicians. Today, the increase in home networking has provided a reason for all of us to acquire a basic understanding of the most common networking devices such as modems, network adapters, network control devices, radio frequency identification devices, and pagers.

Modems. Data and telecommunications networks commonly use transmission media of differing types and capacities at various stages of the communications process. For example many computer systems communicate over analog phone lines. This requires the conversion, or *modulation*, of the computer's digital signal to an analog signal. A computer system receiving an analog signal must *demodulate* the signal back to a digital form. The process of modulation and demodulation is performed by a modem, whose name is derived from its abilities: *modulation* and *demo*dulation.

A **modem** modulates and demodulates signals from one form to another and can be either an internal or external device. Internal modems exist as circuit boards inside a computer; networking cables are connected directly to the computer. External modems exist as separate tabletop boxes; they typically have lights that flash to indicate network activity. Networking cables are connected to the external modem, which, in turn, is connected to the computer.

There are a variety of different types of modems that handle different types of modulation and demodulation. Dial-up modems are most familiar to computer users, since they come standard on PCs and support traditional narrowband Internet connections. These devices not only connect computers over an analog phone line, but also provide other services. Using special software, modems can automatically dial telephone numbers, originate message sending, answer incoming calls, and even record messages. Most dial-up modems also have the ability to send and receive faxes.

Whereas dial-up modems support connections to narrowband networks, other special-purpose modems support connections to broadband networks. A *cable modem* provides Internet access over a cable television network for faster data transmission rates than a traditional dial-up connection (see Figure 5.18). A cable modem is typically an external device that has two connections: one to the cable wall outlet and the other to a computer or computer network device. Although a cable modem modulates and demodulates signals as a dial-up modem does, it is a much more complex device.

A *DSL modem* connects digital devices using a digital signal over *plain old telephone service (POTS)* lines. Digital Subscriber Line (DSL) is a service provided by phone companies that offers relatively inexpensive high-speed access to the Internet for business and residential use. DSL is able to achieve higher speeds than dial-up connections by using a digital signal rather than an analog one. The DSL

FIGURE 5.18 • Cable Modem

A cable modem provides Internet access over a cable television network for faster data transmission rates than a traditional dial-up connection.

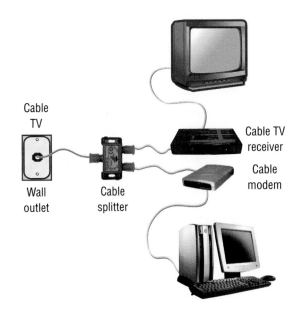

digital signal shares the bandwidth of the phone line with the analog signal of your telephone, so that you can talk on the phone while you are connected to the Internet. Although a DSL modem does not modulate a digital signal to analog, it does other types of signal modulation in order to take maximum advantage of the shared medium.

Network Adapters. Computers can connect to networks and the Internet either by modem, network adapter, or a combination of both. A **network adapter** is a computer circuit board, PC Card, or USB device installed in a computing device so that it can be connected to a network. Network adapters come in two basic varieties: network interface cards and wireless adapters. A network interface card (NIC) is a circuit board or PC Card that, when installed, provides a port for the device to connect to a wired network with traditional network cables. Wireless adaptors can be a circuit board, PC Card, or an external device that connects through a USB port that provides an external antenna with which to send and receive network radio signals (see Figure 5.19). In addition to connecting devices to computer networks, network adapters are used to connect devices to cable modems and DSL modems.

Network Control Devices. For multiple computers to communicate, special devices are required to control the flow of bits over the network medium and ensure that information that is sent reaches its destination quickly and securely. A number of different network control devices handle this responsibility, each with a unique purpose. Here are brief descriptions of those that are most commonly used.

- *Hubs* are small electronic boxes that are used as a central point for connecting a series of computers. A hub sends the signal from each computer to all of the other computers on the network.
- *Switches* are a fundamental part of most networks. They make it possible for several users to send information over a network at the same time without slowing each other down.
- *Repeaters* connect multiple network segments, listening to each segment and repeating the signal heard on one segment onto every other segment connected to the repeater. As mentioned earlier, repeaters are also helpful in situations where a weak signal requires a boost to continue on the medium.
- *Bridges* connect two or more network segments, as a repeater does, but bridges also help regulate traffic.
- A *gateway* is a network point that acts as an entrance to another network.
- *Routers* are advanced networking components that can divide a single network into two logically separate networks. Although network traffic crosses bridges in its search to find every node on a network, it does not cross routers, because the router forms a logical boundary for the network. Routers are also used to interconnect various types of networks, which has led to their widespread deployment in connecting devices around the world to the Internet.
- A *wireless access point* is connected to a wired network and receives and transmits data to wireless adapters installed in computers. It allows wireless devices to connect to a network.
- A *firewall* is a device or software that filters the information coming onto a network to protect the network computers from hackers, viruses, and other unwanted network traffic.

Sometimes network control devices can be combined into a single unit. For example, a home computer network might incorporate a device that includes a router, used to connect to broadband Internet; a switch, used to share Internet access over a wired network and connect computers; a wireless access point, used to connect wireless devices; and a firewall, used to protect the network (see Figure 5.20).

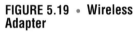

FIGURE 5.19 • Wireless Adapter

This wireless adapter connects to a PC or notebook computer via the USB port.

FIGURE 5.20 • **The Linksys Wireless Access Point Router with 4-Port Switch**

This combination access point/router/switch provides wireless or cable-connected broadband to network users while controlling network traffic.

Radio Frequency Identification (RFID) Devices. A *Radio frequency identification (RFID) device* is a tiny microprocessor combined with an antenna (see Figure 5.21) that is able to broadcast identifying information to an RFID reader. Primarily used to track merchandise from supplier to retailer to customer it is anticipated that RFID will eventually replace the bar code identification system. The most common type of RFID tag consists of a small processor, as small as a grain of sand, embedded on a paper tag connected to conductive carbon ink that acts as an antenna. The tag itself is not self-powered, but gets its power from the magnetic field used by the reader, and uses that power to transmit data to the reader. Wal-Mart has asked its suppliers to include RFID tags on all shipping crates and pallets by 2005.[9] With the cost per tag dipping to $0.05, it is anticipated that RFID tags will become as prevalent as bar code tags. Clothing designer Benetton is embedding RFID tags in all of its clothing.[10] The tags save time when taking inventory, and also can be used to set off alarms if the clothes are illegally taken from a warehouse or store.

FIGURE 5.21 • **Radio frequency ID**

RFID tags include a processor and antena in a tiny package that can be embedded in merchandise for identification.

With the backing of huge retailers like Wal-Mart, it is clear that RFID technology is poised to take off. There are two issues that might slow the development of this technology. The current manufacturing processes are unable to support the demands of manufacturing chips for every item of merchandise. Manufacturers find it improbable that they will be able to meet Wal-Mart's demands of 1 billion tags by 2005.[11] Also, privacy activists are concerned about the ramifications of leaving RFID tags embedded in merchandise after the purchase. Would it be possible for someone to point an RFID reader at a residence and effectively take inventory of all items within the home? Such concern has caused Wal-Mart to hold off on its plans to use RFID on its retail shelves, and confine its use to pallette-level inventory. However, some companies, such as Benetton, continue to embed RFID tags into their products in a manner that doesn't accomodate convenient removal.

Besides its use in retail inventory control, RFID is being used in a number of other areas where automatic identification is useful. Here are some examples:

• Tiny RFID devices are being injected under the skin of pets, where they remain for the lifetime of the pet to assist in tracking the pet should it become lost.

- RFID is used in tagging and tracking wildlife for scientific research.
- RFID is being used to identify people in controlling access to secure locations and information.
- The ScripTalk talking prescription reader[12] uses RFID labels on perscription medicine bottles and a reader that speaks the name of the medicine to assist the blind, elderly, and visually-impaired.
- In parking lot control, RFID tags are being affixed to authorized vehicles to automatically raise the gate upon approach.
- Championchip USA[13] provides RFID tags for marathons, such as the Boston Marathon, that are attached to runner's shoes to determine who crosses the finish line first.

Pagers. *Pagers* are small lightweight devices that receive signals from transmitters. Different pagers have varying levels of ability. The most basic pager simply beeps, flashes, or vibrates to get the attention of the user. More sophisticated pagers accept numeric or text messages. Some pagers allow the owner to listen to voice messages, or send messages as well as receive messages.

There are different types of paging systems. National and regional systems set up transmission towers, much like cell phone networks, to cover large geographic areas. On-site paging systems use small desktop transmitters to send pages over a small wireless network that covers a range of up to 2 miles.

On-site paging systems are finding a variety of uses in businesses and organizations that require on-site messaging. Pagers are being used in businesses to assist in customer service. For instance, in restaurants, emergency rooms, and golf courses, pagers can be given to customers and used to indicate when a table, doctor, or tee time is available (see the Job Technology box). Pagers can also be used to call servers when food is ready to be served, or to call store managers to a check out counter for a price check or check validation. Pagers can eliminate the need for invasive and annoying public address announcements, while supporting finely tuned orchestration between staff members and the provision of high-quality service to the customer.

Industrial Telecommunications Media and Devices

So far, we have introduced devices that most computer users encounter at some point while working with or setting up computer networks. Larger organizations require industrial strength media and devices to manage large volumes of network traffic. Large companies will often lease dedicated lines from telecommunications companies to maintain long-distance connections. Unlike a *switched line* that maintains a connection only as long as the receiver is "off the hook," a *dedicated line* leaves the connection open continuously to support a data network connection.

To handle large quantities of data, businesses may lease a T1 line. A *T1 carrier* line supports high data transmission rates by carrying twenty-four 64-Kbps signals on one line. It has a bandwidth of approximately 1.5 Mbps. *T3 lines* carry 672 signals on one line and are used by telecommunications companies; some act as the Internet's backbone.

Managing industrial-level network traffic takes a considerable amount of orchestration. Signals sent over these high-speed lines must be processed in a manner that takes full advantage of the medium. Three devices are commonly used to control and protect industrial-level telecommunications:

- Multiplexer. A multiplexer sends multiple signals or streams of information over a medium at the same time in the form of a single, complex signal. A demultiplexer at the receiving end recovers the separate signals. Often a multiplexer and demultiplexer are combined into one device.
- Communications Processor. Sometimes called a front-end processor, this device is devoted to handling communications to and from a large computer network.

JOB /\\/\\/\\ TECHNOLOGY

Your Table Is Ready!

Paging systems have greatly assisted the restaurant and hospitality industry in streamlining processes and increasing customer satisfaction. One thing the public will simply not put up with in this era of high productivity, are long lines and extensive waits with nothing to do. It is not unusual for a hostess to hand customers a pager and send them to the lounge or even off for a stroll around the neighborhood for a little shopping while they wait for a table. This is a tremendous service to customers, but can be costly to the restaurant if customers walk off with the paging device. At $80 a crack, a few pagers lost each month adds up to thousands of dollars a year.

To address this problem pager manufacturers are coming up with less-expensive pagers for the restaurant market. Long Range Systems makes lightweight, inexpensive pagers shaped like drink coasters that light up like a disco dance floor when your table is ready. For around $3,000, you can purchase a kit that includes a pager transmitter and 40 "Coaster Call" pagers that stack conveniently on a charger. If you own a seafood restaurant, you might opt for the "Lobster Call" pager. Shaped like a small red lobster, this pager vibrates and blinks when your table is ready, and stacks on a charger when not in use.

Pagers can also be used to call servers. For instance Long Range Systems' Coaster Light is provided to customers in dinner theaters and comedy clubs to allow them to page a server without disturbing others.

Johnny Carino's chain of Country Italian restaurants is using cell phone paging technology to save on the overhead of pagers. When you walk in, the hostess takes your cell phone number. When your table is ready the paging transmitter automatically phones your cell phone and plays a prerecorded message letting you know that your table is ready.

Paging systems have other services to assist restaurant owners. For example, an antitheft feature that causes the pager to vibrate when taken out of range of the transmitter, jogging the memory of the customer to return the pager.

Questions

1. What situations have you encountered that would benefit from pager technology?
2. Can pagers play a role in your chosen career? How or why not?
3. Why would a restaurant owner choose pager technology over cell phone paging systems?

Sources
1. *"Coaster With a Message: Your Table Is Ready,"* Jeffrey Selingo, The New York Times, *June 26, 2003, www. nytimes.com.*
2. *"At Johnny Carino's, Cell-phone paging system the right call,"* Alan Liddle, Nation's Restaurant News, *January 21, 2002.*
3. *Long Range Systems Web site, www.pager.net.*

Like a receptionist handling visitors at an office complex, communications processors direct the flow of incoming and outgoing telecommunications.
- Encryption Devices. An *encryption device* is installed at the sending computer to alter outgoing communications according to an encoding scheme that makes the communications unintelligible during transport. A *decryption device* is installed at the receiving computer to decode incoming data and return it to its original state. Encryption protects private data from being accessed by anyone but the intended recipient.

Often a business or organization with high demands on its telecommunications system will hire a telecommunications company to manage their systems. Telecommunications companies, such as Sprint and MCI, offer many industrial- and business-level networking solutions for every type and size of industrial network need. A list and description of all of the industrial-level telecommunications technologies and options could fill this book. Most of these technologies are only helpful to know and understand if you intend on being a telecommunications specialist yourself.

Networking Software

So far we have discussed the hardware components of a computer network. As we have learned in previous chapters, hardware is useless without the software necessary to drive it; and so it is with networks. *Networking software* performs a number of important functions in a computer network. It monitors the load, or amount of traffic, on the network to ensure that user's needs are being met. It provides error checking and message formatting. In some cases, when there is a problem, the software can indicate what is wrong and suggest possible solutions. Networking software can also provide data security and privacy. Since networking software's main purpose is to support the functioning of the network, it is considered utility software. In its role as a utility, networking software runs mostly unnoticed by network users—with the exception of the network administrator.

A *network administrator* is a person responsible for setting up and maintaining the network, implementing network policies, and assigning user access permissions. A large organization might employ dozens of network administrators to support a network. With the increasing popularity of home networks, many nontechnical computer users are finding themselves placed in the role of network administrator at home. For example, a mother may find herself setting up a home network in a manner that filters out adult Web content from her children's computers. This section discusses a variety of commonly used network utilities.

Network Operating Systems. In Chapter 3 you learned that all computers have operating systems that control many functions. When an application program requires data from a disk drive, it goes through the operating system. Consider a scenario where many computers are accessing resources such as disk drives, printers, and other devices over a network. How does an application program request data from a disk drive on the network? The answer is through the network operating system.

A *network operating system (NOS)* is systems software that controls the computer systems and devices on a network and allows them to communicate with each other. A NOS performs the same types of functions for the network as operating system software performs for a computer, such as memory and task management, and coordination of hardware. When network equipment such as printers and disk drives are required, the network operating system makes sure that these resources are correctly used. Network operating systems come preinstalled on midrange and mainframe servers. All of today's personal computer operating systems, Windows, Mac, and Linux, function as NOSs as well.

Network Management Software. In addition to network operating systems, there are a number of useful software tools and utilities for managing networks. With network management software, a manager on a networked desktop can monitor the use of individual computers and shared hardware (such as printers), scan for viruses, and ensure compliance with software licenses. Network management software also simplifies the process of updating files and programs on computers on the network. Changes can be made through a communications server instead of being made on each individual computer. Some of the many benefits of network management software include fewer hours spent on routine tasks (such as installing new software), faster response to problems, and greater overall network control.

Network Device Software. Routers, switches, firewalls, modems, and other network control devices have software interfaces that allow you to change device settings. Once the device is connected to the network, its software interface can be accessed from a network computer. A router's software can be used to divide up a physical network into multiple virtual networks. A firewall's software can be used to specify filter criteria. Software for a modem might allow you to enable or disable call waiting.

Communications Protocols and Standards. In Chapter 4, you learned that a *protocol* is an agreed-upon format for transmitting data between two devices. In

Chapter 2, you learned that a *standard* is an agreed-upon way of doing something within an industry. In the world of networking, protocols and standards are both essential for enabling devices to communicate with each other. Protocols are used to define the format of the communications between devices, and standards are used to provide the physical specifications of devices and how they interconnect. In Chapter 4, you also learned that the Internet uses the TCP/IP protocols. TCP/IP has become the protocol used for many private networks as well.

Ethernet is the most widely used network standard for private networks. This standard defines the types of network interface cards, control devices, cables, and software that are required to create an Ethernet network. Other network standards, such as *Token Ring*, use unique hardware and software that does not work with Ethernet. Special devices, such as routers or gateways, are required to connect networks that use different standards.

Network media, such as cables or radio signals, combine with network devices and software to connect computers together to enable the sharing of resources such as storage devices, printers, and files. This section has provided you with descriptions of network components. Now, let's put the puzzle pieces together to see how these components combine in functional network scenarios.

NETWORKSAND**DISTRIBUTED**COMPUTING

EXPANDYOUR **KNOWLEDGE**

To learn more about networks, go to www.course.com/swt. Click the link "Expand Your Knowledge" and then complete the lab entitled, "Networking Basics."

Most of us are familiar with the benefits of sharing information between computers from our experience with the Internet and Web. Information sharing and communications are just two of the benefits of networking.

Within a private network computing resources are shared in order to maximize computing power. We have learned that a computer includes devices for input, processing, storage, and output. In a computer network these components can be distributed throughout the network. For instance, you may do your work on a terminal that connects you to a server shared by all employees in the organization. In such a scenario the input and output devices are on your desk, but the processing and storage are handled at some other location. You may store your files on a network drive that exists on a file server and send your print jobs to a printer in a shared area of your office (see Figure 5.22).

FIGURE 5.22 • Distributed network

On a distributed network you may store your files on a network drive that exists on a file server and send your print jobs to a printer in a shared area of your office.

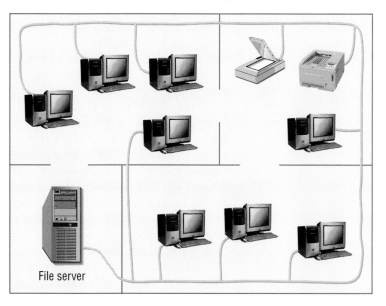

File server

Computer Networking Concepts

Devices attached to a network are called *nodes*. Personal computers attached to a network are often called *workstations*. Workstations typically have access to two types of resources: local and network resources. *Local* resources are the files, drives, and perhaps a printer or other peripheral device that are accessible to the workstation on or off the network; local resources are part of the workstation or connected directly to the workstation. *Network* resources, also called *remote* resources, are resources that the workstation can access only while connected to the network; network resources exist on other nodes.

Network resources are often installed on a workstation in a manner that makes it difficult to tell which resources are local and which are on the network. For example, you might save a document to the F: drive. This drive could exist on your own workstation or any other workstation on the network. When you click the Netscape icon to start the program, that program might be loaded from the local hard drive or from some other computer on the network. Hiding the underlying network structure from the user makes it transparent and uncomplicated to use. *Transparency* is desirable in situations where users are not technically inclined and might be confused by being made aware of the complicated underlying structure.

Distributed Computing. *Distributed computing* refers to computing that involves multiple remote computers that work together to solve a computation problem or perform information processing. Large businesses and organizations, sometimes called *enterprises*, make extensive use of distributed computing. In enterprises, distributed computing generally has meant putting various steps in business processes at the most efficient places in a network of computers. The user interface processing is done on the PC at the user's location, business processing is done on a remote computer, and database access and processing is done on another computer that provides centralized access for many business processes. Typically, this kind of distributed computing uses the client/server communications model.

In Chapter 4 you learned that the Internet uses client/server systems to serve up Internet resources such as Web pages and e-mail. Private networks also make use of client/server systems to serve up data, files, and applications. *Database servers* store organizational databases, and respond to user queries with requested information. *File servers* store organizational and user files, delivering them to workstations on request. *Application servers* store programs such as word processors and spreadsheets, and deliver them to workstations to run when users click the program icon.

An excellent example of the advantages of distributed computing is provided by Hewlett-Packard (HP). HP is working to save corporations money on PCs with new innovative distributed computing technology.[14] HP's new concept takes advantage of the fact that of the many PCs installed in an enterprise, typically around 30 percent, are not being used at any given time. In an organization with 1,000 PCs, 300 of those PCs are not really needed. Rather than yanking 300 PCs off employees' desks and asking employees to share, HP supplies stripped-down network PCs, called thin clients, that cost less than half that of a full-blown PC. A *thin client* includes a keyboard, a mouse, a display, and a small system unit that supplies only enough computing power to connect the device to a server over the network. Thin clients connect to clusters of "blade" computers. Blade computers are like PC motherboards that are rack-mounted together in groups of up to 20 to a case (see Figure 5.23). In this type of system, rather than purchasing 1,000 PCs, an organization can purchase 1,000 inexpensive thin clients that will connect to a blade server that supports up to 700 users simultaneously. This system, paired with a file server on which to store user files, is significantly less costly than 1,000 regular PCs, but offers identical services to users.

FIGURE 5.23 · Client/server technology

HP's blade server includes a separate circuit board that handles the processing for each thin client workstation.

Logical Network Design. Building networks involves two types of design: logical and physical. Earlier in this chapter, we discussed physical components of a network such as cables, and devices. A logical model, called a network topology, shows how network components are organized and arranged. The number of possible ways to logically arrange the nodes, or computer systems and devices on a network, may seem limitless. In actuality, there are four major types of network topologies:

- The *ring* network topology arranges computers and computer devices in a ring or circle. With a ring network, there is no central coordinating computer. Messages are routed around the ring from one device or computer to another.
- The *bus* network topology consists of one main cable or telecommunications line with devices attached to it. Each device is connected with every other device through the main bus cable and can communicate directly with all other devices on the network.
- The *star* network topology connects devices together through a central device called a hub.
- The *hybrid* network topology combines two or more of the preceding network topologies. A *star bus* topology is the most common and versatile network topology in use today. Star networks are created in individual areas of an organization and joined by bus lines throughout the organization.

Figure 5.24 illustrates the four most common network topologies. Bear in mind that theses figures represent models and not the actual network. The actual network that would be based on these models would have lines of varying lengths that typically follow the angles of a room's walls. Figure 5.22 shows an

FIGURE 5.24 • **Network topologies**

The four basic types of network topology are (a) ring, (b) bus, (c) star, and (d) hybrid (star bus).

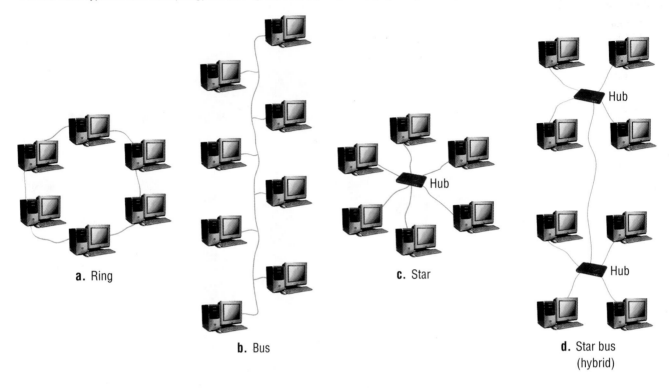

a. Ring

b. Bus

c. Star

d. Star bus (hybrid)

example of a more typical bus topology. Also note that star bus networks can have many stars joined by bus lines, with each star residing in different rooms or buildings.

When network engineers set out to create a new network, they begin with a logical model using one or more of the standard topologies. From the logical design, it is easy to determine the hardware requirements. Today's network designs typically incorporate wireless access points as well as these traditional topologies.

Network Security. Networks enable us to share files and computing resources with other users. It stands to reason that some files and resources will need to be made private and off limits to some network users. For this reason, networks implement a login process to restrict access to the network. Not only does the login process keep unwanted users off the system, but it also allows the system administrator to implement user-level access restrictions. Network users typically have access to only their own files, and sometimes to files shared by a user group to which they belong. Sensitive system files are typically only accessible to network administrators.

Most private networks have usage policies and sometimes require new users to sign a network-usage agreement. The agreement states that the network user is aware of network policies and understands that breaking the policies will lead to serious consquences.

ROBOT FIDO "FETCHES" SECURITY LEAKS

In answer to the security problems posed by wireless networks, a group of security experts created a hacker robot "dog" to look for areas where a network is vulnerable. Powered by batteries, the robot roams company corridors using an 802.11b card to sniff out security breaches and then sends the information back to its "owner." It is expected that the government will also employ the "dog" for espionage purposes.

Source:
"Robot 'guard dog' protects Wi-Fi setups"
By Declan McCullagh
CNET News.com
http://news.com.com/2100-1039_3-5059541.html?tag=fd_top
August 4, 2003
Cited on August 4, 2003

In a college environment, serious consequences may be loss of network access or even expulsion. In a professional environment, employees might lose their job for violating network policies. There are a significant number of cases of employees being fired for inappropriate use of corporate e-mail and Internet access. In some cases, the employees are unaware of the policies they have violated. When beginning a new job and gaining access to the corporate network, make sure to ask what is and is not allowed on the network.

Network Types

A network is classified by its size in terms of the amount of users it serves and the geographic area it covers. From a small, mobile personal area network (PAN) that serves an individual user, to global international networks that serve large corporations, to the Internet, which serves the entire world population, different types of networks are uniquely designed to accommodate the specific needs of their environment. Types of networks include personal area networks, local area networks, virtual private networks, metropolitan areas networks, and wide area networks.

Personal Area Network (PAN). A **personal area network (PAN)** is the interconnection of personal information technology devices within the range of an individual (typically around 32 ft). PAN is the most recently classified network type and has arisen with the popularity of mobile computing devices. The Bluetooth networking standard discussed earlier brought attention to the conveniences offered by PAN technology.

The concept of PAN has its roots in a somewhat different area of technology research. In 1996, Thomas Zimmerman of the MIT Media Lab coined the term personal area network in a paper titled "Personal Area Networks: Near-field Intrabody Communication."[15] Mr. Zimmerman's PAN, which was later adopted by IBM's research and development team, doesn't use portable devices to pass information, but rather uses the body itself (see Figure 5.25). Zimmerman's PAN uses a small transceiver, about the size of a thick credit card, and the natural salinity of the human body to conduct an electrical current through a person's body to carry data. The current is so tiny that the user cannot feel it, but can carry up to 400,000 bits per second. The data is transferred to other PAN users or devices through touch. Imagine passing someone your electronic business card simply by shaking hands!

Zimmerman's technology is still in the research phase at IBM research labs. In the meantime, the PAN concept has been broadened to include wireless mobile devices. Bluetooth has claimed dominance of the PAN market with its low-cost (less than $5) wireless chipset that allows personal mobile devices to communicate wirelessly. According to the Bluetooth SIG, over 1,000 Bluetooth products have been officially registered, and over 2,000 companies are involved in developing new devices.[16]

FIGURE 5.25 • **Personal area network**

Zimmerman's PAN doesn't use portable devices to pass information, but rather uses the body itself.

Local Area Network (LAN). Whereas a PAN provides coupling between pairs of mobile devices, a LAN provides connections between numerous wired or wireless devices. A network that connects computer systems and devices within the same geographical area is a **local area network (LAN)**. A local area network can be a ring, a star, a bus, or a hybrid network. There are more local area networks than any other network type. LANs are used in homes, businesses, and other institutions and organizations.

Local area networks can be built around personal computers or servers. Devices connect to LANs through network interface cards or wireless network adapters. Larger networks make use of servers to store databases, files, and programs. When a person on the network uses a program or data stored on the server, the server transfers the necessary programs or data to the user's computer. A server can be a computer of any size, from a personal computer to a mainframe.

Ethernet is a popular communications standard often used with local area networks. The Ethernet standard is designed for LANs that use bus or star topology; the standard helps ensure compatibility among devices so that many people can attach to a common cable to share network facilities and resources. For LANs that use a ring topology, token-ring protocols have been defined. Like Ethernet, token-ring protocols ease the connection of devices into a LAN.

Since the rise in popularity of the Internet and Web, many LANs are incorporating familiar Internet technologies to create intranets. An **intranet** uses the protocols of the Internet and the Web—TCP/IP and HTTP, along with Internet services such as Web browsers—within the confines of a private network (see Figure 5.26). In an intranet, employees might access confidential documents using a Web browser, while those same documents remain secure from the outside world.

Enterprises typically allow users within their intranet to access the public Internet through firewalls that screen messages to maintain the security of the network. An intranet may be extended beyond the confines of the LAN to connect with other networks to create a virtual private network. A **virtual private network (VPN)** uses a technology called *tunneling* to securely send private network data over the Internet. A VPN may be used to connect an organization's networks dispersed around the world into one large intranet.

Intranet content can be extended to specific individuals outside the network, such as customers, partners, or suppliers, in an arrangement called an *extranet*. Extranets are sometimes implemented through a simple login procedure on a Web server.

VPNs can also be used by enterprises to allow employees to access the corporate intranet from home and while on the road. A large business or organization might hire an *enterprise service provider (ESP)* to set up a *network access server (NAS)*. Users are provided with software and a toll-free number to use to connect to the NAS, VPN, and ultimately the corporate intranet. Some services are setup so that if you have access to the Internet, then you also have secure access to your private intranet.

Metropolitan Area Network (MAN). A **metropolitan area network (MAN)** connects networks within a city or metropolitan size area into a larger high-speed network. Many cities supply local businesses with access to a MAN to improve local commerce and communications. Often a MAN acts as a stepping stone to larger networks, such as the Internet.

Wide Area Network (WAN). A **wide area network (WAN)** connects LANs between cities, cross country, and around the world using microwave and satellite transmission or telephone lines. A LAN becomes a WAN when it extends beyond one geographic location to another geographic location (see Figure 5.27). When you make a long-distance phone call, you are using a wide area network. AT&T, MCI, and other telecommunications companies are examples of companies that offer WAN services to the public. Companies, organizations, and government agencies, also design and implement WANs for private use. These WANs usually consist of privately owned LANs connected over a dedicated line provided by a telecommunications company. For example, your college may maintain a

FIGURE 5.26 • **Intranet**

In an intranet, a Web server provides confidential data to LAN users, while keeping the data safe from those outside the organization through the use of a firewall.

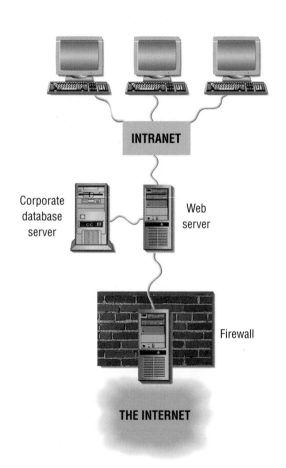

FIGURE 5.27 • Wide area network (WAN)

A WAN connects LANs between cities, cross country, and around the world using microwave and satellite transmission or telephone lines.

LAN that covers the campus. The college network engineers may have laid fiber-optic cable across campus and connected it to networks in each building to provide high-speed networking to students, faculty, and staff. This network is owned and controlled by the college. If your college should decide to open a branch campus across the state, administrators may decide to join the LAN of the main campus with the LAN of the branch campus. Using a dedicated line leased from the phone company, your college creates a WAN by joining the two LANs.

The West Virginia Judicial System set up a WAN that connects its 55 county courthouses and 10 regional jails. It uses the network to conduct arraignments. Defendants, judges, and magistrates all meet from different locations using video conferencing equipment and software. Since prisoners no longer need to be physically present in the courtroom, the state was able to close 45 small county jails that were in disrepair and consolidate prisoners in 10 large regional prisons. It also saved the state the expense and danger of transporting prisoners between the courthouse and the prison. The state calculated that it saved 24,000 prisoner transportation miles in the first year of operation.

Global Area Networks (GAN). A WAN that crosses an international border is considered a **global area network (GAN)** or international network. In Chapter 4, we discussed the world's largest international network, the Internet. As an increasing number of businesses are entering global markets, private global networks are becoming more prevalent.

However, a GAN has additional challenges in international telecommunications to overcome. In addition to requiring sophisticated equipment and software, global area networks must meet specific national and international laws regulating the electronic flow of data across international boundaries, often called *transborder data flow*. Some countries have strict laws restricting the use of telecommunications and databases, making normal business transactions such as payroll costly, slow, or even impossible. Other countries have few laws restricting the use of telecommunications or databases. Other governments and companies can avoid their own country's laws by processing data within the boundaries of countries, sometimes called data havens, that have few restrictions on telecommunications or databases. For example, the popular file-sharing service, Kazaa, has been able to escape prosecution (unlike Napster) because it maintains its servers in Denmark, has its domain registered in Australia, and runs its software from the South Pacific island nation of Vanuatu, a well-known tax haven.[17]

Despite the obstacles, there are numerous private and public international networks. United Parcel Service, for example, covers over 200 countries with their international network, called UPSnet. UPSnet allows drivers to use handheld computers to send real-time information about pickups and deliveries to central data centers. In addition to the 77,000 handheld computers for drivers, UPSnet is based on five mainframes, 60,000 personal computers, several satellite dishes, and enough fiber-optic cable to wrap around the earth 25 times. The huge network allows data to be retrieved by customers to track packages or to be used by the company for faster billing, better fleet planning, and improved customer service.

Home Networks

Like televisions, telephones, and automobiles, personal computers have become such an integral part of many people's lives that many households have more than one. As PC prices continue to decrease, it is increasingly common to find one PC per individual in a household. Whether the individuals are family members or cohabitating friends, they can benefit from connecting their computers in a home network. Home networks allow residents to:

- Share a single Internet connection
- Share a single printer between computers
- Share files such as images, music, and programs
- Back up copies of important files to another PC for safekeeping
- Participate in multiplayer games
- Share media output from devices such as a DVD player or Webcam

Setting up a home network can be an intimidating challenge. The computer industry has recognized home networking as one of the most important and lucrative markets of this century and has made available many new technologies that vastly improve the ease with which a home network can be installed.

Home Networking Technologies. Many of the technologies discussed in this chapter are applicable to home networks. Home networks are typically based on Ethernet standards and can be wired or wireless. Some technically inclined people may opt to run twisted-pair wires through the walls and attic space of their homes to set up a business-quality network. However, most home users are taking advantage of more convenient setups, such as:

- Phone Line Network. *Phone-line networking*, also called *HomePNA* (for phone-line networking alliance), takes advantage of existing phone wiring in a residence. Computers share the phone line with telephones, utilizing different frequencies so that both can be used simultaneously. "If you can plug in a phone, you can network your home" is the slogan of the Home Phoneline Networking Alliance.[18]
- Power Line Network. *Power-line networking*, also called *HomePLC* (for power-line communication), takes advantage of the home's existing power lines and electrical outlets to connect computers. As with Home PNA, HomePLC divides up the frequencies of the household electrical system and uses some for network communications and the others for electrical current.
- Wireless Network. Recent developments in wireless networking have made this perhaps the cheapest and easiest network to install. With speeds up to 54 Mbps, home wireless networks easily support everything a typical home user may want to do on a network.

Setting up a Wireless Home Network. The low price and ease of installation of wireless networks are making it the obvious choice for most home networks. The 802.11g protocol is currently most popular, but is sure to be replaced by even faster protocols in the near future.

To set up a wireless home network you need a wireless access point and a network adapter (see Figure 5.28). A wireless access point is a device that controls the flow of data between devices and allows you to set security so that only your computers can access the wireless network. If you intend to share a broadband Internet connection (cable modem or DSL) over your wireless network, you should get a wireless access point-router. Either device costs between $60 and $100. You also need a network adapter for each device on the network. You can get a USB wireless adapter for PCs and a wireless adapter PC card for notebook and handheld computers. Adapters cost between $40 and $70. Some new notebook computers are being sold with embedded wireless adapters. This new trend may someday eliminate the need to purchase external wireless adapters.[19]

Access points and network adapters come with software that is easy to install and works with your operating system to automatically configure your network. By following simple instructions, you can have your home network set up within an hour.

FIGURE 5.28 • **Wireless home network**

A typical wireless home network uses a wireless access point/router to connect the network to an ISP. Wireless adapters connected to each computer communicate with the access point.

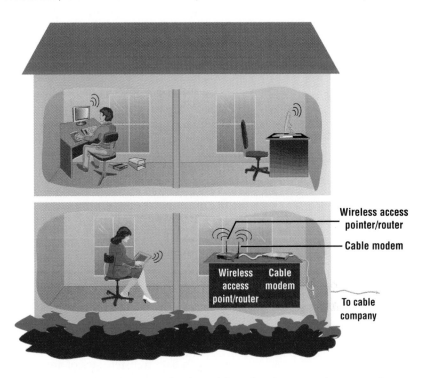

Once your computers are communicating with each other over the network, network users must determine what resources to make available to others on the network. Today's operating systems provide methods for specifying which drives, folders, directories, files, and printers you wish to share over the network. How you share and access network resources varies from operating system to operating system.

Connecting to the Internet. The most common reason to set up a home network is to share an Internet connection. There are several options for connecting to the Internet, including dial-up connection, cable modem, Digital Subscriber Line, digital satellite service, and power-line broadband.

A **dial-up connection** is a narrowband Internet service, with data transfer rates of around 50 Kbps, provided by any one of hundreds of Internet service providers. Customers are provided with a local or toll-free phone number along with a username and password. The computer's modem dials the number, establishes a connection to the ISP, and logs on. The positive aspects of a dial-up connection is that there is little or no up-front investment for equipment (dial-up modems are standard equipment on today's PCs), and monthly rates are low, typically between $10 and $24. The negative aspects of a dial-up connection are that it is slow and ties up your phone line.

A **cable modem connection** is a broadband Internet service, with data transfer rates of around 2 Mbps, provided by cable television providers. Here the Internet signal is carried along the same cable as the television signals. A cable TV receiver receives the frequencies reserved for television, and a cable modem receives the frequencies used for Internet. A cable splitter is used for customers who use the cable for both television and the Internet. The splitter takes one cable and splits the signal to travel over two separate cables. Cable modems can be installed by professionals or for users who have existing cable service, a self-installation kit can be purchased. The self-installation kit typically includes a cable splitter, an Ethernet network card for your computer, a cable modem, and cables. Cable modems can be connected directly to a computer's Ethernet card, or to a router that shares the signal with multiple computers. In Figure 5.28, the cable modem is connected to a wireless access point/router.

Cable modems use less bandwidth for upstream data—the data your computer sends over the connection, and more bandwidth for downstream data—the data that comes to your computer over the connection. This meshes with most usage patterns, and provides faster Web page delivery. The positive aspects of a cable modem connection are fast data transfer rates and an always-on Internet connection. The negative aspects include cost—around $100 to get setup and $40 per month. Special promotional offers may reduce initial costs. Cable modem network lines are shared by neighbors within a neighborhood. Some concerns have been raised over the ability of the cable to support the Internet needs of everyone in a given neighborhood.

A **Digital Subscriber Line (DSL) connection** is broadband access, with data transfer rates of around 1.5 Mbps, provided by the phone company, or ISPs working in conjunction with the phone company. This service is very similar to a cable modem, except that here your telephone line is split to carry signals to both a DSL modem and your telephone. Like a cable modem, and unlike a dial-up connection, a DSL line provides an always-on connection. There is no dialing up and users are able to use the Internet and talk on the phone simultaneously. As with a cable modem a DSL modem is connected to a computer through an Ethernet card or to a router to share the signal between multiple computers. DSL modems share the same benefits and drawbacks as cable modems, with the exception of being slightly slower and more expensive on average.

A *digital satellite service (DSS)* connection is a wireless broadband Internet service, with data transfer rates of around 400 Kbps, provided to your home by companies such as EarthLink and StarBand. Satellite service is much slower and more expensive than either cable modem or DSL (see Figure 5.29). For this reason, it is typically used in situations where neither cable broadband nor DSL is available. Satellite Internet is installed by professionals in much the same manner as cable modems and DSL. Although DSS offers an always-on connection, users may lose their signal during stormy weather.

Although not yet widely offered, the power companies of the world are poised to offer broadband Internet over the power grids through a *powerline broadband* connection.[20] The advantages of powerline broadband are somewhat obvious: the power grid is the most pervasive network in the world, reaching many places where telephone and cable lines do not. Connecting a computer to the Internet would be as easy as plugging a powerline modem into a wall outlet. Powerline Internet access will be provided at speeds of up to 1 Mbps.

Narrowband, dial-up connections, can be shared across a home network by setting up one computer on the network as the Internet connection server. This computer does the dialing and shares its Internet connection with the other computers on the network. Since dial-up connections are slow, performance suffers when more than one user is online simultaneously. For this reason, it is much more common to find home networks sharing broadband connections. By connecting the broadband modem to a LAN router or wireless access point router, all computers on the network share an always-on connection to the Internet. The higher data transfer rates of broadband make it possible to share the connection with two, three, or even four computers.

Home Network Security. Broadband, always-on, connections are vulnerable to hackers. *Hackers* are individuals who attempt to gain access to private computers and networks belonging to others. Hackers may be interested in stealing files from your computer, using your high-speed Internet connection, or vandalizing your files and computer system. Whenever your computer is connected to the Internet, it is important to use a firewall that blocks unwanted entry onto your system.

FIGURE 5.29 • Internet service provider (ISP) speed comparison
Today's broadband Internet access options offer connections 25 to 35 times faster than traditional dial-up connections.

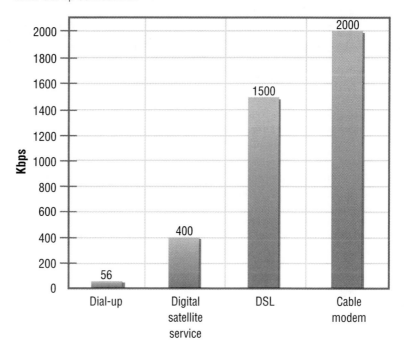

Internet service provider

Firewalls can be purchased as a hardware device or as software installed on your computer. Some operating systems include firewall software and other security features. Network users should also make sure that disk drives and files that are set to be shared with others on the network are password protected.

Wireless networks have additional security concerns. Since wireless signals go through walls (as illustrated in Figure 5.28), it is likely that your wireless network is accessible to people outside your home, and even to next-door neighbors. Wireless access points come with multiple layers of security that can be enabled to make sure that your private wireless network stays private. For example, access points:

- Can be set so that they do not broadcast their identification—information that is needed by computers to connect to the network.
- Can be set so that they only connect to specific network adapters.
- Can encrypt the signal so that it is unintelligible to outsiders.

A considerable number of security features are built into wireless access points. However, most of these features are disabled by default in order to make for easy network setup. Unless users take the time to enable these security features, their home networks may be accessible to neighbors and passersby (read about war driving in the "Community Technology" box).

NETWORKINGAPPLICATIONS**AND**BENEFITS

In homes, computer networks provide convenience and cost savings for personal computer users. In businesses and organizations, computer networks play a key role in supporting information management and work practices that empower groups to be more productive. Computer networks create lines of communication between organization members, allowing individuals to communicate from remote locations. They supply an electronic thoroughfare over which business

COMMUNITY /\/\/\ TECHNOLOGY

War Driving

The recent growth in unsecured wireless networks has brought about a new style of hacking called war driving. In war driving, one or two people cruise neighborhoods in a car with an 802.11 wireless notebook computer. Their goal is to find and connect to an unprotected wireless network. Once found a hacker can take advantage of the network connection by:

- Using the network connection to access the Internet—stealing bandwith from the broadband wireless connection
- Attempting to access, steal, or vandalize data and information on network computers
- Using a "packet sniffer" program to listen in on network conversations—reading data packets being sent over the network

The term "war driving" is derived from the 1983 movie *War Games*. In *War Games*, Matthew Broderick's character demonstrated the popular hacking technique of the day in which he used his modem to randomly dial phone numbers in search of an unprotected data network. Matthew unknowingly hacks the U.S. Department of Defense network and accidentally starts a nuclear war. After the movie, the hacking technique became known as "war dialing" the expression from which "war driving" is derived.

Drive-by networkers typically use notebook computers, rooftop antennas, and Wi-Fi sniffer software, such as NetStumbler, which detects the presence of a Wi-Fi network signal. Groups of war driver hobbyists have organized to create catalogues of available public and private Wi-Fi access points in given regions. GPS technology is sometimes used to pinpoint locations of Wi-Fi networks. The World Wide WarDrive is an annual event involving thousands of drive-by networkers who documented 25,000 access points in 2002.

An interesting related trend, called "warchalking," has its roots in the hobo code used during the great depression. Migrant hobos would mark properties with symbols providing information about the property for other hobos. For instance, three parallel diagonal slashes indicated that the property was not a safe place. In warchalking, mobile computer users mark urban sidewalks with chalk to indicate access to a Wi-Fi network. The symbol)(indicates that a Wi-Fi network is accessible in this location; Y indicates a network is present but secured.

War driving is not just a hobby for hackers. It is also a technique used by network administrators to search for security holes in their own wireless networks. Network administrators will roam the halls and property of their organization with handheld devices running Wi-Fi sniffer software in search of overlooked security holes or rogue access points that have been set up by network users without authority.

Questions

1. Do you think that war driving is an ethical activity? Should there be laws against it?
2. Who is responsible for leaving so many wireless networks unprotected?
3. What can the Wi-Fi industry do to improve the situation?

Sources
1. *"Wireless Hunters on the Prowl," Xeni Jardin,* Wired News, *July 2, 2003, http://wired.com/news/wireless/0,1382,59460,00. html.*
2. *"Wi-Fi Users: Chalk This Way," Paul Boutin,* Wired News, *July 3, 2002, http://wired.com/news/wireless/0,1382,53638,00.html.*
3. *The Warchalking Web site, www.warchalking.org, accessed July 4, 2003.*
4. *"Stealing wireless bandwidth is easy," David Strom,* David Strom's Web Informant, *October 2001, www.strom.com/ awards/268.html.*
5. *www.wardriving.com.*

documents stream from department to department. They supply access to a central store of shared information. This section will explore specific applications and benefits of computer networking and telecommunications.

Information and Software Management

Businesses and organizations use computer networks to streamline business practices and apply proper information-management strategies. For example, file and data servers act as centralized data stores that allow all the organization's members to work from a common dataset, reducing or eliminating the dangers of data redundancy. An application server allows system administrators to install and maintain only one copy of software on the server rather than hundreds of installed applications on workstations.

Collaboration

Through *workgroup software*, sometimes called *groupware* network users can collaborate over the network. A number of workgroup software products and tools have been developed to facilitate the sharing of ideas and documents around the office or the world. Lotus Notes, for example, is a workgroup software package that allows people to communicate with each other, access data and files from shared databases, and route forms and projects electronically, instead of using paper and standard mail.

Communications

Networks are all about communication. All of the communications technologies discussed in Chapter 4 that are available on the Internet, e-mail instant messaging, chat, and the others are also available over a private network. In addition, many businesses are channeling their voice phone signals over their data networks using a protocol called Voice over Internet Protocol. *Voice over Internet Protocol (VoIP)* allows businesses and organizations to save money and complexity by merging phone and data networks into one network (see the Job Technology box).

A new type of voice communications technology that takes advantage of VoIP is being offered by Vocera Communications. The Vocera Communications System makes use of a wireless LAN and lightweight communications devices similar to the original Star Trek communicator, clipped to a lapel or pocket, or worn on a lanyard around the neck. The Vocera device (which they call a badge, shown in Figure 5.30) uses speech recognition to support hands-free communications. It is activated when you speak a command word. For instance, to initiate a conversation with Jim and Mary, the user says "Vocera, get me Jim and Mary." Jim and Mary's badges alert them to your page and create a three-way connection for hands-free, wireless voice communications. The system allows users to be tracked geographically around a site and supports text messaging. The device is being marketed in several industries, including hospitals where immediate communication among the staff can mean the difference between life and death.

FIGURE 5.30 • The Vocera Communications badge

Using VoIP technology, this hands-free device allows users to communicate.

Telecommuting

Having evolved throughout the 1980s and 1990s, telecommuting is a reality today because of improved network systems. **Telecommuting** allows employees to work at home using a personal computer or terminal connected to the office computer via a modem (see Figure 5.31). Telecommuters can also connect to corporate networks and databases to access information ranging from daily sales reports to client phone numbers and addresses. Telecommuting has led to the rise of the *virtual office*, where managers use cellular phones, pagers, and portable computers to work out of their homes, cars, or at remote job sites. It has also led to the rise of *telecommuting centers*—office space owned or leased by employers, equipped with computers, and other necessary office equipment, that is shared by telecommuting employees. Some jobs require only partial presence in the office, perhaps only a few hours a week. In such cases, employers can provide shared workspace that employees can use as needed. Telecommuting often increases employee satisfaction, while providing companies with lower office space requirements and a flexible approach to work.

FIGURE 5.31 • Telecommuting

Telecommuting often increases employee satisfaction, while providing companies with lower office space requirements and a flexible approach to work.

Electronic Data Interchange (EDI)

Connecting corporate computer systems among organizations is the idea behind electronic data interchange (EDI). *EDI* uses network systems and follows standards and procedures that allow output from one system to be processed directly as input to other systems, without human intervention. With EDI, the computers of customers, retailers, manufacturers, and suppliers can be linked. For example, as the cashier scans the bar code of the new blue jeans that you are purchasing, the inventory count of that item is decreased by one. The effect of the decrease may bring the total inventory amount for that item below a set threshold, indicating that more jeans need to be ordered. Since the retail store's computer system is connected to the manufacturer's computer system, the order for more jeans can be made without any human involvement. The manufacturer's computer system receives the order and places the order in the queue to be processed. The manufacturer's computer system may be connected to their suppliers' computer systems. So as they begin running low on indigo dye, for example, an order for more is automatically generated and delivered to the dye producer.

This technology eliminates the need for paper documents and substantially cuts down on costly errors. Customer orders and inquiries are made from the customer's computer to the manufacturer's computer. The manufacturer's computer can then determine when new supplies are needed and can automatically place orders by connecting with the supplier's computer.

For some industries, EDI is becoming a necessity. For many large companies, including General Motors and Dow Chemical, computer input often originates as output from another computer system. Some companies will only do business with suppli-

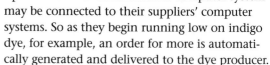

DID I TURN OFF THE STOVE?

By late 2004, people will be able to keep track of their children or their briefcases, check on pets, and tell whether or not they left the iron on through their own wireless communications networks. Developed by Apple cofounder Steve Wozniak, the networks may extend up to 100 miles using the same 900-MHz radio frequencies that cell phones do. The technology will also allow some form of instant, two-way communications.

Source:
"Wireless networks could get personal"
By Benny Evangelista
San Francisco Chronicle
www.sfgate.com/cgi-bin/article.cgi?file=/chronicle/archive/2003/07/21/
BU291111.DTL&type=tech
July 21, 2003
Cited on Monday, July 21, 2003

VoIP and the NFL

NFL Films is a large film and video production company that is named for its work in producing NFL shows and films. NFL Films has won 82 Emmy awards, and produces more than 400 hours of original programming each year. With a staff of around 400, NFL Films is a full-function production company that employs cinematographers, sound engineers, composers, narrators, and musicians to create films that sometimes extend beyond the NFL. For example, they have produced numerous commercial productions, including "We Must. We Can. We Will." a video documentary for the Christopher Reeves Paralysis Foundation.

NFL Films is unique in that it entire "script-to-screen" production is done under one roof. When designing its new 200,000-square-foot state-of-the-art production facility in Mount Laurel, New Jersey, NFL Films decided to do what many businesses are doing and implement a Voice over IP (VoIP) network. Cisco Systems assisted NFL Films in converging its data and phone networks into one digital IP network, saving them $400,000 in telephone system installation and $100,000 in annual costs for running a traditional telephone system.

Cost savings is just one of the benefits of VoIP. NFL Films is enjoying many additional benefits. Their audio and video editors working in 20 studios appreciate the control that they have over the communications network. All communications take place through the computer-based network. By logging onto a PC, employees automatically access custom personalized interfaces over PC speakers or a handset, including speed-dial and voice mail access, along with e-mail. "IP phones are just a lot more feature-rich and user-friendly than standard phones," says Steve Eager, director of network systems administration at NFL Films.

Another great benefit of VoIP is that come Super Bowl time, NFL Films packs up 75 IP phones, 65 PCs, and switching and routing gear, and sets up camp in mobile offices outside the stadium. Rather than a four or five day ordeal of working with the local phone company to set up an elaborate and costly communications network, NFL Films requests two T1 lines and has their own network set up and connected in a day. The IP network is then used for voice communications and video transfer to headquarters and customers like SportsLine.com and Superbowl.com. The staff has the convenience of working with the same communications equipment on the road and at home.

Questions

1. What makes NFL Films a good candidate for VoIP?
2. What challenges do you think NFL Films faced when they switched to VoIP?
3. What other types of businesses would most benefit from VoIP?

Sources
1. *"NFL Films brings VoIP to the Super Bowl,"* Phil Hochmuth, Network World, *January 27, 2003.*
2. *"Enhanced Communications with IP Telephony,"* Fred Sandsmark, Cisco Systems Business Industries, http://business.cisco.com/prod/tree.taf%3Fasset_id=92833&ID=48298&ListID=44756&public_view=true&kbns=1.html accessed July 5, 2003.
3. NFL Films Web site, www.nflfilms.com accessed July 5, 2003.

ers and vendors using compatible EDI systems, regardless of the expense or the effort involved. As more industries demand that businesses have this ability to stay competitive, EDI will cause massive changes in the work activities of companies. Companies will have to change the way they deal with processes as simple as billing and ordering, while new industries will emerge to help build the networks needed to support EDI.

The applications and benefits of computer networks are as limitless as the methods of collaboration used in every business process, creative endeavor, and organizational project. Computer networks are used to bring creative minds together, and provide access to information, entertainment, and communications from anyplace, anytime. Computer networks are used to create communities and build team spirit. Computer networks support people working together striving towards personal and professional goals.

Action Plan

1. **How can Amanda find out what Internet services are available in her area? Once informed, what criteria should Amanda use in choosing an ISP?**

   Amanda should begin by checking with her phone company to see if she is eligible for DSL or some other broadband Internet service, and with her cable TV provider to see if they offer cable modem service. If only one of these services is available to her, then the choice is clear. Otherwise, she should compare the data transfer rates of these two services and talk to her friends to get their recommendations in order to decide which service provides the fastest and most reliable connection. If neither service is available, Amanda should look into satellite Internet access. It may also be possible that Amanda's power company makes the Internet available through the power line.

2. **What type of home network should Amanda set up to accommodate her own needs and those of her housemate? What equipment will she need to purchase?**

   Since Amanda will be sharing her Internet connection with her housemate, she needs to set up a home network. In order to save the trouble of running cables, Amanda chooses to go with a wireless network. She will need to purchase a wireless access point router to connect to the modem provided by her Internet service provider, and wireless adapters, one for each computer. Amanda might also want to invest in a Bluetooth-enabled phone and headset for wireless, hands-free phone use.

3. **What security precautions should Amanda take to insure the security of her home network and the Microserve corporate network?**

   Amanda should purchase either an external firewall device or firewall software to keep hackers from gaining access to her system. She also needs to make sure that she configures her wireless access point so that it is not broadcasting the network ID, and accepts signals only from the network adapters used on the two computers in the house. Amanda can also set up the wireless access point signal so that it is encrypted. Finally Amanda needs to make sure that she logs off Microserve's virtual private network when she is away from her desk so that her housemate and others can't sit down at her computer and access her corporate account in her absence.

Summary

LEARNING OBJECTIVE 1
Understand the fundamentals of data communications and the criteria for choosing a communications medium.

Communication takes place between sender and receiver by way of a signal that travels through a communications medium. Telecommunications refers to the electronic transmission of signals for communication. Data communications is a type of telecommunications that involves sending and receiving bits and bytes that represent data. A computer network connects computers for data communications.

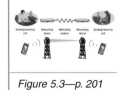

Figure 5.3—p. 201

Telecommunications involves three components: networking media, devices, and software. A data-bearing signal travels over the media between devices that act as relay points. Network software controls the devices to manage telecommunications signals in an economic and efficient manner.

Telecommunications networks manipulate both analog and digital signals. The transmission speed of a given medium is dictated by the signal frequency, measured in hertz, and described in terms of the number of bits per second (bps) that the medium can deliver. The range of frequencies that can be sent over a given medium is known as its bandwidth.

LEARNING OBJECTIVE 2
Explain how networking media, devices, and software work together to provide data networking services.

Network media include cables and wireless signals. The most common types of cables used in telecommunications are twisted-pair cables, coaxial cable, and fiber-optic cable. Microwave transmission sends signals through the air from tower to tower across the land or up to satellites that retransmit the signal to another location on earth. Global positioning systems use a constellation of satellites and trilateration to pinpoint the location of a GPS receiver on earth.

Figure 5.9—p. 207

Wireless Fidelity (Wi-Fi) uses radio signals to connect computers to a network, which is typically connected to the Internet. Bluetooth-enabled devices use radio signals to communicate between personal and mobile devices. Infrared transmission uses infrared light to transfer data between devices at close range without wires. Cellular transmission divides geographic areas into honeycomb-like cells and places a transceiver tower at the center of each cell to support cell phone communications.

Networking devices include modems, network adapters, network control devices, RFID devices, and pagers. Modems connect computers to various types of communications media. Network adapters are circuit boards, cards, or external devices that allow a computer to connect to a computer network. Hubs, switches, repeaters, bridges, gateways, and routers are used to control computer network traffic. Each of these devices performs a specialized task that assists with the flow of data across a network or between networks. A wireless access point connects wireless devices to a Wi-Fi network. A firewall can be either a device or software that filters the information coming onto a network to protect network computers from hackers, viruses, and other unwanted network traffic. A radio frequency identification (RFID) device is a tiny microprocessor combined with an antenna that is able to broadcast identifying information to an RFID reader.

Several other communications devices and media are designed for industrial use. T1 and T3 carrier lines are used to support high demand network traffic. Multiplexers and communications processors assist in managing the flow of information in networks with large quantities of network traffic. Encryption devices secure network traffic by encrypting data on the network so that it is unintelligible to all but intended receivers.

A network operating system (NOS) is installed on all network workstations, and controls the computer systems and devices on a network, enabling them to communicate with each other.

LEARNING OBJECTIVE 3
List the different classifications of computer networks and their defining characteristics and understand how to set up a wireless home network.

Many large businesses and organizations use the client/server network architecture. Server computers are used to distribute data, files, and programs to users, or clients, on the network. Computers connected to a network are called workstations, or nodes. A workstation has access to the local resources and network, or remote resources. The design of the wiring that connects computers to the network is called the network topology. Network topologies include ring, bus, star, and combinations of these such as the popular star bus topology.

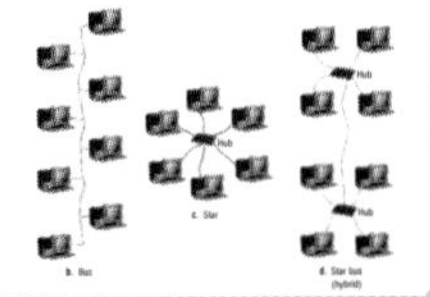

Networks are classified based on size. From smallest to largest they are PAN, LAN, MAN, WAM, GAN. A personal area network (PAN) is the interconnection of information technology devices within the range of an individual. A network that connects computer systems and devices within the same geographical area is a local area network (LAN). A

Figure 5.24—p. 224

metropolitan area network (MAN) connects networks within a city or metropolitan size area into a larger high-speed network. Wide area networks (WANs) tie together geographically dispersed LANs. WANs that cross international borders are called global area networks (GANs) or international networks. An intranet is a private network, set up in an organization, based on Internet protocols. When intranets include specific outside parties, it becomes an extranet. Intranets sometimes use the Internet to connect geographically dispersed networks in a virtual private network (VPN) using tunneling technology.

Home networks are used to share hardware, files, and a common Internet connection. Homes connect to the Internet through an Internet service provider (ISP) that supplies a dial-up, cable modem, DSL, or satellite connection. A modem, which provides the link between the ISP and the home computer, can be connected to a single computer or all computers within the home network. Home network technologies include phone line networks (HomePNA), power line networks (Home PLC), and wireless networks. Wireless home networks require a wireless access point and a wireless adapter for each computer on the network. Wireless networks require additional setup to ensure that the signals sent and received are secure and not accessible to others outside the network.

LEARNING OBJECTIVE 4
Appreciate the benefits of computer networks in homes, organizations, and businesses.

Computer networks allow for convenient management and distribution of information and programs. Software designed to facilitate teamwork, called groupware, allows groups to be more productive. Networks provide multiple platforms for communications between network users. They also can be extended to make private corporate information available to employees at home, to support telecommuting. Telecommuting allows employees to work at home, providing flexibility and freedom to the employee and cost savings to the employer. Through electronic data interchange, or EDI, networks owned by different organizations can be joined and programmed to communicate so that the output of one system is processed as input by the other. EDI allows organizations to automate many time-consuming tasks.

Figure 5.30—p. 234

Test Yourself

LEARNING OBJECTIVE 1: Understand the fundamentals of data communications and the criteria for choosing a communications medium.

1. A networking _____ is anything that carries an electronic signal and interfaces between a sending device and a receiving device.

2. The range of signal frequencies that can be sent over a given medium at the same time is known as the ____.
    a. hertz
    b. bps
    c. bandwidth
    d. broadband

3. True or False: A digital signal continuously changes over a range of values over time.

LEARNING OBJECTIVE 2: Explain how networking media, devices, and software work together to provide data networking services.

4. True or False: For exceptionally high data transmission rates one should look to fiber-optic cabling.

5. A(n) _____ tells you the exact location of the receiver on the earth's surface.

6. ____ enables a wide assortment of digital devices to communicate wirelessly over short distances.
    a. Bluetooth
    b. Wi-Fi
    c. Fiber optics
    d. Microwave transmission

7. A network _____ is a computer circuit board, PC Card, or USB device installed in a computing device so that it can be connected to a network.

8. A network ____ is a person responsible for setting up and maintaining the network, implementing

network policies, and assigning user access permissions.
a. technician
b. supervisor
c. engineer
d. administrator

LEARNING OBJECTIVE 3: List the different classifications of computer networks and their defining characteristics and understand how to set up a wireless home network.

9. Ring, bus, and star are examples of network ____.
a. types
b. topologies
c. protocols
d. nodes

10. True or false: A private network made accessible to select outsiders is called an intranet.

11. A(n) ____ is often used by enterprises to allow employees to access the corporate intranet from home and while on the road.
a. virtual private network (VPN)
b. extranet
c. metropolitan area network (MAN)
d. router

12. The ease of installation of a(n) _____ network is making it the obvious choice for most home networks.

13. A cable modem and DSL are both examples of _____ Internet connections.

LEARNING OBJECTIVE 4: Appreciate the benefits of computer networks in homes, organizations, and businesses.

14. ____ allows businesses and organizations to save money and complexity by merging phone and data networks into one network.
a. Groupware
b. Voice over Internet Protocol (VoIP)
c. Instant messaging
d. Telecommuting

15. Employees that work from a home office rather than an office building are taking advantage of ____.
a. their employer
b. home networking
c. telecommuting
d. electronic data interchange (EDI)

16. True or false: EDI uses network systems and follows standards and procedures that allow output from one system to be processed directly as input to other systems, without human intervention.

Test Yourself Solutions: **1.** medium, **2.** c., **3.** F, **4.** T, **5.** global positioning system (GPS), **6.** a., **7.** adapter, **8.** d., **9.** b., **10.** f., **11.** a., **12.** wireless, **13.** broadband **14.** b., **15.** c., **16.** T

Key Terms

analog signal, p. 202
bandwidth, p. 203
Bluetooth, p. 212
broadband, p. 204
cable modem connection, p. 229
coaxial cable, p. 207
communications satellite, p. 208
dial-up connection, p. 229
digital signal, p. 202
Digital Subscriber Line (DSL), p. 230
Ethernet, p. 221

fiber-optic cable, p. 207
global area networks (GAN), p. 227
global positioning system (GPS), p. 210
intranet, p. 226
local area network (LAN), p. 225
metropolitan area network (MAN), p. 226
microwave transmission, p. 208
modem, p. 215
network adapter, p. 216

networking media, p. 201
personal area network (PAN), p. 225
telecommunications, p. 201
telecommuting, p. 233
twisted-pair cable, p. 206
virtual private network (VPN), p. 226
wide area network (WAN), p. 226
Wireless Fidelity (Wi-Fi), p. 211

Questions

Review Questions

1. Besides a sender and receiver, what other components are required for communication to take place?

2. How do analog and digital signals differ?

3. What do you need to keep in mind when deciding on a networking medium?

4. List the three types of cables discussed in this chapter in order of bandwidth.

5. Name three advantages and one disadvantage of using fiber-optic cable as compared to coaxial and twisted pair.

6. Under what conditions might a company consider using a telecommunications satellite over microwave towers?

7. What are the fundamental differences between Wi-Fi and Bluetooth technologies?

8. Name two personal computer devices that are used to connect to networks.

9. What concerns do privacy advocates have about RFID?

10. What is the purpose of a firewall?

11. What is meant by distributed computing?

12. What is the difference between local resources and remote resources on a network workstation?

13. List four network topologies.

14. List the five network types in order of size.

15. What is the most popular type of network?

16. How does an intranet differ from the Internet?

17. What unique concerns are associated with global area networks?

18. What equipment is required to set up a wireless home network?

19. What options are available for accessing the Internet from home?

20. List five benefits of computer networks.

Discussion Questions

21. What are some negative effects of insufficient bandwidth for residential networks and professional business networks?

22. What personal and professional benefits are afforded by Bluetooth technology? What effect would Bluetooth have on the life of a person in your future profession?

23. How does a client/server network system assist in managing information in a large organization?

24. Envision yourself in your future career. What role might telecommuting play in your weekly activities? Will you be able to do some or all of your work from a home office? How?

25. What role does teamwork play in your career area? How can a computer network assist team members in their work?

Exercises

Try It Yourself

1. Sit down at a network computer on campus. Use a file management utility (such as My Computer on Microsoft Windows) to determine which disk drives are local resources and which are network resources. What other local and network resources are available on the computer? Printers? Scanners? If you are unsure, ask a computer lab assistant or network administrator. Use a word

processor to create a document that lists the location of the computer lab that you used and who manages the network (either a group or person). Include a two-column table listing local resources in the left column and network resources in the right. Use proper column headings and make your document look like an official report.

2. Find the Web page of the organization that provides your campus network. Find the network us-

age policy or agreement for your campus network. Use a word processor to list the five most interesting activities *not* allowed on your campus network and your rationale for why these rules might exist. Why is a network usage policy necessary?

3. Visit the Web site of the department of your major (or intended major). Create a document that lists the computing environment provided to you by the department. Does your department have its own computer lab, or are students expected to use campus labs? Why do you think this is? Does your field require special computing or networking hardware or software?

4. Use a spreadsheet and the Web to compare the costs of setting up a wired Ethernet network compared to setting up a wireless network. The Ethernet network should include three 10/100 Fast Ethernet Adapters, a 10/100 Fast Ethernet Hub (4 port), and three 50 foot Category 5 (Cat5) RJ-45 cables. Your wireless network should include an 802.11b wireless access point and three 802.11b wireless network adapters (USB). You might start your research at www.cdw.com. Which network is cheapest? Which network is fastest? Which network would you prefer? Why?

5. Conduct a Web search on "Bluetooth." Research several informative pages on the topic with at least one positive and one negative perspective. Write a two-page paper on how Bluetooth is being used, along with a summary of positive and negative comments about it.

6. Conduct a Web search on "Network Security," following the links to network security Web sites in an effort to determine what issues are of greatest concern in network security. What appear to be the top five concerns in the field of network security? Rank them in order of importance, and include a brief description of each.

Virtual Classroom Activities

For the following exercises, do not use face-to-face or telephone communications with your group members. Use only Internet communications.

7. Select a U.S. college, and visit the college's Web site. Find information about computer access provided by the college. Does the college provide public computer labs? Are the dorms networked? How can notebook computers be connected to the campus network? Use a word processor to list interesting statistics, such as how many computer labs are available, how many computers are in each lab, what types of computers, and so on. Include anything that you find interesting and unique about the college's network setup. Each group member should distribute his or her findings to the group. Then, hold a group discussion and vote to determine which college has the best setup.

8. If you have set up or maintain a home computer network, create a document that lists the networking difficulties that you have experienced along with the benefits that the network has provided. Include in your document a detailed description of the type of network you have and the equipment you use. If you have no experience with home networking, interview someone who does, and write up his or her comments. Swap stories with other group members and write a summary of shared experiences.

Teamwork

9. Scour the Web in search of the cheapest 802.11g wireless network setup. The wireless setup should include the components discussed in this chapter (see the "Setting up a Wireless Home Network" section), must accommodate two desktop PCs and two notebook computers, and should connect all network users to a cable modem Internet connection. The team member who comes up with the cheapest network that meets the requirements wins! Make sure to include shipping cost.

10. The team should place itself in the role of system administrators of a corporate network. Each team member should work independently to design a network-usage policy that restricts employees from wasting time on the corporate network for personal needs, while not overly restricting them. You should address issues such as personal e-mail, personal Web browsing, access to the network from home, and so on. After listing individual ideas for important issues and policies, the team should get together and share their ideas. Work to merge everyone's policies into one cohesive corporate network usage policy. Do not include policies that do not have full team support, but rather list those separately for further discussion in class.

Learning Check

To check your knowledge of each of the chapter objectives, use this chart to find related end-of-chapter content.

Learning Objective	Key Terms		Questions	Exercises
Learning Objective 1 Understand the fundamentals of data communications and the criteria for choosing a communications medium.	analog signal bandwidth broadband digital signal	networking medium telecommunications	1, 2, 3	4
Learning Objective 2 Explain how networking media, devices, and software work together to provide data networking services.	Bluetooth coaxial cable communications satellite Ethernet fiber-optic cable global positioning system (GPS)	network adapter microwave transmission twisted-pair cable Wireless Fidelity (Wi-Fi)	4, 5, 6, 7, 8, 9, 10	3, 4, 5, 7, 9
Learning Objective 3 List the different classifications of computer networks and their defining characteristics and understand how to set up a wireless home network.	cable modem, dial-up connection, Digital Subscriber Line (DSL), global area networks (GAN), intranet, local area network (LAN),	metropolitan area network (MAN), personal area network (PAN), virtual private network (VPN), wide area network (WAN),	11, 12, 13, 14, 15, 16, 17, 18, 19	1, 2, 3, 4, 5, 6, 7, 8, 9, 10
Learning Objective 4 Appreciate the benefits of computer networks in homes, organizations, and businesses.	telecommuting		20	3, 5, 7

Endnotes

1. Staff, "Sprint is helping us build on success", *Sprint News & Events,* accessed August 9, 2003, *www.sprintbmo. com/bizpark/page/segment/news_resources/news_ detail.jsp?article_id=5121.*

2. Fusco, Patricia, "FCC National Broadband Policy", *ISP-Planet,* November 7, 2001, *www.isp-planet.com/ politics/2001/national_broadband_policy.html,* accessed June, 15, 2003.

3. "Multimedia Network allows Drew University to offer Telemedicine Services to Urban Population" Case Study from Nortel Networks, accessed August 12, 2003 at *http://a2032.g.akamai.net/7/2032/5107/20021004180555/ www.nortelnetworks.com/solutions/education/collateral/bc_ drew.pdf.*

4. *www.aerovironment.com/area-telecom/telecom.html,* and *www.skytowerglobal.com/begin.html* accessed July 1, 2003.

5. Batista, Elisa, "A Kiddie GPS for the Masses?", *Wired News,* October 12, 2002, *www.wired.com.*

6. "Polynesian Island of Niue the First Free Wireless Nation," *Business Wire,* June 23, 2003.

7. *www.bluetooth.com/sig/about.asp.*

8. "Nortel Networks' Companion Product, integrated with Rauland-Borg's Responder® IV System, allowed Sunny-brooks 700-bed wing to deliver high quality patient care, with fewer staff." Case Study from Nortel Networks, accessed August 12, 2003 at *http://a1904.g. akamai.net/7/1904/5107/20020706034927/www.nortel networks.com/solutions/health/collateral/raulandborg.pdf.*

9. Vijayan, Jaikumar, and Brewin, Bob, "Wal-Mart Backs RFID Technology", *ComputerWorld,* June 16, 2003, *www.computerworld.com/softwaretopics/erp/story/ 0,10801,82155,00.html?nas=EB-82155.*

10. Batista, Elisa, "What Your Clothes Say About You", *Wired News,* March 12, 2003, *www.wired.com/news/ wireless/0,1382,58006,00.html.*

11. Brewin, Bib, "Wal-Mart's Plan Poses Challenges for Chip Makers", *Computerworld,* June 16, 2003, *www. computerworld.com/softwaretopics/erp/story/0,10801,82152, 00.html.*

12. Skytek RFID Engineering Web site accessed August 10, 2003, *www.skyetek.com/applications/.*

13. Championchip USA Web site accessed August 10, 2003, *www.championchip.com/home/index.php.*

14. Lohr, Steve, "Hewlett Says Plan for PC's Is Corporate Money-Saver", *NYTimes/Technology,* June 3, 2003.

15. *www.almaden.ibm.com/cs/user/pan/pan.html;* also *www.research.ibm.com/topics/popups/smart/mobile/html/ pan.html.*

16. Shillingford, Joia, "Hotspots and hot topics at FT conference", *Financial Times (FT.com),* June 4, 2003.

17. Woody, Tod, "The Race to Kill Kazaa", Wired Magazine, February 2003, also at *www.wired.com/wired/archive/ 11.02/kazaa.html.*

18. *www.homepna.org/.*

19. Spooner, John, "Intel introduces the Centrino family", *ZDNet News,* January 8, 2003, *zdnet.com.com/ 2100-1103-979655.html?tag=nl.*

20. Lawsky, David, "Electric Companies Plug Homes Into the Internet", *Reuters,* June 11, 2003, *www.reuters.com/ newsArticle.jhtml?type=internetNews&storyID=2910744 &src=eDialog/GetContent.*

DatabaseSystems

Technology 360°

Jeanne Jansen never thought that her hobby would turn into money. As a young girl, she and her mother would spend hours on the sewing machine making dresses and other clothes. What was once a necessity to save money soon became fun. After college, Jeanne got a job working for an upscale retail store. In her spare time, Jeanne started designing sports apparel. She now has a large room full of cloth, buttons, fasteners, and designs for sports shorts and tops. But keeping track of everything has been a problem. Jeanne is also thinking about starting a small business to design and sell women's running and biking clothes. Eventually, she would like to quit her job. Jeanne currently has a personal computer with word processing, spreadsheet, and database programs.

1. How can Jeanne keep track of materials and designs stored in her sewing room?
2. If she starts a small business, how will she be able to pay her employees, pay her bills, and keep track of other business transactions?

Check out Jeanne's *Action Plan* at the conclusion of this chapter.

After completing Chapter 6, you will be able to:

LEARNING OBJECTIVES	CHAPTER CONTENT
1. Understand basic data management concepts.	**Basic Data Management Concepts**
2. Describe different database models, including the hierarchical, network, and relational models, and database characteristics.	**Organizing Data in a Database**
3. Discuss the different types of database management systems and their design and use by individuals and organizations.	**Database Management Systems**
4. Describe how organizations use database systems to perform routine processing, provide information, and provide decision support, and how they use data warehouses, marts, and mining.	**Using Database Systems in Organizations**
5. Discuss additional database systems, including object-oriented and distributed systems.	**Emerging Database Trends**
6. Describe the role of the database administrator (DBA) and database policies and security practices.	**Managing Databases**

Introduction

Everyone and every organization need a way to store data and to have the ability to convert raw data into important information. Databases serve this function. Without databases, today's businesses could not survive. Databases are also used in medicine, science, engineering, the military, and most other fields. Databases are also useful to individuals for keeping track of items in an apartment, music in a CD collection, and expenses used to prepare a budget and complete a tax return. In order to use a database, you must first understand basic data management concepts.

BASICDATAMANAGEMENTCONCEPTS

One of the goals of an effective computer system is to provide people with timely, accurate, and relevant information—information that is based on data. An important resource for any organization is its collection of data.

A database can help individuals and organizations maximize their use of the right data as a valuable resource. Databases also help individuals and organizations achieve their goals. Database software, for example, has done what decades of activism and fieldwork has failed to do: help Birute Galdikas save the orangutan from extinction.[1] Galdikas has spent decades in the field observing orangutans, taking notes, and trying to devise ways to convince the world of the importance of saving the Bornean orangutan from extinction (see Figure 6.1). Today, Galdikas is using a state-of-the-art database software package. With a generous donation from an ex-NASA official worth about $300,000, she is sorting through a mountain of data. Orangutans are more difficult to track and understand than other primates. Unlike gorillas or chimpanzees, orangutans do not move in groups. The adults get together to breed only about once every 8 years or so. With tens of thousands of data points, sophisticated database software is needed to make sense of the data. The database software, called TowerView, has been used by corporations to filter mountains of data to find trends and business opportunities. Similar software was used by NASA to track space probes, including Voyager and Galileo. Using the TowerView database software package, Galdikas is now investigating breeding patterns and other behaviors of orangutans.

As we saw in Chapter 1, a *database* is a collection of data organized to meet users' needs. Throughout your career, you will directly or indirectly access a variety of databases ranging from a simple list of music in your collection to a fully integrated database at work. In his book *Spinning Straw into Gold: The Magic of Turning Data into Money*, John Miglautsch describes how database marketing can result in higher profits.[2] Miglautsch stresses the importance of marketing only to customers who have a high profit potential.

You usually access databases using software called a **database management system (DBMS)**. A DBMS consists of a group of programs that manipulate the database and provide an interface between the database and the user or the database and application programs. A database, a DBMS, and the application programs that utilize the data in the database make up a *database system* or database environment.

Understanding basic database system concepts can enhance your ability to use the power of a computerized database system to support individual and organizational goals (see the Job Technology box). Individuals, for example, can use database concepts to keep a record of expenses for tax returns. Direct mail order companies face the difficult question of how many times to send a new catalogue to current and potential customers.[3] Printing and mailing costs can be 25 percent or more of total expenses. If a company has too many catalogue mailings, it can be very expensive. If there are too few mailings, sales could suffer. How many times to mail catalogues to customers is a key decision that has a direct impact on profitability. The German company, Rhenania, faced this important decision. The company, which sells CDs, books, and related products, mails catalogues to customers 18 times each year. The

FIGURE 6.1 • Saving endangered species

Birute Galdikas is using the state-of-the-art database software package, TowerView, to investigate breeding patterns and other behaviors of orangutans. Her work is instrumental in saving the Bornean orangutan from extinction.

Marketing Database Gives Entertainment UK the Upper Hand

When residents of the United Kingdom purchase music and video CDs and DVDs, there is a one in four chance that Entertainment UK supplied the product they purchased (see Figure 6.2). Entertainment UK links the recording industry and the public through their two divisions:

- Entertainment UK. Wholesale supplier to retailers like Tesco, Woolworth's, and Safeway
- Entertainment UK Direct. Retail supplier to the public through the Internet, kiosks, catalogues, digital TV, or special in-store orders

Entertainment UK uses the MicroStrategy database and analysis software to enhance its business operations. The company collects data from all of its customers and retailers and combines it into one powerful database system. The MicroStrategy software enables Entertainment UK marketing specialists to query the data using Web-based tools, and to see which items are selling, which promotions are working, and what price is optimal for each product. It includes a library of over 150 analytical functions that provide insight into problem areas and opportunities. Marketing specialists can use the software to create visually pleasing presentations and reports to assist their retail suppliers in choosing the products best suited for their client base.

Ian McKee, a manager at Entertainment UK, states, "Entertainment UK provides just-in-time stock control on a sale or return basis so it is critical that we have accurate market information to make good decisions quickly. Our role as a distributor is to be the hub of the supply chain, sharing this market knowledge with our suppliers and customers to maximize sales by ensuring the right products are on the right shelves at the right time."

Questions

1. Describe how the database approach was used in this situation. A just-in-time inventory approach is difficult to manage for items whose consumption rate is not easily predictable. In the entertainment industry where the market fluctuates daily, it becomes nearly impossible to maintain. How can suppliers like Entertainment UK predict the market to know what to deliver just in time?
2. Acting as a middleman between the record/video producers and the public places Entertainment UK in a position to offer both sides special services. We've heard about the services Entertainment UK provides for its clients, the retailers and consumers. What services can Entertainment UK provide for the record/video producers? Is Entertainment UK a valuable middleman, or would consumers and the music/video producers be better off doing away with the middleman and dealing directly with each other? Why?

Sources
1. *"Entertainment UK Charts Performance with MicroStrategy Software," from MicroStrategy's "Success Stories" Web site, www.microstrategy.com, accessed May 4, 2002.*
2. *Entertainment UK Web site, www.entuk.com/index2.html, accessed May 4, 2002.*
3. *"Even small call centers can benefit from specialist products,"* Business Info Magazine, *February 2, 2002, www.entuk.com/coverage.php?coverageID=10.*

FIGURE 6.2 • **The Entertainment UK warehouse**

As a major wholesale supplier, Entertainment UK uses databases to handle order processing and inventory.

company used a database system to obtain important customer preference information. The information from the database was fed into a statistical analysis program, which revealed that profits could be maximized if the company sent out catalogues between 20 and 25 times each year. In contrast, Port City Metals Services in Tulsa, Oklahoma, uses a database management system to identify its best customers and to identify potential customers with the same characteristics.[4] The company fabricates steel parts for manufacturing companies. Understanding database concepts is critical to getting the most out of an organization's data.[5]

Data Management for Individuals and Organizations

Individuals use databases to keep track of valuables for possible insurance claims, develop monthly budgets, store phone numbers and addresses, and keep track of important dates. Without data and the ability to process it, an organization would not be able to successfully complete most activities. It would not be able to generate reports to support decision makers to help achieve organizational goals. Businesses would find it difficult to pay employees, send out bills, order new inventory, or produce information to assist managers in the decision-making process. Recall that data consists of raw facts, like record sales or weather statistics. In order for data to be transformed into useful information, it must first be organized in some meaningful way.

The Hierarchy of Data

Recall from Chapter 2 that, in a computer, a byte is used to represent a character, which is the basic building block of information. Characters can be uppercase letters (A, B, C, . . . Z), lowercase letters (a, b, c, . . . z), numeric digits (0, 1, 2, . . . 9), or special symbols (., !, [+], [-], /, . . .).

In a database, characters are put together to form a field. A **field** is typically a name, number, or combination of characters that in some way describes an aspect of an object (an individual, a music CD, employee, a shelf, a truck) or activity (a sale). Every field has a *field name* and can have either a fixed or variable length. For example, EmployeeNumber is a field name for an employee number that is a fixed 8 characters long. PartDescription is the field name for part description, where the length of the description can vary, depending on the part.

A collection of related fields is a **record**. You can create a more complete description of an object or activity by combining fields that represent various characteristics of objects or activities into records. For instance, an employee record is a collection of fields about one employee. One field would be the employee's name, another her address, and still others her phone number, pay rate, earnings made to date, and so forth.

A collection of related records is a **file**, also called a *table* in some databases. For example, an employee file is a collection of all of an organization's employee records. Likewise, an inventory file is a collection of all inventory records for a particular organization. Employee and inventory files are relatively permanent files. These are examples of **master files**, permanent files that are updated over time. Organizations also have temporary files that hold data that needs to be processed, such as the business transactions of paying employees or taking sales orders. These are called **transaction files**, temporary files that contain data representing transactions or actions that must be taken. A file containing the number of hours employees worked last week or the sales orders from yesterday are examples of transaction files. They must be processed to pay employees or fill orders. Transaction files often cause changes to master files. An inventory master file containing the current amount of an inventory item will have to be adjusted (reduced in this case) to reflect new sales of the inventory item contained in the order transaction file. If a customer orders five cookbooks from an online bookstore, the online bookstore must subtract five cookbooks from its inventory master file to keep the master file current and accurate.

At the highest level of this hierarchy is a **database**, a collection of integrated and related files. Together, characters, fields, records, files, and databases form the *hierarchy of data* (see Figure 6.3). Characters are combined to make a field, fields are combined to make a record, records are combined to make a file, and files are combined to make a database. It is important to remember that a database houses not only all of these levels of data but the relationships among them.

FIGURE 6.3 • The hierarchy of data
The hierarchy of data represents the idea that characters are combined to make a field, fields are combined to make a record, records are combined to make a file, and files are combined to make a database.

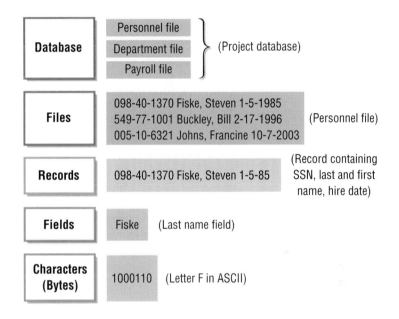

Data Entities, Attributes, and Keys

Databases use entities, attributes, and keys to store data and information. An **entity** is a generalized class of people, places, or things (objects) for which data is collected, stored, and maintained. Examples of entities include music CDs, the contents of an apartment, employees, inventory, and customers. Most organizations store data about entities.

An **attribute** is a characteristic of an entity. For example, employee number, last name, first name, hire date, and department number are attributes for an employee (see Figure 6.4). Inventory number, description, number of units on hand, and location of the inventory item in the warehouse are examples of attributes for items in inventory; customer number, name, address, phone number, credit rating, and contact person are examples of attributes for customers. Attributes are usually selected to capture the relevant characteristics of entities such as employees or customers. The specific value of an attribute, called a *data item*, can be found in the fields of the record describing an entity.

As discussed, a collection of fields about a specific object is a record. A **key** is a field in a record that is used to identify the record. A *primary key* uniquely identifies the record. No other record can have the same key. The primary key is the

FIGURE 6.4 • Attributes and keys

The attributes include employee number, last name, first name, hire date, and department number. The key field, called a primary key, is the Employee number.

Employee number	Last name	First name	Hire date	Dept. number	
005-10-6321	Johns	Francine	10-7-65	257	
549-77-1001	Buckley	Bill	2-17-79	650	Entities (records)
098-40-1370	Fiske	Steven	1-5-85	598	

Primary key field

Attributes (fields)

main or principal key used to distinguish records so that they can be accessed, organized, and manipulated. In employee records such as the ones shown in Figure 6.4, the employee number is an example of a primary key.

Once we have identified a unique primary key for each record, it can be used to relate data in a database. For example, we could have an employee file containing a record for each employee that contains the employee number, pay rate, deductions to gross pay, years employed by the organization, and similar permanent employment data. We could also have an hours-worked file that contains the employee number and hours worked for employees who worked this week. Using the employee number as the primary key, both files can be related and used to compute and print the paychecks for each employee working this week. Multiplying pay rate in the employee file times the hours worked in the hours-worked file and subtracting any deductions gives the employee's pay for this week.

Simple Approaches to Data Management

There are a number of simple ways to manage data. For example, simple data management software packages are easy to use and update. You can use personal information managers (PIMs) to keep track of phone numbers, addresses, Web sites, and e-mail addresses (see Figure 6.5). A PIM also contains a calendar, where you can enter appointments. A home budget software package is another example of a simple data management system. You can enter expense items, and the software will compute totals and compare your actual expenses to your budget. Although these data management systems are simple to use, their structure can be very difficult or impossible to change. For example, the home budget program might limit you to a certain number of income and expense categories. With these simple approaches to data management, the same data can be stored in several different places. For example, information about a brokerage or investment company may appear both in a PIM and a budget program. However, it can be difficult or impossible to share data among various applications. As a result, most organizations decide to develop their own databases using the database approach.

FIGURE 6.5 • **The AMF personal information manager for businesses**

A personal information manager helps people keep track of phone numbers, addresses, Web sites, and e-mail addresses. It also contains a calendar for entering appointments.

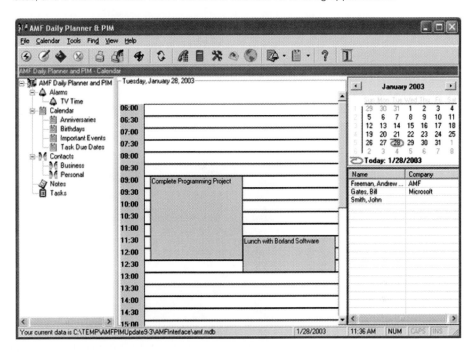

The Database Approach to Data Management

In a *database approach* to data management, multiple application programs share a pool of related data. Rather than each application having its own separate data files, each shares a collection of data files that are maintained in a central location in the database. The grocer Smart & Final Stores, for example, uses the database approach to allow multiple applications to run from a common database system.[6] According to Zeke Judge, chief information officer for the company, "It was just really complex. The data that accounting had looked different than the data that marketing had, which would look different from this or that or the other." Smart & Final uses the database approach to store customer receipts from 230 stores in a digital format. Storing data in one centralized database is more efficient and less prone to errors or mistakes.

DNA DATA LEADS TO POSITIVE ID

Identifying remains from the Word Trade Center collapse on 9/11 was impossible, involving as it did comparing small scraps of DNA to that stored in 22 different databases created for different purposes. A software developer created a system that could link to the other databases, as well as create virtual DNA profiles to compare against both the remains and DNA samples from surviving family members. By July 2003, 1,518 victims had been identified—779 by DNA alone.

Source:
"An Emphasis on Compassion"
By Thea Singer
MIT Technology Review
www.mittechnologyreview.com/articles/wo_singer082203.asp?p=1
August 22, 2003
Cited on August 27, 2003

The database approach can also provide an organization with increased flexibility in the use of data because it offers the ability to share data and information resources. As a part of a homeland security effort, the U.S. State Department is sharing its database of 50 million visa applications with the FBI to help identify possible terrorists.[7] Sharing data and information resources can be a critical factor in coordinating organization-wide responses across diverse functional areas of an organization. Partially as a result of the threat of terrorism, some governments are increasingly using the database approach to track unwanted people and prevent them from entering their country.[8] The U.S.

government, for example, is planning on using fingerprinting databases to track tens of thousands of suspected terrorists or visitors of "national security concern" as they enter the country. The database contains visual images of fingerprints (see Figure 6.6). The National Security Entry-Exit Registration System will attempt to close the borders to suspected terrorists by comparing the fingerprints of entering visitors against a comprehensive database. During the first year, about 200,000 visitors are expected to be fingerprinted and screened by the system.

FIGURE 6.6 • Fingerprinting databases

The U.S. government is planning to use fingerprinting databases to track suspected terrorists or visitors of "national security concern." The database contains visual images of fingerprints.

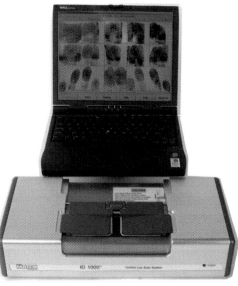

Using the database approach to data management requires a *database management system (DBMS)*. Recall that a DBMS consists of a group of programs that can be used as an interface between a database and the user or the database and application programs. Typically, this software acts as a buffer between the application programs and the database itself. Figure 6.7 illustrates the database approach. With the database approach, a centralized database system contains all the data for the organization or individual. The DBMS interacts directly with the database and passes data to various applications. A DBMS also reduces data redundancy because the data is stored only once. This means that less storage is required. Many modern databases are organization-wide, encompassing much of the data of the entire organization. Table 6.1 lists some of the primary advantages of the database approach. Disadvantages can be the high cost of database software and the need for a specialized staff in some cases.

FIGURE 6.7 • The database approach to data management

In the database approach, a centralized database system contains all the data for the organization or individual. The DBMS interacts directly with the database and passes data to various applications.

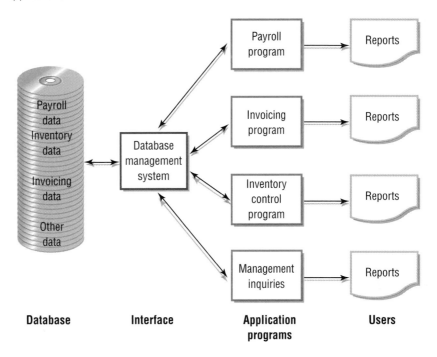

| Database | Interface | Application programs | Users |

TABLE 6.1 Advantages of the Database Approach

Advantages	Explanation
Reduced data redundancy	The database approach can reduce or eliminate data redundancy. Data is organized by the DBMS and stored in only one location. This results in more efficient utilization of system storage space.
Improved data integrity	Before DBMSs, some changes to data were not reflected in all copies of the data kept in separate files. This is prevented with the database approach because there are not separate files that contain copies of the same piece of data.
Easier modification and updating	With the database approach, the DBMS coordinates updates and data modifications. Programmers and users do not have to know where the data is physically stored. Data is stored and modified once. Modification and updating is also easier because the data is stored at only one location in most cases.
Data and program independence	The DBMS organizes the data independently of the application program. With the database approach, the application program is not affected by the location or type of data. Introduction of new types of data not relevant to a particular application does not require the rewriting of that application to maintain compatibility with the data file.
Better access to data and information	Most DBMSs have software that makes it easy to store and retrieve data from a database. In most cases, simple information commands can be given to get important information. Relationships between records can be more easily investigated and exploited, and applications can be more easily combined.
Standardization of data access	A primary feature of the database approach is a standardized, uniform approach to database access. This means that all application programs use the same overall procedures to retrieve data and information.
Better overall protection of the data	The use of and access to centrally located data is easier to monitor and control. Security codes and passwords can ensure privacy by allowing only authorized people to have access to particular data and information in the database.
Shared data and information resources	The cost of hardware, software, and personnel can be spread over a large number of applications and users.

COMMUNITY TECHNOLOGY

In Life Sciences Too Much Data Can Be an Opportunity and a Problem

Life scientists are deluged with data, and the data in genomic research will one day help save lives and prolong life (see Figure 6.8). But the data is not in one place. According to Joanna Batstone, director of IBM's

FIGURE 6.8 • The importance of human genome research reverberates in mouse genome studies

Through the use of extensive research databases scientists all over the world have access to the most up-to-date data available relating to the mouse genome and human genome projects.

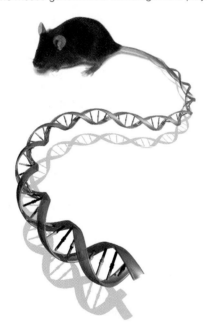

Life Sciences Solutions Department, "Data can reside on different continents and departments. Not only do scientists generate more of their own data, they have to look at other peoples' as well." Britain, which has the largest national store of forensic DNA samples, is now going to have the largest DNA medical database. Over 20 universities will be involved in collecting DNA samples in England.

Increasingly, scientists will have free access to vast databases.[9] This is due to the fact that the value of scientific data diminishes quickly over time. According to Dr. Eric Lander, who was involved in the effort to map the human genome, "It was insane to try to privatize basic research data since, at most, you can only get a few years advantage. Economically, such data is a wasting asset."

Questions

1. How can scientists access and use data that resides in different locations and in different databases?
2. How would you sort through a mountain of scientific data?
3. What other areas or fields face the opportunities and problems of a large amount of data?

Sources
1. *"Managing the Life Science Data Deluge,"* Peter Gynne, Geonomics and Proteomics, *May 01, 2003, p. 39.*
2. *"A Healthy Investment,"* Clare Wilson, New Scientist, *May 10, 2003, p. 25.*

ORGANIZING DATA IN A DATABASE

EXPAND YOUR KNOWLEDGE

To learn how to create a database and use it to answer queries, go to www.course.com/swt. Click the link "Expand Your Knowledge" and then complete the lab entitled, "Databases."

Because many of today's organizations are large and complex, it is critical to keep data organized so that it can be effectively utilized. A museum, for example, needs to organize its database to make sure it can catalogue and retrieve all of its items or pieces. Without a good organization of the database, it would be difficult or impossible for the museum to know exactly what items were part of its collection and where each item was located. This type of information could be critical if the museum has a break-in, and an insurance company needs to determine what may have been stolen. It is also critical during audits of the museum's assets.

A database should be designed to store all data relevant to the organization and provide quick access and easy modification. When building a database, careful consideration must be given to these questions:

- Content. What data is to be collected and at what cost?
- Access. What data is to be provided to which users when appropriate?
- Logical Structure. How is the data to be arranged so that it makes sense to a given user?
- Physical Organization. Where is the data to be physically located?
- Management and Coordination. Who is responsible for maintaining an accurate database system?

Database Models

The structure of the relationships in most databases follows one of three logical database models: hierarchical, network, and relational. Although hierarchical and network models are still being used today, relational models are the most popular.

Hierarchical and Network Models. In many situations, data follows a hierarchical or tree-like structure. A **hierarchical database model** is one in which the data is organized in a top-down or inverted tree-like structure. Data about a fundraising project for a university with three departments (A, B, and C) can follow this type of model (see Figure 6.9). Data about the project would form the beginning, or root, of the hierarchical database model. For a given project in an organization, a number of departments within the organization might be involved. In this case, Departments A, B, and C are involved with Project 1. In addition, certain employees from each department, in this case, Employees 1 through 6, will be involved in the project. The various departments and employees are represented as branches beneath the project. When this type of data is displayed in a logical fashion, it appears in a hierarchical model.

FIGURE 6.9 • A hierarchical data model

Project 1 is the top, or root, element. Departments A, B, and C are under this element, with Employees 1 through 6 beneath them as follows: Employees 1 and 2 under Department A, Employees 3 and 4 under Department B, and Employees 5 and 6 under Department C. There is a one-to-many relationship among the elements of this model.

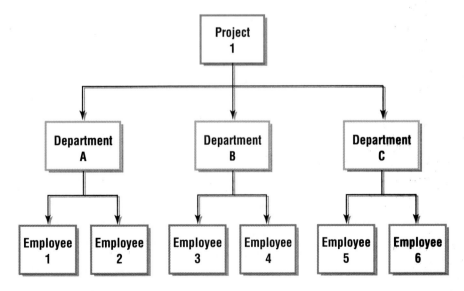

A **network model** is an extension of the hierarchical model. Instead of having only various levels of one-to-many relationships, however, the network model is an owner-member relationship in which a member may have many owners (see Figure 6.10).

FIGURE 6.10 • A network data model

In this network model, there are two projects at the top. Departments A, B, and C are under Project 1; Departments B and C are under Project 2. There is a many-to-many relationship among the elements of this model.

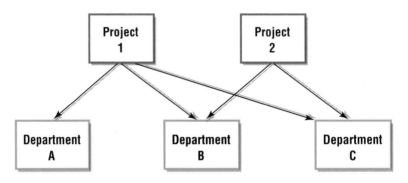

Consider two projects that require work from three departments. The projects (Projects 1 and 2) are placed at the top of the network. Below that, the various departments (Departments A, B, and C) required to do work on the projects would be listed. Then, lines could be drawn that reveal which departments work on which projects. For instance, you can see that Department B performs work on both Project 1 and Project 2; hence, it is a member that is "owned" by Projects 1 and 2.

The primary advantage of the hierarchical model is processing efficiency. A hierarchical database system can take less time to manipulate than other database models, because the data relationships are less complex. Network models offer more flexibility than hierarchical models in terms of organizing data. Network models, however, are more difficult to develop and use because of the complexity of the data relationships. Although hierarchical and network models are sometimes used, they are not as popular as relational database models, discussed next.

Relational Models. Relational models have become the most popular database models, and use of these models will continue to increase in the future. The overall purpose of the relational model is to describe data using a standard tabular format. In a database structured according to the **relational model**, all data elements are placed in two-dimensional tables called *relations* that are the logical equivalent of files.

The tables in relational databases organize data in rows and columns, simplifying data access and manipulation (see Figure 6.11). It is normally easier for people to understand the relational model than hierarchical and network models.

In the relational model, each row of a table, called a *tuple*, represents a record or collection of related facts. The columns of the table are called *attributes*, which we discussed earlier. Each attribute can take on only certain values. The allowable values for attributes or columns are called the *domain*. The domain for a particular attribute indicates what values can be placed in each of the columns of the relational table. For instance, the domain for an attribute such as gender would be limited to male or female. A domain for pay rate would not include negative numbers. Defining a domain can increase data accuracy. For example, a pay rate of -$5.00 could not be entered into the database, because it is a negative number and not in the domain for the attribute Payrate.

FIGURE 6.11 • A relational data model

In the relational model, all data elements are placed in two-dimensional tables or relations. As long as they share at least one common element, these relations can be linked to produce useful information.

DATA TABLE 1: PROJECT TABLE

Project number	Description	Dept. number
155	Payroll	257
498	Widgets	632
226	Sales Manual	598

DATA TABLE 2: DEPARTMENT TABLE

Dept. number	Dept. name	Manager SSN
257	Accounting	421-55-9993
632	Manufacturing	765-00-3192
598	Marketing	098-40-1370

DATA TABLE 3: MANAGER TABLE

SSN	Last name	First name	Hire date	Dept. number
005-10-6321	Johns	Francine	10-7-2003	257
549-77-1001	Buckley	Bill	2-17-1996	650
098-40-1370	Fiske	Steven	1-5-1985	598

Once data has been placed into a relational database, data inquiries and manipulations can be made. Basic data manipulations include selecting, projecting, and joining. *Selecting* involves eliminating rows according to certain criteria. Suppose a project table contains the project number, description, and department number for all projects being performed by an organization, as in Figure 6.11. A president of the company might want to find the department number for Project 226, which is a sales manual project. Using selection, the president can see only the data for number 226 and determine that the department number for the department completing the sales manual project is 598.

Projecting involves eliminating columns in a table. For example, we might have a Department table that contains the department number, department name, and the Social Security number (SSN) of the manager in charge of the project. The sales manager might want to create a new table showing only the department number and the Social Security number of the manager in charge of the sales manual project. Projection can be used to eliminate the department name column and create a new table containing only department number and SSN.

Joining involves combining two or more tables. For example, we can combine the Project table and the Department table to get a new table with the project number, project description, department number, department name, and the Social Security number for the manager in charge of the project.

One of the primary advantages of a relational database is that it allows tables to be linked, as shown in Figure 6.12. As long as the tables share at least one common data element, the tables in a relational database can be *linked* to provide useful information and reports. Being able to link tables to each other through common data elements is one of the keys to the flexibility and power of relational databases. Suppose that the president of a company wants to find out the name of the manager of the sales manual project and how long the manager has been

FIGURE 6.12 • Linking data tables to answer an inquiry

In finding the name and hiring date of the manager working on the sales manual project, the president needs three tables, Project, Department, and Manager. The project description (Sales Manual) leads to the department number (598) in the Project table, which leads to the manager's SSN (098-40-1370) in the Department table, which leads to the manager's name (FISKE) and hiring date (1-5-1985) in the Manager table.

PROJECT TABLE

Project number	Description	Dept. number
155	Payroll	257
498	Widgets	632
226	Sales Manual	598

DEPARTMENT TABLE

Dept. number	Dept. name	Manager SSN
257	Accounting	421-55-9993
632	Manufacturing	765-00-3192
598	Marketing	098-40-1370

MANAGER TABLE

SSN	Last name	First name	Hire date	Dept. number
005-10-6321	Johns	Francine	10-7-2003	257
549-77-1001	Buckley	Bill	2-17-1996	650
098-40-1370	Fiske	Steven	1-5-1985	598

with the company. The president would make the inquiry to the database, perhaps via a desktop personal computer. The DBMS would start with the project description and search the Project table to find out the project's department number. It would then use the department number to search the Department table for the department manager's Social Security number. The department number is also in the Department table, and is the common element that allows the Project table and the Department table to be linked. The DBMS then uses the manager's Social Security number to search the Manager table for the manager's hire date. The final result: the manager's name and hire date are presented to the president as a response to the inquiry. Linking tables is especially useful when information is needed from multiple tables, as in our example. The manager's Social Security number, for example, is only maintained in the Manager table. If the Social Security number is needed, it can be obtained by linking to the Manager table.

Data Analysis. Having the ability to link tables becomes very important when trying to ensure that the content of a database is "good." Good data should be nonredundant, flexible, simple, and adaptable to a number of different applications. The purpose of data analysis is to develop data with these characteristics. **Data analysis** is a process that involves evaluating data to identify problems with the content of a database. Consider a database for a fitness center that contains the attributes name, phone number, sex, dues paid, and date paid (see Figure 6.13). As the records in Figure 6.13 show, Brown and Thomas paid their dues in September. Thomas has paid his dues in two installments. Note that no primary key uniquely identifies each record. As we will see next, this is a problem that must be corrected.

FIGURE 6.13 • Fitness Center Dues

These database entries for a fitness center contain the name, phone number, sex, dues paid, and date paid.

Name	Phone	Sex	Dues Paid	Date Paid
Brown, A.	468-3342	Female	$30	September 15th
Thomas, S.	468-8788	Male	$15	September 15th
Thomas, S.	468-5238	Male	$15	September 15th

This database was designed to keep track of the dues that fitness center members paid in September. Because Thomas has paid dues twice, the data in the database is now redundant. The name, phone number, and sex for Thomas are repeated in two records. Notice that the data in the database is also inconsistent: Thomas has changed his phone number, but only one of the records reflects this change. Further reducing this database's reliability is the fact that no primary key exists to uniquely identify Thomas' record. The first Thomas could be Sim Thomas, but the second might be Steve Thomas. These problems and irregularities in data are called anomalies. Data anomalies often result in incorrect information, causing database users to be misinformed about actual conditions. These anomalies and others must be corrected.

To solve these problems, we can add a primary key, called member number, and put the data into two tables: a Fitness Center Members table with sex, phone number, and related information, and a Dues Paid table with dues paid and date paid (see Figures 6.14a and b). As you can see in Figures 6.14a and 6.14b, both tables include the member number attribute so they can be linked.

With the relations in Figures 6.14a and b, we have reduced the redundancy and eliminated the potential problem of having two different phone numbers for the same fitness center member. Also note that the member number gives each record in the Fitness Center Members table a primary key. Because we have two dues paid ($15 each) with the same member number (SN656), we know this is the same person, not two different people.

WHEN DATABASES GO BAD

The downside to databases is that when information is incomplete or inaccurate, the decisions made from them can be wrong. In response to 3,000 complaints, California's state insurance commissioner charged insurance companies with using inaccurate data to cancel, charge a higher premium for, or deny homeowner's insurance. The commissioner will conduct a series of audits to determine whether or not database information is being abused.

Source:
"Judge tosses insurance database rule"
By Dan Fost, Chronicle Staff Writer
San Francisco Chronicle
www.sfgate.com/cgi-bin/article.cgi?file=/chronicle/archive/2003/08/26/
BU213633.DTL&type=tech
August 26, 2003
Cited on August 27, 2003

The process of correcting data problems or anomalies is called *normalization*. It insures that the database contains "good data." Normalization normally involves breaking one file or table into two or more tables in order to correct the data problem or anomaly, as we did in Figures 6.14a and b. Normalization is a very important technique in database management and is yet another advantage to using a relational database. The details of normalization, however, are beyond the scope of this text.

Database Characteristics

The information needs of individuals or organizations have an impact on what type of data is collected and what type of database

FIGURE 6.14 • Data analysis at a fitness center

To solve data problems, we add a primary key, called member number, and put the data into two tables: a Fitness Center Members table with sex, phone number, and related information, and a Dues Paid table with dues paid and date paid.

a.   FITNESS CENTER MEMBERS TABLE

Member no.	Name	Phone	Sex
SN123	Brown, A.	468-3342	Female
SN656	Thomas, S.	468-5238	Male

b.   FITNESS CENTER DUES PAID TABLE

Member no.	Dues paid	Date paid
SN123	$30	September 15th
SN656	$15	September 15th
SN656	$15	September 25th

model is used. Important characteristics of databases include the amount of data, the volatility of the data, and how immediately the data needs to be updated.

- The database size or *amount* depends on the number of records or files in the database. The size determines the overall storage requirement for the database.
- *Volatility* of data is a measure of the changes, such as additions, deletions, or modifications, typically required in a given period of time.
- *Immediacy* is a measure of how rapidly changes must be made to data. Some applications, such as providing concert ticket reservations, require immediate updating and processing so that two customers are not booked for the same seat. Other applications, such as payroll, can be done once a week or less frequently and do not require immediate processing. If an application demands immediacy, it also demands rapid recovery facilities in the event the computer system shuts down temporarily.

The above characteristics are important for any individual or organization. They determine the requirements of the database and the database system that is needed for the amount of data, the volatility of the data, and the possible need for rapid changes. These characteristics are important in selecting and designing a database management system, discussed next.

DATABASEMANAGEMENTSYSTEMS

Creating and implementing the right database system ensures that the database will support individual and organizational goals. For example, an effective database management system can help doctors provide better patient care—a key goal

FedEx Corporation: Simplifying International Shipping

In the late 1990s, FedEx CIO Robert B. Carter discovered that many customers were frustrated and intimidated by the complexities of shipping their products overseas. Global trade regulations, import duties and taxes, import or export forms, product restrictions, embargoes, and special licensing requirements can all make international trade and overseas shipping an ordeal. So, to provide more customer assistance, Carter assembled a team to develop a new database system for overseas shipping.

FedEx systems analysts decided that the most convenient method for making this data available to their customers was to post it on the company's Web site. They designed a Web site with forms and wizard assistance that customers could use to walk through procedures, enter the necessary queries, and determine the documentation needed for the overseas delivery. The designers and programmers also linked the Web forms with the database and provided a suite of applications to access pertinent database information and create a Web page to display it.

After three years of programming, testing, and debugging, the system was launched on time and on budget. The resulting product was named FedEx Global Trade Manager, a free Web-based guide to an international shipping database for small and midsized businesses (see Figure 6.15). The application helps shippers understand global trade regulations and prepare the appropriate import or export forms based on the items being shipped and the countries of origin and destination. It also alerts users to restrictions on shipping certain items, lets them know if a country is under a trade embargo, and provides information on special licensing requirements.

Donald Broughton, a transportation analyst at A.G. Edwards & Sons in St. Louis, says that although FedEx was the first company to offer such a service, other companies, including Atlanta-based United Parcel Service, now have similar tools.

Questions

1. Do you think the FedEx project was a financial success for the company? Why?
2. How was the FedEx system able to help customers? Would you pay additional for such a service? How much, if any?
3. How might this type of application be used in another industry or field?

Sources
1. "Breakthrough on fedex.com Gives Businesses Power to Estimate Costs of Global Shipping," Staff, *Business Wire,* June 11, 2002.
2. Linda Rosencrance, "Computerworld Premier 100, Best in Class: FedEx Corp," Staff, *Computerworld, March 11, 2002, www.computerworld.com.*
3. FedEx Global Trade Manager Web site, *www.fedex.com/us/ international/, accessed July 2002.*

FIGURE 6.15 • FedEx Global Trade Manager database

The FedEx Global Trade Manager, a free Web-based guide to international shipping for small and midsized businesses, helps shippers understand global trade regulations and prepare the appropriate import or export forms based on the items being shipped and the countries of origin and destination.

EXPAND YOUR
KNOWLEDGE

To learn more about database systems,
go to www.course.com/swt. Click
the link "Expand Your Knowledge"
and then complete the lab entitled,
"Advanced Databases."

of any hospital.[10] At the George Washington University Hospital, the DBMS also helped to streamline paperwork. "The flow of events is based on patient care as the primary mover, not paperwork," says Andrew Robottom, George Washington University's director of the emergency department.

Creating and implementing the right database system involves determining how data is stored and retrieved, how people will see and use the database, how the database will be created and maintained, and how reports and documents will be generated. But how do we actually create, implement, use, and update a database? What type of database is needed?

Overview of Database Types

Database management systems can range from small, inexpensive software packages to sophisticated systems costing hundreds of thousands of dollars. A few popular alternatives include flat file, single user, multiuser, and general-purpose and special-purpose systems.

Flat File. A *flat file* has no relationship between its records and is often used to store and manipulate a single table or file. Flat files don't use any of the database models discussed earlier. Many spreadsheet and word-processing programs have flat file capabilities (see Figure 6.16). These software packages can sort tables and make simple calculations and comparisons.

FIGURE 6.16 • Flat file capabilities in Excel
Many spreadsheet programs have flat file capabilities.

	A	B	C	D	E	F	G
1	Order ID	Product	Unit Price	Quantity	Discount		
2	10248	Queso Cabrales	$14.00	12	0.00%		
3	10248	Singaporean Hokkien Fried Mee	$9.80	10	0.00%		
4	10248	Mozzarella di Giovanni	$34.80	5	0.00%		
5	10249	Tofu	$18.60	9	0.00%		
6	10249	Manjimup Dried Apples	$42.40	40	0.00%		
7	10250	Jack's New England Clam Chowder	$7.70	10	0.00%		
8	10250	Manjimup Dried Apples	$42.40	35	15.00%		
9	10250	Louisiana Fiery Hot Pepper Sauce	$16.80	15	15.00%		
10	10251	Gustaf's Knäckebröd	$16.80	6	5.00%		
11	10251	Ravioli Angelo	$15.60	15	5.00%		
12	10251	Louisiana Fiery Hot Pepper Sauce	$16.80	20	0.00%		
13	10252	Sir Rodney's Marmalade	$64.80	40	5.00%		
14	10252	Geitost	$2.00	25	5.00%		
15	10252	Camembert Pierrot	$27.20	40	0.00%		
16	10253	Gorgonzola Telino	$10.00	20	0.00%		
17	10253	Chartreuse verte	$14.40	42	0.00%		
18	10253	Maxilaku	$16.00	40	0.00%		
19	10254	Guaraná Fantástica	$3.60	15	15.00%		

Single User. Databases for personal computers are most often for a single user. Only one person can use the database at any time. Quicken is an example of a single user DBMS used by many people to store and manipulate financial data (see Figure 6.17).

FIGURE 6.17 • Quicken is a single-user DBMS

Quicken is an example of a single user DBMS used by many people to store and manipulate financial data.

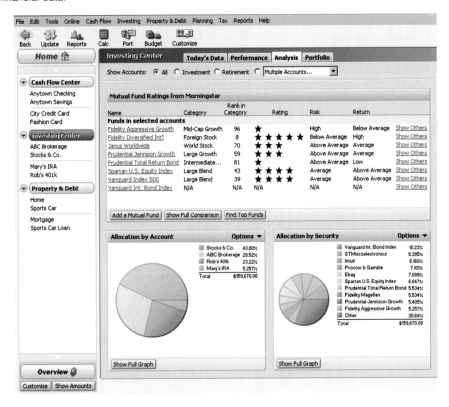

Multiuser. Networked computer systems need multiuser DBMSs. These more powerful, expensive systems allow dozens or hundreds of people to access the same database system at the same time. Popular vendors for multiuser database systems include Oracle, Sybase, Microsoft, and IBM.

General-Purpose and Special-Purpose. A *general-purpose database* can be used for a large number of applications. Oracle, Sybase, and IBM databases are examples of general-purpose databases that can be used by businesses, the military, charitable organizations, scientific researchers, and most other organizations for many different types of applications. In contrast, a *special-purpose database* is designed for one purpose or a limited number of applications. For example, with over a million entries, the American Theological Library Association database is one of the largest special-purpose databases containing articles and references on religion and theology.[11] This theological database would not be appropriate for storing business transactions or the results of scientific research.

Some special-purpose databases store personal information, such as names and addresses in *personal information managers (PIM)*. Others store financial data or tax information. Quicken, for example, is a comprehensive database for individuals that stores income, expense, and asset information. The software can be used to develop budgets, pay bills, and prepare tax records. Another example of a special-purpose database is Quick Books, which is an accounting program for small businesses. In many cases, the overall structure of the database and the reports that can be generated are already developed for easy use. MindManager is a special-purpose database used to organize projects and people's thoughts and ideas (see Figure 6.18).[12]

FIGURE 6.18 • ePortal map from Mindjet MindManager

Mindjet MindManager is a visual tool for brainstorming and planning that can be used to create special-purpose databases.

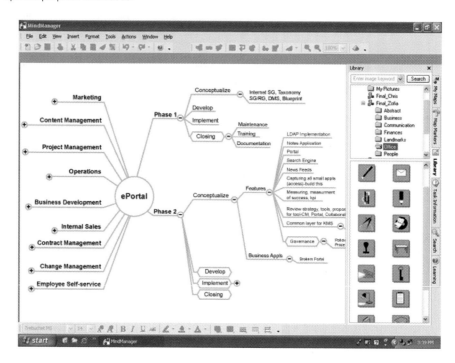

Database Design

Before data can be stored, manipulated, and retrieved, the database must be logically designed. At a minimum, this requires field, record, and table (or file) design. All database management systems have the ability to perform these important design functions. In addition, other aspects of the database can be designed, including the input and output interfaces.

Field Design. As mentioned earlier, a field is typically a name, number, or a combination of characters. The purpose of *field design* is to specify the type, size, format, and other aspects of each field. Some popular field types include:

- Numeric. A *numeric field* contains numbers that can be used in making calculations. The number of CD-RW disks you purchase at a computer store and the price are examples of numeric fields. The hours you work at a local restaurant and your age are examples of numeric data. Numeric data can include real numbers, which may contain a decimal point, such as the price of a new bicycle, $349.95, and integers, which are whole numbers without decimal points, such as your age or the number of CD-RW disks you purchase.
- Alphanumeric. *Alphanumeric*, or character-type, data includes characters or numbers that will not be manipulated or used in calculations. Examples include your name, your street address, your Social Security number, and the color of your hair.
- Date. Databases allow you to enter dates, such as 06/12/04, into the database. Once entered, *dates* can be sorted or even used in computations, such figuring out how many days occur between two dates.
- Logical. A *logical* piece of data contains items, such as "yes" or "no." Only these logical operators can be included in the field. For example, a university database might include a field that tracks whether students have met their English requirements for graduation. The field can contain a "yes" or a "no."

- Computed. A *computed* field, sometimes called a calculated field, is determined from other fields, instead of being entered into the database. Gross pay from a job, for example, is a computed field. It is determined by multiplying your hourly rate times the number of hours you worked. Other computed fields include grade point average, your total bill at a restaurant, and the total energy expended in a scientific experiment.

Record and Table Design. Recall that a record is a collection of related fields, and a table (or file) is a collection of related records. In any database, we must identify the exact fields that are contained in each record, and the types of records that may be included in each table. For example, you might want to develop a database for your music CD collection. Each record in the database could contain an item number that you specify, the artist, the name of the CD, when the CD was produced, when you purchased the CD, the general condition of the CD, and where you store the CD. Similar record designs can be specified for a database of the members in a volunteer group that builds homes, a list of items in your apartment for insurance purposes in case of a fire or theft, the results of a scientific experiment in your nutrition class, and the required courses you must complete to graduate.

Database tables can contain a few or literally thousands of records and fields. Tables can be organized in a variety of ways, and different tables can be related as we discussed earlier in the section on relational databases. We can sort on one or more fields to help organize a table. For a table containing the first and last names of members of a student group, we could sort on last name as the primary sorting key and the first name as the secondary sorting key. Adams would be sorted before Brill, and Crystal Adams would appear before Jake Adams. As mentioned before, tables can also be selected, joined, and projected.

Input and Output Interface Design. Designing effective interfaces is a convenient and powerful database design feature in most database management systems. For entering data into a database, we can design easy to understand forms that users can fill out for each record (see Figure 6.19). After users completely enter data into a field, we can have the database automatically go to the next field, without requiring the user to hit the return or enter key for each field.

FIGURE 6.19 • Input and output design

For entering data into a database, we can design easy to understand forms that users can fill out for each record.

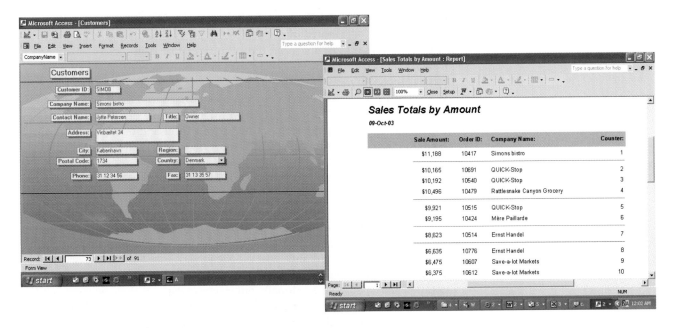

Reports and other outputs from the database can also be designed to be powerful and packed with useful information. A university can have a report that lists only those students who haven't paid their fees; a civil engineering firm could design a report that lists stress points in an old bridge; and a medical blood test report could be designed to include a column with all tests that are outside of normal ranges. Figure 6.19 shows sales totals by amount. These types of reports are an important aspect of providing information support to administrators, military generals, engineers, doctors, and corporate executives.

Using Databases with Other Software

Database management systems are often used in conjunction with other software packages or the Internet. A database management system can act as a front-end application or a back-end application. A *front-end application* is one that directly interacts with people or users. A *back-end application* interacts with other programs or applications; it only indirectly interacts with people or users. Some instructors, for example, use a database as a front-end to a spreadsheet program that contains student grades. The instructor and several teaching assistants can enter student grades into the database. The data is then transferred to a spreadsheet program that computes a student's grade. Researchers often use a database as a front end to a statistical analysis program. The researchers enter the results of experiments or surveys into a database. The data is then transferred to a statistical analysis program to test hypothesis or compute correlation coefficients. Using a database as a front end can increase data accuracy and avoid data corruption in spreadsheet programs, statistical analysis programs, or other back-end applications.

Databases can also be used as the back-end application. A call center operator may use a software package to enter questions from callers needing help or information. The software then interacts with one or more databases (the back end) to get the requested information. When people request information from a Web site on the Internet, the Web site can interact with a database (again the back end) that supplies the desired information. For example, you can connect to a library Web site to find if the library has a book you want to read. The library Web site then interacts with a database that contains a catalogue of library books and articles to determine if the book you want is available.

Data Accuracy and Integrity

As first discussed in Chapter 1, to be of value, data must be accurate. **Data integrity** means that data stored in the database is accurate and up to date. There are many possibilities for inaccuracies in today's information-rich society. Many people have been unable to get credit cards, car loans, or home mortgages because data stored about them by credit bureaus was wrong. In a manufacturing company, a clerk might enter the hours an employee worked as 4 hours instead of 40 hours. In some cases, a retail store may report that someone didn't pay his or her bills, when the bills were paid in full. A survey of a thousand electric utility companies found that customer databases were only 45.6 percent accurate.[13] These types of errors were caused by inaccurate data being entered into a database. The results are inaccurate output. This is called **garbage in, garbage out (GIGO)**.

In other cases, data is simply old and no longer valid. Managers have made multimillion-dollar decisions based on out-of-date data. A manager might decide to build a new manufacturing plant based on old sales data that was much higher than today's numbers. A nurse may give the wrong drugs to a patient because the prescribed treatment was old and reflected the patient's past situation, or a surgeon might amputate the wrong leg because of a mistake in the patient's records.

In other cases, people intentionally enter wrong data for their own gain. In the corporate scandals of the early 2000s, a number of executives and accountants falsified records to inflate profits or hide expenses to get higher bonuses

FIGURE 6.20 • **Damaging data integrity**

In the corporate scandals of the early 2000s, a number of executives and accountants falsified records to inflate profits or hide expenses to get higher bonuses based on the company's stock performance.

based on the company's stock performance (see Figure 6.20). Some medical researchers have falsified research results to get more articles published, which often results in getting tenure, a promotion, or salary increases.

Database management systems must be programmed to detect and eliminate data inaccuracies whenever possible. Databases can be programmed to check for inconsistent data. For example, if the combined expenses of various departments or branches are greater than the total expenses reported on a company's income statement, something is probably wrong. If everyone in a department was reported to have worked only 4 hours last week, a clerical error has probably been made. It is likely that 4 hours was entered into the database instead of 40 hours. Although it's not possible to eliminate all data inaccuracies, good database design and development requires that checks and balances be set up to detect and eliminate errors whenever possible.

Storage and Retrieval of Data

As described earlier, one function of a DBMS is to provide an interface between an application program and the database. When an application program needs data, it goes to the DBMS. Suppose that to calculate the total price of a product, an inventory-pricing program needs price data on all the components of the product. The application program seeks this data from the DBMS. In doing so, the application program follows a **logical access path (LAP)**. Next, the DBMS, working in conjunction with various systems software programs accesses a storage device, such as disk, where the data is stored. When the DBMS goes to this storage device to retrieve the data, it follows a **physical access path (PAP)** to the physical location of the price. In the pricing example, the DBMS might go to a disk drive to retrieve the price data for each component part. The general relationship between the logical access path used by the application and the physical access path used by the DBMS is shown in Figure 6.21.

FIGURE 6.21 • **Logical and physical access paths**

When an application program seeks data from a DBMS, it follows a logical access path. A DBMS follows a physical access path when it retrieves data from a storage device, such as disk.

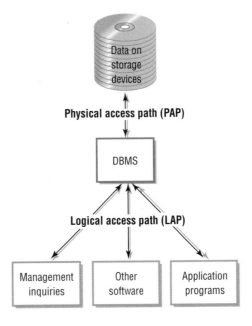

This same process is used if someone wants to get information from the database. First, a person requests the data from the DBMS. For example, a manager might give a command, such as LIST ALL PARTS FOR WHICH PRICE IS GREATER THAN 10 DOLLARS. This command is the LAP. Then, the DBMS goes to a hard disk to get the information for the manager. This is the PAP.

Because the DBMS is responsible for access to a database, one of the first steps in installing and using a database involves telling the DBMS the logical and physical structure of the data and relationships among the data in the database. This description is called a **schema** (as in schematic diagram). A schema can be part of the database or a separate schema file. The DBMS can reference a schema to find where to access the requested data in relation to another piece of data.

Updating a Database

Databases are updated by adding, modifying, and deleting records. Paleontologists looking for dinosaur bones can add records to their database at each new dig (see Figure 6.22). A university can modify your student records to include courses you just completed last semester along with your new GPA. A company can delete customers who paid their bills completely from their accounts receivables table, which lists all customers who still owe the company money from past sales. Continual database updating is absolutely essential to maintain a high degree of data accuracy and integrity. As mentioned earlier, a front-end application can be used to enter the changes, which are then transferred to the database (the back end).

FIGURE 6.22 • A paleontological database

A paleontologist looking for dinosaur bones can add records to her database at each new dig. If you were to search the database for information on a particular type of fossil, you would have access to the most current data. The U.S. Geological Survey National Paleontogological database is an example of this type of database.

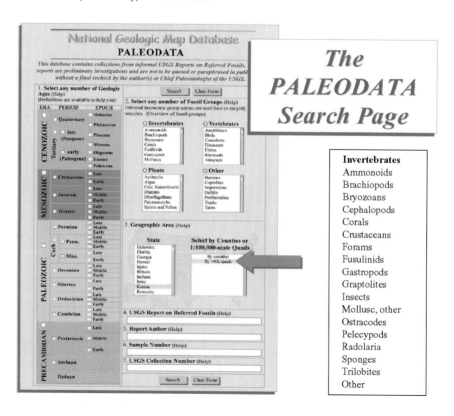

Providing a User View

A DBMS also acts as a user interface by providing a view of the database. A user view is the portion of the database a user can access. To create different user views, subschemas are developed. A **subschema** is a file that contains a description of a subset of the database and identifies which users can perform modifications on the data items in that subset. Whereas a schema is a description of the entire database, a subschema shows only some of the records and their relationships in the database. Normally, programmers or managers only have a need to view or access a subset of the database. For example, a sales representative might only need data describing customers in her region, not the sales data for the entire nation. A subschema could be used to limit her view to data from her region. The use of subschemas mean that the underlying structure of the database can change, but the view the user sees might not change. For example, even if all of the data on the southern region changed, the northeast region sales representative's view would not change if she accessed data on her region.

A number of subschemas can be developed for different people or users and various application programs. Typically, the database user or application will access the subschema, which then accesses the schema (see Figure 6.23). Subschemas can also provide additional security because programmers and other users are typically allowed to view only certain parts of the database.

FIGURE 6.23 • **The use of schemas and subschemas**
A number of subschemas can be developed for different users. Subschemas can provide security because users are typically allowed to view only certain parts of the database.

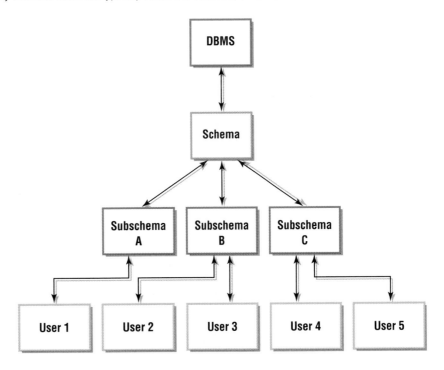

Creation and Modification of the Database

Schemas and subschemas are entered into the DBMS (usually by database personnel) via a data definition language. A **data definition language (DDL)** is a collection of instructions and commands used to define and describe data and data relationships in a specific database.

A DDL allows the database's creator to describe the data and the data relationships that are to be contained in the schema and the many subschemas. In general, a DDL describes logical access paths and logical records in the database. Figure 6.24 shows a simplified example of a DDL used to develop a general schema. The Xs in Figure 6.24 reveal where specific information concerning the database is to be entered. File description, area description, record description, and set description are terms the DDL defines and uses in this example. Other terms and commands can be used, depending on the particular DBMS employed.

Another important step in creating a database is to establish a data dictionary, a detailed description of all data used in the database. The **data dictionary** includes information, such as the name of the data item, who prepared the data, who approved the data, the date, a description, other names, the range of values for the data, the data type (numeric or alphanumeric), and the number of positions or space needed for the data. Figure 6.25 shows a typical data dictionary entry.

For example, the information in a data dictionary for an inventory item part number can include the name of the person who made the data dictionary entry (D. Bordwell) and the date the entry was made (August 4), the name of the person who approved the entry (J. Edwards) and the approval date (October 13), the version number (3.1), the number of pages used for the entry (1 page), the part name (PARTNO), other part names that may be used (PTNO), the range of values (part numbers can range from 100 to 5,000), the type of data

FIGURE 6.24 • **Using a data definition language to define a schema**

In general, a data definition language (DDL) describes logical access paths and logical records in the database.

```
SCHEMA DESCRIPTION
SCHEMA NAME IS XXXX
AUTHOR     XXXX
FILE DESCRIPTION
   FILE NAME IS XXXX
      ASSIGN XXXX
   FILE NAME IS XXXX
      ASSIGN XXXX
AREA DESCRIPTION
   AREA NAME IS XXXX
RECORD DESCRIPTION
   RECORD NAME IS XXXX
   RECORD ID IS XXXX
   LOCATION MODE IS XXXX
   WITHIN XXXX AREA FROM XXXX THRU XXXX
SET DESCRIPTION
   SET NAME IS XXXX
   ORDER IS XXXX
   MODE IS XXXX
   MEMBER IS XXXX
   •
   •
   •
```

FIGURE 6.25 • **A typical data dictionary entry**

The data dictionary includes information, such as the name of the data item, who prepared the data, who approved the data, the date, a description, other names, the range of values for the data, the data type (numeric or alphanumeric), and the number of positions or space needed for the data.

```
          NORTHWESTERN MANUFACTURING

PREPARED BY:        D. BORDWELL
DATE:               04 AUGUST
APPROVED BY:        J. EDWARDS        DATE: 13 OCTOBER
DATE:               13 OCTOBER
VERSION:            3.1
PAGE:               1 OF 1

DATA ELEMENT NAME:  PARTNO
DESCRIPTION:        INVENTORY PART NUMBER
OTHER NAMES:        PTNO
VALUE RANGE:        100 TO 5000
DATA TYPE:          NUMERIC
POSITONS:           4 POSITIONS OF COLUMNS
```

(numeric), and the storage required (four numeric positions are required for the part number). Some of the typical uses of a data dictionary are to:

- Provide a standard definition of terms and data elements. This can help in the programming process by providing consistent terms and variables to be used for all programs. Programmers know what data elements are already captured in the database and how they relate to other data elements.
- Assist programmers in designing and writing programs. Programmers do not need to know which storage devices are used to store needed data. Using the data dictionary, programmers specify the required data elements. The DBMS locates the necessary data.
- Simplify database modification. If for any reason a data element needs to be changed or deleted, the data dictionary would point to those specific programs that utilize the data element that may need modification.

A data dictionary helps achieve the advantages of the database approach in three ways:

- Reduced data redundancy. By providing standard definitions of all data, it is less likely that the same data item will be stored in different places under different names. For example, a data dictionary would reduce the likelihood that the same part number would be stored as two different items, such as PTNO and PARTNO.
- Increased data security. It is more difficult for unauthorized people to gain access to sensitive data and information.
- Faster program development. With a data dictionary, programmers can develop programs faster. They don't have to develop names, descriptions, value ranges, and other data attributes for data items because the data dictionary does that for them. Programmers don't have to check to make sure that the same name is not being used for another purpose or that the same date item doesn't have two or more names. With some programs requiring hundreds or thousands of data names, this can save a significant amount of time.
- Easier modification of data and information. The data dictionary and the database approach make modifications to data easier because users don't need to know where the data is stored. The person making the change indicates the new value of the variable or item, such as part number, that is to be changed. The database system locates the data and makes the necessary change.

Manipulating Data and Generating Reports

Once a DBMS has been installed, the system can be used via specific commands in various programming languages or queried using a data manipulation language. In general, a **data manipulation language (DML)** is a specific language, provided with the DBMS, that allows people and other database users to access, modify, and make queries about data contained in the database and to generate reports. Many databases use **query by example (QBE)** to give you ideas and examples of how queries can be made. QBE makes manipulating databases much easier and faster than learning formal DMLs such as SQL, which is discussed next.

In the 1970s, D.D. Chamberlain and others at the IBM Research Laboratory in San Jose, California, developed a standardized data manipulation language, called **Structured Query Language (SQL)**, pronounced "sequel." In 1986, the American National Standards Institute (ANSI) adopted SQL as the standard query language for relational databases. Since ANSI's acceptance of SQL, there has been increased interest in making SQL an integral part of relational databases on both mainframe and personal computers. The following EMPLOYEE query is written in SQL.

```
SELECT * FROM EMPLOYEE WHERE JOB_CLASSIFICATION = 'C2'
```

The * tells the program to include all columns from the EMPLOYEE table. As discussed in Chapter 3, SQL is an example of a fourth-generation programming language. SQL is easy for nonprogrammers to understand and use; note the English-like programming commands.

SQL lets programmers learn one powerful query language and use it on systems ranging from PCs to the largest mainframe computers.[14] Programmers and database users also find SQL valuable because SQL statements can be embedded into many programming languages, such as the widely used language COBOL. Today, all popular databases use SQL.[15]

Because SQL uses standardized and simplified procedures for retrieving, storing, and manipulating data in a database system, the popular database query language can be easy to understand and use. Programs that include embedded data manipulation languages such as SQL make it easier for end users to create their own reports. A few SQL commands include:

```
CREATE
UPDATE
DELETE
SELECT
JOIN
```

USINGDATABASESYSTEMSINORGANIZATIONS

We have explored a number of database applications in this chapter, from an individual entering a list of music CDs to large corporations keeping track of business operations. In this section, we will take a closer look at how databases are used in organizations, including transaction processing, information and decision support, and a variety of other areas.

Routine Processing

Most organizations have a need to process routine transactions. A museum, for example, has to pay its employees. A small business needs to send out bills quickly to maintain a healthy cash flow, and a religious organization might want to send out a monthly newsletter. These are all routine processing activities that can be implemented with a database system.

In business, the system used to perform routing processing is called a *transaction processing system (TPS)*. The TPS sends out bills, pays suppliers, prints paychecks for employees, keeps track of inventory levels, and performs routine accounting and financial activities, such as producing a balance sheet, which lists assets and liabilities.

Information and Decision Support

The ability of a database system to produce information and decision support can help people and organizations achieve their goals. Today, speedy and flexible military operations require accurate, timely, and relevant information. Stock, futures, and options organizations have made billions by getting information and decision support from databases, and great advances in medical practices have been realized through databases, enhancing health and lengthening life. Manipulating the data in a database into valuable information has helped many people to achieve their goals. To achieve better customer satisfaction Hilton Hotels is using its vast database system to customize service.[16] The new database system provides

JOB TECHNOLOGY

State Street Corp. Speeds Financial Trading with State-of-the-Art Financial Database System

Most stock traders rely on professional service providers to handle the accounting and settlement of financial transfers required to complete a stock sale. A high percentage of these firms rely on State Street Corporation for this service. With more than $6.3 trillion in assets and in excess of $808 billion under its management, State Street Corporation is a world leader in financial services.

Surprisingly, until recently, this financial megacorporation employed low-tech methods for communicating with its clients. The old system of requesting a trade involved faxing the trade request to the financial service to handle. Often faxed trade requests would arrive at State Street Corporation with critical information missing. Using its old system, State Street was often forced to delay a settlement while a staffer confirmed, by phone or fax, the missing information, says John A. Fiore, State Street's executive vice president and CIO. That much manual intervention was tremendously expensive in an operation that makes up as much as two-thirds of State Street's total revenue stream.

Fiore and his team of developers set out to improve the system. A detailed investigation of the current system showed that a large percentage of the follow-up calls were redundant; repeated requests for the same information from the same clients. State Street's solution was to store the relevant information from its regular clients in its own system so that any missing data could be automatically entered and the request processed without human intervention.

To accomplish this goal, State Street personnel had to develop a database to store client information,

which would increase in size with each new client, and develop a program that would read incoming fax requests, determine what, if any, information was missing, supply the missing information using data from the database, and pass along the request for processing.

The resulting Financial Transaction Management (FTM) system now automatically processes more than 80 percent of the requests that flow through it by identifying the source of the fax and automatically filling in missing information. Of the trades that are now processed through FTM, less than 20 percent must be handled manually.

Questions

1. How important is a database system like the one described here to other financial services firms? How has this system improved life for the employees that monitor incoming trade requests? How has it changed their job descriptions?

2. How might the success of this new database system be measured?

3. How could other organizations use this approach to make operations faster and more efficient?

Sources
1. *"State Street Corp.," Kevin Fogarty,* Computerworld, *March 11, 2002, www.computerworld.com.*
2. *"State Street's Chief Information Officer Honored as 2002 Premier 100 IT Leader by Computerworld," Staff,* Business Wire, *January 2, 2002.*
3. *State Street Web site, www.statestreet.com, accessed July 2002.*

detailed information about Hilton customers. A receptionist at a Hilton hotel in New York, for example, might apologize to a customer for not having her room during a recent stay at a Hilton Hotel in Orlando cleaned up as desired. The new system, called OnQ, allows Hilton to store and retrieve a tremendous amount of detailed customer satisfaction information. OnQ will also help Hilton make better decisions based on its database. The receptionist at the Hilton Hotel in New York, for example, might make a decision to offer a customer a special rate or provide additional service based on the customer's stay in Orlando

as a result of the data contained in OnQ. Hilton hopes that this information support will improve the customer experience and increase profits in the long run.

Data Warehouses, Data Marts, and Data Mining

To realize the potential of a database to provide information and decision support, a number of technologies have been developed. A **data warehouse** is a database that holds important information from a variety of sources. It is usually a subset of multiple databases maintained by an organization or individual (see Figure 6.26). The first data warehouses were developed at PacTel Celluar, Aetna Casualty, and Blue Cross/Blue Shield in the 1980s by William Inmon, who is considered by some to be the first person to develop a data warehouse. Today, data warehouses are used by a large number of companies and organizations. Ace Hardware Corporation, for example, uses a data warehouse to analyze pricing trends.[17] According to the company's data warehouse designer, "We had one store that only sold one wheelbarrow a year, but when he lowered the price, he sold four in one month." The price reduction was suggested by the data warehouse.

FIGURE 6.26 • **Data warehouse**

A data warehouse stores important information from multiple databases. You can analyze the data in a data warehouse to uncover trends or develop new strategies.

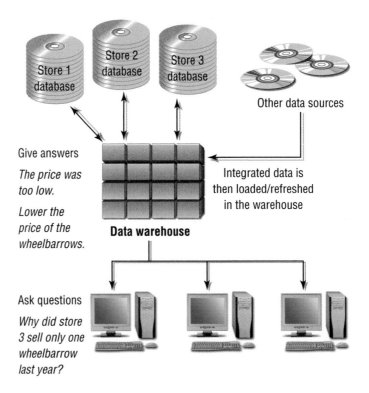

Data warehousing involves taking data from the main database and storing it in another database so that it can be analyzed to uncover trends or suggest new strategies. With a data warehouse, you can perform complex analyses without slowing input to the main database. The primary advantage of data warehousing is the ability to relate data in new, innovative ways. However, replicated databases and data warehouses increase data redundancy, which makes data integrity and accuracy harder to control.

A **data mart** is a small data warehouse, often developed for a specific person or purpose. It can be generated from a data warehouse using a database manage-

CRYSTAL BALL FOR CRIME

Researchers from Pittsburgh's Carnegie Mellon University analyzed an electronic database of over six million crimes collected over the past 10 years in the cities of Pittsburgh, Pennsylvania and Rochester, New York. Besides identifying broad trends, the team created a list of indicators that point to changes in crime patterns. Using this they built a computer model that predicted crime with 80 to 90 percent accuracy within areas as small as an individual police beat.

Source:
"Computer model forecasts crime sprees"
By Emily Singer
New Scientist
www.newscientist.com/news/news.jsp?id=ns99994050
August 17, 2003
Cited on August 18, 2003

ment system (see Figure 6.27). **Data mining** is the process of extracting information from a data warehouse or a data mart. The DBMS can be used to generate a variety of reports that people and organizations can use to help them achieve their goals. The FBI, for example, is using the ClearForest database package to support data warehousing and data mining of the Terrorism Intelligence Database.[18] According to FBI director Robert Mueller, "We are now focused on implementing a data warehousing capability that can bring together our information into databases that can be accessed by agents throughout the world as well as our analysts as soon as a piece of information is developed." Data mining has also been used in the airline-passenger profiling system used to block suspected terrorists from flying and the Terrorism Information Awareness Program, which attempts to detect patterns of terrorist activity.[19]

FIGURE 6.27 • Generating business intelligence from data warehouses and data marts

Data warehouses are generated from a database and other sources; a data mart is a small data warehouse, often developed for a specific person or purpose. Data mining can be used to generate business intelligence.

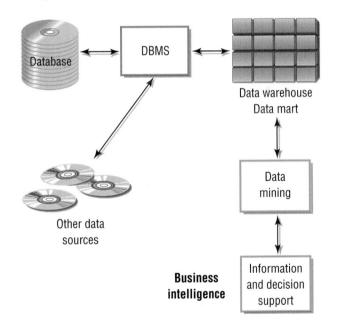

In a business setting, data mining can yield outstanding results. Often called *business intelligence*, a term first coined by a consultant at Gartner Group, the business use of use data mining can help increase efficiency, reduce costs, or increase profits. The business-intelligence approach was first used by Procter & Gamble in 1985 to analyze data from checkout scanners. Today, a number of companies use the business intelligence approach. BankFinancial Corporation of Chicago uses it to help target promotions to bank customers.[20] Owens & Minor, a large medical supplies company, uses business intelligence software to analyze sales data.[21] According to Scott Wiener, chief technology officer at Certive Corporation, "Today, the most

POWER GRID CAN WORK SMARTER, NOT HARDER

After the multistate power outage in August 2003, a consortium from several universities devised a flexible system that collects data on usage off the Internet from all over the country. After analyzing it for patterns, the system then predicts where demand will rise minutes, even hours, ahead of time. Networks can then move power around in advance of demand. Installation of this system is a fraction of the $100 billion estimated for grid replacement.

Source:
"Smarter grid could warn of impending blackouts"
By Charles J. Murray
EE Times
www.eetimes.com/sys/news/OEG20030825S0050
August 25, 2003
Cited on August 27, 2003

innovative business-intelligence technology is able to recommend the optimal course of action based on business rules, representing the first step in automated decision making."[22] Wiener predicts that business-intelligence software may eliminate a large number of midlevel managers. Companies like Ben and Jerry's ice cream store process huge amounts of data.[23] The company collects data on all 190,000 pints it produces in its factories each day, with all the data being shipped to the company's headquarters in Burlington, Vermont, which is a few miles from its first store that was opened over 25 years ago. In the marketing department, the massive amount of data is analyzed. Using business-intelligence software, the company is able to cut costs and improve customer satisfaction (see Figure 6.28). The software allows Ben and Jerry's to match the over 200 calls and e-mails received each week with ice cream products and supplies. Today, the company can quickly determine if there was a bad batch of milk or eggs. The company can also determine if sales of Chocolate Chip Cookie Dough is gaining on the No. 1 selling Cherry Garcia.

FIGURE 6.28 • Business intelligence software

Ben and Jerry's uses business intelligence software to cut costs and improve customer satisfaction. With the software, Ben and Jerry's can match calls and e-mails received each week with ice cream products and supplies.

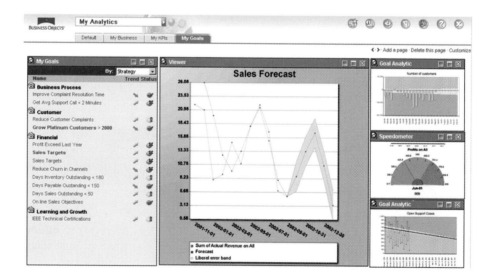

EMERGING DATABASE TRENDS

As individuals and organizations are realizing the power of databases, they are coming up with new and imaginative ways to use and manage them. For example, some organizations that use object-oriented programming also want an object-oriented database system. In other cases, there is a need to coordinate databases at different locations and to access a database through the Internet. People and organizations also have a need to store audio and video files in an organized database. These and similar trends are explored in this section.

Object-Oriented Databases

An **object-oriented database** uses the same overall approach of objected-oriented programming, first discussed in Chapter 3. With this approach, the data and the processing instructions are stored in the database. For example, an object-oriented database could store both monthly expenses and the instructions needed to compute a monthly budget from the monthly expenses. A traditional DBMS might only store the monthly expenses. An object-oriented database uses an **object-oriented database management system (OODBMS)**. A number of computer vendors sell or lease OODBMSs, including eXcelon, Versant, Poet, and Objectivity.[24]

Object-oriented databases also offer the ability to reuse and modify existing objects to develop new database applications. Using existing and already tested objects for new database applications can result in fewer errors. An object-oriented database used by a national football team to pay employees could be modified to pay student interns who work part time or during the summer. Object-oriented databases are used by a number of organizations. Versant's OODBMS, for example, is being used by companies in the telecommunications, financial services, transportation, and defense industries.[25] J.D. Edwards is using an object-oriented database to help its customers make fast and efficient forecasts of future sales and to determine if they have enough materials and supplies to meet future demand for products and services.[26] With the object-oriented database, customers can quickly get a variety of reports on available inventory and supplies. CERN, the European Organization for Nuclear Research, is developing an object-oriented database from Objectivity.[27] The object-oriented database will hold a huge 5 petabytes of raw data obtained from a particle accelerator to help scientists gain insights into the structure of matter. The data will be collected and stored over the next 10 to 15 years.

Distributed Databases

With a **distributed database**, the actual data may be spread across several databases at different locations. Distributed databases connect data at different locations via telecommunications devices. A user in the Milwaukee branch of a shoe manufacturer, for example, might make a request for data that is physically located at corporate headquarters in Milan, Italy. The user does not have to know where the data is physically stored. He or she makes a request for data, and the DBMS determines where the data is physically located and retrieves it (see Figure 6.29).

Distributed databases give corporations more flexibility in how databases are organized and used. Local offices can create, manage, and use their own databases, and people at other offices can access and share the data in the local databases. Giving local sites a more direct way to access highly used data can improve organizational effectiveness and efficiency.

A distributed database creates additional challenges in maintaining data security, accuracy, timeliness, and conformance to standards. Distributed databases allow more users direct access at different user sites; thus, controlling who accesses and changes data is sometimes difficult. Also, because distributed databases rely on telecommunications lines to transport data, access to data can be slower. To reduce the demand on telecommunications lines, some organizations build a replicated database. A *replicated database* is a database that holds a duplicate set of frequently used data. At the beginning of the day, an organization sends a copy of important data to each distributed processing location. At the end of the day, the different sites send the changed data back to be stored in the main database.

FIGURE 6.29 • The use of a distributed database

For a shoe manufacturer, computers may be located at corporate headquarters, in the research and development center, the warehouse, and in a company-owned retail store. Telecommunications systems link the computers so that users at all locations can access the same distributed database no matter where the data is actually stored.

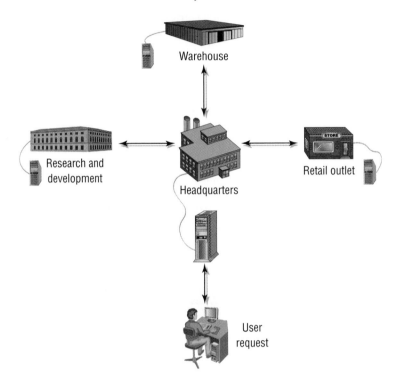

Database Systems, the Internet, and Networks

Anyone with even limited experience with the Internet knows that there is a vast amount of raw data and important information available on the Web. In most cases, a traditional database, such as a relational database, is used. As mentioned before, the database is often the back-end application. From a user's perspective, the traditional database is invisible and behind the scenes. The Web is then used as the front end. All requests made to the database are done through the Internet (see Figure 6.30).

Some people are investigating the seamless integration of traditional databases with the Internet. The result is often called a *Semantic Web*.[28] According to Tim Berners-Lee, creator of the World Wide Web (WWW), "The Semantic Web is about taking the relational database and webbing it." A Semantic Web would allow people to access and manipulate a number of traditional databases at the same time through the Internet.

FIGURE 6.30 • Database access through the Internet

When database access is provided through the Internet, the Web is used as the front end. The database is the back-end application. From a user's perspective, the traditional database is invisible and behind the scenes.

SEEK AND IT WILL BE FOUND FOR YOU

The man who started Borders Group (Borders Books) and Webvan has launched a new company that offers unlimited access to a database of magazine articles from participating publishers. The site is interactive to the extent that after a researcher has signed up and performed a few searches, the system analyzes previous searches and automatically lists any articles on similar topics for the researcher.

Source:
"Serial Founder Tries His Hand at Another Start-Up"
By Seth Sutel, Associated Press
The Los Angeles Times
www.latimes.com/technology/la-fi-borders28jul28,1,4784165.story?
coll=la-headlines-technology
July 28, 2003
Cited on July 28, 2003

A number of Internet development tools can be used to provide interaction with a traditional database. Most of these tools were introduced in Chapter 4. HTML, XML, and other Web development tools can all be employed to develop a Web site to be a front-end interface to a traditional database system. Simplest-Shop, for example, uses the Web to sell compact discs on the Internet.[29] There is a wealth of information on each compact disc, including product reviews (see Figure 6.31). When you look at the company's Web site, it looks as if the company has a large number of employees, but a collection of Web tools has allowed one person, Calin Uioreanu from Romania, to do everything as a side business. He is a full-time software engineer.

FIGURE 6.31 • Simplest-Shop
When you look at the Simplest-Shop Web site, it looks as if the company has a large number of employees. But Web tools have allowed one person to do everything as a side business.

In addition to the Internet, organizations are gaining access to databases through networks. Catholic Health, for example, has developed a network to allow physicians to access patient information from remote locations.[30] Perry Manufacturing in North Carolina uses a network to allow its managers to have access to e-mail and other information stored on its database.

Visual, Audio, and Other Database Systems

In addition to raw data, organizations are increasingly finding a need to store large amounts of visual and audio data in an organized fashion. Music companies, for example, need the ability to store and manipulate sound from recording studios. Purdue University has developed an audio database and processing software to give singers a voice makeover.[31] The database software can correct pitch errors and modify voice patterns to introduce vibrato and other vocal characteristics. According to the project director, "we look at the results from good singers and those of bad singers, and try to understand those differences." Drug companies often need the ability to analyze a large number of visual images from laboratories.[32] The German Federal Institute of Risk in Berlin, for example, stores and analyzes the affects of chemicals in animal studies to determine if the chemicals are safe for animals and humans. The Institute uses an image database and analysis system from SciMagix, an imaging company in California. The PetroView database and analysis tool allows petroleum engineers to analyze geographic information to help them determine where to drill for oil and gas.[33] A visual-fingerprint database was used to solve a 40-year-old murder case in California.[34] The fingerprint database was a $640 million project started in 1995.

Combining and analyzing data from separate and totally different databases is an increasingly important database challenge. Global businesses, for example, sometimes need to analyze sales and accounting data stored around the world in different database systems. Companies like IBM and others are developing *virtual database systems* to allow different databases to work together as a unified database system.[35] Using an IBM virtual database system, a Canadian bioresearch firm was able to integrate data from different databases that used different file formats and types. DiscoveryLink, one of IBM's projects, is allowing biomedical data from different sources to be integrated. According to Raimond Winslow, professor of biomedical engineering and computer science and director of the Center for Cardiovascular Bioinformatics and Modeling at Johns Hopkins University, "Information tools [such as DiscoveryLink provides] ways in which you can mine these huge data sets." The Centers for Disease Control (CDC) also have the problem of integrating different databases.[36] The CDC has more than 100 databases on various diseases. Searching these databases for data and information on diseases such as severe acute respiratory syndrome (SARS) can be difficult.

In addition to visual, audio, and virtual databases, there are a number of other special-purpose database systems. The Interactive Age Check database developed in England, for example, will help companies verify a person's age online.[37] The age verification database can be used to help prevent fraud and protect children. Currently, the main use of the database system is to confirm age-restricted, credit-card sales on the Internet.

MANAGINGDATABASES

EXPAND YOUR **KNOWLEDGE**

To learn more about backup, go to www.course.com/swt. Click the link "Expand Your Knowledge" and then complete the lab entitled, "Backing up Your Computer."

Managing a database is complex and requires great skill. Hiring a good database administrator (DBA), concentrating on important and strategic aspects of databases, training database users, and developing good security procedures are all important.

Database Administration

Databases and database management systems are typically installed and coordinated by an individual or group who performs a function called database administration. *Database administration* involves managing one of the most valuable resources of any organization: its data. In brief, **database administrators (DBAs)** are responsible for all aspects of the database. Most database administrators are responsible for the following areas:

- Overall design and coordination of the database
- Development and maintenance of schemas and subschemas
- Development and maintenance of the data dictionary
- Implementation of the DBMS
- System and user documentation
- User support and training

- Overall operation of the DBMS
- Testing and maintaining the DBMS
- Establishing emergency or failure-recovery procedures

A database administrator (DBA) must work well with both programmers and nonprogramming users of the database. The programmers, part of the computer systems department, are responsible for developing programs for users who need access to the database. Programmers also do other required database tasks. The nonprogramming users consist of employees outside the computer systems department who need to use the database. As you might expect, some of the nonprogramming users are more sophisticated than others and are able to develop their own routines using a data manipulation language to access the database.

Newer database management systems can help the database administrator monitor and control the database. Some DBMSs, like IBM's DB2 for example, have the ability to monitor a database's performance and to make changes or adjustments to increase productivity and efficiency. In a sense, these types of database management systems are self-managing.

Database Use, Policies, and Security

With the proliferation of low-cost hardware and off-the-shelf database and other software packages, traditional end users are now developing computer systems to solve their own problems. *End-user computing* may be broadly defined as the development and use of application programs and computer systems by non-computer-systems professionals. Concerns with end-user computing are generally related to issues of training and control. As we've seen, data contained within an organization's databases is usually critical to the basic functioning of the organization. It is often proprietary in nature, confidential, and of strategic importance. Therefore, the following end-user computing issues must be addressed in terms of database policies and use:

- What data can users read, update, or write in a database?
- Under what circumstances can data be transferred from a personal computer or small computer system to the large mainframe system? (This data transfer is called uploading.)
- Under what circumstances can data be transferred from the large mainframe system to personal computers or small computer systems? (This type of data transfer is called downloading.)
- What procedures are needed to guarantee proper database use?

Most users want to have access to as much data stored in the database as possible. Because data can be confidential, policies must be developed to specify what data can be retrieved by each user. In addition, specifications regarding what data users can view, upload, download, and modify need to be written. For example, a law firm may not want to have sensitive client data downloaded to a personal computer from a mainframe to keep this important data protected from competing firms or lawyers working with the other party in litigation. In general, procedures for all interactions with the mainframe database need to be specified. In most cases, the data that can be accessed depends on the individual's position in the organization. Training programs are needed to inform all employees, including managers and decision makers, of the many procedures and policies regarding the database.

Because there are so many users of any one database, potential data security and invasion of privacy problems have become increasingly important. According to Dan Morrison, partner at the Mishcon DeReya law firm in England, "Some firms have suffered heavy losses because of database theft and at least one company has been forced out of business after a rival firm used a stolen database to undercut its prices."[38]

Technology 360°

⇗ Action Plan

1. **How can Jeanne keep track of materials and designs stored in her sewing room?**

   To keep a list of what is in her sewing room, Jeanne could use the database or flat file capabilities of a spreadsheet or word-processing program. She could also use a general database system designed for a personal computer or a specialized database system for small businesses to keep track of this information. Since Jeanne is thinking about starting a small business, a specialized database system would likely be the best option for Jeanne.

2. **If she starts a small business, how will she be able to pay her employees, pay her bills, and keep track of other business transactions?**

   Starting a small business requires more than the database capabilities of a spreadsheet or word-processing program. Jeanne could develop everything she needs for a small business using a general database program, such as Microsoft Access, but she should also consider a specialized database system for small businesses, such as Quick Books.

Summary

LEARNING OBJECTIVE 1

Understand basic data management concepts.

Data is one of the most valuable resources an organization possesses. Data is organized into a hierarchy that builds from the smallest element to the largest. The smallest element is the bit. A group of characters, such as a name or number, is called a field. A collection of related fields is a record; a collection of related records is called a file. The database, at the top of the hierarchy, is an integrated collection of records and files.

An entity is a generalized class of objects for which data is collected, stored, and maintained. An attribute is a characteristic of an entity. Specific values of attributes, called data items, can be found in the fields of the record describing an entity. A primary key uniquely identifies a record.

The database approach has a number of benefits, including: reduced data redundancy, improved data consistency and integrity, easier modification and updating, data and program independence, standardization of data access, and more efficient program development. A DBMS consists of a group of programs that perform the manipulation of the database and provide an interface between the database and the user of the database and application programs.

Figure 6.3—p. 249

LEARNING OBJECTIVE 2

Describe different database models, including the hierarchical, network, and relational models, and database characteristics.

Databases typically use one of three common models: hierarchical, network, and relational. The hierarchical model has one main record type at the top with subordinate records below. The network model is an owner-member relationship in which each member may have more than one owner. The newest, most flexible structure is the relational model. Instead of a hierarchy of predefined relationships, data is set up in two-dimensional tables. Tables can be linked by common data elements, which are used to access data when the database is queried. Each row is called a tuple, and represents a record. Columns of the tables are called attributes, and allowable values for these attributes are called the domain. Basic data manipulations include selecting, projecting, and joining.

Data analysis is used to uncover problems with the content of the database. Problems and irregularities in data are called anomalies. The process of correcting anomalies is called normalization. Normalization involves breaking one file into two or more tables in order to reduce redundancy and inconsistency in the data.

Figure 6.11—p. 257

LEARNING OBJECTIVE 3
Discuss the different types of database management systems and their design and use by individuals and organizations.

A DBMS is a group of programs used as an interface between a database and application programs. Database types include flat file, single-user, multiuser, and special-purpose databases. When an application program requests data from the database, it follows a logical access path (LAP). The actual retrieval of the data follows a physical access path (PAP). Schemas are used to describe the entire database, its record types, and their relationships to the DBMS.

Subschemas are used to define a user view, the portion of the database a user can access or manipulate. Schemas and subschemas are entered into the computer via a data definition language (DDL), which describes the data and relationships in a specific database. Another tool used in database management is the data dictionary, which contains detailed descriptions of all data in the database.

Figure 6.21—p. 267

Once a DBMS has been installed, the database may be accessed, modified, and queried via a data manipulation language (DML). A more specialized DML is the query language; the most common are Query by Example (QBE) and Structured Query Language (SQL). QBE and SQL are used in several popular database packages today.

LEARNING OBJECTIVE 4
Describe how organizations use database systems to perform routine processing, provide information, and provide decision support, and how they use data warehouses, marts, and mining.

Most organizations use a database system to send out bills, pay suppliers, print paychecks, and perform other routine transaction processing activities.

Perhaps the biggest potential of a database system is to provide information and decision support. The data contained in a database can be filtered and manipulated to provide critical information to a wide range of organizations.

Information is usually obtained and decision support is usually provided using data warehouses, data marts, and data mining. A data warehouse is a database that holds important information from a variety of sources. A data warehouse normally contains a subset of the data stored in the database system. A data mart is a small data warehouse. Data mining is the process of extracting information from data warehouses and data marts.

Figure 6.27—p. 275

LEARNING OBJECTIVE 5
Discuss additional database systems, including object-oriented and distributed systems.

Object-oriented databases store data as objects, which contain both the data and the processing instructions needed to complete the database transaction. The objects can be retrieved and related by an object-oriented database management system (OODBMS). Object-oriented databases offer the capability to reuse and modify existing objects to develop new database applications.

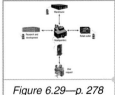

Figure 6.29—p. 278

A distributed database allows data to be spread across several databases at different locations.

Database systems are often used in conjunction with the Internet and networks. In many cases, the Internet or network is used as the front end, where requests for information and data are made. The database management system is the back end, providing the needed information and data.

An increasing amount of the data used by organizations is in the form of visual images, which can be stored in image databases. Audio databases are used to store audio data, including voice and music. Some organizations are using virtual databases that can integrate separate databases into a unified system that acts like a single database.

LEARNING OBJECTIVE 6
Describe the role of the database administrator (DBA) and database policies and security practices.
Management of the database is part of database administration. Database administrators (DBAs) are responsible for database use, policies, and security. They help control DBMS design, implementation, and maintenance. They also establish security and control measures, and many other aspects of database use and control.

Test Yourself

LEARNING OBJECTIVE 1: Understand basic data management concepts.

1. A(n) _____ consists of a group of programs that perform the actual manipulation of the database.

2. In the hierarchy of data, characters that are put together form a:
    a. file
    b. field
    c. record
    d. database

3. True or False: Employee and inventory files are examples of transaction files.

4. True or False: A primary key uniquely identifies a record.

LEARNING OBJECTIVE 2: Describe different database models, including the hierarchical, network, and relational models, and database characteristics.

5. A(n) _____ is one in which the data is organized in a top-down or inverted tree-like structure.

6. What type of database model places data in two-dimensional tables?
    a. hierarchical
    b. network
    c. entity
    d. relational

7. _____ is a process that involves evaluating data to uncover problems with the content of a database.

LEARNING OBJECTIVE 3: Discuss the different types of database management systems and their design and use by individuals and organizations.

8. True or False: A database that can be used to store and manipulate a single table in a spreadsheet or word-processing program is called a single user database.

9. A situation where inaccurate input causes inaccurate output in a database is often called _____.

10. True or False: A physical access path (PAP) involves the database management system going to a storage device to retrieve the needed data.

11. What are the commands that are used to change a database?
   a. the data definition language
   b. the physical access language
   c. the data manipulation language
   d. the logical access language

LEARNING OBJECTIVE 4: Describe how organizations use database systems to perform routine processing, provide information, and provide decision support, and how they use data warehouses, marts, and mining.

12. A(n) _____ is typically a subset of an organization's database.

13. True or False: A data mart is a small data warehouse.

14. What is the process of extracting information from a data warehouse or data mart?
   a. logical access
   b. physical access
   c. decision support
   d. data mining

LEARNING OBJECTIVE 5: Discuss additional database systems, including object-oriented and distributed systems.

15. eXcelon, Versant, and Poet are examples of what type of database?
   a. object-oriented
   b. distributed
   c. visual
   d. audio

16. With a(n) _____ the actual data may be spread across several databases at different locations.

17. With many databases, the Internet is used as a _____ to receive requests made to the database system.

LEARNING OBJECTIVE 6: Describe the role of the database administrator (DBA) and database policies and security practices.

18. True or False: Database systems are typically installed and coordinated by the chief information officer.

19. The _____ must work well with both programmers and nonprogramming users of the database.

Test Yourself Solutions: **1.** database management system, **2.** b., **3.** F, **4.** T, **5.** hierarchical model, **6.** d., **7.** Data analysis, **8.** F, **9.** garbage in, garbage out (GIGO), **10.** T, **11.** c., **12.** data warehouse, **13.** T, **14.** d., **15.** a., **16.** distributed database, **17.** front end, **18.** F, **19.** database administrator (DBA)

Key Terms

attribute, p. 249
data analysis, p. 258
database, p. 249
database administrators (DBAs), p. 280
database management system (DBMS), p. 246
data definition language (DDL), p. 269
data dictionary, p. 270
data integrity, p. 266
data manipulation language (DML), p. 271
data mart, p. 274
data mining, p. 275

data warehouse, p. 274
distributed database, p. 277
entity, p. 249
field, p. 248
file, p. 248
garbage in, garbage out (GIGO), p. 266
hierarchical database model, p. 255
key, p. 249
logical access path (LAP), p. 267
master file, p. 248
network model, p. 256

object-oriented database, p. 277
object-oriented database management system (OODBMS), p. 277
physical access path (PAP), p. 267
query by example, p. 271
record, p. 248
relational model, p. 256
schema, p. 268
Structured Query Language (SQL), p. 271
subschema, p. 269
transaction file, p. 248

Questions

Review Questions

1. What is a database management system?

2. Describe the hierarchy of data.

3. What are entities and attributes? What is a key?

4. What is a primary key?

5. Describe simple approaches to data management.

6. What are the advantages of the database approach?

7. Describe the following three types of database models: hierarchical model, network model, and relational model.

8. Describe the characteristics of a relational database model.

9. What are the important characteristics of databases?

10. What is a flat file? What is a single-user database?

11. What are logical access paths and physical access paths?

12. What is the purpose of a data definition language (DDL)? A data dictionary?

13. What is query by example? What is SQL?

14. How are databases used in organizations?

15. What is a data warehouse? What is a data mart?

16. How is data mining used by organizations?

17. What is a distributed database system?

18. What is an object-oriented database system?

19. How are the Internet and networks used with database systems?

20. List and describe the newer types of database systems. What types of data might they house?

21. Explain the responsibilities of a database administrator.

Discussion Questions

22. Why is a database a necessary component of a computer system? Why is the selection of DBMS software so important to organizations?

23. What databases on your campus contain your name? Off-campus? What is your primary key on campus?

24. What is a data model and what is data modeling?

25. Why is the relational database model more popular than the hierarchical and network models?

26. How could you use a database management system in your personal life? What types of database systems would be most useful to you?

Exercises

Try It Yourself

1. You are a database administrator in the Computer Systems department of a large university. Your organization is currently using a relational database system in applications. Given the trends in database management systems, use your word-processing program to write a letter to your supervisor(s) outlining the need to migrate toward object-oriented database management systems (OODBMSs). Discuss the advantages of OODBMSs over relational database systems, and discuss the disadvantages of migrating to an OODBMS.

2. A university needs to design and implement a relational database to maintain records for students and courses. Some of the essential data fields are student identification number, student name, student address, major, credits completed, course number, course name, faculty member teaching the course, student GPA (grade point average), and grades. Using the chapter material on designing a database, show the logical structure of the relational tables for this proposed database. In your design, include any additional fields that you feel are necessary for this database, and show

the primary keys in your tables. Fill in the database tables with sample data for demonstration purposes (10 records). Once your design is complete, implement your design for a university database using a relational DBMS.

3. A video movie rental store is using a relational database to store the following information on movie rentals to answer customer questions: movie ID number, movie title, year made, movie type (comedy, drama, horror, science fiction, or western), rating (G, PG, PG-13, R, or X), and quantity on hand. Develop a database to store this information for 30 movies. Using the database, create another database with only movies rated PG-13. Develop a report of all horror movies.

4. Based upon the database design from Exercise 3, design a data-entry screen that could be used to enter information into this database. Also include some examples of typical queries the salespeople would use to respond to customers' requests.

Virtual Classroom Activities

For the following exercises, do not use face-to-face or telephone communications with your group members. Use only Internet communications.

5. With distance learning, students from around the world can take the same course. It is also possible to have several different instructors located around the world. With your group, develop a brief report that describes how several instructors at different locations could integrate their databases of assignments, tests, and student grades.

6. On the Internet, research one database system that you could use, such as Access or Quicken. Write a paper describing the features of each database system. Using a spreadsheet program, summarize the costs of each database system. All group members should participate in developing the paper and spreadsheet without any face-to-face meetings.

Teamwork

7. In a team of three or four classmates, interview three users, programmers, or system analysts from different organizations that use DBMSs to determine what DBMSs they are using. How did these people choose the DBMSs that they are using? What do they like about their DBMSs and what could be improved? Considering the information obtained from these people, select one DBMS and briefly present your selection and the rationale for your selection to the class.

8. Using the Internet or your school library, research object-oriented databases. Use a database system to summarize your findings. At a minimum, your database should have columns on the database name, the cost to purchase or lease, and a brief description.

Learning Check

To check your knowledge of each of the chapter objectives, use this chart to find related end-of-chapter content.

	Learning Objective	Key Terms		Questions	Exercises
	Learning Objective 1 Understand basic data management concepts.	database database management system entity field	file key master file record transaction file	1, 2, 3, 4, 5, 6, 23	2, 5, 7

(continued)

	Learning Objective	Key Terms		Questions	Exercises
	Learning Objective 2 Describe different database models, including the hierarchical, network, and relational models, and database characteristics.	data analysis hierarchical model network model normalization relational model		7, 8, 9, 10, 24, 25, 26	1, 3, 6, 7
	Learning Objective 3 Discuss the different types of database management systems and their design and use by individuals and organizations	data definition language (DDL) data dictionary data integrity data manipulation language (DML) garbage-in garbage-out (GIGO)	logical access path (LAP) physical access path (PAP) query by example (QBE) schema structured query language (SQL) subschema	11, 12, 13, 14, 23	2, 3, 4, 6
	Learning Objective 4 Describe how organizations use database systems to perform routine processing, provide information, and provide decision support, and how they use data warehouses, marts, and mining.	data mart data mining data warehouse		15, 16, 17, 24, 27	2, 5
	Learning Objective 5 Discuss additional database systems, including object-oriented and distributed systems.	distributed database object-oriented database objected-oriented database management system		18, 19, 20, 21	1, 5, 8
	Learning Objective 6 Describe the role of the database administrator (DBA) and database policies and security practices.	database administrator		22	

Endnotes

1. Hawn, Carleen, "Please Feedback the Animals," *Forbes*, October 29, 2002, p. 168.

2. Schell, Ernie, "Spinning Straw into Gold," *Catalog Age*, May 01, 2003, p. 6.

3. Elsner, Ralf, et al, "Optimizing Rhenania's Mail Order Business," *Interfaces*, January 2003, p. 50.

4. Krol, Carol, "Looking to Expand," *BtoB*, May 5, 2003, p. 32.

5. Staff, "Database Market's Future," *VAR Business*, July 22, 2002, p. 41.

6. Sliwa, Carol, "Grocer's Digital Receipts Pay Off," *Computerworld*, July 8, 2002, p. 1.

7. Datz, Todd, "State to Share Data with FBI," *CIO*, May 15, 2003.

8. Davis, Ann, Plan to Fingerprint Visitors," *The Wall Street Journal*, July 31, 2002.

9. Hamilton, David, "Biological Databases Are Becoming Freely Available," *The Wall Street Journal*, May 19, 2003, p. R12.

10. Lais, Sami, "Connecting to Patients," *Computerworld*, December 16, 2002, p. 46.

11. Wunderlich, Clifford, "ALTA Religion Database," *Library Journal Reviews*, May 15, 2003, p. 137.

12. Mossberg, Walter, "Mindjet Can Help You Map Out A Project," *The Wall Street Journal*, September 26, 2002, p. B1.

13. Staff, "Most Utilities Fall Short on Customer Data Accuracy," *Utility Weekly*, May 2003, p. 3.

14. Foley, John, "SQL Server: The Sequel," *Information Week*, November 18, 2002, p. 45.

15. Dyck, Timothy, "SQL Databases," *PC Magazine,"* March 26, 2002, p. 122.

16. Binkley, Christina, "Soon, the Desk Clerk Will Know All About You," *The Wall Street Journal*, May 8, 2003, p. D4.

17. Betts, Mitch, "Unexpected Insights," *Computerworld*, April 14, 2003, p. 34.

18. Verton, Dan, "FBI Begins Knowledge Management Face Lift," *Computerworld*, April 21, 2003, p. 10.

19. Davis, Ann, "Data Collection is Up Sharply Following 9/11," *The Wall Street Journal*, May 22, 2003, p. B1.

20. Anthes, Gary, "The Forrest is Clear," *Computerworld*, April 14, 2003, p. 31.

21. Leon, Mark, "Keys to the Kingdom," *Computerworld* April 14, 2003, p. 42.

22. Siener, Scott, "Total Automation," *Computerworld*, April 14, 2003, p. 52.

23. Scholsser, Julie, "Looking for Intelligence in Ice Cream," *Fortune*, March 17, 2003, p. 114.

24. Staff, "Rewards of Persistence," *ComputerWire*, May 01, 2002.

25. Vaas, Lisa, "Tools Give Insights Into Databases," *eWeek*, January 27, 2003, p. 9.

26. Bacheldor, Beth, "Object-Oriented Database Speeds Queries," *InformationWeek*, March 10, 2003, p. 49.

27. Whiting, Rick, "CERN Project Will Collect Hundreds of Petabytes of Data," *InformationWeek*, February 11, 2002, p. 44.

28. Thibodeau, Patrick, "The Web's Nest Leap," *Computerworld*, April 21, 2003, p. 34.

29. Loftus, Peter, "Smooth Talk," *The Wall Street Journal*, March 31, 2003, p. R9.

30. Radding, Alan, "SSL Virtual Private Networks are Simplier to Set Up," *Computerworld*, April 28, 2003, p. 28.

31. Johnson, Colin, "Tech Gives Tone-Deaf a Voice Makeover," *Electronic Engineering Times*, May 5, 2003, p. 51.

32. Derra, Skip, "Image Analysis Software Shows Its Flexibility," *Drug Discovery and Development*, March 01, 2003, p. 61.

33. Staff, "Software System Allows Geographic Display, Analysis of Upstream Activity," *Offshore*, February 2003, p. 58.

34. Worthen, Ben, "Database Cracks Murder Case," *CIO*, May 1, 2003.

35. Vaas, Lisa, "Virtual Databases Make Sense our of Varied Data," *eWeek*, March 31, 2003, p. 12.

36. Dignan, Larry, "Diagnosis Disconnected," *Baseline*, May 5, 2003.

37. Thomas, Daniel, "Online Age Verification," *Computer Weekly*, May 06, 2003, p. 14.

38. Goodwin, Bill, "Police Hamstrung by UK's Outdated Computer Laws," *Computer Weekly*, March 06, 2003, p. 3.

E-commerce

The Forrero name is well known as a maker of fine hand-crafted leather products. You can find Forrero products in many gift shops around the country. Alejandro Forrero is the youngest of many generations of leather artisans and is currently completing his college education, which he plans on using to the benefit of the family business. The computer course that Alejandro is taking has got him thinking about new possibilities for the family business. Currently, Forrero products are marketed at wholesale prices only to retail clothing and gift shops, which then sell them to consumers at twice the wholesale cost. Alejandro is considering the possibility of selling Forrero leather products direct to consumers on the Web. A professionally designed Web site would provide great publicity for the company, the family would be able to make more money per sale, and they would be able to offer better prices to their customers. Selling direct to consumers through the Web could dramatically change the family business! He's excited to share the idea with his parents, but wants to do it right and make them proud. He'll need to do some research and write a proposal that provides details on the costs and benefits of taking the family business online.

1. What will it take to put the Forrero family business online?
2. What benefits might the Forrero family enjoy from an online presence? Do these benefits outweigh the costs?
3. Besides taking the business online what other ways might e-commerce technology assist the Forrero family business?

Check out Alejandro's *Action Plan* at the conclusion of this chapter.

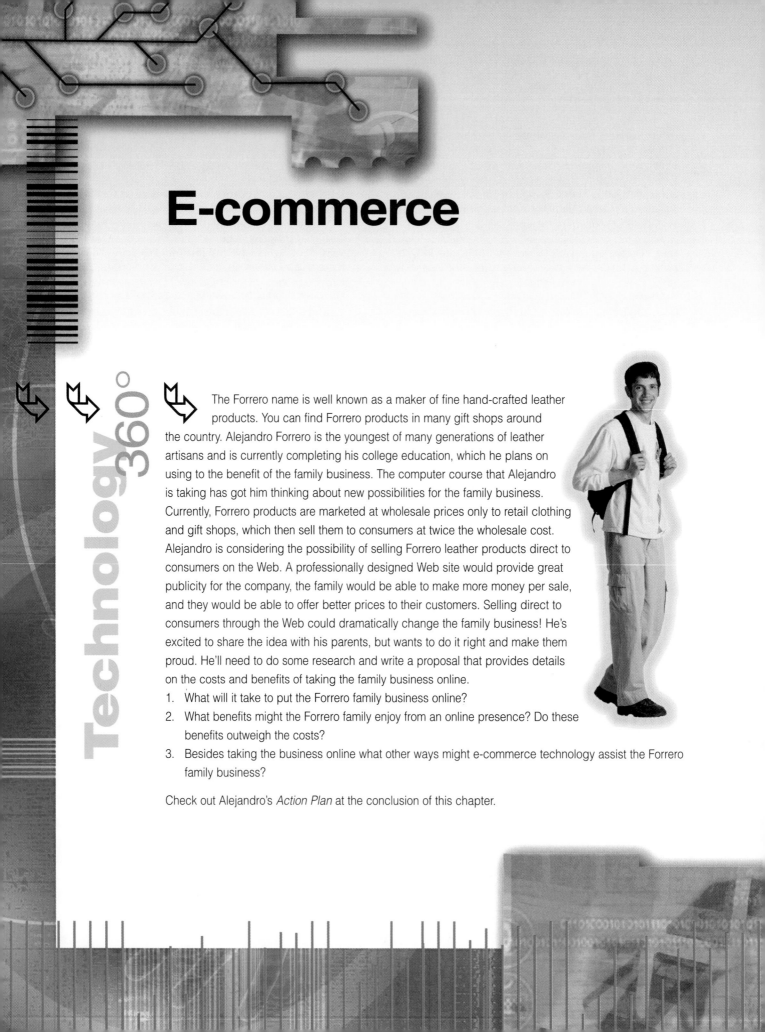

After completing Chapter 7, you will be able to:

LEARNING OBJECTIVES	CHAPTER CONTENT
1. Define e-commerce and understand its role as a transaction processing system.	**The Roots of E-commerce**
2. Define the three types of e-commerce and mobile commerce, listing the benefits and challenges associated with each.	**Overview of Electronic and Mobile Commerce**
3. Discuss several examples of how e-commerce and mobile commerce are being used to provide services.	**E-commerce Applications**
4. List the components of an e-commerce system and explain how they function together to provide e-commerce services.	**E-commerce Implementation**

Introduction

E-commerce has provided a fresh platform for doing business that has changed the way businesses and consumers think about shopping and conducting business. Because of e-commerce and mobile commerce, buyers and sellers are turning to their computers to buy and sell products and are enjoying the benefits. Conducting business online offers convenience and savings to both buyers and sellers. This chapter explores the impact of e-commerce on consumers and businesses, what it takes to set up a successful e-commerce Web site, and the challenges and issues faced by e-commerce participants.

The 1990s was a decade of amazing growth for the Internet. During this decade, the Internet expanded from supporting primarily research for scholars to providing a platform on which to conduct business. The first half of the decade saw the gradual transition of the Internet from a government-owned entity to a public-owned entity. The release of the first Web browser in 1993 made the Internet accessible to the public. The Internet boom really began in 1994 with the birth of Amazon.com and the first online shopping malls, radio stations, cyberbanks, and a host of other commercial ventures. Figure 7.1 illustrates some of the landmark Internet developments that opened the Internet to businesses.

FIGURE 7.1 • 1990s Internet timeline

Landmark Internet developments in the 1990s led businesses to the Web.[1]

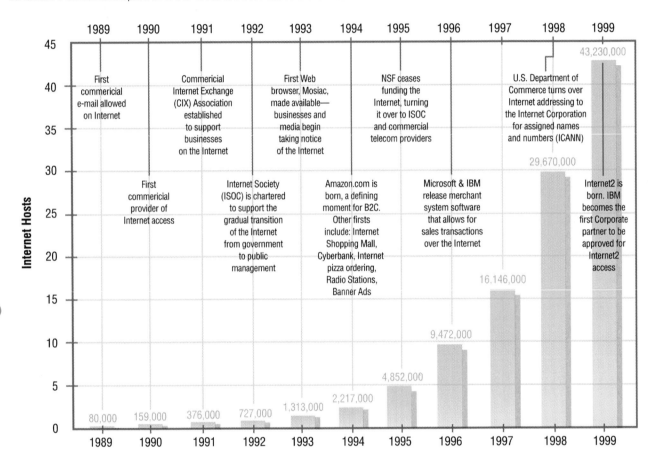

The Internet and Web provided communication unrivaled by any previous network. When the Internet opened for commerce it changed the business landscape dramatically. This new method of carrying out business transactions electronically over the Internet and Web was called e-commerce.

THEROOTSOFE-COMMERCE

Electronic commerce, or **e-commerce**, refers to systems that support electronically executed transactions. Notice that even though the Internet and Web were responsible for the boom in electronic commerce, the words Internet and Web are not part of the definition of e-commerce. Many electronically executed transactions take place off the Internet, on private networks. In fact, the activity of electronically executing transactions predates the Internet.

E-commerce History

Computer use expanded from scientific applications to business applications in 1959 with the production of the Electronic Recording Machine Accounting (ERMA) system. At that time, banks were literally swamped with the growing volume of checks that needed to be processed. ERMA automated the process using magnetic ink recognition and reduced a bank's staffing needs. With ERMA installed, a staff of nine could accomplish what previously required a staff of 50. The success of ERMA led to increased use of computer systems in a variety of industries. Computers were used to keep accounting ledgers, administer payroll, create management reports, and schedule production. Businesses and organizations began focusing on computer-based information systems as a means to streamline business processes.

In the 1970s and 1980s, businesses extended their computer-based information systems beyond their corporate walls to connect with other companies' systems using electronic data interchange (EDI). EDI uses private communications networks called value-added networks (VANs) to transmit standardized transaction data between business partners and suppliers (see Figure 7.2). Businesses began to realize that automating transactions using EDI drastically reduced the amount of paperwork and the need for human intervention. This was the beginning of e-commerce, even if it would take another 20 years for the term to be coined.

FIGURE 7.2 • Electronic data interchange (EDI)

EDI uses private communications networks called value-added networks (VANs) to transmit standardized transaction data between business partners and suppliers.

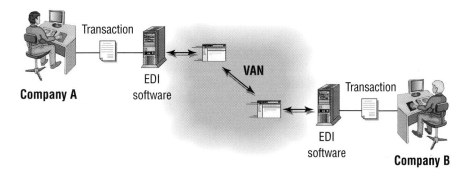

Even though it improved business-to-business transactions, EDI had some problems and was costly. Only businesses that paid for a VAN connection could participate. For e-commerce to really take off, businesses and people needed an inexpensive universal network to which everyone could connect—the Internet. The Internet provided the ideal platform for conducting EDI transactions as well as other forms of transaction processing between businesses. The invention of the Web provided the first opportunity for businesses to conduct transactions with consumers over a computer network. Doing business online was embraced by businesses and consumers alike. The far-reaching implications of the Web as a tool for executing business transactions soon became clear.

To fully understand the benefits of e-commerce, we first need to examine the roots of e-commerce and its fundamental purpose: to execute transactions.

Transaction Processing

E-commerce is a form of transaction processing system (TPS). Recall from Chapter 1 that a TPS supports and records transactions. The transaction information collected by the TPS is fundamental to the operation of other information systems that support important decision making. For example, the company contracted to provide food services for your campus uses a TPS to collect sales information from the cashier's point-of-sale terminal in the school cafeteria (see Figure 7.3). That sales information is then processed by another information system, such as an MIS, to determine which food items are selling best. Items that don't sell may be discontinued and replaced with new items. Through this approach, the food service provider can use the transaction information to continuously improve its service to customers.

FIGURE 7.3 • The value of transaction processing

The transaction data collected through point-of-sale terminals can be used to assess which products are selling well and which are not.

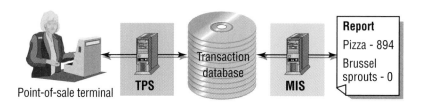

Transaction processing takes place in many different environments and the systems that support them must be created to suit the environment. The electronic checkout system at Amazon.com is a TPS, as is the checkout system at your local book store. The payroll system that calculates an employee's pay and cuts a check is also a TPS. Transaction processing includes capturing input data, making calculations, storing information in a database, and producing various forms of output such as receipts and purchase orders.

There are two methods of processing transactions: batch and online. In *batch processing*, transactions are collected over time and processed together in batches. Batch processing is useful in situations where transactions take place away from the computer system, or when processing would slow down the collection of transaction data. For example, a sales representative operating from a booth at a trade show might record orders on a laptop computer and enter the orders into the main system in a batch upon returning to the home office and connecting to the corporate network.

With *online transaction processing* the processing takes place at the point of sale. For example, as you pay for your concert ticket, the seat you choose is marked as reserved in the concert hall database and your payment is recorded in the day's earnings. Online transaction processing is critical to time-sensitive transactions such as selling concert tickets and making flight reservations, as well as for college class registration systems. If the transaction isn't processed immediately, seats could become double-booked or classes filled to overcapacity.

The Transaction Processing Cycle

E-commerce and all other forms of transaction processing systems share a common set of activities called the *transaction processing cycle*. The stages of the transaction processing cycle are shown in Figure 7.4. They include the following:

- *Data collection* is the process of capturing transaction related data. For example, an order processing system would need to know the item number, quantity, and payment method.
- *Data editing* is the process of checking the validity of the data entered. For example, an invalid credit-card number would be caught in the data-editing stage of the transaction processing cycle.

- *Data correction* is implemented if an error is found in the entered data. Typically, a descriptive error message is displayed along with a request for a correction: "the credit-card number you entered is invalid; please check the number and try again."
- *Data manipulation* involves processing the transaction data. A TPS is typically only required to do simple processing such as adding up the value of the items being purchased, calculating taxes, and determining if the items requested are in inventory, along with performing any other calculations necessary to allow the transaction to proceed.
- *Data storage* is the activity of altering databases to reflect the transaction.

FIGURE 7.4 • The transaction processing cycle

Data processing activities of a transaction processing system.

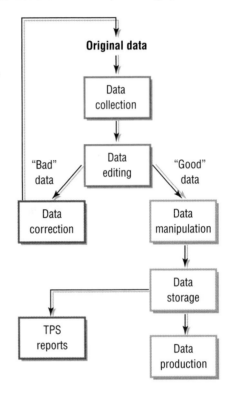

To conclude the transaction, documents may be produced or displayed. For example, after making an online purchase, verification is displayed on the screen, an electronic receipt is sent to your e-mail address, and a document called a *picking list* is produced in the warehouse that tells the workers what to pack and where to ship it.

Different Transaction Processing for Different Needs

There are a variety of transaction processing systems and subsystems that serve many functions within an organization. The two important categories of TPS are order processing systems and purchasing systems. An *order processing system* supports the sales of goods or services to customers and arranges for shipment of products. A *purchasing system* supports the purchase of goods and raw materials from suppliers for the manufacturing of products. Each of these systems is composed of subsystems that interact to address the needs of an organization. Figure 7.5 illustrates how TPSs interact within an organization to address its needs. Notice how the inventory control system acts to connect the order processing system and purchasing system.

FIGURE 7.5 • **Transaction processing system interaction**

Transaction processing typically makes use of many interconnected systems and subsystems.

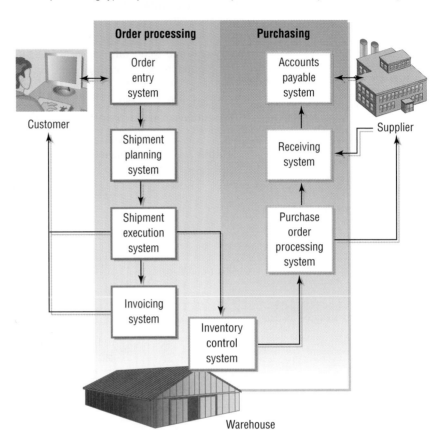

OVERVIEW OF ELECTRONIC AND MOBILE COMMERCE

Just as there are different types of transaction processing systems, there are also different types of e-commerce: business-to-consumer, business-to-business, and consumer-to-consumer. In this section, we will look at e-commerce from the buyer's and seller's perspective, including the benefits and challenges of effectively conducting e-commerce. The section concludes with an introduction to the latest form of e-commerce called mobile commerce, or m-commerce.

Types of E-commerce

What Web site comes to mind when you think of e-commerce? If you're like most Web users, Amazon.com is the first Web site you think of. Amazon.com is the longest running e-commerce success story. Founded on a great idea—selling books online—and a deep understanding of both technology and business, Amazon.com has succeeded where thousands of others have failed. With annual net sales that surpass traditional retailers such as Sears, Amazon.com is proof that success can be found in doing business on the Web.

Amazon.com is an example of business-to-consumer e-commerce. **Business-to-consumer e-commerce**, or **B2C**, makes use of the Web to connect individual consumers directly with sellers to purchase products (see Figure 7.6). B2C e-commerce is sometimes called *e-tailing*, a take-off on the term retailing, since it is the electronic equivalent of a *brick-and-mortar* retail store. Although B2C is the most visible form of e-commerce, it does not generate as much transaction traffic as business-to-business e-commerce.

FIGURE 7.6 • Business-to-consumer e-commerce

Peapod Inc. provides a B2C service that allows customers in select cities to order groceries on the Web for delivery at home.

Business-to-business e-commerce, or **B2B**, supports transactions between businesses across private networks, the Internet, and the Web. Since businesses conduct frequent and high-volume transactions, B2B e-commerce is especially valuable. Figure 7.7 illustrates the dramatic difference between B2C and B2B sales since 1999. With most businesses scrambling to automate their transactions through e-commerce, B2B e-commerce sales are expected to surpass $2.7 trillion in 2004. Businesses make use of B2B e-commerce to purchase:

FIGURE 7.7 • E-commerce revenues

The phenomenal growth in e-commerce revenues since 1999 is due mostly to B2B activity.[2]

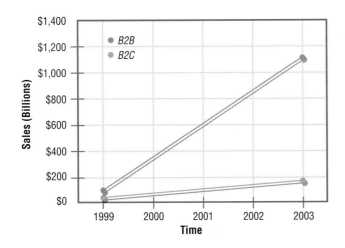

- Raw materials for production of products
- Tools, parts, and machinery for the production line
- Office furnishings, equipment, and products
- Transportation and shipping services

Many B2B transactions take place over EDI networks. As mentioned earlier, there is a growing trend for EDI transactions to take place over the Internet, rather than over private networks. In 2002, Wal-Mart requested that its 10,000 suppliers implement Internet-based EDI—changing from the previously used private network.[3] The suppliers were given one year to comply. EDI allows Wal-Mart to place product orders directly to supplier's information systems without human intervention. In some cases, these orders can be automatically placed by software that recognizes when inventory becomes low. The convenience of automating B2B transactions saves the buyer and seller significant time and money.

The third form of e-commerce is epitomized by the popular trend of private parties selling their belongings on eBay. **Consumer-to-consumer e-commerce**, or **C2C**, uses the Web to connect individuals who wish to sell their personal belongings with people shopping for used items. Although eBay supports all forms of e-commerce, many credit it for the increasing popularity of C2C e-commerce.

E-commerce from the Buyer's Perspective

The process of buying or acquiring goods or services takes place in six distinct stages (see Figure 7.8):

1. Realizing a need
2. Researching a product
3. Selecting a vendor
4. Providing payment
5. Accepting delivery
6. Using product support

FIGURE 7.8 • **The six stages of buying goods**
E-commerce can assist consumers with each of the six stages of the buying process.

1. Realizing a need

2. Researching a product

3. Selecting a vendor

The six stages of buying goods

6. Using product support

5. Accepting delivery

4. Providing payment

E-commerce can assist buyers with each of these stages of buying. Consider the following scenario.

Stage 1: Realizing a need. You spy an ad on the Web for a satellite radio system that offers over 100 channels of music, sports, and information. Wow, 100 stations to tune in wherever you drive! That's something you simply must have.

Stage 2: Researching a product. Running a Web search on "Satellite Radio," you learn that acquiring a satellite radio will require the purchase of a receiver, antenna, and a monthly service subscription.

Stage 3: Selecting a vendor. Upon further Web research you discover that since this is new technology, there aren't a lot of choices for service and hardware. Between the two digital radio broadcasting networks, you choose the service that is $9.99 per month over the one priced at $12.95 per month. Out of several receivers, you select an all-inclusive package that includes a portable receiver that can be connected to your car stereo system and home stereo system. With the manufacturer's name and part number in hand you search the Web for the vendor offering the best price, best reputation, and fastest and cheapest delivery. You find price quotes ranging from $187.84 to $215.98—including shipping. Fortunately, the vendor offering the lowest price also has a good reputation and is highly recommended by the 574 customers who have ranked its service.

Stage 4: Providing payment. You proceed to the vendor's Web site and, finding that there are units in stock that can be shipped immediately, you place the item in your electronic shopping cart and proceed to check out. You provide the vendor with your shipping information and credit-card number using the electronic checkout form, and the transaction is approved and completed.

Stage 5: Accepting delivery. Three days later a package arrives at your doorstep. After installation and setup, you're enjoying CD quality music piped to your automobile from a satellite while cruising down Main Street.

Stage 6: Using product support. Should your new digital receiver break down while under warranty, or if you have questions about setting it up, you could visit the manufacturer's Web site to gather information or arrange an exchange.

Consider the benefits that e-commerce provided you over traditional forms of shopping. Without the Web, you might or might not have heard about satellite radio. Without the Web, you would have had to rely on trade magazines or store salespeople as resources for information about the product. Perhaps the biggest advantage offered by the Web is the ability to comparison shop (see Figure 7.9). Without the Web, you would have been at the mercy of local merchants, who may or may not take advantage of monopoly power with unreasonable price mark-ups.

On the other hand, shopping locally provides the advantage of taking possession of the product at the point of purchase. Local retailers may also offer benefits that are difficult to duplicate over the Web such as demonstrations, installation, and the

FIGURE 7.9 • Comparison shopping on the Web
E-commerce empowers buyers with strong support of comparison shopping to find the best deal.

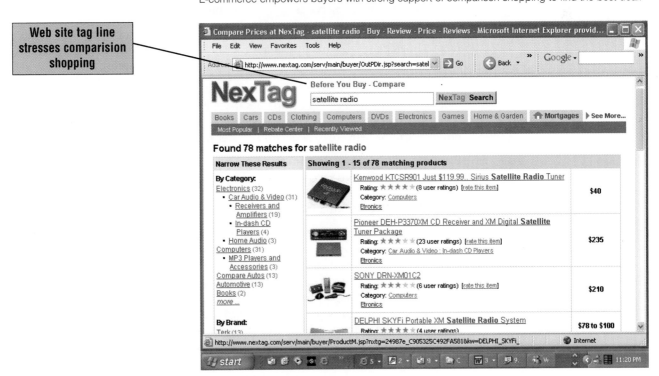

ability to exchange a faulty product for a new one without shipping delays. One of the challenges of e-commerce then is to offer online shoppers all the benefits found with local merchants with the added convenience of shopping from home.

E-commerce from the Seller's Perspective

Sellers strive to influence and support the stages of the buying process using the following business practices:

1. Market research to identify customer needs
2. Manufacturing products or supplying services that meet customer needs
3. Marketing and advertising to make customers aware of available products and services
4. Providing a method for acquiring payments
5. Making arrangements for delivery of the product
6. Providing after-sales support

Consider how e-commerce supports these methods for marketing and selling:

Business Practice 1: Market research to identify customer needs. Sellers may monitor the flow of Web traffic, and solicit customer opinions using Web-based forms in order to conduct market research.

Business Practice 2: Manufacturing products or supplying services that meet customer needs. B2B e-commerce is used to acquire raw materials for the manufacturing of products. Often the products sold or services provided are complemented by or even dependent on Web technology. For example, software, e-books, digital music, and movies can all be delivered via the Internet. Airlines, shipping companies, and banks provide free and valuable services to their customers on the Web.

Business Practice 3: Marketing and advertising to make customers aware of available products and services. Sellers actively use the Web for advertising, as you saw in the satellite radio example, in order to make customers aware of products and services they may desire.

Business Practice 4: Providing a method for acquiring payments. Banks provide merchant accounts to e-tailers for safe and secure credit-card transactions over the Web (we'll have more to say on this later in the chapter).

Business Practice 5: Making arrangements for delivery of the product. E-tailers work with shipping companies like UPS to provide several shipping options to customers at varying price levels. As noted earlier, some services and products can be delivered via download over the Internet.

Business Practice 6: Providing after-sales support. E-tailers and manufacturers may provide product support on their Web site, or through telephone, e-mail, or online chat. Manufacturers' warranties are typically the same for items purchased online and in a local store.

From the seller's perspective, the process of producing and selling goods is sometimes referred to as supply chain management. *Supply chain management* involves three areas of focus: demand planning, supply planning, and demand fulfillment. *Demand planning* involves analyzing buying patterns and forecasting customer demand. *Supply planning* involves producing and making logistical arrangements to ensure that you are able to meet the forecasted demand. *Demand fulfillment* is the process of getting the product or service to the customer. E-commerce is ideally suited for streamlining these processes, saving sellers time and money, while providing more accurate information.

HOLD MY CALLS AND BUY ME TICKETS TO THE CONCERT

A number of electronics firms have formed a consortium to develop software for cell phones that will anticipate needs, in essence functioning as a personal valet. By memorizing behavior patterns, the software will learn to make assumptions, give advice, even make purchases by keying off a calendar and the information it gathers about a user's habits.

Source:
"Smart cellphone would spend your money"
By Duncan Graham-Rowe
Newscientist.com
www.newscientist.com/hottopics/tech/article.jsp?id=99993818&sub= Gadgets%20and%20Inventions
June 15, 2003
Cited on August 4, 2003

M-commerce Technology

Mobile commerce, or **m-commerce**, is a form of e-commerce that takes place over wireless mobile devices such as handheld computers and cell phones. Although most of the principles and practices of e-commerce extend to m-commerce, m-commerce presents additional unique opportunities and challenges.

M-commerce depends on the use and proliferation of mobile communications and computing devices. Imagine subscribing to a music service that provides you with the ability to download songs to your cell phone, which you can then listen to through a wireless headset and transfer to your home stereo. Other m-commerce examples include using your cell phone or handheld computer to trade stocks, purchase concert tickets, have flowers delivered, call a cab, or book a flight.

Although m-commerce may be accessed through Internet-connected handheld computers, the growing popularity of cell phones and advances in cell phone technology are what is really driving m-commerce research and development. The next-generation cell phones being marketed today, sometimes referred to as smart phones, include the computational power and functionality required for m-commerce. They have computational power near or equal to a handheld computer, high-resolution color displays, the ability to connect to the Internet, and the ability to send and receive text messages, and sometimes photos, over the Internet. The ability to transmit data to and receive data from individuals on the Internet or wirelessly between devices is essential for m-commerce. M-commerce transactions can take place over the Internet between a cell phone and a Web server, through SMS text messaging, or wirelessly at close range between a cell phone and another device.

In addition to taking advantage of next generation cell phone technology, m-commerce makes use of other technologies and standards such as:

- Wireless Application Protocol (WAP). A communication standard used by developers to create m-commerce applications.
- Wireless Markup Language (WML). A part of WAP that is similar to HTML and is used to create Web pages designed to fit on the small displays of mobile devices.
- Bluetooth. Enables wireless, close range, device-to-device communications (see Chapter 5).

M-commerce technology received a big boost when industry leaders set aside competitive attitudes to join together in support of the open standards on which m-commerce is built. The *Open Mobile Alliance (OMA)* comprises hundreds of the world's leading mobile operators, device and network suppliers, information technology companies, and content providers, which have joined together to create standards and ensure interoperability between mobile devices.[4]

Benefits and Challenges of E-commerce

E-commerce offers advantages to both buyers and sellers. Buyers enjoy the convenience of shopping from their desktop—or, in the case of m-commerce, anywhere, anytime, on a cell phone or PDA. Sellers value e-commerce because it dramatically extends their markets. Farmyard Nurseries provides a dramatic example. Prior to e-commerce, this small nursery that grows a wide variety of specialty plants in Llandysul, West Wales, did the majority of its business (90 percent) with local residents. A year after expanding to the Web, Farmyard Nurseries found that the majority of its business now came from the rest of Wales (36 percent) and the United Kingdom (37 percent), with distribution beginning to extend around the world (see Figure 7.10).[5]

FIGURE 7.10 • **E-commerce can dramatically extend a business's market**

Farmyard Nurseries' customers consisted of mostly local residents before e-commerce, but expanded to include customers from all over the world after implementing e-commerce.

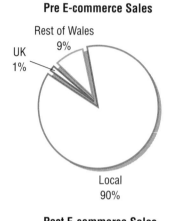

Pre E-commerce Sales

Rest of Wales 9%

UK 1%

Local 90%

Post E-commerce Sales

UK 37%

Rest of Wales 36%

World 2%

Local 25%

B2C e-commerce levels the playing field between large and small businesses, making it much easier for new companies to enter a market and for small businesses to gain market share from large businesses. The Web is an equalizer in that it allows businesses to win over customers with high-quality services and low prices, rather than through size and monopoly power. Consider, for instance, a young entrepreneur who decides to open a small hardware store. What chance for success would you give such a business considering that local competition consists of the two largest superwarehouse, home-improvement chains in the world? Could the small private business compete with the superstores' discount prices and wide selection? What if the young entrepreneur specialized in unique and hard-to-find items on a professionally managed e-commerce site? This would expand the potential customer base for this business from people in the local community to the entire Internet population. Certainly, the chances for this small business would improve in the online environment.

In some cases, e-commerce has extended a lifeline to businesses selling products or services that are made obsolete by technology. For example, realizing that film is on its way out, to be replaced by digital cameras, Kodak worked to change its image from that of a film company to that of a picture company.[6] They put their efforts and investments into digital camera technology and an online presence, where they provide products and tools for digital photographers (see Figure 7.11). The Kodak Web site includes tools and space for visitors to display their digital photos. Kodak discovered that by providing methods for people to share photographs on the Web, they create a greater demand for professional prints of those photos, enlargements, and other specialized services such as photo T-shirts and coffee mugs. Kodak hopes that the additional revenue generated by these digital photo services will make up for the lost revenue from film.

FIGURE 7.11 • The Kodak Web site

Kodak reinvented itself as a picture company by investing in digital camera technology and establishing an online presence, where they provide products and tools for digital photographers.

Although there are many advantages to e-commerce, there are some challenges. Established businesses that wish to expand to the Internet need to alter systems and business practices to accommodate the new method of transaction processing that e-commerce requires. The larger and more established the business, the more costly this change can be. Issues of network security, privacy, and reliability are constant concerns for e-commerce buyers and sellers; these issues are discussed at the close of this chapter.

Finally, there are social concerns. Not everyone has equal access to the technology of e-commerce. People with low incomes and people living in less developed, Third World countries often don't have computers, mobile telephones, and Internet access. Many people in the United States and European Union do not have high-speed, broadband Internet access. The differences between those who have access to technology and those who do not are deepened with the increased use of e-commerce—those without access to the Internet are denied the benefits of e-commerce technology. In addition, accessibility advocates warn that as we move to increasingly smaller devices for day-to-day business, we must make accommodations for individuals who are unable to manipulate such small devices due to old age, poor vision, or other physical limitations.

E-COMMERCEAPPLICATIONS

E-commerce is playing an increasingly important role in our personal and professional lives. It allows us to discover new and interesting products that may not be available in our own community. For items that are available locally, it allows us to find better deals. We use e-commerce to monitor our bank accounts and transfer electronic funds. Businesses use e-commerce to streamline transaction processes and reach new customers. This section provides a categorical view of e-commerce and m-commerce applications from both the buyer's and seller's perspective.

Retail E-commerce: Shopping Online

As previously discussed, e-tailing has dramatically influenced the way people shop by providing customers with product information and the ability to comparison shop for most products. For example, consider the portable Nomad "Muvo" MP3 player from Creative Labs Corp. One model stores 128 MB of MP3 files (about 4 hours of music) in a device that is 1.4" × 2.9" and weighs only 1 oz. Doing a quick search and compare on the Muvo at www.cnet.com brings up an online merchant selling this item at 25 percent less than a local retailer. Price battles continually rage on the Web to the benefit of consumers. Web sites such as mySimon.com, Deal-Time.com PriceSCAN.com, PriceGrabber.com, and NexTag.com provide product price quotations from numerous e-tailers to help you to find the best deal (see Figure 7.12). It may still be that the best deal is found at your local warehouse store.

FIGURE 7.12 • mySimon

At mySimon, product price quotations from many e-tailers help people find the best deal on many different products.

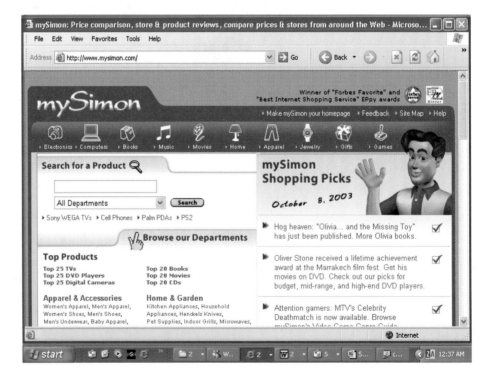

JOB TECHNOLOGY

Lands' End Masters Selling Clothes Online

Of the items that sell well on the Web, clothing is not one. Although electronics and personal computer manufacturers may credit the Web for more than 25 percent of total sales, Web sales make up less than 2 percent of all apparel sales. What's more, 30 percent of all apparel bought online is returned. This has led some clothing merchants to all but forsake the Web as a tool for selling their products. Not so for Lands' End.

Although many companies experienced serious financial losses after the economic downturn that began in 2000, Lands' End, the well-known direct merchant, experienced record earnings. President and chief executive officer David F. Dyer credits the company's success to the business principles to which they adhere. Roughly stated, they include the following:

1. Do everything possible to make better products.
2. Price products fairly and honestly.
3. Accept any return for any reason at any time.
4. Ship products faster than anyone else.
5. Believe that what is best for the customer is best for all of us.

Lands' End uses technology extensively to support its business principles. Its streamlined information and communications systems allow the company to quickly fill orders, shipping within 36 hours of taking the order even during its busiest holiday rush. It is able to keep inventory levels low, avoiding, as much as possible, the necessity of liquidation sales. Lands' End started out as a successful direct marketing business selling its clothing solely through mass mailings of catalogues. In 1995, Lands' End was one of the first clothing retailers to expand its operations to the Web. Its direct marketing experience gave it an edge in this new marketplace. Today, landsend.com is the world's largest (in business volume) apparel Web site, maintaining Web sites in seven countries that support six languages. It has also been a leader in developing new ways to enhance the shopping experience and to foster one-on-one relationships with its customers.

For example:

- "My Virtual Model," an innovative Java program, allows customers to create a 3-D model on which to try clothes (see Figure 7.13).
- Instant personal help online using a chat utility that links customers directly to a customer service representative. The customer service representative can take control of the customer's browser window to show that person Web pages of merchandise in order to assist the customer with his or her purchase.
- Land's End "Shop with a friend" Web service allows two shoppers sitting at two different computers to browse the site together, chat with each other, and add items to a single shopping basket.
- "Lands' End Custom" allows customers to order custom-crafted clothes created just for them.

FIGURE 7.13 • Lands' End Virtual Model

Making the most of 3-D virtual imagery available to e-tailors, Land's End offers consumers the ability to create a model that is built like them—including body type, hair, and facial features—to model potential clothing purchases.

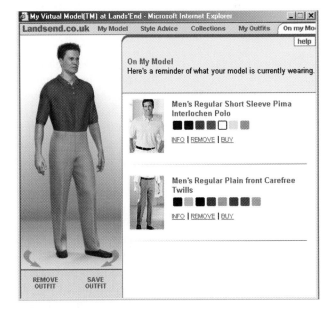

Through technical innovation, Lands' End has been able to streamline its operations to reduce overhead and provide customers with an online shopping experience that it hopes will be easier and more pleasant than shopping at the mall.

Questions

1. What services can a brick-and-mortar clothing store offer that are difficult to duplicate on the Web?
2. Are there any services that can be offered by a Web-based clothing merchant that would be difficult to offer in a brick-and-mortar store?
3. What types of issues may arise while shopping at landsend.com that might frustrate or concern customers? How do these issues compare to those encountered when shopping at a brick-and-mortar business?

Sources
1. *"Lands' End to Beat Goal," The New York Times, February 15, 2002, Section C; p. 16.*
2. *www.landsend.com accessed February 18, 2002.*

Some items are easier to sell online than others. Some purchases are determined not by holding a product in your hands, but by the description or demonstration of the product. Such is the case with books, digital music, computer software, and games—items that sell easily on the Web. Tangibles, such as DVD players, blue jeans, and automobiles are more difficult to sell online (see the "Job Technology" box). However, examining tangible items online has become significantly easier recently with the development of 3-D virtual imagery. 3-D virtual imagery, introduced in Chapter 4, allows a Web user to rotate objects on the screen and view them from every angle. This technology has been a tremendous help to businesses selling tangible products online.

There are several approaches to e-tailing. A business can set up its own electronic storefront, as did Lands' End, and provide visitors access to an electronic catalogue of products, an electronic shopping cart for items they wish to purchase, and an electronic checkout procedure. Another e-tailing option is to lease space in a cybermall. A *cybermall* is a Web site that allows visitors to browse through a wide variety of products from varying e-tailers.

Online Clearing Houses, Web Auctions, and Marketplaces

Online clearinghouses, Web auctions, and *marketplaces* provide a platform for businesses and individuals to sell their products and belongings. Online clearinghouses such as www.ubid.com, provide a method for manufacturers to liquidate stock and consumers to find a good deal. Outdated or overstocked items are put on the virtual auction block for customers to bid on. Users place bids on the objects. The highest bidder(s) when the auction closes gets the merchandise—often for less than 50 percent of the advertised retail price. Credit-card numbers are collected at the time that bids are placed. A good rule to keep in mind is don't place a bid on an item unless you are prepared to buy it.

The most popular auction/marketplace is eBay.com. eBay provides a public platform for global trading where practically anyone can buy, sell, or trade practically anything. EBay offers a wide variety of features and services that enable members to buy and sell on the site quickly and conveniently. Buyers have the option to purchase items in auction-style format, or they can purchase items at a fixed price through a feature called Buy It Now. On any given day, more than 12 million items are listed on eBay across 18,000 categories. In 2002, eBay members transacted $14.87 billion in annualized gross merchandise sales (the value of goods sold on eBay).

Although eBay sells millions of everyday items annually, some items are so unique that they capture the attention of the press. For example, the sale of Bridgeville, a town in Northern California, for $1.8 million on eBay made the front page of some newspapers in December 2002.[7] More unique items of interest sold on eBay are listed at www.whattheheck.com/ebay/.

Auction houses such as eBay do not accept liability for problems that buyers or sellers may experience in their transactions. Participants should be aware that the possibility of fraud is very real in any such Internet dealings.

B2B Global Supply Management and Electronic Exchanges

By now you know that the Internet serves as an ideal way for businesses to connect. The real challenge lies in organizing relationships between businesses. For example, let's pretend that you have a great idea for a new product, such as a new lightweight, motorized, campus scooter. You have test marketed the product, which students on campus greeted with great enthusiasm, you've found a wealthy investor, and you are ready to go into production. You have a list of parts required for the manufacturing of your scooter. But how do you go about finding suppliers that are both reputable and inexpensive? The solution for your scooter manufacturing business, is the same as for any business: Global supply management.

Global supply management (GSM) provides methods for businesses to find the best deals on the global market for raw materials and supplies needed to manufacture their products. There are many GSM products and services available on the Web that promise to lower a businesses costs by providing connections to a wide variety of reputable suppliers along with negotiation tools that will allow a business to be assured that it is getting the best deal. FreeMarkets.com, a GSM company, advertises that its services and software can cut total supply costs by 45 percent.

Some businesses are joining together with others in their industry to pool resources in Web-based electronic exchanges. An *electronic exchange* is an industry-specific Web resource created to provide a convenient centralized platform for B2B e-commerce among manufacturers, suppliers, and customers. Electronic exchanges promote cooperation between competing companies for greater industry-wide efficiency and effectiveness. Through an electronic exchange, a manufacturer has access to a wide variety of industry-specific suppliers and services. Once business relationships are established between members, the electronic exchange provides the framework for fast and efficient transactions.

Covisint (www.covisint.com) is an electronic exchange for automotive manufacturers. Founded by DaimlerChrysler AG, Ford Motor Company, General Motors, Nissan, and Renault, Covisint has created alliances between automotive manufactures and suppliers and contracted several of the largest technology providers to create "the most successful business-to-business electronic exchange the world has ever seen".[8] Covisint members are provided with access to online catalogues and auctions, tools that assist in quality management and problem solving, and an industry portal (see Figure 7.14). The industry portal is software installed on a member's computer system that provides secure access to the electronic exchange's services. The Covisint portal provides tools for finding suppliers and managing e-commerce transactions, library services, and messaging facilities for suppliers and manufacturers.

FIGURE 7.14 • The Covisint portal

The Covisint portal provides convenient access to valuable automotive industry resources.

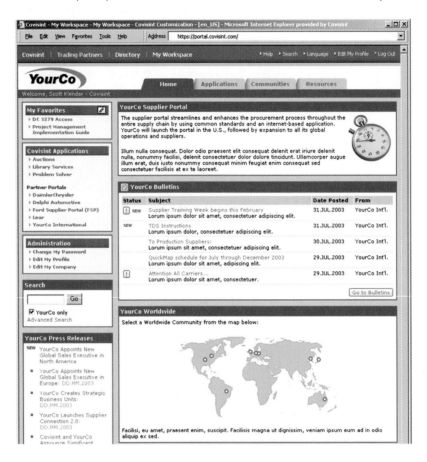

Marketing

Internet users are well aware of marketing on the Internet. Banner ads threaten to overshadow Web content, pop-up ads accumulate on our desktops as we visit Web pages, and our e-mail boxes are brimming with spam. Although some Internet marketing is intrusive, there are positive aspects of e-commerce marketing to focus on.

E-commerce has affected the marketing process perhaps more than any other area of business. The Web is used for:

- Unsolicited advertising, to make buyers aware of products
- Access to product information (call it solicited advertising) through business Web sites, which allow buyers to find information about products that they are actively pursuing
- Market research, to find out what consumers want

Of these areas of Web marketing, perhaps the most helpful to consumers is the ability to find product information online.

Access to Product Information. In some cases Web-based product research leads to e-commerce purchases. For example, consider the earlier example of purchasing a satellite radio system for a car. In others, it leads to more traditional-style purchases. For example, you might use online research to prepare to purchase a car to go with your satellite radio system, but make the actual purchase at a traditional dealership. When shopping for a car, most people use the Web to compare and contrast a variety of makes and models in order to narrow down the field. Web sites such as Edmunds.com, CarSmart.com, and FightingChance.com provide tools for learning about the automotive market and preparing for your purchase. Auto manufacturers provide their own Web sites that include thorough descriptions and photos of their models and model options. Some auto shoppers find the Web site of ConsumerReports, a nonprofit consumer watchdog group, (consumereports.org) worth the subscription fee to access its vehicle ratings. Upon deciding on a make and model, the purchaser may even get some price quotes on the Web (www.pricequotes.com). Ultimately, however, the person will visit a local auto dealer to test drive and make a final decision.

The ability to get better deals and make informed decisions is turning many people into Web researchers. Many patients are turning up in doctor's offices with printed pages of Web content describing their malady, guessing at a diagnosis, and requesting specific prescription medication. Whether dealing with an auto salesperson, a mechanic, a loan officer, a financial advisor, or any number of professionals, the Web empowers us with knowledge in areas previously reserved for professionals and better equips us to ask intelligent questions and confront those who may otherwise take advantage of us.

Market Research. Traditional marketing research takes place by observing what products customers purchase, or interviewing customers to find out how they feel about specific products. Interviews may take place on the street, by phone, by mail, and by paying focus-group participants to try a product and provide their opinions. Through *market segmentation*, customer opinions are divided into categories of race, gender, and age to determine which segment a product appeals to most. Although this method of market research is useful, it has some significant shortcomings. For one, it is expensive for those doing the research and inconvenient for those being interviewed. These restrictions make it difficult for market researchers to obtain the views of a representative cross-section of the population. Another problem is that market segmentation caters to a majority and may exclude individuals who think differently from their peers.

E-commerce allows market segmentation to take place at the level of each individual consumer. E-commerce tools make it possible to follow a visitor around a Web site, monitor which areas and products draw the visitor's attention, and monitor how much time the visitor spends in each area. This data is often collected without the customer's knowledge—so it is in no way an inconvenience and requires very little investment on the e-tailer's part. With the use of cookies, an e-tailer can maintain a history of customer preferences and highlight products that have proven historically to best hold the customer's interest. For example, a person who purchases a Harry Potter book at Amazon.com will be greeted by advertisements for other Harry Potter products on future visits as well as ads for other items that Harry Potter fans tend to purchase.

It is also possible to develop a customer profile based on broader Internet browsing patterns. Marketing companies such as DoubleClick, provide advertising servers that display banner ads and pop-up ads on client Web sites (see Figure 7.15). For example, *The New York Times* (www.nytimes.com) and the *Washington Post* (www.washingtonpost.com), along with most other free online services, have hired DoubleClick to handle their sponsors' Web advertisements.

CUSTOM-TAILORED ADS

A new service in cyber marketing is customizing ads to the viewer. Riding on the coattails of bid-for-placement services, Google and Overture now offer content publishers a way to have the ads they sell pop up when search criteria dovetail with their advertiser's product. If someone searches a newspaper Web site for a book review, the search engine scans a database of ads and pops up one for a related product—such as a bookstore, or maybe an e-publisher.

Source:
"If You Liked the Web Page, You'll Love the Ad"
By Bob Tedeschi
The New York Times
www.nytimes.com/2003/08/04/technology/04ECOM.html
August 4, 2003
Cited on August 4, 2003

FIGURE 7.15 • Web ads

DoubleClick provides banner ads for most Web sites that use banner ads. Google's approach to sponsorship and advertising, called AdWords, does away with the intrusive and bandwith-consuming banner ads used by most other sponsored Web sites. Compare the banner ads in this screen shot from Yahoo! with the AdWords advertisements at Google.

Each time you visit these sites, DoubleClick inserts an advertisement from a sponsor into space provided on the Web site. Often, a different ad will be in the banner each time you visit.

Web advertising and marketing companies collect large amounts of data that can be mined to determine buying patterns and trends. This provides a significantly more detailed level of market research than traditional methods can provide.

Banking, Finance, and Investment

Since banks have moved online, managing money has become easier. Online banking provides convenient access to bank balance information, the ability to transfer funds, automatic bill payment, and account histories. Most bank Web sites provide a way to link your online financial records with financial software on your home PC, such as Quicken, in order to make use of advanced tools that assist with financial management.

Electronic funds transfer has become the norm for paying bills and receiving paychecks. The Web helps us to manage such transfers. Most banks include an automatic bill payment service that can be configured from the bank's Web site. You can also set up automatic payments at the Web sites of companies to whom you are making payments or through third-party services that will perform the transfers for you for a small monthly fee. Electronic bill payments save companies so much money that many are considering requiring it of their customers. British Telecommunications (BT) is encouraging its customers to pay bills online after learning that it would save 45 cents per bill. If BT could get 90 percent of its more than 21 million customers signed up and paying bills online, it could save close to $110 million annually.[9]

Investing activities have also moved to the Web. Online brokerages offer low-cost stock trades (between $5–$10 per trade) and tools to assist you in your investment decisions (see Figure 7.16). Online brokerages are able to execute trades fast, allowing customers to buy or sell at the moment of opportunity. Ameritrade offers a 10-second guarantee: "qualifying S&P 100® Internet equity market trades that take longer than 10 seconds to execute are commission-free!" states the Ameritrade Web site.[10] Most services offer helpful software that provides free quotes and streaming news for a first look at the stories that shape the market. Customers are also provided with market research tools to help them in their

COMMUNITY /\/\/\ TECHNOLOGY

The Customer-Sensitive Approach to Web Advertising

Google (www.google.com), the very popular Web search engine, is working to find new ways of marketing products and services to their users—methods that don't infringe on Web page load time or valuable screen real estate. Google is renowned for its clean design that is free of obnoxious ads. In early 2002, Google banned the use of pop-up ads on its Web site. Google also refrains from using any form of banner ad. So, how does Google make money? Through an approach that they call "AdWords" (see Figure 7.15).

AdWords is a unique, text-only, approach to Web marketing. You won't see any advertisements on Google's home page. It's only when the results of your search are displayed that you will see advertisements—that is, if you look closely. In a narrow column on the right edge of the page you will find a list of text-only advertisements under the heading "Sponsored Links." The key selling feature of these advertisements is that they are directly related to the search keywords entered by the user. So, in a manner of speaking, they are a service to the user.

Businesses interested in advertising on Google with AdWords purchase product-relevant keywords. Pricing for AdWords is based on the value of the keyword and on the position in the list of sponsors that the ad is to be placed; first position in the list holds the highest value. Google offers an alternate package named AdWords Select that uses cost-per-click (CPC) pricing; the sponsor pays only when a customer clicks the ad, regardless of how many times it is shown. In this scenario, your click-through rate and CPC together determine where your ads are shown, so better ads rise to the top. Google offers one other advertising option: Premium Sponsorship Advertising. Premium sponsors pay premium rates to have links to their products or services appear in the first two places of the actual search results.

None of the advertising options that Google offers slows the delivery of search results, nor do they consume a high percentage of screen real estate. Because the advertisements are tied to search keywords, they are more likely to yield results for the sponsors. Overall, Google has developed a winning Web marketing strategy that assists both its sponsors and its users.

Questions

1. How much advertising is too much? Everyone has a different threshold of tolerance for advertising. What is your limit? Can you tolerate one banner ad per Web page? More? How about pop-up advertisement windows?

2. What other types of Web sites, besides search engines, might be able to offer user-targeted advertising like AdWords?

3. Is the future of the Web more likely to resemble network television or public TV? What exterior forces can be applied to sway the Web one way or another?

Sources

1. "The Future of Web Advertising," by James Lewin, www. itworld.com/nl/ebiz_ent/03042002/, February 5, 2002.

2. "No, Google Hasn't Sold Out," by Chris Sherman, http:// siliconvalley.internet.com/news/article/0,2198,3531_989811,00. html, March 12, 2002.

3. "Up Close With Google AdWords," by Danny Sulivan, http://searchenginewatch.com/sereport/02/03-adwords.html, March 4, 2002.

4. "Intrusive ads a sign of online advertising evolution, analysts say," by Brian Sullivan, www.computerworld.com/storyba/ 0,4125,NAV47_STO68452,00.html, February 19, 2002.

5. www.google.com accessed July 18, 2003.

FIGURE 7.16 • Investing online

Most online trading services provide a simple form to buy and sell stocks.

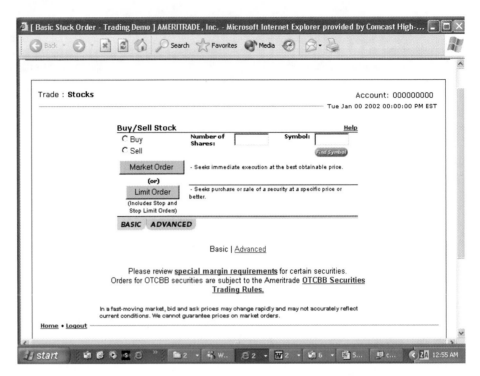

decision making process. The most popular online brokerages include Ameritrade (Datek), Bidwell & Co, Brown & Co., Charles Schwab & Co, and Dreyfus. For more information about online trading look at www.investingonline.org/.

M-commerce Applications

Imagine getting a text message on your cell phone the moment your favorite musical artist releases a new single, with an option to download and listen to it. Or, while driving to a friend's for dinner, using your cell phone to find out if there is a florist anywhere along your route with a good deal on a dozen roses for the host. This is m-commerce as it will be someday. You can see why many businesses are interested in this new area.

Three methods are currently being pursued for m-commerce service delivery. The first utilizes the cell phone's ability to run applications and access the Web. The second uses a cell phone's Short Message Service (SMS) text messaging and Multimedia Messaging Service (MMS). The third uses short-range wireless technology, such as Bluetooth, and a portable device's ability to use it to communicate with other devices such as cash registers.

M-commerce between Cell Phone and Web. Web-based and application-based m-commerce allow the mobile user to interact with a seller's e-commerce system over the Internet or Web (see Figure 7.17). Because smart phones have the ability to run Java applications, users can download an m-commerce application to their cell phone and use it to purchase products or services. For example, Sprint has recently joined with Sony to provide music services over cell phones.[11] In the near future, your Sprint cell phone may come with an application that allows you to browse a catalog of CD tracks, purchase and download your favorites, and listen to them on your cell phone through headphones.

Many m-commerce applications can be accessed through your mobile Web browser, in much the same way that you access e-commerce applications through

FIGURE 7.17 • Web-based m-commerce

Web-based m-commerce makes use of mobile Web browsers in cell phones to support traditional e-commerce applications.

regular Web browsers. Web developers for m-commerce use Wireless Markup Language (WML) to create small Web pages specially designed to fit the mobile display and provide easy navigation through the mobile device user interface. M-commerce Web sites typically focus on delivering services that are useful to users on the go.

M-commerce through SMS Text Messaging. M-commerce is also making use of cell phone text messaging. Texting, as this is called, can be used to order merchandise or services, or for advertisements. Mobile spam over SMS texting is raising concerns in the United Kingdom, where texting has been in use longer than in the US. It is estimated that more than half of British firms are using text messaging as a marketing tool.[12] U.S. firms are likely to follow suit. In the United Kingdom, text messaging service charges are picked up by the sender. Here in the United States, however, many services require the receiver to pick up the bill, making mobile spam all the more disconcerting. Some believe that an "opt-in" approach to mobile spam is the solution. "Text messaging is a double-edged sword. It can ruin your brand if you misuse it or be deadly effective in creating customer loyalty if used correctly," says Pamir Gelenbe, Director of Development at FlyTXT, a U.K. text marketing firm.

M-commerce through Short-Range Wireless Data Communications. Short-range wireless technology is being used to enable some interesting m-commerce applications. Smart phones with Bluetooth technology are being considered as a practical approach to a cashless society. The concept of a

BUY A BALLPARK HOT DOG—ON CREDIT

Using a device that attaches to a handheld, non-brick-and-mortar vendors operating hot dog stands or pushcarts can now process credit cards wirelessly. The device takes data off any card with a magnetic strip and can display, store, or transmit it. It can be programmed for specific applications from taking attendance at colleges and universities (students swipe their ID through it upon entering class), to collecting data on prospects at sales conventions.

Source:
"Scanning Devices takes a swipe at wireless credit processing"
By Elizabeth Dinan
Mass High Tech, The Journal of New England Technology
www.masshightech.com/displayarticledetail.asp?art_id=63094&cat_id=96
July 21, 2003
Cited July 21, 2003

JOB /\/\/ TECHNOLOGY

Dylan's Candy Bar

A new chain of upscale trendy candy shops has recently opened in Long Island, Orlando, and Houston. Owned by Dylan Lauren (daughter of Ralph) and Jeff Rubin, Dylan's Candy Bar claims to be "The most unique and unrivaled candy and sweets store, home to thousands of candies from all over the world!" Dylan's sells much more than candy. Their inventory includes items from four categories: Candy Couture (apparel), Candy Baskets, Candy Creations (topiaries), and Candy Spa. Besides the brick-and-mortar shops that are advertised as "creating a unique and completely unmatched shopping experience in an architecturally significant and artistically awing environment" Dylan's is making strong use of e-commerce and m-commerce to sell products.

Dylanscandybar.com provides a means for customers to purchase Dylan's products online, but Dylan's has taken it one step farther by launching what they call an "mmm-commerce wireless campaign." For example, you can purchase and download candy-themed ringtones, such as "I Want Candy" by Bow Wow Wow, and "Sugar, Sugar" by the Archies, for $2.99. You can also send an m-commerce candygram from the Dylan's Web site. Type in a friend's cell phone number, select a message, and click the button to deliver the text message. You can use the messages to send a Dylan's gift certificate, or to invite a friend to meet you at Dylan's.

Dylan's has contracted Youie corporation to set up their m-commerce services. Youie is in the business of creating and distributing what they call wireless infotainment. Shane Igoe, president of Youie thinks that ringtone and text message marketing is effective with teenagers and young adults. "The ringtones and SMS messages are a very effective viral marketing tool as they drive traffic not only back to the Web site but directly into the stores." Dylan's next m-commerce service will allow customers to send personalized messages with a related ringtone, plus a lollipop gift certificate to a friend from Web or cell phone for $3.99.

Questions

1. Are cell phone users likely to be annoyed when they receive text messages from Dylan's mmm-commerce service? Why or Why not?
2. What other businesses might benefit from using this m-commerce model?
3. How would customers react if they got unsolicited text advertisements from Dylan's on their cell phone? Under what conditions would text advertising work?

Sources
1. *"Mmm-commerce—How Sweet Can It Be?" by Beth Cox, e-commerce guide.com, June 23, 2003, http://ecommerce. internet.com/news/insights/trends/article/ 0,,10417_ 2226311,00.html.*
2. *www.dylanscandybar.com.*
3. *www.youie.com/.*

cashless society has been a dream for quite some time. In such a society, no one would need to carry wallets or money. Transactions take place through automatic debits and credits to consumer and merchant accounts. As a form of m-commerce, such transactions can indeed take place using a small device, such as a cell phone, and wireless data transmission, such as those provided by Bluetooth or infrared. Referred to as a *proximity payment system*, devices such as Vivo, shown in Figure 7.18, allow customers to transfer funds wirelessly between their mobile device and a point-of-sale terminal.

E-commerce and m-commerce applications are limited only by what we can imagine. Although each application is suited to a unique service or product, all applications provide extended service to buyers and increased revenues to sellers.

FIGURE 7.18 • **Proximity payment system**

Proximity payment systems, such as the Vivo device shown here, take consumers one step closer to a cashless society.

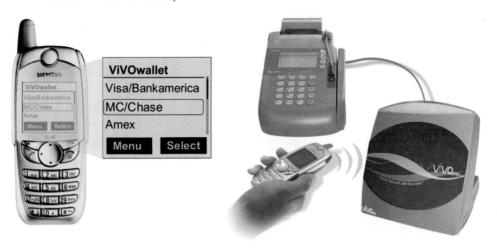

E-COMMERCEIMPLEMENTATION

Implementing e-commerce requires a significant amount of investment and expertise. When a company decides to invest in e-commerce, it places itself at considerable risk. Since e-commerce is highly visible to the public, if it is executed poorly, it could tarnish the reputation of an otherwise well-respected company. E-commerce requires significant amounts of hardware and networking capabilities to accommodate heavy traffic, and expertise in system administration, software development, Web design, and graphics design. Anything less than a professional approach in any of these areas could mean embarrassment for the company. For this reason, companies typically either hire specialists in these areas or contract the work out to professional e-commerce hosting companies.

An **e-commerce host** is a company that takes on some or all of the responsibility of setting up and maintaining an e-commerce system for a business or organization. Hosting services range in price from $7.95 per month to thousands of dollars per month, depending on the size of the business and the services offered by the host (see Figure 7.19). Companies like ValueWeb provide everything needed for a simple e-commerce online business, online catalogue, shopping cart, and transaction processing for $49.95 per month. Large companies with more complicated systems might contract IBM or Sprint to work with their business to develop Web e-commerce solutions at a considerably higher cost.

FIGURE 7.19 • **E-commerce Host**

A typical e-commerce host will set up and maintain an e-commerce system for around $49.95 per month.

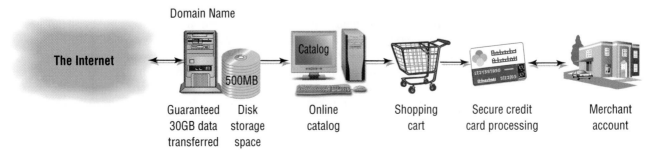

The Internet — Domain Name — Guaranteed 30GB data transferred — Disk storage space 500MB — Online catalog — Shopping cart — Secure credit card processing — Merchant account

Regardless of whether you are creating and implementing your own e-commerce Web site or contracting the work out to a professional e-commerce hosting company, you need to understand the basics of e-commerce infrastructure, hardware and networking, and software issues. You also need to have a grasp of how to build Web site traffic, electronic payment systems, international markets, and security and privacy issues.

Infrastructure

E-commerce typically requires significant changes in an organization's infrastructure. Changes may be required in personnel, manufacturing processes, storage, shipping, information systems, and organizational procedures.

A business that uses e-commerce needs to employ people who are technically savvy and able to understand how technology can assist in meeting the goals of the organization. Knowledge of the technology is necessary even for a small business using an e-commerce hosting company to maintain a Web site. An e-commerce hosting company is only responsible for providing the tools of e-commerce, not for the success of the business. Small-business owners greatly benefit from acquiring technical knowledge. Large business owners and managers benefit as well, but usually enhance their knowledge through a team of experts assigned to support e-commerce operations.

Organizations expanding to the Web find that all areas of the business are affected to some degree: manufacturing, financial departments, sales, and customer service all need to adapt procedures to support doing business online. Wayne Cross found this to be the case when he began using e-commerce to support his resort, the Springs Retreat, outside Melbourne, Australia.[13] The Springs Retreat offers accommodations, a restaurant, a café, conference facilities, a spa, and a golf course and is staffed by 12 full-time employees. Wayne Cross, the managing director, took advantage of state-provided financial incentives and invested them in a high profile Web site. The Web site (www.thesprings.com.au), which provides information and reservation services, is marketed in print and television media. The Web site has generated an additional $85,000 in revenue for the resort and saved $33,760 in 2001. The extra business is keeping the Springs' staff hopping, but fortunately other areas of the business are now less demanding. For example, the success of the Web site has eliminated the need for printed marketing material, producing additional savings in materials and time. Online reservations made at the Web site and outsourced to a reservations service, saves the staff time in reservation processing.

B2C e-commerce often connects manufacturers directly with consumers, cutting out the middleman. This usually means drastic changes in manufacturing, storage, and shipping. Rather than shipping bulk products to retailers, B2C e-commerce requires the shipment of individual products direct to consumers. This may result in minor changes to manufacturing processes and major changes in shipping and storage practices. An extreme example can be found in Izumiya Co. Ltd. of Japan.[14] Izumiya is a retail chain, offering food, clothing, books, furniture, and housewares, that provides an amazing service for Japan's residents (see Figure 7.20). You're in Japan, it's an hour before dinner, and you realize that you don't have enough sushi to accommodate your dinner guests! Log on to www.izumiya.co.jp/, and they can have sushi or any other item in their inventory on your doorstep within an hour. Such a service requires significant support from inventory management systems, storage facilities, distribution networks, and support staff. To handle online orders, an entirely new system is needed, one that works in harmony with the existing system that services in-store customers.

FIGURE 7.20 • B2C e-commerce

Izumiya provides 1-hour grocery delivery service to Japan's residents' doorsteps.

Hardware and Networking

Web-based e-commerce requires enough computing power and network bandwidth to support the Web traffic your site generates. Underestimating the amount of Web traffic will lead to network stalls and long wait times that leave visitors frustrated. A typical e-commerce Web site employs one or more server computers and a high-speed Internet connection. Businesses that choose to outsource to a Web hosting company are typically provided with guarantees that include operation 24 hours a day, 7 days week, and that accommodates a specific number of users. For example, Rackspace Managed Hosting (www.rackspace.com) uses *load-balancing* among servers so that if one goes down, the others pick up the slack. It also has an uninterruptible power supply, backed up by a diesel generator to keep the system up and running in case of power failure. The ValueWeb e-commerce hosting package described earlier provides a transfer allowance of 30 GB per month. ValueWeb claims that for an average Web page, it would take about 100,000 visitors in a month to reach a 5-GB data transfer allowance. Both Rackspace and ValueWeb provide their customers with guarantees of service up to a specified level of traffic.

Software

Several categories of software are associated with e-commerce, from the low-level software that controls the functioning of the Web server to high-level software used to design Web pages and graphics. To succeed at e-commerce, you need to understand Web server software and utility programs, e-commerce software, Web site design tools, graphics applications, Web site development tools, and Web services.

Web Server Software. The primary purpose of *Web server software* is to respond to requests for Web pages from browsers. For e-commerce applications, Web servers also provide security by encrypting sensitive transaction data such as credit-card information. Web servers work with custom-designed programs and databases to provide e-commerce functionality. The two most popular Web server applications are Apache and Microsoft Internet Information Services (IIS).

Web Server Utility Programs. *Web server utility programs* provide statistical information about server usage and Web site traffic patterns. This information can be used to gauge the success of a Web site, its products, and its services.

E-commerce Software. *E-commerce software* is designed specifically to support e-commerce activities. It includes:

- *Catalog management software* for organizing a product line into a convenient format for Web navigation
- *Electronic shopping cart software* for allowing visitors to collect items to purchase
- *Payment software* to facilitate payment for the selected merchandise and arrange shipping

Web Site Design Tools. Web site design tools are typically what-you-see-is-what-you-get (WYSIWYG) applications or wizards that make it simple to graphically lay out a Web page design. It is highly desirable for a Web site to have a consistent look and feel. Typically, design tools allow you to develop a standard template to be used in creating all Web site pages within a site.

Graphics Applications. Graphics applications are particularly important in Web site design. Graphics applications allow the Web developer to design and create the graphic elements that give a Web site its style and overall appearance. Menus, menu buttons, corporate logos, backgrounds, and other graphic elements combine to give a Web site a professional look. Businesses are wise to hire professional Web graphic designers when coming up with the initial design of a Web site.

Web Site Development Tools. Web site development tools include *application programming interface's (API's)* that allow software engineers to develop Web-driven programs. Using programming languages such as Java, C++, or Perl, software engineers develop applications that allow Web pages to be custom created and delivered as users call up a URL. *Web-driven* programs allow users to interact with Web sites to access useful information and services. Often, Web-driven programs access data from a secure corporate database.

Amazon.com uses Web-driven programs to create personalized Web pages on the fly (see Figure 7.21). For example, if you frequent Amazon.com, it will custom

FIGURE 7.21 • Personalized Web pages

Amazon.com uses Web-driven programs to create personalized Web pages on the fly.

create its home page each time you visit, highlighting those items of interest to you. When you search for products using the keyword search engine, the results pages is created by a Web application accessing the Amazon inventory database.

Web Services. **Web Services** are programs that automate tasks by communicating with each other over the Web. Recall from Chapter 5 that when computers combine resources over a network to solve problems it is called distributed computing. Although the concept of distributed computing has been a part of networking for some time, until now, there has been no framework for easily developing distributed computing applications for the Web. Web Services provide that framework. Web service development is based on Extensible Markup Language (XML) and other languages and protocols used to organize and deliver structured data and govern the communication between applications.

Through Web Services, systems developers are able to provide tools for automating trivial or repetitive tasks that traditionally require human interaction. For example, Microsoft has developed a Calendar Service that allows users to share their appointment books with others on the Web. Using this service, you could easily make appointments with your dentist, hair stylist, or mechanic through your Web browser without the need to speak with a receptionist (see Figure 7.22).

FIGURE 7.22 • Web Services

A Calendar Web Service running on your home PC could interact with the Calendar Web Service installed on a computer in the dentist's office to allow you to make an appointment without the need to speak to a receptionist.

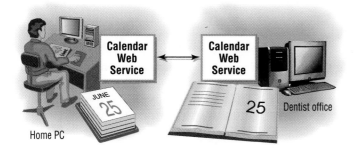

Web Services are becoming increasingly important in transaction processing, because they are ideal for automating the exchange of information between computer systems. For example, a manufacturer could use a Web Service to order materials from a supplier. The Web Service on the supplier's system could then notify the manufacturer of whether or not the item is in stock and when to expect delivery.

Three significant technology companies, Microsoft, IBM, and Sun, are investing heavily in Web Services development. Microsoft offers a Web Services development platform called .Net (pronounced dot net). IBM offers a development platform called WebSphere, and Sun offers the Java Web Services Developer Pack (Java WSDP). These development platforms provide tools for program developers to more easily develop Web Services using a variety of programming languages. The Web Services Interoperability Organization (WS-I) has been established to promote Web Services interoperability across platforms, operating systems, and programming languages. It includes dozens of big technology companies, including Hewlett-Packard and Oracle. By 2005, Web Services technology and interfaces are expected to be a standard part of application integration, and commercial Web Services are expected to drive most e-commerce applications.

Building Traffic

The expression "if you build it, they will come," does not hold true in e-commerce. A new e-commerce Web site is just one among billions of Web sites, and will remain undiscovered unless brought to the attention of the online community. Once a Web site gains attention, it must provide content that keeps users coming back for more. A stagnant Web site will quickly lose visitors. E-commerce companies use several approaches to build traffic to their Web sites. These include the 3Cs approach, keywords and search engines, partnerships, and marketing to build Web site traffic.

The 3Cs Approach. Many B2C e-commerce businesses use the *3Cs approach* for capturing the interest of the online community: content, community, and commerce. The underlying assumption behind this approach is that people prefer Web

sites that offer free and useful information and services over those that offer only a sales pitch. A 3Cs Web site provides useful content to the public. For example, a Web site sponsored by a health food company might offer valuable suggestions for good health, references on medical research, and a calculator that allows visitors to calculate daily caloric needs. The Web site might be updated weekly to keep users coming back for more. As the Web site builds traffic, an online, health-minded community is formed. This community can be nurtured by providing a free membership option. Members provide you with information to receive e-mail news bulletins, and have access to other special members-only privileges. A bulletin board or chat utility that visitors can use to communicate could help foster a feeling of community. Finally, in addition to the content and community being provided, the sponsor can offer its visitors a catalog of products to assist them in meeting their health objectives. The General Nutrition Center Web site (www.gnc.com) in Figure 7.23 provides a good example of the 3Cs approach and other traffic-building tactics.

FIGURE 7.23 • **Building Web site traffic**

General Nutrition Center (GNC) uses smart strategies to build traffic to their Web site. It follows the 3Cs approach by offering content, community, and commerce to its visitors.

Keywords and Search Engines. People discover many Web sites through the use of search engines. There are steps that business owners can take to better ensure that their company's Web site appears in search results. To begin with, a business should choose its name and its product names in a manner that best describes its purpose and features. A hair salon with the name "Quality Hair Stylings" would be recognized by a search engine for what it is much more easily than one with the name "Haute Headz."

Second, a business should select a descriptive domain name; if possible, one that is the same or similar to the business name—www.qualityhairstylings.com. Domain names can be acquired from one of the accredited registrars listed at www.icann.org/registrars/ accredited-list.html.

Third, business-related keywords can be listed in the HTML code of a Web page in a meta tag. *Meta tags* are read by search engines and Web servers, but are not displayed on the page by a Web browser. Here is the meta tag from www.hersheys.com:

```
<META NAME="keywords" content="hershey chocolate kisses,
american candies samples, reese's peanut butter cup, chocolate
products, visit hershey, baking recipes, dessert recipes,
chocolate chip cookies, hershey foods corporation jobs, her-
shey's web sites, fundraising, hershey park, hershey's new
products, hershey coupons, hershey's sweet treats, chocolate
food snacks, milton snavely hershey, chocolate factory, cocoa
bean, gum &#38; mints, confectionery, fun kids games, hal-
loween, trick or treats, candy stores, chocolate gifts, hershey
syrup, chocolate world, investments, hershey souvenirs">
```

Some search engines rely on meta tags to define the important keywords on the Web page. Web page URLs are stored in the search engine database according to the terms listed in the meta tag. Searches run on keywords such as "halloween" or any of the other keywords listed in the hersheys.com meta tag would return the Hershey URL.

Most search engines use a combination of techniques and information, which include meta tags, to classify Web sites, as discussed in Chapter 4. To ensure that your site is listed in a search engine or directory, you can use a link at the site that allows you to submit your URL. For example, at Yahoo.com, there is a link at the bottom of the page for "How to Suggest a Site."

Partnerships. It pays to make friends. Online e-tailers who sell complementary products often form partnerships and advertise each other's Web sites. For example, Jeep teamed with Paramount Pictures in a marketing partnership during the run of Lara Croft: *Tomb Raider—The Cradle of Life*. The hero of the story drove a custom Jeep Wrangler Rubicon, so during the run of the movie, Jeep included movie promotions on its site, while Jeep promotions ran on the *Tomb Raider* site.

Marketing. If a business is unable to generate traffic to its Web site using free methods, such as search engines and partnerships, it will often invest in advertising. Marketing companies can be hired to advertise a Web site online using banner ads, pop-up ads, and e-mail. Search engines, such as Google, offer paid advertising services (described earlier) that make your Web site more likely to be noticed than the hundreds of other links that are displayed as the result of a search. Web sites are also advertised offline using traditional advertising media such as magazines and newspapers, radio, and television.

Electronic Payment Systems

In most e-commerce transactions, the customer pays with either a credit-card number (B2C) or a merchant account number (B2B). Using a secure encrypted connection, the buyer enters the account information in a Web form and submits it. The merchant's Web server passes the information along to the payment processing system, which checks the validity of the account number and balance in the account. If the credit-card checks out the transaction is processed (see Figure 7.24). The only difference between online credit-card processing and in-store processing is that laws require online retailers to wait until shipping the product to deduct funds from the credit card. Because of this, e-tailers will put a hold on the funds until the product is shipped, at which times the funds are transferred.

For individuals who do not have a credit card or do not wish to provide their credit-card information to merchants online, or in the case of C2C, where the

FIGURE 7.24 • **Online credit-card transaction**

Online vendors use payment processing systems to check credit and arrange for the transfer of funds.

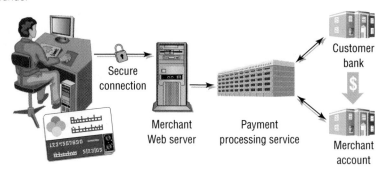

seller does not have the ability to process credit-card transactions, there is electronic cash. **Electronic cash** (**e-cash** or **digital cash**) is a Web Service that provides a private and secure method of transferring funds from a bank account or credit card to online vendors or individuals for e-commerce transactions. PayPal is the best-known e-cash provider. Owned by eBay, PayPal allows members (membership is free) to transfer funds into their PayPal account from a bank account or credit card (see Figure 7.25). The funds in your PayPal account are e-cash that you can use for purchases from on-line vendors or purchases made on eBay. You can also e-mail PayPal e-cash to individuals. For instance, say you're short of cash at a lunch outing with a friend. You can get your friend to pick up your tab and reimburse him through PayPal when you get back to your computer. Your friend receives an e-mail from PayPal in your name with instructions for how to transfer the cash into his bank account.

E-cash has two fundamental benefits. It provides:

- Privacy by hiding your account information from vendors—the e-cash provider is the only one who knows this information
- A method for e-commerce transactions in circumstances where the seller cannot process a credit card or the buyer does not own a credit card

FIGURE 7.25 • **E-cash**

E-cash systems such as PayPal allow users to purchase products online without providing the vendor with a credit-card number. You can also use e-cash to transfer funds between individuals.

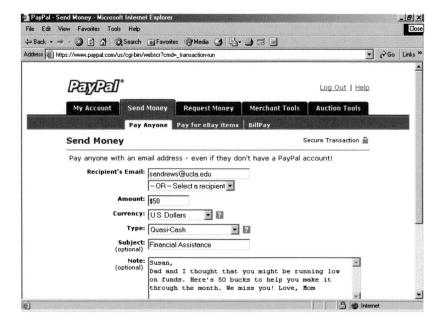

COMMUNITY TECHNOLOGY

Taxing E-commerce

Whether or not to tax Internet use and sales over the Internet has been a hotly debated issue since the first Web-based e-commerce transaction. There is currently a moratorium on taxing Internet access, and it is against the law for states to tax purchases made from out-of-state vendors. In other words, Internet sales are protected by the same laws that govern out-of-state catalog and phone sales, which are also tax-free.

States would love to have money generated by an Internet access tax. Prior to the moratorium, Wisconsin collected $55 million over 2 years in Internet access tax. Such funds would have done wonders for pulling states out of the economic hardships they faced during 2003.

Some feel that allowing tax-free sales over the Internet is unfair to local small businesses. Will customers forsake their neighborhood retailers and order online in order to escape state sales taxes? Representative William Delahunt, a Massachusetts Democrat thinks so: "By failing to ensure sales tax parity between remote sellers and Main Street merchants, we are putting at risk the thousands of small businesses that sustain our economy and contribute so much to our neighborhoods and communities".

Others counter that Internet sales make up only 1 percent of U.S. retail sales. As a new and growing re-source, e-commerce needs all the help it can get. Taxing the Internet and Internet sales would hinder the growth of a very promising area of our national economy.

The Internet tax issue becomes more complicated when you consider international sales. The European Union (EU) has recently authorized a tax on the sales of electronically delivered goods and services from non-EU countries to European customers. This value-added tax (VAT) is intended to "eliminate a long-standing competitive distortion by ensuring that both non-EU suppliers and EU suppliers are subject to the same rules." The tax does not affect B2B sales.

Questions

1. Do you think Internet sales should be taxed? Why or why not?
2. If you were the owner of a small local bookstore, what would you do to compete with Amazon.com?
3. Is the EU right to tax Internet sales from outsiders?

Sources
1. *"House subcommittee approves Internet tax moratorium,"* by Grant Gross, IDG News Service, *May 22, 2003,* www.idg.net/go.cgi?id=804822.
2. *"EU's online sales tax takes effect,"* Scarlet Pruitt, IDG News Service, *July 1, 2003,* www.nwfusion.com/news/2003/0701eusonlin.html.

In spite of these benefits, e-cash has a major drawback: Most large online vendors do not support it. It is primarily used for C2C transactions and with small businesses that cannot process credit cards.

Several software vendors have created electronic wallet applications to make online transactions more convenient. An *electronic wallet*, or *e-wallet*, is an application that encrypts and stores your credit-card information, e-cash information, bank account information, name, address—essentially, all the personal information required for e-commerce transactions—securely on your computer. The convenience provided by e-wallets is significant; rather than having to fill out forms with each online purchase, you simply click a button that withdraws the funds from your e-wallet. However, in the several years that e-wallet applications have been available, there has been no agreed-upon standard for the technology, so online merchants have been unwilling to support it.

Smartcards, credit cards with embedded microchips, are playing an increasing role in e-commerce payment methods. The Blue smartcard from American Express is used with a card reader connected to your PC to make secure e-commerce purchases. When making a purchase at a supporting merchant's Web site, a swipe of

the card sends a temporary transaction number, rather than your credit-card number, to the vendor for processing. The chip on the Blue card also works in conjunction with software provided by American Express and installed on your PC. The smartcard stores your Web and financial information, and the software allows you to access and manage it. Smartcards like the Blue card provide higher levels of security and privacy than traditional credit cards. Account information is only available to the card holder, and transactions can only be made with a card swipe. Customers can use the free USB reader provided by American Express, or purchase a special computer keyboard with an integrated card reader for use with the Blue card (see Figure 7.26). This method of making online purchases is much more secure than typing in a number, since users without physical possession of the card are unable to use it. With traditional credit cards, anyone with knowledge of the card number and expiration date can use it to make purchases online.

FIGURE 7.26 • A keyboard and smartcard reader
This keyboard and smartcard reader allows Web users to make online purchases with the swipe of a card.

MasterCard has teamed with Nokia to place smartcard technology in smart phones in a service they call PayPass.[15] A trial of the technology in Dallas allows participants to pay for products and services at several Dallas businesses by simply waving their cell phone over a reader at the checkout counter.

Companies such as Seimens, Mobileway[16], and Simpay[17] are designing ways to pay for m-commerce services over your cell phone. Simpay's system debits a cell phone user's account to pay for digital goods such as ringtones, MP3 music files, games, or parking meter payments.

International Markets

Taking a business online automatically turns your business into a global enterprise. Internet users of all nationalities will have access to your products and may wish to purchase them. Business owners need to determine if and how to market their products in the global market. Recent trends have indicated that business outside the United States can be lucrative. Amazon.com anticipates that its international sales will match its domestic sales by 2005.[18] Marketing in a global marketplace requires additional considerations.

The first consideration of a global e-commerce strategy is to make sure that visitors of all nationalities and cultures feel at home and comfortable while viewing your Web content. Although English is widely spoken and understood around the world, local references and colloquialisms may confuse and alienate international visitors.

A costly approach is to create multiple versions of your Web site, each in a different language and catering to a different cultural bias (see Figure 7.27). Lands' End, for example, has launched Web sites in the United Kingdom (www.landsend.co.uk), Japan (www.landsend.co.jp), Germany (www.landsend.de), France (fr.landsend.com), Ireland (www.landsend.ie), and Italy (www.landsend.it). This process, called *localization*, requires hiring international Web developers to assist with translation and cultural issues. Each time the Web site is updated, this may require editing all of the associated international Web sites.

FIGURE 7.27 • Localization

Some e-businesses create multiple versions of their Web site, each in a different language and catering to a different cultural bias.

Once an international market is courted and won over, the e-tailer must be able to carry out transactions in foreign currency, including pricing items accordingly, applying the correct national taxes (see the "Community Technology: Taxing E-commerce" box), and accommodating the possibly complex issues of international shipping. E-commerce hosting companies can assist with some of the transaction details. Shipping companies also assist e-businesses with the complications of international shipping. FedEx, for example, provides a free service called "FedEx Global Trade Manager."[19] The application helps shippers understand global trade regulations and prepare the appropriate import or export forms based on the commodity being shipped and the countries of origin and destination.

E-commerce Security Issues

Figure 7.28 displays a typical Web form used to submit bank account information to PayPal. Would you feel comfortable filling out and submitting this form? If you were to submit this form would it be possible for a hacker to intercept your account information on its way to PayPal? Are you certain that the Web server is really owned and protected by PayPal? How can PayPal tell that the account information you are providing is really yours? There are significant and legitimate concerns regarding e-commerce privacy and security. Security concerns arise from the dangers of carrying out electronic funds transfers over a public network without buyer and seller identity verification. In addition, e-businesses are vulnerable to hacker attacks that can put them temporarily or permanently out of business. We discuss identity verification, securing data, attacks and vulnerabilities, and business resumption planning next.

FIGURE 7.28 • Web form for submitting bank account information
Is it safe to provide your bank information using this form?

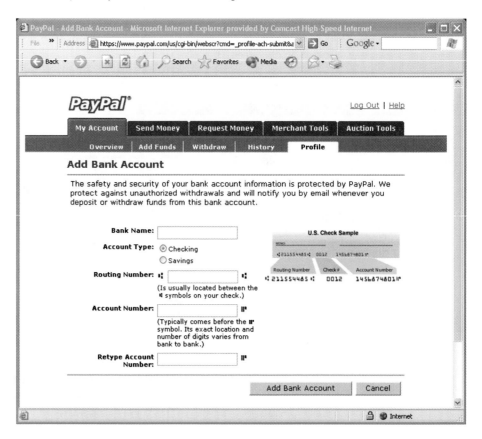

Identity Verification. Since e-commerce transactions occur electronically, and at times automatically, it is important that the identities of the two or more participants in a transaction are positively verified. Consumers need to make sure that they are giving their credit-card number to a legitimate and trustworthy business, and businesses need to confirm that the customer is the owner of the credit card being used. Transaction data must be accessed only by intended parties, and not be intercepted by outsiders. A variety of technologies are available to assist individuals and businesses in meeting these goals, including digital certificates and encryption.

A **Digital certificate** is a type of electronic business card that is attached to Internet transaction data to verify the sender of the data. Digital certificates are provided by *certification authorities* such as VeriSign (www.verisign.com) and Thawte (www.thawte.com). They can be used to verify the sender of e-mail and other forms of Internet communication. Digital certificates for use in encrypting Web communications and credit-card transactions cost the provider between $350 and $1,400, depending on the level of security and type of communications. Certificates cost more for e-commerce than for nonbusiness use. Digital certificates for personal e-mail are provided by Thawte for free.

A digital certificate contains the owner's name, a serial number, an expiration date, and a public key. The public key is used in encrypting messages and digital certificates. **Encryption** uses high-level mathematical functions and computer algorithms to encode data so that it is unintelligible to all but the intended recipient. Through the use of a public key, a large number, and a private key, kept by the certification authority, an encrypted message can be decrypted back into its original state.

Securing Data in Transit. Digital certificates combined with *Secure Sockets Layer (SSL)* technology allow for encrypted communications to occur between Web browser and Web server (see Figure 7.29). This combination of technology is what is used to secure usernames, passwords, and credit-card information when they are typed into a Web form and sent to a Web server. The presence of an SSL connection is usually indicated by a URL that uses "https://" rather than "http://"; also, a closed lock icon will appear in the browser window.

FIGURE 7.29 • Secure Sockets Layer (SSL)

SSL encrypts data sent over the Web and verifies the identity of the Web server.

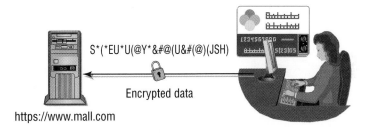

S*(*EU*U(@Y*&#@(U&#(@)(JSH)

Encrypted data

https://www.mall.com

Spoofing. Consumers need to be wary of spoofing scams. **Spoofing** is a technique used to impersonate others on the Internet. E-mail can be spoofed. For example, someone could send e-mail from his or her computer to another party and have it look as though it came from you—thus, the need for digital certificates.

Web sites can also be spoofed. The practice of creating commercial Web sites that look just like the real thing but are run by scam artists is known as *brand spoofing*. For example, users of PayPal have received e-mail spoofed to make it appear as though it came from PayPal. Recall that PayPal is a popular e-cash provider. The e-mail stated that due to a "recent system flush," the customer's billing and personal information was "temporarily unavailable" and asked that customers verify their identity by visiting www.paypal-billingnetwork.net. The e-mail was signed by "Jhon Krepp" from the "PayPal Billing Department." The referenced Web site was spoofed to look just like PayPal's regular Web site. Unwitting customers visited the Web site and filled out and submitted a form that included their credit-card and bank account numbers. The Web site was set up by

scam artists who escaped with the account information before the fraud was uncovered.[20] If the users who were taken in by this scam had noticed that the form they were about to submit was not protected with SSL—it said http and not https—they would have been tipped off that the Web site was not what it claimed to be. SSL connections verify the identity of the Web server.

Denial of Service Attacks. Denial of service attacks are a constant concern to businesses that rely on their Web sites to be up and running at all times. **Denial of service (DOS) attacks** use many computers to request Web pages from the same Web server at the same time. The server is unable to keep up with all the requests and is made unavailable to real customers wishing to do business. Hackers often enlist the help of zombie computers to launch such attacks. *Zombie computers* are computers on the Internet that are either hacked into or under the influence of a virus or worm, and are made to carry out Internet activities on the hacker's behalf—often unknown to the owner of the computer. The August 2003 worm called MSBlast is an example of a denial of service attack that used zombie computers. MSBlast was spread through an e-mail attachment that, when opened, distributed itself to everyone in the user's e-mail system. Once the worm was released into the user's computer, it was set to use the computer as a zombie to run a denial of service attack on the Windows Update Web site at midnight August 13. Microsoft, expecting hundreds of thousands of hits on its Web server, simply shut the server down and foiled the worm's plans. However, with the Windows update server shut down, Microsoft had to arrange other means to get a security patch to their users. All in all, the worm was very successful in disrupting e-mail and Web services.

Business Resumption Planning. Transaction processing systems, especially order processing systems, are so important to a business that great pains are taken to ensure that they stay up and running. Web businesses are particularly vulnerable since every minute that the Web site is out of commission could mean losses of thousands of dollars. *Business resumption planning (BRP)* takes into account every conceivable disaster that could negatively impact the system and provides courses of action to minimize their effects. Through the use of backup power systems, backup computer systems, and security software, BRP takes into account natural disasters such as flood, fire, and earthquake, and man-made disasters such as employee strikes and accidental or intentional sabotage. The goal of business resumption planning is to protect data and keep key systems operational until order is resumed.

Action Plan

1. What will it take to put the Forrero family business online?

The Forrero's need to make changes in infrastructure to support sales directly to consumers in addition to bulk sales to retailers. This will most likely require additional personnel. Alejandro can act as the director of e-commerce operations once he graduates and can implement needed changes in the manufacturing, storage, and shipment procedures.

The Forrero's can outsource the set up and maintenance of the Web site to an e-commerce hosting company at a cost of under $100 per month. They may need to contract with a graphic artist and Web designer to design a Web site that has a professional appearance. The Forreros may also wish to invest in advertisements for their new Web site.

2. What benefits might the Forrero family enjoy from an online presence? Do these benefits outweigh the costs?

By taking their business online, the Forreros' business will acquire greatly increased international exposure. Online sales will represent a new source of revenue for the business. These sales can be used to fund the Forreros' overall e-commerce investment. The Forreros' Web site will increase the Forrero brand-name recognition, improving sales in retail gift shops on which the business depends. Although these benefits seem significant, it will take time to build traffic to the Web site and reap the associated rewards. If the Forreros take it slowly, investing minimally at first, and reinvesting the revenues back into the system, an e-commerce venture should pay off.

3. Besides taking the business online what other ways might e-commerce assist the Forrero family business?

The Forreros can streamline transactions and save time and money by using the e-commerce systems of their suppliers, and implementing an e-commerce system with their retail buyers. Retailers will appreciate efforts to streamline the ordering process, giving Forrero an advantage over the competition.

Summary

LEARNING OBJECTIVE 1

Define e-commerce and understand its role as a transaction processing system.

E-commerce refers to systems that support electronically executed transactions over the Internet, Web, or a private network. Prior to the Internet, e-commerce took place using electronic data interchange (EDI), over private value-added networks (VANs). Today e-commerce takes place mostly over the Internet and Web. E-commerce is a form of transaction processing system. A transaction processing system (TPS) supports and records transactions and is at the heart of most businesses. All transaction processing systems share a common set of activities called the transaction processing cycle. This includes data collection, data editing, data correction, data manipulation, data storage, and document and report production. There are different TPSs for different needs. An order processing system supports the sales of goods or services to customers and arranges for shipment of products. A purchasing system supports the purchasing of goods and raw materials from suppliers for the manufacturing of products.

Figure 7.3—p. 294

LEARNING OBJECTIVE 2
Define the three types of e-commerce and mobile commerce, listing the benefits and challenges associated with each.

The three main types of e-commerce are business-to-consumer (B2C), business-to-business (B2B), and consumer-to-consumer (C2C). B2C, sometimes called e-tailing, involves retailers selling products to consumers. B2B services often take place privately between manufacturers and suppliers. C2C Web sites allow consumers to sell items and trade items with each other. Of these three types of e-commerce, B2B supports the greatest number of business transactions.

E-commerce supports the six stages of buying a product: (1) realizing a need, (2) researching a product, (3) selecting a vendor, (4) providing payment, (5) accepting delivery of the product, and (6) taking advantage of product support. It also supports the seller's efforts to support these stages. The seller's considerations are sometimes referred to as supply chain management. Supply chain management involves three areas of focus: demand planning, supply planning, and demand fulfillment.

Figure 7.8—p. 298

Mobile commerce, or m-commerce, is a form of e-commerce that takes place over wireless mobile devices such as smart phones. M-commerce uses a smart phone's Internet capabilities for commerce. Through text messaging, Web applications, and short-range wireless networking, smart phones can access m-commerce services. M-commerce developers use special protocols and languages such as the Wireless Application Protocol (WAP) and Wireless Markup Language (WML) to create m-commerce applications that can run on small handheld displays.

LEARNING OBJECTIVE 3
Discuss several examples of how e-commerce and mobile commerce are being used to provide services.

Retail Web sites allow consumers to comparison shop to find the best deals. Wholesale Web sites provide a way for suppliers to do business with manufacturers and retailers. Clearinghouses provide good deals to consumers on overstocked or outdated items and assist businesses in clearing their inventory. Web auctions sell merchandise to the highest bidders, and online marketplaces provide a method for consumers to sell their own possessions.

Manufacturers join together in global supply management services and industry-specific electronic exchanges to combine resources to connect with suppliers. E-commerce has made market research much easier and less intrusive, but somewhat worrisome to privacy advocates. E-commerce brings convenience to banking and investing by allowing people to monitor their finances and make investments online.

Figure 7.13—p. 305

The m-commerce application offering the most promise in the market is digital goods, such as ringtones, MP3 music, and games. Using cell phones for proximity payments, wirelessly transferring funds from a cell phone to a cash register, will require significant social changes.

LEARNING OBJECTIVE 4
List the components of an e-commerce system and explain how they function together to provide e-commerce services.

E-commerce requires investment in networking, hardware, and a wide variety of software. It requires changes in infrastructure and can include hiring of specialists such as system administrators, Web designers, and graphic artists. Many firms decide to outsource their e-commerce operations to e-commerce hosting businesses.

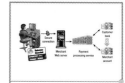

Figure 7.24—p. 322

Hardware and networking services for e-commerce must be robust and trustworthy so that service is never interrupted. Software required for e-commerce includes Web server software to deliver Web pages and services, Web server utilities to provide statistical information about Web traffic, e-commerce software to provide a merchandise catalogue, shopping cart, and checkout services, and the software used to design Web pages, graphics, and Web applications. Web Services use new technology, such as XML, to support distributed computing that allows applications to talk to each other over the Internet, automating many processes.

Businesses use a variety of techniques to build traffic to a Web site. Providing interesting content, building community, and providing commerce (the 3Cs) is one technique. Choosing appropriate names for a business, products, and domain helps search engines recognize a Web site for what it is. Keywords can be included in a Web page's meta tags, which are visible to search engines but not to people viewing the Web page. E-tailers can also profit from forming alliances with others on the Web and promoting each other's Web sites.

E-commerce electronic payment systems typically handle credit-card transactions. E-cash supports financial transactions over the Web without the need for credit cards; an electronic wallet stores transaction information in an encrypted file on your PC. Smartcards store financial information in a microprocessor embedded in a credit card. They provide a more secure and convenient method of carrying out e-commerce transactions.

E-commerce sites that participate in the global market must provide Web sites that cater to the needs of various cultures. Consumers and e-tailers should be aware of security issues associated with e-commerce, including identity verification and methods of securing transaction data transmitted over the Internet. Business resumption planning takes into account every conceivable disaster that could have a negative impact on the system and provides courses of action to minimize their effects.

Test Yourself

LEARNING OBJECTIVE 1: Define e-commerce and understand its role as a transaction processing system.

1. _____ refers to systems that support electronically executed transactions over the Internet, Web, or a private network.

2. Prior to the Internet, electronic transactions between businesses were often carried out using _____ over a value added network.
   a. order processing system
   b. electronic data interchange (EDI)
   c. business resumption planning
   d. source data automation

3. True or False: An airline's flight reservation system is likely to use the online method of transaction processing.

LEARNING OBJECTIVE 2: Define the three types of e-commerce and mobile commerce, listing the benefits and challenges associated with each.

4. _____, is a form of e-commerce that takes place over wireless mobile devices such as smart phones.

5. Individuals selling personal items to other individuals on eBay is an example of
   a. B2B
   b. C2C
   c. e-tail
   d. B2C

6. True or False: B2C consumes a larger segment of e-commerce transactions than B2B.

LEARNING OBJECTIVE 3: Discuss several examples of how e-commerce and mobile commerce are being used to provide services.

7. A(n)_____ is a Web site that allows visitors to browse through a wide variety of products from varying e-tailers.

8. An industry-specific Web resource created to provide a convenient centralized platform for B2B e-commerce between manufacturers, suppliers, and customers is called a(n):
   a. Web portal
   b. Web auction
   c. electronic exchange
   d. online marketplace

9. True or False: E-commerce supports a more detailed level of market segmentation than traditional market research.

LEARNING OBJECTIVE 4: List the components of an e-commerce system and explain how they function together to provide e-commerce services.

10. A(n) _____ is a company that takes on some or all of the responsibility of setting up and maintaining an e-commerce system for a business or organization.

11. _____ are programs that automate tasks by communicating with each other over the Web.
    a. Web Services
    b. Electronic exchanges
    c. Web-driven programs
    d. 3C programs

12. True or False: E-cash is most useful for C2C e-commerce.

Test Yourself Solutions: 1. E-commerce, 2. b., 3. T, 4. M-commerce, 5. b., 6. F, 7. cybermall, 8. c., 9. T, 10. e-commerce host, 11. a., 12. T

Key Terms

business-to-business
  e-commerce (B2B), p. 297
business-to-consumer
  e-commerce (B2C), p. 296
consumer-to-consumer
  e-commerce (C2C), p. 297
denial of service (DOS)
  attacks, p. 328

digital certificate, p. 327
e-commerce host, p. 315
electronic cash (e-cash,
  digital cash), p. 322
electronic commerce
  (e-commerce), p. 292
encryption, p. 327

mobile commerce
  (m-commerce), p. 301
smartcards, p. 323
spoofing, p. 327
Web Services, p. 319

Questions

Review Questions

1. What types of transactions benefit from batch processing?

2. What types of transactions benefit from online processing?

3. List the steps of the transaction processing cycle.

4. What takes place in the data editing stage of the transaction processing cycle?

5. What types of documents or displays might a TPS produce?

6. What is the difference between e-commerce and m-commerce?

7. Name the three types of e-commerce and provide examples of each.

8. What are the six stages of buying?

9. What are the three areas of supply chain management?

10. What device is closely associated with m-commerce? What next-generation features of this device are used in m-commerce?

11. List five methods of selling items on the Web.

12. What are the three methods of providing m-commerce services?

13. What is a problematic application of m-commerce?

14. What is the primary benefit of Web Services?

15. List the types of software associated with implementing e-commerce.

16. What is a primary hardware and network concern of an e-commerce vendor?

17. List four methods of building traffic to a Web site.

18. List two benefits of e-cash.

19. How can smartcards make shopping on the Web more secure?

20. What are the goals of business resumption planning?

Discussion Questions

21. Describe benefits that e-commerce provides for buyers and sellers.

22. Describe challenges that e-commerce faces.

23. List five types of e-commerce applications and provide examples of each.

24. What are the benefits of joining an electronic exchange for both suppliers and manufacturers?

25. What are the pros and cons of online marketing?

26. How can e-commerce affect the infrastructure of an organization?

27. What are the security risks for buyers who participate in e-commerce?

28. What are the security risks for sellers who participate in e-commerce?

Exercises

Try It Yourself

1. Write a proposal for a new e-commerce Web site to sell a product or service of your choosing.
   a. Select a business name that is creative and descriptive.
   b. Use www.enameco.com (or any of the accredited registrars at www.icann.org/registrars/accredited-list.html) to find an available domain name for your Web site that is logical and descriptive.
   c. Describe the product(s) you intend to sell and why you think that it will sell well on the Web.
   d. Describe the type of content (one of the 3Cs) that you will provide to visitors to keep them coming back to your Web site.
   e. Describe what tools you will make available to build community (another of the 3Cs).
   f. List other types of online businesses that sell complementary products and would make good partners for your business.
   g. List 12 keywords that you would want search engines to associate with your product Web site.

2. Surf the Web to find two Web sites (other than www.gnc.com) that follows the 3Cs approach to Web development. Use a word-processing program to describe what elements of each Web site contribute to content, community, and commerce. Provide your opinion on which Web site does a better job of making you want to visit again, and why.

3. Use a paint or graphics program to design a logo and Web page template for an imaginary e-commerce Web site. Include a Web site menu for navigation around the Web site.

4. Search the Web on the keyword: m-commerce. Write a description of an interesting m-commerce application you discover.

5. Consider an electronics device that you might like to purchase over the next year (for example, a smart phone, digital camera, MP3 player, and so on). Use www.mysimon.com to learn more about the product and determine your preferred vendor. Write a couple paragraphs explaining your logic for choosing the device and vendor. Include the features of the particular product that you found attractive, and why, out of all the vendors selling this product, you decided on the one you did.

6. Consider an electronics device that you might like to purchase over the next year (for example, a smart phone, digital camera, MP3 player, and so on). Use www.ubid.com and www.ebay.com to shop for the item. After finding a good deal, search for the same item (using manufacturer and product name along with model number) on the Web using a standard search engine or www.mysimon.com. Were you able to find the same item? If so, was the deal you found at eBay or uBid as good as you originally thought? Write a summary of your findings.

Virtual Classroom Activities

For the following exercises, do not use face-to-face or telephone communications with your group members. Use only Internet communications.

7. Each group member should select an object that he or she is interested in shopping for online. Be very specific in regard to the item's specifications (for example, a 3.2 megapixel digital camera, a pair of black leather moccasins with beads, and so on). Compile everyone's choices into a list and conduct a Web scavenger hunt. The person who finds the most items at the lowest total cost is the winner.

8. List the group members alphabetically and assign member numbers according to the ordering. Each group member should use www.paypal.com to e-mail the next group member $1. The last group member should e-mail the first group member. You'll need to set up a PayPal account and add funds to it from your checking account or credit card prior to sending the e-cash. After collecting each other's dollar, each group member should write a review of the PayPal service. You can delete your account information on Paypal after this experiment if you so desire.

Teamwork

9. Team members should each set out to find the best monthly price on e-commerce hosting. You can start by looking to www.cnet.com under Internet Services > E-commerce hosting. The service should include e-commerce software (for example, Miva), a merchant account, a payment gateway service, 500 MB of space, a 30 GB data transfer rate, 24-hour technical support, and data backup services.

10. Each team member should share a favorite online place to shop with the group. Compile a list of all Web sites and have all team members explore and rank the list of Web sites in order from best to worst. Each team member should create a document listing the Web sites in order of preference with a paragraph explaining what aspects of the favored Web site sold him or her on the site. Include comments on the 3Cs.

 # Learning Check

To check your knowledge of each of the chapter objectives, use this chart to find related end-of-chapter content.

	Learning Objective	Key Terms	Questions	Exercises
	Learning Objective 1 Define e-commerce and understand its role as a transaction processing system.	e-commerce	1, 2, 3, 4, 5	
	Learning Objective 2 Define the three types of e-commerce and mobile commerce, listing the benefits and challenges associated with each.	B2B, B2C, C2C, m-commerce	6, 7, 8, 9, 10, 21, 22	

	Learning Objective	Key Terms		Questions	Exercises
	Learning Objective 3 Discuss several examples of how e-commerce and mobile commerce are being used to provide services.			11, 12, 13, 14, 23, 24, 25	4, 5, 6, 7, 10
	Learning Objective 4 List the components of an e-commerce system and explain how they function together to provide e-commerce services.	denial of service (DOS) attacks, digital certificate, e-commerce host, electronic cash, encryption,	smartcards, spoofing, Web Services	15, 16, 17, 18, 19, 20, 26, 27, 28	1, 2, 3, 8, 9

Endnotes

1   Internet Software Consortium, "Internet Domain Survey Number of Internet Hosts," *www.isc.org/ds/host-count-history.html*, accessed October 16, 2003.

2   Lindberg, Bertil C., "The Growth of E-Commerce," *http://home.earthlink.net/~lindberg_b/GECGrwth.htm*, accessed December 9, 2003.

3   Ody, Penelope, "Wal-Mart hooks up to AS2 Web-based data exchange," *Retail Week*, March 7, 2003.

4   *www.openmobilealliance.org/*

5   "Farmyard Nurseries: specialist plant nursery sees business blossom on the Internet." A Case Study sponsored by eCommerce Innovation Centre (eCIC) *www.ecommerce.ac.uk* at Cardiff University. The study is available at *www.ecommerce.ac.uk/pdf/fnmaster.pdf*.

6   Juhnke, Art, "Still in the Picture," *CIO Web Business Magazine*, August 1, 1999, *www.cio.com/archive/webbusiness/080199_kodak.html*.

7   Chmielewski, Dawn, "Calif. town sold in auction on eBay for $1.7 million," *The Houston Chronicle*, December 28, 2002.

8   *www.covisint.com/about/alliances/*

9   Sullivan, Brian, "BT Pushing Online Customer Bill-Paying," *Computerworld*, June 17, 2002, *www.computerworld.com*.

10 *www.ameritrade.com/html/be_guarantee.html*, accessed July 18, 2003.

11 "Sprint and Sony Music Entertainment Announce Broad Strategic Partnership to Distribute Mobile Entertainment Content," June 30, 2003 news release from Sprint, *http://144.226.116.29/PR/CDA/PR_CDA_Press_Releases_Detail/0,3681,1111663,00.html*.

12 "Mobile spam on the rise," BBC News, July, 8 2002, *http://news.bbc.co.uk/1/hi/sci/tech/2116070.stm*.

13 "Case Study: The Springs Retreat," *http://mmv.vic.gov.au/Web/MMV/MMV.nsf/ImageLookup/Ecommerce/$file/18%20Springretreat.pdf*, accessed July 18, 2003.

14 "Izumiya: fastest, lowest-cost online grocery service in Japan," IBM E-commerce case study, *www-3.ibm.com/ software/success/cssdb.nsf/CS/NAVO-5ATNPQ?OpenDocument&Site=wsecom*, accessed July 18, 2003.

15 Leon, Mark, "Wallet in your cell phone? After a run in Orlando, the companies hold a trial of the PayPass system in the Lone Star State," *M-commerce Times*, May 14, 2003, *www.mcommercetimes.com/Services/334*.

16 "Siemens and Mobileway have launched an over-the-air micro payment service that lets wireless subscribers pay for Java downloads to their mobile phones as they go," *M-commerce Times*, May 12, 2003, *www.mcommercetimes.com/Solutions/332*.

17 "The group that aims to boost m-commerce by devising a standard for mobile phone payments has a new brand name," *M-commerce Times*, June 24, 2003, *www.mcommerce times.com/Industry/341*.

18 Wakabayashi, Daisuke, "Amazon Sees International Sales Catching U.S.," *Reuters*, July 1, 2003, *www.reuters.com/newsArticle.jhtml?type=internetNews&storyID=3017577&src=eDialog/GetContent*.

19 "Breakthrough on fedex.com Gives Businesses Power To Estimate Costs of Global Shipping," Business Wire, June 11, 2002.

20 Roberts, Paul, "The fake site is the latest of several 'brand spoofing' scams," IDG News Service, July 9, 2003, *www.computerworld.com/securitytopics/security/cybercrime/story/0,10801,82888,00.html?nas=EB-82888*.

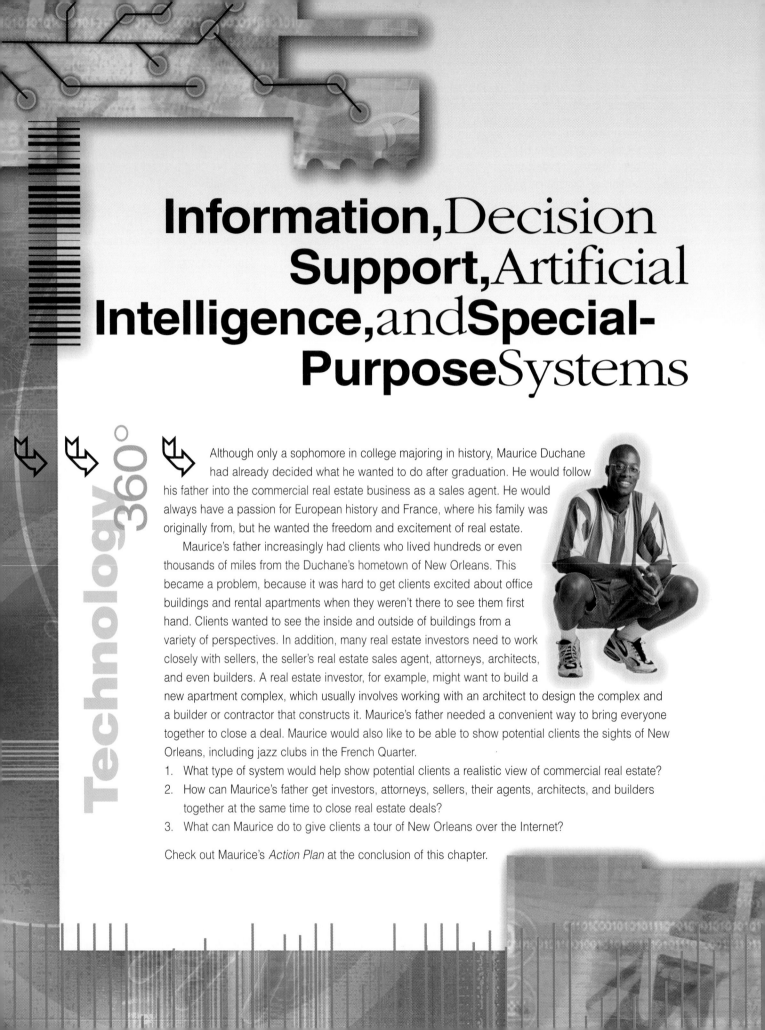

Information, Decision Support, Artificial Intelligence, and Special-Purpose Systems

Although only a sophomore in college majoring in history, Maurice Duchane had already decided what he wanted to do after graduation. He would follow his father into the commercial real estate business as a sales agent. He would always have a passion for European history and France, where his family was originally from, but he wanted the freedom and excitement of real estate.

Maurice's father increasingly had clients who lived hundreds or even thousands of miles from the Duchane's hometown of New Orleans. This became a problem, because it was hard to get clients excited about office buildings and rental apartments when they weren't there to see them first hand. Clients wanted to see the inside and outside of buildings from a variety of perspectives. In addition, many real estate investors need to work closely with sellers, the seller's real estate sales agent, attorneys, architects, and even builders. A real estate investor, for example, might want to build a new apartment complex, which usually involves working with an architect to design the complex and a builder or contractor that constructs it. Maurice's father needed a convenient way to bring everyone together to close a deal. Maurice would also like to be able to show potential clients the sights of New Orleans, including jazz clubs in the French Quarter.

1. What type of system would help show potential clients a realistic view of commercial real estate?
2. How can Maurice's father get investors, attorneys, sellers, their agents, architects, and builders together at the same time to close real estate deals?
3. What can Maurice do to give clients a tour of New Orleans over the Internet?

Check out Maurice's *Action Plan* at the conclusion of this chapter.

After completing Chapter 8, you will be able to:

LEARNING OBJECTIVES	CHAPTER CONTENT
1. Define the stages of decision making and problem solving.	**Decision Making and Problem Solving**
2. Discuss the use of management information systems in providing reports to help solve structured problems.	**Management Information Systems**
3. Describe how decision support systems are used to solve nonprogrammed and unstructured problems.	**Decision Support Systems**
4. Explain how a group decision support system can help people and organizations collaborate on team projects.	**The Group Decision Support System**
5. Discuss the uses of artificial intelligence and special-purpose systems.	**Artificial Intelligence and Special-Purpose Systems**

Introduction

Decisions lie at the heart of just about everything we do. You can't get through a day without making many decisions—some large, some small. In our careers, some decisions can have great significance and affect many other people. A doctor who makes the right diagnosis and prescribes the right treatment can improve lives and sometimes save them. The decisions made by scientists, engineers, and technicians at NASA have life and death consequences for astronauts. Management information and decision support systems can provide a wealth of information to help people make better decisions. Business executives, engineers, environmental specialists, military personnel, music producers, scientists, librarians, and people in most careers can benefit from getting better reports and decision support from computer systems.

Increasingly, people work in small teams. Meetings can be a big waste of time or a productive tool to accomplish organizational objectives. Group decision support systems can help people work effectively in groups, avoiding the pitfalls of negative group behavior, while taking advantage of working in teams. In addition, artificial intelligence and special-purpose systems can help individuals and organizations achieve their goals. Expert systems, for example, can be used to diagnose complex medical problems, saving lives in some cases. Knowing a little about what these systems can do and how they function can help you use them more effectively.

Although people can use computer systems to do tasks more efficiently and less expensively, the true potential of computer systems is providing information to help people and organizations make better decisions. In criminology, police and investigators use computer systems to help solve crimes, and in engineering, engineers use computer systems to design better electric circuits. In business, computer systems help sales representatives target customers with the greatest potential. In this chapter, we will explore how computer systems can provide a wealth of information and decision support to individuals and organizations, regardless of their field or career. To understand how computer systems can provide decision support, you first need a basic understanding of decision making and problem solving.

DECISIONMAKINGANDPROBLEMSOLVING

To be recognized by your friends and coworkers as a "real problem solver" is to be paid one of the highest compliments possible. In general, problem solving is the most critical activity an individual or organization undertakes (see Figure 8.1). But what is problem solving, and what does it involve? The process of problem solving begins with decision making. **Decision making** is a process that takes place in three stages: intelligence, design, and choice. Personal and professional decisions can typically be placed in one of these three stages as we shall see next.

FIGURE 8.1 • White House decision making and strategy session
Presidential decisions reflect not only the thoughts of one man, but often those of his advisors as well. As history shows us, presidential problem solving and decision making can have critical outcomes for the country.

The first stage in the decision-making process is the **intelligence stage**. During this stage, a person or group of people identify and define potential problems or opportunities. Information is gathered that relates to the cause and scope of the problem or opportunity. The problem or opportunity environment is investigated, and things that might constrain the solution are identified. For example, a food cooperative in Hawaii might want to ship tropical fruit to stores in Michigan. Exploring the shipping possibilities is done during the intelligence stage.

PRESCRIPTION FOR ACCURACY

When a pharmacist or nurse misreads a doctor's handwritten notes, the results can be both costly and deadly. To combat that, a New York insurance company is increasing reimbursements to hospitals willing to install an electronic prescription system designed to detect dosing errors and patient allergies to drugs. A study in Boston revealed that such a system resulted in a 55 percent reduction in prescription errors.

Source:
"Rx for Poor Penmanship at Hand for Doctors?"
By Seema Mehta, Times Staff Writer
The Los Angeles Times
www.latimes.com/technology/la-me-handwriting11aug11235417,1,4255311.story?
coll=la-headlines-technology
August 11, 2003
Cited on August 11, 2003

The perishability of the fruit and the maximum price consumers in Michigan are willing to pay for the fruit are constraints. Aspects of the environment that must be considered in this case include federal and state regulations regarding the shipment of food products.

In the **design stage**, alternative solutions to the problem are developed. In addition, the feasibility and implications of these alternatives are evaluated. In our tropical fruit example, the alternative methods of shipment, including the transportation times and costs associated with each, would be considered. During this stage, it might be determined that shipment by freighter to California and then by truck to Michigan is not feasible because the fruit would spoil in the time this method would take.

The last stage of the decision-making phase, the **choice stage**, requires selecting a course of action. In our tropical fruit example, the Hawaiian food cooperative might select the method of shipping by air to Michigan as its solution. The choice stage would conclude with the selection of the actual air carrier to do the shipping. As we will see later, a number of factors influence choice; the apparently easy act of choosing is not as simple as it might first appear. Bayer, the large drug company, explored whether or not to investigate a gene that might have an impact on asthma.[1] The company developed a software model—in essence, a decision support system—that shortened the analysis time by 6 months. In the end, Bayer decided to explore the gene as a possible cause of asthma. According to the head of the scientific development department of a competing company, "This is revolutionary. You can change genes with the stroke of a keypad. We've never had the tools like these, to look at the complexity of disease." Decision software like the software Bayer used can save companies months of work and millions of dollars by helping to select the right course of action.

Problem solving includes and goes beyond decision making. In Figure 8.2, you can see that the problem-solving process includes implementation and monitoring, in addition to all three phases of decision making.

In the **implementation stage** of the problem-solving process, action is taken to put the solution into effect. For example, if the Hawaiian food cooperative's decision is to ship the tropical fruit to Michigan as air freight using a specific air freight company, implementation involves informing the farming staff of the new activity, contracting with the air freight company, getting the fruit to the airport, and actually shipping the product to Michigan.

The final stage of the problem-solving process is called the **monitoring stage**. In this stage, the decision makers evaluate the implementation of the solution to determine whether the anticipated results were achieved and to modify the process in light of new information learned during the implementation stage. Notice that the monitoring stage involves a feedback and adjustment process. For example, after the first shipment of fruit, the Hawaiian food cooperative might learn that the chosen air freight firm routinely makes a stopover in Portland, Oregon, where the

FIGURE 8.2 • The problem-solving process

The three phases of decision making—intelligence, design, and choice—combine with implementation and monitoring to result in problem solving.

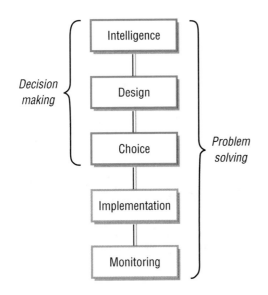

plane sits exposed on the runway for a number of hours while loading additional cargo. If this unforeseen exposure to temperature and humidity adversely affects the fruit, the food cooperative might have to readjust its solution to select a new air freight firm that does not make such a stopover, or perhaps it would consider a change in fruit packaging.

Individuals and organizations can use a reactive or proactive approach to problem solving. With a reactive problem-solving approach, the problem solver waits until a problem surfaces or becomes apparent before any action is taken. The Hawaiian fruit cooperative, for example might wait until a problem with rotting fruit occurs before taking any action. With a proactive problem-solving approach, the problem solver seeks out potential problems before they become serious. For example, an FBI agent could predict a future terrorist attack using credible intelligence information, which could save thousands of lives and millions or even billions of dollars in damage. Both reactive and proactive problem solvers can turn problems into opportunities, but taking a proactive approach means you can identify opportunities earlier and exploit them faster. In reality, most organizations and individuals use a combination of reactive and proactive problem-solving approaches.

Programmed versus Nonprogrammed Decisions

In the choice stage, a number of factors influence the decision maker's selection of a solution. One factor is whether or not the decision can be programmed. **Programmed decisions** are ones that are made using a rule, procedure, or quantitative method. Programmed decisions are easy to automate using traditional computer systems (see Figure 8.3). It is simple, for example, for a music store to program a computer to order more CDs of a popular artist when inventory levels fall to 10 units or less. *Management information systems* are often used to support programmed deci-

FIGURE 8.3 • Programmed and nonprogrammed decisions

Inventory control decisions, illustrated in the screen on the left, are typically programmed decisions. In contrast, some medical decisions are nonprogrammed decisions, as illustrated by the screen on the right.

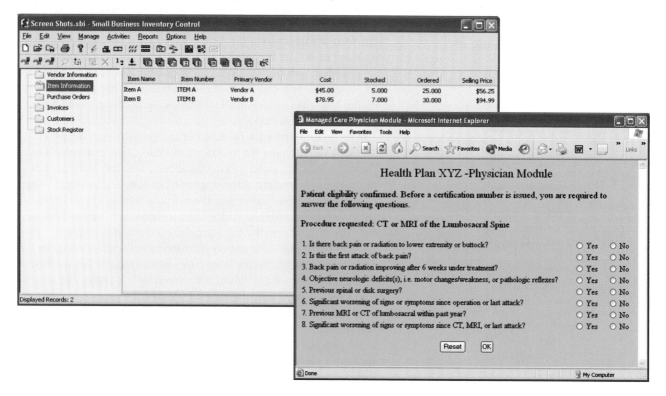

JOB TECHNOLOGY

Continental Airlines Uses an Optimization Program to Slash Costs

Schedule disruptions and delays are not uncommon in the airline industry. Unexpected events, bad weather, mechanical problems, and crew availability are all causes of flight delays. Before September 11, 2001, 15 to 20 percent of all domestic flights were delayed by more than 15 minutes. This number dramatically increased after September 11, until the percent of delayed flights increased to about 27 percent, inconveniencing about 160 million passengers. These delays are costly for the airlines and the people flying.

Using a computer optimization program, Continental Airlines has been able to develop better schedules for its flight crews. The program, called CrewSolver, minimizes total costs, while satisfying flight requirements. Continental estimates that the system will save the airline about $40 million annually. The

U.S. Department of Transportation ranked Continental as first in on-time performance for a 12-month period ending in August 2002.

Questions

1. What is an optimization DSS? How can it save an organization money?
2. Describe the objective and the constraints CrewSolver might have used.
3. What other industries or fields might be able to benefit from optimization?

Sources
1. *"A New Era for Crew Recovery,"* by Gang Yu, et al., Interfaces, *January 2003, p. 5.*
2. *"Right On Queue,"* Derek Atkins, et al., OR/MS Today, *April 2003, p. 26.*

---

sions by providing reports on problems that are routine and where the relationships are well defined; these types of problems are called *structured problems*.

Nonprogrammed decisions, however, deal with unusual or exceptional situations. In many cases, these decisions are difficult to represent as a rule, procedure, or quantitative method (see Figure 8.3). Determining what research projects a genetics company should fund and pursue is an example of a nonprogrammed decision. Determining the appropriate training program for a new employee, deciding whether to buy a townhouse or rent an apartment, and weighing the benefits and disadvantages of various diets for cancer patients are additional examples of nonprogrammed decisions. Each of these decisions contains many unique characteristics for which the application of rules or procedures is not so obvious. Today, *decision support systems* and *expert systems* are being used to solve a variety of nonprogrammed decisions, where the problem is not routine and rules and relationships are not well defined. These are called *unstructured problems*.

Optimization and Heuristic Approaches

Optimization and heuristic approaches are popular problem-solving methods used in decision support systems. An **optimization model** will find the best solution, usually the one that will best help individuals or organizations meet their goals. For example, an optimization model can find the best way to schedule nurses at a hospital or the appropriate number of products an organization should produce to meet a profit goal, given certain conditions and assumptions. Optimization models utilize problem constraints. A limit on the number of available work hours in a manufacturing facility is an example of a problem constraint. Schindler, the world's largest escalator company, used an optimization technique

to plan maintenance programs.[2] One important decision that Schindler and many other companies face is how much preventative maintenance to perform. Good preventative maintenance can save a company from making emergency repairs, which involves sending maintenance teams and equipment to office buildings and retail stores. However, too much preventative maintenance is a waste of money. Using a quantitative optimization program, software that runs calculations to find the best solution (see Figure 8.4), Schindler was able to save about $1 million annually in total maintenance costs.

FIGURE 8.4 • Optimization as an approach to problem solving

Using a quantitative optimization program, such as Excel Solver, can save organizations time and money.

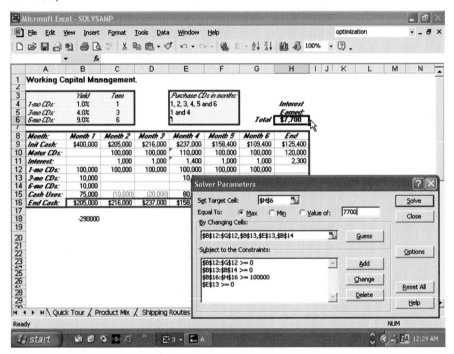

Heuristics, often referred to as "rules of thumb"—commonly accepted guidelines or procedures that usually find a good solution, but usually not the optimal solution—are very often used in the decision-making process. An example of a heuristic rule in the military is to "get there first with the most firepower." A heuristic procedure used by baseball team managers is to place those batters most likely to get on base at the top of the lineup, followed by the "power hitters," who'll drive them in to score. An example of a heuristic used in business is to order four months' supply of inventory for a particular item when the inventory level drops to 20 units or less. Even though this heuristic may not minimize total inventory costs, it may be a very good rule of thumb that produces advantageous results by avoiding stockouts without too much excess inventory. Trend Micro, a provider of antivirus software, has developed an antispam product that is based on heuristics.[3] The heuristic has a 90 to 95 percent success rate in blocking spam.

NEW KINGPIN TO CUSTOMER SERVICE

Faster service equals happier customers, and Wi-Fi systems are giving some businesses a profitable edge. Restaurants are using it to transmit orders to the kitchen. At a national department store, sales staff can track down any garment at any branch, and some grocery stores have equipped their shopping carts with a wireless system so shoppers can order items from service counters in advance. Casinos are also using Wi-Fi to verify winnings and speed hotel checkin.

Source:
"Wi-Fi Moves from Storeroom to Store"
By Roy Furchgott
The New York Times
www.nytimes.com/2003/08/25/technology/25WIFI.html
August 25, 2003
Cited on August 25, 2003

MANAGEMENTINFORMATIONSYSTEMS

In the preceding section, we noted that **management information systems (MISs)** are often used to support programmed decisions made in response to structured problems. The primary purpose of an MIS is to help individuals and organizations achieve their goals by providing reports and information to make better decisions. Individuals, for example, might want to get reports from their doctor on the results of a routine physical exam. A swimming coach at a university might want a report showing all swimmers who have grades below a certain GPA. Filtering and analyzing highly detailed data can produce these reports.

Inputs to a Management Information System

Data entering the MIS can be considered to originate from either internal or external sources. The most significant internal source of data for the MIS is the TPS. External sources include other organizations, governmental agencies, foreign countries, and outside individuals. New federal regulations from the IRS on how public and private organizations report their activities is an example of an external source of information.

One of the major activities of the TPS is to capture and store the data resulting from ongoing transactions. With every transaction, various TPS applications make changes to and update the organization's files and databases. Databases also supply the data needed for the MIS. A database containing research results on new drugs, for example, can be used by a pharmaceutical company to produce a variety of reports about which drugs seem to be working as expected. Outputs of a MIS—various reports—are discussed next.

Outputs of a Management Information System

The output of most management information systems is a collection of reports. These reports provide a structure to unorganized data (see Figure 8.5) and include scheduled reports, demand reports, and exception reports.

Scheduled Reports. **Scheduled reports** are produced periodically or on a schedule, such as daily, weekly, or monthly. An investor can receive monthly statements summarizing the performance of her stock and bond holdings (see Figure 8.6). The scheduled report can show the current month's market value and the previous month's market value to show the investor the performance for the month. A university student receives a report at the end of each semester or quarter summarizing his or her grades. A production manager could monitor and control labor and job costs by using a weekly summary report that lists total payroll costs. Xcel Energy has developed an online reporting system for its customers in Colorado to help them control their electricity bills.[4] The program, called InfoSmart, allows customers to analyze their energy use. "This is one instance where knowledge truly does equal power," says Debbie Mukherjee, product portfolio manager at Xcel. The

FIGURE 8.5 • MIS provide structure to information

Management information systems provide reports and information to help people make better decisions. Without the structure provided by an MIS, people working in organizations could drown in a sea of paper.

FIGURE 8.6 • **Scheduled reports**

A scheduled report can summarize stock and bond positions every month.

MONTHLY PORTFOLIO PERFORMANCE

Name	Symbol	Quote	Shares	Current market value	Previous market value
Fiserve Inc.	FISV	$28.86	8	$230.88	$245.21
The Sports Authority	TSA	$25.23	11	$277.53	$251.55
Oracle	ORCL	$12.19	15	$182.85	$176.20
Total				$691.26	$685.55

FIGURE 8.7 • **Inventory demand report**

An executive might look at this Inventory Demand Report to learn the inventory level for green Trek Antelope 800 bicycles with a 20-inch frame.

INVENTORY DEMAND REPORT

Model	Size	Color	Quantity in stock
Antelope 800	20 inch frame	Green	4

FIGURE 8.8 • **Exception report**

This exception report from a medical lab shows only blood test results that are out of range.

EXCEPTION REPORT

Facility: Dallas Primary Care
Physician: Welch
Patient: Ben Bechtold

Test Name	Units	Results	Range	Flag (H–high; L–low)
Sodium	mEq/L	133	(135–146)	L
Cholesterol	mg/dL	265	(140–200)	H

scheduled reports allow customers to determine the energy efficiency of their homes and major appliances. It also shows them how their energy use compares to other homes in their area.

A *key-indicator report*, a special type of scheduled report, summarizes the previous day's critical activities, and is typically available at the beginning of each workday. The President of the United States, for example, receives daily reports in the morning on national security, terrorism, the economy, and many other areas. Key-indicator reports can summarize inventory levels, production activity, sales volume, and the like. Key-indicator reports allow people to take quick, corrective action when it is most needed.

Demand Reports. **Demand reports** are developed to give certain information at a person's request. In other words, these reports are produced on demand. An executive, for example, may want to know the inventory level for a particular item, such as the number of Antelope 800 Trek bicycles with a 20-inch frame that are in stock (see Figure 8.7). A demand report can be generated to give the requested information. You can get a statement of your credit from one of the credit bureaus on demand. Kodak is using a management information system to send important sales information to its sales reps.[5] According to James Sanford, senior manager of sales communication and strategy, "Like a lot of companies, Kodak was good at collecting data but not very good at sharing and updating that data." The MIS allows sales reps to get demand reports on new products, pricing and special promotions, and customers. The demand reports can be critical to closing sales and making deals. Finding the right classes and professors can be critical for college students. Today, students can get demand reports on both.[6] Students in Idaho and other states, for example, can go to the Rate-MyProfessor Internet site to get ratings of faculty members. Other examples of demand reports include reports requested by executives to show the hours worked by a particular employee, total sales for a product for the year, and so on.

Exception Reports. **Exception reports** are reports that are automatically produced when a situation is unusual or requires action. For example, a patient will get an exception report from a clinic only if a blood test shows a possible problem (see Figure 8.8). A manager might set a parameter that generates a report of all inventory items with fewer than 50 units on hand. The exception report generated by this parameter would contain only those items with fewer than 50 units in inventory. Comerica, a Detroit-based bank, uses exception reports to get a list of customer inquiries that have been open for a period of time without some progress or closure.[7] According to the senior vice president of the company, "We'll be able to see who's doing real well, and reward those folks. And we'll be able to see who's not engaged yet, and help them." As with key-indicator reports, exception reports are most often used to monitor aspects critical to an organization's success. In general, when an exception report is produced, an appropriate individual or executive takes action.

Determining parameters, or trigger points, for an exception report should be done carefully. Trigger points that are set too low may result in an abundance of exception reports; trigger points that are too high could mean problems that need action are overlooked. For example, if the mayor of a large city wants a report that contains all city construction projects over their budget by $100 or more, he may find that almost every project exceeds its budget by at least this amount. The $100 trigger point is probably too low. A trigger point of $5,000 might be more appropriate.

DECISIONSUPPORTSYSTEMS

A **decision support system (DSS)** is an organized collection of people, procedures, software, databases, and devices used to support problem-specific decision making. The focus of a DSS is on decision-making effectiveness when faced with unstructured or semistructured problems. For a TV producer, it could be better ratings through a more comprehensive analysis of viewer desires. For a business, it could mean higher profits, lower costs, and better products and services.

Overall, a decision support system should assist people and organizations with all aspects of decision making. Moreover, the DSS approach realizes that people, not machines, make decisions. DSS technology is used primarily to support making decisions that can solve problems and help achieve individual and organizational goals. For example, in addition to being trained to diagnose disease, today's healthcare providers also have to be trained in how to handle a terrorist attack. The U.S. Department of Human and Health Services (HHS) has developed a decision support system, called ePocrates (see Figure 8.9), to send alerts to doctors and other medical providers in the event of a bioterrorist event.[8] The DSS can tailor information sent to different types of doctors in different locations. In other situations, DSS are even used to monitor, detect, and correct problems with computer systems.[9]

FIGURE 8.9 • Doctor using ePocrates on a handheld device

Products like ePocrates offer doctors instant access to medical information and aid in the treatment and diagnosis of patients.

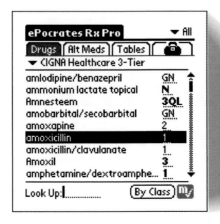

Characteristics of a Decision Support System

Decision support systems have a number of characteristics.

Handle a Range of Data. Decision support systems can handle a range of data from small amounts to large amounts. For instance, advanced database management systems have allowed people to search databases of any size for information when using a DSS. A DSS is also flexible enough to solve problems where only a small amount of data is required.

Obtain and Process Data from Different Sources. Some data sources may reside in databases on personal computers; others could be located on different mainframe systems or networks. DSSs have the capability to access data external to the organization and integrate this data with internal data.

Provide Report and Presentation Flexibility. One of the reasons that DSSs were developed was that TPS and MIS were not flexible enough to meet the full variety of decision makers' problem or information needs. Whereas other information systems produce primarily fixed-format reports, DSSs have more widely varied formats. People can get the information they want, presented in a format that suits their needs. Furthermore, output can be presented on computer screens or produced on printers, depending on the needs and desires of the problem solvers. One diabetes Web site, for example, developed a DSS to provide customized treatment plans and reports (see Figure 8.10).[10]

FIGURE 8.10 • Diabetes Assistant DSS
This diabetes Web site developed a DSS to provide customized treatment plans and reports to patients.

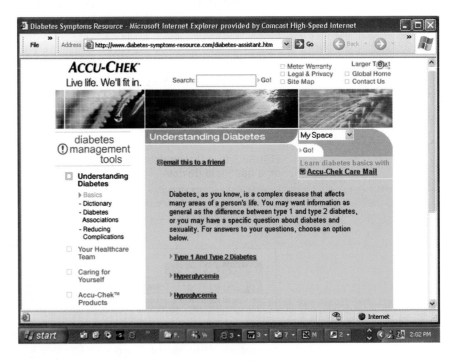

Have Both Textual and Graphical Orientation. A decision support system can provide whatever orientation a person prefers, be it textual or graphical. Some pre-

COMPUTER HEAL THYSELF

The desire to help businesses cut the expenses involved in computer ownership is driving a special branch of research at both IBM and Hewlett-Packard: self-repairing computers. The research is working toward systems that can self-regulate—repair themselves, adjust to flows in demand, fend off hacker attacks, and diagnose their own problems—in the same manner that the human nervous system can self-regulate.

Source:
"Self-Repairing Computers: Striving for dependability"
By Armando Fox and David Patterson
Scientific American
www.scientificamerican.com/article.cfm?articleID=
000860F3-E14D-1EB7-BDC0809EC588EEDF&catID=9
May 12, 2003
Cited on September 8, 2003

fer a straight text interface, but others may want a decision support system that helps them make attractive, informative graphical presentations on computer screens and in printed documents. Today's decision support systems can produce text, tables, line drawings, pie charts, trend lines, and more. By using their preferred orientation, people can both use a DSS to get a better understanding of a situation, if required, and to convey this understanding to others.

Perform Complex Analyses and Comparisons. DSSs can perform complex, sophisticated analysis and comparisons using advanced software packages Marketing research surveys, for example, can be analyzed in a variety of ways using analysis programs that are part of a DSS. Many of the analytical programs associated with a DSS are actually stand-alone programs. The DSS provides a means of bringing these together. As futures and options trading is becoming totally electronic, many trading firms are using DSS software to perform sophisticated analysis and make substantial profits for traders and investors.[11] Some DSS trading software is programmed to place "buy" and "sell" orders automatically without a trader manually entering a trade, based on parameters set by the trader.

Support Optimization and Heuristic Approaches. For smaller problems, decision support systems have the capability to find the best (optimal) solution. For more complex problems, heuristics are used. With heuristics, the computer system can determine a very good, but not necessarily the optimal-solution. The state of California, for example, ordered 19 drug companies to distribute about $150 million of scarce drugs to about 150 California hospitals and clinics as a result of the settlement of a drug case.[12] A DSS heuristic was developed to distribute about 90 percent of the drugs required by the court decision. This heuristic approach was able to distribute more than 125 different drugs in 20 drug categories as required by law. By supporting all types of decision-making approaches, a DSS gives the decision maker a great deal of flexibility in getting computer support for decision-making activities.

Perform What-if and Goal-seeking Analysis. **What-if analysis** is the process of making hypothetical changes to problem data and observing the impact on the results. Consider an emergency disaster plan. What-if analysis could determine the consequences of a hurricane slamming into New Orleans with heavy flooding or the consequences of the hurricane hitting the Mississippi coast instead. With what-if analysis, a person can make changes to problem data—such as changing where the hurricane hits—and immediately see the impact on the results—the difference in the damage done and the lives lost (see Figure 8.11). **Goal-seeking analysis** is the process of determining what problem data is required for a given result. For example, suppose a financial manager has a goal to earn a return of 9 percent on any investment, and she is considering an investment with a certain monthly net income. Goal seeking allows the manager to determine what monthly net income (problem data) is needed to have a return of 9 percent (problem result).

FIGURE 8.11 • **The value of what-if analysis**
What-if analysis could determine the consequences of a hurricane slamming into New Orleans with heavy flooding or the consequences of the hurricane hitting the Mississippi coast instead.

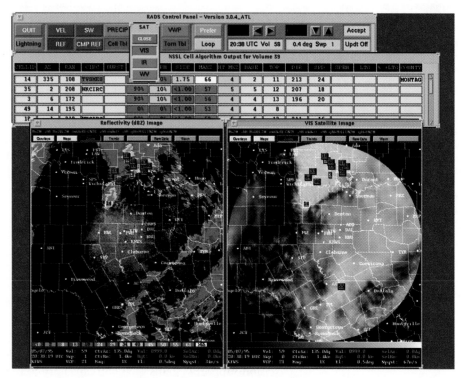

Simulation. With simulation, the DSS attempts to mimic an event that could happen in the future. Simulation uses chance, or probability. For example, there is a certain chance, or probability, that it will rain tomorrow or during the next several months. Sometimes, a problem is so complex that a normal decision support system is just too difficult to develop. One popular alternative is to develop a computer simulation that allows people to analyze various possibilities and scenarios.[13] Corporate executives and military commanders often use computer simulations to allow them to try different strategies in different situations. Corporate executives, for example, can try different marketing decisions in various market conditions. Military commanders often use computer war games to fine-tune their military strategies in different war conditions. Weather forecasters can use a DSS simulation to forecast the chance of a drought, a hurricane, or flooding in certain regions. The Federal Reserve Bank uses simulation to help it organize and structure work teams.[14]

Of course, not all DSSs work the same or have all of these characteristics, which are summarized in Table 8.1. Some are small in scope and only take advantage of some of the characteristics. For example, the Louisiana State University AgCenter, developed a DSS based on an Excel spreadsheet to help farmers decide what to plant to maximize their revenues.[15] Other small-scale DSSs can provide patients and their families with important medical records and reports, which can be critical to patient involvement and recovery from disease.[16] Geisinger Health Systems, for example, is providing patients and their family members access to important health records and reports through the Internet. "Not only did it help with my dad, it gave me peace of mind," says the daughter of one patient.

TABLE 8.1 • **Characteristics of Decision Support Systems**

DSS Characteristics	
Large amounts of data	Perform sophisticated analysis
Different data sources	Graphical orientation
Report and presentation flexibility	Optimization and heuristic approach
Geared toward individual decision-making styles	What-if? and goal-seeking analysis
Modular format	Simulation

THE GROUP DECISION SUPPORT SYSTEM

The DSS approach has resulted in better decision making for all kinds of individual users. However, many DSS approaches and techniques are not suitable for a group decision-making environment. Although not all people are involved in committee meetings and group decision-making sessions, some people can spend more than half of their decision-making time in a group setting. Such people need effective approaches to assist with group decision making. A **group decision support system (GDSS)**, also called a *computerized collaborative work system*, consists of the hardware, software, people, databases, and procedures needed to provide effective support in group decision-making settings (see Figure 8.12). A group of petroleum engineers located around the world, for example, might be collaborating on a new refinery. A GDSS can be used to help the engineers design the new refinery by providing a means to communicate with each other and share design ideas. Mathcard Enterprise is a GDSS for engineers.[17] The software allows engineers to create, share, and reuse calculations.

FIGURE 8.12 • **Group decision support system**

High-tech rooms like the one shown here create a group dynamic that allows people to come together to explore solutions to complex problems.

Characteristics of a GDSS

A GDSS has a number of unique characteristics that go beyond the traditional DSS. These systems try to build on the advantages of individual support systems, while responding to the fact that new and additional approaches are needed in a group decision-making environment. Some GDSSs have the ability to allow the exchange of information and expertise among people without meetings or direct face-to-face interaction. Here are some characteristics of a typical GDSS.

Special Design. The GDSS approach acknowledges that special procedures, devices, and approaches are needed in group decision-making settings. These procedures must foster creative thinking, effective communication, and good group decision-making techniques. Today, a number of specialized software packages can be used to support all aspects of group decision making. Often called *groupware*, these packages allow two or more individuals in a group to effectively work together.[18] These packages were first introduced in Chapter 3.

Ease of Use. Like an individual DSS, a GDSS must be easy to learn and use. People will seldom use systems that are complex and hard to operate. Many groups have less tolerance than individual decision makers for poorly developed systems.

Flexibility. Two or more decision makers working on the same problem may have different decision-making styles and preferences. Each person makes decisions in a unique way, in part due to different experiences and styles of thinking. An effective GDSS must not only support the different approaches that people use to make decisions, but also find a means to integrate their different perspectives into a common view of the task at hand.

Anonymous Input. Many GDSSs allow anonymous input, where the person giving the input is not known to other group members. This allows the group decision makers to concentrate on the merits of the input without considering who gave it. In a business setting, input given by a top-level manager is given the same consideration as input from employees or other members of the group. Some studies have shown that groups using anonymous input can make better decisions and produce superior results compared to groups that do not use anonymous input.

Reduction of Negative Group Behavior. One key characteristic of any GDSS is the ability to suppress or eliminate group behavior that is counterproductive or harmful to effective decision making. In some group settings, dominant individuals can take over the discussion, which can prevent other members of the group from presenting creative alternatives. In other cases, one or two group members can sidetrack or subvert the group into areas that are nonproductive and do not help solve the problem at hand. Other times, a group may assume that they have made the right decision without examining alternatives—a phenomenon called *groupthink*. If group sessions are poorly planned and executed, the result can be a tremendous amount of wasted time. Today, many GDSS designers are developing software and hardware systems that will reduce these types of problems. Procedures for effectively planning and managing group meetings can be incorporated into the GDSS approach.

Support of Positive Group Behavior. A number of positive, highly effective group decision-making approaches have resulted in superior overall decision making. GDSS designers are now incorporating many of these approaches into specific hardware and software packages.

JOB ∿ TECHNOLOGY

Using a Group Decision Support System to Harness the Knowledge of Shearman & Sterling

The global law firm Shearman & Sterling has a reputation for successfully managing big business transactions. The firm represented Viacom in its $36 billion acquisition of CBS, the largest broadcast deal in history. It also facilitated the $189 billion merger of SmithKline Beecham and Glaxo Wellcome, creating the world's largest pharmaceutical company. The firm's portfolio includes more than the depth of big clients; it also contains considerable breadth, with more than 1,000 lawyers located in all of the world's financial capitals—making it one of the few truly global law firms.

In designing its information system, the firm strove to save its lawyers from wasting time "reinventing the wheel" for each new case they handle. Recognizing the value of its collective brainpower, Shearman & Sterling developed a group decision support system to allow its lawyers to work together on cases. The GDSS assisted teams of lawyers in capturing, cataloging, and indexing its rapidly accumulating pool of information. Today, its lawyers are able to search through thousands of case histories on their company notebook computers from anywhere in the world in a fraction of the time that it once took to comb through a law library.

In addition, Shearman & Sterling provides its lawyers with a number of decision support tools. Over the years, the firm has built a powerful system of collaborative work spaces using Lotus Notes, Lotus Domino, Lotus Sametime, and Lotus QuickPlace, enabling its attorneys to share documents and other information on client cases. Legal teams can share schedules, depositions, witness lists, and related cases using this groupware. They can also use their notebook computers for virtual group meetings to brainstorm over the case at hand. A lawyer in need of advice can consult with other firm members online or can seek out and consult with a specialist in a particular legal area.

Shearman & Sterling have proved that even in the most traditional and time-honored professions, computer systems can assist people in being more productive.

Questions

1. How can a group decision support system assist people in other professions with their decision making?
2. What challenges does Shearman & Sterling face in its attempt to catalog and index the knowledge of its lawyers?

Sources
1. *"Shearman & Sterling shares knowledge to think big and think fast," IBM Software Success Stories Web site, www3.ibm.com; accessed May 1, 2002.*
2. *"Lotus ties Notes, Domino to Java for Web services," Jennifer Disabatino, Computerworld, May 1, 2002, www.computerworld.com.*
3. *Shearman & Sterling Web site, www.shearmanand sterling.com, accessed May 1, 2002.*

The *Delphi approach* is used when group decision makers are geographically dispersed throughout the country or the world. This approach encourages diversity among group members and fosters creativity and original thinking in decision making. Another approach, called *brainstorming*, which often consists of members offering ideas "off the top of their heads," fosters creativity and free thinking. The *group consensus approach* forces the group to reach a unanimous decision. With the *nominal group technique (NGT)* each decision maker can participate. This technique encourages feedback from individual group members. The final NGT decision is made by a voting approach similar to the one used to elect public officials.

GDSS Software or Groupware

GDSS software offers many useful tools for group work. For example, compound documents that can include information from spreadsheet programs, database packages, word processors, and other applications can be created, used, and shared by the group. Compound documents can even include multimedia data, such as audio and video clips. Compound documents are stored in a single file, while traditional documents require separate files for each different application (say, one for word processing, one for graphics, and so on.) Many groupware programs also allow compound documents to include applications from different software companies.

GDSS software, often called **groupware**, helps with joint work group scheduling, communication, and management. One popular groupware package, Lotus Notes, can capture, store, manipulate, and distribute memos and communications that are developed during group projects. By using groupware, all group members can share information to accomplish joint work, even when group members are located around the globe. An accounting firm, for example, can use groupware to coordinate group work and consulting. Groupware can be used to post thousands of notes on bulletin boards on a variety of subjects. The same system can be used in countries around the world. Using groupware gives every employee rapid access to a vast source of information. Artificial intelligence and special-purpose systems, discussed next, can also give people access to vast sources of information.

ARTIFICIALINTELLIGENCEANDSPECIAL-PURPOSESYSTEMS

At a Dartmouth College conference in 1956, John McCarthy proposed the use of the term **artificial intelligence (AI)** to describe computers with the ability to mimic or duplicate the functions of the human brain. Many AI pioneers attended this first AI conference; a few predicted that computers would be as "smart" as people by the 1960s. The prediction never materialized, but the benefits of artificial intelligence can be seen today. Advances in AI have led to systems that work like the human brain to recognize complex patterns.

An Overview of Artificial Intelligence

Science fiction novels and popular movies have featured scenarios of computer systems and intelligent machines taking over the world (see Figure 8.13). The movie *A.I.* explored fictional machines with human characteristics, a futuristic glimpse of what might be. Fictional accounts of human-like computers are entertaining, but we are far from creating computer systems that can completely replace human decision makers. Even so, today we are seeing the direct application of many computer systems that use the notion of AI. These systems are helping to make medical diagnoses, explore for natural resources, determine what is wrong with mechanical devices, and assist in designing and developing other computer systems. Garry Kasparov, perhaps one of the best-known chess masters of recent times, has competed numerous times with artificial intelligence software embedded in a computer. One of his first AI matches was against an IBM computer called Deep Blue in 1997.[19] In this match, the computer defeated the human being. More recently, Kasparov competed against a personal computer with AI software developed in Israel, called Deep Junior. This match, in 2003, was a 3-3 tie, but Kasparov picked up something the machine would have no interest in, $700,000. In this section, we explore the exciting applications of artificial intelligence and look at what the future might hold.

FIGURE 8.13 • Timeline of AI in the movies

Many popular movies have featured scenarios of computer systems and intelligent machines taking over the world. We seem to be both fascinated and scared by the idea of artificial intelligence.

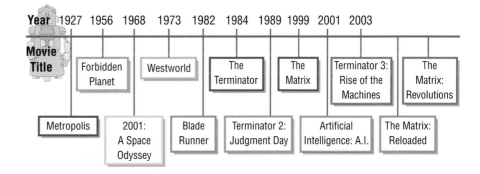

Artificial Intelligence in Perspective

Artificial intelligence systems include the people, procedures, hardware, software, data, and knowledge needed to develop computer systems and machines that demonstrate characteristics of intelligence. Researchers, scientists, and experts on how humans think are often involved in developing these systems. The objective in developing contemporary AI systems is not to replace human decision making completely, but to replicate it for certain types of well-defined problems. As with other computer systems, the overall purpose of artificial intelligence applications is to help individuals and organizations achieve their goals.

The Difference between Natural and Artificial Intelligence

Since the term *artificial intelligence* was coined in the 1950s, experts have disagreed about the difference between natural and artificial intelligence. For instance, is there a difference between carbon-based life (human or animal life) and silicon-based life (a computer chip) in terms of behavior? Today, there are profound differences, but those differences are declining in number, as shown in Table 8.2. One of the driving forces behind AI research is an attempt to understand how human beings actually reason and think. It is believed that the ability to create machines that can reason will only be possible once we truly understand our own processes for doing so.

TABLE 8.2 • A Comparison of Natural and Artificial Intelligence

Attributes	Natural Intelligence (human)	Artificial Intelligence (machine)
Acquire a large amount of external information	High	Low
Use sensors (eyes, ears, touch, smell)	High	Low
Be creative and imaginative	High	Low
Learn from experience	High	Low
Be forgetful	High	Low
Make complex calculations	Low	High
Be adaptive	High	Low
Use a variety of information sources	High	Low
Transfer information	Low	High

Components of Artificial Intelligence

AI is a broad field that includes several key branches, such as robotics, vision systems, natural language processing, learning systems, neural networks, genetic algorithms, intelligent agents, and expert systems (see Figure 8.14). Many of these areas are related; advances in one can occur simultaneously with advances in another, or result in advances in others.

FIGURE 8.14 • A conceptual model of artificial intelligence

The broad field of AI includes several key branches that are related. Advances in one branch can occur simultaneously with advances in another, or result in advances in others.

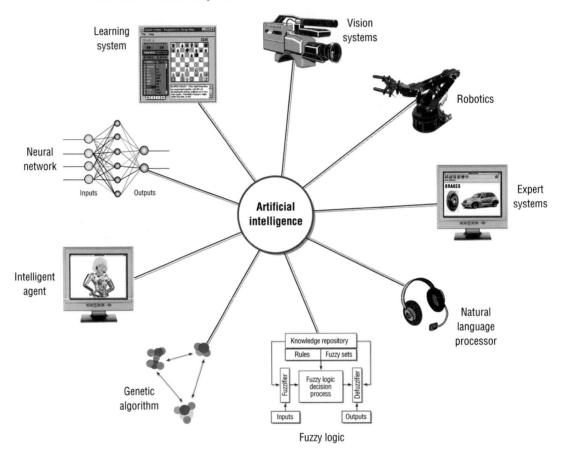

Robotics

Robotics involves developing mechanical or computer devices to perform tasks that require a high degree of precision or are tedious or hazardous for humans. Contemporary robotics combines both high-precision machine capabilities and sophisticated controlling software. The controlling software in robots is what is most important in terms of AI. One robot uses technology based on the whiskers of a rat to navigate through close spaces.[20] Known as Whiskerbot, the robot uses whisker-like sensors to determine the closeness, size, and texture of objects it touches.

There are many applications of robots, and research into these unique devices continues (see Figure 8.15). Manufacturers use robots to assemble and paint products. The U.S. Army is involved in developing medical robotics to allow doctors to perform surgery in combat areas via remote control. Not only does this technique make it safer for doctors in combat situations, it allows them to "be" in several places at once. The Da Vinci Surgical System, for example, allows doctors to operate using a robotic arm.[21] Sitting at a console, the surgeon can replace a heart valve or remove a tumor. The robotic arm can be accurately controlled and requires only a small incision in the patient, making surgery more precise and the recovery easier. Dr. Makimoto, chief of technology at Sony Corporation has predicted that in 50 years, robot football players will be able to beat the best human football teams.[22] "Some think it's a crazy idea but robot engineers are very serious about this!" says Dr. Makimoto.

FIGURE 8.15 • MIT's Kismet robot and its creator

Robot engineering has surpassed physical applications. Here the Kismet robot mimics the emotions of its creator.

Vision Systems

Another area of AI involves vision systems. **Vision systems** include hardware and software that permit computers to capture, store, and manipulate visual images and pictures. A California wine bottle manufacturer uses a computerized vision system to inspect wine bottles for flaws.[23] The vision system saves the bottle producer both time and money. The company produces about 2 million wine bottles per day. The U.S. Justice Department makes use of vision systems to perform fingerprint analysis, with almost the same level of precision as human experts. The speed with which the system can search through the huge database of fingerprints has brought a quick resolution to many unsolved mysteries.

FIGURE 8.16 • ASIMO (advanced step in innovative mobility)

Honda's ASIMO robot has eyes and a vision system sophisticated enough that it can use light switches, turn door knobs, and work at tables.

FIGURE 8.17 • Speech recognition technology

Speech recognition technology allows professionals to be experts in their fields, without needing to be expert typists.

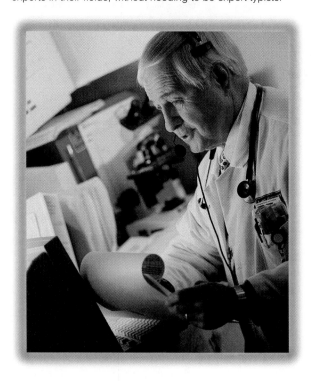

Vision systems can be used to give robots "sight" (see Figure 8.16). A sophisticated robot and vision software are used to attach the rear windscreen on Jaguar-S-Type cars.[24] The vision system guides robots to correctly and accurately install the windshields on the luxury cars. Generally, robots with vision systems can recognize black and white and some gray-level shades, but do not have good color or three-dimensional vision. Other systems concentrate on only a few key features in an image, ignoring the rest. It may take years before a robot or other computer system can "see" in full color and draw conclusions from what it sees, the way humans do.

Natural Language Processing

Natural language processing, often referred to as speech recognition, allows a computer to understand and react to statements and commands made in a "natural" language, such as English. With natural language processing, it is possible to speak into a microphone connected to a computer and have the computer convert the electrical impulses generated from the voice into text files or program commands. TD Waterhouse uses a natural-language-processing search engine that allows customers to get their questions answered through the brokerage firm's call center.[25] Perhaps you've encountered natural-language-processing systems when using directory assistance, or making collect or calling card calls.

Three major challenges of natural language processing require artificial intelligence solutions. The first is interpreting ambiguous words, words that sound alike but are spelled differently. The second is sentence parsing, which involves determining where one word ends and the next begins. The third challenge is being able to interpret the unique ways in which people pronounce words. Although researchers have not completely overcome these challenges, speech recognition technology has advanced enough that many computer users are considering it as an alternative to typing (see Figure 8.17).

Learning Systems

Another part of AI deals with **learning systems**, a combination of software and hardware that allows the computer to change how it functions or reacts to situations based on feedback it receives. For example, a number of computerized games have learning abilities. If the computer does not win a particular game, it remembers not to make the same moves under the same conditions. Learning systems software requires feedback on the results of its actions or decisions. At a minimum, the feedback needs to indicate whether the results are desirable (winning a game) or undesirable (losing a game). The feedback is then used to alter what the system will do in the future.

Neural Networks

An increasingly important aspect of AI involves neural networks. A **neural network** is a computer system that can act like or simulate the functioning of a human brain. The systems use massively parallel processors in an architecture that is based on the human brain's own meshlike structure. Neural networks can process many pieces of data at once and can learn to recognize patterns. The systems then program themselves to solve related problems on their own. Some of the specific features of neural networks include:

- The ability to retrieve information even if some of the neural nodes fail
- Fast modification of stored data as a result of new information
- The ability to discover relationships and trends in large databases
- The ability to solve complex problems for which all of the information is not present

Neural networks excel at pattern recognition, and this ability can be used in a wide array of situations. For example, neural network computers can be used to read bank check bar codes despite smears or poor-quality printing. Neural networks can also recognize patterns in data such as stock market prices. Neural network software designed for investors looks for stock market patterns and advises brokers when to buy or sell. Another software package, called Falcon Fraud Manager, is used to protect more than 450 million credit-card accounts. Some hospitals use neural networks to determine a patient's likelihood of contracting cancer or other diseases. The speed of genomic research can be increased with software that includes neural network features, such as Numerical Algorithms Group's (NAG) data mining software.[26] Fujitsu Laboratories used neural networks to improve motor coordination and movement in its robots.[27] The neural network software gives the robot a smooth walk and allows it to get up if it falls.

Fuzzy Logic

Computers typically work with numerical certainty; certain input values will always result in the same output. However, in the real world, as you know from experience, certainty is not always the case. To handle this dilemma, a specialty research area in computer science, called **fuzzy logic** or **fuzzy sets**, has been developed. Fuzzy logic deals in probabilities rather than absolutes. Research into fuzzy sets has been going on for decades. A simple example of fuzzy logic might be one in which cumulative probabilities do not add up to 100 percent, a state that occurs frequently in medical diagnosis. Another example of fuzzy logic involves unclear terms, like "tall" or "many." Fuzzy logic theory allows people to incorporate interpretations and relationships that are not completely precise or known. Infrared Technologies of Oak Ridge, Tennessee, has developed a large infrared oven used to produce automotive brake parts using fuzzy logic to control the temperature of the ovens.[28]

Genetic Algorithms

A **genetic algorithm** is an approach to solving large, complex problems where a number of algorithms or models change and evolve until the best one emerges. The approach is based on the theory of evolution, which requires variation and natural selection. The first step in developing a genetic algorithm solution is to

COMMUNITY TECHNOLOGY

Good Morning Computer!

Julia awakens to her favorite music, which starts quietly and builds gradually to gently bring her to consciousness. "Good morning computer," she says, and the computer brings up the room lighting to a low ambiance, and starts the coffee maker in the kitchen. "Computer, what's on my agenda?" she asks. The computer responds with "You have a 9:00 A.M. appointment with Bob Martin . . . ." "E-mail to Bob Martin," Julia commands. "Bob, I'm running a little late. I'll see you around 9:15.—Computer, send message."

Sound like science fiction? Not at all. This technology already exists, and some of it may already be on your PC. Both Microsoft and Apple have integrated speech recognition systems into their current software. Microsoft integrated speech recognition into Office XP. Apple has integrated speech recognition into its Mac OS X operating system. All that is required is a sound card—standard equipment on PCs and Macs—and a microphone.

Microsoft speech recognition requires training; a process of reading standard sample text into the microphone so the system can learn how you pronounce vowel and consonant combinations. The Mac system claims that no training is necessary. You can speak to running applications that support speech recognition, but you cannot yet speak to the operating system. It is anticipated that the next versions of both Windows and Mac operating systems will remedy this shortcoming.

Speech recognition includes two modes, command mode and dictation mode. In command mode, predefined keywords are used for common commands such as "send message." Dictation mode is used for free form dictation, such as "I'm running a little late, see you soon!" Efforts are underway to provide speech recognition systems in automobiles to allow drivers to control mobile phones, radios, or navigation systems with voice commands. Speech recognition is being incorporated into increasing numbers of electronic devices. Major technology corporations such as Microsoft, Apple, and IBM are investing heavily in speech recognition research and development. With this kind of industry-wide activity, there is little doubt that all of us will soon be chatting with our computers.

Questions
1. Name three situations where speech recognition would provide much-needed assistance.
2. Name three situations where speech recognition would be impractical.
3. How do you think the public will respond to speech recognition as an alternative to typing? Will users be quick to throw away their keyboards, or might it take some time before speech recognition gains acceptance? Why?

Sources
1. *"Speech Recognition Grapples with 'Real-World' Conditions,"* Richard Mullen, New Technology Week, *August 18, 2003.*
2. *Apple Web site, accessed September 15, 2003, www.apple.com/macosx/jaguar/speech.html.*
3. *Microsoft Web site, accessed September 15, 2003, www.microsoft.com/office/evaluation/indepth/speech.asp.*

change or vary a number of competing solutions to a problem. This can be done by changing the parts of a program or combining different program segments into a new program. If you think of program segments as building blocks similar to genetic material, this process is similar to the evolution of species, where the genetic makeup of a plant or animal mutates or changes over time (see Figure 8.18). The second step is to select only the best models or algorithms, which continue to evolve. Programs or program segments that are not as good

FIGURE 8.18 • Genetic algorithms

If you think of program segments as building blocks similar to genetic material, the process of a genetic algorithm is similar to the evolution of species, where the genetic makeup of a plant or animal mutates or changes over time.

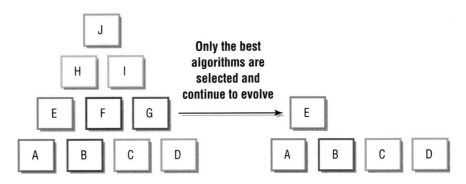

as others are discarded. This part of the process is similar to natural selection, where only the best or fittest members of a species survive and continue to evolve. This process of variation and natural selection continues until the genetic algorithm yields the best possible solution to the original problem. For example, some investment firms use genetic algorithms to help select the best stocks or bonds.[29] According to Doug Case, the CIO for Advanced Investment Technology, "We all have the same data, and the question is what are we going to do with it. AI can deal with that data and handle these disorderly global markets. There's even a chance that as AI filters down to amateur stock pickers, the result may be warp-speed markets where using this technology will be a must." Genetic algorithms are also used in computer science and mathematics.[30]

Intelligent Agents

An **intelligent agent** (also called an intelligent robot or bot, an abbreviation for robot) consists of programs and a knowledge base used to perform a specific task for a person, a process, or another program. Like an agent who searches for the best endorsement deals for a top athlete, an intelligent agent often searches to find the best price, the best schedule, or the best solution to a problem. Often used to search the vast resources of the Internet, intelligent agents can help people find information on an important topic or the best price for a new digital camera. Intelligent agents, like Cybelle and others, can be found at www.agentland. com (see Figure 8.19). Intelligent agents have been used by the U.S. Army to route security clearance information for soldiers to the correct departments and individuals.[31] What used to take days when done manually now takes hours. Intelligent agents can

HEADHUNTERS TRACK DOWN EXECS ONLINE

Search engines are already an industry, but now niche market companies are springing up that focus on narrow bands of information. Executive recruiters, for instance, can hunt for "passive" job candidates on a system that visits 1.5 million corporate Web sites four times a year and scans press items hourly to maintain their database of over 15 million executives. The system's clients can access potential candidates by name, job title, schooling, ethnicity, location, or company.

"Competition fierce for search engines that get to specifics"
By Chris Gaither, Boston Globe Staff
Boston Globe
www.boston.com/business/articles/2003/09/08/competition_fierce_for_search_engines_that_get_to_specifics/
September 8, 2003
Cited on September 8, 2003

FIGURE 8.19 • Internet-based intelligent agent

Intelligent agents on the Internet can help people find information easily in various areas or on diverse topics.

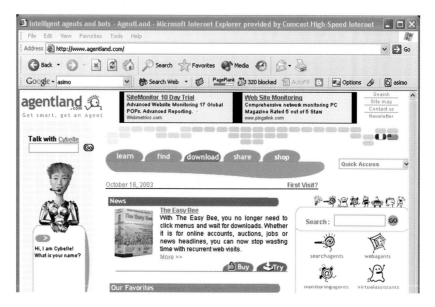

also be used to make travel arrangements, monitor incoming e-mail for viruses or junk mail, and coordinate the meetings and schedules of busy executives. In one application, an intelligent agent called eGenius was used to help with online training.[32] The software is a spin-off of work done at the University of Western Australia. According to Brian Sharpe, managing director of the company, "It employs intelligent agents that look ahead in the training environment. It knows where you are in the sequence of curriculum, so it will start to queue your content up, transferring it before you need it." Staples uses intelligent agents to find job candidates.[33] The intelligent agent searches a 12-million person database by title, company, gender, and other factors to find the best job candidates.

Expert Systems

An **expert system (ES)** acts or behaves like a human expert in a field or area. Charles Bailey, one of the original members of the Library and Information Technology Association, developed one of the first expert systems in the mid-1980s to search the University of Houston's library to retrieve requested resources and citations.[34] Computerized expert systems have been developed to diagnose diseases given a patient's symptoms, suggest the cause of a mechanical failure of an engine, predict future weather events, and assist in designing new products and systems.

Like human experts, computerized expert systems use heuristics, or "rules of thumb," to arrive at conclusions or make suggestions. However, one challenge for expert system developers is capturing knowledge and relationships that are not precise or exact.[35]

Like the other systems thus far discussed, expert systems support decision making. Mortgage financing companies, for example, use expert systems to perform credit evaluations on customers applying for loans. The system analyzes various types of data to determine whether or not applicants are qualified. The decision made by the expert system helps speed the financier's up-front decision making. She can more quickly notify those rejected for a loan, as well as provide faster financing for those rated financially sound. By working in this capacity, the expert system can act like a colleague or partner in providing information and assistance with decisions. Some gambling casinos use expert system software developed by Systems Research & Development to catch gambling cheats.[36] The CIA is testing the software to see whether it can be used to detect possible terrorists when they make hotel or airline reservations. Hospitals, pharmacies, and other healthcare providers can use expert systems like CaseAlert by MEDecision to determine possible high-risk or high-cost patients.[37]

Specialized Systems

In addition to the management information, decision support, and artificial intelligence systems discussed in the preceding sections, there are a number of specialized computer systems that benefit individuals and organizations. These specialized systems include virtual reality systems, geographic information systems, game theory systems, and a variety of other specialized systems.

Virtual Reality Systems. Virtual reality is a computer-simulated environment or event. The original idea was to have a three-dimensional world totally created by a computer system (see Figure 8.20). By using a special headset with a computer simulated view and stereo sound, you could become immersed in the computer simulation as if it were the real world. Other devices, such as special gloves and motion detectors, could change the world you are seeing and hearing through the headset. These computer simulations were used to totally

FIGURE 8.20 • Virtual reality systems
Virtual reality systems use computers to simulate an environment or event. In the virtual world shown in this image people are able to explore ancient Rome as it existed centuries ago.

immerse you in another (virtual) world to play realistic games or take a tour of a building. The computer simulation made you feel like you were actually fighting an enemy or walking around inside a building.

Today, virtual reality is used to describe a computer simulation that is generated on the Internet or using a computer system. These forms of virtual reality allow you to take a tour of a home or condo anywhere around the world, see inside the human body, or be on stage with a rock band.

There are a number of important uses of virtual reality. In medicine, doctors can use virtual reality to perform sophisticated surgical operations thousands of miles away from the patient. The doctor can see the patient on the computer screen, and give commands to control medical equipment to perform the surgery. In some cases, hand movements that the doctor makes are recreated hundreds or thousands of miles away to allow an operation to be performed on a patient. Virtual reality technology can also be used to link stroke patients to physical therapists.[38] Patients put on special gloves and other virtual-reality devices at home that are linked to the physical therapist's office. The physical therapist can see whether the patient is performing the correct exercises without having to travel to the patient's home or hospital room. Using virtual reality can cut costs and motivate patients to exercise regularly. According to Grigore Burdea, director of Rutgers University's Center for Advanced Information Processing, "There's tremendous potential here to have the therapy monitored at a distance and to have it done at home." An architect can use virtual reality to show a real estate investor the outside and inside of a building before it is constructed. Using virtual reality, the investor can view the grounds, landscaping, and rooms of the proposed building. A theater company can use virtual reality to help design a set for a new play, and a history teacher can use virtual reality to allow students to view an ancient battle or important historical event.

Geographic Information Systems. A **geographic information system (GIS)** is capable of storing, manipulating, and displaying geographic or special information, including maps of locations or regions around the world (see Figure 8.21). Although many software products have seen declining revenues in recent years, the use of GIS software is increasing by more than 14 percent per year on average.[39] A 911 operator can use a GIS to quickly determine the specific location of a caller with an emergency. The GIS converts the caller's phone number to the specific address of the caller and the directions for the police or an ambulance to get to the caller in a minimum amount of time. A business can use a GIS to display sales information for a specific region of the country. Higher sales can be displayed in red, and lower sales can be displayed in green or blue. This can give sales representatives a visual image of where to find sales opportunities and target their efforts. The military can use a GIS to target enemy forces on a battlefield. Using a GIS, along with other GPSs (global positioning systems), a tank group can quickly identify enemy positions and equipment in a constantly and rapidly changing battle situation. This helps a military force devastate an enemy position while avoiding friendly-fire casualties. GISs are also used in urban planning, social work, criminology and law enforcement, and a variety of other fields.

Game Theory Systems. **Game theory** involves developing strategies for people, organizations, or even countries who are competing against each other. Two competing businesses in the same market can use game theory to determine the

FIGURE 8.21 • Geographic information system
Geographic information systems store, manipulate, and display geographic or special information, including maps of locations or regions around the world. This is a GIS map demonstrating carbon monoxide emissions.

best strategy to achieve their goals. The military can use game theory to determine the best military strategy to win a conflict against another country, and individual investors can use game theory to determine the best investment strategies when competing against other investors in a government auction of bonds. Groundbreaking mathematical work was done on game theory by John Nash, and made popular in the book and film *A Beautiful Mind*.[40] Game theory has also been used to develop approaches to deal with terrorism.

Other Specialized Systems. In addition to the preceding applications, there are a number of other exciting special-purpose systems. Actuality Systems makes what some think are the world's highest-resolution 3-D images.[41] The system uses a clear crystal that is about 20 inches in diameter. Images are displayed inside the crystal, which you can walk around to get different views.

Informatics combines traditional disciplines, like science and medicine, with computer systems and technology. *Bioinformatics*, for example, combines biology and computer science. Also called computational biology, bioinformatics has been used to help map the human genome and conduct research on biological organisms. Using sophisticated databases and artificial intelligence, bioinformatics is being used to help unlock the secrets of the human genome, which could eventually prevent diseases and save lives. Stanford University has a course on bioinformatics and offers a bioinformatics certification. *Medical informatics* combines traditional medical research with computer science. Journals, such as *Healthcare Informatics*, report research on ways to reduce medical errors and improve healthcare delivery by using computer systems and technology in medicine. The University of

Geographic Information System Saves Trees

The gypsy moth, *Lymantria dispar*, is one of North America's most devastating forest pests. It was accidentally introduced near Boston by E. Leopold Trouvelot, in the late 1860s. About 10 years after this introduction, the first outbreaks began in Trouvelot's neighborhood, and in 1890 the state and federal government began attempts to eradicate the gypsy moth. These attempts ultimately failed, and since that time, the gypsy moth has continued to spread. The gypsy moth is known to feed on the foliage of hundreds of species of plants in North America, but its most common hosts are oaks and aspen. When densities reach very high levels, trees may become completely defoliated. Several successive years of defoliation, along with other stresses, may ultimately result in the death of a tree.

In 1999 the USDA Forest Service, along with state and federal participants, implemented the National Gypsy Moth Slow the Spread (STS) Project across the 1,200-mile gypsy moth frontier from North Carolina through the Upper Peninsula of Michigan. At the heart of the STS is a Web-based geographic information system (GIS) that supplies participants with valuable data gathered from the transition zone. Using this information, rangers can easily determine where a new infestation is taking place and treat the area while the infestation can be controlled. The GIS compiles and stores data from the entire project.

The USDA Forest Service refers to the GIS as its decision support system, since it assists the rangers in deciding what areas need closer examination, and ultimately which areas need treatment. By using a GIS, they are able to see the patterns of new infestation and decide on an informed defensive action. The GIS brings data, numbers, locations, and quantities to life and effectively supports strategic planning.

Whether an organization is tracking moths or customer sales in retail outlet stores, GISs assist managers in deciding what strategies are working and where to focus their attention.

Questions

1. How would the management of the STS project differ if the Internet and the GIS were not available?
2. The STS project GIS is a Web-based data access tool. It allows system users to view data but not to enter data. Would it be even more helpful if it could be used to enter data into the system? If so, how?
3. How might a GIS be used to serve the needs of a retail marketing firm?

Sources
1. *Slow the Spread Web site, www.ento.vt.edu/STS/, accessed May 4, 2002.*
2. *"Gypsy Moth in North America," National Forest Service Web site, www.fs.fed.us/ne/morgantown/4557/gmoth/, accessed May 4, 2002.*

Edinburgh has a School of Informatics. The school has courses in the structure, behavior, and interactions of natural and artificial computational systems. The program combines artificial intelligence, computer science, engineering, and science.

The Segway Human Transporter™ is another example of a special-purpose system.[42] Using sophisticated software, sensors, and gyroscopes, the device can transport standing people through warehouses, offices, and downtown sidewalks (see Figure 8.22).

FIGURE 8.22 • A special-purpose personal transportation system
Segway is an alternate form of transportation that is just beginning to establish a role in our society.

Special-purpose bar codes are also being introduced in a variety of settings.[43] In Accenture's Office of the Future, each consultant and office space has a bar code. Instead of having permanent offices, Accenture assigns consultants to offices as needed. The bar codes help to make sure that a consultant's work, mail, and other materials are delivered to the right office space when they are needed. Accenture estimates that it saves about $8 million a year in rent by not having permanent office spaces sitting idle for its consultants. "A can of peas has its own bar code, why not us?" says Doug Picker of Symbol Technologies, a company that makes mobile bar code systems.

Action Plan

Technology 360°

1. What type of system would help show potential clients a realistic view of commercial real estate?

Although there are a variety of tools that can be used, virtual reality on an Internet site is an excellent choice to show clients the inside and outside of buildings. Virtual reality technology allows potential clients or investors to take a "virtual tour" of the building and landscape.

2. How can Maurice's father get investors, attorneys, sellers, their agents, architects, and builders together at the same time to close real estate deals?

A group decision support system could help get everyone together. Groupware, such as Lotus Notes, can be used to facilitate group meetings and work. Spreadsheets, legal documents, and real estate analysis can be shared using this approach. In addition, a GIS can be used by investors, attorneys, sellers, and their agents to analyze different real estate possibilities.

3. What can Maurice do to give clients a tour of New Orleans over the Internet?

Using virtual reality, Maurice can build an Internet site that shows clients the French Quarter and various points of interest in New Orleans. This Internet site can also be linked to other Internet sites developed by the city and other companies and organizations.

Summary

LEARNING OBJECTIVE 1
Define the stages of decision making and problem solving.

The true potential of computer systems is providing information to help people and organizations make better decisions. Decision making is divided into three phases: intelligence, design, and choice. Problem solving takes decision making a step further, and involves taking action by implementing the choice made by the decision maker and monitoring the effects of the decision.

Figure 8.2—p. 339

The types of decisions made by an organization can range from structured, programmed decisions to unstructured, nonprogrammed decisions. In some instances, when the optimal solution to a problem must be determined, optimization models assist in finding the best solution. In other cases, a solution that meets a basic set of criteria may be acceptable, although not optimal. This heuristic approach is often used because it is more cost-effective than the optimization approach. In addition, individuals and organizations can use a reactive or proactive approach to problem solving. With a reactive problem-solving approach, the problem solver waits until a problem surfaces or becomes apparent before taking any action. With a proactive problem-solving approach, the problem solver seeks out potential problems before they become serious.

LEARNING OBJECTIVE 2
Discuss the use of management information systems in providing reports to help solve structured problems.

A management information system is an organized collection of people, procedures, databases, and devices that provide managers and decision makers with information to help achieve organizational goals. An MIS can help an organization achieve its goals by providing managers with insight into the regular operations of the organization so that they can control, organize, and plan more effectively and efficiently. The output of most management information systems is a collection of reports that are distributed to managers. These reports include scheduled reports, demand reports, and exception reports. Scheduled reports are produced periodically or on a schedule, such as daily, weekly, or monthly. A key-indicator report is a special type of scheduled report that summarizes the previous day's critical activities. Demand reports are developed to give certain information at a manager's request. Exception reports are reports that are automatically produced when a situation is unusual or requires management action.

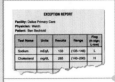

Figure 8.8—p. 345

LEARNING OBJECTIVE 3
Describe how decision support systems are used to solve nonprogrammed and unstructured problems.

A decision support system (DSS) is an organized collection of people, procedures, software, databases, and devices working to support managerial decision making. DSSs provide assistance through all phases of the decision-making process. Decision support systems can handle a large amount of data, obtain and process data from different sources, provide report and presentation flexibility, have both textual and graphical orientation, perform complex and sophisticated analysis, support optimization and heuristic approaches, and perform what-if and goal-seeking analysis.

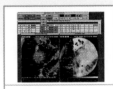

Figure 8.11—p. 348

LEARNING OBJECTIVE 4
Explain how a group decision support system can help people and organizations collaborate on team projects.

A group decision support system (GDSS), also called a computerized collaborative work system, consists of hardware, software, people, databases, and procedures needed to provide effective support in group decision-making settings. GDSSs are typically easy to learn and use, and can offer specific or general decision-making support.

A GDSS also has some unique components, such as compound documents, groupware, and telecommunications links. Groupware is specially designed software that helps generate lists of decision alternatives and performs data analysis. These packages let people work on joint documents and files over a network. The characteristics of a GDSS include special design, ease of use, flexibility, anonymous input, reduced negative behavior, and support of positive group behavior.

Figure 8.12—p. 350

LEARNING OBJECTIVE 5
Discuss the uses of artificial intelligence and special-purpose systems.

Artificial intelligence (AI) is a broad field that includes several key components, including robotics, vision systems, natural language processing, learning systems, neural networks, fuzzy logic, genetic algorithms, intelligent agents, and expert systems.

Robotics involves developing mechanical or computer devices to perform tasks that require a high degree of precision or are tedious or hazardous for humans. Vision systems include hardware and software that permit computers to capture, store, and manipulate images and pictures. Natural language processing allows the computer to understand and react to statements and commands made in a "natural" language, such as English. Learning systems use a combination of software and hardware that allows the computer to change how it functions or reacts to situations based on feedback it receives. A neural network is a computer system that can act like or simulate the functioning of a human brain. A genetic algorithm is an approach to solving large, complex

Figure 8.14—p. 355

problems, where the algorithms or models change and evolve until the best one emerges. Expert systems act or behave like a human expert in a field or area. Fuzzy logic entails dealing with ambiguous criteria or probabilities and events that are not mutually exclusive. An intelligent agent consists of programs and a knowledge base used to perform a specific task for a person, a process, or another program. Like an agent who searches for the best endorsement deals for a top athlete, an intelligent agent often searches to find the best price, the best schedule, or the best solution to a problem.

There are a number of special-purpose systems, including virtual reality, geographic information, game theory, and other special-purpose systems. Virtual reality is a computer-simulated environment or event. It can be used to design buildings, help the military, or play exciting games. A geographic information system is capable of storing, manipulating, and displaying geographic information, including maps of locations or regions around the world. Game theory involves developing strategies for people, organizations, or even countries competing against each other.

Test Yourself

LEARNING OBJECTIVE 1: Define the stages of decision making and problem solving.

1. With the _____ approach, the problem solver waits until a problem surfaces before any action is taken.

2. True or false: Problem solving is a component of the decision-making approach.

3. The first stage in the decision-making process is:
   a. design
   b. choice
   c. intelligence
   d. goal seeking

4. The final stage of the problem-solving process is _____.

5. True or False: A programmed decision is easy to computerize using traditional computer systems.

6. What is commonly referred to as a "rule of thumb"?
   a. heuristic
   b. optimization
   c. goal seek
   d. nonprogrammed decision

LEARNING OBJECTIVE 2: Discuss the use of management information systems in providing reports to help solve structured problems.

7. True or False: Data entering the MIS can be considered to originate from either internal or external sources.

8. What types of reports are produced periodically?

   a. demand
   b. scheduled
   c. heuristic
   d. optimization

9. A(n) _____ is a special type of scheduled report that summarizes the previous day's critical activities.

10. True or False: An exception report is automatically produced when a situation is unusual or requires management action.

LEARNING OBJECTIVE 3: Describe how decision support systems are used to solve nonprogrammed and unstructured problems.

11. A(n) _____ is used when people or organizations face unstructured or semistructured problems.

12. What is the process of determining the problem data required for a given result?
    a. heuristic
    b. optimizing
    c. goal-seeking
    d. simulation

13. True or False: With heuristics, the DSS attempts to mimic an event that could happen in the future.

14. What type of system has both a textual and graphical orientation?
    a. transaction processing system
    b. management information system
    c. neural network system
    d. decision support system

15. _____ is the process of making hypothetical changes to problem data and observing the impact on the results.

LEARNING OBJECTIVE 4: Explain how a group decision support system can help people and organizations collaborate on team projects.

16. What type of software is used to allow two or more individuals to work together effectively in a group?
    a. groupware
    b. decisionware
    c. cooperative software
    d. teamware

17. The _____ approach is used when decision makers are geographically dispersed throughout the country or the world.

18. True or False: Anonymous input in a GDSS is used to make sure that the person giving input is not known to other group members.

LEARNING OBJECTIVE 5: Discuss the uses of artificial intelligence and special-purpose systems.

19. _____ allows the computer to understand and react to statements and commands made in English or a similar language.

20. What type of artificial intelligence is used to simulate or act like the functioning of the human brain?
    a. fuzzy logic
    b. expert systems
    c. neural networks
    d. genetic algorithms

21. True or False: A neural network is an approach to solving problems where a number of models change and evolve until the best one emerges.

22. A(n) _____ acts like a human expert in a field or area.

23. True or False: Game theory involves developing strategies for people, organizations, or even countries competing against each other.

Test Yourself Solutions: 1. reactive approach, 2. F, 3. c., 4. monitoring, 5. T, 6. a., 7. T, 8. b., 9. key-indicator, 10. T, 11. decision support systems, 12. c., 13. F, 14. d., 15. What-if analysis, 16. a., 17. Delphi, 18. T, 19. Natural language processing, 20. c., 21. F, 22. expert system, 23. T

Key Terms

artificial intelligence (AI),
   p. 353
artificial intelligence systems,
   p. 354
choice stage, p. 339
decision making, p. 338
decision support system
   (DSS), p. 345
demand reports, p. 344
design stage, p. 339
exception reports, p. 345
expert system (ES), p. 360
fuzzy logic, p. 359
fuzzy sets, p. 359
game theory, p. 364

geographic information
   system, p. 363
genetic algorithm, p. 359
goal-seeking analysis, p. 348
group decision support
   system (GDSS), p. 349
groupware, p. 352
heuristics, p. 341
implementation stage, p. 339
informatics, p. 365
intelligence stage, p. 338
intelligent agents, p. 360
learning systems, p. 357
management information
   systems (MIS), p. 342

monitoring stage, p. 339
natural language processing,
   p. 346
neural network, p. 358
nonprogrammed decisions,
   p. 340
optimization model, p. 341
problem solving, p. 339
programmed decisions, p. 340
robotics, p. 354
scheduled reports, p. 343
virtual reality, p. 362
vision systems, p. 346
what-if analysis, p. 348

Questions

Review Questions

1. Describe the stages of decision making.

2. What is the overall purpose of the design stage?

3. Describe the stages of problem solving.

4. What is a programmed decision?

5. What is the heuristic approach?

6. What is a management information system (MIS)?

7. What are the inputs to an MIS?

8. Describe the outputs of management information systems.

9. What is the difference between a scheduled report and a demand report?

10. What is a key-indicator report?

11. Define a decision support system. What are its characteristics?

12. Describe what-if analysis.

13. How can goal-seeking analysis be used?

14. Describe the overall approach of simulation.

15. What is a group decision support system (GDSS)?

16. List five characteristics of a GDSS.

17. What is groupthink?

18. What is the group consensus approach?

19. Describe the use of groupware.

20. What are the components of artificial intelligence?

21. What is the difference between artificial and natural intelligence?

22. What is robotics? What are neural networks?

23. What are the capabilities of an expert system?

24. What is virtual reality? What is a geographic information system?

Discussion Questions

25. Think of an important decision you made in the last few years. Describe the results of decision-making and problem-solving steps you used.

26. Discuss the difference between scheduled, demand, and exception reports.

27. How can MISs be used to help individuals and organizations make better decisions?

28. What functions do decision support systems (DSS) support in organizations?

29. List one or two career areas that interest you. Describe how a DSS might be used to help you achieve your career goals.

30. How is decision making in a group environment different from individual decision making, and why are information systems that assist in the group environment different? What are the advantages and disadvantages of making decisions as a group?

31. What are the characteristics of intelligent behavior?

32. How could robots be used in the military or law enforcement?

33. Give an example of how expert systems can be used in a field of interest to you.

34. What type of college or university courses might benefit from virtual reality?

Exercises

Try It Yourself

1. You have been asked to set up some reports to help your school better plan course offerings. Your school's registration system collects data not only on what classes students have enrolled in, but also on what classes students tried to enroll in but were denied enrollment because the class was full. Using the data in Table 8.3, create two reports:

(1) an exception report listing all courses that more than three students couldn't get into because the class was full, and (2) a scheduled report listing the students who are enrolled in each class (a class roster). This scheduled report will be printed out every day during registration and can also be used on demand after registration is over.

TABLE 8.3 • Data for Try It Yourself Exercise 1

Course#	StudentID	Status	Date	Reason
370	5987	Enroll	10/13/96	
370	9237	Enroll	10/15/96	
567	1629	Enroll	10/14/96	
567	2863	Denied	10/15/96	Full
567	4631	Enroll	10/14/96	
567	4731	Denied	10/15/96	Full
567	5987	Enroll	10/13/96	
567	9237	Denied	10/15/96	Full
567	9832	Enroll	10/13/96	
963	3958	Denied	10/13/96	Full
963	5678	Denied	10/13/96	Full
963	9832	Denied	10/13/96	Full

2. A university has designed and implemented a database to maintain records for students and courses. Some of the essential fields are student identification number, student name, student address, majors, credits completed, course number, course name, faculty member teaching the course, student GPA, and grades. Using this database, design and implement a decision support system query for department heads and administrators to determine the number of credit hours that are generated by each instructor. Course credit hours are calculated by multiplying course credits times the number of students. Instructor credit hours are calculated by adding together the credit hours for each course. Administrators can use this information as a method of determining the number of course sections and the workload of instructors. You can use a database management system or spreadsheet to design the report.

3. Use the Internet to explore the decisions that are required for your chosen career area or field. Also use the Internet to explore expert systems. Using your word-processing program, describe how you could develop an expert system for your career area or field. Develop 10 heuristics, or "rules of thumb," that show how your expert system could make decisions given certain conditions or situations.

4. Investigate the use of game theory on the Internet. Use your word-processing program to describe how you could use game theory in your career area or field.

Virtual Classroom Activities

To complete the following exercises, do not use face-to-face or telephone communications with your group members. Use only Internet communications.

5. As discussed in the chapter, a nonprogrammed decision can involve unusual or exceptional situations. Your virtual classroom group should first list three nonprogrammed decisions that a freshman in college might encounter. For each nonprogrammed decision, develop a brief description of factors to consider during the intelligence and design phases of decision making to help the freshman make the best decision.

6. Groupware is often used to help groups make decisions. Using the Internet, investigate the use of groupware in two or more areas or organizations. The members of your virtual classroom group should summarize the features, advantages, and disadvantages of each groupware product.

Teamwork

7. Your team is to design an information system for a local bookstore chain. Currently there is a system installed to process sales transactions, but an integrated information system does not exist. Andy Masters, president of the local bookstore, is planning on expanding from four stores to ten within the next year. To manage this growth, and to keep track of the regular operations of the business, he wants to have a management information system that links together all stores. Prepare a brief memo to Andy explaining five different reports that the information system should produce. Include at least one demand and exception report. Your group should create a layout of the bookstore's new management information system using presentation graphics software.

8. Your team should develop a spreadsheet to be used to estimate the expenses to move off campus next year. The model must allow input of a variety of rent amounts, food costs, transportation costs, and so on, as well as tuition and books. Each team member should put in his or her current estimated costs. Assume that tuition and books are fixed at this year's amounts. After finding an average of the group members' current costs, perform two what-if scenarios. For the first, assume no change in costs but 2 percent inflation. For the second, assume 5 percent inflation. Do the projection for a year.

Create a word-processed document to explain your model to a novice student who might use it to guide decision making for next year.

9. Your team should brainstorm at least five ideas for expert systems that would be useful on campus.

Try to develop rules you might use to make decisions (say, to choose classes for a semester). This exercise will show the difficulty of using multiple experts to build a knowledge base and the difficulty in defining rules for a knowledge base.

Learning Check

To check your knowledge of each of the chapter objectives, use this chart to find related end-of-chapter content.

Learning Objective	Key Terms		Questions	Exercises
Learning Objective 1 Define the stages of decision making and problem solving.	choice stage decision making design stage heuristics implementation stage intelligence stage	monitoring stage nonprogrammed decisions optimization model problem solving programmed decisions	1, 2, 3, 4, 5, 25	5
Learning Objective 2 Discuss the use of management information systems in providing reports to help solve structured problems.	demand report, exception report, scheduled report,		6, 7, 8, 9, 10, 26, 27	1, 7
Learning Objective 3 Describe how decision support systems are used to solve non-programmed and unstructured problems.	decision support system goal-seeking what-if analysis		11, 12, 13, 14, 28, 29	2
Learning Objective 4 Explain how a group decision support system can help people and organizations collaborate on team projects.	group decision support system (GDSS) groupware		15, 16, 17, 18, 19, 30	6, 8
Learning Objective 5 Discuss the uses of artificial intelligence and special-purpose systems.	artificial intelligence artificial intelligence systems expert systems fuzzy logic game theory genetic algorithms geographic informa- tion systems	informatics intelligent agents learning systems natural language processing neural networks robotics virtual reality vision systems	20, 21, 22, 23, 24, 31, 32, 33, 34	3, 4, 9

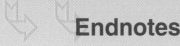

Endnotes

1. Barrett, Amy, "Feeding the Pipeline," *Business Week*, May 12, 2003, p. 78.

2. Blakeley, Fred et al., "Optimizing Perodic Maintenance," *Interfaces*, January, 2003, p. 67.

3. Savage, Marcia, "Trend Micro Deputs Heuristical Anti-spam Solution," Asia *Computer Weekly*, March 17, 2003.

4. Draper, Heather, "Xcel Site Turns Up the Heat on Waste," *Rocky Mountain News*, March 3, 2003, p. 1B.

5. King, Julia, "Sealing the Deal and Collecting Their Due," *Computerworld*, March 31, 2003, p. 52.

6. Giegerich, Steve, "Putting Professors to the Test," *Summit Daily News*, February 20, 2003, p. B1.

7. Nelson, Kristi, "Referral System Leads to Connectivity," Bank System & Technology, March 1, 2003, p. 16.

8. Brewin, Bob, "Feds Test Network to Send Alerts," *Computerworld*, March 31, 2003, p. 19.

9. Grimes, Seth, "Autonomic Computing – Major Vendors are Applying Decision Support Techniques to Service-Centric Computing," *Intelligent Enterprise*, November 15, 2002, p. 18.

10. Bulkeley, William, "Diabetes Web Site To Provide Customized Treatment Plans," *The Wall Street Journal*, May 14, 2003, p. D3.

11. Tan, Kopin, "Technology Transforms Options Traders," *The Wall Street Journal*, April 30, 2003, p. C14.

12. Swamnathan, J. "Decision Support for Allocating Scarce Drugs," *Interfaces*, March 2003, p. 1.

13. Gomes, Lee, "How High-Tech Games Can Fail to Simulate," *The Wall Street Journal*, March 31, 2003, p. B1.

14. So, Kut et al, "Models for Improving Team Productivity at the Federal Reserve Bank," *Interfaces*, March 2003, p. 25.

15. Staff, "Computer Program Aids Farm Bill Decisions," *Southwest Farm Press*, May 16, 2002.

16. Rundle, Rhonda, "Healthcare Providers Let Patients View Records Online," *The Wall Street Journal*, June 25, 2002, p. B1.

17. Strassbery, Dan, "Software Facilitates Sharing of Engineering Calculations," *EDN*, March 6, 2003, p. 17.

18. Schultz, Keith, "Lotus Notes and Domino 6," *New Architect*, January 1, 2003, p. 40.

19. Bentley, Ross, "Man Versus Machine," *Computer Weekly*, March 20, 2003, p. 24.

20. Staff, "Rat's Whiskers Help to Make Better Robots," *Factory Equipment News*, May 2003.

21. Huber, Peter, "The Dexterous Robot," *Forbes*, February 18, 2002, p. 88.

22. Staff, "Robot Football Players Will Give Boot to Beckham," *Electronics Weekly*, May 14, 2003, p. 1.

23. Staff, "Machine Vision and Infrared Lighting Track Production," *Vision Systems Design*, April 2003, p. 29.

24. Staff, "A Vision of Robots Soldering On," *Automation*, April 2003, p. 14.

25. Mearin, Lucas, "Brokerage Launches Search Engine to Aid Call Center," *Computerworld*, March 18, 2002, p. 10.

26. "NAG Data Mining Components Speed Application Development," *Worldwide Database*, March 2002.

27. Ball, Richard, "Fujitsu Walking Robots Gets in Brains from Neural Networks," *Electronics Weekly*, April 9, 2003, p. 19.

28. Staff, "Infrared Oven Constructed," *Industrial Heating*, March 2002, p. 56.

29. Pethokoukis, James, "Robotrading," *U.S. News and World Report*, January 28, 2002, p. 23.

30. Ke-zhang, et al, "Recognition of Digital Curves Scanned from Paper Drawings Using Genetic Algorithms," *Pattern Recognition*, January 2003, p. 123.

31. Overby, Stephanie, "The New, New Intelligence," *CIO Magazine*, January 1, 2003, p. 35.

32. Wilson, Eric, "Getting Smart with E Learning," *Sydney Morning Herald*, September 3, 2002, p. 9.

33. Tischelle, George, "Searching For That One," *Information Week*, February 17, 2003, p. 58.

34. Staff, "The Imagineer," *Library Journal*, March 15, 2003, p. 18.

35. "Fuzzy Logic Software Corporation Announces Closing the Share Purchase Agreement," *Business Wire*, February 25, 2002.

36. Disabantino, Jennifer, "CIA-Backed Analysis Tool Eyed for Passenger Checks," *Computerworld*, January 1, 2002, p. 12.

37. Kohler, Tracey, "MEDexision's CaseAlert Software to be Used in Innovative Medicaid Disease Management Program," *PR Wire*, February 21, 2002.

38. Blough, Kay, "Virtual Reality to Aid Stroke Therapy," *Information Week Online*, February 19, 2002.

39. Staff, "GIS Software Market Sees Dynamic Growth," *Electric Light & Power*, February, 2003, p. 6.

40. Begley, Sharon, "A Beautiful Science: Getting the Math Right Can Thwart Terrorism," *The Wall Street Journal*, May 10, 2003, p. B1.

41. Kay, Russell, "3-D Vision Speaks Volumes," *Computerworld*, April 1, 2002, p. 44.

42. Machrone, Bill, "Segue – From Ginger to Segway," *PC Magazine*, January 29, 2002, p. 53.

43. Hwang, Suein, "In Office of the Future, We'll All Be Scanned Like a Can of Peas," *The Wall Street Journal*, April 10, 2002, p. B1.

SystemsDevelopment

Technology 360°

Joe Pena was hired less than two years ago, and he is already a regional sales manager for a company that offers discounted long-distance and Internet service. The company is aggressively trying to compete with AT&T, MCI, and Sprint. It is offering Joe generous commissions for each customer he can convert to an Internet subscriber. Large bonuses at the end of the year will sweeten the deal for Joe if he meets his sales numbers. Joe would like the company to develop a new sales program that would help identify potential new customers using the company's existing database. Joe recently met Maria Jones, a systems analyst with the company, at a party. He would like her help in developing a system to help him identify new customers.

1. How should Joe approach his company to get a new sales program developed?
2. If the company decides to develop a new sales program for sales managers and representatives, how should Joe be involved in the process?
3. What role would Maria and people like her play in developing a new sales program?

Check out Joe's *Action Plan* at the end of this chapter.

LEARNING OBJECTIVES	CHAPTER CONTENT
1. Describe the participants in and importance of the systems development life cycle.	**An Overview of Systems Development**
2. Discuss the use of CASE, project management, and other systems development tools.	**Tools for Systems Development**
3. Understand how systems development projects are initiated.	**Systems Investigation**
4. Describe how an existing system can be evaluated.	**Systems Analysis**
5. Discuss what is involved in planning a new system.	**Systems Design**
6. List the steps for placing a new or modified system into operation.	**Systems Implementation**
7. Describe the importance of updating and monitoring a new or modified system.	**Systems Maintenance and Review**

Introduction

Throughout this book, you have seen how computer systems have been used to help people and organizations in a variety of settings. You have seen the use of computer systems in engineering, science, the arts, business, library studies, sociology, criminology, architecture, music, the military, and many, many other fields. But how are these computer systems acquired or developed? And how can the people and organizations that use these systems make sure they help them achieve their goals? The answer is systems development.

This chapter introduces the systems development process, including systems investigation, analysis, design, implementation, maintenance, and review. In this chapter, you will see how you can be involved in systems development to advance your career and help your company or organization. You will also see how computer systems professionals, including systems analysts and computer programmers, work together to develop effective computer systems. In addition, you will see how you can be involved in the systems development process to get the systems and software you need. In the pages that follow, you will see how systems development can be used to realize the true potential of computer systems in almost every field or discipline.

Systems development is the activity of creating new or modifying existing systems. It refers to all aspects of the process—from identifying problems to be solved or opportunities to be exploited to the evaluation and possible refinement of the chosen solution. Throughout this book, you have seen the results of systems development. You have seen how computer systems have been developed to help employees balance life and work, people vote during elections, scientists discover distant planets, environmentalists save endangered species, teachers deliver distance learning classes, executives use business intelligence to increase profits, people make effective group decisions, and so much more. All of these uses of computer systems are a direct result of the systems development process discussed in this chapter.

AN OVERVIEW OF SYSTEMS DEVELOPMENT

Systems development efforts can range from a small project, such as purchasing an inexpensive computer program, to a major undertaking, such as installing a $50 million system, including hardware, software, communications systems, databases, and new computer systems personnel. For example, Adnan Osmani, a 16-year-old student in Dublin Ireland, developed his own Internet browser without spending a large amount of money or requiring sophisticated computer equipment.[1] "I just wanted it faster for myself," Osmani said. Osmani won about $3,500 and the top prize at Ireland's Young Scientist Exhibition, which was sponsored by an Irish telecommunications company. In contrast, Fresh-Direct, an online food company, raised $120 million to develop a high-quality Internet-based food ordering and delivery system.[2] The project includes a systems development effort to create the necessary software and Web site. In an even bigger systems development project, the U.S. Naval Sea Systems Command used systems development to streamline its purchasing process.[3] The military operation has an annual budget of $19 billion. As a result of the project, the Naval department was able to cut buying time by 85 percent from about 270 days to about 30 days. The U.S. Congress allocated $1.35 billion to the Internal Revenue Service (IRS) to upgrade its computer systems.[4] Congress and U.S. citizens hope the money spent will make it easier for people to contact and interact with the IRS.

Organizations have used different approaches to developing computer systems. In some cases, these approaches are formalized and captured in volumes of documents that describe what is to be done. In other cases, less formal approaches are used. The steps of systems development may vary from one organization to the next, but most approaches have five common phases: investigation, analysis, design, implementation, and maintenance and review, as shown in Figure 9.1.

The systems development process is typically called a **systems development life cycle (SDLC)** because the activities associated with it are ongoing. Systems investigation and analysis looks at the existing system and determines if the existing system can and should be improved. Systems design and implementation involves modifying an existing system or developing a new one and placing it into operation. Finally, maintenance and review makes sure that the new or modified system is operating as intended. As each system is being built, the project has timelines and deadlines, until at last the system is installed and accepted. The life of the system continues as it is maintained and reviewed. If the system needs significant improvement beyond the scope of maintenance—if it needs to be replaced due to a new generation of technology, or if there is a major change in the computer systems needs of the organization—a new systems development project will be initiated, and the cycle will start over. A number of companies use a standard SDLC. Some are very similar to the one shown in Figure 9.1. The consulting company Recho, for example, uses an SDLC that includes information collection, user requirements, detailed system analysis, design, programming, testing, implementation, and maintenance.[5] In contrast, Paragon Development Systems uses an SDLC that includes planning, procurement (the purchasing process), deployment, management, support, and retirement.[6]

FIGURE 9.1 • The systems development life cycle (SDLC)

The systems development life cycle (SDLC) involves working through a number of steps to go from the initial idea to a finished system. Sometimes information learned in a particular phase requires cycling back to a previous phase.

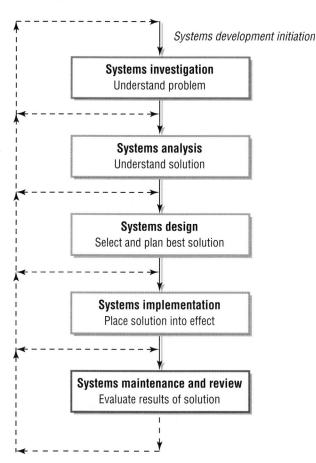

As shown in Figure 9.1, a particular system under development may move from one phase of the SDLC to the next, and then back to a previous phase, and so on. In an ideal world, it would be unnecessary to return to a previous phase to correct errors or make adjustments. In reality, however, activities in a later phase of the SDLC may uncover a need to change the results of previous steps. For example, a medical researcher might realize during implementation of a new software system that the current computers are too slow. This might require that hardware and software be upgraded, which could restart the systems design phase. Thus, although it is described as a series of steps, the SDLC is more likely to cycle back and forth between steps to continuously rebuild and refine a system. At each step, there are checkpoints to determine if the step has been successfully completed, if additional work is needed, and if the systems development process should continue.

Even with the steps of systems development, many systems development efforts fail to achieve their goals. Organizations have lost hundreds of millions of dollars on failed systems development efforts. In addition, an organization's clients or customers can also suffer losses. In one classic case, a major stock exchange tried to implement a new computerized trading system. Companies and individuals that interacted with the new computerized trading system had to spend money to change their systems to work with the new trading system. When the new trading system didn't work and was never implemented, the companies and individuals that interacted with the stock exchange had to change back to their old systems, wasting a tremendous amount of time and money.

Participants in Systems Development

Effective systems development requires a team effort. The team usually consists of system stakeholders, users, managers, systems development specialists, and various support personnel. This team, called the development team, is responsible for determining the objectives of the computer system and delivering to the organization a system that meets these objectives. **System stakeholders** are individuals who, either themselves or through the area of the organization which they represent, will ultimately benefit from the systems development project.

Users are a specific type of stakeholder. Users are individuals who will be interacting with the system on a regular basis. They can be employees, managers, customers, suppliers, vendors, and others.[7] Physicians, for example, were actively

The Impact of Anthropology on Systems Development

Throughout this book, you have seen how computer systems have had a huge impact on almost every field or career area. But these fields and career areas can also have a huge impact on the systems development process used to create new computer systems. Tracey Lovejoy, an anthropologist, has studied how people go about their daily lives. She has observed, studied, and recorded the behavior of people at school, work, and home. But Tracey does not work for a university. She works for Microsoft, the software company.

Tracey uses ethnographic research, which analyzes the behavior of people and groups on a daily basis, to study people's needs for community support, communications, relationships, and many other variables. Margaret Mead used ethnographic research to gather the material in her book *Coming of Age in Samoa*. Tracey uses ethnographic research to help design and develop future Microsoft products and services, "Rather than designing a product and teaching the consumer to change their behavior to use that product, it's important to understand the consumer's behavior and design that product based on what they do already." To conduct her research, Tracey often follows travelers on cab rides, through airport terminals and baggage claim areas, and

to hotels and meetings. Microsoft hopes to use this research to design the next generation of operating systems. Ethnographic studies done a few years ago motivated Microsoft to redo its Internet connection wizard in Windows XP. Ethnography was also used to design Microsoft's tablet PC. The researchers investigated the cultural, social, and logistical aspects of note taking.

Questions

1. How is ethnography used to develop future operating systems?
2. What operating system are you using? How could your operating system be improved to make it easier to use and more effective?
3. In addition to anthropology, what other fields can have an impact on how software or computer systems are built, to make them easier to use or more effective?

Sources
1. *"Look Who's Watching," Alison Wellner-Stein*, Continental, *April 2003, pp. 39.*
2. *"Anthropology in the Face of History," Mary Carmichael,* Newsweek, *June 23, 2003, p. 11.*
3. *"Retail Anthropology," Staff* Retail Week, *June 14, 2003, p. 17.*

FIGURE 9.2 • A surgical training system

Doctors who are specialists in gastroenterology can use this virtual reality training system to practice new probing techniques.

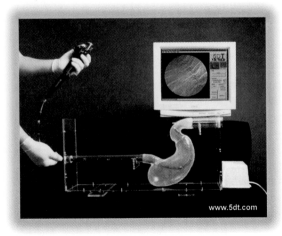

www.5dt.com

involved in developing a 3-D system for surgery.[8] The new system allows doctors to practice surgeries on simulations of a patient's internal organs before actually doing the surgery, preventing mistakes and saving lives (see Figure 9.2). One systems development approach, called *agile modeling*, calls for very active participation of customers and other stakeholders in the systems development process.[9]

Managers are people within an organization most capable of initiating and maintaining change. For large-scale systems development projects, where the investment in and value of a system can be quite high, it is common to have senior-level managers as part of the development team. The director of a World War II museum, for example, may be involved in developing a new museum database system that contains data and information on all of the World War II exhibits and artifacts stored in the museum.

Systems development specialists are typically computer systems personnel. Depending on the nature of the systems project, the development team might include the project leader, systems analysts, and software programmers, among others. A *project leader* is the individual in charge of the systems development effort. This person coordinates all aspects of the systems development effort and is responsible for its success. A **systems analyst** is a professional who specializes in analyzing and designing systems. Systems analysts play important roles while interacting with the system stakeholders and users, management, software programmers, and other computer systems support personnel (see Figure 9.3). Like an architect developing blueprints for a new building, a systems analyst develops detailed plans for the new or modified system. The *software programmer*, sometimes called a computer programmer or software engineer, is responsible for modifying existing programs or developing new programs to satisfy user requirements. Like a contractor constructing a new building or renovating an existing one, the programmer takes the plans from the systems analyst and builds or modifies the necessary software.

The other support personnel on the development team are mostly technical specialists, either computer systems department employees or outside consultants, including database and telecommunications experts, knowledge engineers, and other personnel such as vendor or supplier representatives. Some specialize

FIGURE 9.3 • Participants in systems development
The systems analyst plays an important role in the development team, and is often the only person who sees the system in its totality. The arrows in this figure do not mean that there is no direct communication between other team members. Instead, these arrows represent the pivotal role of the systems analyst—an individual who is often called upon to be an interface, facilitator, moderator, negotiator, and interpreter for development activities.

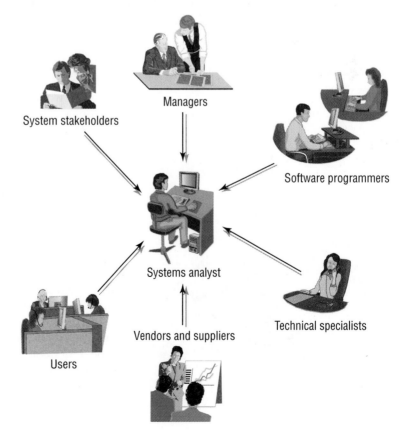

in building new systems, while others might specialize in implementing computer systems or testing them. Depending on the magnitude of the systems development project and the number of computer systems development specialists on the team, the team may also include one or more computer systems managers. *Computer systems management* can include the chief information officer (CIO) and other computer systems executives.

Why Start a Systems Development Project?

Many organizations seek to initiate systems development projects that will provide a competitive advantage. Organizations are always seeking a competitive advantage. For example, music companies are always looking for the next big hit. Software companies are always exploring ways to make new products that people will flock to. Each movie studio wants to be the one with the next big box office hit. Oil companies want to maximize their profits. Figuring out how to gain a competitive advantage usually requires creative and critical analysis.

Creative analysis involves the investigation of new approaches to existing problems. Fuji and Kodak are hoping to achieve a competitive advantage by developing online photo-sharing services.[10] The services are aimed at camera-enabled cell phone users who don't know what to do with the photos after they snap them with their cell phone (see Figure 9.4). Allstate Financial Group created a Web site called Access-Allstate to allow 350,000 sales reps to get information about Allstate insurance, retirement, and investment products.[11] It provided a competitive advantage because sales reps could rapidly respond to customer needs. Before the Web site, Allstate sales reps had to call the company for information. By looking at problems in new or different ways and by introducing innovative methods to solve them, many organizations have gained significant competitive advantage. Typically, these new solutions are inspired by people and things not directly related to the problem.

Critical analysis means being skeptical and doubtful, and requires questioning whether or not the current computer system is still effective and efficient. Critical analysis can result in finding a better way of doing things, and ways that can result in a competitive advantage. The bankrupt United Airlines, for example, looked critically at its operation and decided that providing e-mail on many of its flights would attract more business customers, generate additional revenue, and give the company a competitive advantage.[12] As part of the resulting systems development project, United is hiring Verizon to provide the in-flight e-mail services.

The systems development process often begins with gathering information on users' needs. Questioning users about their needs and being skeptical and doubtful about initial responses can result in better systems and more accurate predictions of how those systems will work. Too often, system stakeholders and users specify certain system requirements because they assume the only way to meet their needs is through those requirements. But often, their needs might best be met through an alternate approach. For example, a movie producer might decide to hire a team of stuntmen for an action scene because this is how he has done it for decades. However, a new computerized imaging system might be able to digitally generate the scenes he wants at less expense. All too often, problem solutions are selected before a complete understanding of the nature of the problem itself is obtained.

FIGURE 9.4 • Competing in a changing market

FujiFilm and Kodak have created online photo-sharing services aimed at digital camera users and camera-enabled cell phone users who don't know what to do with photos after they snap them.

End-User Systems Development

End users often decide to develop their own systems to achieve a competitive advantage. *End-user systems development* is the development of computer systems by individuals outside of the formal computer systems planning and departmental structure. The increased availability and use of general-purpose information technology and the flexibility of many packaged software programs have allowed non-computer-systems employees to independently develop computer systems that meet their needs. These employees feel that, by bypassing the formal requisitioning of developmental resources from the computer systems department, they could develop systems more quickly. In addition, these individuals often feel that they have better insight into their own needs and could develop systems better suited to their purposes. Macromedia, for example, has an end-user systems development tool called Contribute that is designed to make it easy for people to develop and edit Web pages.[13] Such a Web development tool can be used to give specific people and groups the ability to edit specified Web sites (see Figure 9.5). In addition, many end users are increasingly developing computer systems or solving computer-related problems for others.[14] Dennis Christensen's coworkers often call him to fix computer glitches, printer problems, or e-mail stoppages. Christensen is a marketing manager for a Michigan credit bureau and not a computer systems person.

End-user-developed systems range from the very small (a software routine to merge form letters) to those of significant organizational value (such as customer contact databases). Like all projects, some end-user-developed systems fail, while others are successful. Initially, computer systems professionals discounted the value of these projects and basically ignored them. As the number and magnitude of these projects increased, however, computer systems professionals began to realize that for the good of the entire organization, their involvement with these projects needed to increase.

Today, the term end-user systems development is more commonly used to describe any systems development project in which the primary effort is undertaken by some combination of system stakeholders and users. Rather than ignoring these initiatives, astute computer systems professionals encourage them by offering guidance and support. Technical assistance, communication of standards, and the sharing of "best practices" throughout the organization are just some of the ways computer systems professionals work with motivated managers and employees undertaking their own systems development. In this way, end-user-developed systems can be structured to be complementary to, rather than in conflict with, existing and emerging computer systems. In addition, this open communication between computer systems professionals and potential system stakeholders and users allows the computer systems professionals to identify specific initiatives that should be elevated in status so that additional organizational resources are provided for their development.

FIGURE 9.5 • End user development with Macromedia Contribute

As the Internet stretches and expands, more and more end users are driven to develop their own Web pages. This development is made easier by products like Macromedia Contribute.

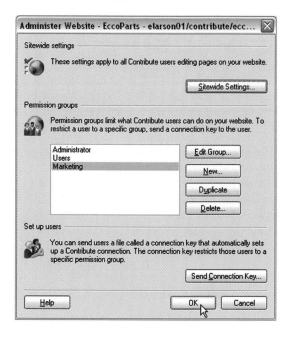

TOOLSFOR**SYSTEMS**DEVELOPMENT

Systems development tools can greatly simplify the systems development process. In the strictest sense, a tool can be almost any instrument, from a pencil to a large, complex machine. Systems development tools most often used include computer-aided software engineering tools, flowcharts, decision tables, project management tools, prototyping, outsourcing, and object-oriented systems development.

Computer-Aided Software Engineering

One type of systems development tool consists of software programs that help automate various aspects of the systems development process. Software engineering, a formal way of conducting systems development, typically employs software-based systems development tools called **computer-aided software engineering (CASE)** tools. CASE tools automate many of the tasks required in a systems development effort (see Figure 9.6).

FIGURE 9.6 • CASE tools

CASE tools can be used to diagram and develop new computer systems.

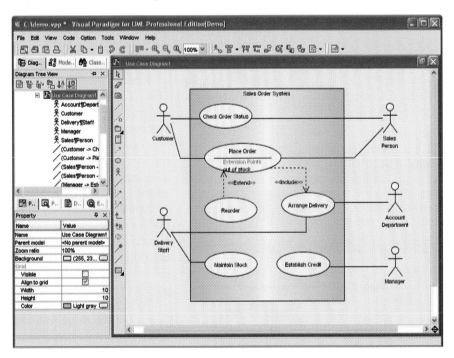

As with any team, coordinating the efforts of members of a systems development team can be a problem. To help address coordination problems, many mainframe and network CASE tools allow more than one person to work on the same system at the same time via a multiuser interface. The multiuser interface coordinates and integrates the work performed by all members of the same design team. With this facility, one person working on one aspect of systems development can automatically share his or her results with someone working on another aspect of the same system.[15]

Flowcharts

Like a road map, a **flowchart** reveals the path from a starting point to the final destination. Flowcharts can display any amount of detail. Through the use of symbols, flowcharts show the logical relationships between system components. Some of the more commonly used flowcharting symbols are shown in Figure 9.7.

When developing a system, a general flowchart is used to describe the overall purpose and structure of the system. This is usually called the system flowchart or application flowchart. An *application flowchart* for a simplified payroll application is shown in Figure 9.8. Inputs include an employee file that contains an employee's pay rate and a time file that contains the hours the employee worked during the week. The payroll program multiplies the pay rate times the hours

FIGURE 9.7 • Some basic flowcharting symbols

The symbols in a flowchart show the logical relationships between system components.
These are some of the more commonly used flowcharting symbols.

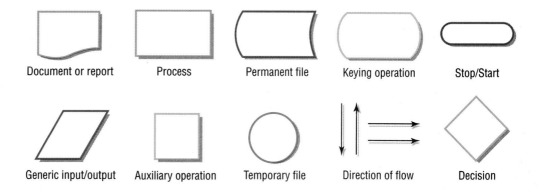

FIGURE 9.8 • An application flowchart of a simplified payroll application

Circles in this application flowchart show that inputs include an employee file and a time file. The
process square labeled "Payroll program" represents the operations of multiplying the pay rate times
the hours worked and subtracting deductions to compute the employee's paycheck.

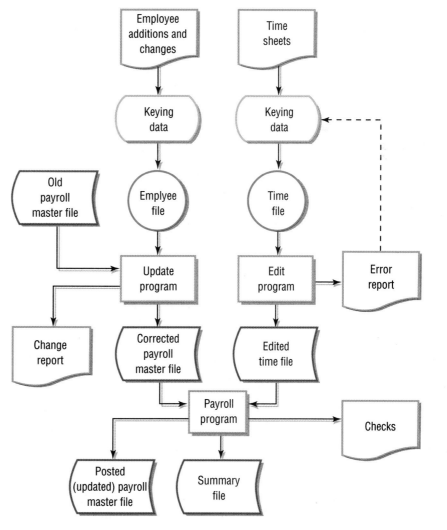

worked and subtracts any deductions to compute the paycheck for the employee. More detailed flowcharts, called *program flowcharts*, are needed to reveal how each software program is to be developed.

Flowcharts have a number of limitations. They were originally developed to help programmers and analysts design and document computer systems and programs. As programs became larger, flowcharts became more difficult to implement. You can imagine how difficult it would be to develop a detailed program flowchart for a program containing more than 50,000 program statements. As a result, many organizations are now reducing the amount of flowcharting they use.

Decision Tables

A **decision table** can be used as an alternative to or in conjunction with flowcharts. When there are a large number of branches or paths within a software program, decision tables are particularly useful; in fact, in these cases, decision tables are preferable to flowcharts. In general, a decision table displays the various conditions that could exist and the different actions that the computer should take as a result of these conditions. A decision table that would aid decisions regarding airline reservations is shown in Figure 9.9.

FIGURE 9.9 • A decision table for an airline reservation application

A decision table displays the various conditions that could exist and the different actions that the computer should take as a result of these conditions.

Airline reservation application	Rule number			
	1	2	3	4
Condition statements				
First-class requested	Y	Y	N	N
First-class available	Y	N	N	N
Tourist-class requested	N	N	Y	Y
Tourist-class available	N	N	Y	N
Actions taken				
First-class ticket issued	X			
Tourist-class ticket issued			X	
First-class wait listed		X		
Tourist-class wait listed				X

Name of decision table

Rule numbers

Condition statement

Actual conditions

Action statement

Action taken

EXPAND YOUR KNOWLEDGE

To learn more about project management tools, go to www.course.com/swt. Click the link "Expand Your Knowledge," and then complete the lab entitled, "Project Management."

Project Management Tools

Although the steps of systems development seem straightforward, larger projects can become complex, requiring literally hundreds or thousands of separate activities. For these types of systems development efforts, project management becomes essential. The casino company Harrah's Entertainment, for example, is offering its computer systems personnel project management training that is specific to its casino operations.[16] The overall purpose of **project management** is to plan, monitor, and control necessary development activities. Even for smaller systems development projects, some type of project management must be undertaken. America West, for example, struggled after the September 11, 2001, terrorist attack.[17] The airline industry has lost $18 billion since September 11th and may lose another $10 billion before they recover. According to Joe Beery, chief information officer at America West, "The rigors, constraints and milestones that you have to meet to move forward with new programs have now become much more intense."

Two techniques frequently used in project management are Program Evaluation and Review Technique (PERT) and Gantt charting. PERT is a formalized approach that involves creating three time estimates for an activity: the shortest possible time, the most likely time, and the longest possible time. A formula is then applied to come up with a single PERT time estimate. A Gantt chart is a graphical tool used for planning, monitoring, and coordinating projects. A Gantt chart is essentially a grid that lists activities and deadlines. Each time a task is completed, a darkened line is placed in the proper grid cell to indicate completion of a task (see Figure 9.10).

FIGURE 9.10 • Gantt chart

A Gantt chart shows progress through systems development activities by putting a bar through appropriate cells.

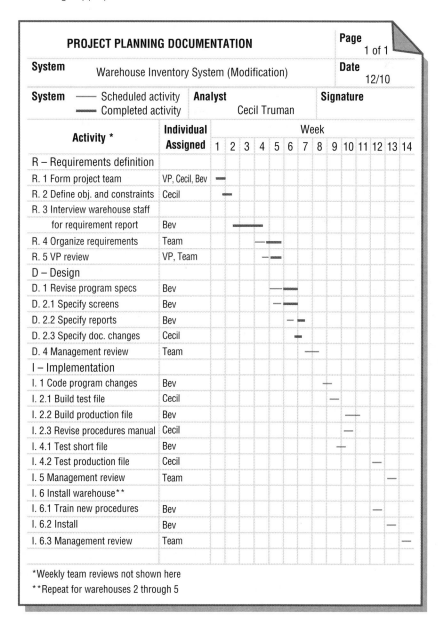

PROJECT PLANNING DOCUMENTATION — Page 1 of 1

System: Warehouse Inventory System (Modification) — Date 12/10

System —— Scheduled activity / —— Completed activity — Analyst: Cecil Truman — Signature

Activity *	Individual Assigned	Week 1	2	3	4	5	6	7	8	9	10	11	12	13	14
R – Requirements definition															
R. 1 Form project team	VP, Cecil, Bev	—													
R. 2 Define obj. and constraints	Cecil		—												
R. 3 Interview warehouse staff for requirement report	Bev			—											
R. 4 Organize requirements	Team					—									
R. 5 VP review	VP, Team						—								
D – Design															
D. 1 Revise program specs	Bev						—								
D. 2.1 Specify screens	Bev						—								
D. 2.2 Specify reports	Bev						—								
D. 2.3 Specify doc. changes	Cecil							—							
D. 4 Management review	Team								—						
I – Implementation															
I. 1 Code program changes	Bev								—						
I. 2.1 Build test file	Cecil								—						
I. 2.2 Build production file	Bev									—					
I. 2.3 Revise procedures manual	Cecil									—					
I. 4.1 Test short file	Bev									—					
I. 4.2 Test production file	Cecil											—			
I. 5 Management review	Team											—			
I. 6 Install warehouse**															
I. 6.1 Train new procedures	Bev											—			
I. 6.2 Install	Bev											—			
I. 6.3 Management review	Team												—		

*Weekly team reviews not shown here

**Repeat for warehouses 2 through 5

Both PERT and Gantt techniques can be automated using project management software, such as Microsoft Project. This type of software monitors all project activities and determines if activities and the entire project are on time and within budget. Project management software also has workgroup capabilities, having the ability to handle multiple projects and enabling a team of people to interact with the same software. Project management software helps people determine the best way to reduce project completion time at the least cost (see Figure 9.11). Reducing project completion time is called project crashing. This project management software feature can be very useful if a project starts to fall behind schedule or realizes cost overruns.

FIGURE 9.11 • Project crashing in Microsoft Project

By applying PERT and Gantt techniques, people can use project management software to create and implement plans that reduce the time needed to complete a project.

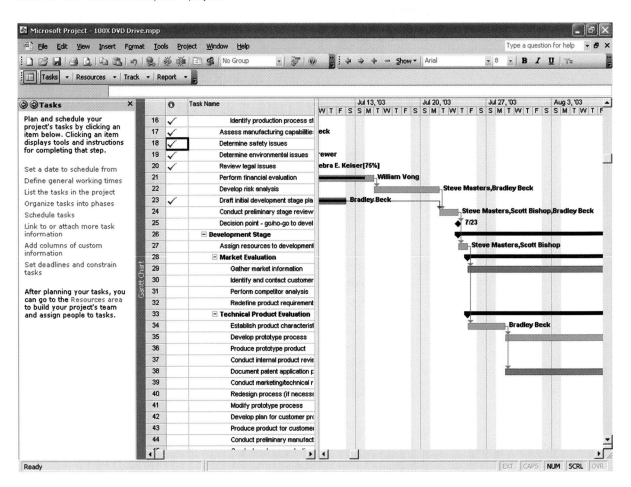

Prototyping

A different technique for systems development uses a phased or iterative approach. With the iterative approach to systems development, each phase of the SDLC is repeated several times (iterated). During each iteration, requirements and alternative solutions to the problem are analyzed, solutions are designed, and some portion of the system is implemented and subject to a user review (see Figure 9.12).

FIGURE 9.12 • An iterative approach to systems development

During an iteration, each phase of the SDLC is repeated several times. System requirements and alternate solutions to the problem are analyzed, solutions are designed, and some portion of the system is implemented and subjected to a user review.

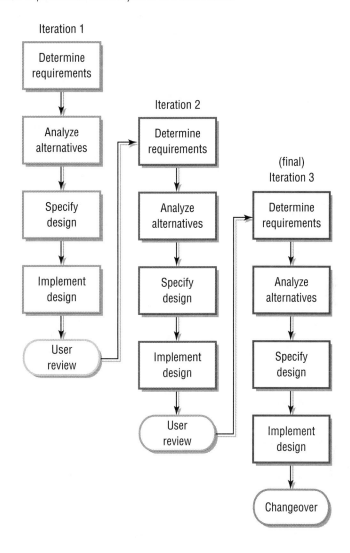

A prominent example of an iterative technique for systems development is prototyping. **Prototyping** typically involves the creation of some preliminary model or version of a major subsystem, or a small or "scaled-down" version of the entire system. For example, a prototype might be developed to show sample report formats and input screens using a graphics program. Once developed and refined, the prototype reports and input screens developed in the graphics program are used as models for the actual system, which may be developed using a programming language such as C++ or Visual Basic. In many cases, prototyping continues until the complete system is developed.

The iterative approach using prototypes has the following sequence of steps:

1. Investigate, analyze, and define the problem.
2. Build the initial version or prototype of the system. The builder could be the user or someone from the computer systems department. The initial version is usually built quickly (days or weeks) and may be a working prototype.
3. Put the prototype into operation. After giving the prototype to the user(s), they will utilize the initial version and evaluate it.

4. Refine and modify the prototype. User(s) provide feedback to the system builder about possible additions, deletions, and modifications. Users will almost always want additions to system capabilities. They want to know, "If the system can do this, can't it also do this?" The builder then incorporates suggestions into a second version of the system. The iterative process now cycles between Steps 2, 3, and 4, producing successive refinements to the system.

The first preliminary model is refined to form second- and third-generation models, and so on until the complete system is developed (see Figure 9.13). Research has shown that system investigation, design, and implementation are the phases that benefit the most from the prototyping approach. According to Porus Munshi, a computer systems consultant, "Rapid prototyping is the cornerstone of innovation. In the dilemma between perfecting a design and experimenting, go for the experiment every time."[18]

To gain a better understanding of the use of prototyping, consider a company that sells and services vending equipment in Wisconsin, Illinois, and Indiana. The company wants to develop a new sales application for its five sales representatives to show revenues from their areas. The company decides to use prototyping and starts by developing a program that simply prints sample sales reports. No data is entered into the program at this time. After studying the sales reports for a week, sales representatives and sales management suggest several changes. These changes are made in the program, which is then expanded to accept some data from the sales ordering program and print two sample reports for each representative using actual data. The sales representatives and sales managers evaluate how effective the two actual reports are for their own particular purposes and make further suggestions. The changes are made and additional input data and reports are added to the application. This iterative process, typical of prototyping, continues until the new application is complete and satisfies the needs of both the sales representatives and sales management.

Advantages and disadvantages of the prototyping approach are shown in Table 9.1. Although some important steps may be omitted, a system can usually be developed faster by using prototyping than by using the traditional systems development process.

Outsourcing. Many organizations and countries hire an outside consulting firm that specializes in systems development to take over some or all of its computer systems development activities. This approach, called **outsourcing**, is gaining in popularity. WorldCom, for example, was given an outsourcing deal worth $20 million to develop a cellular phone system in Baghdad, Iraq by the U.S. Department of Defense.[19]

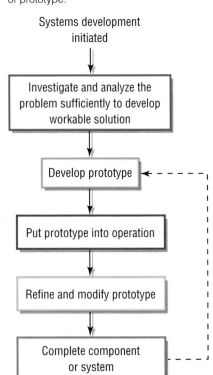

FIGURE 9.13 • Prototyping

Prototyping is a popular technique in systems development. User and stakeholder feedback is used to refine each generation of prototype.

TABLE 9.1 • Advantages and Disadvantages of Prototyping Compared to the Traditional Systems Development Process

Advantages	Disadvantages
A prototype can be developed faster than the traditional systems development process.	Some important steps may be forgotten or overlooked, including testing, training, and documentation.
Errors and possible problems can be located in less time.	There is no formal ending process with prototyping. It can go on for a very long time.
Users can try the system early in the process and provide important feedback.	

Reducing costs, obtaining state-of-the-art technology, eliminating staffing and personnel problems, and increasing technological flexibility are reasons that organizations have used the outsourcing approach. American Express, for example, hired IBM for about $4 billion over 7 years to manage its Web site, network servers, data storage, and help-desk operations.[20] The deal also moved about 2,000 American Express employees to IBM's Global Services division. In another outsourcing deal, AT&T has agreed to pay Accenture, a computer consulting company, about $2.6 billion to provide guidance on cutting costs and improving efficiency for AT&T's long-distance division. Weyerhaeuser, a wood products company, used outsourcing for many of its IS personnel.[21] It hired EDS and transferred many of its employees to EDS.

There are, however, disadvantages to the outsourcing approach. Organizations using outsourcing may be asked to sign complicated and restrictive legal contracts that may be difficult to change. Internal expertise and loyalty can suffer under an outsourcing arrangement. When an organization uses outsourcing, key computer systems personnel with expertise in technical and organizational functions are no longer needed. Once these computer systems employees leave, the organization loses their experience with the organization and their expertise in computer systems. In addition, outsourcing large and complex projects can be very expensive in the long run.

Outsourcing can be very costly. Because of a faulty sales ordering system that had been outsourced, the aviation parts company, Aviall, lost about $70 million in sales.[22] Aviall decided to develop its own systems for $40 million and saw a $430 million increase in sales. For other companies, it can be difficult to achieve a competitive advantage when competitors are using the same outsourcing company. When the outsourcing is done offshore or in a foreign country, some people have raised security concerns.[23] A Gartner, Inc. study estimates that about 80 percent of U.S. companies outsource critical activities to India, Russia, Pakistan, and China. Some believe that this figure is even higher.

Object-Oriented Systems Development

Object-oriented (OO) systems development is a continuation of object-oriented programming.[24] OO development follows a defined system development life cycle, much like the SDLC. The life cycle phases can be, and usually are, completed with lots of iterations. Object-oriented systems development typically involves:

1. Defining requirements. This means defining all of the objects that are part of the user's work environment using a process called object-oriented analysis. Analysis involves studying the organization and building a model of the objects that are part of the organization (such as a customer, an order, or a payment).
2. Designing the system. This means defining all of the objects in the system and how they interact, using a process called object-oriented design.
3. Implementation and programming. Programming involves writing statements that define system objects, using a process called object-oriented implementation or programming. Implementation is where the object model begun during analysis and completed during design is turned into a set of interacting objects in the system. Object-oriented programming languages are designed to allow the programmer to create classes of objects in the computer system that correspond to the objects in the organization. Objects such as customer, order, and payment are defined as certain computer system elements, such as a customer screen, an order-entry menu, or a dollar sign icon. Then scenarios are created. Each scenario is like a script, which documents the way the objects behave when the system is used for a certain task. Programmers then write program statements that define objects and show how these objects interact for certain tasks.

4. Evaluation. The initial implementation is evaluated by users and improved. Additional scenarios and objects are added and the cycle repeats.
5. Operation. Finally, a complete, tested, and approved system is available for use.

The object-oriented approach can be used during all phases of systems development, from investigation to maintenance and review. Consider a kayak rental business in Maui, Hawaii, where the owner wants to computerize its operations. This business has many system objects, including the kayak rental clerk, renting kayaks to customers, and adding new kayaks into the rental program. These objects can be diagrammed (see Figure 9.14). As you can see, the kayak rental clerk rents kayaks to customers and adds new kayaks to the current inventory of kayaks available for rent. The stick figure is an example of an *actor*, and the ovals each represent an event, called a *use case*. In our example, the actor (the kayak rental clerk) interacts with two use cases (rent kayaks to customers and add new kayaks to inventory).

Although it is still necessary to go through systems investigation and analysis to determine organizational objectives and system requirements, systems design and implementation are often easier and cost less in object-oriented (OO) systems development because existing programming modules can be used. Also, maintenance can be simplified if programming objects can be reused to upgrade existing software and systems. Finally, because system objects are self-contained units, they can be changed or replaced without interfering with the rest of the system. These benefits are the main reasons for the interest in object-oriented systems development.

Object-oriented systems development and the other tools discussed in the preceding sections are used throughout the systems development life cycle, beginning with systems investigation, discussed next.

FIGURE 9.14 • **Diagram for a kayak rental program**

A kayak rental business has many system objects, including the kayak rental clerk, renting kayaks to customers, and adding new kayaks into the rental program. This figure illustrates one way to diagram these objects.

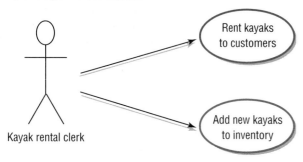

Kayak rental clerk

Rent kayaks to customers

Add new kayaks to inventory

SYSTEMSINVESTIGATION

Systems investigation is usually the first step in the development of a new or modified computer system. The overall purpose of **systems investigation** is to determine whether or not the objectives met by the existing system are satisfying the goals of the organization. In systems investigation, potential problems and opportunities are identified. Investigation attempts to reveal the cause and scope of the problem or opportunity. In general, systems investigation attempts to uncover answers to the following types of questions:

• What primary problems might a new or enhanced system solve?
• What opportunities might a new or enhanced system provide?
• What new hardware, software, databases, telecommunications, personnel, or procedures will improve an existing system, or are required in a new system?
• What are the potential costs?
• What are the associated risks?

The systems investigation phase consists of two steps: initiating the investigation and conducting a feasibility study.

Lenox Initiates Systems Development and Sees Improved Customer Satisfaction

Bob Palmer, vice president of information technology at Lenox Collections, a division of Lenox Inc., decided to initiate a systems development effort to improve the company's Internet site. As a result of systems investigation, he and a team of developers set out to revamp LenoxCollections.com. Palmer and the development had four goals:

1. Reduce the number of clicks in the checkout process
2. More closely align the site with the company's catalog
3. Provide consumers with more information about their purchases
4. Update the site design

What happened after systems development was initiated? The team invested 17 months in the project, with the design phase taking 14 months, followed by 3 months of development. By being thorough in the design of the Web site and supportive systems, Palmer and his team could be assured that the development process would progress smoothly and quickly, and maintenance of the system would be minimal.

Palmer says the work has already paid for itself. LenoxCollections.com saw a 115 percent sales increase in one quarter.

Palmer's team took the experience gained from LenoxCollections.com and applied it to other Lenox Web sites. He says that about 70 percent of the code used on LenoxCollections.com was reusable, allowing his team to put up a site for U.K.-based retailer Brooks & Bentley in less than 3 months. Palmer says his development team can now quickly implement new features when customers request them. "Now that we've got the basics right, additional features aren't difficult to add," he says.

Questions

1. What were the goals and what was involved in this project?
2. Find an example of a poor-quality Web site that embarrasses the organization that it represents. What features make it a bad Web site? What features are likely to motivate customers to return to a Web site and make additional purchases?

Sources
1. *"Lenox Inc.," Michael Meehan,* Computerworld, *March 11, 2002, www.computerworld.com.*
2. *"EasyAsk Wins Lenox, J. Jill, and SmartBargains; LenoxCollections.com Signs as EasyAsk's First Search Advisor Customer," Staff,* Business Wire, *April 15, 2002.*
3. *LenoxCollections.com Web site, www.lenoxcollections.com, accessed July 2002.*

Initiating Systems Investigation

Systems investigation can be initiated in a number of ways by managers inside the organization, requests from clients or customers outside the organization, as a result of new governmental regulations, and many other ways. Since the 1980s, as people learned more about the capabilities and limitations of computer systems, systems development requests began to be initiated by stakeholders outside the computer department, including users and nonusers of the system, from customers, suppliers, and government agencies to employees and managers. For example, customer needs can trigger new systems development efforts. Marriott International decided to launch a major systems development project to provide wireless Internet connection to its major hotels to satisfy customer demands

(see Figure 9.15). According to Lou Paladeau, vice president for Marriott's Technology Development department, "Customers are making decisions about where they stay based on where this technology is available. If you don't have it, you're not getting them in the door." Marriott is using Wi-Fi at their hotels, including Courtyard and Residence Inn facilities.

FIGURE 9.15 • Customer needs can initiate new systems development efforts

In hotel lobbies all over the world, people are using Wi-Fi to access the Internet with their laptops, cell phones, and PDAs. Satisfying customer demands was the reason Marriott International launched a systems development project to provide wireless Internet access at its major hotels.

In some cases, one systems development project initiates changes to other systems or companies. Aventis Pharmaceuticals, for example, embarked on a systems development project to upgrade its e-mail system.[25] The upgrade caused a complete redevelopment of the company's global hardware and software systems, including operating systems. The new systems development project took more than 3 years to complete. Peugeot Citroen initiated a systems development effort to use software to improve how its car bodies are manufactured.[26] Like many systems development efforts, the Peugeot Citroen project had an impact on the companies that supplied it with car parts. The company believes that the systems development project resulted in an additional $130 million in increased profits.

Feasibility Analysis

A key part of the systems investigation phase is feasibility analysis, which investigates the problem to be solved or opportunity to be met. Feasibility analysis involves an investigation into technical, economic, legal, opera-

tional, and schedule feasibility (see Table 9.2). **Technical feasibility** is concerned with whether or not hardware, software, and other system components can be acquired or developed to solve the problem. Quicken Loans, Inc., for example, is investigating the technical feasibility of using new hardware and software to simplify the loan process.[27] According to a company representative, "We are trying to make applying for mortgages as easy as applying for a credit card." **Economic feasibility** determines if the project makes financial sense and whether predicted benefits offset the cost and time needed to obtain them. Putnam Lovell Securities investigated the economic feasibility of sending financial research reports to its customers and executives electronically instead of through the mail.[28] Economic feasibility can involve analyzing cash flows and costs. **Legal feasibility** determines whether laws or regulations may prevent or limit a systems development project. For example, an Internet site that allowed users to share music without paying musicians or music producers was sued. Legal feasibility involves an analysis of existing and future laws to determine the likelihood of legal action against the systems development project and the possible consequences.

TABLE 9.2 • Types of Feasibility

Type of Feasibility	Description
Technical feasibility	Determines whether or not hardware, software, and other system components can be acquired or developed
Economic feasibility	Determines if the project makes financial sense
Legal feasibility	Determines whether laws or regulations may prevent or limit a systems development project
Operational feasibility	Measure of whether or not the project can be put into action or operation
Schedule feasibility	Determines if the project can be completed in a reasonable amount of time

Operational feasibility is a measure of whether or not the project can be put into action or operation. Operational feasibility includes both physical and motivational considerations. Motivational considerations (acceptance of change) are very important, because new systems affect people and may have unintended consequences. As a result, power and politics may come into play. Some people may resist the new system. Because of deadly hospital errors, a healthcare consortium called the Leapfrog Group is looking into the operational feasibility of developing a new computerized physician-order entry system.[29] The new system would require that all prescriptions and every order a doctor gives to staff be entered into the computer. The computer would then check for drug allergies and interactions between drugs. If operationally feasible, the new system could save lives and lawsuits. Finally, **schedule feasibility** determines if the project can be completed in a reasonable amount of time—a process that involves balancing the time requirements of the project with other projects. In some cases, additional resources can be expended to shorten project completion dates. The solution to a problem, for instance, might be technically complex and time-consuming to develop; the logistics of controlling a system might require numerous employees and bring significant labor costs.

If a systems development project is determined to be worthwhile and feasible, systems analysis will formally begin.

SYSTEMSANALYSIS

After a project has been approved for further study during systems investigation, the next step is to perform a detailed analysis of the existing system, whether or not it is currently computer-based. **Systems analysis** attempts to understand how the existing system helps solve the problem identified in systems investigation and answer the question, "What must the computer system do to solve the problem?" The process involves understanding the broader aspects of the system that would be required to solve the problem and address the limitations of the existing system, as identified in systems investigation. The overall emphasis of analysis is to gather data on the existing system and the requirements for the new system, and to consider alternative solutions to the problem within these constraints and the feasibility of these solutions. The primary result of systems analysis is a listing of systems requirements and priorities.

General Analysis Considerations

Systems analysis starts by clarifying the overall goals of the individual or organization and determining how the existing or proposed computer system helps meet these goals. A university, for example, might want to develop a fundraising database that contains information on all of the people, trusts, and organizations that have made financial contributions or donations to the university. This goal can be translated into one or more informational needs. One need might be to create and maintain an accurate list of all projects funded by donations made to the university. Another need might be to produce a list of all donors who contributed more than $1,000 over the last year. The list can be used to generate personalized thank you letters.

Analysis of a small organization's computer system can be fairly straightforward. On the other hand, evaluating an existing computer system for a large organization can be a long, tedious process. As a result, large organizations evaluating a major computer system normally follow a formalized analysis procedure involving: collecting appropriate data, analyzing the data, and determining new system requirements and project priorities (see Figure 9.16)

Data Collection

The purpose of data collection is to seek additional information about the problems or needs identified during systems investigation. In many cases, the strengths and weaknesses of the existing system are uncovered.

Data collection involves identifying and locating the various sources of data. In general, there are both internal sources and external sources (see Table 9.3). Notice that many of both the internal and external sources are stakeholders.

Once data collection sources have been identified, data collection begins. Figure 9.17 shows the steps involved. Once data is collected, it is often necessary to clarify

FIGURE 9.16 • The sequence of systems analysis activities

Large organizations follow a formalized analysis procedure that involves collecting appropriate data, analyzing the data, and determining new system requirements and project priorities.

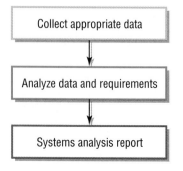

TABLE 9.3 • **Internal and External Sources of Data for Systems Analysis**

Internal Sources	External Sources
Users, stakeholders, and managers	Customers
Organizational charts	Suppliers
Forms and documents, including input documents from accounting and other transactions	Stockholders
Procedure manuals and written policies	Local, state, and federal government agencies
Financial reports	Competitors
Computer documents, including computer systems manuals	Outside organizations, such as environmental associations
Other measures of existing processes	Trade journals, books, and periodicals related to the organization
	External consultants and other commercial groups

FIGURE 9.17 • **The steps of data collection**

After data sources have been identified, interviews, direct observation, outputs, questionnaires, and other data collection methods are used to collect the data. Often, it is necessary to clarify what the data means.

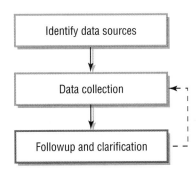

what it means. Data collection may require a number of tools and techniques, such as interviews, direct observation, outputs, questionnaires, and other data collection methods.

Interviews. In a *structured interview*, questions are written in advance. In an *unstructured interview*, the questions are not written in advance; the interviewer relies on experience in asking the best questions to uncover the inherent problems and weaknesses of the existing system. An advantage of the unstructured interview is that it allows the interviewer to ask follow-up or clarifying questions immediately.

Direct Observation. With *direct observation*, one or more members of the analysis team directly observe the existing system in action. One of the best ways to understand how the existing system functions is to literally work with users to discover how data flows in certain tasks. This entails direct observation of users' work procedures, their reports, current screens (if a computer system is already in use), and so on. From this observation, members of the analysis team determine which forms and procedures are adequate and which are inadequate and need improvement. Direct observation, however, requires a certain amount of skill. The observer must be able to see what is really happening and not be influenced by his or her own attitudes or feelings. This approach can reveal important problems and opportunities, information that would be difficult to obtain using other data collection methods.

Outputs. Outputs from the existing system, both manual and computerized, are obtained during data collection. These outputs can be obtained from various records, the organization's transaction processing and decision support systems, and other sources. These outputs can include memos, letters, organization charts (see Figure 9.18), payroll documents, inventory reports, and bills that have been sent or have not been paid. These outputs, or a lack of them, are important in analyzing problems with the existing system or unmet opportunities.

FIGURE 9.18 • Outputs from existing systems

An organization chart can be an important source of information.

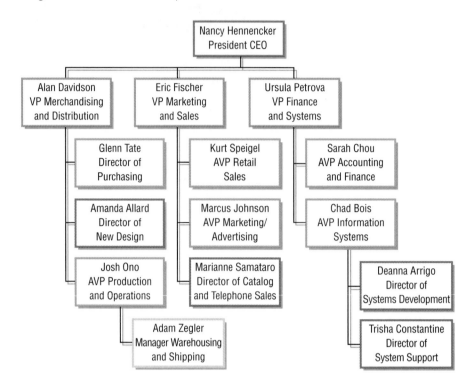

Questionnaires. When many data sources are spread over a wide geographic area, questionnaires may be the best approach. Like interviews, questionnaires can be either structured or unstructured. In most cases, a preliminary study is conducted to fine-tune the questionnaire. A follow-up questionnaire can capture the opinions of those who do not respond to the original questionnaire.

Other Data Collection Methods. A number of other data collection techniques can be employed. In some cases, telephone calls are an excellent method. In other cases, activities may be simulated to see how the existing system reacts. Simulated sales orders, customer complaints, and data-flow bottlenecks may be created to see how the existing system responds to these situations. *Statistical sampling*, which involves taking a random sample of data, is another technique. For example, suppose that we want to collect data that describes 10,000 sales orders received over the last few years. Analyzing each of the 10,000 sales orders is too time-consuming, so statistical sampling can be used to collect a random sample of 100 or 200 sales orders from the entire batch. The characteristics of this sample are then assumed to apply to the 10,000 sales orders.

Data Analysis

The data collected in its raw form is usually not adequate to determine the effectiveness and efficiency of an existing system, nor the requirements for a new system. The next step is to use data analysis to put the collected data into a form that is usable by the members of the development team participating in systems analysis. Two commonly used data analysis tools are application flowcharts and CASE tools, which were discussed earlier.

Requirements Analysis

The overall purpose of **requirements analysis** is to determine user, stakeholder, and organizational needs. For an accounts payable application, the stakeholders could include suppliers and members of the purchasing department. Questions that should be asked during requirements analysis include the following: Are these stakeholders satisfied with the current accounts payable application? What improvements could be made to satisfy suppliers and help the Purchasing Department?

Numerous tools and techniques can be used to capture systems requirements, including asking directly, critical success factors, joint application development, and rapid application development. The Milan, Italy, clothes designer Prada, for example, performed requirements analysis and determined that its salespeople needed to do a better job greeting customers and understanding their needs.30 The resulting system provided salespeople with a handheld computer that they could use to access customer preferences and shopping habits. The device could scan sales tags of Prada merchandise and access the Internet to get information on the styles available, fabrics that were used, and the accessories that could be purchased for the scanned item.

Asking Directly. One of the most basic techniques used in requirements analysis is asking directly. *Asking directly* is an approach that asks users and stakeholders about what they want and expect from a new or modified system. This approach works best for stable systems in which stakeholders or users have a clear understanding of the system's functions. Unfortunately, many individuals do not know exactly or are unable to adequately articulate what they want or need. The role of the systems analyst during the analysis phase is to exercise critical and creative thinking skills, questioning statements and assumptions, in order to understand and convey these individual requirements so that the new or modified system will best meet users' and stakeholders' requirements.

Critical Success Factors. Another approach uses *critical success factors (CSF)*. Users and stakeholders are asked to list only those factors or items that are critical to the success of their area or the organization. A CSF for a lawyer might be exceptional legal research. A CSF for a sales representative could be a list of customers currently buying a certain type of product. Starting from these CSFs, the system inputs, outputs, performance, and other specific requirements can be determined. One study found that different CSFs might be important during different phases of a systems development project.[31]

Joint Application Development. *Joint application development (JAD)* can be used in place of traditional data collection and requirements analysis procedures. Originally developed by IBM Canada in the 1970s, JAD involves group meetings in which users, stakeholders, and computer systems professionals work together to analyze existing systems, propose possible solutions, and define the requirements of a new or modified system. JAD groups consist of both problem holders and solution providers. A group normally requires one or more top-level executives who initiate the JAD process, a group leader for the meetings, people who will use the system, and one or more individuals who act as secretaries and clerks to record what is accomplished and to provide general support for the sessions (see Figure 9.19). Many organizations have found that groups can develop better requirements than individuals working independently and have assessed JAD as a very successful development technique.

FIGURE 9.19 • Joint application development

Joint application development includes a group leader for the meetings, people who will use the system, and one or more individuals who act as secretaries and clerks to record what is accomplished and to provide general support for the sessions.

Rapid Application Development. Another efficient approach to determine and define systems requirements of a group is called rapid application development. *Rapid application development (RAD)* combines JAD, prototyping, and other techniques in order to quickly and accurately determine the requirements for a system. RAD involves a process in which a developer first builds a working model, or prototype, of the system to help a group of stakeholders, users, or managers identify how well the system meets their requirements. The prototypes are then refined to more closely align with stated requirements. Rational Software, a division of IBM, has RAD tools to make developing large Java programs and applications easier and faster.[32]

SYSTEMSDESIGN

The purpose of **systems design** is to select and plan a system that meets the requirements needed to deliver the problem solution. This can often require involving outside companies and vendors, especially if additional hardware and software are needed. Systems design results in a new or modified system, and thus results in change. If the problems are minor, only small modifications are required. On the other hand, major changes may be suggested by systems analysis. In these cases, major investments in additional hardware, software, and personnel may be necessary. For example, There, Inc., a California company, spent more than $17 million designing an online simulation that lets people chat, interact, and flirt with avatars, lifelike people on the Internet.[33] The company hopes that the four-year systems development project will generate revenues from subscriptions and companies that want to advertise their products on its Web site. For some projects, systems design can take more time and resources than the other phases of systems development. The first step of systems design is to generate systems design alternatives, discussed next.

JOB TECHNOLOGY

General Motors Reduces Dealer Costs with Procurement System

GM's 7,500 dealers spend an estimated $1 billion on various materials and supplies, such as office supplies, computers, and tools. These expenses are passed on to the consumer in the form of higher sticker prices, which hurts GM by reducing sales and market share.

GM's systems analysts worked with two outside companies to develop a system that would reduce the costs of materials, supplies, and equipment needed by its dealers. The resulting system includes Covisint LLC, an automotive purchasing exchange, and Reynolds & Reynolds Co., the developer of GM DealerWorld, the Internet portal all GM dealers currently use.

Now, when a dealer needs to purchase business materials, rather than going to the yellow pages, the dealer can call up this private marketplace online, which sells only items an automotive dealer might be interested in at a discounted price. GM expects the dealer purchasing site to help boost the retailers' profits, allowing them to invest more in their outlets and sell more cars and trucks. The day that the new system was publicly announced, GM shares on the New York Stock Exchange rose by $1.28.

Questions

1. What type of information did GM need to collect from dealers to determine the need for the new system? Once the need was established, what type of information did GM need to collect from dealers to develop an effective system?

2. Besides the automotive industry, what other industries might benefit from a system such as this?

Sources
1. *"GM Creates Web Site Designed to Drive Down Costs at Dealerships,"* Ed Garsten, The Associated Press State & Local Wire, June 17, 2002.
2. *"GM Dealers to Get Online Purchasing: Lower Prices Promised,"* Alison Fitzgerald, National Post *(f/k/a* The Financial Post*),* June 18, 2002, Pg. FP14.
3. *"GM Unveils Dealer Buying Site,"* Staff, Journal of Commerce — JoC Online, June 18, 2002, www.joc.com/.
4. *"GM Set to Launch Procurement Web Site for Dealers,"* Linda Rosencrance, Computerworld, June 17, 2002, www.idg.net/ic_876602_4914_1-2787.html.
5. *"GM Site Offers Dealers Plenty of Bargains,"* Margaret Kane, ZDNet News, June 17, 2002; GM Web site, www.media.gm.com/news/releases/020617_dealerships.html, accessed July 2002.

Generating Systems Design Alternatives

The first step of design is to investigate the various alternatives for all components of the new system, which can include hardware, software, databases, telecommunications, personnel, and more. When additional hardware is not required, alternative designs are often generated without input from vendors. A *vendor* is a company that provides computer hardware, equipment, supplies, and a variety of services. Vendors include hardware companies, such as IBM and Dell, software companies, including Microsoft, database companies, such as Oracle, and a variety of other companies.

A museum might not need a vendor if it wants to modify one of its databases to include the estimated value of each item in the museum and where each item is located in the museum. This modification will likely require someone on the museum staff working with the database management system without the need for input from outside vendors. However, if the new system is a complex one, the original development team may want to involve additional personnel in generating alternative designs. If new hardware and software are to be acquired from an outside vendor, various requests can be made of the vendor.

A *request for information (RFI)* asks a computer systems vendor to provide information about its products or services, and a *request for quotes (RFQ)* asks a computer systems company to give prices for its products or services. The **request for proposal (RFP)** is generated during systems development when an organization wants a computer systems vendor to submit a bid for a new or modified system. It often results in a formal bid that is used to determine who gets a contract for new or modified systems. The RFP specifies, in detail, required resources such as hardware and software. It communicates these needs to one or more vendors, and it provides a way to evaluate whether or not the vendor has delivered what was expected. In some cases, the RFP is made a part of the vendor contract. The table of contents of a typical RFP is shown in Figure 9.20. The RFP process can be automated. Wachovia Bank, for example, purchased a software package, called The RFP Machine from Pragmatech Software, to improve the quality of its RFPs and to reduce the time it takes to produce them.[34] The RFP Machine stores important data needed to generate RFPs and automates the process of producing RFP documents.

FIGURE 9.20 • A typical table of contents for a request for proposal (RFP)

The RFP specifies required resources such as hardware and software. It communicates these needs to one or more vendors, and it provides a way to evaluate whether or not the vendor has delivered what was expected.

JOHNSON & FLORIN, INC.
REQUEST FOR PROPOSAL

Table of Contents

Cover page (with company name and contact person)
Brief description of the company
Overview of the existing computer system
Summary of computer-related needs and/or problems
Objectives of the project
Description of what is needed
Hardware requirements
Software requirements
Personnel requirements
Communications requirements
Procedures to be developed
Training requirements
Maintenance requirements
Evaluation procedures (how vendors will be judged)
Proposal format (description of how vendors should respond)
Important dates (when tasks are to be completed)
Summary

Evaluating and Selecting a Systems Design

The next step in systems design is to evaluate the various design alternatives and select the design that will offer the best problem solution in support of organizational goals. For a simple design, such as a new graphics program for a commercial artist, one person can complete the system design. A moderate design project can involve a number of people inside the organization. To modify a database or an existing software program at a tax preparation company, programmers from inside the organization can be used. For larger, more complex system designs that require new hardware and software, evaluation and selection can involve both a preliminary evaluation and a final evaluation before a design is selected. These more complex designs often require input from computer vendors in addition to people from within the organization.

The Preliminary Evaluation. A preliminary evaluation begins after all proposals have been submitted. The purpose of the preliminary evaluation is to dismiss some of the proposals. Several vendors can usually be eliminated by investigating their proposals and comparing them to the original criteria. The remaining vendors are asked to make a formal presentation to the analysis team. Furthermore, the vendors should be asked to supply a list of organizations using their equipment for a similar purpose. The organization then contacts these references and asks them to evaluate the hardware, software, and vendor.

The Final Evaluation. For simple or smaller systems development projects, final evaluation can involve one person making the final evaluation. A nutritionist, for example, might need a statistical analysis program to compare weight loss produced by the Atkins diet over a 6-month period with the results of other popular diets for a study she is conducting. Final evaluation for her might involve comparing the statistical tests that are available in several statistical analysis programs, such as SPSS and SAS. For larger systems development efforts, final evaluation often involves an analysis of several computer vendors. For these situations, final evaluation involves a detailed investigation of the proposals offered by each of the remaining vendors. The vendors should be asked to make a final presentation and to fully demonstrate the system. The demonstration should be as close to actual operating conditions as possible.

After the final presentations and demonstrations have been given, the organization makes the final evaluation and selection. Cost comparisons, hardware performance, delivery dates, price, modularity, backup facilities, available software training, and maintenance factors are considered. Although it is good to compare computer speeds, storage capacities, and other similar characteristics, it is also necessary to carefully analyze if the characteristics of the proposed systems meet the objectives set for the system and how it will help the organization solve problems and obtain goals. Figure 9.21 illustrates the evaluation process. As the organization grows closer to making a final decision about the system, the number of possible alternatives decreases.

The Contract

When large computer systems are purchased, the hardware vendor often requires a contract. Most computer vendors provide standard contracts; however, these contracts are designed to protect the vendor, not necessarily the organization buying the computer equipment. Developing a good contract can be one of the most important steps in systems design if new computer facilities are to be acquired.

More and more organizations are developing their own contracts, stipulating exactly what they expect from the system vendor and what interaction will occur between the vendor and the organization. All equipment specifications, software, training, installation, maintenance, and so on are clearly stated.

FIGURE 9.21 • The stages in preliminary and final design

Note that the number of possible alternatives decreases as the organization grows closer to making a final decision.

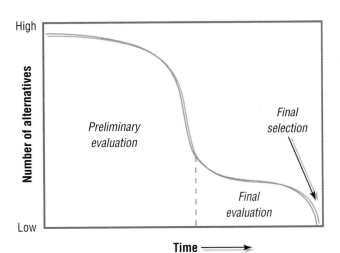

Furthermore, deadlines for the various stages or milestones of installation and implementation are stipulated, as well as actions to be taken by the vendor in case of delays or problems. Some organizations include penalty clauses in the contract, in case the vendor is unable to meet its obligation by the specified date. Typically, the request for proposal (RFP) becomes part of the contract. This saves a considerable amount of time in developing the contract, because the RFP specifies in detail what is expected from the system vendor or vendors.

SYSTEMSIMPLEMENTATION

FIGURE 9.22 • Typical steps in systems implementation
To realize the full potential of new or modified systems, organizations must carefully analyze the tradeoffs at each step in the implementation process.

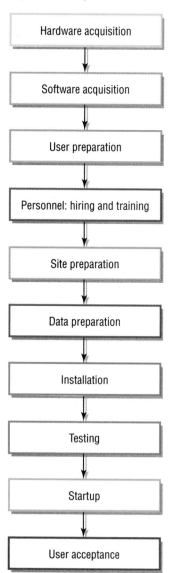

Hardware acquisition

Software acquisition

User preparation

Personnel: hiring and training

Site preparation

Data preparation

Installation

Testing

Startup

User acceptance

After the computer system has been designed, a number of tasks must be completed before the system is installed and ready to operate. This process, called **systems implementation**, includes hardware acquisition, software acquisition or development, user preparation, hiring and training of personnel, site and data preparation, installation, testing, startup, and user acceptance. The typical sequence of these systems implementation activities is shown in Figure 9.22. In many cases, some of the steps of systems implementation can be performed at the same time. For example, while hardware is being acquired, software can be developed and new computer personnel can be hired.

At each step shown in Figure 9.22, there are choices and tradeoffs to be made, which involve analyzing the benefits of the various choices. Unfortunately, many organizations do not take full advantage of these steps or carefully analyze the tradeoffs, and hence never realize the full potential of new or modified systems. The hassles and carelessness that often cause these steps to be overlooked must be avoided if organizations are to achieve their objectives and get the most from the new or modified computer system.

Acquiring Hardware

Although you can build your own computer using commonly available hardware components or have someone build a computer for you, most people and organizations acquire hardware and computers by purchasing, leasing, or renting computer resources from a computer systems vendor. As mentioned before, a computer systems vendor is a company that offers hardware, software, telecommunications systems, databases, computer systems personnel, or other computer-related resources to other organizations and individuals. Types of computer systems vendors include:

- General computer manufacturers
- Small computer manufacturers
- Peripheral equipment manufacturers
- Computer dealers and distributors
- Leasing companies, which lease or rent computers and computer equipment to others for a fee
- Time-sharing companies, which share the time of a large computer system to others for a fee
- Software companies

The National Institute of Meteorology in Spain, for example, purchased an $8 million supercomputer from Cray, Inc.[35] The supercomputer will be used for weather forecasting and climate modeling. In addition to buying, leasing, or renting computer hardware, it is also possible for an organization to pay only for the computing that it uses.[36] Called "pay as you go computing" or "utility computing," this approach means that an organization pays only for the computer power it uses. This is similar to paying only for the electricity you use. J.P. Morgan, for

COMMUNITY  TECHNOLOGY

When Systems Implementation Can Disrupt Customer Service

Comcast, the third largest cable provider in the United States, found itself in a tough spot when its partner Excite@Home declared bankruptcy. Excite@Home had been responsible for supplying 950,000 Comcast customers with high-speed Internet access via Comcast's cable. Comcast paid $160 million to keep the Excite service running through the end of February 2002, at which point it hoped a new system to provide high-speed Internet access would be in place.

The development of the new system was an 18-month process that had its share of problems. Dave Watson, vice president for marketing at Comcast said that some customers experienced a "small" delay in receiving e-mail. But some customers said the delays were more substantial than the company indicated. They claimed that they were unable to send or receive e-mail for days. "It is a total nightmare," said Michael Gunther, a Comcast customer in Summit, New Jersey, noting that it had become a regular habit for him to call Comcast customer service: "I had to put them on speed dial because I talk to them more than I talk to my wife." Most frustrating of all, some customers said, was that their calls to customer service were not answered, were met with busy signals, or were answered by technicians who lacked the expertise to solve their problems. Comcast gambled that its monopoly in the market would sustain its customer base through the hardships of the transition; a gamble that paid off.

After months of gradually transferring customers to its own network, service returned to normal for Comcast customers; the overwhelming number of calls to customer service dwindled. Comcast had survived the ordeal. In fact, Comcast did more than survive—it prospered. By transforming itself into an independent broadband Internet service provider (see Figure 9.23), Comcast made itself more attractive to other players in the industry and profited from the resulting mergers, acquisitions, and partnerships.

Questions

1. How do systems development projects affect customers and employees during and after the process?

2. Was there anything Comcast could have done to improve customer service during its systems development project?

3. How can companies prepare for the effects of a system development process prior to implementation?

Sources

1. "Comcast Says Its Transition to Internet Network Is Done," Matt Richtel, The New York Times, *March 2, 2002,* www.nytimes.com
2. "Comcast Copes with Internet Problems," Matt Richtel, The New York Times, *January 4, 2002, www.nytimes.com.*
3. "Law Firm Lovell & Stewart Announces Securities Fraud Class Action Lawsuit against AT&T Corp. Alleging Misstatements and Omissions Regarding Excite@Home," Business Wire, *March 5, 2002.*
4. "Seeing the AT&T-Comcast Deal in a Different Light," Richard J. Martin, Business Week, *Readers Report; Number 3785, p. 19.*
5. Comcast Web site, www.comcast.com, accessed July 2002.

FIGURE 9.23 • **Comcast high-speed Internet**

For Comcast, the nation's third largest cable provider, entering the Internet market was risky and fraught with problems, but it was ultimately a worthwhile venture.

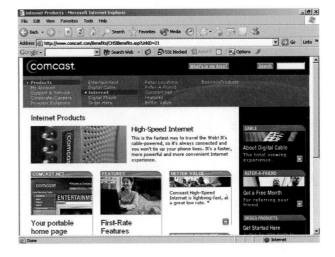

NO ONE'S HOME, BUT THE LIGHTS CAN BE TURNED ON

A "green and wired" condo complex in Sweden has incorporated tech-nology into the design from the groundwater up. Besides decontami-nating its own soil, recycling water, and generating power from renew-able resources, the 27 units each come with laptops and are wired with sensors and broadband Web access. Owners can control temper-ature, entry, and lighting; access security cameras; and open or close windows—from anywhere with an Internet connection.

Source:
"It Takes Tech to Tango"
By Raul Barreneche
Popular Science
www.popsci.com/popsci/hometech/article/0,12543,448268-1,00.html
May 2003
Cited on August 28, 2003

example, is using this approach by buying only the computer resources it needs from IBM. These computer resources can include hardware, software, telecommunications, databases, and more. Hewlett-Packard has a "capacity-on-demand" approach, where organizations pay according to the computer resources actually used, including processors, storage devices, and network facilities.[37]

It is also possible to purchase used computer equipment.[38] Todd Lutwak, director for eBay's information systems marketplace, expects the company will sell more than $1 billion of used computer-related equipment annually.

Selecting and Acquiring Software: Make, Buy, or Rent

As with hardware, software can be acquired in several ways. As previously discussed, software can be purchased from external developers or developed in-house. Some-times, developing software in-house produces the most effective result. For example, the Neves Corvo mine developed sophisticated mining software that allowed the mine operators to increase production from copper, tin, and zinc deposits in south-ern Portugal.[39] The software allows the Geology Department of Neves Corvo, a joint venture of Rio Tinto and the Portuguese government, to display 3-D models of the mines instead of 2-D models from older software. Similarly, NASA developed a soft-ware program called DAC for space exploration to analyze how a spacecraft enters distant environments and atmospheres (see Figure 9.24).[40] The award-winning soft-ware has been used for the Mars Global Surveyor and the Mars Odyssey missions.

Software can also be rented.[41] Salesforce.com, for example, rents software online that helps organiza-tions manage their sales force and internal staff.

In some cases, organizations use a blend of exter-nal and internal software development. That is, off-the-shelf or proprietary software programs are modi-fied or customized by in-house personnel.

Some of the reasons that an organization might pur-chase or lease externally developed software include lower costs, less risk regarding the features and perform-ance of the package, and ease of installation. The amount of development effort is also less when software is purchased, compared to in-house development. Even if software is purchased, it cannot be used unconditionally. For example, you may not be able to copy it as many times as you like to be used on other computers. Pur-chased software may require users to *authorize* it before it can be used. A popular income tax preparation program for individuals, for example, at one time required that you authorize the software before it could be used to print the final tax return. The software can only be authorized for use on one computer. In other cases, a software company will require the user to sign a *license agreement* that specifies how the soft-ware can be used (see Figure 9.25). Larger organizations can purchase a license agreement that allows software to be installed on multiple computers. A university, for example, can purchase a license to run Microsoft Word and Excel on a hundred

FIGURE 9.24 • NASA DAC software

NASA's award winning DAC software is used to analyze how a spacecraft enters distant environments and atmospheres.

FIGURE 9.25 • **Software license agreement**

Many software packages must be authorized before they can be used. Shown here is a standard end-user license agreement for the Microsoft Encarta Reference Library, an encyclopedia application. To sign the agreement, you select the option "I accept the terms in the License Agreement," and click the Next button.

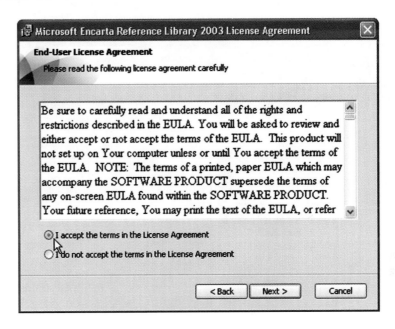

PCs in the university's PC labs. In addition to traditional software companies, software can be also acquired from an application service provider. An *application service provider (ASP)* is a company that provides software and support, such as computer personnel to run the software.

Another option is to make or develop software internally. This requires in-house software development, during which the organization's computer systems personnel are responsible for all aspects of developing the necessary programs. Some of the advantages of in-house developed software include meeting user and organizational requirements, and having more features and increased flexibility in terms of customization and changes. Software developed within the organization also has greater potential for providing a competitive advantage. In-house developed software programs are not easy for competitors to duplicate in the short term. Chapter 10 discusses the in-house development process in detail.

Acquiring Database and Telecommunications Systems

Acquiring or upgrading database systems can be one of the most important parts of a systems development effort. Acquiring a database system can be closely linked to the systems development process, since many systems development projects involve a new or modified database system. Because databases are a blend of hardware and software, many of the approaches discussed for acquiring hardware and software also apply to database systems. For example, an upgraded inventory control system may require database capabilities, including more hard disk storage or a new DBMS. Additional storage hardware would have to be acquired from a computer systems vendor. New or upgraded software could be purchased or developed in-house.

Telecommunications is one of the fastest growing applications for today's businesses and individuals. The Nasdaq Stock Market, for example, is investing $50 million in a new network system to streamline operations and cut costs (see Figure 9.26).[42] According to the chief information officer for Nasdaq, "We're

FIGURE 9.26 • The Nasdaq home page

Nasdaq invests heavily in systems development projects to streamline operations and get important information to their traders and customers. The Nasdaq Web site offers up-to-the minute information on stocks, business services, and financial news.

going to be able to take a lot of circuits out of our network and save costs." Like database systems, telecommunications systems require a blend of hardware and software. The Internal Revenue Service (IRS) hired a new chief information officer to oversee its large systems development effort to improve network security and other aspects of the IRS computer system.[43]

For personal computer systems, the primary piece of telecommunications hardware that people often acquire is a modem. For client/server and mainframe systems, the hardware can include multiplexers, concentrators, communications processors, and a variety of network equipment. Communications software also has to be acquired from a software company or developed in-house. You acquire telecommunications hardware and software in much the same way that you acquire computer system hardware and software.

YOU'VE GOT MAIL—FROM YOUR LAUNDRY

USA Technologies has developed a system called eSuds.net specifically for laundry rooms on college campuses. Washers and dryers are connected to a hub that collects information on usage, availability, sales, and even service of the machines, all accessible through a Web site. Students can go online to see if any machines are empty, see what cycle they're on, or even add fabric softener to their load. When their laundry is done, the machine sends them an e-mail.

Source:
"Wired Students Clean Up Act"
By Jennifer Uscher
Popular Science
www.popsci.com/popsci/internet/article/0,12543,399085,00.html
August 2003
Cited on August 28, 2003

User Preparation

User preparation is the process of readying managers and decision makers, employees, and other users and stakeholders for the new or modified system. System developers need to provide users with the proper preparation and training to make sure they use the computer system correctly, efficiently, and effectively. User preparation can include, marketing, training, documentation, and support.

Without question, training users is an essential part of user preparation, whether they are trained by internal training personnel or by external training firms. In some cases, companies that provide software will provide user training at no charge or at a reasonable price. Training can be negotiated during the selection of new software. Some companies conduct user training throughout the systems development process. Fears and apprehensions about the new system must be eliminated through these training programs. Old and new employees should be acquainted with the system's capabilities and limitations (see Figure 9.27).

FIGURE 9.27 • User preparation

User preparation is the process of readying managers and decision makers, employees, users, and stakeholders for the new or modified system.

Computer Systems Personnel: Hiring and Training

Depending on the size of the new system, a number of computer systems personnel may have to be hired and, in some cases, trained. A computer systems manager, computer programmers, data entry operators, and similar personnel may be needed for the new system. When chicken processor Tyson acquired IBP, a meat-packing conglomerate, a massive systems development project was initiated to integrate the

information systems of the two firms.[44] The multimillion-dollar project required additional personnel. It also required the existing personnel to work longer hours.

As with users, the eventual success of any system depends on how it is used by the computer systems personnel within the organization. Training programs should be conducted for the computer systems personnel who will be using or dealing with the computer system. These programs will be similar to those for the users, although they may be more detailed in terms of technical aspects of the systems. Effective training will help computer systems personnel use the new system to perform their jobs and help them provide support to the other users in the organization.

Site Preparation

The actual location of the new system needs to be prepared in a process called **site preparation**. For a small system, this may simply mean rearranging the furniture in an office to make room for a personal computer. For a larger system, this process is not so easy. Larger systems may require special wiring and air conditioning. One or two rooms may have to be completely renovated. Additional furniture may have to be purchased. A special floor may have to be built, under which the cables connecting the various computer components are placed, and a new security system may have to be installed to protect the equipment. For larger systems, additional electrical circuits may also be required.

Data Preparation

If an organization is about to computerize, all manual files must be converted into computer files in a process called **data preparation**. For old, computerized files, *data conversion* may be required to transform the existing computerized files into the proper format to be used by the new system. All of the permanent data must be placed on a permanent storage device, such as magnetic tape or disk. Usually the organization hires some temporary, part-time data-entry operators or a service company to convert manual data. Once the information has been converted into computer files, the data-entry operators or the service company are no longer needed. A computerized database system or other software will be used to maintain and update these computer files.

Installation

Installation is the process of physically placing the computer equipment on the site and making it operational. For a small systems development project, this might require making room on top of a desk for a new PC, plugging it into a wall outlet, and following the manufacturer's instructions to turn it on. For a larger project with a mainframe computer system, installation usually involves the computer manufacturer. Although it is normally the responsibility of the manufacturer to install the computer equipment for larger systems development projects, someone from the organization (usually the chief information officer or the computer systems manager) should oversee this process, making sure that all of the equipment specified in the contract is installed at the proper location. After the system is installed, the manufacturer performs several tests to ensure that the equipment is operating as it should.

Testing

Testing involves the entire computer system. It requires testing each of the individual programs (unit testing), testing the entire system of programs (system testing), testing the application with a large amount of data (volume testing), and

FIGURE 9.28 • Types of testing

Testing involves the entire computer system and requires testing each of the individual programs, the entire system of programs, the application with a large amount of data, and all related systems together, as well as conducting any tests required by the user.

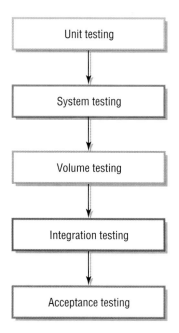

testing all related systems together (integration testing), as well as conducting any tests required by the user (acceptance testing). The sequence in which these testing activities normally occur is shown in Figure 9.28.

Unit testing is accomplished by developing test data that will force the computer to execute every statement in the program. In addition, each program is tested with abnormal data to determine how it will handle problems with bad data.

System testing requires the testing of all of the programs together. It is not uncommon for the output from one program to become the input for another. In these cases, system testing ensures that the output data from one program can be used as input for another program within the system.

Volume testing is performed to ensure that the entire system can handle a large amount of data under normal operating conditions.

Integration testing ensures that the new program(s) can interact with other major applications. It also makes sure that data flows efficiently and without error to other applications. For example, a new tax preparation program may require data input from a personal accounting program. Integration testing would be done to ensure smooth data flow between the new and existing applications. Integration testing is typically done after unit and system testing.

Finally, **acceptance testing** makes sure that the new or modified system is operating as intended. Run times, the amount of memory required, disk access methods, and more can be tested during this phase. Acceptance testing makes sure that the objectives of the new or modified system are met. Involving users in acceptance testing may help them better understand and effectively interact with the new system. Acceptance testing is the final check of the new or modified system before startup. Pioneer HI-Bred International, for example, performed acceptance testing for a new crop management system that will help farmers anticipate crop growth, disease outbreaks, and insect infestations.[45] The new system uses handheld computers and global positioning systems to collect data and feed it into a large crop database. Once data is collected, the database makes it available to farmers.

Startup

Startup begins with the final tested computer system. When startup is finished, the system will be fully operational. Different startup approaches include direct conversion, phase in and parallel conversion, and pilot conversion (see Figure 9.29).

Direct conversion involves stopping the old system and starting the new system on a given date. This is usually the least desirable approach because of the potential for problems and errors when the old system is completely shut off and the new system is turned on at the same instant.

The **phase-in approach** is a popular technique preferred by many organizations. In this approach, the new system is slowly phased in, while the old one is slowly phased out. During this process, parts of the old system and new system are running at the same time, in parallel. This is called a *parallel conversion*. When everyone is confident that the new system is performing as expected, the old system is completely phased out. This process is repeated for each application until the new system is running every application.

Pilot startup involves running a pilot or small version of the new system along with the old. After the pilot runs without errors or problems, the old system is stopped and the new system is fully operational. With pilot startup, small pilots can be introduced until the complete new system is operational. For example, a state prison system with a number of correctional facilities throughout the state could use the pilot startup approach and install a new computerized security system at one of the facilities. When this pilot program at the pilot facility runs without errors or problems, the new security system can be implemented at other prisons throughout the state.

FIGURE 9.29 • **Startup approaches**

Startup begins with the final tested computer system. When startup is finished, the system will be fully operational.

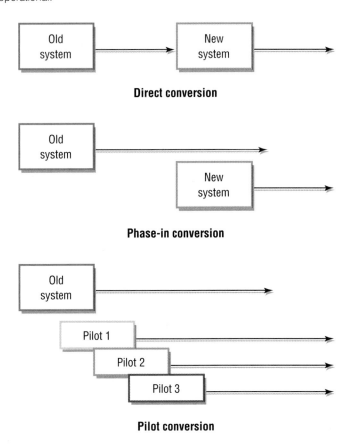

User Acceptance and Documentation

User acceptance and documentation is usually done for larger systems development projects that require new computers or servers. Smaller systems development projects, such as a musician acquiring new software to blend several music tracks into a finished song, usually don't require user acceptance and documentation.

A **user acceptance document** is a formal agreement signed by the user that a phase of the installation or the complete system is approved. This is a legal document that usually removes or reduces the vendor's liability or responsibility for problems that occur after the user acceptance document has been signed. Because this document is so important, many organizations get legal assistance before they sign the acceptance document. Stakeholders may also be involved in acceptance to make sure that the benefits to them are indeed realized.

The system should also be fully documented. *Documentation* includes all flowcharts, diagrams, and other written materials that describe the new or modified system. In general, there are two types of documentation. *Systems documentation* describes the technical aspects of the new or modified system. It can be used by the chief information officer (CIO), systems analysts, programmers, and other computer-related staff. *User documentation* describes how the system can be used by noncomputer personnel. A manual on how to use a spreadsheet program or an operating system is an example of user documentation. If a company develops a new game for a PC that simulates a cartoon character, user documentation is needed to describe to people (users) how the new game is to be played. If another company develops new reports for managers, user documentation is needed to describe how managers can develop and use the new reports.

SYSTEMSMAINTENANCE**AND**REVIEW

The final steps of systems development are systems maintenance and review. **Systems maintenance** involves checking, changing, and enhancing the system to make it more useful in achieving user and organizational goals. In some cases, an organization will encounter major problems that involve recycling through the entire systems development process. In other situations, minor modifications will be sufficient.

Causes of Maintenance

Maintenance can involve all aspects of the system, including hardware, software, databases, telecommunications, personnel, and other system components. Older hardware, for example, may be too slow and without enough storage capacity. Older software can also require maintenance. Once a program is written, it should ideally require little or no maintenance, but old programs require maintenance to make them faster or enhance their capabilities. In addition, new federal regulations or new computer technology may require that computer programs be modified. Experience shows that frequent, minor maintenance to a program, if properly done, can prevent major system failures later on. Today, the maintenance function is becoming more automated. The Home Depot, for example, is using new maintenance tools and software that will allow the large chain to maintain and upgrade software centrally.[46] The Home Depot is expected to have about 90,000 computers using the new approach by the end of 2004.

Some of the major causes of the need for systems maintenance are:

- New requests from stakeholders, users, and managers
- Bugs or errors in the program
- Technical and hardware problems
- Corporate mergers and acquisitions
- Governmental regulations that require changes in programs

When it comes to making necessary changes, most organizations modify their existing programs instead of developing new ones. That is, as new systems needs are identified, most often the burden of fulfilling these needs falls upon the existing system. Old programs are repeatedly modified to meet ever-changing needs. Over time, these modifications tend to interfere with the system's overall structure, reducing its efficiency and making further modifications more burdensome.

The Financial Implications of Maintenance

The cost of maintenance is staggering. For older programs, the total cost of maintenance can be up to five times greater than the total cost of development. In other words, a program that originally cost $50,000 to develop may cost $250,000 to maintain over its lifetime. The average programmer can spend from 50 percent to over 75 percent of his or her time maintaining existing programs as opposed to developing new ones. Furthermore, as programs get older, total maintenance expenditures in time and money increase, as illustrated in Figure 9.30. With the use of newer programming languages and approaches, including object-oriented programming, maintenance costs are expected to decline. Even so, many organizations have literally millions of dollars invested in applications written in older languages, such as COBOL, that are both expensive and time-consuming to maintain.

The financial implications of maintenance make it important to keep track of why systems are maintained, in addition to tracking the cost. For this reason, documentation of maintenance tasks is crucial. A determining factor in the decision to replace a system is the point at which it is costing more to fix it than to enhance or replace it.

FIGURE 9.30 • **Maintenance costs as a function of age**

As programs get older, total maintenance expenditures in time and money increase.

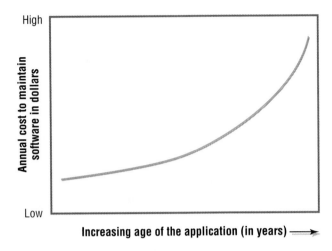

Systems Review

Systems review, the final phase of the systems development life cycle, is the process of analyzing systems to make sure that they are operating as intended. All aspects of the system are reviewed, including hardware, software, database systems, networks and Internet, people, and procedures. Systems review often involves comparing the expected performance and benefits of the system as it was designed with the actual performance and benefits of the system in operation. There are two types of review procedures:

- Event-driven review
- Time-driven review

An **event-driven review** is one that is triggered or caused by a problem or opportunity such as an error, a corporate merger, or a new government regulation. In some cases, an individual or organization will wait until a large or important problem or opportunity occurs before a change is made. In this case, minor problems may be ignored. Today, some organizations use a *continuous improvement* approach to systems development. With this approach, an organization makes changes to a system when even small problems or opportunities occur. Although this approach can keep the system current and responsive, doing the repeated design and implementation can be time-consuming and expensive.

A **time-driven review** is one that is started after a specified amount of time. Many application programs are reviewed every 6 months to a year. With this approach, an existing system is monitored on a schedule. If problems or opportunities are uncovered, a new systems development cycle may be initiated. A computer-assisted bicycle design program may be reviewed once a year to make sure that it is still operating as expected. If not, changes are made.

Many organizations use both approaches. A computerized program to choreograph new dance routines for a theater production company, for example, might be reviewed once a year for opportunities to display new dance moves. This is a time-driven approach. In addition, the dance program might be redone if errors or program crashes make the software difficult to use. This is an event-driven approach.

Action Plan

1. How should Joe approach his company to get the new sales program developed?

Joe should follow corporate procedures if they exist. He should demonstrate how such a program can help the company achieve its goals of getting new subscribers and increasing revenue.

2. If the company decides to develop a new sales program for sales managers and representatives, how should Joe be involved in the process?

If the company decides to undertake systems development to create a new sales program, Joe's involvement will be critical. Joe will need to help the people in the computer systems department determine exactly what reports and output would help him and other sales managers and sales representatives. Joe should also be involved during the process to make sure that his needs will be satisfied by the new program.

3. What role would Maria and people like her play in developing a new sales program?

As a systems analyst, Maria could help in developing plans and documents for a new sales program, including CASE documents, flowcharts, and so on. If she is involved in the project, she might even work with Joe in determining his needs and desires for the new program. She would also work with programmers. Working with users and programmers is the classic role of the systems analyst.

Summary

LEARNING OBJECTIVE 1

Describe the participants in and importance of the systems development life cycle.

The systems development process is called a systems development life cycle (SDLC) because the activities associated with it are ongoing. The five phases of the SDLC are investigation, analysis, design, implementation, and maintenance and review.

The systems development team consists of stakeholders, users, managers, systems development specialists, and various support personnel. The development team is responsible for determining the objectives of the computer system and delivering to the organization a system that meets its objectives.

Many organizations seek to initiate systems development projects that will provide a competitive advantage. This usually requires creative and critical analysis. Creative analysis involves the investigation of new approaches to existing problems. Critical analysis means being skeptical and doubtful, and requires questioning whether or not the existing system is effective and efficient.

Figure 9.1—p. 377

End-user systems development is a term that was originally used to describe the development of computer systems by individuals outside of the formal computer systems planning and departmental structure. The proliferation of general-purpose information technology and the flexibility of many packaged software programs have allowed noncomputer systems employees to independently develop computer systems that meet their needs.

LEARNING OBJECTIVE 2
Discuss the use of CASE, project management, and other systems development tools.
Some common tools and techniques for systems development include CASE tools, flowcharts, decision tables, project management tools, prototyping, outsourcing, and object-oriented systems development. Some formalized systems development approaches have come to be called software engineering. These approaches typically employ the use of software-based systems development tools called computer-aided software engineering (CASE) tools that automate many of the tasks required in a systems development effort. Like a road map, a flowchart reveals the path from a starting point to the final destination. A decision table can be used as an alternative to or in conjunction with flowcharts. When there are a large number of branches or paths within a software program, decision tables are preferable to flowcharts. The overall purpose of project management is to plan, monitor, and control necessary development activities. A prominent technique for systems development is prototyping, which typically involves the creation of some preliminary models or versions of major subsystems, or "scaled-down" versions of the entire system. Many organizations hire an outside consulting firm that specializes in systems development to take over some or all of its computer systems development activities. This approach is called outsourcing. Object-oriented (OO) systems development combines a modular approach to structured systems development with the power of object-oriented modeling and programming. OO development follows a defined system development life cycle, much like the SDLC.

Figure 9.8—p. 383

LEARNING OBJECTIVE 3
Understand how systems development projects are initiated.
Systems investigation is usually the first step in the development of a new or modified computer system. The overall purpose of systems investigation is to determine whether or not the objectives met by the existing system are satisfying the goals of the individual or organization. Systems investigation is designed to assess the feasibility of implementing systems solutions, including their technical, economic, legal, operational, and schedule feasibility.

Table 9.2—p. 393

LEARNING OBJECTIVE 4
Describe how an existing system can be evaluated.
Systems analysis is the examination of existing systems. This step is undertaken once approval for further study is received. The additional study of a selected system attempts to further understand the systems' weaknesses and potential improvement areas. Data collection methods include observation, interviews, and questionnaires. Data analysis manipulates the data collected. The analysis includes flowcharts, CASE tools, and other approaches. The overall purpose of requirements analysis is to determine user and organizational needs. Asking directly or using critical success factors can be used to complete requirements analysis. Joint application development (JAD) can be used in place of traditional data collection and requirements analysis procedures. Another efficient approach to determine and define systems requirements from a group is called rapid application development. Rapid application development (RAD) combines JAD, prototyping, and other structured techniques in order to quickly and accurately determine the requirements of the system.

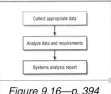

Figure 9.16—p. 394

LEARNING OBJECTIVE 5:
Discuss what is involved in planning a new system.
The purpose of systems design is to prepare the detailed design needs for a new system or modifications to the existing system. Organizations often develop a request for information (RFI) to get information from

computer systems vendors. If new hardware or software will be purchased from a vendor, a formal request for proposal (RFP) is needed. The RFP outlines the company's needs; in response, the vendor provides a written reply. The final phase of system design is evaluation and selection of alternatives. A preliminary evaluation begins after all proposals have been submitted. The purpose is to dismiss some of the proposals. The final evaluation can include presentations and demonstrations from the final computer systems vendors. Although most computer systems vendors provide standard contracts for new hardware, software, and systems, organizations today are increasingly developing their own contracts.

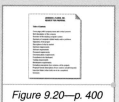
Figure 9.20—p. 400

LEARNING OBJECTIVE 6
List the steps for placing a new or modified system into operation.
Systems implementation includes hardware acquisition, software acquisition or development, user preparation, hiring and training of personnel, site and data preparation, installation, testing, startup, and user acceptance. Hardware acquisition requires purchasing, leasing, or renting computer resources from a vendor. Types of vendors include small and general computer manufacturers, peripheral equipment manufacturers, leasing companies, time-sharing companies, software companies, dealers, distributors, service companies, and others. Software can be purchased from external vendors or developed in-house—a decision termed the make-or-buy decision. User preparation involves readying managers, employees, and other users for the new system. New IS personnel may need to be hired, and users must be well trained in the system's functions. Preparation of the physical site of the system must be done, and any existing data to be used in the new system will require conversion to the new format. Hardware installation is done during the implementation step, as is testing. Testing includes program (unit) testing, systems testing, volume testing, integration testing, and acceptance testing. Startup begins with the final tested computer system. Startup approaches include direct conversion, phase in, and pilot startup. Direct conversion involves stopping the old system and starting the new system on a given date. The phase-in approach involves gradually phasing the old system out and the new system in. Pilot startup involves running a pilot or small version of the new software along with the old. Users typically perform an acceptance test to be sure that the capabilities promised were actually delivered.

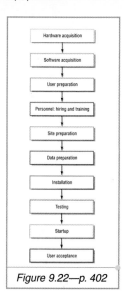
Figure 9.22—p. 402

LEARNING OBJECTIVE 7
Describe the importance of updating and monitoring a new or modified system.
Systems maintenance involves checking, changing, and enhancing the system to make it more useful in achieving user and organizational goals. Maintenance is critical for the continued smooth operation of the system. The costs of performing maintenance can well exceed the original cost of acquiring the system. Maintenance can vary from a small change to a large one.

Systems review is the process of analyzing systems to make sure that they are operating as intended. The two types of review procedures are event-driven review and time-driven review. An event-driven review is one that is triggered or caused by a problem or opportunity. A time-driven review is one that is started after a specified amount of time.

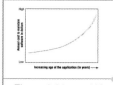
Figure 9.30—p. 412

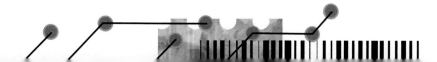

Test Yourself

LEARNING OBJECTIVE 1: Describe the participants in and importance of the systems development life cycle.

1. _____ are individuals who will ultimately benefit from systems development.

2. Who interacts with the users and others to develop detailed plans for the new or modified systems, like an architect developing blueprints for a new building?
   a. systems analyst
   b. programmer
   c. stakeholder
   d. chief information officer

3. True or False: Developing a competitive advantage typically requires critical and creative analysis.

4. _____ is a term that was originally used to describe the development of computer systems by individuals outside the formal computer systems department.

LEARNING OBJECTIVE 2: Discuss the use of CASE, project management, and other systems development tools.

5. True or False: CASE tools are used by one person at a time to make sure that results are consistent and accurate.

6. The _____ is a general flowchart needed to reveal the overall purpose and structure of an application.

7. What systems development tool is appropriate for programs that have a large number of branches or paths?
   a. flowchart
   b. PERT diagram
   c. decision table
   d. Gantt chart

8. The overall purpose of _____ is to plan, monitor, and control necessary development activities.

9. Use case diagrams are often used with:
   a. flowcharts
   b. object-oriented systems development
   c. PERT
   d. Gantt

LEARNING OBJECTIVE 3: Understand how systems development projects are initiated.

10. _____ is concerned with whether or not hardware, software, and other systems components can be acquired or developed to solve the problem.

11. True or False: Operational feasibility determines if the project can be completed in a reasonable amount of time.

LEARNING OBJECTIVE 4: Describe how an existing system can be evaluated.

12. The purpose of _____ is to seek additional information about the problems or needs identified during systems investigation.

13. What technique was developed by IBM and uses group meetings in which users, stakeholders, and computer systems personnel work together to analyze the existing system?
   a. joint application development
   b. rapid application development
   c. critical success factors
   d. prototyping

14. True or False: Rapid application development involves a process in which a developer first builds a working model of the system to help a group of stakeholders, users, or managers identify how well the prototype meets their requirements.

LEARNING OBJECTIVE 5: Discuss what is involved in planning a new system.

15. What asks computer systems vendors to provide information about its products or services?
   a. request for information
   b. request for proposal
   c. asking directly
   d. critical success factors

16. A(n) _____ begins after all proposals have been submitted by vendors.

17. True or False: More and more organizations are developing their own contracts, stipulating exactly what they expect from the system vendor and what interaction will occur between the vendor and the organization.

LEARNING OBJECTIVE 6: List the steps for placing a new or modified system into operation.

18. _____ includes hardware acquisition, software acquisition or development, user preparation, hiring and training of personnel, site and data preparation, installation, testing, startup, and user acceptance.

19. True or False: Site preparation is the process of physically placing the computer equipment on the site and making it operational.

20. What requires the testing of all of the programs together?
    a. unit testing
    b. system testing
    c. integration testing
    d. acceptance testing

LEARNING OBJECTIVE 7: Describe the importance of updating and monitoring a new or modified system.

21. _____ involves checking, changing, and enhancing the system to make it more useful in achieving user and organizational goals.

22. True or False: Systems review can include an event-driven review and a time-driven review.

Test Yourself Solutions: **1.** Stakeholders, **2.** a., **3.** T, **4.** End-user systems development, **5.** F, **6.** application or system flowchart, **7.** c., **8.** project management, **9.** b., **10.** Technical feasibility, **11.** F, **12.** data collection, **13.** a., **14.** T, **15.** a., **16.** preliminary evaluation, **17.** T, **18.** Systems implementation, **19.** F, **20.** b., **21.** systems maintenance, **22.** T

Key Terms

acceptance testing, p. 409
computer-aided software engineering (CASE) tools, p. 382
data preparation, p. 408
decision table, p. 384
direct conversion, p. 409
economic feasibility, p. 393
event-driven review, p. 412
flowcharts, p. 382
installation, p. 408
integration testing, p. 409
legal feasibility, p. 393
object-oriented systems development, p. 389
operational feasibility, p. 393

outsourcing, p. 388
phase-in approach, p. 409
pilot startup, p. 409
project management, p. 384
prototyping, p. 387
request for proposal (RFP), p. 400
requirements analysis, p. 397
schedule feasibility, p. 393
site preparation, p. 408
startup, p. 409
system testing, p. 409
systems analysis, p. 394
systems analyst, p. 378
systems design, p. 398
systems development, p. 376

systems development life cycle (SDLC), p. 376
systems implementation, p. 402
systems investigation, p. 390
systems maintenance, p. 411
systems review, p. 412
system stakeholder, p. 377
technical feasibility, p. 393
testing, p. 408
time-driven review, p. 412
unit testing, p. 409
user acceptance document, p. 410
user preparation, p. 407
volume testing, p. 409

Questions

Review Questions

1. What are the phases of the systems development life cycle? What tasks are performed in each phase?

2. Who are the participants in systems development?

3. Give an example of how an organization can achieve a competitive advantage.

4. What is end-user systems development?

5. What is an application flowchart?

6. Describe when a decision table should be used.

7. What is prototyping? What are the steps involved in developing a prototype?

8. Describe the object-oriented systems development approach.

9. What is the purpose of systems investigation?

10. What is technical feasibility? What is economic feasibility?

11. What is the difference between operational and schedule feasibility?

12. What is systems analysis? What steps are included in systems analysis?

13. What tools and techniques are used for data collection and analysis?

14. What are joint application development and rapid application development?

15. What is the purpose of systems design?

16. What is a request for proposal (RFP) and why is it important?

17. What are the preliminary and final evaluation steps in systems design?

18. What is systems implementation?

19. List the types of information systems vendors.

20. What steps are involved in testing the information system?

21. What are some of the causes of the need for systems maintenance?

22. What is systems review and what are the two types of review procedures?

Discussion Questions

23. Why is the term *systems development life cycle* used to describe the process of systems development?

24. For what types of system development projects might prototyping be especially useful? What might be some of the characteristics of a system developed with a prototyping technique?

25. Describe the different types of feasibility. Give an example of each.

26. Describe the various methods used to perform requirements analysis and when each should be used.

27. What is the difference between a request for information and a request for proposals? Give examples of each.

28. Assume that you are responsible for the site preparation of the building where a new computer system will be installed. What are some of the equipment, improvement, and other considerations that you would have during this process?

29. You have been put in charge of reviewing the new system at your organization. What factors would you consider and how might you evaluate these factors?

Exercises

Try It Yourself

1. You are developing a new computer system for The Fitness Center, a company that has five fitness centers in your metropolitan area, with about 650 members and 30 employees in each location. Both members and fitness consultants will use the system to keep track of participation in various fitness activities, such as free weights, volleyball, swimming, stair climbers, and aerobic classes. Prepare a brief memo detailing the required participants in the development team for this systems development project. Describe in your memo how you would determine the requirements for the new system. Using a graphics program, develop a chart that shows how participants are organized and their responsibilities in the development team.

2. Using the Internet, search for fitness centers. Describe these fitness centers. Using your word-processing program, write a brief report describing what you learned about how computer systems are likely used at these fitness centers. What types of systems development tools would be useful for these fitness centers?

3. A consultant has recommended that the management of The Fitness Center not only design a new system, but design it well to avoid maintenance costs. Use your spreadsheet and its graphing capabilities to produce a graph that supports the consultant's recommendation.

Virtual Classroom Activities

For the following exercises, do not use face-to-face or telephone communications with your group members. Use only Internet communications.

4. Pick a career area or field that is of interest to your group. Develop a report that describes how a computer system could be developed for this career area or field. Each group member should develop a separate part of the report.

5. Describe a new or modified computer system that would make life easier for students at your college or university. Develop a plan to implement the new system.

Teamwork

6. Effective systems development requires a team effort. The team usually consists of system stakeholders and users, managers, system development specialists, and various support personnel. This team, called the development team, is responsible for determining the objectives of the computer system and delivering to the organization a system that meets these objectives. Have each team member choose a different role to play: chief information officer, systems analyst, senior-level management, or system stakeholder or user. Someone from this group should also be chosen as project leader. Having created the team, develop a profile of the "organization" for which you will develop a system. What is the name of the organization? How many employees does it have? Where is it located? What are its main activities? What are its products or services? Who are its customers and members? Create a document using a word-processing program that will give someone who knows nothing about this organization an understanding of the nature of the organization.

7. Using the organization you created in Exercise 6, go through the steps of design for a new computer system.

8. Describe how the organization should implement and maintain the new system.

Learning Check

To check your knowledge of each of the chapter objectives, use this chart to find related end-of-chapter content.

Learning Objective	Key Terms	Questions	Exercises
Learning Objective 1 Describe the participants and importance of the systems development life cycle.	systems analyst systems development systems development life cycle system stakeholder	1, 2, 3, 4, 23	1, 6
Learning Objective 2 Discuss the use of CASE, project management, and other systems development tools.	computer-aided software engineering decision table flowchart project management prototyping object-oriented systems development outsourcing	5, 6, 7, 8, 24	1, 6
Learning Objective 3 Understand how systems development projects are initiated.	legal feasibility operational feasibility schedule feasibility systems investigation technical feasibility, economic feasibility	9, 10, 11, 25	2
Learning Objective 4 Describe how an existing system can be evaluated.	requirements analysis systems analysis	12, 13, 14, 26	1
Learning Objective 5 Discuss what is involved in planning a new system.	request for proposal (RFP) systems design	15, 16, 17, 27	4, 7
Learning Objective 6 List the steps of placing a new or modified system into operation.	acceptance testing systems data preparation implementation direct conversion system testing installation testing integration testing unit testing phase-in approach user preparation pilot startup user acceptance site preparation document	18, 19, 20, 28	5, 8
Learning Objective 7 Describe the importance of updating and monitoring a new or modified system.	event-driven review systems maintenance systems review time-driven review	21, 22, 29	3, 8

Endnotes

1 Marks, Debra, "Teenage Web Wiz Aspires to Create a Better Browser," *The Wall Street Journal*, May 14, 2003, p. B5B.

2 Kirkpatrick, David, "The Online Grocer Version 2.0," *Fortune*, November 25, 2002, p. 217.

3 Hamblen, Matt, "NavSea's ROI Ship Comes in," *Computerworld*, March 24, 2003, p. 46.

4 Weiss, Todd, "New CIO Takes Reins of IRS Tech Upgrade," *Computerworld*, June 2, 2003, p. 14.

5 Recho Web site at *www.recho.com* accessed on March 23, 2002.

6 PDS Web site at *http://pdspc.com* accessed on March 23, 2002.

7 Friedman, Andrew et al, "Developing Stakeholder Theory," *The Journal of Management Studies*," January 2002, p. 1.

8 Demaitre, Eugene, "The Greater Good," *Computerworld*, June 2, 2003, p. 25.

9 Ambler, Scott, "Know the User Before Implementing a System," *Computing Canada*, February 1, 2002, p. 13.

10 Bandler, James, et al, "Fuji, Kodak Creating Virtual Scrapbook," *Rocky Mountain News*, June 16, 2003, p. 2B.

11 Grimes, Brad, "Microsoft.NET," *PC Magazine*, March 25, 2003, p. 74.

12 Carey, Susan, "United to Install In-Flight E-Mail," *The Wall Street Journal*, June 17, 2003, p. D1.

13 Wildstrom, Sthephen, "You, Too, Can Be a Webmaster," *Business Week*, February 3, 2003, p. 29.

14 Sandberg, Jared, "The Unofficial Techies," *The Wall Street Journal*, May 28, 2003, p. B1.

15 Liu, Xiaohua, "Multiuser Collaborative Work in a Virtual Environment Based CASE Tool," *Information and Software Technology*, April 1, 2003, p. 253.

16 Dash, Julekha, "Project and Relationship Management Skills," *Computerworld*, January 14, 2002, p. 30.

17 Verton, Dan, "Struggling Airlines Scrutinize IT Projects," *Computerworld*, April 7, 2003, p. 1.

18 Munshi, Porus, "Prototyping All the Way to Perfection," *Businessline*, June 23, 2003, p. 1.

19 Brewin, Bob, "WorldCom Wins $20M Bid to Build Baghdad Cell Network," *Computerworld*, May 26, 2003, p. 14.

20 Greenemeier, Larry, "American Express, IBM Sign $4B Deal," *Information Week Online*, February, 26, 2002.

21 Ulfelder, Steve, "Opting for Outsourcing," *Comuterworld*, April 28, 2002, p. 30.

22 Melymuka, Kathleen, "When The Chips Were Down," *Computerworld*, May 26, 2003, p. 41.

23 Verton, Dan, "Offshore Coding Work Raises Security Concerns," *Computerworld*, May 5, 2003, p. 1.

24 Lehmann, Hans, "An Object-Oriented Architecture Model for International Information Systems," *Journal of Global Information Management*, July 2003, p. 1.

25 Mitchell, Robert, "E-Mail Upgrade," *Computerworld*, April 7, 2003, p. 25.

26 Patchong, Alain, et al, "Improving Car Body Production," *Interfaces*, January 2003, p. 36.

27 Vijayan, Jaikumar, "Mortgage Vendor Signs on to E-Signatures," *Computerworld*, January 21, 2002, p. 8.

28 Kerstetter, Jim, "The Web at Your Service," *Business Week*, March 18, 2002, p. EB13.

29 Landro, Laura, "Deadly Hospital Errors Prompt Group to Push for Technological Help," *The Wall Street Journal*, March 15, 2002, p. B1.

30 Brown, Jeanette, "Prada Gets Personal," *Business Week*, March 18, 2002, p. EB8.

31 Ang, James et al, "A Multiple-Case Design Methodology for Studying MRP Success and CSFs," *Information & Management*, January 2002, p. 271.

32 Sliwa, Carol, "Rational Software Set to Roll Out Rapid Development Tool," *Computerworld*, May 19, 2003. p. 7.

33 Clark, Don, "The Affluent Avatar," *The Wall Street Journal*, January 8, 2003, p. B1.

34 Amato-McCoy, Deena, "Wachovia Discovers Cure for RFP Blues," *Bank Systems & Technology*, February, 2002, p. 44.

35 Staff, Cray Wins $8.4M Supercomputer Deal," *Computerwire*, November 8, 2002.

36 McWilliams, Gary, "Pay As You Go," *The Wall Street Journal*, March 32, 2003, p. R8.

37 Hoffman, Thomas, "HP Takes New Pricing Path," *Computerworld*, May 26, 2003, p. 1.

38 Meehan, Michael, "IT Managers Turn to eBay to Cut Costs," *Computerworld*, May 6, 2002, p. 14.

39 Badenhorst, Colin, et al, "Operating Strategies," *Engineering and Mining Journal*, March 1, 2003, p. 3.

40 Rosenberg, Barry, "Modeling and Simulation Win NASA's Software of the Year," *Aviation Week & Space Technology*, January 13, 2003, p. 426.

41 Clark, Don, "Renting Software Online," *The Wall Street Journal*, June 3, 2003, p. B1.

42 Mearian, Lucas, "Nasdaq's CIO Looks to Streamline Systems," *Computerworld*, June 2, 2003, p. 19.

43 Weiss, Todd, "New CIO Takes Reins of IRS Tech Upgrade," *Computerworld*, June 2, 2003, p. 14.

44 Cope, James, "Tyson IT Staff Faces Meaty Integration Job," *Computerworld*, January 14, 2002, p. 10.

45 Staff, Handheld Computers, GPS Help Growers See What's Coming," *The Corn and Soybean Digest*, May 8, 2003.

46 Meehan, Michael, "Home Depot Seeks Remote Control of Desktops," *Computerworld*, January 7, 2002, pp. 12.

Designing
SoftwareSolutions

Susan Bishop started working as a clinical nurse at The Children's Hospital in Boston when she was fresh out of college three years ago. She loves children and her work makes her feel as though she is making a big difference in the lives of her patients and their families. After two years of investing 150 percent of herself in her work, she earned the respect of her colleagues and the hospital administrators and was promoted to supervisor of the newborn ICU.

After a year as supervisor, Susan has grown confident in her job and has learned the strengths and weaknesses of her unit. One weakness she has noticed is in employee morale. Some of the employees have confided in her that they are unhappy with the scheduling. They feel as though they have little or no input when it comes to work schedules. Some feel as though "favored" employees consistently get the best shifts, while others get a raw deal. Susan would like to create a scheduling program that would take individual staff preferences into account while remaining unbiased and fair to all.

Susan has a friend who works as a computer programmer for the hospital. She knows from casual conversation with him that the programming staff is short-handed and has a long list of jobs awaiting their attention. Perhaps Susan can do some of the work involved in designing a scheduling program herself. She might be able to convince her friend to help her with the job without going through the formal process and long wait associated with requesting a new system.

1. What first step should Susan take to begin the program development process?
2. How much of the program development process can Susan handle without her friend, the computer programmer?
3. If the output of Susan's scheduling program is a weekly schedule that satisfies the nurses and technicians in Susan's unit, what will be required as input?

Check out Susan's *Action Plan* at the conclusion of this chapter.

LEARNING OBJECTIVES	CHAPTER CONTENT
1. Define software development and provide examples of how non-programmers are involved in the software development process.	**Overview of Software Development**
2. Discuss issues related to problem analysis and the process of developing a program specification.	**Problem Analysis—Defining Program Specifications**
3. Compare and contrast program design approaches, and list the tools and methods used to create an algorithm.	**Program Design—Defining the Program Logic**
4. Discuss the steps and issues related to creating an executable program from an algorithm.	**Program Implementation—Coding the Program**
5. Describe the methods used to guarantee that a program is ready for use and determine if there are concerns or problems regarding the program after it is formally released.	**Program Testing, Debugging, and Maintenance**

Introduction

Software development is the process of developing software solutions to address a specific need or problem. Professionals from all fields are finding themselves either called upon or inspired to participate in software development. The ability to create your own software, or assist in the development of software in your profession, gives you additional power over the computer. It allows you to go beyond mass-produced software to develop solutions for your own unique needs. In addition, you will find that the organized process for problem solving used by computer programmers can be applied to non-computer-related problems. This chapter presents the logical approach to problem solving as used in software development of all types.

In Chapter 9, we discussed system development and how hardware, software, computer networks, databases, people, and procedures combine to create systems for processing information. At the heart of all such information systems is the software—the sequence of instructions that governs the processing. None of the technology described in this textbook would be possible without those instructions.

Software is designed to solve problems and supply services. All of the useful software that is commonplace today began as someone's solution to a problem.

- Dan Bricklin, a Harvard student working on an MBA, dreamed of an easier way to do the complicated calculations required in his studies. He invented VisiCalc, the first spreadsheet application.[1]
- Douglas Engelbart, a graduate student in electrical engineering at UC Berkeley, tired of being held back by traditional computer interfaces, dreamed of flying through two-dimensional graphical information spaces displayed on the screens. He invented the mouse and graphical user interface.[2]
- Tim Berners-Lee needed a method of organizing the hundreds of notes that he had accumulated over the years. The hyperlink system he designed for the task provided the building blocks of the Web.[3]

Traditionally, people have relied solely on computer programmers to design software for users. However, in recent years, users have become increasingly involved in the software development process. There are several reasons for this. First, users often understand the problems that software is to address better than the programmers. Second, users have become more technically savvy and desire more control over their computing applications. Third, the tools people use to create software are getting easier to use. Last, professional programmers are not able to keep up with the needs of users; many helpful software programs are going undeveloped simply for the lack of time.

Some experts believe that we are at the "tipping point" that will lead to a new paradigm in computing.[4] A tipping point occurs as gradual advances build up in technology, and await one final new development to dramatically change the technological landscape. For example the Web browser was the catalyst that "tipped" us into the Web generation after years of development in networking and internetworking technologies. Web services along with tools that empower users to develop their own applications are about to "tip" us into a new generation of computing where users take on much of their own program development. This chapter is not intended to teach you how to program. The goal of this chapter is to show you the basic problem-solving skills used in software development. This knowledge will empower you to:

1. Understand the power and limitations of the computer so that you can use software more intelligently
2. Assist in the development of software in your career—professionals in all fields who have an understanding of software development are highly valued
3. See software development as an activity for all, not just computer programmers, and perhaps even inspire you to want to write your own software

OVERVIEW OF SOFTWARE DEVELOPMENT

Software development, also called *program development*, *computer programming*, and *software engineering*, is the process of developing computer programs to address a specific need or problem. A **software developer**, also called a *software engineer* or a *computer programmer*, is an individual who designs and implements software solutions. The goals of software development are often posed as problems.

Table 10.1 provides examples of problems solved by software. Although you can hardly call "needing a video game" a problem (in the general sense of the word), designing a game is a challenging problem to be solved by a game designer.

TABLE 10.1 • **Examples of Problems Solved through Software**

Problem	Software Solution
Personal budget in shambles	Personal finance software to organize budget
Spam	E-mail filter software to sift out spam based on keywords found in known spam messages
Slow Internet connections do not support multimedia over the Web	Browser plug-in program to deliver compressed and streamed media
Design an exciting multiplayer video game based on the movie *The Matrix*	Enter the Matrix video game software for GameCube, PlayStation2, and Xbox gaming consoles

Software is developed for a wide range of problems at varying levels of complexity. Some people become involved in casual computer programming without having made a conscience effort to do so. Other people set out to develop software using application generators that allow them to write programs without learning a programming language. In businesses and organizations employees participate in program development at various levels. This section provides an overview of how individuals not trained in computer programming are becoming engaged in software development and computer programming.

SPORTS TRAINING + TECHNOLOGY = WINNERS

Athletes in every sport are adding technology to muscle in their training and the result is improved performances. One application monitors an individual's heart, hormone, nervous, and energy systems in real time so the athlete can tell whether their training needs to be stepped up or slowed down. Another uses digital imaging to analyze and measure the differences between performances, thereby showing the athlete exactly what needs to be done to improve.

Source:
"The Tech Edge in Training"
By Jane Black
Business Week Online
www.businessweek.com/technology/content/apr2003/
tc20030415_3555_tc109.htm
April 15, 2003
Cited on September 8, 2003

Casual Computer Programming

Casual computer programming refers to the activity of individuals who become involved in computer programming with little or no forethought or training. People become involved in writing programs in a number of ways. For example, creating a spreadsheet can involve a form of programming. Mini-programs, called functions, are used in spreadsheets to make calculations based on the contents of cells—boxes within the spreadsheet that contain data. Consider the budget spreadsheet in Figure 10.1. Cell C2 (the intersection of column C and row 2) contains the following function:

```
=IF(D7>D6,"This Job is OVER Budget!","This Job is under
             budget.")
```

This function reads and compares the contents of cells D6 and D7. If the contents of cell D7 (Total Spent) is greater than the contents of cell D6 (Quoted Price), the function prints "This Job is OVER Budget!" If not, the function prints "This Job is under budget." Spreadsheets incorporate casual programming.

FIGURE 10.1 • **Casual programming with spreadsheets**

Some applications offer users the opportunity to create mini-programs to control the software's behavior, such as using functions in a spreadsheet.

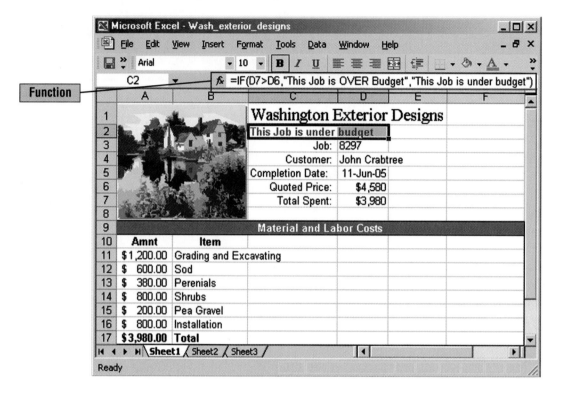

Many people create personal Web sites to share information with family, friends, or the public. To make their Web sites more attractive, interesting, and useful some people include small JavaScript programs to add animation and interactive features. Web sites such as the one at http://javascript.internet.com/ provide JavaScript applications to download for free, making it easy to add functionality to your own Web site. Some useful and popular JavaScript programs include:

- A guest book for visitors to sign and let you know they've visited your Web site
- An e-mail form that sends the URL of the Web site to anyone the visitor chooses
- Animations, such as a pair of eyeballs that follow the mouse cursor when it is moved
- Changing backgrounds, and other animated graphic designs
- Image slide show presentations set to run automatically or controlled by the visitor
- Clocks and scrolling news tickers
- Calculators of every kind
- Games

Application Generators

Application generators are programs that allow you to create other programs without using a formal programming language. An application generator automates the process of writing source code and compiling to machine code, allowing software developers to create programs using a simple user interface (see Figure 10.2). A software developer provides the application generator with data specifications and a description of how the data is to be input, processed, and output, typically through a step-by-step process. Application generators are used to write specific kinds of applications. For example, the MultiMedia Database and Authoring (MMD) tool, by Capella Computers Ltd.[5], is an application generator used by developers to create large complex multimedia applications. The tool uses a database to store multimedia files and allows a developer to create multimedia programs for online product catalogs, educational tutorials, and other multimedia presentations.

FIGURE 10.2 • Application generator

An application generator automates the process of writing source code and compiling to machine code, allowing software developers to create programs using a simple user interface.

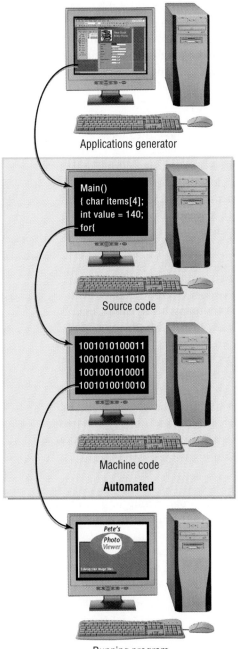

Applications generator

Source code

Machine code

Automated

Running program

JOB TECHNOLOGY

Lego Programming

The Lifelong Kindergarten research group at MIT designs new technologies for primary and secondary education to nurture playfully inventive learners. The group has come out with several projects that help children learn computer programming and the fundamentals of programming logic with games and toys. One such project is called building-block programming. The group has created a programming language that allows children to create fun computer programs by manipulating blocks on the screen. Each block contains a mini-program with an interesting function. By connecting the blocks together children create fun programs that differ depending on how the blocks are arranged.

The designers took the idea one step farther and built physical building blocks with electronics inside, each with a unique function. Each block includes an input and output link that when clicked together allow the blocks to interact to create cool active robots and interactive kinetic sculptures. In the process of playing with these blocks, the children are learning about programming, engineering, and design.

These programmable blocks were so popular with children that the LEGO company heard about them and used them as the basis of their Mindstorms product line. LEGO Mindstorms kits let children design and program robots with special LEGO blocks; the children use a computer to make the robots do what they want them to (see Figure 10.3). For example, they can create a robotic rover that navigates around obstacles and follows a trail. Although created for and used by children ages 9 and up, these kits are used in many college-level robotics courses to teach the basics of robotics.

Questions

1. If children begin to view programming as a fun activity, how will that affect the future of technological innovation?

2. The Lifelong Kindergarten group focuses on bringing their technology to poor neighborhoods. How might this technology make a difference in the life of an underprivileged child?

3. Besides learning the basics of computer programming what other skills do children gain from playing with these toys?

Sources
1. *"Tomorrow's Toys", The Osgood File, CBS Radio Network, January 1, 2003, www.acfnewsource.org/science/tomorrows_toys.html.*
2. *MIT's Lifelong Kindergarten Web site, accessed September 29, 2003, at www.lego.com/eng/products/next/.*
3. *Lego Robotics Web site, accessed September 29, 2003, at www.lego.com/eng/products/next/.*

FIGURE 10.3 • Lego Mindstorms

LEGO Mindstorms kits brings computer programming to a child's level with programmable robots that work with special LEGO blocks and a computer.

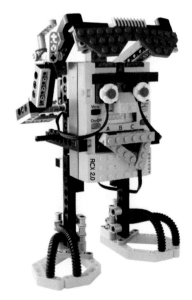

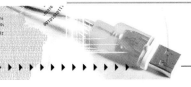

NEW TOOLS FOR THE DRUG TRADE

It currently takes 17 years and $800 million to bring a new drug from dis-
covery to market. Researchers must wade through a terabyte of information published daily on the human genome, reactions to diseases, and
interventions on a molecular level. New application tools from a company
in New Zealand and grid computing, however, can sort through this unstructured data in a fraction of the time, lowering drug ETAs to 10 years,
and the cost to $100 million.

Source:
"Computer modelling future of medicine"
By Adam Gifford
The New Zealand Herald
www.nzherald.co.nz/storydisplay.cfm?storyID=3521371&thesection=
business&038;thesubsection=technology&038;thesecondsubsection=information
September 3, 2003
Cited on September 3, 2003

The Gusbase Windows application generator, by Group Unispec[6], is used to create
data input applications for handheld computers. Using this tool, software developers
create forms to install on handheld devices
so that workers who need to collect data
in the field can do so more conveniently.
When the worker returns to home base, the
data collected is transferred from the handheld device to the main computer system.

Application generators are part of the
continuing trend in computer programming to move away from ones and zeros to
more natural and convenient ways to create
software. They are an example of the
fourth-generation languages (4GLs) that
were discussed in Chapter 3. Although
these tools do not require knowledge of a
programming language, they do require an
understanding of programming logic and problem solving, which are discussed
in this chapter.

Some educators believe programming logic and computer-based problem solving should be a part of the primary school curriculum along with reading, writing, and arithmetic. The Media Lab at MIT has a research group dedicated to creating fun ways for children to learn programming logic (see the "Job Technology"
box). It is very likely that when they grow up children born today will be com-
manding computers in a very different way than we do—a way that utilizes their
learned understanding of computer logic.

Software Development in Organizations

Software may be developed to function independently or as a component of a
larger system. For example, we use a media player to listen to music and view
video on a PC. The media player is a self-contained system that works independently to provide a service. If you visit the Rhapsody Music Service to purchase and
download music to add to your collection, you will interact with an order processing program that acts as a component of the larger Rhapsody Music Service
system. That larger system includes a Web server, a music database, a customer
database, personnel, policies, and procedures.

Businesses and organizations often develop special-purpose systems that function as part of a larger whole, like Rhapsody's music service. In Chapter 9, you
learned about developing systems that include hardware, software, databases, and
other components through a process called the systems development life cycle
(SDLC). Developing the software for such systems is an important task that requires participation in some form from all who will be affected by the system:
users, managers, systems development specialists, computer programmers, and
other stakeholders.

Software development is a subprocess within systems development. In creating a large information system, much preparation takes place before computer
programmers begin to write the software. A new service at Emory University in
Atlanta illustrates the relationship between systems development and program
development. Recently, Emory University provided its students with the ability to
pick their own roommates.[7] Using an online roommate-selection system, which

works much like a computer dating service, incoming freshmen fill out and submit a personality questionnaire (see Figure 10.4). The software compares student responses and provides each student with a list of others with like interests. Students contact each other via e-mail to finalize the arrangement.

FIGURE 10.4 · Finding the perfect match

Personality profiling software is only one component of the larger system that includes networking, databases, and hardware, along with people and procedures designed to allow students to select their own college roommate.

The systems development process for developing a roommate-selection system would consider all of the needs of such a system. For example, the decision to deliver this system over the Web is made during systems development. Other questions considered during systems development include:

- Would the system require a new server computer to handle the additional Internet traffic that will be generated?
- What questions should be included in the questionnaire?
- Would a new domain name be needed for the roommate-selection Web site?
- What type of database system would be required for storing the student data?
- What kind of privacy issues would need to be addressed?
- What policies would need to be in place?
- Would the system require additional technical staff or a reduction in housing staff?

The answers to these questions are provided through interviews with students, school administrators, lawyers, system administrators, and other specialists. Computer programmers are then provided with the specifications for how the software for this system should behave. Armed with this information, the programmer can then logically design software that meets the detailed specifications. The software ties together all the components of the system.

As mentioned in Chapter 9, software can be developed in-house or by an outside developer. In the case of the roommate-selection system, Emory University decided to use a software package developed by the WebRoomz company; WebRoomz designs software specifically for the purpose of pairing up roommates, and has provided many universities with its product.

The Program Development Life Cycle

Once program specifications are provided to a programmer or programming team, the activity of developing the software begins. It is estimated that most software projects fail. Research shows that more than 80 percent are unsuccessful due to being over budget, late, missing functionality or a combination of all three.[8] Software developers have found that one way to minimize these problems is by using an organized development process. Many software developers use a sequence of steps known as the program development life cycle. The *program development life cycle* provides a five-step sequence of activities for developing and maintaining programming code that include problem analysis, program design, program implementation, testing and debugging, and maintenance. The final stage of the cycle, maintenance, leads back to the first stage, problem analysis, to provide for future versions of the software that address problems or add more features (see Figure 10.5). Like the systems development life cycle, the program development life cycle often requires the software developer to revisit earlier stages to address unforseen complications. You can find an example of the cyclic nature of programming in Web browsers. Internet Explorer 6 is in its sixth iteration of the program development life cycle.

Although not all program development follows this traditional development process, most software developers recognize the importance of planning. The more time spent planning, the fewer problems will be faced later in the development process. This is particularly true for large projects. We will use the program development life cycle as an organizational foundation for our discussion of the software development process—beginning with problem analysis.

FIGURE 10.5 • The program development life cycle
The program development life cycle is used to organize the process of developing and maintaining software.

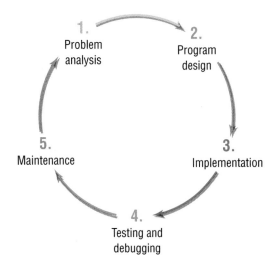

1. Problem analysis
2. Program design
3. Implementation
4. Testing and debugging
5. Maintenance

PROBLEMANALYSIS—DEFININGPROGRAMSPECIFICATIONS

The first and most important stage of software development is problem analysis. During **problem analysis**, the problem requirements are studied in order to create detailed specifications for the computer program. The result of the problem analysis is a **program specification**; a document that defines the requirements of the program in terms of input, processing, and output (see Figure 10.6). Here we focus on what the program does rather than on how it does it. Therefore, the emphasis is on data in terms of input and output, and on the objectives that the program is being created to fulfill. The problem analysis stage lays the foundation on which all the other stages build. Misunderstandings or errors in this stage will be magnified into substantial wastes of effort in later stages. Time must be invested to thoroughly understand the details of problem requirements.

FIGURE 10.6 • Program specification

The program specification defines the requirements of the program in terms of input, processing, and output.

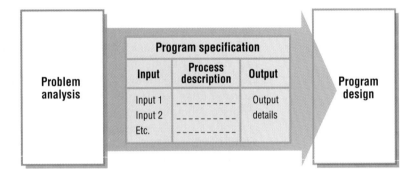

Understanding Problem Requirements

You gain a thorough understanding of problem requirements by reducing a problem down to its most basic elements. A problem description usually begins as a vague idea. Let's consider an example that focuses on the responsibilities of a disk jockey (DJ). A DJ is judged by the music he or she provides and the timing and sequence of song delivery. A full-time DJ might invest hours each day creating song sequences to provide hours of entertainment and dance music. The song delivery must be paced according to style and tempo. New songs are added frequently, while old songs are retired. DJs who work the same crowd night after night need to vary their sequences to keep the regulars interested. A software solution to the DJ problem that automates the task of creating song sequences would be a valuable tool.

This description of the DJ problem is typical of problem descriptions that lead to software development. To thoroughly understand this problem's requirements, you need to refine this vague description. The first step in problem analysis is defining the goals, or output, of the program. We might state the goal of our DJ program as follows:

The DJ program will provide a list of 100 songs in a sequence that is appealing to audiences.

Even though somewhat vague, this problem statement sums up the longer problem description nicely and provides a starting point for further discussion of the problem. From here, we can ask, "What input and processes will produce the above result?" In this stage of software development, we are not interested in the details of the processing, but rather the details of the data, in terms of both input and output.

In a sense, we are developing an expert system. We need to find out how DJs make selections for song sequences. Through interviews with DJs, we may learn that songs are placed in a sequence based on tempo, style, era, and popularity. Using this information, we can fill in the input and output portions of our program specification as shown in Figure 10.7.

FIGURE 10.7 • Input/output specifications for the DJ program

A program specification typically begins by defining the input and output of the software.

DJ Program Specification		
Input	**Process description**	**Output**
All the songs that are available to play including the following specifications: title, artist, tempo, style, era, and popularity rating of each song.	?	A list of 100 songs in a sequence that is appealing to audiences.

DJs may find that certain sequence patterns are more successful than others and develop "recipes" that guide their selection of songs. For example, a DJ may decide to include a slower tempo song every fifth song. Top notch DJs might have a very detailed recipe, as shown in Figure 10.8, that defines the style, tempo, era,

FIGURE 10.8 • Providing a process description

The DJ's recipe can serve as the process description in our program specification, and provides us with more detail for input specifications.

DJ's mix secret recipe	
Song 1	Era: Current Category: Top 10 Tempo: 120-140 Style: Old Skool
Song 2	Era: Current Category: Top 10 Tempo: 100-120 Style: Funk
Song 3	Era: 70's Category: Top 10 Tempo: 80-100 Style: Techno
Song 4	Era: Current Category: Top 10 Tempo: 120-160 Style: Romance
	etc...

Input parameters

Style	Era
• Acid Jazz	• 30s
• Big Band	• 40s
• Disco	• 50s
• Funk	• 60s
• Hi NRG	• 70s
• Hip-Hop	• 80s
• House	• 90s
• Latin Jazz	• 00s
• Old Skool	• Current
• Pop	
• Reggae	**Category**
• Romance	• Top 10
• Salsa	• On Charts
• Ska	• Unknown
• Techno	• Personal Fav

Tempo

Number representing beats per minute. Typically between 60 and 160 — 60 being the slowest tempo.

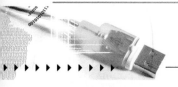

and popularity category for each song in the sequence. Our program could use such a recipe as a description of the process that transforms the input into output.

In learning of the DJ's recipe, we also discover more details about the input. For example, there can be 15 different styles and 9 different eras. Data, such as these, that are manipulated by a program, are called variables. A *variable* is a named data component that can be set to different values. In our DJ example, the variable Era can hold the value 30s, 40s, 50s, and so on.

At this point, the problem analysis for our DJ example is complete. We have defined input variables in detail, provided a description of the output, and provided rules for creating the output from the input. This information can be compiled into a complete program description. From the very beginning of software development, software developers work closely with the users of the software to assist in designing the program specifications. The program specifications for the DJ program could not have been written without interviewing the DJ.

Program Delivery

Often the details of program delivery are included in the program specification. *Program delivery* defines where the program will be installed, who will have access to the program, and the type of user interface. For example, a florist may request a flower delivery scheduling program that is accessible over the Web. Program delivery should be considered in the earliest stages of program development, since it can influence the way that the program is designed. A program might be delivered as a single-user installation or a multiple-user installation on a private network or the Internet.

Delivering applications over the Web is rapidly becoming the preferred form of delivery—primarily because the Web supports multiple computer platforms, which eliminates program installation issues. An *Infoworld* survey report found that Web applications have become the industry standard. An overwhelming 80 percent of software developers surveyed responded that "Web applications are part of their server development;" and 53 percent said "they prefer to give their applications a Web-style user interface," over the 33 percent who responded that they prefer traditional installed graphical user interfaces.[9]

PROGRAMDESIGN—DEFININGTHEPROGRAMLOGIC

Once program specifications are defined, software developers begin designing the program. In the **program design** stage of development, a formal algorithm is designed to satisfy the requirements of the program specification. An **algorithm**, sometimes called *program logic*, is a step-by-step problem-solving process that arrives at a solution in a finite amount of time. Most of the work of computer programming is performed in this stage. First the programmer determines if the problem can be solved by a computer—whether the program is feasible. Once it is determined that the program specifications are feasible, software developers determine the best program design approach for the problem specification. The design approach that is chosen determines the types of tools that the programmer will use to design the program. The programmer uses descriptive languages and tools to design and describe a detailed chart for the functioning of the software. The end product, if designed well, should be effortless to translate into program source code. This section discusses computability, program design approaches, and tools for developing algorithms.

Computability

Some types of problems are easy to solve with a computer program; others are not. In Chapter 8, we learned about programmed and nonprogrammed decisions. Programmed decisions are easy to address with software solutions, whereas some types of nonprogrammed decisions are significantly more difficult. *Computability* refers to how likely or feasible it is that a problem can be solved by a computer. You learned in Chapter 2 that computers perform arithmetic and logic operations. Arithmetic operations are operations involving math. Logic operations involve comparisons; for example, is one number greater than, less than, or equal to another number? You've also learned that computers are ideal for storing, displaying, printing, and transferring large amounts of data. Consider the roommate selection program again. Many of the computer's abilities were combined to provide this service. The database *stored* student information, and the processor *logically* compared the resulting data, *calculating* the percentage of similar character traits, to determine which students were compatible.

Although it is relatively easy to list all of the things computers are capable of doing, it may be more difficult to list things computers are incapable of doing—or list things it is difficult for computers to do (see Table 10.2). Can a computer help you decide which restaurant you should go to for lunch? Sure! It can be programmed with a list of your favorite restaurants, along with the primary attributes of each, and then present you with a list of questions regarding your current state of mind; it would then use your responses to provide an intelligent recommendation. Or, it could simply make a random selection on your behalf. Can a computer wash your car? Sure! Computers control many of the automated robotic car wash systems used today.

TABLE 10.2 • **Computable and Noncomputable Problems**

Computable	Noncomputable
Provided with information from the most recent U.S. census, how many females between ages 31 and 40 reside in Colorado?	What percentage of females between ages 31 and 40 in Colorado are leading a satisfying life?
Provided with my monthly income and expenditures, how much money will I have left at the end of the month?	Provided with current federal financial records, will the federal budget be in deficit in 2010?
Do the frequency patterns of one recorded sound match the frequency patterns of a second recorded sound?	Is this song good?

Can a computer think like a human being? In some ways, yes; in other ways, no. Chapter 8 explored this notion during the discussion of artificial intelligence. A computer does not possess the creative capabilities of the human mind. It does not inherently have an imagination, intuition, or common sense. Due to these limitations, you would probably not want a computer to design a logo for your new business, or for that matter, a jingle. Although computers can do such things, the result is usually not appealing to the human judge. Fortunately, activities that involve these purely human characteristics are things that we find interesting and fulfilling to do ourselves.

Even within the activities at which computers excel—math and logic—there are some problems that may seem simple, but require significant amounts of processing. For example, let's imagine that you are planning a vacation. You plan to visit your cousin in Las Vegas, an old friend in Denver, and your brother in Phoenix, and then return home. Depending on the order of your visits, you could save significantly on miles and time. Which route will take you to these three cities and back home in the least amount of miles? With a pencil and paper, you might map out every possible order of visits and add the miles. You would find that you can make your visits in six possible orders, and it wouldn't take long with a calculator to figure out which route is shortest. With only three cities to visit, this problem is fairly simple; however, when you add more cities, this problem gets complex very quickly. To visit four cities takes 24 comparisons, for five cities, 120 comparisons, for 10 cities over 3 million comparisons.

This example, called the traveling salesman problem, is well known in computer programming. The traveling salesman problem is an example of problems that get very complex as the input value increases. Problems of this type are said to exhibit *exponential growth*. In 2001, researchers at Rice University and Princeton University produced a traveling salesman solution for 15,112 cities in Germany.[10] The computation was carried out on a network of 110 processors that worked for 10 continuous weeks to come up with the solution.

It is considered an optimization problem, since its goal is to find the best route between towns. This type of optimization problem has many important applications. For example, you might be asked to arrange efficient school bus routes to pick up the children in a school district. Airlines face very challenging routing schedules, where saving miles and time means huge financial savings. Manufacturers can save money by determining the best path for an automated laser to follow when drilling holes in a circuit board. A short-cut solution to the traveling salesman problem—one that does not mean comparing every possible path—could be useful in many applications. Computer scientists use the traveling salesman problem to challenge their problem solving abilities. Some have come up with approaches to improve the speed with which a computer can solve this problem. Still, the problem is considered one that is difficult for a computer to handle.

Although the traveling salesman problem meets the requirements of computability, it is a type of problem that is deceivingly complex. Such problem solutions are time-consuming for computers and almost completely impractical to attempt to solve without a computer.

Program Design Approaches

Once it is determined that the goals of the program specification are feasible, the programmer must decide which approach to use for programming design. Design approaches are closely tied to the programming language that will be used to code the program. The programming language, in turn, is often determined by the programmer's skill areas. In larger organizations, the programming language is often determined by the programming platform endorsed by the team of programmers and used in the existing system. The two most general approaches to programming design are structured design and object-oriented design.

Structured Design. **Structured design** divides a program specification into subproblems. Using the divide and conquer approach, structured design provides a solution to the program specification by solving all of its subproblems. Structured design makes use of a main module that controls the execution of the program. The main module calls *subroutines* or *procedures*, which are designed to solve subproblems, in sequence. Each subroutine can then call other subroutines in sequence. Figure 10.9 illustrates the structured design approach for a gas station pump program that accepts credit-card payments. A *structured chart*, such as this one, uses boxes to represent subroutines. For example, the "Cash customers" box in the figure may contain instructions to display a message that sends the customer to the cashier to pay prior to pumping. The sequence of steps that the main module carries out are listed from left to right below the main module box. If a subroutine has subroutines, they are also listed from left to right. The technique of breaking a problem and its solution into small sequential steps makes large, unwieldy problems manageable. Solutions are easier to test, and problems are easier to find. The code modules can be reused in other solutions that have similar subproblems.

FIGURE 10.9 • Structured design

This gas pump program design utilizes structured design, which divides a program specification into subproblems, and by solving each subproblem, provides an overall solution to the program specification.

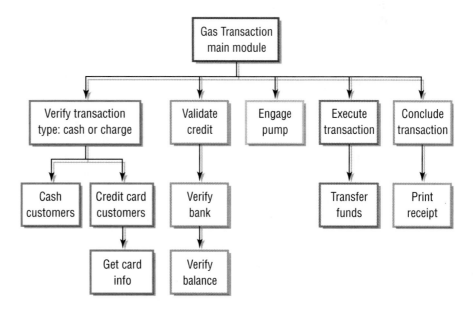

COMMUNITY /\/\/\ TECHNOLOGY

Improving Human-Computer Interaction through Common Sense

Computer programmers and users often find themselves having to "think like a computer" in order to get computers to do what they want. However, soon computers may get better at "thinking like people." In 1984, artificial intelligence pioneer Doug Lenat began formalizing human common sense and entering it into a computer program he named Cyc (short for encyclopedia). Lenat's goal was to develop a rational computer program that could make independent assertions. He has labored years to codify facts such as "Once people die, they stop buying things." He uses a form of symbolic logic called predicate calculus (see Figure 10.10) to classify and show the properties of information in a standard way. Now, 19 years later, with over 600 person-years and $60 million invested, the Cyc knowledge base contains over 3 million rules of thumb that the average person knows about the world, plus about 300,000 terms or concepts. Lenat's intelligent child is ready to begin earning its keep.

What service can Cyc provide to computer users? "I see this more as a power source rather than a single application." Lenat states. "[For any given application], you need common-sense knowledge and domain knowledge.

FIGURE 10.10 • Knowledge Sample

An example of predicate calculus used to help Cyc understand that "Animals sleep at home."[11]

```
(ForAll ?x (ForAll ?S
(ForAll ?PLACE
(implies (and
(isa ?x Animal)
(isa ?S SleepingEvent)
(performer ?S ?x)
(location ?S ?PLACE))
(home ?x ?PLACE)))))
```

This says that if x is an animal and is the performer of a sleeping event, then the place where that event takes place is the home of x.

We are building in the common-sense knowledge." For example Cyc could serve as a smart Web search engine that finds what you want because it understands content, instead of just matching keywords. When searching on the keywords "Rock climbing," Cyc would understand that you probably are looking for sport-related content, and not Web pages about igneous rock and climbing ivy, which both match the keywords.

Among the many applications that are making use of Cyc's unique ability, one of the most promising is in the development of "smart" interfaces that respond to user commands more intuitively. Rather than clicking an option in a menu, you could type in or speak what you wish to happen. Cyc would empower the computer to understand statements or commands such as "Computer, when do I have a 2-hour block of time available?" Cyc could be instrumental in breaking through the human-computer barrier. If Cyc's common sense were applied to program development, programmers might no longer need to think like a computer, because the computer would be thinking more like a human.

Questions

1. How will the introduction of common sense into computer systems affect human-computer relations? Will users be more or less likely to become frustrated with a PC that exhibits common sense?
2. Besides Web searching, what applications do you think would benefit from a computer with common sense?
3. What most frustrates you about using computers? Could Cyc help?

Sources
1. *"Computerizing Common Sense," Gary H. Anthes,* ComputerWorld, *April 8, 2002, www.computerworld.com/news/2002/story/0,11280,69881,00.html.*
2. *"Wise Up, Dumb Machine," Mitchell Leslie,* Stanford Magazine, *March/April 2002, www.stanfordalumni.org/news/magazine/2002/marapr/departments/brightideas.html.*
3. *"A.I. Reboots", Michael Hilzik,* MIT Technology Review, *March 2002, www.technologyreview.com/articles/print_version/hiltzik0302.asp.*
4. *Cycorp Web site: www.cyc.com.*

Object-oriented Design. Earlier chapters introduced the concepts of *object-oriented*. The object-oriented approach to viewing and solving problems originated in computer programming and is a very popular method for designing software solutions. In **object-oriented design**, the solution to the program specification is derived from the interaction of objects. An *object* is composed of *attributes*, which are identifying characteristics such as variables, and *methods*, which are actions that the object can carry out. Figure 10.11 provides an example of object-oriented design as applied to the gas pump example. Here the job of accepting credit-card payment for a gas purchase at the pump involves three objects: a transaction object, a credit-card object, and a pump object. Examine the attributes of each object shown in the top portion of the circle. These are the variables that were identified in the program specification. The methods of each object, shown in the bottom half of each circle, hold the functionality of the object, the actions that the object is programmed to carry out. Methods of one object can interact with methods of another object. This interaction between objects is what creates the solution to the program specification.

FIGURE 10.11 • Object-oriented design

This gas pump program design utilizes object-oriented design. It shows three objects, with attributes and methods, interacting with each other.

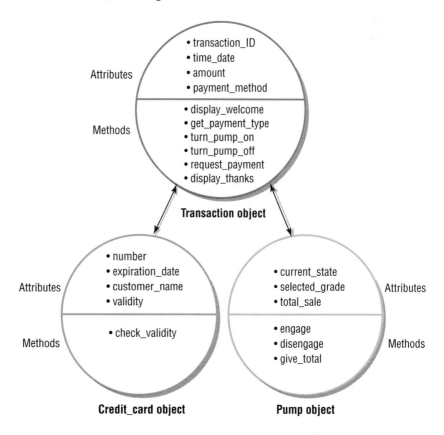

Of the methods in Figure 10.11, which one would you guess is activated first? It seems likely that the gas pump routine would use the following sequence of methods:

1. transaction.display_welcome
2. get_payment_type → credit_card.check_validity
3. transaction.turn_pump_on → pump.engage
4. pump.give_total → transaction.request_payment
5. transaction.turn_pump_off → pump.disengage
6. transaction.display_thanks

Object-oriented design takes a little getting used to, but the advantages are significant. Notice in our example how all data and actions associated with an object are contained within the object itself. This is known as *encapsulation*. Encapsulation makes it possible to pluck an object from one application and use it in another. For example, if we were asked to write an algorithm for the transactions that take place in the mini-mart associated with the gas station, we could reuse the credit_card object, and with slight modifications to the transaction object, have a new program ready to go in no time. Since such convenience is not offered in traditional structured design many programmers are turning to object-oriented design as a faster, more efficient method of developing software. Note, however, that structured design is often used within the methods of objects.

Event-Driven Programs

Most programs that involve human interaction are designed with a graphical user interface and are event-driven. An *event-driven* program sits idle until an event, such as a mouse click or key press, occurs and launches a set of computer instructions. For example, a Web browser will sit idle until you click a link on a Web page, which launches a set of instructions in the Web browser that fetches a new Web page or initiates some other action (see Figure 10.12). Event-driven programming is a by-product of the graphical user interface.

FIGURE 10.12 • **Event-driven program**

Web pages such as the ESPN site are poised for action with links that launch a cascade of information, videos, or other content when clicked.

Algorithm Development Tools

Even seemingly simple programs, such as the gas pump program, become complex as they are refined into the detailed steps of an algorithm. Therefore, it is helpful to have organizational tools to assist in the process of refinement. Many such tools are available to programmers. The most popular tools are pseudocode, flowcharts, and the Unified Modeling Language.

Pseudocode. **Pseudocode** is a form of notation that describes the detailed steps of an algorithm in a fashion similar to a programming language, but in a more natural language without the formal syntax requirements of a programming language. Pseudocode describes solutions to problems at a highly detailed level, using programming methods that are common to all programming languages. Table 10.3 illustrates the use of pseudocode in a portion of the gas pump program. It also provides a look at the equivalent programming language statements in C++. Note the differences between the two.

TABLE 10.3 • Pseudocode versus Program Code

Pseudocode	C++ Program Source Code

If payment_method is cash
   display See Cashier
or if payment_method is credit
   read_credit_card
	If (payment_method == cash){
	   cout << See Cashier \n;
	}
	elseif (paymeny_method == credit){
	   read_credit_card();
	}

Flowcharts. As you saw in Chapter 9, a *flowchart* is a graphical diagram that reveals the path from a starting point to the final destination. Flowcharts have been used to illustrate programming logic since the early days of programming. They are best suited for structured program design; other tools, such as UML (discussed next), are better at supporting object-oriented design. Flowcharts are also ideal for illustrating standard programming structures that are common to all programming languages and that are the building blocks of programming logic.

To handle anything beyond the simplest problems, programs need to be able to take different actions based on decisions. They also need to be able to go back and repeat actions. Two common programming structures that accommodate decisions and repetition are selection and looping. In *selection*, a path is chosen based on a condition within the program. The pseudocode in Table 10.3 illustrates selection. Programmers sometimes call selection "if-then" statements; "if" a condition exists, "then" do action 1, "if" some other condition exists, "then" do action 2, and so on. Figure 10.13 illustrates how a flowchart is used to represent selection.

FIGURE 10.13 • A selection structure
This flow chart illustrates a selection based on the payment method chosen. If the payment method selected is Cash, then "See Cashier" is displayed. Otherwise, if credit is selected, a sequence of instructions is launched to read the credit card and proceed with the transaction.

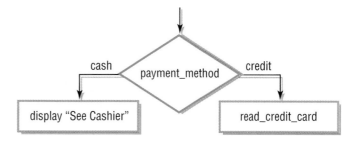

In a program *loop*, an action is repeated as long as some condition exists in the program. For example, a gas pump may be controlled with the statement "while the pump handle is squeezed, pump gas;" when the handle ceases to be squeezed, the pumping stops. Programmers often refer to looping as "while" statements.

Unified Modeling Language. The *Unified Modeling Language (UML)* provides tools for creating object-oriented models for software solutions. Just as flowcharts have been used for generating structured design algorithms, UML is becoming very popular for generating object-oriented design algorithms.

UML is much more powerful than flowcharts. To see why, consider the construction trade. In construction, as in programming, there are those in design, the architects, and those who use the designs, the builders. Communication between the architect and builder is critical to the success of a construction project. Architects and builders use a common language expressed in a building blueprint to make sure that there is a shared understanding of the plan. UML provides a similar tool during software development for systems analysts and business analysts (the designers), and computer programmers (the builders).

UML provides a high-level description of a system through *use-case diagrams*, which were discussed in Chapter 9 (remember the Kayak rental clerk in Figure 9.14). Powerful UML tools, such as Rational Rose software from IBM, allow programmers to refine use-case diagrams into object diagrams, such as the objects described earlier in our gas pump example (see Figure 10.11). The refinement can continue all the way down to a level where the UML tool will actually create the programming language code for the software.

UML tools, such as those provided by Rational Rose, will become increasingly popular since they empower users to create software through a natural progression of refinement, rather than by struggling with the details of a programming language (see Figure 10.14). These tools also dramatically reduce program development errors by allowing software users to more specifically describe their needs to software developers.

FIGURE 10.14 • Rational Rose

Rational Rose software empowers users to create software using a GUI interface, rather than by struggling with the details of a programming language.

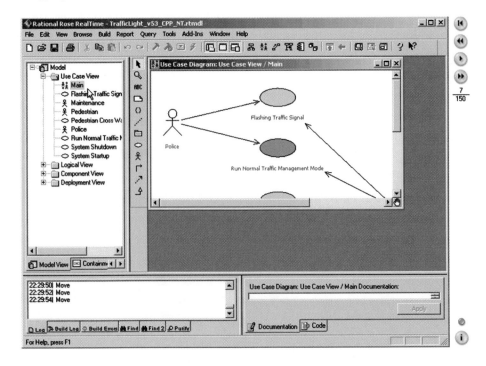

PROGRAMIMPLEMENTATION—**CODING**THE**PROGRAM**

EXPANDYOUR
KNOWLEDGE

To learn more about visual programming, go to www.course.com/swt. Click the link "Expand Your Knowledge," and then complete the lab entitled, "Visual Programming."

At this point in the software development process, the developer or development team has a very detailed plan for the design of the software. It is time to implement the program in a language that the computer can understand. In **program implementation**, the algorithm developed in the program design stage is translated into a computer programming language to create a working, executable program. Figure 10.15 illustrates the deliverable items that link the stages of the development process.

The implementation stage requires some knowledge of a programming language (programming languages were discussed in Chapter 3). This stage can be automated if the developer is using an application generator as discussed in the first section of this chapter. In most cases, though, this stage is carried out by computer programmers. The programmer or systems analyst selects a programming language that supports the design style used in developing the algorithm: object-oriented or structured. The choice of user interface and program delivery method also affect the choice of programming languages. Some programming languages provide convenient tools for developing graphical user interfaces. Furthermore, there are special considerations for programs that are delivered over the Web.

FIGURE 10.15 • Program implementation deliverables
Deliverable objects, shown in the arrows, join each stage of the software development process.

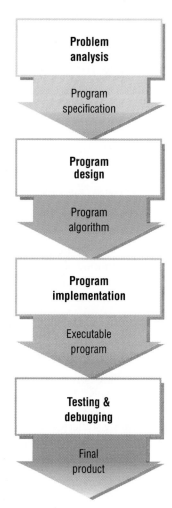

From Algorithm to Source Code

Algorithms are written so that they use the structures common to most programming languages. If the algorithms provided are thorough, it becomes a simple matter to turn them into a program by using the syntax rules of a programming language. You may recall from Chapter 3 that a programming language's syntax is the rules of the programming language—how to write commands and use the symbols of the language. Consider the translation of the pseudocode algorithm into C++ programming code shown in Figure 10.16.

FIGURE 10.16 • From algorithm to programming language

A simple password algorithm is translated into the C++ programming language.

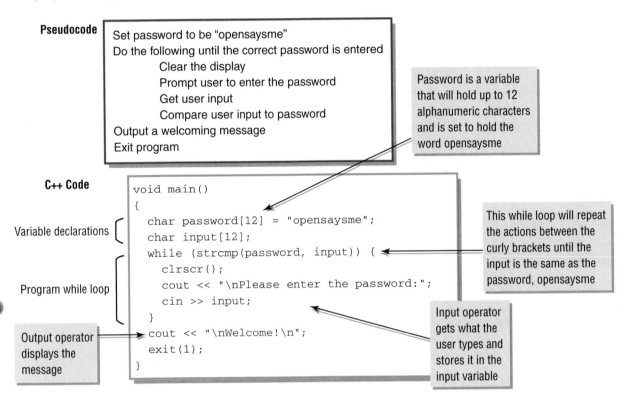

Notice the similarities and differences between the the pseudocode and programming language code in the figure. The C++ syntax requires curly brackets to indicate the beginning and end of code segments. You can see that they are used to indicate the beginning and end of the main code section and the while loop. Programs typically start out with variable declarations, which define variable names and sometimes assign a value to them. Here, the declaration assigns the value "opensaysme" to the password variable. You may notice that each program statement ends with a semicolon; this is a basic part of C++ syntax. The while loop is based on a comparison of the input to the password. The loop clears the screen, displays "Please enter the password", and retrieves the password that is entered.

This example illustrates the relationship between pseudocode and programming source code, and also illustrates the details of programming language syntax. As you can see, learning a programming language requires learning the rules and commands of the language, which carry out common programming operations.

Software developers typically use software to build software. A *software development kit*, more formally referred to as an integrated programming environment (IDE), is a software package that assists programmers with the development of software using a particular programming language. Many of these kits include drag-and-drop graphical user interfaces—they are often called visual programming languages. The programmer can use a visual programming language to create a graphical user interface by dragging and dropping buttons, text boxes, list boxes, and other GUI objects onto the application interface, as you can see in Figure 10.17. However, don't let the GUI interface and ease of drag-and-drop fool you. Visual programming still requires knowledge and use of a formal programming language.

FIGURE 10.17 • The .NET software development kit

The .NET software development kit includes tools that assist programmers in developing applications for Microsoft Windows and the Web.

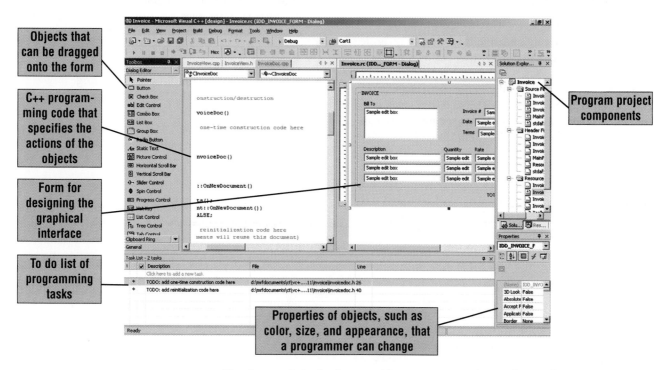

Development tools also provide syntax correction and completion services that assist the programmer with using the language syntax correctly as the code is being entered, debugging tools that assist with finding errors in the programming syntax and logic, and compilers and interpreters to turn the source code into an executable program.

From Source Code to Executable Program

Once the programmer has completed writing the source code for a program, the code is translated to object code to be run on the computer. In a typical software development kit, going from source code to executable program is a simple matter of clicking a button. For example, you might choose "make program" from a menu, or click a "compile" button on a toolbar. In either case, the compiler or interpreter will progress through the source code line by line, checking to make sure that the programming language was used correctly, and if so, translating it to an executable program that can be run.

JOB ⁄ⁿⁿⁿ TECHNOLOGY

Extreme Programming

The latest rage in programming techniques is called extreme programming (XP). Extreme programming makes use of the traditional program development life cycle with many minor adjustments that add up to faster software development that meets the customer's needs more thoroughly.

Programmers work closely with users in XP development. Users write up characteristics that they desire in the software—XP calls these "user stories." Developers design software tests based on the user stories prior to writing any code (XP is also called test-driven programming). The project is then broken into small incremental objects, using the object-oriented design approach, and divided among programming teams. One of the unique qualities of XP development is that programmers work in two-person teams. If a team gets stuck, they may swap jobs with another team. The program is written in small increments with frequent tests to see if what has been written so far works. The user/customer is involved in each iteration of programming and is a full-time member of the development team. Coding and testing take place in rapid succession until each team's work is complete and combined together for final tests.

Big name companies such as Hewlett-Packard, IBM, and Sabre—even Domino's Pizza—are turning to the XP approach in the hope of improving productivity. What was once a fringe, grassroots movement has now become a solid programming practice of major technology companies. It is no wonder that companies are looking for an improved approach to programming. Consider the following statistics:

- 15 percent of information technology projects fail and are canceled, costing $38 billion each year.
- Products that are released contain only 52 percent of the features requested.
- Projects are chronically late with only 18 percent delivered by the quoted deadline.
- Released products contain bugs that range anywhere from 1 in 100 to 1 in 1,000 lines of code.

Extreme programming has set out to change these statistics and reclaim the public trust in software developers.

Questions

1. What benefit does working in pairs provide for the development process?
2. Why do you think traditional software development ends up providing only 52 percent of the requested features?
3. Provide an example of how extreme programming might benefit other professional processes.

Sources
1. "The New X-Men", Martha Baer, Wired, September 2003.
2. "Extreme Programming: A gentle introduction", www. extremeprogramming.org/ accessed September 29, 2003.

Often the compiling process will not be successful on the first attempt. The compiler will produce *syntax error* messages that indicate the location in your code where a syntax error was found. For example, the error message might say "; missing at line 256". Scrolling down the source code to line 256 you will find that indeed you did forget to place a semicolon at the end of the command as required by the language.

The larger the program, the more room for errors. Programmers typically develop a program incrementally or in sections, compiling and testing it frequently (see the "Job Technology" box). It's much easier to find one syntax error in 40 lines of code, than it is to find 20 errors in 800 lines of code. Consider Microsoft Windows XP, which weighs in at a hefty 40 million lines of code.[12] Think about how difficult it might be to track down a few errors among 40 million lines of code.

After coding, compiling, running, and evaluating, many times, with incremental additions and improvements each time, the completed program will eventually compile without any errors, at which point it is ready to be run and evaluated.

Running the Program

Once a program is compiled into an executable form the programmer runs it to evaluate whether or not it meets the specifications. A program that passes a compiler's syntax evaluation may run, but still have problems (see Figure 10.18). A **logic error** is the result of a poor algorithm that contains a flaw in reasoning that causes the program to crash, behave in an unexpected fashion, or not effectively solve the problem for which it was designed. Logic errors are often difficult to track down since no explicit error message indicates what part of the code is causing the error. The process of tracking down and correcting logic errors in a program is called **debugging**. Testing and debugging are discussed in the next section.

FIGURE 10.18 • Why a program might not work: Syntax and logic errors

This C++ code contains a syntax error that would produce errors during the compiling process, and a logic error that would cause the program to loop forever since password will never be the same as input.

```
void main()
{
  char password[12] = "opensaysme";
  char input[12];
  while (strcmp(password, input)) {
   clrscr();
   cout << "\nPlease enter the password:";
   cin >> password;
  )
  cout << "\nWelcome!\n";
  exit(1);
}
```

Syntax error – should be curly bracket

Logic error – should store user input in input variable, not password variable

Error Handling

Once a program appears to run as intended, programmers typically focus on error handling. *Error handling*, also called *exception handling*, is code that checks data items to make sure that they are valid and reasonable. For example, what happens if a user types "H" in a textbox that asks for "weekly hours worked"? Will the program attempt to calculate the person's paycheck based on H weekly hours? Will the program crash, freeze, or lock up? A program *crash* occurs when the program executes commands that cause the computer to malfunction or shut down. A program *freeze* or *lock-up* occurs when a program executes commands that cause the computer to cease responding to user input; the program becomes frozen in its current state.

A sizable percentage of program code is typically dedicated to error handling. Some of this code is manually written by the programmer to provide useful error messages to the user. For example, when H is entered as weekly hours, a message

box might appear that states "Please type a numeric value between 0 and 40." Other error-handling routines are provided by the programming language and automatically kick in when data threatens to crash the program. For example, if a command is written to read data from a database, but the database is not found, the program may automatically inform the user that the database cannot be found.

PROGRAMTESTING,**DEBUGGING**,AND**MAINTENANCE**

Program testing and debugging takes place in every stage of software development. In the problem analysis stage, testing of possible solutions to the problem provides a method of determining feasibility. In the program development stage, developers often use paper and pencil to follow data through a proposed algorithm to determine if the algorithm will produce the desired result. Testing and debugging were continual processes in the program implementation stage as we coded, compiled, ran, and evaluated our code repeatedly. These stages have brought us to the point where we believe that we have a program that meets the requirements of the problem specification. In the **program testing and debugging** stage, we run stringent tests on the program to determine if it is ready for release. There are two phases of program testing and debugging: alpha testing and beta testing.

Alpha Testing

Alpha testing refers to the first stage of testing that is implemented by the software developer. Testing begins by running test data through the software and observing the results. As an example, consider a teacher's grade book program. The software developer inputs scores earned by a student into the software, and the software outputs a final grade. Table 10.4 describes the program specifications for a grade book application.

TABLE 10.4 • Grade Book Program Specification

Input	Processing	Output
	Final grade is calculated as:	Final grade
2 assignment scores	Assignments 25 percent	
2 quiz scores	Quizzes 25 percent	
1 final exam score	Final exam 50 percent	

The algorithm for this program would first average the assignment scores, then average the quiz scores, and then use the equation (assignment_average $\times$ .25) + (quiz_average $\times$ .25) + (final_exam_score x .5) to determine the final grade. Using a calculator, the alpha tester would manually calculate what the output should be for a variety of inputs (see Table 10.5).

After manually calculating the solutions, the alpha tester will run the test data on the program to confirm that it provides the correct output. Some alpha testing makes use of programs that automatically feed a program input and check the output. Automation makes it possible to more quickly and thoroughly test a program with a greater number of data sets. Testing is typically not as simple as the above example. Software typically has many functions, each of which must be tested (see "Job Technology" box).

JOB TECHNOLOGY

Software Tester

If you have an eye for detail, a natural ability with computers, and a passion to make the world a better place through computing, then you may be cut out for a career as a software tester. The software testing field is rapidly growing and providing good paying opportunities for individuals with a knack for computers. You don't necessarily need any programming training or experience. What you do need is a passion for detecting errors in programs and fixing them.

Most software testing makes use of automated tools, such as those manufactured by Mercury and Rational. The tester runs the testing tools, which control the software being tested, to find all possible results from the software and compare them to the desired results. The tools themselves are fairly sophisticated and take some training to run. There are a wide variety of software tester positions that range from programming to being a very observant user.

Software testing can be financially lucrative. The more you know about software development the better

salary you can earn. With an increasing emphasis on security and reliability, software testing is expected to grow to be a several billion dollar industry within the next few years.

Questions

1. Name five applications where software testing could be a matter of life or death.
2. Have you had an experience that shows a lack of software testing? What was it?
3. Why is software testing more important now than it was 5 years ago?

Sources
1. *"Software Testing as a Career," Narayana Murthy, Indian Institute of Information Technology Web site, accessed October 1, 2003, at www.iiitb.ac.in/ss/Publications/TOI/Software%20 Testing%20as%20a%20Career.htm.*
2. *"Welcome to the world of software testing," Gurmit Singh, Personal Web site accessed October 1, 2003, www.geocities. com/gurmitleo/articles/.*

TABLE 10.5 • Sample Data and Output for Alpha Testing

Input	Output
Test Data 1: 70, 80, 90, 70, 80	Solution 1: 79
Test Data 2: 100, 100, 90, 90, 100	Solution 2: 97.5
Etc.	

After testing a program under typical conditions, an alpha tester will begin interacting with the software in unpredictable and unspecified ways to test the program's error-handling ability.

If logic errors are detected during the testing process, the development process shifts back to the design stage where corrections to the original algorithms can take place. If program bugs, such as program crashes, are detected the code goes back to the implementation stage where debugging takes place (see Figure 10.19). The program may bounce back and forth between alpha testers and programmers several times before it is finally cleared for beta testing.

FIGURE 10.19 • Program testing

Program errors found during the testing stage send the program back to one of the previous stages.

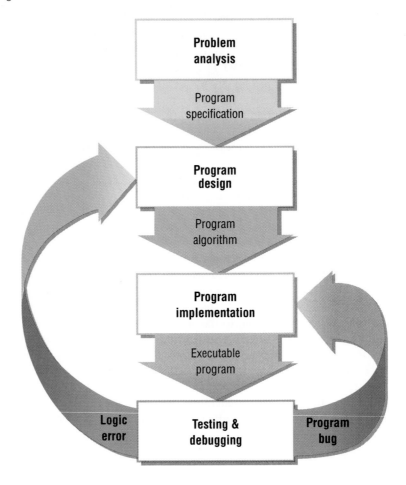

Usability

During the testing stage and often during the development of the user interface, developers run an intense battery of usability tests. **Usability** refers to how easy a program is to use. Five major usability issues are studied in designing and testing a program's user interface:

- Learnability. How easy it is for users to learn how to use the functions of the software?
- Efficiency. How much effort is required on the part of the user to carry out tasks with the software?
- Memorability. How quickly can the user remember how to use the software after being away from it for a while?
- Errors. How many errors is the user likely to make during normal use of the software and in what range of severity?
- Satisfaction. How pleasant does the user feel the software is to use?

Usability has a direct relationship to productivity. Software that is unnecessarily difficult to use wastes the user's time and can cost companies lots of money. For this reason, many software development projects invest as much as 10 percent of the total budget on usability testing.[13]

Beta Testing

Beta testing, the second level of program testing, uses a select group of end users to try out the program and provide feedback. Software that is released for beta testing is in its last stage of development. Beta testers are charged with the responsibility of giving final clearance to the project. Beta testing allows the software to be tested on a wide variety of computers and conditions. Beta testers are typically asked to use the software as they normally would, and report any problems that arise.

Sometimes, beta versions of usually expensive software are released to the public for free. The software is programmed to work only for the beta testing period, typically a few months. Beta release software comes with a long list of disclaimers that essentially say that if this software destroys your computer, it isn't the software manufacturer's fault. However, if the software manufacturer is well known and respected, the public is usually willing to accept the risk. It should be noted that regular software comes with a similar disclaimer (see the "Community Technology" box). Such beta tests provide customers with free use of products, while building future customers for the product when it is formally released.

Once beta testing is complete, and the product has been improved upon by the alpha and beta test processes, the software is ready for formal release. For commercial software projects, formal release is when the software is packaged and distributed to retailers, or made available for purchase online. For software developed as part of system development, formal release takes place when the system is put in to use in the organization. For software created by an individual for personal use, one individual is the programmer, alpha tester, beta tester, and end user. In this case, formal release would take place when all the bugs are worked out and the program is in regular use.

No program is ever really finished. There is always room for improvement. Software is continuously evaluated, and sometimes brought back into the shop for an overhaul. When software gets to this stage of development it has left the testing and debugging stage, has been formally released, and has entered the maintenance stage.

Maintenance

Programs that are formally released and in regular use are in their maintenance stage. During **software maintenance**, programs are evaluated under normal use and improved upon with reversions and revisions, if deemed necessary. A reversion of a program makes only minor improvements in the program, and usually consists of some minor bug fixes. A revision is a more drastic modification of the program that may include new features, or a new look and feel. Popular software packages are typically around for many revisions.

Often, software manufacturers publish patches to fix bugs that are found in the software after it is released and prior to the next revision or reversion. Patches are typically free to registered users and downloadable from the software manufacturer's Web site. For operating systems, such as Microsoft Windows, several patches between reversions are typically published to address security issues, compatibility issues, and bugs. Microsoft collects patches together in "service packs," and automates the process of downloading and installing each service pack through a service called Windows Update.

COMMUNITY /\/\/ TECHNOLOGY

Trustworthy Computing

People don't trust computer software. We don't trust computer programs to run correctly, and we are not surprised when they crash. In general, we accommodate flaws in software much more than we accommodate flaws in other products. Why? It's new technology! There are bound to be a few bugs.

Society's lack of trust in computer software is slowing advances of technology into key financial areas. Electronic wallets have not gained public acceptance because the public will not trust software to store valuable private information such as credit-card numbers. Some businesses hesitate to conduct online transactions due to fears of software failure, inadequate security, and privacy issues.

The warranty that accompanies software packages does little to instill confidence. Consider this warranty statement that accompanies a popular software product:

IN NO EVENT SHALL MICROSOFT OR ITS SUPPLIERS BE LIABLE FOR ANY SPECIAL, INCIDENTAL, INDIRECT, OR CONSEQUENTIAL DAMAGES WHATSOEVER (INCLUDING, WITHOUT LIMITATION, DAMAGES FOR LOSS OF BUSINESS PROFITS, BUSINESS INTERRUPTION, LOSS OF BUSINESS INFORMATION, OR ANY OTHER PECUNIARY LOSS) ARISING OUT OF THE USE OF OR INABILITY TO USE THE SOFTWARE PRODUCT

This statement is typical of all software warranties that users agree to—without much thought—upon installation of the software.

Microsoft has recognized that consumer trust must be won back in order to expand their operations. "We will have to make the computing ecosystem sufficiently trustworthy that people don't worry about its fallibility or unreliability the way they do today . . . It may take us 10 to 15 years to get there." wrote Microsoft's CTO Craig Mundie in a white paper outlining Microsoft's "trustworthy computing" initiative.

The trustworthy computing initiative was launched with a well-publicized e-mail from Bill Gates to Microsoft employees with the subject "Trustworthy Computing." In the e-mail Gates outlined an approach to building customer trust through focusing on three areas:

- Availability. Software runs reliably without crashing.
- Security. Data that is manipulated and stored by software is protected from harm and used or modified only in appropriate ways.
- Privacy. Users' personal information is protected from outside view including the software manufacturer.

Although some people believe Microsoft's strategy is a ploy to comfort consumers and reinvigorate the PC market, Craig Mundie has put his money where his mouth is. He bet Google CEO Eric Schmidt that by 2030, passengers would trust software to the extent that they will board computer piloted airline flights. The hope is that if people trust software with their life, then perhaps, they will trust it with their money.

Questions

1. How often do you experience software failure? In what form?
2. How much do you trust software? Would you trust it to pilot your flight?
3. Will software manufacturers like Microsoft be successful in winning consumer trust?

Sources
1. *"Trustworthy Computing", e-mail from Bill Gates to Microsoft employees, January 15, 2002, www.wired.com/news/ business/0,1367,49826,00.html.*
2. *Anti-Trustworthy Computing, Paul Boutin, salon.com, www. salon.com/tech/feature/2002/04/09/trustworthy/.*
3. *Microsoft's Visual Basic 6 software warranty.*

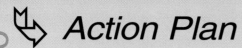 *Action Plan*

1. What first step should Susan take to begin the program development process?

Susan should begin by analyzing the problem, determining the important factors, and developing a program specification that includes what will be needed as input, what will be presented as output, and the goals of the program.

2. How much of the program development process can Susan handle without her friend, the computer programmer?

Susan can analyze the problem and design a solution without any formal knowledge of a programming language. By providing her programmer friend with detailed program specifications and a detailed algorithm, Susan has completed most of the time-consuming effort involved in program development. This project might even inspire Susan to learn a program language herself, so that she can develop future programs for her unit without anyone's help.

3. If the output of Susan's scheduling program is a weekly schedule that satisfies the nurses and technicians in Susan's unit, what will be required as input?

Susan will need to develop a questionnaire to find out the scheduling preferences of the nurses and technicians in her unit. The responses to the questionnaire along with the personnel information of each person on the staff would be inputs to this system. Susan would also need to define the shifts, the number of shifts in a 24-hour period, and the start and stop times of each shift. The staff might agree that those on the staff the longest should have some preference over newer staff members. Years-on-staff might be another input value.

Summary

LEARNING OBJECTIVE 1

Define software development and provide examples of how nonprogrammers are involved in the software development process.

Software development is the process of developing computer programs to address a specific need or problem. A software developer is an individual who designs and implements software solutions. Programs are developed for a wide range of problems at varying levels of complexity. Casual programming refers to programming done by individuals who become involved in computer programming with little or no forethought or training. Another way to develop software is through application generators that allow users to write programs without learning a programming language. Much of the software used in large businesses and organizations is custom-designed to meet the needs of the organization. Program development is a subprocess of systems development. Many programmers follow a sequence of steps known as the program development life cycle. The *program development life cycle* provides a five step sequence of activities for developing and maintaining code that includes problem analysis, program design, program implementation, testing and debugging, and maintenance.

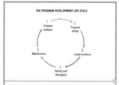

Figure 10.5—p. 431

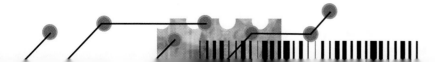

LEARNING OBJECTIVE 2
Discuss issues related to problem analysis and the process of developing a program specification.

In the problem analysis stage, the problem requirements are studied in order to design detailed specifications, called the program specification, for a computer program. In problem analysis the problem is broken down into its essential elements, called variables. The resulting program specification includes a detailed description of the input and output of the program and a general description of the processing. The program delivery method and user interface requirements are also usually defined in this stage.

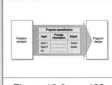

Figure 10.6—p. 432

LEARNING OBJECTIVE 3
Compare and contrast program design approaches, and list the tools and methods used to create an algorithm.

In the program design stage, a formal algorithm is designed to satisfy the requirements of the program specification. The first step in designing a program algorithm is to decide whether the problem is computable, whether it is solvable by a computer. If the program is computable, a design approach is chosen. Program design approaches include structured design and object-oriented design. Algorithms are often defined using pseudocode or flowcharts. Two common structures in programming are selection, in which a path through a program is chosen based on a condition, and looping, in which an action is repeated as long as some condition exists. The Unified Modeling Language (UML) provides tools for creating object-oriented models for creating software solutions.

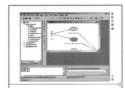

Figure 10.14—p. 442

LEARNING OBJECTIVE 4
Discuss the steps and issues related to creating an executable program from an algorithm.

In program implementation, the algorithm developed in the program design stage is translated into a computer programming language to create a working, executable program. Programmers sometimes use software development kits to assist in developing the source code. Source code is translated into an executable program by a complier or interpreter. Often the compiling process will alert the programmer to syntax errors in the code. Programs can also include logic errors that are difficult to track down. Program errors are called bugs, and the process of tracking them down is called debugging.

Figure 10.17—p. 445

LEARNING OBJECTIVE 5
Describe the methods used to guarantee that a program is ready for use and discover concerns regarding the program after it is formally released.

In the program testing and debugging stage, stringent tests are run on the program to determine if it is ready for release. Alpha testing refers to the first stage of testing that is implemented by the software developer. Developers test programs for usability to make sure that the software is easy to use. In beta testing, the second level of program testing, a select group of end users tries out the program and provides feedback. Once beta testing is complete, and the product has been improved according to beta test results, the software is ready for formal release. During the maintenance stage, programs are evaluated under normal use, and improved upon with reversions and revisions if deemed necessary.

Figure 10.19—p. 450

Test Yourself

LEARNING OBJECTIVE 1: Define software development and provide examples of how nonprogrammers are involved in the software development process.

1. _____ is the process of developing computer programs to address a specific need or problem.

2. _____ are programs that allow you to create other programs without using a formal programming language.
   a. Program development toolkits
   b. Application generators
   c. Visual programming languages
   d. Compilers

3. True or False: Systems development is a subprocess within program development.

LEARNING OBJECTIVE 2: Discuss issues related to problem analysis and the process of developing a program specification.

4. True or False: The goal of the problem analysis stage is to come up with an algorithm for a program solution.

5. A(n) _____ is a named data component that can be set to different values.
   a. constant
   b. input
   c. variable
   d. algorithm

6. The result of the problem analysis is a _____, a document that defines the requirements of the program in terms of input, processing, and output.

LEARNING OBJECTIVE 3: Compare and contrast program design approaches, and list the tools and methods used to create an algorithm.

7. A(n) _____ sometimes called *program logic*, is a step-by-step problem-solving process that arrives at a solution in a finite amount of time.

8. True or False: Object-oriented design is becoming more popular than structured design because of the ability to reuse code modules.

9. Which of the following is not a tool for algorithm development:
   a. pseudocode
   b. debugger
   c. flowchart
   d. UML

LEARNING OBJECTIVE 4: Discuss the steps and issues related to creating an executable program from an algorithm.

10. True or False: Programmers use compilers and interpreters to translate object code into source code.

11. A(n) _____ error is the result of a poor algorithm that contains a flaw in reasoning that either causes the program to crash or behave in an unexpected fashion.
    a. syntax
    b. bug
    c. exception
    d. logic

12. The process of tracking down and correcting logic errors in a program is called _____.

LEARNING OBJECTIVE 5: Describe the methods used to guarantee that a program is ready for use and discover concerns regarding the program after it is formally released.

13. True or False: Alpha testing is implemented by the software developer.

14. _____, the second level of program testing, uses a select group of end users to try out the program and provide feedback.

15. During the _____ stage of software development, programs are evaluated under normal use, and improved upon with reversions and revisions if deemed necessary.
    a. testing and debugging
    b. maintenance
    c. design
    d. implementation

Test Yourself Solutions: 1. Software development, **2.** b., **3.** F, **4.** F, **5.** c., **6.** Program Specification, **7.** algorithm, **8.** T, **9.** b., **10.** F, **11.** d., **12.** debugging, **13.** T, **14.** Beta, **15.** b.

Key Terms

Questions

Review Questions

1. Name the five stages of the program development life cycle.

2. Present an example of casual programming.

3. What is an application generator?

4. What is the goal of the problem analysis stage of software development?

5. What is a variable?

6. Why is program delivery a consideration in problem analysis?

7. What details does a program specification contain?

8. Name three options for program delivery.

9. What is the deliverable object that is produced by the program design stage?

10. What is the main benefit of object-oriented design?

11. What are event-driven programs?

12. How does pseudocode differ from a flowchart?

13. What is the deliverable object that is produced by the program implementation stage?

14. What is a syntax error?

15. How does a syntax error differ from a logic error?

16. What is the purpose of program testing and debugging?

17. What is the purpose of alpha testing?

18. Who is involved in beta testing?

19. What is the purpose of software maintenance?

20. What is the difference between a program revision and a program reversion?

Discussion Questions

21. What is the purpose of software development?

22. How does program development relate to systems development?

23. What types of problems are computers best at solving?

24. What activities do computers find to be most difficult?

25. Give some examples of how programs that you use make use of selection.

26. Give some examples of how programs that you use make use of looping.

27. What benefits does UML provide to developers?

28. What assistance does a software development kit provide to programmers?

29. What development activity might create syntax errors? Why?

30. What program symptoms indicate the existence of a logic error?

Exercises

Try It Yourself

1. Search the Web on the keywords "application generators." Browse through the search results to find the best definition of this expression. Cut and paste the definition into a word-processing document. Provide the URL of the Web site where you got the definition, and list two other Web sites that provide information on application generators. Add a paragraph that provides your thoughts on the likelihood that you will ever use an application generator.

2. Using a spreadsheet, calculate the shortest path for a salesman to travel to visit all four cities in Figure 10.20 and return home. Provide the sequence of cities starting and ending at home and the total distance traveled. How many calculations were necessary to find the shortest path?

FIGURE 10.20 • Exercise 2

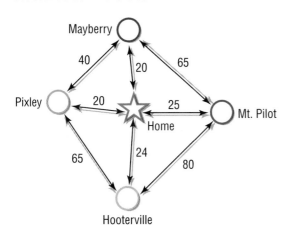

3. Table 10.6 shows a program specification for a miles per gallon (MPG) calculator program that includes input variables and output. This program allows the user to input the starting mileage from the odometer before the trip, the ending mileage from the odometer at the conclusion of the trip, and the number of gallons used for the entire trip. From this input, the program will calculate the miles per gallon achieved on the trip. Write an algorithm in pseudocode to fill in the processing portion of this table.

TABLE 10.6 • Program Specifications for Exercise 3

Input	Processing	Output
Starting_mileage Ending_mileage Gallons_used	?	The miles per gallon (MPG) achieved on the trip

4. Write three test data sets for use in testing the algorithm you wrote for Exercise 3. Include the three inputs and the output achieved for each data set. Use a spreadsheet or calculator to determine the output for each data set.

5. Create a flowchart for an age calculator program that behaves as follows:
    a. The user types in his or her year of birth.
    b. The program, knowing the current year, calculates the age of the user.
    c. If the user is 21 or older, the program displays the message "You may pass!" and exits the program.
    d. If the user is younger than 21, the program repetitively asks the user to enter a number between 1 and 10 until the user enters 7 at which point the program displays "you are wise beyond your years" and exits.

(Hint: this algorithm includes selection and looping)

Virtual Classroom Activities

For the following exercises, do not use face-to-face or telephone communications with your group members. Use only Internet communications.

6. Consider an electronic soft drink machine program. The customer inserts coins or a dollar bill, the program evaluates the amount entered, the customer selects a beverage, and the soft drink machine delivers the product and produces change if necessary. Each team member, using a drawing program (paint, or PowerPoint, or any program that allows you to draw and label simple figures), should individually create an object diagram similar to the one in Figure 10.11. Define objects, their attributes, and methods. Tip: You might

base your design loosely on the gas pump example. Submit your finished work to the group, along with a written rationale for your design. The group should vote on the best design and submit it to the instructor.

7. Have each group member create a structured design diagram for the soft drink machine program similar to the one shown in Figure 10.9. Make sure to cover account error checking. For instance, what happens if the customer does not insert enough money? What happens if the soft drink machine is empty? All members submit their diagram to the group for a vote to see which is most favored. Submit the winner to the teacher.

Teamwork

8. The group is assigned the task of developing a roommate selection program like the one discussed in this chapter. As a group, come up with 10 questions for a questionnaire that you think are useful in deciding roommate compatibility. Remember, you will need to use the responses to these questions to calculate compatibility. You might want to phrase questions in a manner that the user can respond with a number—such as, on a scale of 1 to 10, or "agree/disagree/undecided." As a group decide on the input and output requirements for this program. Divide the work of developing the application between team members, each member taking one or more of the following jobs:

a. Input user interface designer: This person uses a graphics application to design the user interface.

b. Algorithm designer: This person creates an algorithm that will classify each user into a personality profile to use for deciding compatibility.

c. Output designer: This person designs how the results of the program will be displayed.

d. Testing and debugging: This person has each group member submit test data and uses the algorithm to determine which group members are compatible. The group then decides if the program meets the requirements.

Learning Check

To check your knowledge of each of the chapter objectives, use this chart to find related end-of-chapter content.

	Learning Objective	Key Terms	Questions	Exercises
	Learning Objective 1 Define software development and provide examples of how nonprogrammers are involved in the software development process.	application generators, software developer, software development	1, 2, 3, 21 22, 23, 24	1, 2
	Learning Objective 2 Discuss issues related to problem analysis and the process of developing a program specification.	problem analysis, program specification	4, 5, 6, 7, 8	3, 8

(continued)

	Learning Objective	Key Terms	Questions	Exercises
	Learning Objective 3 Compare and contrast program design approaches, and list the tools and methods used to create an algorithm.	algorithm, object-oriented design, program design, pseudocode, structured design	9, 10, 11, 12, 25, 26, 27	3, 4, 5, 6, 7, 8
	Learning Objective 4 Discuss the steps and issues related to creating an executable program from an algorithm.	debugging, logic error, program implementation	13, 14, 15, 28, 29	
	Learning Objective 5 Present the methods used to guarantee that a program is ready for use and discover concerns regarding the program after it is formally released.	beta testing, program testing and debugging, usability, software maintenance	16, 17, 18, 19, 20, 30	8

Endnotes

1 Dan Bricklin's Web site, accessed October 5 at *www.bricklin.com.*

2 "MouseSite" accessed October 6, 2003 at *http://sloan.stanford.edu/MouseSite/.*

3 "Time 100: The most Important People of the 20th Century—Network Designer Tim Berners-Lee", Joshua Quittner, accessed October 5 at *www.time.com/time/time100/scientist/profile/bernerslee.html.*

4 Sapir, Jonathan, "Full Speed Ahead: IT Projects Get a Boost From Users", *Computerworld* online, September 29, 2003, *www.computerworld.com.*

5 Capella Computer Ltd. Web site, *www.capella-mm.com,* accessed September 26, 2003.

6 Group Uni-spec Web site, *www.uni-spec.com/* accessed September 26, 2003.

7 "First Test for Freshmen: Picking Roommates," Tamar Lewin, *The New York Times,* August 7, 2003.

8 "Best Practices for Software Development Projects," Mike Perks, *Computerworld* online, September 29, 2003, *www.computerworld.com.*

9 "Developers show their independent streak," September 29, 2003, *Inforworld* online, *www.infoworld.com.*

10 *www.math.princeton.edu/tsp/.*

11 From *www.computerworld.com/news/2002/story/0,11280,69881,00.html.*

12 Wheeler, David, "More Than a Gigabuck: Estimating GNU/Linux's Size," online research paper, July 29, 2002, *www.dwheeler.com/sloc/redhat71-v1/redhat71sloc.html.*

13 Nielsen, Jakob, "Usability 101," Jakob Nielsen's Alertbox, August 25, 2003, *www.useit.com/alertbox/20030825.html.*

Multimedia Applications**and** Production

Ana Arguello was in her first semester of college. On her own for the first time, she had a real sense of freedom—along with a bit of apprehension. Most of her friends had chosen a major and knew what they wanted to do in life. Ana enjoyed so many things that she had trouble choosing just one area on which to focus. She had always been an expressive, artistic person. She had a good sense of style and real artistic talent. She also played the piano and had received an award in the talent show during her senior year in high school.

Computers had been very much a part of Ana's life. Her mom and dad worked as computer consultants. By the time Ana went to college, she had developed computer skills that surpassed her friends'. She enjoyed the challenge of computer games but often felt steamed that so many were geared towards guys. Ana thought about majoring in a computer-related field, but wondered if she wouldn't be happier majoring in art or music—fields that weren't so male dominated. But, that just seemed like the easy way out.

Deep down, Ana knew what she really wanted to do. She wanted to use her artistic and musical talent to help create video games that would entertain and challenge women and men alike. She was enough of an expert at video games that she understood the components that made for an exciting game. She also had some great ideas for her own games. Could she carve out a place for herself in the video game field? Could she actually make a living at this? She wasn't sure, but she wanted to find out.

1. What skills should Ana develop during college to help her succeed in the video game industry?
2. What major and minor should Ana choose to best prepare for her career?
3. What contacts should Ana make during college that might help her get a job in the industry?

Check out Ana's *Action Plan* at the conclusion of this chapter.

After completing Chapter 11, you will be able to:

LEARNING OBJECTIVES	CHAPTER CONTENT
1. Understand the value and use of digital audio in a variety of career areas and in your life.	**Digital Audio**
2. Describe the many uses of 2-D and 3-D digital graphics and imaging media.	**Digital Graphics**
3. Discuss how interactive media is used to educate and entertain.	**Interactive Media**

Introduction

Digital technology and information systems are tremendously useful in many practical ways. Multimedia brings these systems to life with stunning and vivid graphics, powerful music, and realistic, interactive animated 3-D environments. If technology were alive, multimedia might be considered its heart and soul. Multimedia provides a technical venue for people to express themselves through audio and visual output. This chapter provides an overview of all areas of multimedia, including digital music and audio, digital graphics such as 2-D and 3-D graphics, animation, photography, video, and interactive media such as video games and interactive TV. This chapter looks at state of the art multimedia technologies and how they affect us in our personal and professional lives.

You don't need to be artistically inclined to appreciate and make use of multimedia. A term once used to describe PCs with audio and video capabilities, contemporary **multimedia** has grown to encompass digital devices of all kinds that serve and support digital media such as music, video, and graphics. Digital portable music players, video game consoles, and surround-sound home entertainment systems are all forms of multimedia devices delivering digital media. Multimedia is not only fundamental to today's entertainment industry, but also key to many professions. Designers, engineers, and architects make use of multimedia graphics software to design 3-D products and projects. Desktop publishers and Web designers use multimedia graphics software to develop attractive 2-D print and Web pages. Manufacturers and retailers use multimedia to sell products and support their customers. Scientists use interactive 3-D graphics to simulate inaccessible objects and environments. Multimedia is of use to everyone in one manner or another.

Thousands of multimedia software applications are available for both professional and personal use. Multimedia applications fall into one or more of three categories: digital audio, digital graphics, and interactive multimedia.

DIGITALAUDIO

EXPAND YOUR
KNOWLEDGE

To learn more about working with audio, go to www.course.com/swt. Click the link "Expand Your Knowledge," and then complete the lab entitled, "Working with Audio."

Digital technologies have fundamentally altered the production and distribution mechanisms within the music industry, providing musicians with powerful creative tools, improving the quality of recorded music, and providing listeners with more convenient access. New online forms of music distribution have undermined the recording industry's control of the distribution process and created one of the more complicated legal debates between industry leaders and their customers. But digital audio has had an impact on more than just the music industry. Digital audio affects most other forms of entertainment, and many nonentertainment industries as well.

The process of digitizing sound was explained in Chapter 2. In this section we will build on that discussion, and explain how digital audio is produced, distributed, and used in a variety of professions. Let's begin by looking at how digital audio enriches our personal and professional lives.

The Value of Digital Audio

Digital audio encompasses digital music and digital sound. **Digital music** is any music that is stored digitally, regardless of how it was originally created. **Digital sound** refers to the spoken word, other nonmusic sounds, and sound effects that are stored and sometimes manipulated digitally.

Digital sound and the ability to digitize the sound of our voice have led to breakthroughs in communication. As noted in earlier chapters, digital sound technology has brought us digital cell phone services that provide clearer sound quality and higher levels of privacy. Digital sound is responsible for the gradual merging of phone services with the Internet. Digital sound enables us to command our computers with our voices, and dictate memos that the computer can automatically transcribe.

Many individuals make their living working with digital sound and music. The professional production and editing of digital audio takes place in sound production studios. *Sound production studios* use a wide variety of audio hardware and software to record and produce music and sound recordings. Figure 11.1 shows what a professional sound studio looks like.

Table 11.1 lists the wide array of services provided by sound production studios. Some large studios provide all of these services, but smaller studios may specialize in a specific area. Each service requires specific hardware and software tools. For example recording the soundtrack for a motion picture requires video production tools that allow the sound engineer to view the movie while recording the soundtrack. Studios that specialize in recording music are known simply as *recording studios*. Sound studios that work with motion pictures are typically referred to as *production studios*. As you can see from the list of services in Table 11.1, sound production plays an important role in many media and entertainment industries. Sound production is an important part of music, movies, radio, television, video games, and the Internet.

FIGURE 11.1 • Sound production studio

Sound production studios use a wide variety of audio hardware and software to record and produce music and sound recordings.

TABLE 11.1 • Sound Production Studio Services

Sound Production Services	Description
Music recording	Recording of music performance using multitrack recording equipment
Movie soundtrack production	Recording of musical performance for motion picture accompaniment
Movie sound effects	Addition of special sounds, such as footsteps, breaking glass, and explosions, to motion pictures to lend additional realism and impact
Voice-over recording and dubbing	Voice recordings that are provided behind video or other media productions that may be narrative or synchronized to the lip movements of the actors
Postproduction sound engineering	Includes movie soundtrack production, movie sound effects, voice-over recording and dubbing, and also the overall editing of motion picture soundtracks to create the final product
Radio commercials	Recording of voice, music, and sound effects for radio commercials
Music and sound effects for computer video games	Same services as offered for motion pictures, but applied to video games
Audio for distance learning and training	Recording narration, lectures, and other sound needs for educational software and distance learning
Multimedia and Internet audio	Audio recordings for delivery over the Internet, such as Internet radio and audio accompaniment to Flash and video presentations.
Audio restoration and enhancement	Improving the recorded quality of old or damaged recordings
Forensic audio	Uses digital processing to de-noise, enhance, edit, and detect sounds to assist in criminal investigations

Sound production studios play a large role in motion picture production. Most audio production for motion pictures occurs in postproduction, after the film has been recorded. Musical soundtracks and sound effects are synchronized with the action on the screen and recorded onto the film. *Postproduction sound engineering* involves adding sound tracks, sound effects, and voice-overs to a movie after the movie has been recorded. *Voice-over recording* refers to the voice recordings that are provided behind video or other media productions that may be narrative or synchronized to the lip movements of the actors. Postproduction sound engineering often utilizes surround sound techniques to make the movie experience more realistic. *Surround sound*, also referred to as *3-D audio*, makes use of special sound recording techniques and multiple speakers placed around the audience, so that sound-producing objects can be heard from all directions. Surround sound provides audiences with the illusion that they are in the center of the action.

In addition to the entertainment value of digital sound and music production, there are valuable scientific aspects of sound production work. *Audio restoration and enhancement* is used to improve the quality of old or damaged recordings. *Forensic audio* uses digital processing to de-noise, enhance, edit, and detect sounds to assist in criminal investigations. Details about forensic audio techniques are provided in the "Job Technology" box.

Digital Music Production

Although digital audio processing may have many industrial applications, it is most strongly connected with the music industry. Today's music recording studios are high-tech digital processing centers. Even the most "unplugged"-sounding acoustic music recordings utilize digital sound-processing techniques to enrich and purify the sound so that it sounds as though you are sitting with the musicians.

Music is transformed into digital signals through the process of digitization described in Chapter 2. You'll recall that a sound wave is digitized using an analog-to-digital converter (ADC) that samples, or measures, the sound wave at predetermined time intervals and stores the resulting numbers. Recording studios use ADCs to transform the recorded sound of voices, violins, horns, and other acoustic instruments to digital signals that can then be manipulated. Studios record music using multitrack recording devices. Multitrack recording devices treat each instrument or microphone as a separate input, or track. The engineer uses a *mixing board* (the large panel with many dials, buttons, and sliders in Figure 11.1) to adjust the sound quality of each instrument separately. Multitrack recording allows the instruments to be recorded either all at once or separately. For example, a jazz quintet might decide to record the rhythm section—bass, guitar, and drums—first. After the rhythm section tracks are recorded ("laid down"), the solo instruments and vocals can be added one at a time. Using multitrack recorders, studio engineers are able to mix many separate instrument tracks together to create the finished product. Using digital signal processing, the engineer can mold the sound of each instrument, adjusting the tone quality and adding effects. In what is called the "final mix," after all tracks have been recorded, the engineer plays the recording and applies changes to the volume levels of each track to balance the sound of the instruments and bring listeners' attention to specific instruments at specific times. As the engineer "mixes" the song, the computer stores the settings. The final product is then transferred to CD or some other storage medium.

Digital music instruments, such as synthesizers and samplers, produce musical sounds electronically. A **synthesizer** electronically produces sounds designed to be similar to real instruments or produces new sounds unlike any that a traditional

Forensic Audio

Forensic audio has been helpful in the hunt for Al-Qaeda terrorist leader, Osama bin Laden. Forensic audio specialists studied recorded speeches claiming to have been made by bin Laden to determine the authenticity of the recording. In September 2003, forensic audio specialist Tom Owen studied one such tape and determined with relative certainty that the voice was indeed bin Laden and that it had been recorded recently—thus bin Laden must still be alive. Mr. Owen explained that technology allows officials to make a very-well-educated guess about the tape's authenticity. "You could get a high certainty based on the fact that you have a large sample of the known voice vs. this voice." According to Owen, they use digital audio software and equipment to process the recording and compare the pitch, quality of the voice, rate of speech, and amplitude against previous recordings of the voice.

Among many tools available to forensic audio specialists, the spectrographic sonogram is perhaps the most valuable. A spectrographic sonogram provides a visual fingerprint for various sounds in a recording. For instance, when a tape head engages the tape, it leaves a distinct impression (fingerprint) that can be used to determine if a tape was tampered with. Gunshots, car engines, and voices all have a unique pattern when viewed as a spectrographic sonogram. Figure 11.2 shows the spectrographic sonogram of a human voice.

The process of identifying a recorded human voice is known as voice-print identification. The technique is considered highly reliable and has been used as evidence in more than 7,000 criminal cases. Head of Forensic Tape Analysis Inc, Steve Cain states that "It is very accurate. All you need is about 15 words to make a match."

Questions

1. Close your eyes and consider the sound around you. What might an audio forensics expert assume about you and your environment by analyzing these sounds?

2. Besides voice-print identification, what other sounds might an audio forensics specialist be asked to identify in court?

3. Do you think that it is possible for an audio forensics expert to be tricked? How might this be accomplished?

Sources
1. *"Voice is likely bin Laden's CIA says,"* John Lumpkin, Associated Press, *September 13, 2003.*
2. *"Sound Identification,"* Creative Forensic Services Web site, *accessed September 21, 2003, http://creativeforensic.com/id.html.*
3. *"Bin Laden Tape: Voice Squad Scours Audio for 'Prints,'"* Niles Lathem, The New York Post, *November 14, 2002, www.forensictapeexpert.com/pr02.htm.*

FIGURE 11.2 • Spectrographic sonogram of a human voice
Gunshots, car engines, and voices all have a unique pattern when viewed as a spectrographic sonogram.

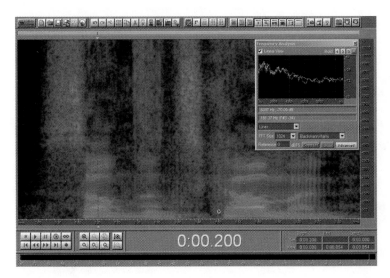

instrument could produce. A **sampler** digitally records real musical instrument sounds and allows them to be played back at various pitches using an electronic keyboard. Synthesized instrument sounds have an electronic quality to them that rarely fool anyone into thinking that they are the actual instrument. In contrast, it is difficult for listeners to tell a sampled sound from the real instrument. Professional-grade synthesizer keyboards, like the one in Figure 11.3, use sampled sounds for the real instruments that they emulate. If you play a middle C on a synthesizer keyboard with the trumpet sound selected, an actual digital recording of a trumpet playing a middle C is produced.

FIGURE 11.3 • Synthesizer keyboard

This Yamaha synthesizer keyboard includes hundreds of digitally sampled instrument sounds and synthesized sounds.

Musicians sometimes use drum machines to record basic drum tracks over which to layer other instrument sounds. *Electronic drum machines* allow the musician to record drum beat patterns by tapping on pressure-sensitive buttons or pads to produce sampled drum sounds that can be played back in a looping pattern. With a little training and practice even a nondrummer can lay down a basic repeating drum pattern; it won't necessarily rival a real drummer's performance, but it can be useful for practice and composition. A **sequencer** is a device that allows musicians to create multitrack recordings with a minimal investment in equipment. Using a sequencer, a musician can first record a drum track, then record a bass track over the drum track, and continue to layer instrument track upon instrument track to produce a recording that sounds like a full band of musicians. Many solo performers make use of both drum machines and sequencers to provide accompaniment for their performance. In this way, one person singing (and perhaps strumming a guitar) can sound like an entire band. Small bands can use sequencers and synthesizers to sound like an entire orchestra.

Synthesizers, samplers, drum machines, and sequencers are only a few examples of the many digital music devices available for creating music. Most music production studios have large racks of interconnected digital audio devices, called outboard devices, to process digital music and audio signals (see Figure 11.4). In

FIGURE 11.4 • Rack-mounted digital audio devices

Most major production studios have large racks of interconnected digital audio devices, called outboard devices, to process digital music and audio signals.

the early 1980s, digital music device manufacturers collaborated to create a protocol to allow their devices to connect together and communicate. The **musical instrument digital interface (MIDI)** protocol was implemented in 1983 to provide a standard language for digital music devices to use in communicating with each other. MIDI commands include basic control commands such as "Note on," "Note off," "Program change" (to change instrument sounds), and others. Using MIDI a musician can connect and control many devices all from a single synthesizer keyboard or computer.

FIGURE 11.5 • Integrated digital studio

The AW4416 includes a 16-channel mixing board, a 64 GB hard drive on which to record, an analog to digital converter, sequencing and sampling software, a CD writer, and other features to take music from performance to a distribution CD.

Integrated digital studios, such as the Yamaha AW4416 shown in Figure 11.5, package many digital recording devices in one unit for convenient home recording. The AW4416 includes a 16-channel mixing board, a 64-GB hard drive on which to record, an analog-to-digital converter, sequencing and sampling software, a CD writer, and many other more-technical features to take music from performance to a distribution CD. A musician could purchase this device for about the same price as the cost of one day in a professional studio—about $1,000 to $2,500.

MIDI cards are available for Windows PCs and are included as standard equipment in most Apple computers to allow computers to be connected to digital music devices. All of the digital music devices described in this section—drum machines, sequencers, samplers, and synthesizers—are available as personal computer software. Most personal computers come equipped with *on-board synthesizers* located on the computers sound card that include all the standard synthesizer keyboard sounds. Using sequencing software, such as Apple's Logic Platinum software, shown in Figure 11.6, a personal computer can become a self-contained recording studio.

Many musicians are connecting their home computers to low-priced home recording equipment to create their own home recording studios. Home recording studios save musicians from having to pay premium rates for premium services that may not be required. Home studios are empowering many musicians to perform, record, produce, and distribute their music

FIGURE 11.6 • Sequencing software

Sequencing software, such as Apple's Logic Platinum software, allows a personal computer to become a self-contained recording studio.

independently. The freedom to record music anytime at home provides a valuable service to musicians for developing new music. As with most of today's new technology, advances in digital music technology is empowering musicians with tools that were previously available only to professionals.

One example of the empowering nature of digital music can be found in downtown Manhattan, in a club called Open Air, where musicians and musician "wannabes" gather Sunday nights for a musical jam session. The unique feature of these performances is that the musicians don't play musical instruments, but perform on notebook computers. The musicians manipulate notebooks equipped with software sequencers, synthesizers, and other digital sound tools, connected to the sound system to create layers of spontaneous sound that combine into an "electronica" symphony. "The music people play here is a prototype for the music of the future" says Rich Panciera, one of the organizers of the weekly session.[1]

Digital Music Distribution

Once music is produced it must be stored on a distribution medium and distributed to customers. Distribution media and channels have been greatly affected by the digitization of music.

Digital Music Media. The days of vinyl records and cassette tapes—both analog media—are for the most part behind us now. These analog media have been displaced by digital music on digital media. The purity of digital sound, combined with the low price and longevity of digital media, make it an obvious choice over traditional analog media.

Today, music is most often distributed on CD, with an increasing trend towards distribution over the Internet. Digital music is burned to CD using a special music format for CD audio. When viewed with a computer's file management tools these files may look like standard computer files with a .cda file extension, but they are stored on the disk in a unique manner, not at all like a computer's file system. These files are designed to be read and manipulated by CD players and computer media players, not by computer users.

There are music file formats specifically designed for computer use. For example Windows PCs support .wav files, and Apple computers use the .aiff music file format. Table 11.2 shows some of the most common audio file formats. Audio

TABLE 11.2 • Popular Music File Formats

File Extension	Format	Description
.aac	Advanced Audio Coding	Apple compressed audio file format. A new compressed file format that is more efficient than MP3. Used with Apple's iTunes music service.
.au	Audio	Audio file format used mostly on UNIX and Apple operating systems.
.cda	Compact Disc Audio	Used to store music on traditional music CDs using a storage technology different from typical computer files.
.mid	MIDI	File format containing MIDI commands to control keyboard synthesizers and other electronic instruments.
.mp3	MP3	A popular compressed audio file format used on file-sharing networks and the Internet.
.ra	Real Audio	Format designed for streaming audio over the Web.
.wav	Waveform Audio	Windows PC audio file format.
.wma	Windows Media Audio	Microsoft Windows compressed audio file format. A new compressed file format that is more efficient than MP3 and provides the distributor with control over copying of the file. Used with most Internet music services other than Apple iTunes.

FILE SWAPPING ALIVE, WELL, AND LEGAL—IN CANADA

While the Recording Industry Association of America (RIAA) struggles to put a lid on P2P file copying, Canada solved the problem five years ago by allowing "private copying" and simultaneously assessing a small tax on blank tapes ($.77 CDN) and CDs ($.29 CDN). To date, the tax has passively accumulated $70 million in income for the Canadian recording industry. An added wrinkle for the RIAA is files shared from a Canadian site are outside their jurisdiction.

Source:
"Blame Canada"
By Jay Currie
Tech Central Station
http://techcentralstation.com/081803C.html
August 18, 2003
Cited on September 16, 2003

files may be distributed over the Internet using any of the listed file formats. The most recognized digital music file format is MP3. The **MP3** file format compresses music files to less than 10 percent of their original size. A 32-MB music file on a music CD can be compressed down to a 3-MB MP3 file. A standard music CD that traditionally held up to 20 standard length songs could hold as many as 200 average size MP3 songs.

Music file formats such as MP3, AAC, and WMA are able to store music in much smaller files using sound compression. *Sound compression* removes those frequencies that are beyond the range of human hearing and in so doing reduces the size of the digital music file. There are varying ranges of file compression. Encoding software that creates MP3 files from standard CD files usually provides a method of selecting the quality of sound desired. For example, you may select from studio quality, CD quality, radio quality, or phone quality sound. The better the quality, the larger the MP3 file.

Digital Music Distribution Channels. The music industry uses the same distribution channels as most other retail industries. Business-to-business (B2B) distribution is commonly conducted between music studios and their customers in motion picture, radio, television, software and other industries. Business-to-consumer (B2C) distribution occurs through retailers selling CDs and online services that allow customers to download music directly to their computers. The various forms of online music distribution were discussed in Chapter 4. They include Internet radio and subscription services that allow customers to download music for a fee, to enjoy while at the computer, to take with them on portable devices, or burn to CDs.

The MP3 music file format provides computer users with music files that are small and easy to share. Soon after the birth of the MP3 format, file-sharing networks, such as Napster, and later many others, sprang up to support the easy sharing of music files over the Internet. The problem with these file sharing networks, however, is that most of the music files being shared are intellectual property protected under copyright laws. Users who supply copyright protected songs to others, and people who accept them, are violating copyright laws and subject to legal action. The availability and simplicity of file-sharing software led many users to believe that there was nothing illegal about sharing music files. A snow-ball effect took place in which an increasing amount of file-sharing caused increasing numbers of users to think that it must be okay, and try it for themselves. The more people who participated, the more everyone felt they were within their rights to share copyright-protected music. By 2003, over 61 million otherwise law-abiding citizens were sharing and accessing music files on the Internet. That is 19 percent of the U.S. population, with the vast majority of music file sharers being between the age of 12 and 24.

Music file-sharing networks provide an illegal distribution stream in the music industry. Each copyrighted song downloaded for free is a song that is not purchased through legitimate means. In 2003, the Recording Industry Association of America (RIAA) began taking file-sharing individuals to court in an effort to crack down on illegal music distribution (see "Community Technology" box). The RIAA represents the vast majority of recording companies and musical artists in the United States. It lists among its responsibilities the protection of intellectual property rights worldwide and the First Amendment rights of artists.[2]

The RIAA has more to be concerned about than illegal file sharing over the Internet. As CD writers become standard on most PCs, increasing amounts of music fans are burning their own music CDs. Friends are making CD copies of their favorite music to share with each other, and on a larger scale, bootleg CDs are being mass produced and sold for profit in other countries. An estimated 2 of every 5 music CDs sold in the world are pirated.[3] In 2002, the sales of blank CD-Rs surpassed the sales of prerecorded music CDs. A paradox now exists: much more music is being distributed than ever before, while music industry recorded sales are plummeting. You can see from Figure 11.7 that prerecorded music CD sales were down 7.2 percent from 2002 to 2003. This decline in sales started in 1999, with the introduction of MP3 file sharing over P2P networks. You might wonder who gets hurt when distribution is hijacked in this manner. The majority of profits from CD sales go to the record companies, with the artists receiving anywhere from as little as 2 percent[4] to as much as 40 percent. The recording industry will need to reinvent itself to accommodate new distribution streams.

FIGURE 11.7 • Music CD sales statistics

Since the birth of MP3 file sharing in 1999, music CD sales have continuously declined.[5]

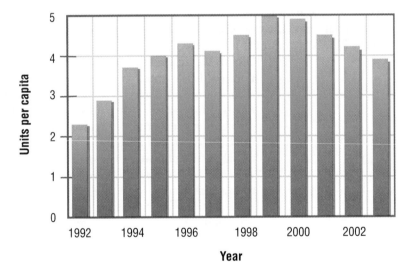

Many of today's online music subscription services are moving to more advanced file compression formats that provide them with control over what members can do with the music files that they download. For example, the new Napster 2.0 music service uses the WMA format, which is encoded in such a way that a downloaded song can only be copied to one other PC.

Future music distribution will include the ability to swap songs with friends over cell phones. The Warner music and Bertelsmann's Music companies have designed a system for cell phone users that supports the sharing of music files between cell phones in a legal manner.[6] The technology will be extended to include video clips. Imagine sending a friend a video clip of highlights from last weekend's big game.

Some groups of musicians are taking control of their own music distribution. Magnatune, at www.magnatune.com, is the result of dozens of musicians joining together to create a new and improved form of online music distribution.[7] Armed with the slogan "We're a record label. But we're not evil," Magnatune distributes music using the open-source approach used by some software companies. They take "donations" when you download music from the Web site of which 50 percent goes to the musicians—a much higher percentage than traditional distribu-

COMMUNITY TECHNOLOGY

The Record Industry versus Its Customers

In September 2003, the Record Industry Association of America (RIAA) stepped up its fight against music file sharing over P2P networks by issuing subpoenas to 261 file swappers and promising to bring thousands more to court. At the same time the RIAA publicized a "Clean Slate Program" that would allow file sharers a method to come clean by submitting a signed and notarized form stating that they had illegally shared files, but will delete those files from their computer and will not share or obtain any more music files illegally.

Twelve-year-old Brianna was one of the first to be fined in this string of cases. The case against Brianna did not help the RIAA's image in the public eye. Brianna lives in a low-rent city housing project on New York's Upper West Side. She was fined $3,000 for making copyrighted music files available to others on a P2P network; the $3,000 is significantly lower than what the RIAA says they will fine others. Regarding the case, Brianna commented "I am sorry for what I have done. I love music and don't want to hurt the artists I love." Brianna's mother assured the record industry that "You can be sure Brianna won't be doing it anymore."

A poll of teenagers between the age 12 and 17 indicates that more than half participate in P2P music swapping. Most feel that they are doing nothing wrong. In interviews of children in this age group conducted by the *New York Times* one child stated, "It shouldn't be illegal, It's not like I'm selling it." Another child commented "Isn't it like recording movies?

They're making a big thing out of nothing." Another child holds the opinion that "It's wrong to be downloading hundreds of songs, but if you only want one or two, it's not that big a deal."

Musicians are caught in the middle as the companies they hold contracts with sue their fans. Some artists, like those in the band Metallica, strongly support the RIAA's crackdown. Others, such as System of a Down, Public Enemy, Moby, and the Dead, are opposed to the RIAA's actions and would prefer that the RIAA treat fans with respect and work with technology instead of against it.

Questions

1. Should free music file sharing be legal? Is it possible for artists and the music industry to support itself without revenues from recorded music sales?
2. Do the teenagers interviewed by the *New York Times* make valid points? Why or why not?
3. What can the RIAA do, short of taking fans to court, that might influence them and keep them from file sharing?

Sources
1. *"Girl, 12, settles piracy suit," Ted Bridis*, The New York Times, *September 10, 2003.*
2. *"Is It Wrong to Share Your Music? (Discuss)," Katie Hafner,* The New York Times, *September 19, 2003.*
3. *"File-Sharing Battle Leaves Musicians Caught in Middle," Neil Strauss,* The New York Times, *September 15, 2003.*

tion models. Listeners are encouraged to share the music files with friends for noncommercial use. People who wish to use the music for commercial use are charged on a sliding scale. For example, to use a song from Magnatune for background music on your wedding video might cost $5, to use it as a soundtrack for a major motion picture might cost $2,600. As the industry searches for solutions to digital distribution we will no doubt see many experiments similar to Magnatune.

Personal Music Hardware and Software

Along with digital music production and distribution comes a host of hardware devices and software to support it. Since most music is available on CD, the CD player remains the most popular digital music player. People use CD players to listen to music at computers, in living rooms, in cars, and while walking about.

However, today's new generation of CD players have additional functionality that allows them to play not only traditional music CDs but also homemade CDs containing MP3 and WMA files. People can create their own mix of artists and songs on a CD-R (recordable CD or CD-RW for re-writable CD), and are no longer bound by song sequences that occur on a store-bought CD.

Some music lovers are doing away with the need for CDs and storing their favorite music directly on their computers. Once on the computer, favorite tracks can be transferred to a portable MP3 player to listen to while away from the computer. The process of transferring music from CD to MP3 is called *ripping* a CD. Ripper software can be used to translate your favorite music CDs (CDA format) to MP3 files on your hard drive. Digital music files can be transferred from one format to another using *encoder software*. Hardware devices such as CD burners and portable MP3 players typically come with their own software to allow you to transfer music files from your computer to the device or media. Portable MP3 players typically support other popular music formats such as Windows WMA format or Apple AAC format. Portable MP3 players range in storage capacity (and price) from small ultraportable players the size of your thumb with 128 MB of memory that store around 30 songs up to players the size of a deck of cards with 40 GB of memory that store an entire CD collection's worth of music—10,000 songs. Figure 11.8 shows the Apple iPod portable MP3 player with a 40-GB capacity.

Jukebox software allows computer users to categorize and organize their digital music files for easy access. Jukebox software also typically includes tools for creating play lists, ripping and burning CDs, and transferring songs to portable devices. *Media players* provide similar functions, but also include video support. The most popular media players are the RealOne Media Player from Real Networks, the Windows Media Player from Microsoft, and the QuickTime Player for Apple; all these players are free downloads.

FIGURE 11.8 • The Apple iPod

The Apple iPod holds up to 10,000 songs in a small package that weighs less than what two CDs weigh.

DIGITALGRAPHICS

EXPAND YOUR **KNOWLEDGE**

To learn more about graphics, go to www.course.com/swt. Click the link "Expand Your Knowledge," and then complete the lab entitled, "Working with Graphics."

Digital Graphics refers to the family of computer-based media applications that support the creation, editing, and viewing of 2-D and 3-D images, animation, and video. At first glance, digital graphics may appear to be the exclusive domain of artists. But, in reality, many people, artists and nonartists alike, are finding themselves called upon or inspired to create digital visual artwork for personal and professional use. This section begins by exploring several ways in which digital graphics may be useful to you, followed by discussions of each of the digital graphics areas: vector graphics, 3-D modeling, animation, photo editing, and video editing.

The Value of Digital graphics

Digital graphics provides us with personal and professional benefits in several ways. It is used as a form of creative expression, as a means of visually presenting information, as a means to communicate and explore ideas, as a form of entertainment, as a tool to assist in the design of real-world objects, and as a method of documenting life.

Creative Expression. *Digital art* is a new form of art that uses computer software as the brush and the computer display as the canvas. The purpose of digital art is the same as traditional studio art: to affect and emotionally move the viewer with visual images. Digital art can employ real or abstract images. The images shown in Figure 11.9 illustrate digital art depicting a surrealistic world in a superrealistic style and abstract computer art. Other artists are taking advantage of aspects of computers that are not available to traditional visual artists. For example, artwork displayed at the HotWired RGB Gallery (http://hotwired.wired.com/rgb/gallery/) is described as an "interactive experiment" that allows users to interact with artwork that may include stills, animation, and sound. Taken a step further, using 3-D media, artists can move beyond the two-dimensional plane to allow the viewer to virtually enter the artwork to further interact with it.

FIGURE 11.9 • Digital art
Digital art can employ real or abstract images.

Photographers and videographers use digital graphics software to edit digital images for the purpose of creative expression. Artists of all genres are using computers in some aspect of their work. Sculptors use computer models to assist in planning their projects. Artists use the Internet as a platform for collaboration, publishing, and selling artwork of all kind.

Amateurs as well as professionals enjoy being creative with computers. Home computer users make use of their computers to create artwork for the home and for friends. It is becoming increasingly common to receive greeting cards made on a PC that incorporate personalized messages and photos. Digital photography makes it easy and inexpensive for nonprofessionals to experiment with and have fun taking artistic pictures and enhancing them with special effects on their home computers.

Presenting Information. Commercial graphics designers depend on graphics software to create visually appealing designs. Web designers are specialists in creating attractive Web page designs. They use graphics software to design buttons, backgrounds, and other stylistic elements that combine to make an appealing Web page. Desktop publishers use *desktop publishing* software to design page layouts for magazines, newspapers, books, and other publications (see Figure 11.10). Other graphics designers use computers to design company logos, product packaging, television and printed advertisements, billboards, and artwork for other commercial needs.

FIGURE 11.10 • Desktop publishing

Some magazines, newspapers, and books are designed using desktop publishing software.

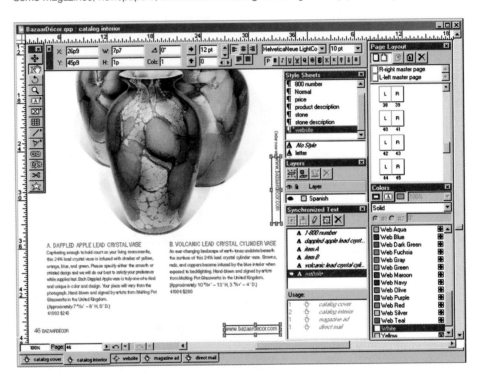

Digital video is being increasingly used to present news and information over the Web. Broadband Internet users can view video clips that present news and sports coverage. RealNetworks (www.real.com) offers free and subscription services that provide news and entertainment video clips. Microsoft offers a competing service from its www.msn.com Web site.[8]

Communicating ideas. Pictures, photographs, illustrations, graphs, animation, and video can communicate ideas in a more powerful manner than the printed or spoken word alone. The political cartoon might be the best example of this point. They quickly and concisely illustrate biting wit in a manner that would be difficult to accomplish with words alone. Professionals from nearly every career area use graphics to make a point. Teachers and others who provide educational presentations may use graphic presentation software, as was discussed in Chapter 3, to provide visual accompaniment to their presentations. Educators may incorporate video or animated simulations during presentations, as shown in Figure 11.11.

Illustrators use graphics software to illustrate children's stories in order to assist in developing a child's imagination. Technical artists illustrate instruction manuals and draw product specifications so customers can more easily assemble and understand the workings of products. All of these professionals use computer-generated graphics to communicate ideas.

Some ideas can be described only in graphic form. Geographic maps are created to graphically represent our world. Maps are now available on the Internet for nearly every location on Earth. GPS technology is used to accurately represent

FIGURE 11.11 •   Digital graphics in education

Educators often use video or animated simulations during a presentation to help drive home a point.

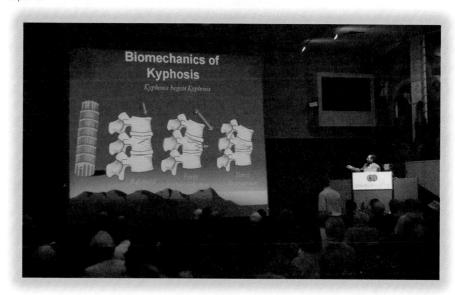

distances and elevations to the inch. Digital topography takes measurements and elevations as input and produces maps, even 3-D maps, from the data.

Exploring New Ideas. **Scientific visualization** involves the use of computer graphics to provide visual representations that improve our understanding of some phenomenon. There is a wide range of applications of scientific visualization, everything from the presentation of football team statistics to predict the winner of the Super Bowl to studying the interaction of subatomic particles. Figure 11.12 shows a visualization of the Earth's magnetic fields. The simulation took a supercomputer several thousand hours to perform and can be run as an animation in order to study the flow of magnetic currents. The gold lines indicate outward magnetic flow, and the blue lines inward magnetic flow. Visualization can be used to represent quantities of raw data as pictures.

FIGURE 11.12 •   Scientific visualization

This visualization of the Earth's magnetic fields can be useful to scientists.

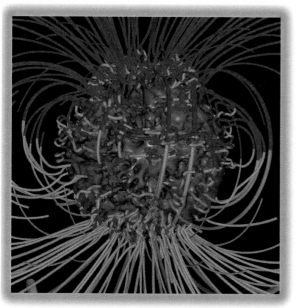

Entertainment. Artists in a variety of entertainment industries make use of digital graphics to produce products for the enjoyment of their audiences. Cartoonists and comic book artists can produce their products much more quickly using graphics software than they can by sketching and coloring. Animators no longer need to work with markers on transparent sheets, drawing hundreds of individual pictures that take only a matter of seconds to play on the screen. Now animators draw cartoon characters on a computer and program them to move across the screen.

The motion picture industry is capitalizing on the power of computing to create effects that are not possible to generate in the real world. Gradually, the motion picture industry is moving towards digital cinema, which will do away with outdated motion picture projection methods in favor of digital projection (see "Community Technology" box).

COMMUNITY TECHNOLOGY

The Digital Cinema

Digital cinema applies digital technology to the production, distribution, and projection of motion pictures, replacing chemicals on film with bits and bytes. Although computers play an important role in the production of today's motion pictures, they are still distributed on old-fashioned reels of film and projected by mechanical projectors. *Digital projection* does away with the reels and mechanical projectors, and projects the movie directly from a computer's hard drive.

The advantages of this approach include savings in distribution costs that add up to a couple million dollars on each movie released, and a long-lasting final product. Large amounts of money are invested in restoring and preserving old classic movies that have degenerated over time. Digital films do not degenerate.

Digital cinema is not only practical for the motion picture industry, but people prefer films delivered through digital projection over traditional projection. One study found that changing to digital projection increased revenues by 40 percent. Digital projection eliminates the dust, scratches, and slight shaking perceptible in the traditional delivery of images from film reels. So why hasn't the movie industry pushed for the upgrade to digital projection?

The movie industry has been slow in moving to digital cinema for several reasons. It is costly to convert old systems to digital systems. It costs an estimated $150,000 to convert a traditional theater into a digital theater. With 35,000 projection booths in the United States, this adds up to a substantial amount of money. There are also concerns over piracy; digital movies are much easier to duplicate than movies on film. Digitizing the theater would mean dramatic changes in the industry's work force. Many people in the industry would lose their jobs, while other more technically trained individuals would gain employment. Moving to a digital cinema is inevitable, but it will take time to fully integrate digital cinema into the industry.

Questions

1. How might the upgrade to digital projection change the motion picture distribution system?
2. What types of jobs might be lost by moving from reels of film to digital distribution?
3. What new technical jobs might be created by the move to digital cinema?

Sources
1. *"Digital Projection of Films Is Coming. Now, Who Pays?" Eric Taub, New York Times, October 13, 2003, www.nytimes.com.*
2. *"How Digital Cinema Works," How Stuff Works Web site, accessed October 14, 2003, http://entertainment.howstuffworks. com/digital-cinema.htm.*

Designing Real-world Objects. **Computer-assisted design (CAD)** software assists designers, engineers, and architects in designing three-dimensional objects from the gear mechanism in a watch to suspension bridges. CAD software provides tools to construct 3-D objects on the computer screen, examine them from all angles, and test their properties. CAD is able to turn designs on the computer into blueprint specifications for manufacturing. CAD is used by urban and regional planners to design neighborhoods, shopping malls, and other large-scale construction. Figure 11.13 shows how CAD software can be used to view 3-D images of products and provide the specifications for creating that product.

CAD is not used just for 3-D manufacturing, however. Professionals in the textile industry rely on computers for designing the graphic patterns for material. Computer systems are used to apply those designs to the fabric.

FIGURE 11.13 • **Computer-assisted design (CAD)**

CAD is able to turn designs on the computer into blueprint specifications for manufacturing.

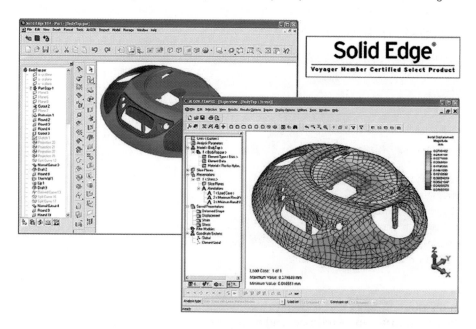

Documenting Life. We use images to preserve our visual memories of life. Photography acts as a witness to the events that mark special moments in our lives. Photo journalists as well as amateurs are moving to digital cameras and image processing for collecting, managing, and manipulating photographs and films for historical and sentimental value. Once digitized, these images are easily copied and shared with others over the Internet.

Vector Graphics Software

Now that we have a proper understanding of the value of digital graphics, we begin our discussion of digital graphics applications with the most fundamental type of digital graphics: vector graphics software. Vector graphics and bitmapped graphics were defined in Chapter 2. We continue that discussion here with details about creating pictures with vector graphics software.

Vector graphics software, sometimes called *drawing software*, provides tools to create, arrange, and layer graphical objects on the screen to create pictures. Vector graphics uses an object-oriented approach that recognizes pictures as being made up of layers of multiple objects, some in the foreground and some in the background. Figure 11.14 illustrates the object-oriented approach of vector graphics. If you examine this image closely, you can see that there are only five primary images in the picture: a butterfly, a blossom, a rainbow fish, a starfish, and a seahorse. There are also five secondary images: a tree leaf, seaweed, a bubble, a palm tree, and a pine tree. The primary and secondary images are copied repeatedly at different sizes, locations, orientations, and levels of transparency and are interwoven together over a background to make a complex picture.

The primary benefit of the object-oriented approach of vector graphics is that objects in the picture can be manipulated independently. Consider the difference between creating a picture using colored markers on paper, and creating a picture using paper cutouts. With markers, once something is drawn, it cannot be moved, and making a mistake means having to start over. With paper cutouts, you have the freedom to arrange the objects on the page anyway you like. You can place the

FIGURE 11.14 • Vector graphics

Vector graphics uses an object-oriented approach that recognizes pictures as being made up of layers of multiple objects. This image uses repeated copies of 10 primary and secondary objects.

objects one atop the other to create layers and the illusion of depth, and if you don't like the way one arrangement looks, you can simply rearrange the items. Working with vector graphics is like working with paper cutouts, with the additional benefit of being able to manipulate the properties of each object. For instance, the repeated images of the butterfly in Figure 11.14 are rotated, resized, and presented at varying levels of transparency.

Vector graphics artists not only view pictures as combinations of objects, but also view the objects in the picture as combinations of objects. Figure 11.15 illustrates the individual vector objects that combine to create a realistic image of a gardenia blossom. When an artist combines objects to create larger objects, vector graphics provides a method to group the objects so that, for example, the artist can treat the completed flower in the figure as one object. The artist can copy, rotate, and manipulate the flower in dozens of ways. Objects can be grouped together, arranged one atop another, and transformed by being moved, stretched, sized, or rotated.

Vector graphics software also provides filtering and effects tools that an artist can use to further manipulate objects in a picture. Filter tools allow you to adjust the color of an object by altering the levels of brightness, contrast, hue, and saturation. Effects tools range from subtle effects, such as changing the sharpness/blurriness of edges within a drawing, to dramatic, such as changing a picture so that it looks as though you are viewing it through a glass block. Figure 11.16 illustrates how the gardenia blossom can be altered with filters and effects.

The most popular vector graphics software packages are Adobe Illustrator and Corel Draw. Both are full-feature, professional-level graphics applications (and sell at professional-level prices). Less expensive vector graphics packages are available from Macromedia, Ulead, and other vendors.

FIGURE 11.15 • Vector objects

Vector objects can be composed of many subobjects grouped together.

FIGURE 11.16 • Vector graphics filters and effects

Vector graphics software allows for easy duplication of objects and provides filters and effects to alter the properties of an image.

3-D Modeling Software

3-D Modeling Software provides graphics tools that allow artists to create pictures of 3-D, realistic models. 3-D modeling takes the object-oriented approach of vector graphics to the next level. The process of changing two-dimensional objects, such as those created with vector graphics applications into 3-D models involves adding shadows and light. 3-D modeling is often referred to as *ray-tracing* since the software must trace beams of light as they would interact with the models in the real world. 3-D modeling also requires that surface textures be defined for models. Surface textures are an important element in the interaction between light and a model. Consider the way light interacts with the models in Figure 11.17. Although this figure looks a lot like a photograph it is actually a computer drawing. Notice the effect of light on the models in this picture. The models are shaded to produce a 3-D effect, and the surfaces of the models provide reflections of the room around them. Also notice, as you view this picture, that the source of the light is apparently coming from somewhere off to your left, perhaps through a window.

FIGURE 11.17 • Ray tracing

Ray tracing uses the software's ability to calculate how light would interact with models in the real world. Notice the shadows and reflections in this computer-generated painting.

LAPTOP LEAPS DIMENSIONS

Japanese electronics maker Sharp has released the first laptop to sport a three-dimensional screen. Retailing at $3,000, the model is initially intended for three-dimensional software program developers, but one designed for consumer use is on the way. The company achieved the effect by sending a different image to each eye at the same time by bending the image in slightly different angles.

Source:
"Sharp Introduces Laptops With 3-D"
AP Wire Service
The Los Angeles Times
www.latimes.com/technology/la-fi-rup12.7sep12,1,3401973.story?
coll=la-headlines-technology
September 12, 2003
Cited on September 13, 2003

3-D digital art creation takes place in a scene on a 3-D stage (see Figure 11.18). The artist starts by defining a light source: the position of the light in the scene, the style of lighting—natural, spotlight, florescent, candle, table lamp, and so on—and the intensity of the light. Models are inserted into the scene either by selecting from a library of predesigned 3-D models, by creating the model from scratch through a process of manipulating virtual wire frames, or by using 3-D scanners to import images of real models into the computer. The artist selects surface textures for each model and positions the models on the stage. Finally, the artist selects a background for the scene, and the software renders the scene. *Rendering* is the process of calculating the light interaction with the virtual 3-D models in the scene and presenting the final drawing in two dimensions to be viewed on the screen or printed.

3-D graphics act as a foundation for other technologies. For example CAD software uses 3-D graphics to design and view manufactured products. Virtual reality uses 3-D graphics to build virtual worlds in which users can interact with the 3-D models. 3-D graphics are the fundamental component in computer-generated animation for video games and motion picture production. Popular 3-D art applications include Adobe Dimensions and Strata 3-D.

FIGURE 11.18 • 3-D graphics production

By placing objects on a 3-D stage, digital artists can define and position the object and the light source.

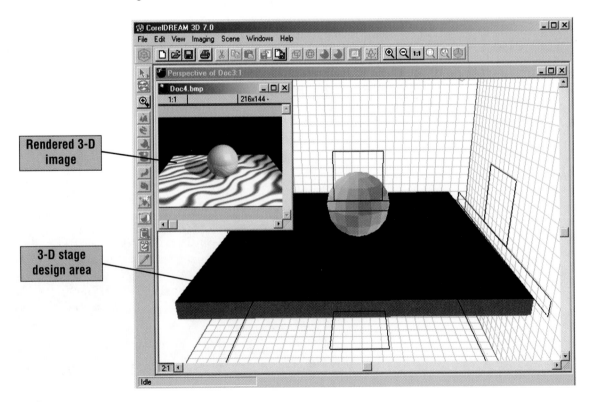

Computer Animation

Digital graphics animation involves displaying digital images in rapid succession to provide the illusion of motion. Graphic animations can be as simple as a stick man jumping rope, or as complex as Disney's major motion pictures *Toy Story*, *Finding Nemo*, and *The Incredibles*—all of which were completely computer generated. Animated graphics employ either 2-D or 3-D objects, with 3-D animations requiring the most advanced graphics software and processing power to create.

2-D Computer Animation. You may have seen simple animations on the Web, simple drawings that repeat the same motion over and over, endlessly. This is the most basic form of animation, called an *animated GIF* (pronounced jiff). Animated GIFs are created with simple tools that allow the artist to draw several images that when played in succession create the illusion of motion (see Figure 11.19). The images are stored in one GIF file, and when viewed in a Web page, they are played sequentially to present the animation. The artist can set the animated GIF to loop endlessly and can control the speed of the sequence. The animated GIF format allows for as many images as are required for the animation; however, the more images loaded into the GIF file, the larger the file becomes and the longer it takes to load.

FIGURE 11.19 • GIF animation software

GIF animation software allows you to import drawings as frames in an animated GIF file.

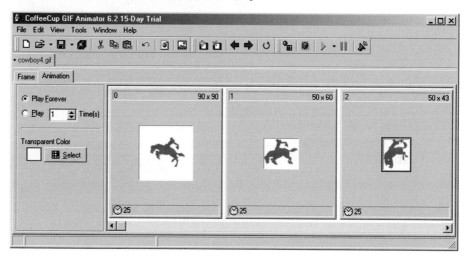

For more complex Web animations, artists must turn to programming languages such as Java, or Web animation development platforms such as Macromedia Flash. Since most animators are not computer programmers, Flash has become the most popular tool for creating animated Web content. Flash provides a timeline tool that is used to cue movement in the animation. Unlike animated GIF tools, Flash automates the frame production process. For example, a picture of a rocket-beetle (see Figure 11.20) can be placed in the upper-left corner of the Flash workspace at time unit 1; at time unit 10, the rocket-beetle could be placed at the right side of the workspace. Flash will "fill in" the movement from left to right evenly over the time between 1 and 10 according to your instructions; for example you might instruct Flash to move the rocket-beetle in an "S" pattern.

FIGURE 11.20 • **Macromedia Flash**

Macromedia Flash provides a timeline tool that is used to cue movement in the animation. In this image, the rocket-bug zooms across the screen over the duration of the timeline.

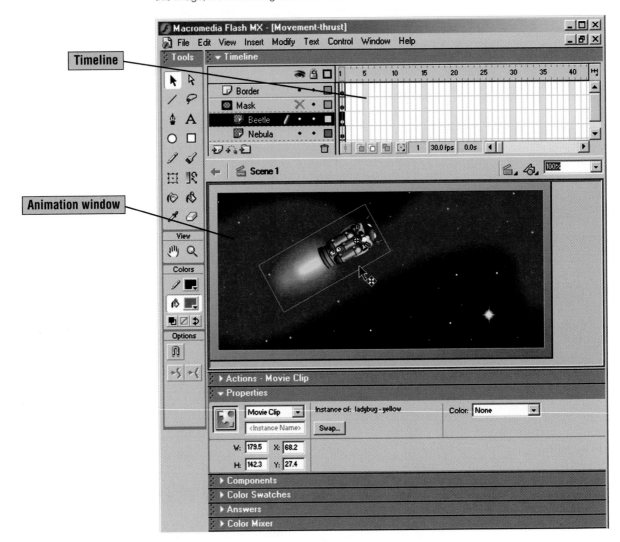

Flash can be used for simple or advanced Web animations and applications. Full-blown animated films can be produced, as well as interactive games. Other tools used to create animations on the Web include Macromedia Shockwave, and Apple Quicktime. *Wired* magazine provides some examples of Web animations (www.wired.com/animation/), and Macromedia provides free Shockwave games (www.shockwave.com/sw/home/).

3-D Computer Animation. 3-D computer animation is much more complex than 2-D computer animation. 3-D *computer animation* includes all of the complexity of 3-D graphic rendering, multiplied by the necessity to render 24 3-D images per second to create the illusion of movement. 3-D animation software is typically packaged with 3-D modeling software. 3-D animation programs, such as LightWave from NewTek and Mental Ray from SoftImage, range in price from $1595 to $13,000.

3-D models of people, animals, and other moving objects, created with the modeling software, are provided with the ability to move using avars. *Avars* are

JOB /\/\/\/\ TECHNOLOGY

How'd They Do That?!—Special Effects

Over the past few years, special effects in motion pictures have become increasingly realistic. In many of today's films it is impossible to tell real life from computer effects, unless you have an understanding of what is possible and impossible under the laws of physics. For the films *The Matrix Reloaded* and *Matrix Revolutions*, old special effects technologies were not going to be enough to pull off what was envisioned by the writers and directors. New technology was required and the best minds in the industry were recruited to develop it.

The first *Matrix* movie made use of an effect that is now referred to as "Bullet Time" (see Figure 11.21). Bullet Time slows the action sequence to a speed in which cameras, in seemingly real time, can pan around a bullet in flight. The effect was used in *The Matrix* to allow Keanu Reeves to dodge bullets. Bullet Time requires the use of over a hundred still cameras positioned around the action. The cameras are triggered in sequence to simulate the action of a movie camera moving around the set. Computer software can manipulate the photographs to control speed and sequence so that the director can seemingly move the camera around stopped or extreme slow motion action. This effect has made a huge impact on film production and is now used in many movies and even television commercials to lend a sense of surrealism to a scene.

FIGURE 11.21 • Special effects
Powerful computers, software, and a host of talented specialists are able to make the impossible look as though it is possible.

The director of *The Matrix Reloaded* wanted to use this effect in a fight scene involving dozens of actors. To do so would require thousands of cameras and impossible amounts of processing power. To tackle this challenge, effects specialist John Gaeta needed to completely digitize Bullet Time, and in doing so ended up reinventing cinematography. The entire fight scene was to be computer generated. Rather than using 3-D graphics software to assemble virtual wire frame forms out of polygons covered with computer-simulated textures, Gaeta invented a new form of modeling called *image-based rendering*. Image-based rendering is similar to sampled sounds in a synthesizer keyboard. Rather than recreating the forms of the actors in the scene, Gaeta fed the details of the actors' physical characteristics into the computer using high resolution photographs. The actors supplied hundreds of facial expressions for digital capture. The result was digital photorealistic actors stored on computer that can be manipulated as animated characters. In *The Matrix Reloaded*, it is impossible to tell when the real actor Keanu Reeves is performing and when it is the computer-generated Keanu Reeves.

In developing image-based rendering, Gaetna became concerned over the potential for this technology to be misused. He wrote then-president Clinton warning him of the possibility of using the procedure for creating mass deception. The obvious irony is in the fact that *The Matrix* is a film in which society is programmed to believe that they exist in a computer-generated world. The effects developed for the movie provide the technology for developing just such a computer-generated world.

Questions
1. How will image-based rendering affect the movie industry?
2. Would the public be susceptible to deceptive computer-generated films passed off as reality?

Sources
1. "Matrix2", Steve Silberman, Wired, *May 2003*
2. "Matrix Reloaded" Pumping Out the Effects, David Haffenreffer, CNNfn, *May 15, 2003*

points on the object that are designed to bend or pivot at specific angles. Avars are used at joints in the model's skeleton to provide articulation—movement at the joints. Avars are also used for muscular movement in the skin. The character Woody, from Disney's *Toy Story* , used 100 avars in his face to depict facial expressions. Avars are controlled either by special input devices manipulated by the artists or through software. Figure 11.22 shows an avar placed on the eyelid of a virtual frog.

FIGURE 11.22 • Animated 3-D Objects
An avar placed on the eyelid of this frog allows for a blinking motion.

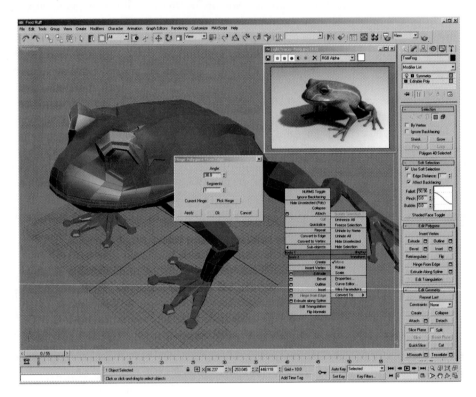

3-D computer animation software is able to move animated characters according to the direction of the artist. Rather than drawing and painting individual frames, animators are more like puppeteers who direct the animated characters around the set. After the action is recorded, rendering computers apply the 3-D effects and lighting to each frame. Even with powerful computers, high-quality rendering, such as that used for major animated motion pictures, takes hours per frame.

Photo-editing Software

So far all that we have discussed is based on vector graphics and the method of creating and editing artwork, graphics, and animation by manipulating objects. Now let's turn our attention to *digital imaging*—working with photographic images. Instead of using vector graphics, digital imaging uses bitmapped, or raster, images. Recall from Chapter 2 that bitmapped images store the color code for each individual pixel in the image. When you work with bitmapped images, you lose the capacity to work with objects. Editing bitmapped images is more like coloring with markers than arranging cutouts.

Photo-editing software includes special tools and effects that are designed for improving or manipulating bitmapped photograph images. Digital photographs are captured as bitmapped images either with a digital camera or a scanner. Photo-editing software provides practical tools for a variety of uses:

- Altering the hue and saturation of the colors in the photograph to give skin tones a healthy glow, or enrich colors in a landscape
- Smoothing surfaces or removing flaws in surfaces
- Removing "red eye"—the effect of the camera flash on the eyes of subjects, which causes eyes to appear red in a photograph
- Smoothing edges or bringing out of focus shots into focus
- Cropping and realigning photos that aren't centered properly

Photo-editing tools also include special effects, such as the ability to transform photos into watercolor paintings. Or you can use edge detection to remove an object from one photo and insert it in another. Unlike vector graphics, when an object is cut out of a bitmapped image, it leaves a hole where the image used to be. The ability to combine photo images to create fictitious photos has made it difficult to trust any photograph at face value (see Figure 11.23). Photos no longer stand up as evidence in the courtroom as they once did.

FIGURE 11.23 • Faked photos
Has SeaWorld really added a giant goldfish to their killer whale performance?

Personal photo-editing software provides easy to use tools for cleaning up photos and integrating them into frames, greeting cards, calendars, and other practical printed forms. This software often includes wizards that walk the user through the photo-editing process. Figure 11.24 illustrates such a program. Professional-grade photo-editing software, such as Adobe Photoshop, provides many tools for retouching and editing photographs to professional standards.

FIGURE 11.24 • **Personal Photo Editing**

Personal photo-editing software provides easy to use tools for cleaning up photos, adding effects, and integrating the photos into frames, greeting cards, calendars, and other practical printed forms.

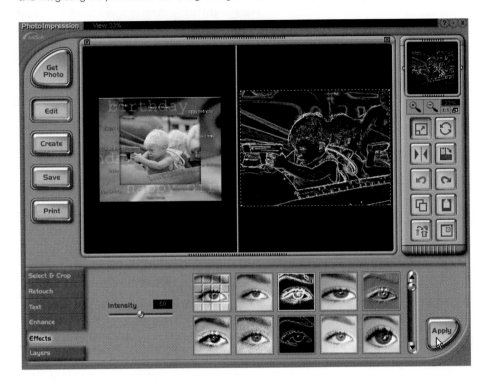

EXPAND YOUR **KNOWLEDGE**

To learn more about video, go to www.course.com/swt. Click the link "Expand Your Knowledge," and then complete the lab entitled, "Working with Video."

Digital Video Editing

With the increase in popularity of digital camcorders, increasing numbers of home PC users are finding it useful to edit their digital videos on their home PC. Much of the footage captured on video tape is often not worth saving. **Video-editing software** allows professional and amateur videographers to edit bad footage out of digital video and rearrange the good footage to produce a professional-quality video production. Popular video-editing software packages include Studio Moviebox for Windows from Pinnacle Systems, Adobe products such as Premier, Video Collection, and After Effects available for both Windows and Apple computers, and Final Cut Pro for Apple.

Digital video can be transferred to a computer directly from a camcorder or read from a DVD or VCR tape. Video takes up a significant amount of space on the hard drive, so most home users do not store many videos on their PC, but rather copy them to CD or DVD after they finish editing.

Video-editing software uses a storyline on which to build a video production. A *storyline* allows the videographer to arrange video scenes sequentially and specify the transition effects between each scene (see Figure 11.25). The videographer can cut scenes out of the video footage and drag the scenes to a position on the storyline. Options for transitions include effects such as dissolving one scene into the next, fading to black, or abruptly starting one scene when the previous scene finishes. Figure 11.25 illustrates the video-editing process. The videographer can add still images, background music, and text to the storyline as well as video scenes. When the storyline is complete, it is saved to one of many possible video formats on hard drive and usually burned to DVD to be viewed on TV.

Digital movies, which might otherwise require hundreds of gigabytes or even terabytes of storage space, are compressed down to less than 10 GB in order to fit onto a DVD. Digital video compression involves analyzing each frame of the

FIGURE 11.25 • Video-editing storyline

Using video-editing software, a videographer arranges scenes and transitions between scenes on a storyline to create a video production.

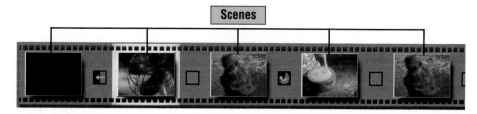

video and storing only the pixels that change from frame to frame. Consider a nightly news show. Such video typically has little or no change in the background behind the news reporter. So, when compressed, the bits that make up the background only need to be stored once for the frames in which they remain unchanged. A video frame might display a million pixels but only have 1,000 pixels that change from the previous frame reducing the storage requirements from a million to a thousand.

Both digital photography and digital video are used in a variety of research and other professional areas. *Forensic graphics* is used to create animations and demonstrative exhibits to use in the court of law in order to explain theories and present evidence. Figure 11.26 shows a forensic graphics storyboard used to reconstruct the spread of an industrial fire. Forensic graphics experts also study photos and videotaped evidence in an effort to solve crimes. For example, video of a convenience store robbery would be studied by a forensic graphics expert to ascertain the identity of the thieves. Video cameras mounted at intersections are increasingly being used to catch drivers who run red lights. Forensic graphics is used to read the license number of the vehicle in the video image.

FIGURE 11.26 • Forensic graphics

Forensic graphics storyboards are used to reconstruct the spread of an industrial fire.

By collecting and studying digital video, athletes and trainers can review the movement of athletes and determine how to perfect their abilities. Digital video is used to study pedestrian and traffic patterns. It is also used by scientists to study the activity of microbes and other organisms. The capturing and study of digital video are useful in many professional endeavors.

INTERACTIVEMEDIA

Interactive media refers to multimedia presentations that involve user interaction for education, training, or entertainment. Interactive media is unique in that it is not created for a passive audience to sit and observe, but rather it is created specifically for the audience to take part in the creative or educational process. Interactive media typically combines both digital audio and digital video media for a full multimedia experience.

When interactive media incorporates 3-D graphic animation, the result is virtual reality. Virtual reality, discussed in Chapter 8, produces a simulated environment in which the human participant can move and manipulate objects. Adding surround sound makes the interactive experience more realistic.

Video games make up a large portion of the interactive media market. Other forms of interactive media provide computer-based tutorials and training, and still others are used in commercial applications to support the sales of products and provide customer support. Interactive media is becoming increasingly important as technology advances to support its large demands for processing speed, storage, and bandwidth. New development tools are being released that better support interactive media over the Internet and Web. This section provides an overview of interactive multimedia and its value in our lives.

Education and Training

Research shows that most individuals are able to comprehend complex ideas more thoroughly and quickly when able to interact with them using multimedia. For example, engineering professors at the University of Missouri turned to interactive multimedia to assist students who were having a difficult time understanding the theories behind stress transformation—the internal stresses and forces that loads place on building materials. They developed an interactive multimedia tool that allowed students to witness the effects of stress on different materials and the associated stress transformation equations. By visually associating the stress placed on virtual objects with the equations, students could more easily understand how abstract concepts relate to the real world. Results from the study showed that when lecture, interactive media, and reading textbooks are compared side by side, students felt that they learned best in lectures and preferred interactive media over textbook reading.[9]

Educational research also shows that everyone learns differently. For this reason many curricula are including multimedia and interactive multimedia components.

One of the most popular tools for developing educational interactive multimedia comes from Macromedia and is called Authorware. **Authorware** is a tool used to produce interactive multimedia educational tu-

PICASSO MEETS DISNEY

Intelligent software under development at the Massachusetts Institute of Technology will evaluate rough-drawn lines on a computer screen and then assign an interpretation. It also updates the assessment as the line changes. Once it assigns an interpretation, it then animates it according to the laws of physics: a rectangle with two circles will morph into a moving car. The software is expected to "revolutionize" teaching children and aid engineers in design.

Source:
"Smart software makes sense of rough sketches"
By Celeste Biever
New Scientist
www.newscientist.com/news/news.jsp?id=ns99994152
September 12, 2003
Cited on September 13, 2003

torials that are packaged on CD, delivered over a network, or delivered over the Web. Authorware works in a fashion similar to video-editing software in that objects are organized on a sequential line, called a flowline, that dictates the order and path of the presentation. Objects can be static pages containing text and pictures, video clips, or learning tools such as quizzes and interactive graphics. Figure 11.27 shows a completed authorware project in a Web browser window. In this particular example, "Introduction to Photography," the student is asked to click different parts of the camera to show that she can recognize them by name. Buttons are used to progress through the lesson. By returning to the main menu, the student can progress through the lessons in a nonlinear fashion.

FIGURE 11.27 • Authorware

Authorware is a tool used to produce interactive multimedia educational tutorials, such as an introduction to photography, that are packaged on CD, delivered over a network, or delivered over the Web.

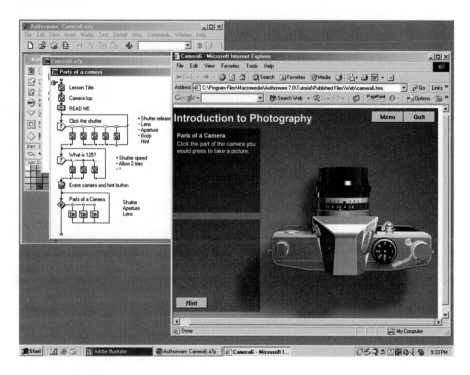

Interactive multimedia is being used in many education environments:

- In the traditional classroom setting. it is used to help students learn difficult concepts.
- In distance learning, it sometimes takes the place of lecture demonstrations.
- In museums, it allows the public to interact with virtual objects and environments that it is not possible to interact with in real life.
- In skills-training, interactive multimedia simulations are used to train pilots and others in a host of skills-based occupations.

Interactive lessons can be presented on PCs or public kiosks. They allow the learner to work at his or her own pace and often in his or her own environment. Learners can use interactive lessons repeatedly until they absorb the concept thoroughly. Often multimedia permits interaction that is not feasible or convenient in real life. For example, software from Mind Avenue (www.mindavenue. com) provided the ability to develop a 3-D interactive Web demonstration of the Wright brothers' first airplane. Web users can learn how the first airplane was constructed, explore the principles that made it fly, and read instructions for flying it. The plane can be rotated 360 degrees for a thorough examination. The user can then manipulate the rudders and elevators, using the arrow keys, to control a simulated flight while witnessing first-hand the early mechanics of flight (see Figure 11.28).

FIGURE 11.28 • Educational interactive mulitmedia

This interactive tutorial allows users to explore how the Wright brothers' first airplane was constructed, learn about the principles that made it fly, and read instructions for flying it.

Commercial Applications of Interactive Multimedia

Companies have jumped on interactive multimedia to offer customers additional services and benefits. Interactive multimedia plays a large role in Web-based e-commerce. Interactive multimedia is the technology that underlies 3-D product viewing, which allows online customers to thoroughly examine products (see Chapter 4). Travelers can take virtual tours of resort destinations prior to booking a room. Web marketers are even using interactive games in banner ads to get users to click.

Interactive multimedia is also used to provide product support and customer training. For example, Mercedes provides its customers with interactive multimedia on CD that allows them to explore the parts and features of their new automobile. In the construction industry, electronic blueprints provide a 3-D view of a home. The owner can click an option to view the home's electrical system and rotate the image to determine how and where to add an additional wall outlet. Interactive 3-D is being used in interior design to place objects within a virtual home and determine what looks best.

Interactive multimedia is playing a large role in attracting customers to Web sites, and once there, it plays a role in keeping them there. The Web site for the Toyota Prius automobile (see Figure 11.29) uses interactive multimedia in nearly every conceivable way, enabling the customer to evaluate the car in every way, short of taking it for an actual test drive. It includes 360-degree interior and exterior views of the car, educational animations that explain the unique gas-electric hybrid engine design, and a wizard that allows you to custom design your own Prius.

FIGURE 11.29 • Commercial use of interactive multimedia

The Toyota Prius Web site uses interactive multimedia to enable visitors to rotate and manipulate the vehicle on the screen, and even take it for a virtual test drive.

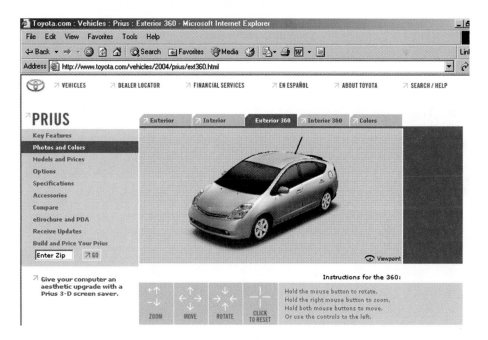

Interactive Multimedia Entertainment

In the area of interactive multimedia entertainment, the computer video game reigns supreme. Video games employ nearly every aspect of digital media discussed in this chapter. Most gaming takes place in living rooms on game consoles wired to television sets, rather than on personal computers. The three gaming consoles on the market today are the Nintendo GameCube (see Figure 11.30), the Sony

FIGURE 11.30 • Video game console

Video game consoles connect to your TV to deliver high-quality 3-D gaming.

Playstation 2 (PS2), and the Microsoft Xbox. **Video game consoles** are high-powered multiprocessor computers designed to support 3-D interactive multimedia. They come equipped with a fast microprocessor that works in conjunction with a graphics coprocessor to support fast-paced gaming action. The microprocessor is specially designed to handle the high demands of live action 3-D rendering. These units also include memory, storage similar to a PC, and an optional Internet connection to connect with gamers in other locations.

The Nintendo GameCube supports many games of interest to a preteen audience, whereas Sony and Microsoft tend to cater to teen and adult gamers. Table 11.3 provides a side-by-side comparison of the features of these three game consoles.

TABLE 11.3 • Console Comparison Chart[10]

	Nintendo GameCube	Sony PlayStation 2	Microsoft Xbox
CPU Speed	485 MHz	295 MHz	733 MHz
Generation	128-bit	128-bit	128-bit
Memory	24 MB SRAM	32 MB	64 MB
Medium	3 inch Optical Disc (1.5 GB)	DVD/CD	DVD/CD
Controller Ports	4	2	4
Hard Drive	No	Future add-on	8GB (built-in)
Internet	optional 56k modem, Ethernet adapter	optional 56k modem, Ethernet adapter	Built-in Ethernet adapter
Graphics Processor	162 MHz	147 MHz	233 MHz
Expansion Ports	serial & parallel ports	USB, Firewire, PCMCIA, Optical/Digital Out	Multi/AV port
DVD Movie Playback	No	Yes	Optional remote control required

The gaming market has ridden a wave of success right through the downturn in the economy that began in 2001, and it doesn't look as though it will slow down anytime soon. Since 1995 and the release of the Sony PlayStation, over 3 billion video game consoles have been sold. In 2002 alone, 30 million game consoles were sold. Global sales for video games are expected to increase from $20.7 billion in 2002 to as much as $30 billion by 2007.

Video game development requires a team effort from specialists in a variety of areas: game designers, artists, sound designers, programmers, and testers.[11] *Game designers* develop the game's theme, storyline, rules, characters, and environment. Designers create a detailed plan called a design document. The document describes every aspect of the game and serves as a central blueprint. *Game artists* use 2-D or 3-D graphics tools to develop game characters and backgrounds. Animators give life to game characters by providing them with the capability of movement through the animation methods described earlier in this chapter. Game *sound designers* provide background music, voices, and sound effects for the game to add realism and mood. Often composers are hired to write music that matches the desired atmosphere for the game. *Game Programmers* take all the pieces—game design, characters, backgrounds, animation, and sound—and encode them into the

VGD SEEKS WC, OBJECT: BUILD NEW WORLDS

Video game developers and wireless companies are wooing one another to create a dynasty of virtual game worlds accessible through a wireless phone. Still needed is middleware—technology platforms that route players around a virtual world and track events there. In anticipation, however, phone manufacturers like Nokia are already producing phones with larger, full-color, 3-D screens, and multiplayer capability for worldwide games.

Source
"New-Generation Phones Got Game"
By Brad King
Wired News
www.wired.com/news/games/0,2101,60417,00.html
September 12, 2003
Cited on September 13, 2003

game software. Game programming involves some of the most complex programming, and requires high levels of math knowledge and considerable programming experience. *Game testers* range from technicians who check the final product for bugs and glitches to game enthusiasts contracted to play the game and provide feedback.

Putting a new game on the market requires a large financial investment and is a big risk—a risk that many developers are willing to take in pursuit of the rewards that come with having a hit. A successful game must engage the user by allowing progress through the game at just the right pace, with action sequences timed at just the right intervals. Successful video games are easy to learn but difficult to master.

In efforts to engage older gamers, games have progressively moved to more violent themes. The popular, but controversial Grand Theft Auto: Vice City sold 8.5 million copies, earning the company $277.4 million in the first 3 months after its release.[12] Some people have become concerned about the effects of prolonged exposure to violence on game users (see Figure 11.31 and the "Community Technology" box).

FIGURE 11.31 • Video game violence

With the popularity of games such as Grand Theft Auto, many people wonder how prolonged exposure to violence might be affecting the young people who play it.

COMMUNITY TECHNOLOGY

Violence and Video Games

There is considerable concern from many sources that playing violent video games desensitizes gamers to acts of violence and may lead to violent behavior. Today's video games are so violent that the U.S. Marines uses them to desensitize recruits, claims former army psychologist Lt. Col. David Grossman. The Marines state that the games are used to develop hand-eye coordination. Grossman argues that "We are teaching children to associate pleasure with human death and suffering. We are rewarding them for killing people. And we are teaching them to like it."

"Our games are like modern-day computer versions of cowboys and Indians," says Todd Hollenshead, maker of "Doom." He compares it to the violence of cartoons like the Road Runner and Wile E. Coyote. He also points out that FBI crime statistics indicate that the violent crime rate has gone down over the past 10 years.

Governments are starting to pass laws against violent games. Washington Governor Gary Locke signed a bill into law that fines retailers $500 for renting violent video games to children. A St. Louis ordinance requires that children under the age of 17 have parental consent to rent, buy, or play such games. However, video-game publishers are working to get these laws overturned.

Questions

1. Do you think violent video games desensitize children to violence? Why or why not?
2. Should there be laws to keep children from purchasing and renting violent video games?
3. Should there be laws to control the level of violence depicted in video games? Why or why not?

Sources
1. *"The Games Kids Play", John Stossel, Abcnews.com, March 22, 2003, http://abcnews.go.com/onair/2020/2020_000322_videogames_feature.html.*
2. *"No Violent Games for You, Kids," Wired News Report, May 21, 2003.*

Interactive TV

Interactive TV has been touted as "the next big thing" in interactive multimedia entertainment. Various features of interactive TV are available to cable subscribers in select areas. **Interactive TV** is a digital television service that includes one or more of the following: video on demand, personal video recorder, local information on TV, purchase over TV, Internet access over TV, and video games over TV. **Video On Demand** (VoD) allows digital cable customers to select from hundreds of movies and programs to watch at anytime they choose. The movie or program is stored using a set-top box and can be paused, rewound, and treated as a DVD. In mid-2003, approximately 40 percent of U.S. cable TV systems were offering VoD, and almost 4 million subscribers were using the service. It is estimated that VoD digital set-top boxes will be in 55 percent of U.S. homes by the end of 2005. *Personal Video Recorders* (PVR), such as Tivo and Replay TV, provide large hard drive storage to record dozens of movies and programs to be watched at your leisure. *Local Information on TV* provides local community news and information. *Purchase over TV*, sometimes called *t-Commerce*, allows viewers to make purchases over their cable TV connection much as computer users make purchases on the Web. *Internet Access over TV*, through services like WebTV, allows viewers to navigate the Web on their television sets. Cable TV services provide access to video games through *Video Games over TV*.

As with the Web, interactive TV has the potential to provide individual targeted marketing. Cable providers are considering ways they can collect customer information in order to provide customers with television commercials that are targeted to individuals' interests. Using *behavioral profiling*, cable TV providers can observe customers' viewing patterns in order to develop an understanding of their interests. Some cable providers consider targeted marketing to be a core part of interactive television.

Microsoft has paved the way for interactive TV with WindowsXP Media Center Edition. This version of Windows runs on Media Center PCs, such as the one from Gateway shown in Figure 11.32, that use a television, or preferably a plasma display. The Media Center PC connects to your television service and acts as an electronic program guide, a Web browser, a television receiver, a personal video recorder (PVR), a DVD player, a digital music player, a personal digital video player, and a digital photograph displayer. Each media is supported by programs that sort, catalog, and schedule your media content.

FIGURE 11.32 • Windows XP Media Center

Windows XP Media Center acts as an electronic program guide, a Web browser, a television receiver, a personal video recorder (PVR), a DVD player, a digital music player, a personal digital video player, and a digital photograph displayer.

Action Plan

1. What skills should Ana develop during college to help her in the video game industry?

Ana's ideas for new games and her experience with art, music, and computers make her an ideal candidate for a position as a game designer. Recall that a game designer supplies the ideas and blueprint for games. Game designers also orchestrate the interaction between artists, sound designers, and computer programmers. Ana should research the specific responsibilities of game designers so that she can start formalizing her game ideas. She might also try to learn as much as she can about successful game designers in the field. Since Ana will be working with digital audio, digital 3-D animation, and computer programming, she should learn as much as she can about all of these areas, keeping in mind that she will be working with others who are experts in these areas. When possible, Ana should begin investing in equipment that is required in the field. She could begin with some entry-level 3-D graphics and animation software that could help her to begin developing game characters and scenes. She can purchase an inexpensive synthesizer keyboard, and take an entry-level computer programming course.

2. What major and minor should Ana choose to best prepare for her career?

Ana has a year or two before she will have to formally declare a major. In that time she should learn the basics of computer programming, 3-D graphic arts, and graphic design—enough to find out which area she enjoys the most. As a game designer, Ana will also require management and communication skills. Depending on what interests her most, computer programming, graphic design, music, or business management, Ana should select a major and minor that will benefit her as a game designer and business person.

3. What contacts should Ana make during college that might help her get a job in the industry?

Ana will need to work with programmers, artists, and musicians. It would be good for her to make friends in these areas and perhaps find others who share her interests. Ana might check out school clubs and organizations centered on technology or graphic arts. She should consider gaining experience in the field through internships.

Summary

LEARNING OBJECTIVE 1
Understand the value and use of digital audio in a variety of career areas and in your life.

Digital audio includes both digital music and digital sound. The professional production and editing of digital audio takes place in sound production studios. Sound production is an important part of music, movies, radio, television, video games, and the Internet. Postproduction dubbing and voice-over recording are used to apply music, sound effects, and voice to films. Audio restoration and enhancement are used to improve the quality of old or damaged recordings. Forensic audio uses digital processing to de-noise, enhance, edit and detect sounds to assist in criminal investigations.

Figure 11.1—p. 463

Digital technology is applied to all aspects of the music industry: creation, production, and distribution. Digital instruments such as synthesizer keyboards, samplers, and drum machines are used in the creation of digital music. A recording studio employs many digital sound production tools, such as sequencers and outboard devices, to record and manipulate digital music. The MIDI (Musical Instrument Digital Interface) protocol was implemented in 1983 to provide a standard language for digital music devices to use in communicating with each other. P2P digital music distribution other the Internet has undermined the recording industry's control of the distribution process and created a complicated debate between industry leaders and their customers. A wide array of digital music software and devices are available today to provide users with more control over their music-listening experience.

LEARNING OBJECTIVE 2
Describe the many uses of 2-D and 3-D digital graphics and imaging media.

Digital graphics refers to media applications that include digital graphics and digital imaging. Digital graphics is used as a form of creative expression, including presenting information in a visually pleasing fashion, communicating and exploring ideas, and assisting in the design of real-world objects, entertaining, and documenting life. Vector graphics software, sometimes called drawing software, provides tools to create, arrange, and layer graphical objects on the screen to create pictures. Vector

Figure 11.17—p. 479

graphics software also provides filtering and effects tools to further manipulate objects in the picture. 3-D modeling software provides graphics tools that allow artists to create pictures of 3-D, realistic models. Ray tracing involves calculating how light would interact with surfaces in a picture to create shadows and reflections. Digital graphics animation involves displaying digital images in rapid succession to provide the illusion of motion. 3-D computer animation includes all of the complexity of 3-D graphic rendering, multiplied by the necessity to render 24 3-D images per second to create the illusion of movement.

Photo-editing software provides editing tools for manipulating digital photographs. Using these tools, photos can be enhanced and repaired. Photo editing also includes special effects, such as the ability to use edge detection to remove an object from one photo and insert it in another. Personal photo-editing software provides easy-to-use tools for cleaning up photos and integrating them into frames, greeting cards, calendars and other practical printed forms. Video-editing software uses a storyline on which to build a video production. The videographer cuts scenes out of the video footage and drags the scenes to a position on the storyline. After cutting and pasting scenes onto the storyline, the videographer defines the transitions between scenes to create a professional-looking video production.

LEARNING OBJECTIVE 3
Discuss how interactive media is used to educate and entertain.

Interactive media refers to multimedia presentations that involve user interaction for education, training, or entertainment. Interactive media is unique because it empowers the audience to take part in the creative or educational process. Authorware is a tool used to produce interactive multimedia educational tutorials that are packaged on CD, delivered over a network, or delivered over the Web. Companies use interactive multimedia to offer customers additional services and benefits.

Figure 11.32—p. 495

Computer video games make up a large portion of the interactive media market. Most gaming takes place on game consoles wired to television sets, rather than on computers. The three big gaming consoles on the market today are Nintendo GameCube, Sony Playstation 2 (PS2), and Microsoft Xbox. Today's gaming consoles are high powered multiprocessor computers designed to support 3-D interactive multimedia. Video game development requires a team effort from specialists in game design, art, sound design, programming, and testing. Interactive TV is likely to be the next big thing in interactive multimedia entertainment. Interactive TV includes digital services such as video on demand, personal video recorder (PVR), purchase over TV, Web TV, and video games over TV.

Test Yourself

LEARNING OBJECTIVE 1: Understand the value and use of digital audio in a variety of career areas and in your life.

1. The professional production and editing of digital audio takes place in _____.

2. The _____ protocol was implemented in 1983 to provide a standard language for digital music devices to use in communicating with each other.
    a. Integrated Digital Studio (IDS)
    b. Digital Music Media (DMM)
    c. Musical Instrument Digital Interface (MIDI)
    d. Compact Disc Audio (CDA)

3. True or False: Sharing copies of copyright protected music is legal.

4. A _____ is a device that allows musicians to create multitrack recordings with a minimal investment in equipment.
    a. drum machine
    b. synthesizer
    c. sequencer
    d. MIDI

LEARNING OBJECTIVE 2: Describe the many uses of 2-D and 3-D digital graphics and imaging media.

5. _____ software, sometimes called *drawing software*, provides tools to create, arrange, and layer, graphical objects on the screen to create pictures.

6. _____ is the process of calculating the light interaction with the virtual 3-D models in a scene and presenting the final drawing in two dimensions to be viewed on the screen or printed.
    a. rendering
    b. animating
    c. compiling
    d. light tracing

7. True or False: Even with powerful computers, high-quality rendering such as that used for major animated motion pictures takes hours per frame.

8. _____ software is able to turn designs on the computer into blueprint specifications for manufacturing.

LEARNING OBJECTIVE 3: Discuss how interactive media is used to educate and entertain.

9. _____ is a tool used to produce interactive multimedia educational tutorials that are packaged on CD, delivered over a network, or delivered over the Web.

10. Microsoft Xbox is a _____.
    a. video game console
    b. home entertainment system
    c. digital cell phone
    d. handheld computer

11. True or False: A media center PC acts as a centralized entertainment control system for the home.

12. True or False: Nearly all digital cable TV users take advantage of video on demand.

Test Yourself Solutions: 1. sound production studio, **2.** c., **3.** F, **4.** c., **5.** Vector graphics, **6.** a., **7.** T, **8.** CAD, **9.** Authorware, **10.** a., **11.** T, **12.** F

Key Terms

3-D modeling software, p. 479
authorware, p. 488
computer-assisted design (CAD), p. 476
digital audio, p. 462
digital graphics, p. 472
digital music, p. 462
digital sound, p. 462

interactive media, p. 488
interactive TV, p. 494
MP3, p. 469
multimedia, p. 462
musical instrument digital interface (MIDI), p. 467
photo-editing software, p. 485
sampler, p. 466

scientific visualization, p. 475
sequencer, p. 466
synthesizer, p. 464
vector graphics software, p. 477
video-editing software, p. 486
video game consoles, p. 492
video on demand, p. 494

Questions

Review Questions

1. Name and define the two subcategories of digital audio.

2. Define multimedia.

3. What services are provided by a sound production studio?

4. What audio services cater to the motion picture industry?

5. What digital tools and instruments do musicians use to create music?

6. Name three methods of transferring music to your computer.

7. How does digital graphics differ from digital imaging?

8. What types of professionals make use of CAD software?

9. How do vector graphics differ from bitmap graphics?

10. What does it mean to render 3-D models?

11. What are animated GIFs, and where do you usually find them?

12. What benefits does Macromedia Flash offer for Web content?

13. What are avars and how do they give life to 3-D animations?

14. Name four forms of interactive media.

15. What is the purpose of authorware?

16. What are some commercial uses of interactive media?

17. What are the three most popular models and manufacturers of video game consoles?

18. What types of specialists are typically involved in video game production?

19. Name five services associated with interactive TV.

20. What is video on demand?

Discussion Questions

21. How is forensic audio used to catch criminals?

22. What is the purpose of MIDI?

23. How has digital music empowered musicians?

24. How has digital music empowered music fans?

25. What is MP3, and why is it so popular?

26. How has digital music affected music distribution?

27. What is scientific visualization and how is it used?

28. What is digital cinema, and how will it affect the motion picture industry?

29. Why are vector graphics considered to be object oriented?

30. Why is the process of 3-D modeling sometimes called ray tracing?

31. What benefits does photo-editing software provide photographers?

32. How is video editing used to create professional-quality video productions?

33. What benefits does Windows XP Media Center offer?

Exercises

Try It Yourself

1. Visit www.yamaha.com/yamahavgn/CDA/Home/ YamahaHome/, click Keyboards and Digital Instruments. Explore the products, then view the MOTIF. On the MOTIF page click MOTIF Synthesizers, then click the link for Media Clips. Listen to the sampled instrument recordings presented there. List your five favorite sounds. Listen to the Acoustic instrument sounds. Do they sound real? Write your impressions in a few paragraphs and submit them to your teacher.

2. Visit www.irtc.org and www.hotwired.com/rgb/ gallary and view the digital artwork that you find there. Write a few paragraphs on which piece most affects you or interests you from each site and why? If none interest you, explain why not.

3. Visit www.mindavenue.com, download and install the Axel player, then go to the Gallery. Try out some of the interactive productions and games. List the five that you feel are the most interesting. Write a paragraph summary of your impression of the technology and its value on the Web.

4. Visit www.pixar.com and view the link that explains Pixar's animation and movie making process. Summarize the steps of the animation process in a word-processing document and submit it to your instructor.

Virtual Classroom Activities

For the following exercises, do not use face-to-face or telephone communications with your group members. Use only Internet communications.

5. Have the group members answer the questions following this exercise. Compile the data to derive statistical information about your group. Add group member song amounts to get a total amount of songs downloaded for your group. Divide that number by 10 (the average number of songs on a CD) to determine how many CDs worth of music has been downloaded by your group. Then, multiple that number by $15 to determine how much money your group has saved and the record industry has lost. Report your findings, without attaching individual names to specific responses, to your instructor. Your instructor can compile the statistics for the entire class.

   Questions:
   a. Do you use file-sharing networks to download music? If yes, approximately how many music files are currently in your collection?
   b. Do you use file-sharing networks to supply music to others?
   c. Do you believe that sharing music in this way should be legal?

6. Using a virtual classroom application or other chat utility, as a group, visit www.worth1000.com. Explore the images you find there and decide which image everyone in the group enjoys most. Share it with your instructor.

Teamwork

7. Try or view a demonstration of the video game Grand Theft Auto by visiting a video game retail store or accessing it in some other way. Learn what the goals are in the game and the details of the challenges. Have a group debate to decide whether or not the game desensitizes users to violence. After everyone has a chance to express their opinions take a vote and submit the results to the instructor.

8. Use a group member's digital camera (or borrow one from a friend) to take a group photo. Distribute the photo electronically to all group members, and using photo-editing software, have a contest to see who can edit the photo in the most interesting way. Submit all entries to the instructor.

Learning Check

To check your knowledge of each of the chapter objectives, use this chart to find related end-of-chapter content.

	Learning Objective	Key Terms		Questions	Exercises
	Learning Objective 1 Understand the value and use of digital audio in a variety of career areas and in your life.	digital audio digital music digital sound MP3 multimedia	musical instrument digital interface (MIDI) sampler sequencer synthesizer	1, 2, 3, 4, 5, 6, 21, 22, 23, 24, 25, 26	1, 5
	Learning Objective 2 Describe the many uses of 2-D and 3-D digital graphics and imaging media.	3-D Modeling Software computer-assisted design (CAD) digital graphics photo-editing software scientific visualization vector graphics software video-editing software		7, 8, 9, 10, 11, 12, 13, 27, 28, 29, 30, 31, 32	2, 4, 6, 8
	Learning Objective 3 Discuss how interactive media is used to educate and entertain.	authorware interactive media interactive TV video game consoles video on demand		14, 15, 16, 17, 18, 19, 20, 33	3, 7

Endnotes

1. Davis, Eric, "Songs in the Key of F12," *Wired*, May 2002.
2. RIAA—About Us Web page, accessed September 14, 2003, www.riaa.com/about/default.asp.
3. "Pirated CD Sales Top 1 Billion," CNN.com, July 10, 2003.
4. Albini, Steve (producer of Nirvana's "In Utero"), "The Problem With Music," Negativeland.com accessed September 14, 2003 at www.negativland.com/albini.html.
5. Liebowitz, Stan, "Will MP3 Downloads Annihilate the Record Industry?" Research Paper, University of Texas, Dallas, June 2003, wwwpub.utdallas.edu/~liebowit/intprop/records.pdf.
6. "Music Labels Unveil Mobile Song-Swapping Technology," Reuters, October 13, 2003.
7. Ulbrich, Chris, "Music Label Cashes in by Sharing," *Wired* News, October 8, 2003, www.wired.com.
8. "Microsoft to Offer Video Service for MSN," Reuters, October 14, 2003.
9. "The Amazing Stress Camera: An Interactive Discovery Experience," Timothy Philpot and Richard Hall, University of Missouri, http://imej.wfu.edu/articles/2003/1/04/index.asp.
10. "Game Console Buying Guide," Viewz.com, Sept 20, 2003, www.viewz.com/shoppingguide/consoleguide.shtml.
11. Crosby, Olivia, "Working so others can play: Jobs in video game development," *Occupational Outlook Quarterly*, accessed September 19, 2003, www.bls.gov/opub/ooq/2000/Summer/art01.pdf.
12. Morris, Chris, "'Grand Theft Auto' Pays for Take Two," Chris Morris, CNNMoney, February 27, 2003, http://money.cnn.com/2003/02/27/commentary/game_over/column_gaming/.

Societal and Ethical Issues in Computer Systems

Technology 360°

John Toh was thrilled to be working in the Department of Environmental Protection for the state of Florida. After graduating in 4 years from a Colorado university, he was ready to start work. After just six months on the job, he had purchased his first personal computer system and was starting to pay off his student loans. John was very excited about owning his own computer after spending countless hours in computer labs at the university. John spent hours on the Internet at home, signing up for all kinds of free services and products on a large number of Internet sites. It was incredible how much you could get on the Internet free of charge.

John's excitement about a new computer, however, was short lived. After a few months, John was receiving almost 30 e-mails a day for travel deals, prescription drugs, stereo equipment, hearing aids, and even get-rich-quick scams. Even worse, though, his computer just stopped working. John wondered if his new computer had become infected with a virus.

1. What can John do to avoid getting unwanted e-mail?
2. How can John check for viruses and prevent virus infections?

Check out John's *Action Plan* at the conclusion of this chapter.

After completing Chapter 12, you will be able to:

LEARNING OBJECTIVES	CHAPTER CONTENT
1. Describe how a computer system can be used as a tool to commit a crime or be the object of a crime and what can be done to prevent computer crime.	**Computer Crime**
2. Discuss privacy issues and describe how to avoid invasion of privacy.	**Privacy**
3. List health and job issues that could have an impact on you and others.	**Issues in the Work Environment**
4. Define and discuss ethical issues in computer systems.	**Ethical Issues in Computer Systems**
5. List common computer-related waste and mistakes, describe how they can be avoided, and describe how computers can be used to help resolve social issues.	**Computer Waste, Mistakes, and Other Social Issues**

Introduction

Individuals and organizations have greatly benefited from the use of computer systems. Yet, computers also generate their share of problems. Some viruses have completely shut down computers. Some people have had serious health problems from working long hours on computer keyboards. Computer crime has cost some companies millions of dollars in losses. Numerous social issues are related to the use of computer systems, including computer crime, invasion of privacy, job and health concerns, computer-related-waste, and computer mistakes. In addition, there are ethical issues to consider when using computers. Although computer systems can have negative impacts on society, they can also help address important societal issues. In this chapter, we will explore all these societal issues.

Computers can be a double-edged sword. On the one hand, they have the potential—often realized—to help people and organizations achieve their goals. On the other hand, they have an equal potential to produce problems of great concern to people, organizations, and society. The potential problems include computer crime, invasion of privacy, negative impact on health, computer waste and mistakes, and other social issues. Let's take a close look at each of these potential problems and what can be done to avoid them. We'll also review some of the positive impacts of computer systems on society.

COMPUTERCRIME

Computer crime is a popular topic that receives a lot of attention in the media; many movies have used computer crime as a significant theme, including *The Net*, *War Games*, and *Enemies of the State*. But computer crime goes beyond fiction and has a serious impact on real individuals and organizations. In less than a second, a computer can process millions of pieces of data. In the same amount of time, computers can also be used to steal thousands or millions of dollars. Compared to the dangers of robbing a bank or retail store with a gun, computer crime is relatively safe. With the right equipment and know-how, a person can commit a computer crime in the privacy of his or her own home. Computer crime is often difficult to detect, the amount stolen or diverted can be substantial, and the crime is "clean" and nonviolent.

The vast, interconnected computer systems of today are a relatively open territory for crime. And, although law enforcement officials work to stay abreast of technology as it develops, they often seem to remain one step behind computer criminals. Officials are learning, however; they are getting tougher, and catching up fast. Five brokerage companies, for example, were fined a total of $8.25 million for not properly saving e-mail related to stock market investigations.[1]

Part of what makes computer crime so unique and hard to combat is its dual nature—it can be both the tool used to commit a crime and the object of that crime.

The Computer as a Tool to Commit Crime

Like using dynamite to open a safe, a computer can be used to gain access to valuable information or as the means to steal thousands of dollars. Just as there are many ways that an ordinary criminal can break into a residence or commercial establishment, there are many ways that a computer security system can be breached for illegal purposes. In general, two capabilities are required to commit most computer crimes. First, the criminal needs to know how to gain access to the computer system. Sometimes this requires knowledge of a username and a password, or the ability to generate fake or authentic codes. Second, the criminal must know how to manipulate the system to produce the desired result.

The Computer as the Object of Crime

A computer can also be the *object* of the crime, rather than the tool used to commit the crime. Millions of dollars of computer time and resources are stolen every year. Each time system access is illegally obtained, data or computer equipment is stolen or destroyed, or software is illegally copied, the computer becomes the object of crime. In one case, a company was fined $1 million for illegally shipping a computer system to Russia.[2]

Hackers and Crackers: Illegal Systems Access and Use. Crimes involving illegal systems access and use of computer services are a concern to the government and all organizations. Computers are sometimes left unattended over weekends without proper security, and university computers are often used for commercial purposes under the pretense of research or other legitimate academic pursuits. Hackers and crackers often illegally access systems.

From the outset of the information technology era, hackers and crackers have plagued computer systems. A **hacker** is a person who knows computer technology and spends time learning and using computer systems. In many cases, hackers are people who are looking for fun and excitement—the "challenge" of beating the system. In contrast, a **cracker** is a criminal hacker, a computer-savvy person who attempts to gain unauthorized or illegal access to other computer systems to harm the system or to make money illegally. In one case, crackers sold thousands of credit card numbers for $50 each to a crime ring. They got the credit-card numbers from unknowing shoppers.[3]

EXPAND YOUR
KNOWLEDGE

To learn more about computer viruses, go to www.course.com/swt. Click the link "Expand Your Knowledge," and then complete the lab entitled, "Keeping Your Computer Virus Free."

Viruses and Worms. The intentional use of illegal and destructive programs to alter or destroy data is as much a crime as destroying tangible goods. The most common of these types of programs are viruses and worms, which are software programs that, when loaded into a computer system, will destroy, interrupt, or cause errors in processing. A **virus** is a program that attaches itself to other programs. A **worm** does not attach itself to other programs. It acts as a free agent, placing copies of itself into other systems, destroying programs, and interrupting the operation of networks and computer systems (see Figure 12.1). Worms spread primarily as e-mail attachments. For example, within 10 minutes of its introduction, the slammer worm had attacked more than 75,000 computers.[4] Thirty minutes later, some believe the worm had disrupted 1 in 5 data packets sent over the Internet. The Sobig worm and many other virus and worm attacks were seen in the summer of 2003. The Sobig worm mails itself to addresses it gets from the victim's computer. The subject line of the e-mail that is sent includes "Your details,"

FIGURE 12.1 • MSblaster.worm
Viruses and worms can destroy data and programs on your computer system.

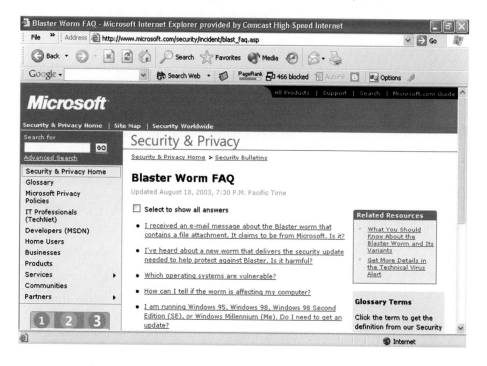

"Thank you!" "That movie," "Wicked screensaver," and others. During a typical month, 200 or more viruses are on the loose around the world.[5] In some cases, a virus or a worm can completely halt the operation of a computer system or network for weeks or longer until the problem is found and repaired. In other cases, a virus or a worm can destroy important data and programs. If there are inadequate backups, the data and programs may never be fully functional again.

The two most common kinds of viruses are application viruses and system viruses. **Application viruses** infect application files, including .exe and .com files, and often add themselves to applications such as word-processing programs and spreadsheet packages. A *macro virus* infects applications that use a macro language, including some word processors and spreadsheet programs. When the application is executed, the virus infects the computer system. Application viruses can be unknowingly sent through e-mail or the Internet to infect hundreds or thousands of computers and networks around the world. Because these types of viruses normally attach themselves to application files, they can often be detected by checking the length or size of the file. If the file is larger than it should be, a virus may be attached.

A **system virus**, also called a *boot-sector virus*, typically infects operating system programs or other system files. These types of viruses usually infect the system as soon as the computer is started or booted. Another type of program that can destroy a system is a **logic bomb**, a program designed to "explode" or execute at a specified time and date. Logic bombs are often disguised by **Trojan horses**, a program that appears to be useful but actually masks the destructive program. Some of these programs execute randomly; other programmers design these bombs to lie inert in software until a certain code is given. In this fashion, the bomb will explode months, or even years, after being "planted."

Viruses are most often obtained from floppy disks, the Internet, or from networks, where the virus is planted and can be unintentionally downloaded. However, viruses can lurk almost anywhere in a system.

A **virus hoax**, which is e-mail sent to people warning them of a virus that doesn't exist, is a related problem. In some cases, a virus hoax is just an inconvenience or nuisance. It just wastes your time. In other cases, it can cause serious problems. If the hoax tells you to delete a "virus" file that is actually an uninfected and important system file and you delete it, you may not be able to run your computer.

Preventing Virus and Worm Attacks. Some viruses and worms attack personal computers, while others attack network and client-server systems.[6] A virus or worm that attacks a network or client-server system is usually more severe because it can affect hundreds or thousands of personal computers and other devices attached to the network. To prevent similar attacks, some companies are hiring ex-criminal hackers to find out how they were able to unleash harmful viruses and worms.[7] Other companies avoid this practice. Intel, the company that supplies chips to PCs, is developing a new chip that will have built-in security features to help detect viruses and worms.[8]

Here are some ways to protect against virus and worm attacks and the harm these attacks can cause:

- Use a Firewall. Organizations and individuals often use firewalls to protect themselves. A **firewall** is software or hardware that protects an organization's computer system from outside attacks. Firewalls are typically placed between the Internet and other outside networks and the organization's computer system (see Figure 12.2).
- Use Virus Scanning Software. A primary way to avoid viruses and worms on a personal computer is to install *virus-scanning software*. McAfee, Symantec, and other companies produce popular virus-scanning software products. Some

FIGURE 12.2 • The Use of firewalls

A firewall protects a computer system from attack.

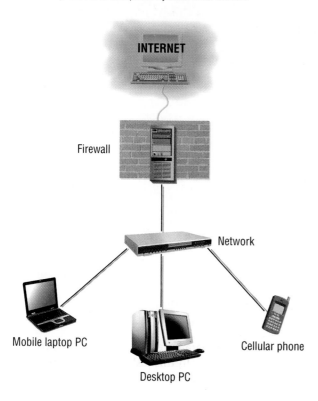

Internet service providers include virus-scanning software as part of their service. To be fully protected, you need to remember to update your virus-scanning software often and scan for viruses on disks you get from others.

- Implement a Known Source Policy and Verify E-mail Attachments. Only accept disks, e-mails, and downloads from people and organizations you know and trust. Even when you receive e-mails from known sources, such as friends and family, you have to be extremely careful. Many of today's worms come from e-mail attachments from an e-mail address you know. Only open e-mail attachments that you are expecting.

- Keep a Backup of Software and Data. With the availability of inexpensive CD and DVD writers, backing up important data is very easy. The importance of keeping a backup copy of software and data can't be overemphasized. If a virus attack does manage to disable your computer system, a backup copy of all software (application and systems software) and data can get you back into operation. Backup software and data is also a good idea in case you have a hard disk failure or other computer problems, not related to a virus. In some cases, a backup is the only way to recover from a computer-related problem.

- Have a Rescue Disk. Because a virus can prevent your computer system from working, it is always a good idea to have a rescue disk. A **rescue disk** is software on a floppy disk, CD ROM, or other disk used to start or boot your computer in case you can't start or boot your computer from your hard disk. A rescue disk is also handy if you have hard disk problems that are not related to a virus.

Scams and Fraud. The same types of scams and fraud that have existed for hundreds of years are now being committed using computer systems and the Internet. In addition, new scams and fraud are being developed every year. Con artists, for example, often advertise false products and services on online auctions.[9] One con artist got $800,000 from about 300 people by falsely advertising Apple Macintosh computers through auction sites. The number of online fraud referrals to state and federal agencies is about 50,000 annually.[10] The Federal Trade Commission (FTC) and numerous state agencies are actively pursuing fraud committed on the Internet. John Ashcroft, U.S. Attorney General, charged over 130 people with scams totaling about $17 million.[11] One person received about $60 million from 15,000 people as a result of an investment scam over the Internet. Some Internet sites sell medical supplements that claim to completely heal almost every imaginable disease.[12] The Federal Trade Commission (FTC) started Operation Cure-All to help people distinguish between good medical advice and "snake-oil" sellers.

Data and Information Theft. Individuals who illegally access systems often do so to steal data and information. Although the highly publicized cases of data theft involve people from outside an organization, insiders with the knowledge to locate, retrieve, and take the right data more often steal data. For example, without a good security system, departing employees might be able to print out all of the organization's account information and relay it to a competing firm.

COMMUNITY TECHNOLOGY

Protecting Your Identity

Identity theft is a serious threat, the threat is growing, and many people have had horrifying experiences with having their identity stolen.[13] If your identity is stolen, it can be extremely difficult to remove your personal information from the public domain. That is why preventing identity theft is so important. Your identity can be stolen on Internet sites, such as career or job sites. Criminals can use bogus job listings to ask you to provide a wealth of private information about yourself. Those eager to find work will often freely provide this type of information. Once a criminal has your information, he or she can create IDs, including driver's licenses using illegal Internet sites or other means.

You can use a number of strategies to prevent identity theft. Experts advise you to be extremely careful in giving your Social Security number and other personal information to others over the phone or the Internet. Credit-card companies, such as Visa, are actively developing software and systems to prevent identity and credit-card theft. The disadvantage of these fraud-detecting systems is that some innocent people can be flagged as possible criminals. In addition, you can use

software from companies such as Anonymizer and Steganos to block people and organizations from electronic snooping while you are on the Internet. The software, however, also prevents the FBI and other federal agencies from legally getting information about people under the Patriot Act.

Questions

1. How can you prevent identity theft?
2. How would you know if your identity had been stolen?
3. What are the disadvantages of the approaches to prevent identity theft?

Sources
1. *"Identity Scams Plague Career Sites,"* Steve Fox, PC World, June 2003, p. 47.
2. *"Creating a Fake Identity,"* Ira Sager, et al., Business Week, September 2, 2002, p. 69.
3. *"When Visa Thinks You're a Thief,"* Ron Lieber, The Wall Street Journal, April 24, 2003, p. D1.
4. *"Web Privacy Services Complicates Feds' Jobs,"* Sean Marciniak, The Wall Street Journal, July 3, 2003, p. B4.

Identity Theft. Stealing someone's personal information, such as their Social Security number, driver's license number, credit-card numbers, date-of-birth, address, and other personal information is called **identity theft**. Care must be taken when using credit cards on the Internet.

Make sure that the URL of the Web server reflects the company name and begins with https:// to ensure that the connection is secure. Once your identity has been stolen, a criminal can use the information to charge goods and services to your credit-card account without your knowledge or consent. Your credit-card accounts can be drained, and your credit can be ruined. You can spend a large amount of time trying to get your money back and your credit restored.

Equipment Theft. The miniaturization of computer systems has similarly affected computer equipment theft. Laptop and handheld computers (and the data and information stored in them) are easy targets for thieves. Computer equipment has also been diverted in its path from buyer to seller. For instance, a computer company might sell a large computer to an intermediary company at a $500,000 discount off list price. This intermediary company could then turn around and sell the same computer to an organization at full list price, pocketing the $500,000 discount. As a result of this simple transaction, the intermediary company made a profit of $500,000. Inadequate hardware acquisition policies, improper management, and blatant politics are all to blame.

Time and Supplies Theft. In addition to computer equipment, people can steal computer time and supplies. Employees using computer systems at work to entertain themselves, to buy stocks and bonds, or to conduct private business transactions are examples of computer time theft. People can also steal computer paper, printer ink, disks, and other computer-related supplies.

Software, Music, and Movie Theft: Intellectual Property Rights. Like data, intellectual property is an asset. Each time you use software, listen to music, or see a movie, you are taking advantage of someone else's intellectual property. **Intellectual property rights** concern the ownership and use of software, music, movies, data, and information. In general, intellectual property rights issues include:

- Who owns the intellectual property (programs, data, music, movies, and information)?
- What rights do users have to use the intellectual property?
- Who places a value on intellectual property?

One study reported that almost 40 percent of business software in use was illegally obtained.[14] Often, people who would never think of plagiarizing an author's written work have no qualms about using and copying software, music, or movies they haven't paid for. Such illegal duplicators are called pirates; the act of illegally duplicating software, music, or movies is called **piracy**. Software and music have long been illegally copied with the use of the Internet and CD and DVD burners.

When the Recording Industry Association of America (RIAA) launched lawsuits against individuals for illegally sharing music, Internet traffic to music-sharing Internet sites such as Kazaa and Morpheus fell dramatically.[15] Sharman Networks, the distributor of Kazaa software, claimed that some entertainment companies were illegally downloading Kazaa software in attempts to locate file sharers.[16] Kazaa also has a pay-for service.

In another example, the movie *Matrix Reloaded* could be downloaded illegally on the Internet a few weeks after it was released (see Figure 12.3).[17] Today, the movie industry is very concerned about movies being copied using the Internet and DVD burners. DVD X Copy, for example, can be used to back up important

FIGURE 12.3 • Software and music piracy
Respectcopyright.org, a Web site sponsored by the Motion Pictures Association of America (MPAA), educates consumers on the value of protecting copyrighted works against piracy.

software and data, and can also be used to copy movies from DVDs.[18] One company, 321 Studios, the maker of DVD X Copy, claims that the software can be used to allow consumers to create backup copies of their movie collection in case the original DVDs are ruined.[19]

Software, music, and movies are typically protected by copyright. A **copyright** means that others can't use or duplicate your work or intellectual property without your consent. Software companies use copyright laws to protect their software and receive payment when other people use their software. The U.S. Naval Academy, for example, disciplined about 85 students for illegally copying and swapping copyrighted music and movies using Naval Academy equipment.[20] Technically, a software purchaser is only granted the right to use the software under certain conditions; they don't really own the software. These conditions usually include making only one backup copy of the software in case problems arise or the original is destroyed. Writers and musicians use copyrights to protect their books and music. Writers and musicians are paid royalties when their books or music are sold or used. The *fair use doctrine* describes when and how copyrighted material can be legally used. The *Digital Millennium Copyright Act* provides global copyright protection.

Electronic Plagiarism. **Electronic Plagiarism** involves using computer systems or the Internet to pass off someone else's work as your own. If you take another person's writing or work and turn it in to a teacher as if it were your own work, you are plagiarizing. If a news reporter uses another reporter's story as his or her own story, it is plagiarism. With the Internet and the ability to easily copy files, plagiarism is becoming easier to commit. Internet sites, for example, sell term papers and research papers to anyone who wants to pay the price.[21] To prevent and detect plagiarism, teachers from grade school to graduate school are starting to search files electronically for duplicate passages.[22]

Electronic Libel. *Electronic Libel* is a written statement about a person that is not true and can cause the person harm, where the written statement is produced using a computer system or over the Internet. Slander and libel, whether done using a computer system, the Internet, or any other means, can result in a lawsuit. The Rocker Management hedge fund, for example, sued 17 investors for libel for posting false information on Internet message boards.[23] The Australian High Court has determined that an Australian businessman could bring a libel case against an individual who posted an article on a U.S. Web site.[24] The author of the article has made an appeal to the United Nations High Commissioner on the basis of his right to free speech. Some insurance companies have started to offer "cyber-liability coverage" to protect clients from libel cases.[25]

Denial-of-Service Attack. A *denial-of-service attack* is caused by a person or group sending an Internet site thousands or millions of access attempts or requests. The result is that the Internet site is overwhelmed, and no one is able to gain access to the Web site. Depending on the Internet site, a denial-of-service attack can be an inconvenience or it can be very damaging. A bank, stock brokerage firm, or a company buying or selling products and services over the Internet can be severely hurt with a denial-of-service attack. In some cases, an attack may not completely shut down a Web site, but result in a *delay-of-service*, where the Web site is very slow to respond.

Preventing Computer-Related Crime

Because of increased computer use today, a greater emphasis is placed on the prevention and detection of computer crime. All over the United States, private users, organizations, employees, and public officials are making individual and group efforts to curb such crime. Deloitte & Touche, for example, uses forensics approaches to help detect employee fraud.[26] On one weekend raid, the company was hired to photograph employee desks, copy employee hard disks, and explore work areas without being detected by employees.

Preventing Unauthorized Access to Computer Systems. There are a number of ways to prevent unauthorized access to computer systems. The primary approaches are to use something you know, something you have, or something about you.

- Something you know. *Usernames* and *passwords* are popular ways of preventing unauthorized access and can be implemented on most computer systems, including personal computers and PDAs (see Figure 12.4). A personal identification number (PIN) is an example of a security procedure that is used when you withdraw funds from a bank or make other financial transactions.

- Something you have. ID cards and badges are often used to authorize access to secure areas, such as computer systems rooms.

- Something about you. A **biometric device** is based on something about you. Devices that can read fingerprints, facial characteristics, and retinal or eye characteristics are examples of biometric devices (see Figure 12.5). The Kennedy International Airport in New York, for example, uses an iris recognition system by Iridian Technologies to screen employees who have access to the tarmac or runways.[27] The U.S. Department of Homeland Security is planning on spending about $400 million on various biometric devices to screen visitors entering U.S. borders.[28]

FIGURE 12.4 • Windows logon screen

From home use to network use operating systems offer you the ability to secure access to your computer with password verification.

FIGURE 12.5 • Face recognition system

A face recognition system is an example of a biometric device.

Using Technology to Fight Computer Crime. Organizations are serious in their efforts to fight computer crime. In many cases, organizations have designed procedures and specialized hardware and software to protect their organizational data and systems. Specialized hardware and software, such as *encryption devices*, can be used to encode data and information to help prevent unauthorized use.

Any organization using a computer system should be actively involved in crime prevention and detection. One of the best ways to become involved is to design protective security systems into a computer system before it is built and placed into operation. Another strategy is to assign the various data-processing tasks to a number of people. Separating computer tasks and responsibilities helps prevent crime because the people involved can act as a check on each other.

A knowledge of some of the methods used to commit crime can help prevent and detect computer crime, and help develop systems resistant to computer crime. Even though the number of potential computer crimes appears to be limitless, the actual methods used to commit these crimes are limited and fall into a few specific categories (see Table 12.1).

TABLE 12.1 • Some Common Methods Used to Commit Computer Crimes

Methods Used to Commit Computer Crime	Examples
Add, delete, or change inputs to the computer system	An employee could change the hours he or she worked from 25 to 40 on a time card or work report.
Modify or develop computer programs that commit the crime	A programmer at a bank could modify a loan program to put a few cents into his or her account when loan payments are deposited by bank customers.
Alter or modify the data files used by the computer system	A high-school student might break into a teacher's office and change a grade on an assignment in the teacher's student grades spreadsheet program.
Operate the computer system in such a way as to commit computer crime	A corporate accountant might force the computer to be operated to hide expenses or inflate revenues to get higher bonuses at the end of the year.
Divert or misuse valid output from the computer system	A secretary at a small property management company might take valid rent checks from property owners and forge them to get extra money.

PRIVACY

Another important social issue involves privacy. Basically, the issue of privacy deals with the collection and use or misuse of data. Data on each of us is constantly being collected and stored. This data is often distributed over easily accessed networks without our knowledge or consent. Concerns of privacy regarding this data must be addressed. This section describes an individual's basic right to privacy, discusses privacy issues, and describes privacy legislation.

The Basic Right to Privacy

In 1890, U.S. Supreme Court Justice Louis Brandeis stated that the "right to be let alone" is one of the most "comprehensive of rights and the most valued by civilized man." With modern computers, the right to privacy is an especially challenging problem. More data and information is produced and used or misused today than ever before.

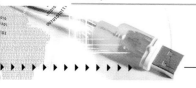

A difficult question yet to be answered is, "Who owns this information and knowledge?" If a public or private organization spends time and resources in obtaining data on you, does the organization own the data, and can it use the data in any way it desires? Government legislation answers these questions to some extent for federal agencies, but many questions remain unanswered for private organizations.

Privacy Issues

Privacy is an important issue to address for the simple reason that data on an individual can be collected, stored, and used without that person's knowledge or consent. When someone is born, takes certain exams, starts working, enrolls in a college course, applies for a driver's license, purchases a car, serves in the military, gets married, buys insurance, gets a library card, applies for a charge card or loan, buys a house, or merely purchases certain products, data is collected and stored somewhere in computer files.

The federal government is perhaps the largest collector of data. There are billions of records on individuals, collected by numerous federal agencies. Other data collectors include state and local governments and profit and nonprofit organizations of all types and sizes. Even supermarket and grocery store checkout systems can collect financial and personal information on customers. By combining customer information obtained through the use of a credit or debit card with product information obtained through bar codes, point-of-sale devices, and coupons, these types of systems provide companies with customer/product profiles. Data from sales and checkout scanners is also used by some companies that specialize in marketing databases to provide organizations with names and information about potential customers. At what point does this practice infringe on privacy? A more obvious infringement of privacy involves cases where people who log on to the Internet have had their hard disks scanned or searched.

The right to privacy at work is an equally important issue. Some experts believe there will be a collision between workers who want to maintain their privacy and companies that demand to know more about their employees. *Employee monitoring* involves an organization collecting data on what employees do at work. Workers may find that they are being closely monitored via computer technology while on their employer's property or networks. These computer-monitoring systems tie directly into computerized workstations; specialized computer programs can keep track of every keystroke made by a user. This type of system can determine what workers are doing every second of the day. It can determine if a person is doing his or her job correctly and how many breaks he or she is taking (see Figure 12.6). An employee's e-mail can be monitored and used against that person in a court of law. Employees can be prosecuted for sexual harassment, stealing company secrets, racial discrimination, and other offenses based on the e-mail an employee sends to others. Many workers consider this type of supervision dehumanizing. Some are even fighting back by using wireless hand-held computers while at restaurants, doing errands, or away from their desks.[29] The wireless computers send signals to the desktop computer at work to make it look as if the employee is hard at work at the office.

FIGURE 12.6 • Employee monitoring
Companies are very interested in knowing just how hard their employees are working, even at the expense of individual privacy.

E-mail, in particular, raises some interesting issues about work privacy. Some employees feel there is not enough privacy guaranteed. In some organizations e-mail has been monitored by managers and others without the knowledge or consent of employees (see Figure 12.7). On the other hand, the use of e-mail among public officials may violate "open meeting" laws. These laws, which apply to many local, state, and federal agencies, prevent public officials from meeting in private about matters that have an impact on the state or local area. So in some parts of society, e-mail is considered not private and open to inspection—essentially public— and in other parts of society, e-mail is considered private, rather than public.

FIGURE 12.7 • E-mail has forever changed how workers and managers communicate
With e-mail, people can communicate in the same building or around the world. E-mail, however, can be monitored and intercepted. The convenience of e-mail must be balanced with the potential for privacy invasion.

How Information about You Is Obtained

Information about you is collected, stored, and used every day. In some cases, you willingly provide information. In other cases, you don't have any control or knowledge that the information is obtained about you. Here are some of the ways that information about you is obtained:

- You willingly give information to others. This can happen when you fill out a warranty card on a product you purchase, enter a contest, or register to use an Internet site.
- You buy products and services. When you purchase groceries, buy clothes, or enroll in a class, a vast amount of information is collected about you. When you use credit cards, it is easy for companies to track your buying habits. Your credit card activity can also reveal a history of your whereabouts.
- You interact with the federal government and state agencies. The federal government and state agencies are perhaps the largest collectors of information about you. If you file a tax return, get married, get a ticket for speeding, file for bankruptcy, or interact with federal or state agencies in other ways, a record of the information is kept in a computer system.
- You use the Internet: Cookies. Recall from Chapter 4 that when you visit some Web sites, the site places a text file, called a *cookie*, on your hard disk. The cookie stores information about you, information you typed into Web forms, and a history of where on the Web site you visited. When you visit the Web site again, the site checks your computer for any existing cookies. If you buy books online, for example, the Internet site can store information about the books you buy, such as mystery novels, in a cookie on your computer's hard disk. When you visit the online bookstore again, it knows your preferences for mystery novels.
- You use the Internet: Spyware and adware. *Spyware* and *adware* can be placed on your computer system without your knowledge or consent, normally through the Internet, to secretly spy on you and collect information. It is not used to help a company serve you by knowing your preferences like a cookie. Some downloaded software may record your Internet habits, deliver advertising, collect private information, or modify your system settings. Pay close attention to the end-user license agreement and installation options. Spyware and adware are there to see who you are and what you are doing, which can sometimes be harmful to you. Marc Heatherington's PC firewall, for example, told him that his PC was sending Internet traffic every few minutes to another Internet site.[30] The site was a marketing firm that was collecting data on Marc's PC and his Internet browsing habits, including IP addresses, Web logs, browser type, and the types and versions of software installed on Marc's PC. Marc had no idea that the spyware was on his computer and sending out information it collected.

In addition to collecting information about you, companies often share your information with or sell it to others. This information can then be combined to produce comprehensive profiles about you that can be used without your knowledge or consent. As a result, you could be bombarded with promotions on travel, debt consolidation, stereo equipment, diet programs, and much more. When these unwanted promotions are sent to you by e-mail, it is called *spam*, first discussed in Chapter 4.

The Impact of Privacy Invasion

Every day, people generate a trail of information without knowing how this information will be used. Yet, the impact of privacy invasion can be very serious.

COMMUNITY /\/\/\ TECHNOLOGY

DoubleClick Tempers Marketing with Customer Privacy

By storing information on the customer's computer, in data packages called cookies, businesses can track a customer's movement around a Web site. By enticing the customer to supply his or her name and other personal information, for instance, by signing up for a "free" user account to access special services, the retailer is able to connect the user profile with a name and to store that information in its database. Through *data mining*, companies can sift through the combined information of any one customer or group of customers to recognize trends and tendencies—and ultimately pitch products and services specifically for that customer's interests.

In general, consumer privacy advocates maintain that consumers have the right to know what information is being stored about them and control how that information is used. Take, for example, the New York–based Internet advertising company DoubleClick. DoubleClick is a marketing company that, among other things, provides Internet-based advertising services through direct e-mail and banner ads on the Web. By placing banner ads on numerous Web sites, DoubleClick can collect a vast amount of customer information from multiple sources to get a complete picture of a person's buying patterns and preferences.

The balance between effective marketing and respect for customer privacy is a difficult one to reach. Like DoubleClick, most e-commerce retailers have published privacy policies by which they are legally bound. Some e-commerce retailers have posted ads that resemble computer-warning messages and have been sued for deceptive advertising.[31] The Federal Trade Commission has ruled that unless otherwise stated, these policies extend to a company's offline data practices as well.

Questions

1. What methods of collecting consumer information were used prior to the Internet? How do you think the Internet has changed marketing approaches in general?
2. Aside from the public concerns over customer profiling, are there any customer benefits to profiling? List some.

Sources
1. *"Putting the Ethics in E-Business," Zachary Tobias,* Computer-World, *November 6, 2000, www.computerworld.com*
2. *"DoubleClick Drops 'Intelligent Targeting' Product,"* Newsbytes, *January 9, 2002, www.washingtonpost.com/wp-dyn/technology*
3. *Brian Krebs, "Online Privacy Policies Apply to Offline Data Practices— FTC,"* Newsbytes, *December 10, 2001*
4. *www.networkadvertising.org, follow links to "About NAI," "Principles", accessed January 27, 2002*
5. *www.doubleclick.net, follow links to "Privacy Policy," accessed January 27, 2002*

In addition, there can be a trade off between security and privacy. Some people and organizations are concerned that the recent moves to tighten security to prevent terrorism can potentially invade individual privacy (see Figure 12.8). The U.S. Patriot Act, for example, gives broad powers to the FBI and other federal agencies to obtain school, health, financial, Web, and other personal information about people suspected of possible terrorist activities.[32] For example, the Patriot Act allows the FBI to collect personal information from libraries and bookstore records without a court order or criminal warrant. The Electronic Privacy Information Center and the American Civil Liberties Union have concerns about the Computer Assisted Passenger Pre-Screening System.[33] The system allows airline companies to collect passenger information during ticketing and reservations for security purposes.

FIGURE 12.8 • Airport security response to terrorism

In the effort to maintain security, the government is enacting tighter security at airports as well as through increased scrutiny, which treads on individual freedom.

Fairness in Information Use

The information market is so lucrative, it seems likely that many companies will continue to store and sell the data they collect on customers, employees, and others. When is this information storage and use fair to the individuals whose data is stored and sold? Do individuals have a right to know about data stored about them and to decide what data is stored and used? For example, the national Do-Not-Call list, started in the fall of 2003, gives people the ability to decide if they want to be called by telemarketers—people can now decide how their telephone number can be used. As shown in Table 12.2, these questions about rights can be broken down into four issues that should be addressed: knowledge, control, notice, and consent.

TABLE 12.2 • The Right to Know and the Ability to Decide

Fairness Issues	Database Storage	Database Usage
The right to know	Knowledge	Notice
The ability to decide	Control	Consent

- Knowledge. Individuals should have knowledge of what data is stored on them. In some cases, individuals are informed that information on them is stored in an organization's database. In others, individuals do not know that their personal information is stored in one or more databases.
- Control. Individuals should have the ability to correct errors in database systems. This is possible with most organizations, although it can be difficult in some cases.

- Notice. When an organization uses personal data for a purpose other the original purpose, individuals should be notified in advance. For example, if a charge card, credit bureau, or grocery store decides to sell information they collected to another organization, individuals should be told in advance.
- Consent. If information on individuals is to be used for other purposes, these individuals should be asked to give their consent before data on them is used. Many organizations do not give individuals the ability to decide if information on them will be sold or used for other purposes.

Federal Privacy Laws and Regulations

In the past few decades, some significant laws have been passed regarding an individual's right to privacy. Not all laws increase privacy. Each year, legislation is introduced that could reduce privacy protection. Some people believe that the Patriot Act, which is designed to prevent terrorism in the United States, might actually decrease privacy protections. The following are a few laws that have an impact on privacy.

- The Fair Credit Reporting Act (FCRA) regulates the operation of credit bureaus. This law specifies how credit bureaus are to collect, store, and use credit information.
- The **Privacy Act** is the major piece of legislation on privacy, enacted by Congress in 1974. The Privacy Act applies only to certain federal agencies, but it serves as a privacy guideline for private organizations as well.
- The Tax Reform Act (TRA) restricts the IRS in obtaining and using certain types of personal information.
- The Electronic Funds Transfer (EFT) Act, which went into effect in 1979 and 1980, outlines the responsibilities of companies using electronic funds transfer systems. This act also covers consumer rights and stipulates customer liability for bank cards (debit cards).
- The Right to Financial Privacy Act places restrictions on the government concerning access to certain records held by financial institutions.
- The Freedom of Information Act permits individuals to have access to personal data contained in federal agency files.
- The Education Privacy Act restricts the collection and use of data for federally funded institutions. This particular act stipulates that only certain types of data may be collected, that parents and students may have access to the data, and that education-related records may be disclosed only to school officials or to state and federal educational agencies.
- The Financial Service Modernization Act requires that financial institutions not sell or share customer information unless permission from the customer is obtained.
- The Computer Matching and Privacy Act regulates the matching of federal computer files to verify information. For example, this act helps the federal government determine if people are eligible for certain federal programs.
- The Health Insurance Portability and Accountability Act requires healthcare organizations to develop policies to keep patient health information private.
- The Patriot Act was passed in the U.S. in 2001 to protect the country against terrorism, but some people believe that it relaxes privacy protections. The act allows the FBI and other federal agencies to get information from telephone companies, financial institutions, medical facilities, and other organizations if it is related to terrorism without your consent and without court orders.

State and International Privacy Laws and Regulations

A number of states either have or are proposing their own privacy legislation. California, for example, has a privacy law that went into effect in July, 2003, that requires companies that do business in California to notify California residences of possible security attacks that could have an adverse impact.[34] Many people believe that the only way to reduce the amount of federal interference and legislation is to have the various states legislate their own privacy laws. Some of the proposed state legislation is more comprehensive and covers more organizations than some federal laws. The use of Social Security numbers and medical records, the disclosure of unlisted telephone numbers by telephone companies and credit reports by credit bureaus, the disclosure of bank and personal financial information, and the use of criminal files are some of the issues being considered by state legislators (see Figure 12.9). Furthermore, many of these proposed legislative actions apply to both public and private organizations. Concerns about privacy are being addressed around the world, not just in the United States. Japan's Lower House has passed a privacy law that requires companies to notify individuals when they collect information about them.[35] The law also prohibits companies from sharing personal information without an individual's prior consent.

FIGURE 12.9 • US Search

It can be very easy for anyone to find out anything about each of us.

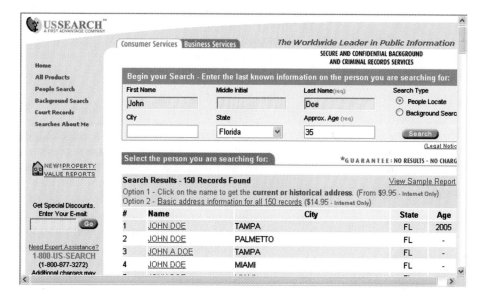

Organizational Privacy Policies

Even though privacy laws for organizations are not very restrictive, most organizations are very sensitive to privacy issues and fairness. They realize that invasion of privacy problems can hurt them. In a business, inadequate privacy protections can turn away customers and dramatically reduce revenues and profits.

Some organizations even have a privacy bill of rights that specifies how the privacy of employees, clients, and customers is to be protected. Corporate privacy policies should address a customer's knowledge, control, notice, and consent over the storage and use of information. It may also cover who has access to private data and when it may be used. In some cases, these privacy policies and controls can be built into software or database management systems. In others, work procedures can establish data access and use restrictions. These policies determine the knowledge, control, notice, and consent factors discussed earlier.

EXPAND YOUR
KNOWLEDGE

To learn more about protecting your
privacy, go to www.course.com/swt.
Click the link "Expand Your Knowledge,"
and then complete the lab entitled,
"Protecting Your Privacy Online."

Protecting Yourself from Privacy Invasion

One of the best ways to protect your privacy is to be careful when sharing information with other people and organizations you don't know or trust. Before you do business with an organization, you can check out its privacy policies, if they have any. But sometimes even checking an organization's credentials doesn't protect you from privacy invasion. One person, for example, purchased computer batteries on the Internet, but he used a unique version of his name.[36] The Internet site had the TRUSTe icon, which assures customers that their privacy is being maintained. Yet, the person started getting journals and other unsolicited ads, all sent to the unique version of his name, meaning that it had come through the Internet battery site.

Software, such as the **Platform for Privacy Preferences**, is being developed to help protect your privacy. This type of software has the potential to alert you to companies that don't have adequate privacy policies according to preferences that you specify. It is being developed primarily for Internet usage.

ISSUESINTHEWORKENVIRONMENT

Computer systems have changed the makeup of the work force. Jobs that require computer systems competency have increased, while many less-skilled positions have been eliminated. Even the simplest tasks have been aided by computers, making cash registers faster, causing order processing to be smoother, and allowing the disabled to participate more actively in the work force. As computers drop in cost and become easier to use, more workers will benefit from the increased productivity and efficiency they provide. But there are work issues, including health and job concerns.

Health Concerns and Issues

There are a number of health concerns in today's work environment. For some people, working with computers can cause occupational stress. Feelings of job insecurity, loss of control, incompetence, and demotion are just a few of the fears people might experience. These fears could become a serious problem for some employees. Some experts believe this fear might cause threatened workers to sabotage computer systems and equipment. If a manager determines that an employee has this type of fear, training and counseling can often help the employee and avoid potential problems.

There are many other potential health problems. As more organizations benefit from computerization, more people will suffer from computer-related problems and hazards. Claims relating to repetitive motion disorder, which can be caused by working with computer keyboards and other equipment, have increased greatly. As discussed in Chapter 1, **repetitive stress injury (RSI)** can cause problems that include tendonitis, tennis elbow, the inability to hold objects, and sharp pain in the fingers. **Carpal tunnel syndrome (CTS)** is the aggravation of the pathway for nerves that travel through the wrist (the carpal tunnel). CTS involves wrist pain, a feeling of tingling and numbness, and difficulty in grasping and holding objects. It may be caused by a number of factors, such as stress, lack of exercise, and the repetitive motion of typing on a computer keyboard. Working long

TECHNOLOGY LEARNING CURVE

Technological devices now permeate every avenue of life from work to play, and consumers are having to develop a certain level of technical proficiency fast. Tech support lines are unreliable or costly, "plug" isn't always "play," and software often comes with glitches. It takes time and energy to do your own troubleshooting and repair—time that's unpaid if you are self-employed, that's unproductive if your are an employee, or that you might prefer to spend another way if at home.

Source:
"Techies by Necessity, Not by Choice"
By Katie Hafner
The New York Times
www.nytimes.com/2003/07/24/technology/circuits/24boot.html
July 25, 2003
Cited on July 25, 2003

hours staring at a computer screen without proper light can cause a variety of vision problems. In some cases, your eyes will get tired, itch, or even burn. In more severe cases, double or blurred vision can result, making it unpleasant to work and reducing your efficiency. In addition to wrists and eyes, you can get a sore back, sore arms, and headaches from long hours working with computer systems without adequate breaks. Even children can get CTS from long sessions with computers.[37]

Other work-related health hazards involve emissions from improperly maintained and used equipment. Some studies show that poorly maintained laser printers may release ozone into the air; others dispute the claim. Most computer manufacturers publish technical information on emissions from their screens, and many organizations pay close attention to this information.

Mental-Health and Related Problems

In additional to physical health concerns, the use of computer systems can cause a variety of mental-health issues and related problems. These include gambling, information overload and stress, and Internet addiction and isolation.

Gambling. Compulsive gambling is a problem for some people using the Internet. According to Media Metrix, illegal gambling is the eighth largest business on the Internet.[38] Although Internet gambling is illegal in the United States, it is not illegal in other countries. As a result, Web sites have surfaced in foreign countries that permit gambling on the Internet. Compulsive gamblers find using the Internet to be much easier than driving to a gambling casino.

Information Overload and Stress. For some people, computer systems and the Internet are a source of information overload and stress. These people have trouble handling the vast amount of information available through today's computer systems. This is especially true for people who are afraid of computer systems or do not have adequate computer skills. For them, a minor computer problem or a simple need to get information can become a nightmare because they don't know how to solve computer problems or perform basic computer functions, such as retrieving an attachment sent via e-mail.

Internet Addiction and Isolation. The use of the Internet can be addictive. Some people spend most of their time connected to the Internet and staring at the computer screen (see Figure 12.10). When this behavior becomes compulsive, it can interfere with normal daily activities, including work, relationships with others, and other activities. Often, Internet addiction means that a person is isolated and doesn't interact with other people, unless they are also online. Some people have used the Americans with Disabilities Act to sue companies for firing them for using the Internet at work for personal purposes, claiming that their Internet usage at work is a mental disorder.[39]

FIGURE 12.10 • Internet addiction
Internet addiction can cause otherwise normal people to become withdrawn and isolated.

Avoiding Health and Related Problems

Many computer-related health problems are minor and caused by a poorly designed work environment. The computer screen may be hard to read, with the problems of glare and poor contrast. Desks and chairs may be uncomfortable. Keyboards and computer screens may be fixed and difficult or impossible to move. The hazardous activities associated with these types of unfavorable conditions are collectively referred to as *work stressors*. Although these problems may not be of major concern to casual users of computer systems, continued stressors such as repetitive motion, awkward posture, and eyestrain may cause more serious and long-term injuries. If nothing else, these problems can limit productivity and performance.

Ergonomics is the applied science of designing and arranging the things we work with, such as computer systems, in a manner that promotes health. The field has suggested a number of approaches to reducing health problems. The slope of the keyboard, the positioning and design of display screens, and the placement and design of computer tables and chairs have been carefully studied. Flexibility is a major component of ergonomics and an important feature of computer devices. People of differing sizes and tastes require different positioning of equipment for best results. Some people, for example, want to have the keyboard in their laps; others prefer to place the keyboard on a solid table. Because of these individual differences, computer designers are attempting to develop systems that provide a great deal of flexibility.

Like other industries, the computer industry is investigating ways to be kinder to the environment. One approach is developing PCs that use less power. To reduce power usage, the EPA has initiated the **Energy Star program**. An Energy Star (see Figure 12.11) personal computer has restrictions on how much power it can consume while being used. Organizations are also starting to recycle laser ink cartridges and rechargeable computer batteries for laptop computers.

Computer systems are also being used to help people with disabilities or other health-related problems. According to Richard Atwood, vice president of CIA Corporation, "All government agencies are required to make their systems and content accessible to disabled users under Section 508."[40] The Royal Blind School in Edinburgh, Scotland uses screen enlargement software to make computers screens easier to read and use.[41] The school also uses an audio software package, called JAWS, to allow students to open and use Microsoft Office applications, write e-mails, and perform other tasks that normally require being able to see a computer screen (see Figure 12.12). Some phone companies can use Web cameras attached to a deaf person's computer. When the person makes a call and uses sign language to communicate, an operator translates the hand signals to a hearing person at the other end of the line.[42]

FIGURE 12.11 • Energy Star program

Computers that have the Energy Star power management features are designed to conserve electricity when not in use.

FIGURE 12.12 • Computers help with disabilities

Increasingly, computer systems are being used to help people with disabilities or other health-related problems.

Job Concerns

The use of computer systems has created job opportunities and career advancement for many people. In addition to computer systems personnel, people in noncomputer careers have greatly benefited from computer systems. People in architecture, medicine, science, music, the arts, business, the military, and many other areas have seen their careers and salaries soar as a result of using computer systems. Yet, the use of computer systems has created a number of job issues and concerns, including job loss, outsourcing, job transfer to overseas companies, and the importation of people to perform computer-related jobs.

Job Loss. Although computer systems have created many new jobs, jobs have also been cut or lost as a result of computer systems and automation. In general, more jobs have been created than lost. Young, college-educated people have benefited the most from the use of computer systems, while older workers not skilled in the use of computer systems have seen their career advancement slow or their jobs eliminated. Continuing education, distance learning, and training offered by companies and organizations can help older people or people with less computer training take advantage of computer systems at work, at home, and in their personal lives.

Outsourcing. *Outsourcing* involves taking jobs that were once performed inside the organization or company and transferring them to outside organizations or companies (see Figure 12.13). Accenture and EDS, for example, are outsourcing companies that will perform some or all of an organization's computer processing activities. For a fee, these companies will write software, manage and run computer systems departments, help an organization acquire hardware and software, manage an organization's Internet site, and handle almost any other activity or task related to acquiring and using a computer system.

FIGURE 12.13 • Outsourcing

Outsourcing involves taking jobs that were once performed inside the organization or company and transferring them to outside organizations or companies.

Transferring Jobs to Overseas Companies. As a result of global communications systems and high-speed Internet connections, companies are increasingly outsourcing computer jobs to overseas companies. The objective is to reduce costs. Some U.S. personal computer manufacturers, for example, have moved their help-desk operations to India or Asia. If you call the PC manufacturer in the United States with a problem, your call can be routed overseas to a foreign company, where your problem will hopefully be solved. Software companies are also transferring jobs to overseas companies. Programmers and systems analysts located around the world are now being used to write software. The finished software can be easily and quickly sent to the software company using high-speed Internet connections. Outsourcing work to companies outside the United States is commonly referred to as hiring offshore. As long as labor costs are less expensive in another country, transferring jobs to overseas companies will continue to be popular.

Importing Workers from Other Countries. Companies often try to hire people from other countries to get additional people skilled in computer systems or to reduce labor costs. In the United States, for example, the H-1B visa program allows companies to hire foreign workers on a temporary basis if the foreign worker has special skills. This can help companies by giving them a larger and sometimes cheaper work force. Some technology workers, on the other hand, believe that it hurts their ability to get work.

ETHICALISSUESINCOMPUTERSYSTEMS

Ethical issues deal with what is generally considered right or wrong. Even with the emphasis on ethical behavior today, we continue to see situations that are unethical, illegal, or both. We begin this section with an introduction to ethical issues in computer systems.

Ethical Issues in Computer Systems

When it comes to computer systems, ethical issues involve the use to which these computer systems are put. These issues involve a number of areas, including accuracy and electronic deception, and access.

Accuracy and Electronic Deception. Numerous problems have been caused by inaccurate data stored in computer systems. An individual's credit can be improperly denied as a result of faulty or dated information. People have been denied a home mortgage, admission to school, and employment because of inaccurate data. Accuracy issues include:

- Who is responsible for data and information accuracy?
- Who is accountable or liable for storing and disseminating inaccurate data and information?
- What safeguards have been established to ensure accuracy?
- What can individuals do to make sure that data stored on them is accurate?

Although data files are usually used correctly and justifiably, there are many potential opportunities for misuse. Organizations have refused to hire individuals because of faulty data files maintained by firms charged with doing background checks. Furthermore, there may be facts that people do not want to become common knowledge, such as treatment for medical problems or past bankruptcy filings.

Electronic Deception involves using computer systems and the Internet to intentionally lie and deceive. In some cases, a man will lie about his age or interests to lure women on Internet dating sites. During the corporate scandals of the early 2000s, some people posted false information about stocks on the Internet, hoping to make a quick profit. Others used computer systems to make corporate profits appear higher than they really were in order to get higher bonuses or a higher value on their stock options at the end of the year. Some people looking for jobs create false resumes and place them on Internet job sites. Today, researchers are investigating if people are more likely to lie and deceive electronically and if there are electronic means to detect these lies and deceptions.

Access. The issue of access deals with the ability of individuals to gain entry into information and computer systems. Some of the specific issues include:

- What information does a person have a right to access?
- What safeguards exist for information use?
- What should be done for people not skilled enough to use computer systems or too poor to afford access to computer systems?

Should an individual, for example, have the right to see and correct private information stored in public and private databases? Perhaps a company has a database on the credit history of past customers. Should all individuals in this database have the right to see and correct this information? A number of federal laws described in this chapter allow this type of access to federal databases, but there is a lack of comprehensive federal law pertaining to private companies.

Should companies have the right to sell sensitive personal information in their databases to others? For years, organizations have rented or sold all or parts of their databases to others. Once your information is sold to another organization, it can be used without your knowledge and in almost any fashion.

Access also depends on literacy and economics. Some individuals who are not trained or skilled in computer systems may not be able to use them wisely. In other words, their lack of computer systems competency prevents them from access. In addition, access to databases requires relatively expensive equipment, such as personal computers and a connection to the Internet. Some individuals without financial resources are unable to gain access to computer systems and the Internet.

Ethical Codes of Conduct

A number of organizations and associations have developed codes of ethics. Ethical codes of conduct can foster ethical behavior in the organization and give confidence to people who interact with the organization, including clients and customers. Some organizations and associations that have developed an ethical code of conduct include:

- Computer Professionals for Social Responsibility (CPSR)
- Association of Information Technology Professionals (AITP)
- The Association for Computing Machinery (ACM)
- The Institute of Electrical and Electronics Engineers (IEEE)
- The British Computer Society (BCS)

COMMUNITY TECHNOLOGY

The Digital Divide

If you are typical of those who purchase this book, you are among a group of individuals who are considered electronically "connected." You communicate with others through e-mail, and rely on the Web for information and entertainment. Your biggest concerns regarding technology may be to find low-cost broadband Internet access, and to reduce the amount of junk mail you find in your e-mail box each day.

Think about the changes that computing and the Internet have brought about in your life. Using your computer you can access information on nearly any subject and communicate with everyone from your classmates to your teacher to the president of your college. Using computers and having access to the Internet provides tremendous advantages that assist us in defining and meeting our personal and professional goals. But where does that leave people who cannot afford a computer and the training to use it?

We use the term *digital divide* to refer to the gap between people who have access to computers and can effectively use new information and communication tools, such as the Internet, and those who do not have computer access or the training to use computers. The digital divide can exist in a number of geographic scopes: local, national, and international.

The digital divide in the U.S., although of significant concern, has been shrinking over the last 3 years. Internet users in the low income range (people earning less than $25,000 a year) soared by 46 percent in 2001, making them the fastest growing segment of Internet users. According to a 2002 study by the U.S. Department of Commerce (USDC), more than half of the nation is online, with two million new Internet users per month. The USDC credits the school system for leveling the playing field, stating that "computers at schools substantially narrow the gap in computer usage rates for children from high and low income families."

The situation with the *global* digital divide is less optimistic. The World Economic Forum Web site states that industrialized countries, with only 15 percent of the world's population, are home to 88 percent of all Internet users. Finland alone has more Internet users than the whole of Latin America. A study by Neilsen/Netratings found that:

- The United States has more computers than the rest of the world combined.
- 41 percent of the global online population is in the United States and Canada.
- 27 percent of the online population lives in Europe, the Middle East, and Africa. (25 percent of European homes are online.)
- 20 percent of the online population logs on from Asia Pacific. (33 percent of all Asian homes are online.)
- Only 4 percent of the world's online population are in South America.

If we are to utilize computers and the Internet to build a global community, it's clear that the more affluent neighborhoods cannot ignore the needs of the underdeveloped countries.

Questions

1. A new neighbor moves in next door. This person is the same age, gender, and race as you with one major difference: the new neighbor has never touched a computer. What professional advantages do you have over your new neighbor? What personal advantages do you have over your new neighbor? Are you inclined to help this person?

2. Name three significant benefits of investing in underdeveloped countries to build an inclusive global economy.

3. Is it possible to include all nations in the global community? What about those that shun technology as being an evil Western tool? What will their role be in the global community?

Sources:

1. *Leapfrog the digital divide," Thea Williams, February 28, 2002, http://australianit.news.com.au/.*
2. *"Five Thoughts About the Digital Divide," Jon Surmacz. September 13, 2001, www.darwinmag.com/.*
3. *"Global Digital Divide Still Very Much in Existence," Michael Pastore, http://cyberatlas.internet.com, accessed March 1, 2002*
4. *"Digital Divide Basics Fact Sheet," Digital Divide Network Staff, Benton Foundation, www.digitaldividenetwork.org, accessed March 1, 2002.*
5. *"A Nation Online: How Americans Are Expanding Their Use of the Internet," a report by the National Telecommunications and Information Administration (NTIA) accessed at www.ntia.doc.gov/ntiahome/dn/index.html, March 1, 2002.*

COMPUTERWASTE,MISTAKES,ANDOTHERSOCIALISSUES

Computer waste and mistakes are major causes of computer problems. Computer waste involves the inappropriate use of computer technology and resources. Computer mistakes refer to errors, failures, and other computer problems that make computer output incorrect or not useful. In this section, we explore the damage that can be done as a result of computer waste and mistakes. In addition, there are other important social issues to consider.

Computer Waste

Computer waste is found in the public sector and the private sector. Some organizations discard old floppy disks and even complete computer systems when they still have value. Others waste organizational resources to build and maintain complex systems never used to their fullest extent. A less dramatic, yet still relevant, example of waste is the amount of time and money wasted by employees playing computer games. The Internet can often waste people's time. It is easy to send copies of e-mail to dozens or hundreds of people, when they may not need to get copies.[43] As a class project, a student sent out 23 e-mails asking for a response.[44] In a few weeks, her e-mail inbox was jammed with over eight thousand responses. The time it took to delete all the messages was tremendous. Unwanted pop-up ads that appear on some Internet sites (see Figure 12.14) are time-consuming to close or delete and can waste a tremendous amount of time for people trying to get work done on the Internet.[45]

FIGURE 12.14 • Pop-up ads are an example of computer waste

Closing or deleting unwanted pop-up ads can waste a tremendous amount of time for someone working on the Internet.

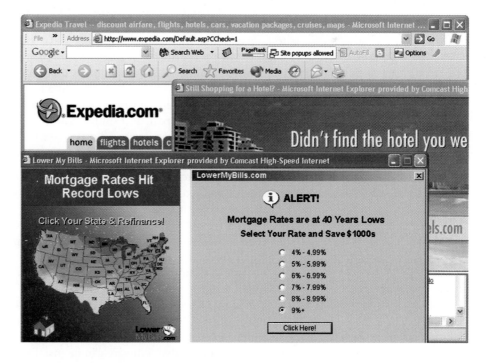

Sometimes the use of information is a nuisance. In other cases, it is more serious. Junk mail, including junk e-mail or *spam* and junk fax, is an example. Because of spam, the computer systems of Bluespring Software, located in Cincinnati, were down for hours, forcing a chief executive officer to miss meetings because his

appointment files could not be used.[46] People who read spam can have their health put in jeopardy if they follow the advice given in the unsolicited e-mail.[47]

Some people receive dozens of unwanted e-mails daily. During a person's lifetime, he or she will receive mail, spam, phone calls, and fax transmissions generated from data files containing names and addresses. This junk correspondence invites people to get credit cards, subscribe to magazines, join a book or record club, or buy encyclopedias, life insurance, vacuum cleaners, or discount clothing—all because their names appear in certain computer files. You can get spam on almost any imaginable product or service. One popular Internet company told the U.S. Senate Commerce Committee that 60 percent to 80 percent of all e-mail received by the company's subscribers was junk or spam.[48] The number of spam e-mails sent each year could reach almost 3 trillion by 2006.[49] The rapid growth of electronic junk mail, such as unsolicited advertisements sent over fax machines or the Internet, is a by-product of enhanced telecommunications.

Some individuals and organizations have fought back against junk phone calls, fax, and spam. Call-back services and automatic number identification are being offered by common communications carriers to help people avoid and identify the source of unwanted phone calls. Federal and state legislators are now passing laws to help curb unwanted spam.[50] A Utah lawyer, for example, has sued over 1,000 companies under Utah's anti-spam laws. U.S. Senator Charles Schumer has proposed a national list of people who don't want to receive unwanted e-mail to help eliminate spam.[51] In December 2003, President Bush signed the Can-Spam bill into law in an effort to regulate spam. The law specifies prison terms as punishment for companies sending e-mails that include misleading subjects.[52] Earth-Link, a large Internet service provider, has a team of people investigating spam senders.[53] In an interesting case, crackers, tired of getting spam, attacked an Internet site sending out spam and shut it down.[54]

In the years to come, laws and software will help curb spam, but here is what you can do to help prevent spam until this happens:

- Know the Source. Only interact with known and respected Internet sites. Don't sign up for free services or products. Avoid contests to win something, such as travel or a free PC.
- Don't Give Away Your Address. According to one study, spammers get 97 percent of their e-mail addresses from addresses posted on Internet sites.[55]
- Don't Try to Unsubcribe from Spam E-Mail. If you try to unsubscribe or opt out of e-mail from a spammer, it will only confirm your e-mail address. It might result in your getting even more spam.
- Use Spam Guards. Some Internet service providers have spam guards to remove spam or to place it in a separate folder or directory to be reviewed or simply deleted.
- Blacklist the Sender. Software can be installed on a computer system that will block (blacklist) the address of spam sites (see Figure 12.15). Any e-mail from this source will be blocked.
- Whitelist the Sender. This approach involves accepting e-mail only from people or locations that you approve and specify.

FIGURE 12.15 • **Spamguard**

Spamguard software blacklists the addresses of spam sites. Any e-mail from these sources will be blocked.

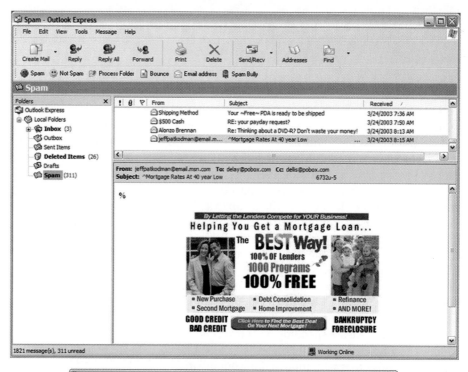

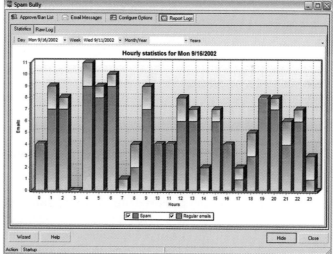

Computer-Related Mistakes

No matter how sophisticated the machine, improperly programmed or operated computers cannot produce meaningful outputs. That is, although computers themselves rarely make mistakes, programmers and other humans responsible for computer systems operations often do. For example, an individual might develop a spreadsheet to analyze home loans or a monthly budget. A mistake in the spreadsheet could be very costly if the homeowner selects the wrong mortgage or spends too much because the budget was wrong. In other cases, a programmer might develop a program that contains errors. In still other cases, a data-entry clerk might enter the wrong data. The speed of computers magnifies any mistake made. As

COMMUNITY TECHNOLOGY

Wasteful Information Systems Running Amok?

Complexity can often result in waste. When computer systems are too complex, they can be difficult to use and almost impossible to integrate with other systems. Companies have wasted millions of dollars trying to get complex systems to work together effectively. Doug Elix, a top IBM executive, has made a plea to the computer industry to work to reduce the complexity of information systems. Elix is an Australian who heads IBM's $35 billion global services division, which accounts for 40 percent of the company's revenue and gross profits. In his address to industry leaders at the World Congress on IT in Adelaide, he stated that technology has become more and more complex to manage, despite incredible advances. "It's staggering to think how much we are spending on integration of complex technology, rather than spending time and money on things that will improve how our organizations perform, or improve the way we live our lives."

According to research company IDC, U.S. companies spent $2.6 trillion on information systems during the last decade, and companies in the Asia-Pacific region spent more than $1.3 trillion. A study by the

Gartner Group found that integrating incompatible programs and systems accounts for 40 percent of all computer systems spending in most organizations. At the current pace, 200 million more information technology workers will be needed to support the billion people, millions of businesses, and one trillion devices that will be connected by the end of this decade. In short, Elix says, "The technology is outstripping the human capacity to manage it."

Questions

1. Why do you think the complexity of computer systems wastes so much time and money?
2. How can organizations persuade technology companies to work together to reduce the cost of technology integration?

Sources
1. *"It's Running Amok, IBM Chief Warns," Ian Grayson,* Australian IT, *March 1, 2002, http://australianit.news.com.au/.*
2. *"IBM: Solve Hi-Tech Complexity," Adrienne Perry,* Infotech Weekly, *March 11, 2002, p.5.*

---

information technology becomes faster, more complex, and more powerful, there is greater risk that organizations and individuals will experience the results of computer-related mistakes.

One major mistake made with computer systems involves poor or inadequate computer systems planning. Numerous negative computer-systems-related consequences have resulted from inadequate systems backup and protection of backup files. Take the example of one organization that was having trouble with its system. From time to time, the system was inadvertently destroying some of the "permanent" data. In order to keep the permanent data available while the organization's computer systems personnel corrected the problem, they decided to store all of the data files on magnetic tape in the same room as the computer for easy access. One fire destroyed both the original files and the backup. In another case, a computer mistake caused thousands of English farmers to not get their support payments.[56]

Preventing Computer-related Waste and Mistakes

Preventing computer-related waste and mistakes like those described should be a goal for any individual or organization. We begin this section by investigating how to prevent computer-related waste.

Preventing Computer-Related Waste. To prevent computer-related waste, individuals should make sure that computer purchases are necessary and cost-justified. For example, to reduce waste, some people print draft manuscripts on the other side of used computer paper. One way that organizations can prevent computer-related waste is to establish procedures regarding efficient disposal of systems and devices that are obsolete or no longer needed (see Figure 12.16). Today, a number of companies have established procedures to avoid computer waste. One company, for example, is in the business of recycling used floppy disks and software. Even the packaging material is recycled. Still another corporation is refurbishing old computer systems for use in developing countries. Some companies donate their used computer systems and devices to schools or charitable organizations. Applying these types of measures to avoid waste is good for the environment, society, and the companies involved.

Establishing policies for system acquisition and use is another way to prevent waste. This is particularly important as more and more individuals and workgroups are requesting computer systems access and use. After the systems have been installed, it is often difficult to monitor how effectively these systems are being used. As a result, some organizations are now developing more stringent policies on the acquisition of computer systems and equipment. Formal justification statements are typically required. In other words, workgroups, managers, and employees who want to acquire computer systems must develop a written document describing how the system would be used and how its cost could be justified in terms of benefits to the organization.

FIGURE 12.16 • Recycling to avoid waste

Organizations can prevent computer related waste by recycling systems and devices. A worker at CP Recovery of Omaha, Nebraska, uses a disc cutter to remove monitor tubes.

Computer-related Mistakes. The variations of computer-related mistakes seem numerous, but the actual types of errors that can occur are relatively few. The major types of errors include those shown in Table 12.3. A number of actions can be taken by individuals and organizations to prevent computer-related mistakes. Individuals can double-check data in database programs and formulas in spreadsheets. Checking entries in tax-preparation and money-management programs is another way to prevent computer-related mistakes. Many individuals use surge protectors or have backup computers in case of problems or mistakes with hardware.

TABLE 12.3 • Types of Computer-related Mistakes

Type of Mistake	Example
Data-entry errors	A military commander might enter the wrong GPS position for enemy troops into the computer. This data-entry error might cause friendly troops to be killed.
Errors in computer programs	A payroll program might multiply a person's pay rate by 1.5 for overtime instead of 2. This programming error will result in a lower paycheck than the employee should receive for overtime work.
Mishandling of computer output	A medical office might send lab results to the wrong person. The person receiving the results will have access to another person's private medical information.
Inadequate planning for and control of equipment malfunctions	An individual's hard drive might fail. If the person has not backed up important files recently, he or she will lose access to important information and have to redo work.
Inadequate planning for and control of electrical problems, humidity problems, and other environmental difficulties	A power outage in an area could shut down an organization's computer system. Without a backup power supply and protection from electrical surges, information and data might be lost and equipment might be ruined.

In many cases, organizations using computers have control standards and procedures for the acquisition and use of computers, with a goal of avoiding mistakes. These organizations realize that good policies and good systems management can save the organization thousands of dollars and improve effectiveness and efficiency.

Other Societal and Ethical Issues

A number of other societal and ethical issues are illegal, offensive, or both. These problems are not trivial. For example, Media Metrix estimates that illegal or black-market business on the Internet, which is about $36 billion annually, occurs at about the same rate as legitimate business activity.[57] On the Internet, illegal or offensive activities include:

- Pornography
- Hate material
- Instructions on how to commit terrorism

Some Internet service providers use filters to block this material. In addition, software can be purchased to block unwanted or undesirable Internet sites, including Cyber Patrol and SurfControl (see Figure 12.17). The *Children's Internet Protection Act* requires schools, libraries, and other organizations that receive federal funds to protect children from obscene material on the Internet.

FIGURE 12.17 • SurfControl

Schools, libraries, and other organizations that receive federal funds are required to protect children from obscene material on the Internet.

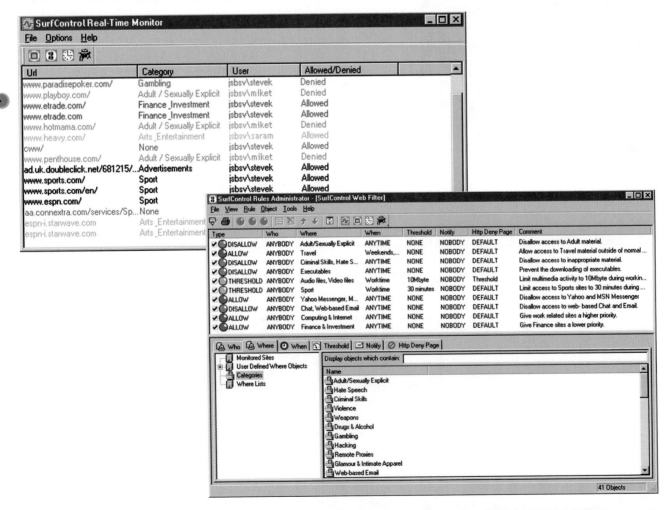

Technology and Society

In this chapter, we have explored some of the potentially negative aspects of computer systems and what can be done to prevent and recover from them. However, in addition to negative societal effects, technology can have some very positive effects on society. For example, technology can have a huge positive impact on seniors. Internet sites such as www.RetiredBrains.com can be used to engage older people and tap into their experience.[58] Computer systems can connect housebound seniors to the world and save their lives if they have emergency health problems. Of course, computers and the Internet can help keep families connected across town or around the world. Technology has also been used to keep track of the very young using satellite-guided wristbands.[59] Like following a trail of bread crumbs, parents are able to follow the movements of their young children using the satellite gadgets. Technology can deliver products, services, and even medical aid around the world. Doctors and healthcare professionals can consult with people who live in distant countries and remote areas. The positive impact of technology on society is almost limitless.

Technology has created a very complex world, and for all of its advantages it has introduced new challenges into our society. Staying educated and engaged is the key to getting the most from technology and making a difference in our world. In addition to helping you achieve your personal and professional goals, technology can be used to help others achieve their goals. Young professionals are signing up with organizations such as Geekcorps and taking their technology skills to Ghana and other underdeveloped countries to make a significant difference to the people of these remote areas (see Figure 12.18).[60] These volunteers are using their time and technology skills to help others succeed. Whatever field you pursue and whatever personal activities you enjoy, technology offers new ways to enhance and improve your life.

FIGURE 12.18 • Helping others with technology

Geekcorps sends out 50 "techies" a year to bring the benefits of technology to communities in remote areas such as Bulgaria, Ghana, Mongolia, and Rwanda.

Action Plan

1. What can John do to avoid getting unwanted e-mail?

John is having a typical problem with spam. To help prevent getting spam in the future, he can: know the source of any e-mail, not give away his e-mail address, not try to unsubscribe from spam e-mail, use spam guards, blacklist senders that have sent spam in the past, and whitelist legitimate e-mail addresses of people and organizations he knows and trusts. If the spam becomes a bigger problem, John can always change his e-mail address and then use these measures aggressively.

2. How can John check for viruses and prevent virus infections?

The best approach to handling viruses is prevention. John should install virus-scanning software by Symantec, McAfee, or another virus-prevention company as soon as possible. John should carefully follow all installation instructions, including how to update the software for the latest virus-scanning features and for the latest virus identification files. He should also carefully follow all instructions for removing any viruses. In the future, John should know and trust the source of the disk or Internet site before he inserts any disk into his computer or downloads any data or software from an Internet site. John should keep a backup of all software and data. He should also have a rescue disk in case a virus completely disables his computer.

Summary

LEARNING OBJECTIVE 1
Describe how a computer system can be used as a tool to commit a crime or be the object of a crime and what can be done to prevent computer crime.

Computers may be used as tools to commit crimes, or they can be the actual object of the crime, both nationally and abroad. Crimes involving illegal system access and use of computer services are a concern to both government and organizations. A hacker is a person who knows computer technology and spends time learning and using computer systems; a criminal hacker, or cracker, is a person who uses his or her knowledge of computers to commit computer crime.

A virus is a program that attaches itself to other programs. A worm does not attach itself to programs, but acts as a free agent to destroy programs or interrupt the operation of computer systems or networks. Application viruses affect word-processing, spreadsheet, and other similar programs; a system virus infects operating system programs. A logic bomb is designed to explode or execute at a specified time and date. Viruses and worms can be prevented by using virus-scanning software, knowing the source of data and software coming into your computer and using software only from trusted sources, keeping a backup of all data and software, and having a rescue disk. Organizations and individuals often use firewalls to protect themselves.

Scams, fraud, data and information theft, identity theft, equipment theft, and time and supplies theft are crimes that have occurred with computer systems. Software, music, and movie theft can also be a problem. Intellectual property rights concern the ownership and use of software, music, movies, data, and information. In general, intellectual property rights issues include: Who owns the intellectual property (programs, data, music, movies, and information)? What rights do users have to use the intellectual property, and who places a value on intellectual property?

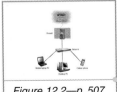

Figure 12.2—p. 507

Electronic plagiarism involves using computer systems or the Internet to take someone's work and pass it off as your own. Electronic libel is a written statement, produced using a computer system or over the Internet, about a person that is not true and can cause the person harm. Libel, whether done using a computer system, the Internet, or any other means can result in a lawsuit. A person or group sending thousands or millions of access attempts or requests to an Internet site causes a denial-of-service attack that overwhelms an Internet site.

Ways to prevent unauthorized or unwanted access to a computer system include using something you know (usernames and passwords), something you have (ID cards and badges), or something about you (biometric information). State and federal laws against computer crime also help to prevent computer-related crime.

LEARNING OBJECTIVE 2
Discuss privacy issues and describe how to avoid invasion of privacy.

Privacy issues center around the collection and use or misuse of stored data. Data is collected on individuals from birth until death, and is stored by numerous governmental agencies and organizations for later access by authorized users. Sometimes the information stored by organizations or the government contains errors that unknowingly cause problems for individuals, such as the denial of credit. Information about you can be obtained by your willingly giving it to others, when you buy products and services, when you interact with government agencies, and when you use the Internet.

The four key issues regarding privacy are knowledge, control, notice, and consent. Individuals should have knowledge of the data that is stored about them and have the ability to correct errors in corporate and organizational databases systems. If information on individuals is to be used for other purposes, these individuals should be asked to give their consent beforehand. Each individual should have the right to know and the ability to decide.

Some legislation attempts to address privacy issues. For instance, the Privacy Act restricts IRS and other government agencies from using certain personal data. Action on privacy-related laws also has occurred at the state and local level, and is a current topic internationally as well. Some companies even have a privacy bill of rights that specifies how the privacy of employees, clients, and customers is to be protected. States have their own privacy laws, and some organizations have privacy policies.

Table 12.2—p. 517

LEARNING OBJECTIVE 3
List health and job issues that could have an impact on you and others.

There are fears and health concerns in today's work environment. Feelings of job insecurity, loss of control, incompetence, and demotions are just a few of these fears. Health problems include claims relating repetitive motion disorder to computer use. Also called repetitive stress injury (RSI), this type of problem can include tendonitis, tennis elbow, the inability to hold objects, sharp pain, and wrist pain related to carpal tunnel syndrome (CTS). Online gambling, information overload and stress, and Internet addiction and isolation are important mental-health issues. Job issues, including job loss and outsourcing, are also of concern to many people.

Figure 12.13—p. 523

LEARNING OBJECTIVE 4
Define and discuss ethical issues in computer systems.

In most organizations, ethics are a concern. Accuracy of information and electronic deception, for example, are concerns to most organizations. Organizations must address who has access rights to information and what safeguards are in place for its protection.

Several organizations have developed ethical codes of conduct related to computer systems. Computer Professionals for Social Responsibility (CPSR), the Association of Information Technology Professionals (AITP), the Association for Computing Machinery (ACM), the Institute of Electrical and Electronics Engineers (IEEE), and the British Computer Society (BCS) have their own ethics codes. In addition, many businesses and nonprofit organizations have an ethical code of conduct.

LEARNING OBJECTIVE 5

List common computer-related waste and mistakes, describe how they can be avoided, and describe how computers can help resolve societal issues.

Computer waste and mistakes are major causes of computer problems. Computer waste, the inappropriate use of computer technology and resources, can occur in both the public and private sectors. Spam is a major source of individual and organizational waste. To avoid spam, you should know the source of Internet sites you visit, don't give away your e-mail address, don't try to unsubscribe from spam, use spam guards, blacklist the senders of spam, and whitelist legitimate senders.

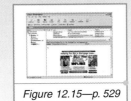

Figure 12.15—p. 529

Computer mistakes relate to errors, failures, and other problems that result in output that is incorrect and without value. The major error types can be put into a few broad categories: data-entry errors, computer program errors, computer output mishandling, equipment malfunctions, and technical/environmental problems.

Although computer systems can be used to create societal and ethical issues that are illegal, offensive, or both, they can also have some very positive effects on society. Technology can help seniors share their work experience, and they can connect house-bound seniors to the world. Technology can deliver products, services, and even medical aid to people living in underdeveloped countries or remote areas.

Test Yourself

LEARNING OBJECTIVE 1: Describe how a computer system can be used as a tool to commit a crime or be the object of a crime and what can be done to prevent computer crime.

1. A(n) _____ is a person who knows computer technology and spends time learning and using computer systems. In many cases, such people are looking for fun and excitement— the "challenge" of beating the system.

2. True or False: A worm acts as a free agent, placing copies of itself into other systems, destroying programs, and interrupting the operation of networks and computer systems.

3. What infects files, including .exe and .com files?
   a. worms
   b. system virus
   c. application virus
   d. Trojan horse

4. A(n) _____ is software or hardware that protects a computer from outside attacks.

5. _____ is stealing someone's personal information, such as a Social Security number and driver's license.

6. True or False: A copyright means that others can't use or duplicate your work or intellectual property without your consent.

7. Taking another person's work and turning it in to a teacher as if it were your own is called:
   a. slander
   b. libel
   c. intellectual property
   d. plagiarism

8. A(n) _____ attack is caused by a person or group sending an Internet site thousands or millions of access attempts or requests.

LEARNING OBJECTIVE 2: Discuss privacy issues and describe how to avoid invasion of privacy.

9. True or False: U.S. Supreme Court Justice Louis Brandeis stated that the "right to be let alone" is one of the most "comprehensive of rights and the most valued by civilized man."

10. The _____ is a major piece of legislation, enacted by Congress in 1974, that applies to certain federal agencies and serves as a guideline for private organizations.

11. True or False: Fairness in information use includes knowledge, notice, control, and consent.

12. Some people believe that the _____ act, which gives the FBI and other federal agencies the power to obtain school, health, financial, Web, and other personal information about people suspected of possible terrorist activities, may reduce individual privacy rights.

13. Software, such as the _____, which has the potential to alert you to companies that don't have adequate privacy policies according to preferences that you specify, is being developed to help protect your privacy on the Internet.

LEARNING OBJECTIVE 3: List health and job issues that could have an impact on you and others.

14. True or False: Cron's Syndrome (CS) is the aggravation of the pathway for nerves that travel through the wrist. CS involves wrist pain, a feeling of tingling and numbness, and difficulty in grasping and holding objects.

15. The study of the design and positioning of computer equipment is called:
    a. computer alignment design
    b. computer-assisted design
    c. ergonomics
    d. sysonomics

16. To reduce power usage, the EPA has initiated the _____ program. A personal computer with this program has restrictions on how much power it can consume while being used.

17. True or False: Outsourcing involves taking jobs that were once performed inside the organization or company and transferring them to outside organizations.

LEARNING OBJECTIVE 4: Define and discuss ethical issues in computer systems.

18. _____ concern the ownership and use of information.

19. True or False: the Association of Information Technology Professionals (AITP) is an example of an organization with an ethical code of conduct.

LEARNING OBJECTIVE 5: List common computer-related waste and mistakes, describe how they can be avoided, and describe how computers can help resolve social issues.

20. Accepting e-mail only from people or locations you approve and specify is called using a:
    a. spam guard
    b. firewall
    c. whitelist
    d. blacklist

Test Yourself Solutions 1. hacker, **2.** T, **3.** b., **4.** firewall, **5.** Identity theft, **6.** T, **7.** d., **8.** denial-of-service, **9.** T, **10.** Privacy Act, **11.** T, **12.** Patriot Act, **13.** Platform for Privacy Preferences, **14.** F, **15.** c., **16.** energy star, **17.** T, **18.** Intellectual property rights, **19.** T, **20.** c.

Key Terms

application virus, p. 506
biometric device, p. 511
carpal tunnel syndrome
    (CTS), p. 520
copyright, p. 510
cracker, p. 505
electronic deception, p. 525
electronic plagiarism, p. 510
Energy Star program, p. 522
ergonomics, p. 522

ethical issues, p. 524
firewall, p. 506
hacker, p. 505
identity theft, p. 508
intellectual property rights,
    p. 509
logic bomb, p. 506
piracy, p. 509
Platform for Privacy
    Preferences, p. 520

privacy, p. 513
Privacy Act, p. 518
repetitive stress injury (RSI),
    p. 520
rescue disk, p. 507
system virus, p. 506
Trojan horse, p. 506
virus, p. 505
virus hoax, p. 506
worm, p. 505

Questions

Review Questions

1. What are some ways a computer is used to commit crimes? How might a computer be the object of crime?

2. What is the difference between a hacker and a cracker? What are the major problems caused by crackers?

3. What is a worm?

4. What is a virus, an application virus, and a system virus?

5. What is software piracy, and why is it common?

6. What are intellectual property rights?

7. What is the difference between electronic plagiarism and libel?

8. What is a biometric device?

9. What issues should be addressed when considering an individual's right to privacy?

10. What is a cookie?

11. What is fairness in information use?

12. What are repetitive motion disorders, and how can they be prevented?

13. Describe the mental-health issues related to computer systems.

14. What is ergonomics?

15. What is the Energy Star program?

16. What are the major job concerns related to computer usage?

17. What are ethical issues? Give an example.

18. Give an example of electronic deception.

19. Differentiate between computer waste and computer mistakes.

20. What is spam?

Discussion Questions

21. What can organizations do to detect and prevent computer crimes?

22. How can you prevent identity theft?

23. Consider this quote: "There's barely a piece of information about people that isn't used for far different purposes than it was initially gathered for, and always without approval." Do you feel this statement is true? Which of the four issues associated with privacy does the quote address? Which of the four is most important to you?

24. Your organization has many employees (including you) who spend most of their days using a computer. What can be done to reduce or prevent the effects of repetitive motion disorder?

25. How can organizations ensure that their computer systems are used in an ethically and morally responsible fashion?

26. Describe how you can avoid computer-related waste and mistakes.

27. Discuss some ways that computer systems can be used to help address social issues.

Exercises

Try It Yourself

1. Using the Internet, search for information about known viruses and worms. Using a database, store the information about different viruses and worms you find. Include columns on the name of the virus or worm, the impact of the virus or worm, possible monetary costs of the virus or worm, and what in-dividuals and organizations can do to prevent this type of virus or worm in the future.

2. With advancements in DNA, it may be possible to identify genes that could possibly cause diseases and even death. Keeping this health information private is important for many individuals. Using your word-processing program, describe what new laws should be enacted to keep DNA information private.

3. Use the Internet to search for ethical codes of conduct for businesses or organizations. Write a brief report on what you find. What features would you like to see in ethical codes of conducts for businesses and organizations?

Virtual Classroom Activities

For the following exercises, do not use face-to-face or telephone communications with your group members. Use only Internet communications.

4. With your virtual classroom group, investigate the cost and waste created by spam. Using the Internet, explore the ways individuals can prevent spam. What software is available to block or prevent spam?

5. Each member of your virtual classroom group should explore a different software package that can be used to prevent viruses and worms. Write a report that describes the different software packages you explored, including the advantages and disadvantages of each package.

Teamwork

6. *The Financial Forum,* your financial newsletter, has done very well—the number of subscribers has tripled since the first issue. Recently, you have begun distributing issues over the Internet. Now, several other companies are interested in buying a list of your subscribers' names and addresses. Before you make any decision, you call a meeting of the *Forum's* managers to create an ethics policy statement. Conduct this "meeting" with your team. Create an ethics policy statement for the organization. Note that you should address the issues discussed in the chapter and what responsibilities computer systems workers who support the computer systems for this organization should have.

7. Have each team member explore a federal or state law that deals with invasion of privacy. Use a word-processing program to summarize what you found. Include what privacy legislation you would like to see in the future to protect your individual privacy.

Learning Check

To check your knowledge of each of the chapter objectives, use this chart to find related end-of-chapter content.

Learning Objective	Key Terms		Questions	Exercises
Learning Objective 1 Describe how a computer system can be used as a tool to commit a crime or be the object of a crime and what can be done to prevent computer crime.	application virus biometric device cracker copyright electronic plagiarism firewall hacker identity theft intellectual property rights	logic bomb piracy rescue disk system virus Trojan horse virus virus hoax worm	1, 2, 3, 4, 5, 6, 7, 8, 21, 22	1, 5

Learning Objective	Key Terms	Questions	Exercises
Learning Objective 2 Discuss privacy issues and describe how to avoid invasion of privacy.	Platform for Privacy Preferences privacy Privacy Act	9, 10, 11, 23	2, 7
Learning Objective 3 List health and job issues that could have an impact on you and others.	carpal tunnel syndrome (CTS) Energy Star ergonomics repetitive stress injury (RSI)	12, 13, 14, 15, 16, 24	2
Learning Objective 4 Define and discuss ethical issues in computer systems.	electronic deception Ethical issues	17, 18, 25	3, 6
Learning Objective 5 List common computer-related waste and mistakes, describe how they can be avoided, and describe how computers can be used to help resolve social issues.		19, 20, 26, 27	4

Endnotes

1 Mearian, Lucas, "Wall Street Firms Fined for Not Saving E-Mails," *Computerworld*, December 9, 2002, p. 7.

2 Staff, "California Firm Fined $1 Million for Illegal Shipment to Russia," *State Department*, January 8, 2003.

3 Borrus, Amy, "To Catch an Identity Thief," *Business Week*, March 31, 2003, p. 91.

4 Staff, "Dawn of the Superworm," *PC World*, May 2003, p. 26.

5 Cobburn, Tavis, "Protect Your PC," *PC World*, July 2002, p. 92.

6 Alwang, Greg et al, "Viruses: New Threats," *PC Magazine*, April 22, 2003, p. 112.

7 Wientraub, Arlene, "Portrait of an Ex-Hacker," *Business Week*, June 9, 2003, p. 116.

8 Clark, Don, "Intel to Build Security Features Into Its Chips," *The Wall Street Journal*, September 10, 2002, p. B4.

9 Stafff, "Scam Artists Prowl Online Auction Sites," *CNN Online*, January 10, 2003.

10 Wilke, John et al, "Online-Auction Fraud is Target of Crackdown," *The Wall Street Journal*, April 30, 2003, p. A3.

11 Sullivan, Andy, "U.S. Arrests 135 in Nationwide Cybercrime Sweep," *Compuserve Online*, May 16, 2003.

12 Kandra, Anne, "Avoid Online Snake Oil Sellers," *PC World*, June 2003, p. 51.

13 Brown, Cherie, "Letters: Credit Nightmare," *The Washington Post*, September 21, 2003, p. W04.

14 Reuteman, Rob, "Piracy Takes a Dip," *Rocky Mountain News*, June 4, 2003, p. 1B.

15 Staff, "Kazaa, Morpheus Activity Down After Lawsuits," *Reuters*, September 30, 2003.

16 Gross, Grant, "Kazza Slams RIAA for Copyright Infringement," *IDG News Service*, September 26, 2003.

17 Staff, "Matrix Sequel Pirated Online," *BBC News*, May 27, 2003.

18 Lewis, Peter, "The Burning Question in DVDs," *Fortune*, March 31, 2003, p. 146.

19 Orwall, Bruce, "Hollywood Is Determined to Prevent Unauthorized Copying of Movies," *The Wall Street Journal*, May 19, 2003, p. R4.

20 Sabar, Ariel, "Naval Academy Disciplines 85 Caught in Internet Music Raid," *Houston Chronicle*, April 16, 2003, p. 13A.

21 Bloom, Adi, "Tens of Thousands of GCSE and A-Level Coursework Essays Are Available on the Internet," *The Times Educational Supplement*, March 21, 2003, pp. 7.

22 Mann, Tony, "Plagiarism and The Internet," *The Times Higher Education Supplement*, May 23, 2003, p. 14.

23 Zuckerman, Gregory, "Hedge Fund Finds Dark Side to Message Boards," *The Wall Street Journal*, April 14, 2003, p. C1.

24 Staff, "Defendant in Dow Jones Libel Case Appeals to UN," *New Media Age*, April 24, 2003, p. 12.

25 Briggs, Robert, "Cyber-Liability Made to Order," *Florida Underwriters*, February 2003, p. 33.

26 Byron, Ellen, "Computer Forensics Sleuths Help Find Fraud," *The Wall Street Journal*, March 18, 2003, p. B1.

27 Grimes, Brad, "Biometric Security," *PC Magazine*, April 22, 2003, p. 72.

28 Verton, Dan, "Feds Plan Biometrics for Border Control," *Computerworld*, May 26, 2003, p. 12.

29 Spencer, Jane, "How to Fake a Hard Day at the Office," *The Wall Street Journal*, May 15, 2003, p. D1.

30 Metz, Cade, "Spyware: It's Lurking on Your Machine," *PC Magazine*, April 22, 2003, p. 85.

31 Morrissey, Brian, "DoubleClick Hit with Deceptive Ad Suit," *InternetNews.com*, July 22, 2003.

32 Walczak, Lee, "The Revolt Against the Patriot Act," *Business Week*, May 19, 2003, p. 51.

33 Vibayan, J. "Proposed Air Passenger Screening System Alarms Privacy Advoates," *Computerworld*, March 31, 2003, p. 10.

34 Sabett, Randy, "California's New Privacy Law," *Information Security*, June 2003, p. 62.

35 Staff, "Japan Lower House Passes Privacy Law," *Direct*, May 6, 2003.

36 Berlind, David, "Reality Check," *ZDNet*, May 28, 2003.

37 Field, Anne, "How to Set Up Ergonomically Correct Workstations for Your Kids," *Business Week*, December 23, 2002, p. 98.

38 Staff, "The Underground Web," *Business Week*, September 2, 2002, p. 67.

39 Staff, "Personal Use of the Internet During Business Hours," *Electronics News*, June 2002.

40 Rapaport, Lowel, "Theory and Practice," *Transform Magazine*, October 1, 2002, p. 48.

41 Presely, Denyse, "Seeing a Way to Online Learning," *The Times Educational Supplement*, April 4, 2003, p. 8.

42 Bergstein, Brain, "As Baby Boomers Age and Disabilities Become More Prevalent," *The Wall Street Journal*, March 17, 2003, p. 2B.

43 Zaslow, Jeffrey, "Offices Try New Rules Banning Blind CC," *The Wall Street Journal*, May 28, 2003, p. D1.

44 Kronholz, June, "Dear World, Please Stop Writing Me," *The Wall Street Journal*, February 13, 2003, p. A1.

45 Ernst, Warren, "Random Pop-Ups," *PC Magazine*, April 22, 2003, p. 76.

46 Woellert, Lorraine, "Slamming Spam," *Business Week*, May 12, 2003, p. 40.

47 Greene, Kelly, "Scientists Battle Spam," *The Wall Street Journal*, Mossberg, Walter, June 12, 2003, p. B1.

48 Staff, "AOL Cites Heavy Spam Level," *The Wall Street Journal*, May 23, 2003, p. A4.

49 Solomon, Melissa, "Spam Attack," *Computerworld*, November 11, 2002, p. 33.

50 Mangalindan, Mylene, "Putting a Lid on Spam," *The Wall Street Journal*, June 6, 2003, p. B1.

51 Magnalindan, Mylene, "Senator Proposes Legislation to Create 'Do-Not-E-mail List," *The Wall Street Journal*, April 28, 2003, p. B3.

52 Lee, Jennifer, "President Signs Law Aiming to Limit Spam," *New York Times*, December 16, 2003, http://www.nytimes.com/2003/12/16/politics/16CND-SPAM.html, accesssed December 22, 2003.

53 Angwin, Julia, "Elusive Spammer Sends Web Service on a Long Chase," *The Wall Street Journal*, May 7, 2003, p. A1.

54 Mangalindan, Mylene, "Giving Spammers a Big Dose of Their Medicine," *The Wall Street Journal*, May 19, 2003, p. A1.

55 Kay, Russell, "Fighting Spam," *Computerworld*, May 12, 2003, p. 33.

56 Tasker, Johann, "System Glich May Delay English Support Money," *Farmers Weekly*, February 21, 2003, p. 17.

57 Staff, "The Underground Web," *Business Week*, September 2, 2002, p. 67.

58 Maher, Kris, "Internet Sites Emerge to Serve Coming Wave of Older Job Seekers," *The Wall Street Journal*, September 30, 2003, p. B14.

59 Mossberg, Walter, "Putting Junior Under Surveillance," *The Wall Street Journal*, September 17, 2003, p. D4.

60 Hall, Mark, "Volunteers Get a Career Boost," *Computerworld*, September 22, 2003, p. 44.

Glossary

3Cs approach — Emphasizing content, community, and commerce on a B2C e-commerce Web site, a strategy for capturing the interest of the online community.

3-D audio — Audio that makes use of special sound recording techniques and multiple speakers placed around the audience, so that sound-producing objects can be heard from all directions; also known as surround sound.

3-D modeling software — Programs that provide graphic tools that allow artists to create pictures of 3-D, realistic models.

acceptance testing — Conducting tests required by the user, to make sure that the new or modified system is operating as intended.

access points — Wireless network sites, also known as hot spots, distributed around a geographic area that broadcast network traffic using radio frequencies to computers equipped with wireless fidelity (Wi-Fi) cards or adapters.

access time — The amount of time it takes for a request for data to be fulfilled by a storage device.

activate — Make software fully operational, which may require registering the program with the software maker.

ActiveX — Microsoft's alternative to the JavaScript Web programming language.

actor — The object that interacts with events, or use cases, in an object-oriented systems development approach.

adware — Software placed on your computer system without your knowledge or consent, normally through the Internet, to secretly spy on you and collect information, especially for advertising purposes.

agile modeling — A systems development approach that calls for very active participation of customers and other stakeholders in the systems development process.

algorithm — A step-by-step problem-solving process that arrives at a solution in a finite amount of time; sometimes called program logic; a detailed procedure or formula for solving a problem.

alpha testing — The first stage of testing that is implemented by the software developer.

alphanumeric — In database fields, character-type data, including characters or numbers that will not be manipulated or used in calculations.

American Standard Code for Information Interchange (ASCII) — A code for representing text characters that the computer industry agreed upon in the early days of computing.

analog — Signals that vary continuously; the opposite of digital.

analog signal — A signal that continuously changes over time.

analog-to-digital converter — A device that translates sound and music to digital signals.

animated GIF — Simple drawings, created with simple software tools, that repeat the same motion over and over endlessly; the most basic form of animation.

Apple — One of the two most popular personal computing platforms. There are no Apple-compatible computers, since Apple has always used its own proprietary hardware.

application flowchart — A general flowchart used to describe the overall purpose and structure of a system; also known as the system flowchart.

application generators — Programs that automate the process of writing source code and compiling to machine code, allowing you to create other programs without using a formal programming language.

application layer — The software portion of the three-layer Internet model, which also includes transport (protocol) and physical (hardware) layers.

application programming interfaces (APIs) — Web site development tools that allow software engineers to develop Web-driven programs.

application servers — Computers that store programs, such as word processors and spreadsheets, and deliver them to workstations to run when users click the program icon.

application service provider (ASP) — A company that provides software and support, such as computer personnel, to run the software.

application software — Programs that apply the power of computers to help perform tasks or solve problems for people, groups, and organizations; along with systems software, one of two basic types of software.

application viruses — Programs that infect application files, including .exe and .com files, and often add themselves to applications such as word-processing programs and spreadsheet packages.

arithmetic logic unit (ALU) — One of three primary elements within a central processing unit (CPU), it contains the circuitry to carry out instructions, such as mathematical calculations and logical comparisons.

artificial intelligence (AI) — A term coined in the 1950s to describe computers with the ability to mimic or duplicate the functions of the human brain; computer systems taking on the characteristics of human intelligence.

artificial intelligence systems — The people, procedures, hardware, software, data, and knowledge needed to develop computer systems and machines that demonstrate characteristics of intelligence.

asking directly — A requirements analysis technique that asks users and stakeholders about what they want and expect from a new or modified system.

assembly languages — Second-generation programming languages that replaced the binary digits of first-generation machine languages with symbols that are more easily understood by human programmers.

assigned research — A form of research in which the topic to explore is given, rather than prompted by curiosity, for the purpose of education.

asynchronous communication — A form of electronic communications that allows participants to leave messages for each other to be read, heard, watched, and responded to at the recipient's convenience, such as by using answering machines, voice mail, and email.

attribute — A characteristic of an entity; in the relational data model, a column of a table; an identifying characteristic, such as a variable, that is associated with an object in object-oriented design.

.audio restoration and enhancement — Sound production work that is done to improve the quality of old or damaged recordings.

authorize — Provide proof of a software's purchase, so that it can be used.

authorware — A popular software tool used to produce interactive multimedia educational tutorials that are packaged on CD, delivered over a network, or delivered over the Web.

avars — Points on a computerized 3-D object that are designed to bend or pivot at specific angles.

avatar — A 3-D representation of a participant in a virtual world environment, which can be used to navigate through the virtual world.

B2B — Business-to-business e-commerce, a system supporting transactions between businesses across private networks, the Internet, and the Web.

B2C — Business-to-consumer e-commerce, the use of the Web to connect individual consumers directly with sellers to purchase products.

back-end application — Software that interacts with other programs or applications, and only indirectly with people or users.

backward-compatible — Capable of supporting previous technology. For example, DVD drives are backward-compatible and thus can play CDs as well as DVDs.

bandwidth — A measure of transmission capacity.

BASIC (Beginners All-purpose Symbolic Instruction Code) — Along with COBOL and FORTRAN, a third-generation, high-level programming language, with increased use of symbolic code.

basic input/output system (BIOS) — A set of instructions, activated by one or more computer chips, to perform additional testing and to control various input/output devices, such as keyboards and display screens.

batch processing — A method of processing transactions by collecting them over time and processing them together in batches.

behavioral profiling — Observing customers' cable TV viewing patterns in order to develop an understanding of their interests.

benchmark — A side-by-side evaluation of competing products' performance.

beta testing — The second level of program testing, which uses a select group of end users to try out the program and provide feedback.

binary — A numbering scheme in which there are only two possible values for each digit: 0 and 1.

binary data — Data that is intended for a processor to process.

binary number system — A computer numbering system consisting of only two numbers, 0 and 1.

bioinformatics — Also called computational biology, a combination of biology and computer science that has been used to help map the human genome and conduct research on biological organisms.

biometric device — A device that can recognize physical traits, such as fingerprints, facial characteristics, or retinal or eye characteristics, and can be used to prevent unauthorized access to a computer system or a security area.

biometrics — The study of measurable biological characteristics, such as eye patterns or fingerprints.

bit — Short for *binary digit*; the smallest unit of information used in computers.

bit-mapped graphics — A representational method that uses bytes to store the color of each pixel in an image. Also known as raster graphics.

bits per second (bps) — A measurement of data transmission speed.

Bluetooth — A low-cost, short-range wireless specification for connecting mobile products; Bluetooth technology enables a wide assortment of digital devices to communicate wirelessly over short distances.

booting — The steps taken to start a computer when it has been powered down.

boot-sector virus — A system virus, a program that infects operating system programs or other system files.

brainstorming — A group decision-making approach that often consists of members offering ideas "off the top of their heads."

brand spoofing — The practice of creating commercial Web sites that look just like the real thing but are run by scam artists.

brick-and-mortar — A term used to refer to a traditional retail store.

bridges — Common network control devices that connect two or more network segments, and help to regulate network traffic.

broadband — A category of bandwidth; exactly how fast broadband media is remains debated, but it is significantly faster than narrowband.

broadcasting — Sending messages, as by e-mail, to large groups.

buddy lists — Also known as contact lists, names of people who are frequent communication partners in chat rooms or via instant messaging.

bulletin board — A central location on the Internet where members of a discussion board can log in to post, read, and reply to messages.

bus — A network topology consisting of one main cable or telecommunications line with devices attached to it.

business intelligence — The business use of data mining to help increase efficiency, reduce costs, or increase profits; a term first coined by a consultant at Gartner Group.

business resumption planning (BRP) — The review of every conceivable disaster that could negatively impact a transaction processing system, and the provision of courses of action to minimize their effects.

business to business (B2B) — A type of electronic commerce or transaction that is conducted between two businesses.

business to consumer (B2C) — A type of electronic commerce or transaction that is conducted between a business and a consumer.

business-to-business e-commerce — A system supporting transactions between businesses over private networks, the Internet, and the Web; also known as simply B2B.

business-to-consumer e-commerce — The use of the Web to connect individual consumers directly with sellers to purchase products; also known as simply B2C or e-tailing.

byte — Eight bits combined, the standard unit of storage in digital electronics.

C2C — Consumer-to-consumer e-commerce, the use of the Web to connect individuals who wish to sell their personal belongings with people shopping for used items.

cable modem — A sophisticated signal-conversion device that provides Internet access over a cable television network; it offers faster data transmission rates than a traditional dial-up connection.

cable modem connection — A broadband Internet service, with data transfer rates of around 2 Mbps, provided by cable television providers.

cache memory — A type of high-speed memory that a processor can access more rapidly than RAM, allowing for quick retrieval of program instructions and data.

calculating — Using arithmetic operations to determine a result.

camcorders — Optical recording devices that capture full-length digital video that can be watched on TV, downloaded to a computer, or transferred to disk or tape.

capacitor — A passive electronic component that stores energy in the form of an electrostatic field; typically used with transistors to process and store bits and bytes.

carpal tunnel syndrome (CTS) — an inflammation of the pathways for nerves that travel through the wrist (the carpal tunnel), that involves wrist pain, a feeling of tingling and numbness, and difficulty in grasping and holding objects; a condition sometimes associated with long hours at the computer keyboard.

casual computer programming — The programming activity of individuals who become involved in computer programming with little or no forethought or training.

catalog management software — E-commerce software for organizing a product line into a convenient format for Web navigation.

CD-RW — Compact disk-rewritable; a type of CD where the data can be written over many times.

central processing unit (CPU) — The group of integrated circuits that work together to perform any system processing, such as arithmetic calculations, logic comparisons, and data access.

certification authorities — Businesses, such as VeriSign, that provide digital certificates.

channels — Also known as chat rooms, the various topic related forums on the Internet for synchronous text messaging between two or more participants.

character recognition software — Software that when combined with a scanner can transform document images into editable word-processing documents.

chat — On the Internet, synchronous text messaging between two or more participants.

chat rooms — Also known as channels, the various topic related forums on the Internet for synchronous text messaging between two or more participants.

Children's Internet Protection Act — A U.S. law enacted in 2000 that requires schools, libraries, and other organizations that receive federal funds to protect children from obscene material on the Internet.

choice stage — The last stage of the decision-making process, during which a course of action is selected.

citation — A formal recognition of the source of a quotation within a paper.

client — The program, in a client/server relationship, that makes a service request.

client servers — Computer systems used to coordinate client computers, usually personal computers, connected to a network.

client/server — A relationship between two computer programs in which one program, the client, makes a service request from another program, the server, which provides the service.

clip art — Drawings and photos, covering a wide variety of objects, offered in presentation graphics or other programs for use in slide presentations and other graphic projects.

clock speed — The rate, typically measured in megahertz or gigahertz, at which a CPU's system clock produces a series of electronic pulses, which is a factor in overall system performance.

CMOS memory — Short for complementary metal oxide semiconductor, it provides semi-permanent storage for system configuration information that may change.

coaxial cable — A type of cable consisting of an inner conductor wire surrounded by insulation, a conductive shield, and a cover; the type of cable provided by cable television services.

COBOL (COmmon Business-Oriented Language) — Along with BASIC and FORTRAN, a third-generation, high-level programming language, with increased use of symbolic code.

cold boot — A computer startup performed by pushing a start button or switch when the computer is not on.

command-based user interface — Access to and command of a computer system by giving the computer text commands to perform basic activities.

communications medium — Anything that carries a signal between a sender and a receiver.

communications processor — A device used to control and protect industrial-level telecommunications, by handling the communications to and from a large computer network; sometimes called a front-end processor.

communications satellite — A microwave station placed in outer space that receives a signal from one point on earth and then rebroadcasts it at a different frequency to a different location.

communications software — Software that connects to other computers through the phone, cable, or satellites.

compact disk read-only memory (CD-ROM) — Commonly referred to as a CD, the first optical media to be mass-marketed to the general public. CDs are read-only—once data has been recorded on one, it cannot be modified.

competitive advantage — A significant and long-term benefit. For example, an athlete might obtain a competitive advantage by using a computer to analyze technique and training methods.

compiler — A language translator that coverts a complete program, such as a COBOL program, into a complete machine-language program.

complex instruction set computer (CISC) — A processor architecture that includes many instructions in its instruction set and very fast system clocks. Intel processors are based on it.

computability — A measure of how likely or feasible it is that a problem can be solved by a computer.

computed — A field determined from other fields, instead of being entered into a database.

computer animation — Animation that includes complex 3-D graphic images, rendered at 24 3-D images per second to create the illusion of movement.

computer keyboard — A common input device, used for entering characters, text, and basic commands.

computer mouse — A common input device, used to direct the computer's activities by selecting and manipulating onscreen symbols, icons, menus, or commands.

computer network — A collection of computing devices connected together to share resources such as files, software, processors, storage, and printers; a specific type of telecommunications network that connects computers and computer systems for data communications.

computer platform — The combination of hardware configuration and system software for a particular computer system.

computer programmers — People who write or create the sets of instructions or statements that become complete programs; software developers, individuals who design and implement software solutions.

computer programming — Software development, the process of developing computer programs to address a specific need or problem.

computer programs — Sets of instructions or statements to the computer that direct the circuitry within the hardware to operate in a certain fashion.

computer system — Any device that supports the activities of input, processing, storage, and output; the hardware, software, the Internet, databases, telecommunications, people, and procedures that comprise the computing experience.

computer systems management — The team of managers that can include the chief information officer (CIO) and other computer systems executives.

computer systems personnel — All the people who manage, run, program, and maintain a computer system.

computer-aided software engineering (CASE) — Software-based tools that automate many of the tasks required in a systems development effort.

computer-assisted design (CAD) — Software that assists designers, engineers, and architects in designing three-dimensional objects.

computerized collaborative work system — The hardware, software, people, databases, and procedures needed to provide effective support in group decision-making settings; also called a group decision support system.

computers — Electronic devices used to perform calculations and other functions at high speed.

computing platform --The processor and operating system that together comprise the computing environment; for example, Intel Pentium processor running Microsoft Windows operating system.

consumer to consumer (C2C) — A type of electronic commerce or online transaction that is conducted between two consumers.

consumer-to-consumer e-commerce — The use of the Web to connect individuals who wish to sell their personal belongings with people shopping for used items; also known as simply C2C.

contact lists — Also known as buddy lists, names of people who are frequent communication partners in chat rooms or via instant messaging.

content streaming — Also known as streaming media, streaming video, or streaming audio, a technique to deliver multimedia without a wait, since the media begins playing while the file is still being delivered.

continuous improvement — An approach to systems development in which an organization makes changes to a system when even small problems or opportunities occur.

contract software — A specific software program developed for a particular company or organization.

control unit — One of three primary elements within a central processing unit (CPU), it sequentially accesses program instructions, decodes them, and also coordinates the flow of data in and out of various system components.

cookie — A text file placed on your hard disk by a Web site you visit, for the purpose of storing information about you and your preferences.

cookies — Small text files that are stored on your computer and retrieved by a Web server each time you visit a Web page.

coprocessors — Special-purpose processors, typically used in larger workstations, that speed processing by executing specific types of instructions, while the CPU works on another processing activity.

copyright — A legal protection of your work or intellectual property from being used or duplicated by others without your consent.

cracker — A criminal hacker, a computer savvy person who attempts to gain unauthorized or illegal access to other computer systems to harm the system or to make money illegally.

crash — A program failure that occurs when the program executes commands that cause the computer to malfunction or shut down.

crawling — The process of continually following all Web links in an attempt to catalog every Web page by topic.

creative analysis — The investigation of new approaches to existing problems.

critical analysis — A skeptical and doubtful approach to problems, such as questioning whether or not the current computer system is still effective and efficient.

critical success factors (CSF) — A requirements analysis approach in which users and stakeholders are asked to list only those factors or items that are critical to the success of their area or the organization.

curiosity-driven — A form of research based on seeking information prompted by a personal thought or question, rather than a topic being assigned, that is responsible for most of the world's great inventions.

custom-developed — Programs built or developed by individuals and organizations to address specific needs.

cybercafes — Also known as Internet cafes, coffee houses and other sites that provide locations where people away from their homes or offices can connect to the Internet.

cybermall — A Web site that allows visitors to browse through a wide variety of products from varying e-tailers.

data — Raw facts, such as an employee's name and the number of hours he or she worked in a week, that computers can convert into valuable information and other useful outputs.

data analysis — A process that involves developing good, nonredundant, adaptable data, and evaluating data to identify problems with the content of a database.

data collection — The transaction processing activity of capturing transaction related data.

data communications — A specialized subset of telecommunications, referring to the electronic collection, processing, and distribution of data, typically between computer system hardware devices.

data conversion — The transformation of existing computerized files into the proper format to be used by a new system.

data correction — The transaction processing activity of correcting any errors found in data.

data definition language (DDL) — A collection of instructions and commands used to define and describe data and data relationships in a specific database.

data dictionary — A detailed description of all data used in a database, including information such as the name of the data item, who prepared the data, and the range of values for the data.

data editing — The transaction processing activity of checking the validity of the data entered.

data files — Computer-stored collections of data and information, such as a word-processing document.

data integrity — Ensuring that data stored in the database is accurate and up to date.

data item — The specific value of an attribute, found in the fields of the record describing an entity.

data manipulation — The transaction processing activity of processing the transaction data.

data manipulation language (DML) — A specific language provided with a database management system, that allows people and other database users to access, modify, and make queries about data contained in the database and to generate reports.

data mart — A small data warehouse, often developed for a specific person or purpose.

data mining — The process of extracting information from a data warehouse or a data mart; sifting through the combined information of any one customer or group of customers to recognize trends and tendencies—and ultimately pitch products and services specifically for that customer's interests.

data preparation — The process of converting manual files into computer files.

data storage — The transaction processing activity of altering databases to reflect a transaction.

data warehouse — A database that holds important information from a variety of sources.

database — A collection of integrated and related files; a collection of data organized to meet users' needs; an organized collection of facts and information.

database administration — The management of all aspects of a database.

database administrators — The persons responsible for managing all aspects of a database, such as overall design and coordination, user support and training, and testing and maintaining the database management system.

database amount — The size of a database, which depends on the number of records or files in it.

database approach — A data management strategy in which multiple application programs share a pool of related data.

database management software — Personal productivity software that can be used to store large tables of information and produce documents and reports.

database management system (DBMS) — A group of programs that manipulate a database and provide an interface between the database and the user or the database and application programs.

database servers — Computers that store organizational databases, and respond to user queries with requested information.

database system — Everything that makes up the database environment, including a database, a database management system, and the application programs that utilize the data in the database.

dates — In database fields, temporal identifiers, such as 06/12/04, that can be sorted or used in computations.

debugging — The process of tracking down and correcting logic errors in a program.

decision making — A process that takes place in three stages: intelligence, design, and choice.

decision support system (DSS) — An organized collection of people, procedures, software, databases, and devices used to support problem-specific decision making; applications used to solve a variety of nonprogrammed decisions, where the problem in not routine and rules and relationships are not well defined.

decision table — A systems development tool, often used as an alternative to or in conjunction with flowcharts, for displaying various conditions that could exist and the different actions the computer should take as a result of these conditions.

dedicated line — A line that leaves the connection open continuously to support a data network connection.

defragmenting — Rearranging files on a hard disk to increase the speed of executing programs and retrieving data on the hard disk.

delay of service — An attack, caused by a person or group sending an Internet site thousands or millions of access attempts or requests, that does not completely shut down the site but causes it to respond very slowly.

Delphi approach — A group decision-making approach that encourages diversity among group members and fosters creativity and original thinking.

demand fulfillment — The supply chain management process of getting the product or service to the customer.

demand planning — The supply chain management activity of analyzing buying patterns and forecasting customer demand.

demand reports — Reports developed to give certain information at a person's request.

demodulate — To convert an analog signal received by a computer to a digital signal, part of the function (along with modulation) of a modem.

denial of service (DOS) attacks — A person or group using many computers to send an Internet site thousands or millions of access attempts or requests, overwhelming it and preventing others from gaining access; the attack potentially makes the server unavailable to real customers wishing to do business.

design stage — The second stage in the decision-making process, during which alternative solutions are developed and the feasibility and implications of these alternatives are evaluated.

desktop — One of the most popular types of personal computers, designed to sit on a desktop.

desktop publishing — Software to design page layouts for magazines, newspapers, books, and other publications.

dial-up connection — A narrowband Internet service, with data transfer rates of around 50 Kbps, provided by a multitude of Internet Service Providers (ISPs).

digital — Signals that exist in one of two possible values; the opposite of analog.

digital art — A new form of art that uses computer software as the brush and the computer display as the canvas.

digital audio — Digital music and digital sound.

digital camera — An optical recording device or special-purpose computer device that captures images through a lens and stores them digitally rather than on film.

digital cash — A Web service that provides a private and secure method of transferring funds from a bank account or credit card to online vendors or individuals for e-commerce transactions; also known as e-cash.

digital certificate — A type of electronic business card that is attached to Internet transaction data to verify the sender of the data.

digital cinema — The application of digital technology to the production, distribution, and projection of motion pictures, replacing chemicals on film with bits and bytes.

digital convergence — The trend to merge multiple digital services into one device.

digital divide — The gap between people who have access to computers and can effectively use new information and communication tools, such as the Internet, and those who do not have computer access or the training to use computers.

digital graphics — Computer-based media applications that support the creation, editing, and viewing of 2-D and 3-D images, animation, and video.

digital graphics animation — The display of digital images in rapid succession to provide the illusion of motion.

digital imaging — Working with photographic images.

Digital Millennium Copyright Act — A U.S. law enacted in 1998 that provides global copyright protection.

digital music — Any music that is stored digitally, regardless of how it was originally created.

digital projection — The projection of a movie directly from a computer's hard drive.

digital satellite service (DSS) — A wireless broadband Internet service, with data transfer rates of around 400 Kbps, provided by companies such as EarthLink and StarBand, typically used in situations where neither cable broadband nor DSL is available.

digital signal — A signal with a discrete state, either high or low.

digital sound — The spoken word, other nonmusic sounds, and sound effects that are stored and sometimes manipulated digitally; sound that is represented as a series of binary numbers and bits.

Digital Subscriber Line (DSL) connection — A broadband Internet access, with data transfer rates of around 1.5 Mbps, provided by the phone company, or Internet Service Providers working with the phone company.

digital video disk (DVD) — An optical storage device that is similar to a CD but has much smaller pits burned onto the disk surface, allowing DVDs to store much more data.

digital-to-analog converter — A device that translates sound and music to analog signals.

digitization — The process of representing data and information using bits, 1s and 0s,.

direct access — A storage medium feature that allows a computer to go directly to a desired piece of data, by positioning the read-write head over the proper track of a revolving disk.

direct conversion — A startup approach that involves stopping the old system and starting the new system on a given date.

direct observation — A data collection technique in which one or more members of the analysis team directly observe the existing system in action.

discussion boards — Online newsgroups that are similar to listservs, except that rather than using e-mail to facilitate discussion, they use a central bulletin board on the Internet.

display resolution — A measure of the number of pixels on the screen, with a larger number of pixels per square inch considered a higher image resolution.

distance education — Conducting classes over the Web with no physical class meetings.

distributed computing — Computing that involves multiple remote computers that work together to solve a computation problem or to perform information processing.

distributed database — A database in which the actual data may be spread across several databases at different locations, connected via telecommunications devices.

documentation — All flowcharts, diagrams, and other written materials that describe the new or modified system.

domain — In the relational data model, the allowable values for attributes or columns.

domain names — The English name associated with a numerical

Internet Protocol (IP) address, such as www.fsu.edu.

dot-per-inch (dpi) — A printer's output resolution; the greater the number of dots printed per inch, the higher the resolution.

drawing software — Programs that provide tools to create, arrange, and layer graphical objects on the screen to create pictures; also called vector graphics software.

drill down — Clicking links through a series of Web pages to find additional information.

DSL modem — Digital Subscriber Line modem, for connecting digital devices using a digital signal over telephone lines, for relatively inexpensive high-speed access to the Internet.

DVD+RW — One of two popular formats for rewritable DVDs.

DVD-RW — One of two popular formats for rewritable DVDs.

dynamic — Referring to an Internet Protocol (IP) address, one that is assigned to computers as needed.

Earth Simulator — A massively parallel processing system built by NEC in Japan to assist scientists in simulating possible planetary futures.

e-cash — Electronic cash, a Web service that provides a private and secure method of transferring funds from a bank account or credit card to online vendors or individuals for e-commerce transactions.

e-commerce — Electronic commerce, the process of conducting business or other transactions online, over the Internet, or using other telecommunications and network systems; systems that support electronically executed transactions.

e-commerce host — A company that takes on some or all of the responsibility of setting up and maintaining an e-commerce system for a business or organization.

e-commerce software — Software designed specifically to support e-commerce activities, including catalog management, shopping cart use, and payment.

economic feasibility — The determination of whether a project makes financial sense and whether predicted benefits offset the cost and time needed to obtain them.

EDI — electronic data interchange, the network systems technology, standards, and procedures that allow output from one system to be processed directly as input to other systems, without human intervention.

electronic cash — A Web service that provides a private and secure method of transferring funds from a bank account or credit card to online vendors or individuals for e-commerce transactions; also known as e-cash or digital cash.

electronic commerce — Also known as e-commerce, the process of conducting business or other transactions online, over the Internet, or using other telecommunications and network systems; systems that support electronically executed transactions.

electronic deception — The use of computer systems and the Internet to intentionally lie and deceive.

electronic drum machines — Musical instruments that allow the musician to record drum beat patterns by tapping on pressure-sensitive buttons or pads to produce sampled drum sounds that can be played back in a looping pattern.

electronic exchange — An industry-specific Web resource created to provide a convenient centralized platform for B2B e-commerce among manufacturers, suppliers, and customers.

electronic libel — A written statement, produced using a computer system or over the Internet, about a person that is not true and can cause the person harm.

electronic plagiarism — The use of computer systems or the Internet to pass off someone else's work as your own.

electronic shopping cart software — E-commerce software for allowing visitors to collect items to purchase.

electronic wallet — An application that encrypts and stores credit-card information, e-cash information, bank account information—all the personal information required for e-commerce transactions—securely on your computer; also known as e-wallet.

e-mail—Electronic mail; the transmission of messages over a network to support asynchronous text-based communications.

e-mail attachment — Typically a binary file or a formatted text file that travels along with an e-mail message but is not part of the e-mail ASCII text message itself.

e-mail body — The component of an e-mail transmission that contains an ASCII text message written by the sender to the recipient.

e-mail header — The component of an e-mail transmission that contains technical information about the message, such as the destination address, source address, subject, and date and time.

embed — Insert an entire application inside another application.

embedded operating systems — Operating systems, like those for many small computers and special-purpose devices, that are embedded in a computer chip.

emoticons — Combinations of keyboard characters to convey underlying sentiments, such as :-) to create a sideways facial expression meaning happy or smiling.

employee monitoring — Collecting data on what employees do at work, which organizations are now often doing via computer technology.

encapsulation — The containment of all data and actions associated with an object within the object itself.

encoder software — Software used to transfer digital music files from one format to another.

encryption — The use of high-level mathematical functions and computer algorithms to encode data so that it is unintelligible to all but the intended recipient.

encryption devices — Devices used to control and protect industrial-level telecommunications, by being installed at the sending computer to alter outgoing communications according to an encoding scheme that makes the communication unintelligible during transport; specialized hardware and software that can be used to encode data and information to help prevent unauthorized computer use.

end-user computing — The development and use of application programs and computer systems

by non-computer-systems professionals.

end-user systems development — The development of computer systems by individuals outside of the formal computer systems planning and departmental structure.

Energy Star program — A program the EPA has initiated to reduce power usage, for example by restricting how much power a personal computer can consume while being used.

enterprise resource planning (ERP) — A set of transaction processing system applications for handling an organization's routine activities, bundled into a unified package.

enterprise service provider (ESP) — A company that provides users, typically large businesses or organizations, server connections and software that allow employees to access a corporate Intranet from outside the office.

enterprises — Large businesses and organizations, which make extensive use of distributed computing.

entity — A generalized class of people, places, or things (objects) for which data is collected, stored, and maintained.

ergonomic keyboard — A set of keys designed so that the user can enter data in a manner that is comfortable and avoids strain on the hands or wrists.

ergonomics — The study of designing and positioning computer equipment to reduce health problems.

ergonomics — The applied science of designing and arranging the things we work with, such as computer systems, in a manner that promotes health.

error handling — The running of code that checks data items to make sure that they are valid and reasonable; also known as exception handling.

e-tailing — B2C e-commerce; a take-off on the term retailing, since it is the electronic equivalent of a brick-and-mortar retail store.

Ethernet — The most widely used network standard for private networks.

ethical issues — Matters dealing with what is generally considered right or wrong.

event-driven — A type of program that sits idle until an event, such

as a mouse click or key press, occurs and launches a set of computer instructions.

event-driven review — A systems review procedure that is triggered or caused by a problem or opportunity such as an error, a corporate merger, or a new government regulation.

e-wallet — Electronic wallet, an application that encrypts and stores credit-card information, e-cash information, bank account information — all the personal information required for e-commerce transactions — securely on your computer.

exception handling — Error handling, the running of code that checks data items to make sure that they are valid and reasonable.

exception reports — Reports automatically produced when a situation is unusual or requires action.

expansion board — Also known as an expansion card, a circuit board often packaged with specialized peripheral devices for installation on a computer's motherboard.

expansion card — Also known as an expansion board, a circuit board often packaged with specialized peripheral devices for installation on a computer's motherboard.

expansion slots — Connecting sites on a computer motherboard where circuit boards can be inserted to add additional system capabilities.

expert system (ES) — A computerized system that acts or behaves like a human expert in a field or area; an information system that can make suggestions and reach conclusions in much the same way that a human expert can; a subfield of artificial intelligence.

exponential growth — Rapidly increasing growth, such as experienced with problems that get very complex as the input value increases.

extranet — An arrangement whereby Intranet content is extended to specific individuals outside the network, such as customers, partners, or suppliers.

fair use doctrine — The legal principle that describes when and how copyrighted material can be legally used.

feedback — Output a computer produces that is used to make adjustments or changes to input or processing activities.

fiber-optic cable — A type of cable that consists of thousands of extremely thin strands of glass or plastic bound together in sheathing; because it transmits signals via light rather than electricity, fiber-optic cable is extremely fast and reliable.

field — A name, number, or combination of characters that in some way describes an aspect of an object.

field design — The specification of type, size, format, and other aspects of each field.

field name — An identifying label applied to a particular field.

fifth generation languages (5GLs) — High-level programming languages used to create artificial intelligence or expert systems applications.

file — A named collection of instructions or data stored in a computer or computer device; a collection of related records; also called a table in some databases.

file servers — Computers that store organizational and user files, delivering them to workstations on request.

firewall — A device or software that filters the information coming onto a network to protect the network computer from hackers, viruses, and other unwanted network traffic.

FireWire — A standard, and a type of expansion card, for fast video transfer from a camera to the computer.

flash BIOS — A basic input/output system recorded on a flash memory chip rather than a ROM chip. Flash memory can store data permanently, like ROM, but can also be updated with new revisions when they become available.

flash memory card — A chip that maintains its data even after system shut down.

flat file — A type of database in which there is no relationship between the records; often used to store and manipulate a single table or file.

flat panel display — A flat, space-saving display that uses liquid crystals between two pieces of glass to form characters and graphic images on a backlit

screen; also known as liquid crystal display (LCD).

FLOPS — Floating-point operations per second, a more precise measure than MIPS of processor performance.

flowchart — A systems development tool or graphical diagram that reveals the path from a starting point to the final destination.

forensic audio — Digital processing to de-noise, enhance, edit, and detect sounds to assist in criminal investigations.

forensic graphics — Art used to create animations and demonstrative exhibits to use in courts of law in order to explain theories and present evidence.

format – A function performed by the operating system on a disk before it can be used.

FORTRAN (FORmula TRANslator) — Along with BASIC and COBOL, a third-generation, high-level programming language, with increased use of symbolic code.

fourth generation language (4GL) — A high-level programming language, such as Structured Query Language (SQL), that is less procedural and more English-like than third-generation languages, allowing for their use by people with little or no training in computers or programming.

frame buffer — A buffer, also know as video RAM, that stores image data after they are read from RAM and before they are written to the display.

frames — Series of bit-mapped images that when shown in quick succession create the illusion of movement.

freeware — Software, usually for personal computers, that is free.

freeze — A program failure that occurs when a program executes commands that cause the computer to cease responding to user input; also known as a lock-up.

front-end application — Software that directly interacts with people or users.

fuzzy logic — A specialty research area in computer science developed to deal with ambiguous criteria or probabilities and events that are not mutually exclusive; also known as fuzzy sets; a form of mathematical logic used in artificial intelligence systems.

fuzzy sets — A specialty research area in computer science developed to deal with ambiguous criteria or probabilities and events that are not mutually exclusive; also known as fuzzy logic.

game artists — Technicians who use 2-D or 3-D graphics tools to develop video game characters and backgrounds.

game designers — Technicians who develop a video game's theme, storyline, rules, characters, and environment.

game programmers — Technicians who take all the pieces, including video game design, characters, backgrounds, animation, and sound, and encode them into the game software.

game testers — Technicians who check the final video game product for bugs and glitches, as well as game enthusiasts contracted to play the game and provide feedback.

game theory — The study of strategies used by people, organizations, or countries who are competing against each other.

gamepad — A specialized input device used to control and manipulate game characters in a virtual world.

garbage in, garbage out (GIGO) — Inaccurate data being entered into a database, resulting in inaccurate output.

gateway — A network point that acts as an entrance to another network.

General Public License (GPL) — A legal arrangement that makes software available for free to its users.

general purpose — Input devices designed for a variety of computer environments, such as the standard keyboard and mouse.

general-purpose computers — Computers that can be programmed and used for a wide variety of tasks or purposes, such as mobile and personal computers.

general-purpose database — A database that can be used for a large number of applications.

genetic algorithm — An approach, based on the theory of evolution, to solving large, complex problems where a number of algorithms or models change and evolve until the best one emerges.

geographic information system (GIS) — An application capable of storing, manipulating, and displaying geographic or special information, including maps of locations or regions around the world.

gigaflop — Billions of floating-point operations per second, a measurement for rating the speed of microprocessors.

gigahertz — Billions of cycles per second, a measurement used to identify CPU clock speed; for example, a 500 GHz processor runs at 500 billion cycles per second.

global area network (GAN) — A wide area network that crosses an international border; an international network.

global positioning system (GPS) — A sophisticated satellite networking system that is able to pinpoint exact locations on earth; a special-purpose computing device, typically installed in an automobile or boat, that uses satellite and mobile communications technology to pinpoint current location.

global supply management (GSM) — A process that provides methods for businesses to find the best deals on the global market for raw materials and supplies needed to manufacture their products.

goal-seeking analysis — The process of determining what problem data is required for a given result.

graphical user interface (GUI) — Access to and command of a computer system by using pictures or icons on the screen and menus, which many people find easier to learn and use compared to a command-based user interface.

graphics tablets and pens — Input tools that allow you to draw with a penlike device on a tablet to create drawings on a display.

group consensus approach — A group decision-making approach that forces the group to reach a unanimous decision.

group decision support system (GDSS) — The hardware, software, people, databases, and procedures needed to provide effective support in group decision-making settings; also called a computerized collaborative work system.

groupthink — A phenomenon in which a group assumes that they have made the right decision without examining alternatives.

groupware — Group decision support system software that helps with joint work group scheduling, communication, and management; software that allows network users to collaborate over the network; also called workgroup software.

hacker — A person who knows computer technology and spends time learning and using computer systems.

handheld computers — A type of small, easy to use mobile computer.

handheld scanners — Compact data input scanning devices that can convert pictures, forms, and text into bit-mapped images.

hard copy — Computer output printed to paper.

hardware — All of the computer equipment used to input raw data, process it into something meaningful, and output the results.

Help — Features of a software package that may include program documentation that explains the program to users.

hertz (Hz) — A measurement of signal frequency, in cycles per second.

heuristics — A problem-solving method used in decision support systems, often referred to as "rules of thumb"—commonly accepted guidelines or procedures that usually find a good, though not optimal, solution.

hierarchical database model — A database model in which the data is organized in a top-down or inverted tree-like structure.

hierarchy of data — The progressive levels of characters, fields, records, files, and databases, such that characters are combined to make a field, fields are combined to make a record, and so forth.

high-capacity diskette — A magnetic storage device, such as the Iomega Zip disk, that stores 69 to 83 times as much data as on a standard floppy disk.

high-level programming language — A third-or-higher-generation programming language that uses English-like statements and commands to promote ease of learning and use.

home page — The main page or starting place for a site on the World Wide Web.

HomePLC — Home power-line communication, networking that takes advantage of a home's existing power lines and electrical outlets to connect computers; also called power-line networking.

HomePNA — Home phone-line networking alliance, networking that takes advantage of existing phone wiring in a residence; also called phone-line networking.

HTML tag — Hypertext Markup Language tag, a specific command indicated with angle brackets (<>) that tells a Web browser how to display items on a page.

hubs — Small electronic boxes that are used as a central point for connecting a series of computers.

human-readable — Information that a person can read and understand.

hybrid — A network topology that combines two or more other network topologies, such as star bus topology.

hyperlink — An element in an electronic document, such as a word, phrase, or an image, that when clicked opens a related document. Hyperlinks are a cornerstone of the World Wide Web.

hypermedia — Pictures or other media that act as a links to related documents.

hypertext — Text that acts as a link to a related document.

Hypertext Markup Language (HTML) — The primary markup language that is used to specify the formatting of a Web page.

Hypertext Transfer Protocol (HTTP) — The protocol used to control communication between Web clients and servers.

IBM-compatible — One of the two most popular personal computing platforms. It includes all PCs manufactured to work like the IBM PC; sometimes called Wintel since these computers typically use the Microsoft Windows operating system and Intel or Intel-compatible processors.

identification numbers — Sets of numbers known by individuals and used to prevent unauthorized access to computer systems, including personal computers and PDAs.

identity theft — The act of stealing someone's personal information, such as their Social Security number, driver's license number, credit-card numbers, and other personal information, and then using that information illegally.

image-based rendering — A form of computer modeling that allows digital photorealistic actors stored on computer to be manipulated as animated characters.

immediacy — A database characteristic, referring to a measure of how rapidly changes must be made to data.

implementation stage — A stage of the problem-solving process, during which action is taken to put the solution into effect.

informatics — The combination of traditional disciplines, like science and medicine, with computer systems and technology.

information — A collection of facts organized in such a way that they have additional value beyond the value of the facts themselves.

information overload — The inability to find the information you need on the ever-growing Web due to an overabundance of unrelated information.

infrared transmission — The sending of signals through the air via light waves, a type of wireless media.

ink-jet printer — A popular type of printer, providing economical but relatively low-print-quality black and white or color output.

input device — A device that helps to capture and enter raw data into a computer system, such as a keyboard, mouse, or touch screen.

input — Information a computer collects, manipulates, and stores. This information can take many different forms.

installation — The process of physically placing computer equipment on the site and making it operational.

instant messaging — A form of chat for one-on-one communications over the Internet.

instruction set — The specific set of instructions that a processor is engineered to carry out.

integrated application packages — An application that contains several basic programs, such as word processing, spreadsheet, and calendar, offering a range of capabilities, but with less power and for less money than the standalone software included in software suites.

integrated circuit — A module, or chip, consisting of multiple electronic components and used to store and process bits and bytes in today's computers.

integrated digital studios — High-tech electronic systems that package many digital recording devices in one unit for convenient home recording.

integration testing — Testing all related systems together, to ensure that the new program(s) can interact with other major applications.

intellectual property rights — Rights associated with the ownership and use of software, music, movies, data, and information.

intelligence stage — The first stage in the decision-making process, during which a person or group of people identify and define potential problems or opportunities.

intelligent agent — An intelligent robot, or bot, consisting of programs and a knowledge base used to perform a specific task for a person, a process, or another program.

interactive media — Multimedia presentations that involve user interaction for education, training, or entertainment, typically by combining both digital audio and digital video for a full multimedia experience.

interactive TV — A digital television service that includes one or more of the following: video on demand, personal video recorder, local information on TV, purchase over TV, Internet access over TV, and video games over TV.

Internet — An international network that allows computers and other devices to be connected to other computers and a vast array of devices and services.

Internet Access over TV — Services, such as WebTV, that allow viewers to navigate the Web on their television sets.

Internet backbone — The collection of the many national and international communications networks owned by major telecommunication companies, such as MCI, AT&T, and Sprint, that provides the hardware over which Internet traffic travels.

Internet cafes — Also known as cybercafes, coffee houses and other sites that provide locations where people away from their homes or offices can connect to the Internet.

Internet hosts — The more than 200 million computers joined together to create the Internet, the world's largest network.

Internet Message Access Protocol (IMAP) — A communication standard used to transfer only the e-mail headers from an e-mail server to a PC.

Internet Protocol — Along with Transmission Control Protocol (TCP), one of the sets of policies, procedures, and standards used on the Internet to enable communications between two devices; defines the format and addressing scheme used for packets.

Internet radio — Radio programming that is similar to local AM and FM radio, except that it is digitally delivered to a computer over the Internet, and there are more choices of stations.

Internet service providers (ISPs) — Companies that provide users access to the Internet through points of presence.

internetwork — Networks joined together to make larger networks, such as today's Internet, so that users on different networks can communicate and share data.

interpreter — A language translator that converts each statement in a programming language into a machine language and executes the statement.

intranet — A private network that uses the protocols of the Internet and the Web, TCP/IP and HTTP, along with Internet services such as Web browsers.

IP address — A unique Internet Protocol address consisting of a series of four numbers (0 to 255) separated by periods, assigned to all devices connected to the Internet.

IrDA ports — Infrared Data Association ports, for using infrared transmission to connect most handheld and notebook computers to desktop computers and other digital devices.

Java — An object-oriented programming language developed by Sun Microsystems that can be used to create programs that run on any operating system and on the Internet.

Java Applets — Small applications developed using the Java programming language.

JavaScript — A programming language developed specifically for the Web and more limited in nature than Java and other high-level programming languages.

joining — A basic data manipulation that involves combining two or more tables.

joint application development (JAD) — A requirements analysis technique that involves group meetings in which users, stakeholders, and computer systems professionals work together to analyze existing systems, propose possible solutions, and define the requirements of a new or modified system.

joystick — A specialized input device, in the form of a swiveling stick, used to control and manipulate game characters in a virtual world.

jukebox software — Software that allows computer users to categorize and organize digital music files for easy access.

key — A field in a record that is used to identify the record.

keyboard — An input device for entering data into a computer.

key-indicator report — A special type of scheduled report that summarizes the previous day's critical activities, and is typically available at the beginning of each workday.

keywords — Words that are specified to a search engine to find information on a topic of interest.

kiosks — Special-purpose computing stations, often equipped with touch-sensitive screens, made available where the public can access location-relevant information.

language translator — System software that converts a statement from a high-level programming language into machine language to be executed by the CPU.

laptop — Also called a notebook, a type of personal computer designed for portability.

laser printers — A popular type of printer that provides the cleanest output and is typically used when professional-quality documents are required.

LCD projectors — Small, portable devices used to project presentations from a computer onto a larger screen.

learning systems — A combination of software and hardware that allows the computer to change how it functions or that reacts to situations based on feedback it receives.

legal feasibility — The determination of whether laws or regulations may prevent or limit a systems development project.

license agreement — A contract that software companies may require users to accept that specifies how the software can be used.

link — A feature of applications that work together through object linking and embedding, such that a change in one application is transferred to another.

linked — In a relational database, the connection of tables that share at least one common data element; allowing tables to be linked can provide useful information and reports and is a primary advantage of a relational database.

Linux — An open-source, GUI-based operating system developed in 1991 by Linus Torvalds, which runs on computer systems ranging from small personal computers to large mainframe systems.

Linux servers — Computer systems using the Linux operating system to operate over a network or the Internet.

liquid crystal display (LCD) — A flat, space-saving panel display that uses liquid crystals between two pieces of glass to form characters and graphic images on a backlit screen; also known as flat panel display.

listservs — Special interest groups that create online communities for discussing topic-related issues via e-mail.

load-balancing — The sharing of system processing among servers so that if one goes down, the others pick up the slack.

local — Along with network, one of two types of resources that workstations typically have access to: the files, drives and printers or other peripheral devices that are accessible to the workstation on or off the network.

local area network (LAN) — A network that connects computer systems and devices within the same geographical area.

Local Information on TV — A feature of interactive TV that provides local community news and information.

localization — The process of creating multiple versions of a Web site, each in a different language and catering to a different cultural bias.

lock-up — A program failure that occurs when a program executes commands that cause the computer to cease responding to user input; also known as a freeze.

logic bomb — A program designed to "explode" or execute at a specified time and date.

logic error — The result of a poor algorithm that contains a flaw in reasoning, causing a program to crash, behave in an unexpected fashion, or not effectively solve the problem for which it was designed.

logical — Database fields limited to certain operators, such as "yes" or "no."

logical access path (LAP) — The way an application program seeks data from the database management system.

logical versus physical access — Two ways of viewing memory access, exemplified by how memory-management programs convert a logical request for data or instructions into the physical location where the data or instructions are stored.

loop — An action repeated as long as some condition exists in the program.

machine cycle — The combination of the instruction phase and the execution phase, which together are required to execute an instruction.

machine cycle time – The amount of time that is required for a computer to carry out one instruction.

machine languages — First-generation programming languages with instructions written in binary code, telling the CPU exactly which circuits to switch on and off.

machine-readable data — Information that is usually stored as bits and bytes and can be read and understood by a computer system.

macro virus — A program that infects applications that use a macro language, including some word processors and spreadsheet programs.

magnetic disk — A thin steel platter (hard disk) or piece of Mylar film (floppy disk) used to store data, with widely varying capacity and portability.

magnetic ink character recognition (MICR) — Use of a special-purpose optical reading device to read magnetic-ink characters, such as those written on the bottom of a check.

magnetic storage — Technology that uses magnetic properties of iron oxide particles to store data more permanently than RAM.

magnetic tape — Mylar film coated with an iron oxide; used as a sequential access storage medium.

mail forwarding — Forwarding e-mail messages to one central account, a strategy to manage multiple e-mail accounts.

mainframe servers — Computer systems typically used by universities and large organizations, which require plenty of processing power and speed.

management information system (MIS) — An organized collection of people, procedures, databases, and devices used to provide routine information to managers and decision makers; it supports programmed decisions by providing reports on structured problems.

managers — The people within an organization who are most capable of initiating and maintaining change.

market segmentation — A method of market research in which customer opinions are divided into categories of race, gender, and age to determine which segment a product appeals to most.

marketplaces — E-commerce sites that provide a public platform for global trading where practically anyone can buy, sell, or trade practically anything.

massively parallel processing — A form of multiprocessing, used in supercomputers, that works by linking a large number of powerful processors to operate together.

master files — Permanent files that are updated over time.

m-commerce — Mobile commerce, a form of e-commerce that takes place over wireless mobile devices such as handheld computers and cell phones.

media cards — Flash memory cards used in media devices such as digital cameras, camcorders, and portable MP3 players.

media players — Media software programs that combine digital music functions with video support; popular media players such as Windows Media Player from Microsoft and QuickTime Player from Apple are free downloads.

megahertz (MHz) — Millions of cycles per second, a measurement used to identify CPU clock speed; for example, a 500 MHz processor runs at 500 million cycles per second.

meta search engine — A tool that allows you to run keyword searches on several search engines at once.

meta tags — Information tags, containing terms such as business-related keywords, that are read by search engines and Web servers, but not displayed on the page by a Web browser.

methods — The actions that objects in object-oriented design can carry out.

metropolitan area network (MAN) — A large, high-speed network connecting a series of smaller networks within a city or metropolitan size area.

microprocessor — A single module, smaller than a fingernail, that holds all of a computer's central processing unit (CPU) circuits and performs system processing.

microwave transmission — Also known as terrestrial microwave, the line-of-sight sending of high-frequency radio signals through the air.

MIDI cards — Musical instrument digital interface expansion boards, available for Windows PCs and included as standard equipment in most Apple computers, that allow computers to be connected to digital music devices.

midrange servers — Also called minicomputers, computer systems that are more powerful than personal computers and are used by small businesses and organizations to perform business functions, scientific research, and more.

MIPS — Millions of instructions per second, indicating the amount of time it takes a processor to execute an instruction, a measure of processor performance.

mixing board — A large panel with many dials, buttons, and sliders that a sound engineer uses to adjust the sound quality of each instrument separately.

mobile commerce — A form of e-commerce that takes place over wireless mobile devices such as handheld computers and cell phones; also known as m-commerce.

mobile computers — Small, portable, and easy to use computer systems, such as personal digital assistants (PDAs), tablet PCs, and palmtop computers.

modem — An external or internal device that converts analog and digital signals from one form to the other.

modulation — The conversion of a computer's digital signal to an analog signal, part of the function (along with demodulation) of a modem.

monitoring stage — The final stage of the problem-solving process, during which the decision makers evaluate the solution's implementation to determine whether the anticipated results were achieved and to modify the process in light of new information learned during the implementation stage.

Moore's Law — A trend, first predicted by Intel cofounder Gordon Moore in 1965 and since proven true, that technological innovations would be capable of doubling the transistor densities in an integrated circuit every 18 months, resulting in increased processor speeds.

motherboard — Also called the system board, the main circuit board of the computer where many of the hardware components are placed, such as the central processing unit, memory, storage, and other supportive chips.

mouse — An input device for entering data into a computer.

MP3 — A digital music file format that compresses music files to less than 10 percent of their original size.

MP3 players — Special-purpose computer devices used for listening to digital music files.

multimedia — Digital devices of all kinds that serve and support digital media such as music, video, and graphics; the computer's ability to present and manipulate visual and audio media such as graphics, animation, video, sound, and music.

multimedia messaging service (MMS) — A service for mobile cell phone users to send pictures, voice recordings, and video clips to other cell phones or e-mail accounts.

multiplexer — A device used to control and protect industrial-level telecommunications, by sending multiple signals or streams of information over a medium at the same time in the form of a single, complex signal.

multiprocessing — The simultaneous operation of more than one processing unit.

Multipurpose Internet Mail Extensions (MIME) — The protocol that e-mail servers follow to govern the transportation of e-mail attachments.

multitasking — Running more than one application at the same time.

multithreading — Running several parts of an application at the same time.

musical instrument digital interface (MIDI) — A protocol, implemented in 1983, that provides a standard language for digital music devices to use in communicating with each other.

narrowband — A category of bandwidth; narrowband is slower than broadband and is more restricted in its applications and uses.

natural language processing — Often referred to as speech recognition, the ability that allows a computer to understand and react to statements and commands made in a "natural" language, such as English.

netiquette — Network etiquette, the informal set of conduct rules for communicating online.

network — Along with local, one of two types of resources that workstations typically have access to: those that the workstation can access only while connected to the network; also called remote resources.

network access server (NAS) — A computer that large businesses or organizations use to access the network.

network adapter — A computer circuit board, PC Card, or USB device installed in a computing device so that it can be connected to a network.

network administrator — Person responsible for setting up and maintaining a network, implementing policies, and assigning user access permissions.

network model — An extension of the hierarchical database model, characterized by an owner-member relationship in which a member may have many owners.

network operating system (NOS) — Operating system software, such as Windows NT and Windows 2000, that controls the computer systems and devices on a network and allows them to communicate with each other; includes security and network management features.

networking devices — Hardware components that together with networking software enable and control communications signals between communications and computer devices.

networking hardware devices — Also known as networking devices, hardware components that together with networking software enable and control communications signals between communications and computer devices.

networking media — Anything that carries an electronic signal and creates an interface between a sending device and a receiving device.

networking software — Software components that work together with hardware components to enable and control communications signals between communications and computer devices.

networks — Interlinked systems that can connect computers and computer equipment in a building, across the country, or around the world.

neural network — A computer system that can act like or simulate the functioning of a human brain, process many pieces of data at once, and learn to recognize patterns; a branch of artificial intelligence.

newsletters — Subscription-based broadcast e-mail communications, such as the *New York Times* newsletter.

nodes — Devices attached to a network.

nominal group technique (NGT) — A group decision-making approach that encourages participation and feedback from each member of the group and reaches a final decision through a vote.

nonprogrammed decisions — Decisions that deal with unusual or exceptional situations, and in many cases are difficult to look at as a matter of a rule, procedure, or quantitative method.

nonvolatile — A characteristic of permanent or secondary memory storage, such that a loss of power to the computer does not cause a loss of data and programs.

normalization — The process of correcting data problems or anomalies to insure that the database contains good data.

notebook — Also called a laptop, a popular type of personal computer designed for its portability.

numeric field — A database field that contains numbers that can be used in making calculations.

object — An element of the object-oriented design approach that is composed of attributes and methods.

object code — The machine-language code necessary for a computer to execute programming instructions.

object linking and embedding (OLE) — A software suite feature that enables users to copy a figure, table, chart, or text from one application and paste it into another application.

object-oriented (OO) systems development — A systems development process that follows a defined life cycle, much like the SDLC, and typically involves defining requirements, designing the system, implementation and programming, evaluation, and operation.

object-oriented database — A database that stores both data and the processing instructions for it.

object-oriented database management system (OODBMS) — A group of programs that manipulates an object-oriented database, providing an interface between the database and the user or the database and application programs.

object-oriented design — An approach to programming design that derives the solution to the program specification from the interaction of objects.

object-oriented programming languages — High-level programming languages, such as Visual Basic .NET, C++, and Java, that group together data, instructions, and other programming procedures.

off-the-shelf — Software mass produced to meet the needs of particular markets.

off-the-shelf software — An existing software program developed for the general market.

off-the-shelf software packages — Software programs developed for the general market; also called general software programs.

on-board synthesizers — Synthesizers located on most personal computers' sound cards that include all the standard synthesizer keyboard sounds.

online clearinghouses — E-commerce sites that provide a method for manufacturers to liquidate stock and consumers to find a good deal.

online transaction process — A method of processing transactions at the point of sale, which is critical for time-sensitive transactions such as making flight reservations.

Open Mobile Alliance — An organization comprised of hundreds of the world's leading mobile operators, device and network suppliers, information technology companies, and content providers, which have joined together to create standards and ensure interoperability between mobile devices.

Open System Interconnection (OSI) — A detailed, seven-layer model for networks, such as the Internet, that provides network technicians and administrators with a deeper understanding of the technology to design and troubleshoot networks.

open-source — Offering users free and open access to source code, such as the Linux operating system does.

open-source software — Software programs that make the source or machine code available to the public, allowing users to make changes to the software or develop new software that integrates with the open-source software.

operating system (OS) — A set of computer programs that runs or controls the computer hardware, acts like a buffer between hardware and application software, and acts as an interface between application programs and users.

operational feasibility — The determination, affected by both physical and motivational considerations, of whether or not a project can be put into action or operation.

optical character recognition (OCR) — Use of a special-purpose reading device to read hand-printed characters.

optical mark recognition (OMR) — Use of a special-purpose reading device to read "bubbled-in" forms, such as those found on exams and ballots.

optical storage — Technology that uses an optical laser to burn pits into the surface of a highly reflective disk, such as a CD or DVD, to store data. Such disks hold significantly more data than a magnetic device.

optimization — A feature of many spreadsheet programs that allows the spreadsheet to maximize or minimize a quantity subject to certain constraints.

optimization model — A popular problem-solving method, used in decision support systems, that identifies the best solution, usually the one that best helps individuals or organizations meet their goals.

order processing system — A type of transaction processing system that supports the sales of goods or services to customers and arranges for shipment of products.

output — Computer produced information, usually in the form of documents, reports, and data for other applications.

output device — A device that displays the results produced by a computer, such as a display screen or printer.

outsourcing — The hiring of an outside consulting firm that specializes in systems development to take over some or all of an organization's computer systems development activities; taking jobs that were once performed inside an organization or company and transferring them to outside organizations or companies.

packet — Data transported over the Internet as a small group of bytes, which includes the data being sent as well as a header containing information about the data, such as its destination, origin, size, and identification number.

packet switching — The dividing of information into small groups of bytes in order to make efficient use of the network.

page scanners — Data input scanning devices that can convert pictures, forms, and text into bit-mapped images.

pagers — Small lightweight devices that receive signals from transmitters.

pages printed per minute (ppm) — A measurement used to compare the speed of printers.

palmtop computers — A type of small, easy to use mobile computer.

parallel conversion — A process during the phase-in startup approach in which parts of the old system and new system are running at the same time.

parallel processing — A form of multiprocessing that works by linking several microprocessors to operate at the same time, or in parallel.

parental control — Applications, such as Net Nanny, that filter out adult content to make Web browsing safe for young users.

passwords — Words known by individuals and used to prevent unauthorized access to computer systems, including personal computers and PDAs.

payment software — E-commerce software to facilitate payment for merchandise and arrange shipping.

PC Cards — Short for PCMCIA cards, small expansion cards typically inserted into notebook computers to support network adapters, modems, and additional storage devices.

PC-based video phones — Devices that provide video phone services through a combination of a headset or speakers with microphone, a video camera or Webcam, video communication software and the multimedia functionality of a PC with an Internet connection.

PCMCIA cards — Usually called PC Cards, small expansion cards typically inserted into notebook computers to support network adapters, modems, and additional storage devices. PCMCIA is an acronym for the standard-developing Personal Computer Memory Card International Association.

PCMCIA slots — The area on notebook computers where PCMCIA cards can be inserted.

peer-to-peer (P2P) — A type of networking communication in which a computer acts as both a client and a server, allowing participants to provide other participants with direct access to a portion of their file system

people — Users and operators—the most important element in most computer systems.

personal area network (PAN) — The interconnection of personal information technology devices within the range of an individual, usually around 32 feet.

personal computers — Systems, typically laptop and desktop, used by individuals and now found in more than half of all U.S. households.

personal digital assistants (PDAs) — A type of small, easy to use mobile computer.

personal information managers (PIMs) — Software that individuals, groups, and organizations can use to store information, such as a list of tasks to complete or a list of names and addresses; a special-purpose database for storing personal information.

Personal Video Recorders — Electronic devices, such as Tivo and Replay TV, which provide large hard drive storage to record dozens of movies and programs to be watched at your leisure.

pervasive communications — The ability to communicate with anyone, anywhere, anytime, through a variety of formats, resulting from advances in wireless and Internet communications.

pervasive computing — The growing spread of computer devices to the point where everything and anything can be used for input and output.

peta — A prefix that represents 2 to the 50th power (roughly a quadrillion, or a thousand million).

phase-in approach — A popular startup technique preferred by many organizations, in which the new system is slowly phased in, while the old one is slowly phased out.

phone-line networking — Networking that takes advantage of existing phone wiring in a residence; also called HomePNA (home phone-line networking alliance).

photo printers — Printers, often used in conjunction with digital cameras, that produce photo-quality images on special photo-quality paper.

photo-editing software — Programs with special tools and effects designed for improving or manipulating bitmapped photograph images.

physical access path (PAP) — The way a database management system, working in conjunction with various systems software programs, retrieves data from a storage device.

physical layer — The hardware portion of the three-layer Internet model, which also includes application (software) and transport (protocol) layers.

pilot startup — A startup approach that involves running a pilot or small version of the new system along with the old.

piracy — The act of illegally duplicating software, music, or movies.

pixels — Short for picture elements, small points organized in a grid to form an image. Pixels are used to determine the quality of displays, printers, scanners, and digital cameras — the higher the pixels the better the quality.

plagiarism — Representing someone else's writing as your own.

plain old telephone service (POTS) — The conventional, analog-based telephone service provided by phone companies.

Platform for Privacy Preference — Software being developed primarily for Internet usage to help protect individuals' privacy; it has the potential to alert an individual to companies that don't have adequate privacy policies according to specified preferences.

plotters — Output devices that produce hard copy for general design work, such as blueprints and schematics.

plug and play (PnP) — An operating system feature that allows users to attach a new hardware device and have it automatically installed and configured by the operating system.

plug-in — An application, such as Macromedia's Flash, that works with a Web browser to offer extended services, such as the ability to view audio, animations, or video.

points of presence (PoPs) — Utility stations that enable Internet users to connect to network service providers, including networking hardware for dial-up connections.

portable operating system — Sometimes called generic, an operating system that can function with different hardware configurations.

ports — On Internet server computers, logical addresses that are associated with a specific service; on personal computers, sockets where you can connect devices, such as displays, keyboards, and printers.

Post Office Protocol (POP) — The standard used to transfer e-mails from an e-mail server to a PC.

postproduction sound engineering — The addition of sound tracks, sound effects, and voice-overs to a movie after the movie has been recorded.

powerline broadband — A broadband Internet access, not yet widely offered, over the power grids; connecting a computer to the Internet would be as easy as plugging a powerline modem into a wall outlet.

power-line networking — Networking that takes advantage of a home's existing power lines and electrical outlets to connect computers; also called HomePLC (home power-line communication).

power-on self test (POST) — A test that is performed during the booting process to make sure that components are working correctly.

presentation graphics — Personal productivity software programs, such as Microsoft PowerPoint, that enable people to create slideshow presentations using built-in features ranging from developing charts and drawings, to formatting text, to inserting movies and sound clips.

primary key — The main or principal database field used to uniquely identify a record so that it can be accessed, organized, and manipulated.

print driver — Software used by the operating system to add a new printer.

privacy — The right to be let alone and not intruded upon without your consent.

Privacy Act — The major piece of legislation on privacy, enacted by Congress in 1974.

problem analysis — The first and most important stage of software development, in which problem requirements are studied in order to create detailed specifications for the computer program; the first of five stages in the program development life cycle, in which problems are clearly defined by breaking them into their fundamental components.

problem solving — A process that combines the three phases of decision making—intelligence, design, and choice—with implementation and monitoring.

procedure — In structured design, a code module or subroutine, which is designed to solve a subproblem.

procedures — The strategies, policies, methods, and rules people use to operate a computer system.

processing — An action a computer takes to convert or transform data into useful outputs.

production studios — Sound production studios that work with motion pictures.

productivity — A measure of the output achieved divided by the input required.

program code — The set of instructions that signal the CPU to perform circuit-switching operations.

program coding — The process of creating a program using a programming language to carry out predetermined algorithms, the third of five phases of the program development life cycle.

program debugging and testing — The process of ensuring that software successfully accomplishes the goals for which it was designed, the fourth of five phases of the program development life cycle.

program delivery — A problem analysis activity that defines where the program will be installed, who will have access to the program, and what type of user interface will be chosen.

program design — The software development stage in which a formal algorithm is designed to satisfy the requirements of the program specification; making use of logical thinking and algorithms to produce a detailed path to defined goals, the second of five phases of the program development life cycle.

program development — Software development, the process of developing software solutions and services, or computer programs, to address a specific need or problem.

program development life cycle — A five-step sequence of activities for developing and maintaining programming code that includes problem analysis, program design, program implementation, testing and debugging, and maintenance.

program documentation — The collection of narrative descriptions produced by a software manufacturer that explains the program's use and implementation, usually included in Help features or menus, on the Internet, or in manuals.

program files — Computer-stored collections of instructions that can be run or executed, such as a word processing program.

program flowcharts — Detailed flowcharts that reveal how each software program in a system is to be developed.

program implementation — The stage in the software development process in which the algorithm developed in the program design stage is translated into a computer programming language to create a working, executable program.

program logic — An algorithm, a step-by-step problem-solving process that arrives at a solution in a finite amount of time.

program maintenance — Observing software in action and improving upon it if and when necessary, the fifth and final stage of the program development life cycle.

program specification — A document, resulting from problem analysis, that defines the requirements of the program in terms of input, processing, and output.

program testing and debugging — The software development stage in which stringent tests on the program are run to determine if it is ready for release.

programmed decisions — Decisions that are made using a rule, procedure, or quantitative method, and that are easy to automate using traditional computer systems.

programmer — An individual who writes or codes the instructions that make up a computer program.

programming — The writing or coding of instructions to create a computer program.

programming language — Coding schemes, used to write both systems and application software, whose primary function is to provide instructions to the computer system.

programming language standard — A set of rules that describes how programming statements and commands should be written.

project leader — The individual in charge of the systems development effort, who coordinates all aspects and is responsible for its success.

project management — The planning, monitoring, and controlling of necessary systems development activities.

projecting — A basic data manipulation, involving eliminating columns in a table.

proprietary — Services or products that are protected by exclusive legal rights and thus, for example, often do not communicate or easily interconnect with each other.

proprietary operating system — A vendor developed operating system intended for use with specific computer hardware.

proprietary software — An program developed or customized by an individual, group, or organization for a specific application.

protocol — Rules that ensure that devices participating in a network are communicating in a uniform and manageable manner; an agreed-upon format for transmitting data between two devices.

prototyping — An iterative technique for systems development that typically involves the creation of some preliminary model or version of a major subsystem, or a small or "scaled-down" version of the entire system.

proximity payment system — A mobile commerce transaction method using devices that allow customers to transfer funds wirelessly between their mobile device and a point-of-sale terminal.

pseudocode — A form of notation that describes the detailed steps of an algorithm in a fashion similar to a programming language, but in a more natural language without the formal syntax requirements of a programming language.

public domain software — Software that is not protected by copyright laws and can be freely copied and used.

Purchase over TV — A feature of interactive TV that allows viewers to make purchases over their cable TV connection, much as computer users make purchases on the Web; sometimes called t-commerce.

purchasing system — A type of transaction processing system that supports the purchase of goods and raw materials from suppliers for the manufacturing of products.

quality — The ability of a product, including services, to meet or exceed customer expectations.

query by example (QBE) — An easy and fast way to make queries about data contained in a database; many databases use this approach to give users ideas and examples of how queries can be made.

radio frequency identification device (RFID) — A tiny microprocessor combined with an antenna that is able to broadcast identifying information to an RFID reader, primarily used to track merchandise from supplier to retailer to customer.

random access memory (RAM) — Temporary storage that is cleared each time a computer is turned off.

rapid application development (RAD) — A requirements analysis approach that combines joint application development, prototyping, and other techniques in order to quickly and accurately determine the requirements for a system.

raster — Bit-mapped graphics, in which bytes are used to store the color of each pixel in an image.

ray-tracing — Creating computerized 3-D models by adding shadows and light, which 3-D modeling software does by tracing beams of light as they would interact with the models in the real world.

readme — Files included with software that often contain last minute updates or disclosures, including how to deal with bugs.

read-only memory (ROM) — Permanent storage for data and instructions that do not change, such as programs and data from the computer manufacturer.

record — A collection of related fields.

recording studios — Sound production studios that specialize in recording music.

recovery disk — A disk that stores an operating system for starting the computer when there is a problem with the hard disk and the computer is not booting correctly.

reduced instruction set computer (RISC) — A processor architecture that, compared to a complex instruction set computer (CISC) architecture, works with a smaller instruction set and slower system clock. Apple Power PC processors are based on it.

refined — Broken down into smaller steps.

register — Secure official authorization for a software program's use from the software maker.

registers — One of three primary elements within a central processing unit (CPU), they hold the bytes that are currently being processed.

relational model — A database model in which all data elements are placed in two-dimensional tables called relations that are the logical equivalent of files.

relations — Two-dimensional tables that are the logical equivalent of files.

remote — Along with local, one of two types of resources that workstations typically have access to: those that the workstation can access only while connected to the network; also called network resources.

removable disk cartridge — A magnetic storage device, such as the Iomega Jaz disk, that contains a hard disk within a removable cartridge, thus combining hard disk storage capacity and floppy disk portability.

rendering — The process of calculating the light interaction with the virtual 3-D models in a scene and presenting the final drawing in two dimensions to be viewed on the screen or printed.

repeaters — Devices used to boost the signal in twisted-pair cable so that it can travel longer distances; repeaters are also used to connect multiple network segments.

repetitive stress injury (RSI) — A potentially computer-related health problem characterized by conditions such as tendonitis, tennis elbow, the inability to hold objects, and sharp pain in the fingers, caused by long hours at the computer keyboard; also known as repetitive motion disorder.

replicated database — A database that holds a duplicate set of frequently used data.

request for information (RFI) — A request directed to a computer systems vendor to provide information about its products or services.

request for proposal (RFP) — A request directed to a computer systems vendor to submit a bid for a new or modified system.

request for quotes (RFQ) — A request directed to a computer systems vendor to give prices for its products or services.

requirements analysis — The process of determining user, stakeholder, and organizational needs.

rescue disk — Software on a floppy disk, CD ROM, or other disk used to start or boot your computer in case you can't start or boot your computer from your hard disk.

restart — A procedure or button on a computer that when clicked performs a warm boot.

ring — A network topology in which computers and computer devices are arranged in a ring or circle.

ripper software — Programs that can be used to translate music CDs to MP3 files on your hard drive.

ripping — The process of transferring music from CD to MP3.

robot — An automated machine or system.

robotics — The development of mechanical or computer devices to perform tasks that require a high degree of precision or that are tedious or hazardous for humans.

routers — Advanced networking components that can divide a single network into two logically separate networks.

routers — Special-purpose computing devices, typically small to large boxes with network ports, that manage network traffic by evaluating messages and routing them to their destination.

sample — To measure a sound wave's amplitude at regular timed intervals.

sampler — A digital music instrument that digitally records real musical instrument sounds and allows them to be played back at various pitches using an electronic keyboard.

schedule feasibility — The determination of whether a project can be completed in a reasonable amount of time.

scheduled reports — Reports produced periodically or on a schedule, such as daily, weekly, or monthly.

schema — A description of the logical and physical structure of the data and relationships among the data in a database; a description of the entire database.

scientific visualization — The use of computer graphics to provide visual representations that improve our understanding of some phenomenon.

search engine — A tool that enables a user to find information on the Web by specifying keywords.

secondary storage — Nonvolatile devices that are used to store data and programs more permanently than RAM, while the computer is turned off.

Secure Sockets Layer (SSL) — Technology that encrypts data sent over the Web and verifies the identity of the Web server; in combination with digital certificates it allows for encrypted communications between Web browser and Web server.

selecting — A basic data manipulation, involving eliminating rows according to certain criteria.

selection — A common programming structure in which a path is chosen based on a condition within the program.

Semantic Web — The seamless integration of traditional databases with the Internet, allowing people to access and manipulate a number of traditional databases at the same time.

sequencer — A device that allows musicians to create multitrack recordings with a minimal investment in equipment.

sequential access — A storage medium feature that makes a computer that needs to read data from, for example, the middle of a reel of magnetic tape, sequentially pass over all of the tape before reaching the desired piece of data. It is one disadvantage of magnetic tape.

server — A computer system with hardware and software operating over a network or the Internet, and often sharing common resources, such as disks and printers; in a client/server relationship, the program that receives a service request and provides the service.

shareware — Software, usually for personal computers, that is inexpensive and can often be tried before purchase from the software developer.

Short Message Service (SMS) — A method for sending short messages, no longer than 160 characters, between cell phones.

signal — The communications element, containing a message comprised of data and information, that is transmitted by way of a medium from a sender to a receiver.

Simple Mail Transfer Protocol (SMTP) — The set of rules that e-mail servers follow to pass e-mail messages back and forth.

single in-line memory module (SIMM) — A circuit board that holds a group of memory chips, or RAM.

site preparation — The process of preparing the actual location so it is ready for a new computer system, which may mean simply rearranging furniture in an office or may require installing special wiring and air conditioning.

smartcards — Credit cards with embedded microchips, which are playing an increasing role in e-commerce payment methods.

software — Programs and instructions given to the computer to execute or run; computer programs that control the workings of the computer hardware, along with the explanatory program documentation.

software developer — An individual who designs and implements software solutions; also called a software engineer or a computer programmer.

software development — The process of developing computer programs to address a specific need or problem; also called program development, computer programming, and software engineering.

software development kit — A software package that assists programmers with the development of software using a particular programming language.

software engineer — A software developer, an individual who designs and implements software solutions.

software engineering — Software development, the process of developing computer programs to address a specific need or problem.

software maintenance — A program development stage in which programs are evaluated under normal use and improved upon with reversions and revisions, if necessary.

software programmer — The person in the systems development process who is responsible for modifying existing programs or developing new programs to satisfy user requirements.

software suite — A collection of application software bundled together into one package, often including word processors, spreadsheets, presentation graphics, and more.

sound compression — The ability to remove those frequencies that are beyond the range of human hearing and in so doing reduce the size of a digital music file.

sound designers — Technicians who provide background music, voices, and sound effects for video games to add realism and mood.

sound production studios — Facilities that use a wide variety of audio hardware and software to record and produce music and sound recordings.

source code — The high-level program code that a language translator converts into object code.

source data automation — The process of automating the entry of data close to where it is created, thus ensuring accuracy and timeliness.

spam — Unsolicited e-mail or an unwanted e-mail promotion that is sent to a large number of people; junk e-mail.

special purpose — Input devices designed for a unique purpose, such as a pill-sized camera that can be swallowed to record images of the digestive system.

special-purpose computers — Computers developed and used for primarily one task or function, such as MP3 players for listening to digital music files.

special-purpose database — A database designed for one purpose or a limited number of applications.

special-purpose device — Technology developed and used for primarily one task or function.

speech recognition — The software to translate human speech into text or commands.

spiders — Automated search programs that follow all Web links in an attempt to catalog every Web page by topic.

spoofing — A technique used to impersonate others on the Internet.

spooling — An operating system's method of storing data temporarily in a buffer or queue area before transferring it to, for example, a slower printer, in order to free the processor for other tasks.

spreadsheet applications — Personal productivity software that stores rows and columns of data and is used for making calculations, analyzing data, and generating graphs.

spyware — Software placed on your computer system without your knowledge or consent, normally through the Internet, to secretly spy on you and collect information.

standalone video phones — Devices that provide video phone service over traditional phone lines.

standard — An agreed-upon way of doing something within an industry.

star — A network topology connecting devices together through a central device called a hub.

star bus — The most common and versatile network topology in use today; it is a hybrid of star networks created in individual areas of an organization and joined by bus lines throughout the organization.

startup — The next to last step in systems implementation, beginning with the final tested computer system and finishing with the fully operational system.

static — When referring to an Internet Protocol (IP) address, one that is permanently assigned to a particular computer.

statistical sampling — A data collection technique that involves taking a random sample of data.

storage capacity — The maximum number of bytes a storage medium can hold.

storage device — The drive that read, writes, and stores data.

storage media — Objects that hold data, such as disks.

stored — Maintained as data.

storyline — A feature of video-editing software that allows the videographer to arrange video scenes sequentially and specify the transition effects between each scene.

structured design — An approach to programming design that divides a program specification into subproblems to be solved.

structured interview — A data collection technique in which an interviewer relies on questions written in advance.

Structured Query Language (SQL) — A standardized data manipulation language adopted as the standard query language for relational databases; a fourth-generation programming language used to perform database queries and manipulations.

stylus — A short, penlike device, without ink, used to select items on a touch screen.

subject directory — A catalog of sites collected and organized by human beings, such as the directory found at Yahoo.com.

subschema — A file that contains a description of a subset of the database and identifies which users can perform modifications on the data items in that subset.

supercomputers — The most powerful and advanced computers, often used for sophisticated and complex calculations.

supply chain management — The process of producing and selling goods, involving demand planning, supply planning, and demand fulfillment.

supply planning — The supply chain management activity of producing and making logistical arrangements to ensure that a company is able to meet the forecasted demand.

surround sound — Audio that makes use of special sound recording techniques and multiple speakers placed around the audience, so that sound-producing objects can be heard from all directions; also known as 3-D audio.

switched line — A line that maintains a network connection only as long as the receiver is active.

switches — Common network control devices that make it possible for several users to send information over a network at the same time without slowing down other users.

symbolic languages — Post-first-generation programming languages, which emphasize the use of symbols that are easily understood by humans.

synchronous communication — Along with asynchronous, one of two forms of electronic communications, allowing participants to communicate in real time as phrases are transmitted, whether spoken or typed, such as by using telephones, online chat, and instant messaging.

syntax — The set of rules each programming language has that dictates how the symbols should be combined into statements capable of conveying meaningful instructions to the CPU.

syntax error — An error in the form of a program's coding, such as a missing semicolon at the end of a command.

synthesizer — A digital music instrument that electronically produces sounds designed to be similar to real instruments or produces new sounds unlike any that a traditional instrument could produce.

system board — Also called the motherboard, the main circuit board in the computer where many of the hardware components are placed, such as the central processing unit, memory, and storage.

system bus — A collection of parallel pathways between the CPU and RAM that supports the transporting of several bytes at a time.

system clock — The CPU component that determines the speed at which the processor can carry out an instruction.

system software — A collection of programs that interact with the computer hardware and application programs.

system stakeholders — The individuals who, either themselves or through the area of the organization which they represent, will ultimately benefit from a systems development project.

system testing — Testing an entire system of programs together.

system virus — A program that infects operating system programs or other system files; also called a boot-sector virus.

systems analysis — A process that attempts to understand how the existing system helps solve the problem identified in systems investigation and answer the question, "What must the computer system do to solve the problem?"

systems analyst — A professional who specializes in analyzing and designing computer systems.

systems design — The selection and planning of a system to meet the requirements outlined during systems analysis, which are needed to deliver a problem solution.

systems development — The activity or process of creating new or modifying existing computer systems.

systems development life cycle (SDLC) — The ongoing activities associated with the systems development process, including investigation, analysis, design, implementation, and maintenance and review.

systems development specialists — Computer systems personnel who might include a project leader, systems analysts, and software programmers.

systems development tools — Instruments such as computer-aided software engineering tools, flowcharts, and decision tables that can greatly simplify the systems development process.

systems documentation — Written materials that describe the technical aspects of a new or modified system.

systems implementation — A process that includes hardware acquisition, software acquisition or development, user preparation, hiring and training of personnel, site and data preparation, installation, testing, startup, and user acceptance, according to the systems design.

systems investigation — The first step in the development of a new or modified computer system, the purpose of which is to determine whether the objectives met by the existing system are satisfying the goals of the organization; the activity of exploring potential problems or opportunities in an existing system or situation.

systems maintenance — One of the final systems development steps, involving the checking, changing, and enhancing of the system to make it more useful in achieving user and organizational goals.

systems maintenance and review — The process of making any necessary changes to the system after it is installed and operational.

systems review — The process of analyzing systems to make sure that they are operating as intended, the final phase of the systems development life cycle.

systems software — Along with application software, one of two basic types of software, consisting of the set of programs that coordinates the activities of the hardware and various computer programs.

T1 carrier — A network line that supports high data transmission rates by carrying twenty-four signals on one line.

T3 lines — Network lines that carry 672 signals on one line and are used by telecommunications companies; some act as the Internet's backbone.

table — A collection of related records; also called a file.

tablet PCs — A type of small, easy to use mobile computer.

t-commerce — A feature of interactive TV that allows viewers to make purchases over their cable TV connection, much as computer users make purchases on the Web; also known as purchase over TV.

TCP/IP — Transmission Control Protocol/Internet Protocol, the two Internet protocols.

technical feasibility — The determination of whether or not hardware, software, and other system components can be acquired or developed to solve the problem.

telecommunications — The electronic transmission of signals for communications.

telecommunications network — A network that connects communications and computing devices.

telecommunications system — An organized collection of people, procedures, and devices used to share and transfer information.

telecommuting — Employees working at home using a personal computer or terminal connected to the office computer via a modem.

telecommuting centers — Office space owned or leased by employers, equipped with computers and other necessary office equipment, that is shared by telecommuting employees.

teraflop — Trillions of floating-point operations per second, a measurement for rating the speed of microprocessors.

testing — Conducting tests on the entire computer system, including each of the individual programs, the entire system of programs, the application with a large amount of data, and all related systems together.

the Web — The World Wide Web, a client/server Internet application that links together related documents from diverse sources providing an easy navigation system with which to find information.

thin client — Stripped-down network PCs, which include a keyboard, mouse, display, and a small system unit that supplies only enough computing power to connect the device to a server over the network.

time-driven review — A systems review procedure that is started after a specified amount of time.

time-sharing — More than one person using a computer system at the same time.

token-ring — A network standard using unique hardware and software that does not work with Ethernet.

top-level domain (TLD) — The final portion, such as .com or .edu, of a domain name, classifying Internet locations by type or, in the case of international Web sites, by location.

touch pad — A touch-sensitive input pad below the spacebar on notebook computers that allows you to control the mouse pointer.

touch screen — An input device that allows users to select screen items by touching them.

trackball — An input device that allows you to control the mouse pointer by rolling a stationary, mounted ball.

TrackPoint — An input nub in the center of the keyboard on notebook computers that allows you to control the mouse pointer.

transaction — An exchange involving goods or services, such as buying medical supplies at a hospital or downloading music on the Internet.

transaction files — Temporary files that contain data representing transactions or actions that must be taken.

transaction processing cycle — The common set of activities, including the collection, editing, correction, manipulation, and storage of data, that e-commerce and all

other forms of transaction processing systems share.

transaction processing system (TPS) — An organized collection of people, procedures, databases, and devices used to record completed transactions; the system used to perform routine processing, such as sending out bills, paying suppliers, and printing employee paychecks.

transborder data flow — Specific national and international laws regulating the electronic flow of data across international boundaries.

transistor — A device made of a semiconducting material, usually silicon, that opens or closes a circuit to alter the flow of electricity.

Transmission Control Protocol(TCP) — Along with Internet Protocol (IP), one of the sets of policies, procedures, and standards used on the Internet to enable communications between two devices.

transparency — A feature of network management, in which the underlying network structure is hidden from the user, promoting ease of use.

transport layer — The protocol portion of the three-layer Internet model, which also includes application (software) and physical (hardware) layers.

Trojan horses — Programs that appear to be useful but actually mask a destructive program.

tunneling — A technology used by virtual private networks to securely send private network data over the Internet.

tuple — In the relational model, each row of a table, representing a record or collection of related facts.

TV-based video phones — Devices that use a set-top box equipped with a video camera and microphone that work in conjunction with a television set and phone line.

twisted-pair cable — A cable consisting of pairs of insulated twisted wires bound together in a sheath; the type of cable that brings telephone service to homes.

ubiquitous computing — A vision of a future so completely saturated with computer technology that we no longer even notice it.

Unified Modeling Language (UML) — A language that provides tools for creating object-oriented models for software solutions.

Uniform Resource Locator (URL) — The unique string of characters, such as http://www.course. com, that indicates where a particular Web page resides on the Internet; a Web address.

unit testing — Testing each of the individual programs in the computer system, which is accomplished by developing test data that will force the computer to execute every statement in the program.

Universal Serial Bus (USB) — A relatively new standard for computer ports that can be used to connect a wide range of devices.

UNIX — A powerful command-based operating system developed in the 1970s by AT&T for minicomputers.

UNIX servers — Computer systems using the UNIX operating system to operate over a network or the Internet.

unstructured interview — A data collection technique in which an interviewer relies on experience, rather than on questions written in advance, to formulate questions designed to uncover the inherent problems and weaknesses of an existing system.

upwardly compatible — Designed to work with previous versions. For example, a new version of a software package that is upwardly compatible can automatically read the files from an older version of the same software.

usability — A measure of how easy a program is to use.

USB storage — Small flash memory modules that plug into the universal serial bus port found on many computers, digital cameras, and MP3 players.

use case — The event than an actor interacts with in an object-oriented systems development approach.

use-case diagrams — Diagrams that represent the events in an object-oriented systems approach; used in Unified Modeling Language to provide a high-level description of a system.

Usenet — A collection of online newsgroups that includes thousands of public discussion forums that are accessible using news reader software that connects to a Usenet server.

user acceptance document — A formal agreement signed by the user that a phase of the installation or the complete system is approved.

user documentation — Written materials that describe how the computer system can be used by non-computer personnel.

user preparation — The process of readying managers and decision makers, employees, and other users and stakeholders for a new systems.

users — A specific type of stakeholder who will be interacting with the system on a regular basis; people who use computers to their benefit.

utility programs — System software that is used to perform important routine tasks, such as to merge and sort sets of data or to keep track of computer jobs being run.

variable — A named data component that can be set to different values.

vector graphics — A representational method that uses bytes to store mathematical formulas that define all the shapes in an image.

vector graphics software — Programs that provide tools to create, arrange, and layer graphical objects on the screen to create pictures; also called drawing software.

vendor — A company that provides computer hardware, equipment, supplies, and a variety of services.

video cameras — Special-purpose computer devices used to take videos, edit them, burn them to disks, and even send them to another person.

video conferencing — Technology that combines video and phone call capabilities along with shared data and document access.

video game consoles — High-powered multiprocessor computers designed to support 3-D interactive multimedia.

Video Games over TV — A feature of interactive TV that provides access to video games.

Video on Demand (VoD) — Technology that allows digital cable customers to select from hundreds of movies and programs to watch at anytime they choose.

video RAM — A buffer, sometimes referred to as a frame buffer, that stores image data after they are read from RAM and before they are written to the display.

video-editing software — Programs that allow professional and amateur videographers to edit bad footage out of digital video and rearrange the good footage to produce a professional video production.

virtual database systems — Virtual constructions that allow different databases to work together as a unified database system.

virtual memory — Also known as virtual storage, an operating system feature that allows users to store and retrieve more data without physically increasing the actual storage capacity of memory.

virtual office — A substitute office, as in workers' homes and cars, or at remote job sites, that can be worked out of using cell phones, pagers, and portable computers.

virtual private network (VPN) — An intranet that is extended beyond the confines of the local area network to connect with other networks; VPNs use a technology called tunneling to securely send private network data over the Internet.

virtual reality — A computer-simulated environment or event.

virtual reality headset — A gogglelike device, with spatial sensors as input devices, that projects output in the form of three-dimensional color images.

virtual storage — Also known as virtual memory, an operating system feature that allows users to store and retrieve more data without physically increasing the actual storage capacity of memory.

virus — A program that attaches itself to other programs.

virus hoax — E-mail sent to people warning them of a virus that doesn't actually exist.

virus-scanning software — Programs that detect viruses and worms on a personal computer.

vision systems — The hardware and software that permit computers to capture, store, and manipulate visual images and pictures.

Visual Basic — One of the first visual programming languages; it can be used to develop applications that run under the Windows operating system.

Visual Basic .NET — A visual programming language; it can be used to develop applications that run under the Windows operating system.

visual languages — Programming languages that use a graphical or visual interface, allowing programmers to "drag and drop" programming objects onto the computer screen.

Voice over Internet Protocol (VoIP) — A networking protocol for channeling voice phone signals over a data network.

voice recognition — A technology, similar to speech recognition, used by security systems to allow only authorized personnel into restricted areas.

voice-over recording — Voice recordings that are provided behind video or other media productions that may be narrative or synchronized to the lip movements of the actors.

volatile — A characteristic of primary memory storage, such that a loss of power to the computer means that the contents of memory is also lost or eliminated; temporary memory storage that is cleared each time the computer is shut down.

volatility — A database characteristic, referring to a measure of the changes, such as additions, deletions, or modifications, typically required in a given period of time.

volume testing — Testing an application with a large amount of data, to ensure that the entire system can handle it under normal operating conditions.

warm boot — A computer startup performed while the computer is currently running, as by clicking the restart button.

Web auctions — E-commerce sites that provide a virtual auction block where users can place bids on items.

Web authoring software — Software that allows users to create HTML documents using word-processor-like programs.

Web based — In reference to e-mail, messages stored on a Web server and viewed using a Web browser.

Web browser — A Web client used to request Web pages from Web servers.

Web conferencing — Online video conferencing, allowing groups to see, hear, text chat, present, and share information in a collaborative manner.

Web portals — Web pages that serve as entry points to the Web.

Web server — A computer that stores and delivers Web pages and other Web services; a computer system used to handle and coordinate traffic on the World Wide Web or the Internet.

Web server software — Software whose primary purpose is to respond to requests for Web pages from browsers.

Web server utility programs — Software programs that provide statistical information about server usage and Web site traffic patterns.

Web Services — Programs that automate tasks by communicating with each other over the Web.

Web-based e-mail — Messages stored on a Web server, and viewed using a Web browser.

Webcams — Typically low-priced video cameras, often used for video conferencing over the Internet.

webcasting — A technology that that provides television-style delivery of information using steaming video and high-speed Internet connections.

Web-driven — Programs that allow users to interact with Web sites to access useful information and services.

what-if analysis — The process of making hypothetical changes to problem data and observing the impact on the results.

wide area network (WAN) — A network connecting local area networks between cities, cross country, and around the world using microwave and satellite transmission or telephone lines.

Wintel — Also known as IBM-compatible, one of two popular personal computing platforms, along with Apple. These computers typically use the Microsoft Windows operating system and Intel or Intel-compatible processors.

wireless access point — A site that is connected to a wired network and receives data from and transmits data to wireless adapters installed in computers.

wireless fidelity (Wi-Fi) — A term used to describe wireless networking devices that use a special protocol and wireless access points distributed around a geographic area.

word processing — Text and document manipulation software, such as Microsoft Word, that is perhaps the most highly used application software for individuals.

wordlength — The number of bits that a CPU can process at one time; the larger the wordlength, the more powerful the computer.

work stressors — Hazardous activities associated with unfavorable work conditions, such as hard-to-read computer screens, uncomfortable desks and chairs, and fixed keyboards, possibly leading to serious and long-term injuries.

workgroup software — Software that allows network users to collaborate over the network; also called groupware.

workstation — A powerful desktop computer used to make sophisticated calculations or graphic manipulations; a personal computer attached to a network.

World Wide Web — Also known as the Web, a client/server Internet application that links together related documents from diverse sources providing an easy navigation system with which to find information; an Internet-access application that uses a graphical interface to ease Internet navigation.

worm — A program that, rather than attaching itself to another program, acts as a free agent, placing copies of itself into other systems, destroying programs, and interrupting the operation of networks and computer systems.

WYSIWYG — Pronounced wizzie-wig, and short for "what you see is what you get." It is a feature of Web-site editing programs, such as Dreamweaver, that allows users to design Web pages that will look the same when published on the Web.

XHTML — A successor to Hypertext Markup Language that embodies the best of HTML and XML in one markup language.

XML — Extensible Markup Language, a promising new markup language for designing data classification to organize the content of Web pages and other documents.

zombie computers — Computers on the Internet that are either hacked into or under the influence of a virus or worm, and are made to carry out Internet activities on the hacker's behalf.

SubjectIndex

CareerIndex

PhotoCredits

Chapter 1
Figure 1.1: Courtesy COMPASS System, Ministry of Transportation Ontario; © David Sailors/CORBIS
Figure 1.3: Courtesy of Intuitive Surgical, Inc.
Figure 1.4: © David Sailors/CORBIS
Figure 1.5: Courtesy of Vicon Motion Systems Ltd.
Figure 1.6: © Getty Images
Figure 1.7: © B. Busco/The Image Bank
Figure 1.8: Courtesy of Intel Corporation
Figure 1.9: Courtesy of Kingston Technology Company, Inc.
Figure 1.10: Courtesy of Seagate Technology; Courtesy of Imation; Courtesy of TDK Corporation; Courtesy of TDK Corporation
Figure 1.11: Courtesy of Logitech, Inc.; Courtesy of Logitech, Inc.
Figure 1.12: Image taken from the CD ROM **Any Body Can Dance**, Courtesy of **YDance** (Scottish Youth Dance)
Figure 1.14: Courtesy of Fujitsu Siemens Computers; Courtesy of IBM Corporation; Courtesy of Fujitsu Siemens Computers; Courtesy of Fujitsu Siemens Computers; Courtesy of Los Alamos National Laboratory
Figure 1.15: Toyota photo
Figure 1.18: © Zigy Kaluzny/Stone
Figure 1.21: Courtesy of National Aeronautics and Space Administration (NASA)
Figure 1.22: Copyright 2002 Course Technology
Figure 1.23: © Yellow Dog Productions/The Image Bank
Figure 1.24: Courtesy of Iridian Technologies, Inc.

Chapter 2
Figure 2.1: Courtesy of Nokia; Courtesy of Siemens AG, Munich/Berlin; Courtesy of RCA/Thomson Consumer Electronics
Figure 2.3: Courtesy of Microsoft® Corporation
Figure 2.4: Courtesy of Microsoft® Corporation
Figure 2.6: Courtesy of Handspring, Inc.

Figure 2.7: Courtesy of Intel Corporation
Figure 2.10: Courtesy of Apple Computer Corporation; Courtesy of Gateway, Inc.; Courtesy of Sun Microsystems, Inc.
Figure 2.11: COPYRIGHT: JAMSTEC/Earth Simulator Center
Figure 2.14: © Goodwin Photography
Figure 2.17: Courtesy of M-Systems Flash Disk Pioneers Ltd.
Figure 2.19: Courtesy of Symbol Technologies, Inc.
Figure 2.20: Courtesy of Brunel University, West London
Figure 2.21: Courtesy of Microsoft® Corporation
Figure 2.22: Courtesy of Microsoft® Corporation
Figure 2.23: Courtesy of Logitech, Inc.
Figure 2.24: Courtesy of First Virtual Communications, Inc.
Figure 2.25: Courtesy of NEC-Mitsubishi Electronics Display of America, Inc.; Courtesy of Sony Electronics Inc.
Figure 2.26: Courtesy of The National Institute for Standards and Technology (NIST)
Figure 2.27: Courtesy of Fujitsu Siemens Computers; Courtesy of Fujitsu Siemens Computers
Figure 2.28: © Goodwin Photography
Figure 2.29: Courtesy of SanDisk Corporation
Figure 2.30: Courtesy of Symbol Technologies, Inc.
Figure 2.31: © AP/WIDE WORLD PHOTOS
Figure 2.32: Courtesy of Microsoft® Corporation

Chapter 3
Figure 3.7: Courtesy of Microsoft® Corporation
Figure 3.17: Courtesy of Microsoft® Corporation
Figure 3.18: Courtesy of Apple Computer Corporation
Figure 3.19: Copyright 2003 Course Technology
Figure 3.20: Screen shot copyright © 2003 Red Hat, Inc. All rights reserved. Reprinted with permission from Red Hat, Inc.

Figure 3.21: Courtesy of Symantec Corporation
Figure 3.22: Courtesy of Symantec Corporation
Figure 3.23: Courtesy of Pixaround
Figure 3.24: Courtesy of Apple Computer Corporation
Figure 3.25: Courtesy of Corel Corporation
Figure 3.30: Box shot courtesy of Microsoft Corporation
Figure 3.31: Courtesy of Autodesk, Inc.; Courtesy of Sibelius USA Inc.; © SPSS® for Mac® OS X, Release 11.0.2 (14 May 2003)
Figure 3.32: Courtesy of IBM Corporation

Chapter 4
Figure 4.1: Courtesy of NASA/JPL/Caltech
Figure 4.2: Courtesy of Daniel Reed, Department of Computer Science, University of Illinois at Urbana-Champaign
Figure 4.4: Courtesy of AT&T
Figure 4.11: © 2003 The New York Times Company. Reprinted by permission
Figure 4.13: Courtesy of Worlds.com
Figure 4.15: Courtesy of Siemens AG, Munich/Berlin
Figure 4.16: Photo of Beamer Videophone, BM-80, provided courtesy of Vialta, Inc.
Figure 4.25: © 2003 Amazon.com, Inc.
Figure 4.26: Courtesy of Macromedia, Inc.
Figure 4.32: © Chris Hardy/San Francisco Chronicle/Corbis
Figure 4.35: Reproduced with permission of Yahoo! Inc.© 2003 by Yahoo! Inc. YAHOO! and the YAHOO! logo are trademarks of Yahoo! inc.

Chapter 5
Figure 5.7: Courtesy of Black Box Corporation
Figure 5.8: Courtesy of Black Box Corporation
Figure 5.9: Courtesy of Anixter, Inc.
Figure 5.11: © Michael Dunning/The Image Bank

Figure 5.12: Courtesy of National Aeronautics and Space Administration (NASA)

Figure 5.13: Courtesy of Garmin, Ltd.

Figure 5.14: Wherify Wireless, Inc.; Wherify Wireless, Inc.

Figure 5.16: *The Bluetooth* word mark and logo are owned by the Bluetooth SIG, Inc. and are reprinted by permission of the Bluetooth SIG, Inc.

Figure 5.19: Courtesy of Linksys

Figure 5.20: Courtesy of Linksys

Figure 5.21: Courtesy of Texas Instruments, Inc.

Figure 5.23: Courtesy of Fujitsu Siemens Computers; Courtesy of Fujitsu Siemens Computers

Figure 5.30: Courtesy of Vocera Communications

Figure 5.31: © Michael Barley/CORBIS

Chapter 6

Figure 6.1: Courtesy of Orangutan Foundation International

Figure 6.2: Courtesy Symbol Technologies, Inc.

Figure 6.5: From AMF's Daily Planner & PIM v9.2, courtesy http://www.AMFsoftware.com

Figure 6.6: Courtesy of Integrated Biometric Technology; Courtesy of Integrated Biometric Technology

Figure 6.8: Courtesy of Daryll Leja, National Human Genome Research Institute (NHGRI)

Figure 6.17: Courtesy of Intuit Inc.

Figure 6.18: Courtesy of Mindjet

Figure 6.20: © AP/WIDE WORLD PHOTOS

Figure 6.22: Courtesy of the U.S Geological Survey National Geologic Map Database Project

Figure 6.28: Courtesy of Business Objects

Chapter 7

Figure 7.6: © Michael Keller/CORBIS; Courtesy of Peapod

Figure 7.10: © Frank Siteman/Stone

Figure 7.14: Courtesy of Covisint

Figure 7.15: Reproduced with permission of Yahoo! Inc.© 2003 by Yahoo! Inc. YAHOO! and the YAHOO! logo are trademarks of Yahoo! inc.

Figure 7.17: Courtesy of AT&T Wireless; © Photographer's Choice/Getty Images

7.20: Courtesy of Izumiya

Figure 7.26: Courtesy of Cherry Corporation

Chapter 8

Figure 8.1: Photo by Eric Draper/White House/Getty Images

Figure 8.3: Courtesy of RyTech Software; reprinted with permission of MatheMEDics, Inc. (http://mathemedics.com)

Figure 8.5: © Jon Feingersh/CORBIS

Figure 8.9: Courtesy of ePocrates, Inc.; © Jim Craigmyle/CORBIS

Figure 8.11: Courtesy of National Severe Storms Laboratory

Figure 8.12: Courtesy of Touchstone Consulting Group, Inc.

Figure 8.14: Courtesy of University of Illinois Pablo Research Group

Figure 8.15: Donna Coveney/MIT

Figure 8.16: Honda Motor Co., Ltd.

Figure 8.17: Courtesy of Scansoft, Inc.

Figure 8.20: UCLA Cultural Virtual Reality Laboratory

Figure 8.21: Tom E. Sellsted and Joan Davenport, City of Yakima, Washington

Figure 8.22: Courtesy of Segway LLC

Chapter 9

Figure 9.2: Fifth Dimension Technologies (www.5dt.com)

Figure 9.5: Courtesy of Macromedia, Inc.

Figure 9.6: Courtesy of Visual-Paradigm.com

Figure 9.11: Courtesy of Microsoft Corporation

Figure 9.15: © Comstock

Figure 9.19: © Steve Chenn/CORBIS

Figure 9.24: Michael J. Aftosmis at NASA Ames Research Center

Figure 9.27: © Getty Images

Chapter 10

Figure 10.3: Courtesy of The LEGO Group

Figure 10.14: Courtesy of IBM Software Group

Chapter 11

Figure 11.1: Courtesy of Westlake Audio

Figure 11.2: Courtesy of Creative Forensic Services

Figure 11.3: Yamaha Motif 6 ES Music Production Synthesizer Workstation. Photo courtesy Yamaha Corporation of America

Figure 11.4: Courtesy of Westlake Audio

Figure 11.5: Yamaha AW4416 Digital Audio Workstation. Photo courtesy Yamaha Corporation of America

Figure 11.6: Courtesy of Apple Computer, Inc.

Figure 11.8: Courtesy of Apple Computer, Inc.

Figure 11.9: Courtesy of Sebastian Proost

Figure 11.10: Reprinted with permission of Quark, Inc. and its affiliates

Figure 11.11: David Young-Wolff/PhotoEdit

Figure 11.12: Research: Gary Glatzmaier, University of California, Santa Cruz; Visualization: Greg Foss, Pittsburgh Supercomputing Center

Figure 11.13: Courtesy of ALGOR, Inc. ALGOR is a registered trademark of ALGOR, Inc.

Figure 11.17: Courtesy of Nate Ryan (www.housepixels.com)

Figure 11.20: Courtesy of Macromedia, Inc.

Figure 11.21: Courtesy of discreet®

Figure 11.22: © CORBIS SYGMA

Figure 11.23: Image courtesy of Andrew Hall (www.worth1000.com)

Figure 11.26: Courtesy of AEC-Michael Bloomenfeld

Figure 11.27: Courtesy of Macromedia, Inc.

Figure 11.28: Courtesy of MindAvenue and the Canadian Aviation Museum

Figure 11.30: © Reuters NewMedia Inc./CORBIS

Figure 11.31: © 2003 Take-Two Interactive Software, Inc. All Rights Reserved.

Figure 11.32: Courtesy of Gateway, Inc.

Chapter 12

Figure 12.3: Courtesy of the Motion Picture Association of America, Inc. (MPAA), www.respectcopyrights.org

Figure 12.4: Courtesy of Microsoft Corporation

Figure 12.5: Courtesy of Identix, Inc.

Figure 12.6: © Tom & Dee Ann McCarthy/CORBIS

Figure 12.7: © Vicky Kasala/Getty Images

Figure 12.8: AP/Wide World Photos

Figure 12.10: © Tom Grill/CORBIS

Figure 12.11: ENERGY STAR® is a registered trademark and is owned by the U.S. Government

Figure 12.12: Courtesy of Freedom Scientific

Figure 12.15: Courtesy of Spam Bully

Figure 12.16: AP/Wide World Photos

Figure 12.17: Courtesy of SurfControl plc

Figure 12.18: Courtesy of David Smith and Geekcorps.org